A History of
Ancient Egypt

A History of
Ancient Egypt

NICOLAS GRIMAL

Translated by Ian Shaw

BLACKWELL
Oxford UK & Cambridge USA

English edition first published 1992
Reprinted 1993, 1994
First published in paperback 1994
Reprinted 1995, 1996, 1997 (twice), 1998 , 1999 (twice)

Blackwell Publishers Ltd
108 Cowley Road, Oxford OX4 1JF, UK

Blackwell Publishers Inc.
350 Main Street
Malden, Massachusetts 02148, USA

British Library Cataloguing in Publication Data
A CIP catalogue record for this book is available from the British Library

Library of Congress Cataloging in Publication Data
Grimal, Nicolas-Christophe
[Histoire de l'Egypte ancienne. English]
A history of ancient Egypt/Nicolas Grimal; translated by Ian Shaw.
p. cm.
Translation of: Histoire de l'Egypte ancienne.
Includes bibliographical references and index.
ISBN 0–631–17472–9 (hb.) — 0–631–19396–0 (pb.)
1. Egypt – History – To 332 B.C. I. Title.
DT83.G7513   1993
932'.01 — dc20   92–9580
CIP

Typeset in 10 on 12pt Sabon
by Best-set Typesetter Ltd, Hong Kong
Printed and bound in Great Britain
by MPG Books Ltd, Bodmin, Cornwall

This book is printed on acid-free paper

Contents

List of Illustrations

FIGURES

TABLES

Translator's Note
and Acknowledgements

This translation of Nicolas Grimal's *Histoire de l'Egypte ancienne* differs from the French edition in a number of ways. The text is illustrated by a different selection of plates, line drawings and tables, and the best available English-language translations have been used in place of French translations of extracts from ancient Egyptian texts. The glossary and chronological appendix were compiled by the translator.

The translator and publishers would like to acknowledge the following for permission to reproduce extracts:

Aris & Phillips Ltd, for lines from Faulkner 1973–7; The British Museum Press, for lines from Faulkner 1985; Oxford University Press, for lines from Gardiner 1961 and 1964; University of California Press, for lines from Lichtheim 1975, 1976, 1980; University of Chicago Press, for lines from Grene 1987.

Introduction

The compilation of a history of pharaonic Egypt is no longer as much of an adventure as it was at the turn of the century, when scientism was at its height and Gaston Maspero wrote his monumental work, *Histoire des Peuples de l'Orient Ancien*. Maspero's work, along with James Henry Breasted's *History of Egypt*, still forms the basis for most modern historical syntheses. It was not so long ago, however, that the combined influence of the Bible and the Classical tradition conspired to produce a rather incoherent view of Egyptian civilization, and the great chronological disputes inherited from the nineteenth century are a continuing legacy of this confusion. The disputes were generally between the adherents of a so-called 'long' chronology, based on a fairly unscientific use of textual sources, and those who proposed a 'short' chronology, which was founded on a less romantic and more archaeological view of history. Now, however, virtually all scholars adhere to the 'short' chronology.

Although there is currently broad agreement on the course of its first two thousand years, recent advances in research have revived the problem of the beginnings of Egyptian history and the origins of pharaonic civilization. Despite the fact that Egyptology is one of the youngest of the historical disciplines (if it is considered to have begun with the work of Champollion 150 years ago), the increasing use of modern scientific methods has placed it in the forefront of research into the origins of civilization.

Pharaonic culture has always been a source of fascination, even to those unable to understand the profundity of a system in which everything gives an impression of permanence and unchanging wisdom. The Greek travellers were particularly guilty of misrepresentation. Unable to convey a true sense of Egypt's basic values to their Greek audience, they tended instead to use Egypt as a vehicle for the ideas which already interested them. They presented it as an impressive and mysterious fountainhead of human thought, where a remarkably advanced level of civilization had been achieved, but they clearly regarded Egyptian civilization simply as a stage in the development towards the perfect Greek version. Their descriptions of Egyptian culture were characterized both by unbridled enthusiasm and by a distinct sense of uncertainty when they were confronted by customs of which they invariably misunderstood the origins.

The Greeks embarked on a systematic exploration of the country: first there were the researches of Herodotus in the fifth century BC, then the works of geography by Diodorus Siculus and Strabo, both of whom familiarized themselves with the Nile valley through a prolonged stay 'in the field'. Six hundred years later Plutarch documented the religious mysteries of Egypt. As well as these contemporary investigations there were others based directly on the original Egyptian sources, which were rediscovered in the Ptolemaic period by the researches of such men as Manetho (*c.*280 BC) and the geographer Claudius Ptolemy (*c.*150 BC).

Even the Romans' appreciation of Egypt was not solely due to the country's wealth, although this was clearly the main attraction for Mark Antony, Julius Caesar, Germanicus, Hadrian, Severus and the rest. The researches of Pliny and Tacitus were similar to those of the Greek historians and geographers who had preceded them. Egypt was regarded as a place of great scholarly achievement by such disciples of Aristotle as Theophrastus, and it served to assuage Rome's great thirst for eastern values. The first evidence of increasing eastern influence on Rome dates to the beginning of the second century BC, when Cato persuaded the Senate to issue a decree forbidding Bacchanalian rites, which were considered to be a thinly disguised excuse for the celebration of increasingly popular foreign religious cults. At the cost of a few thousand lives, traditional Roman values were thus temporarily saved from the uncontrollable spread of the East.

The Greek cities continued to submit to the Roman *imperium*, which had inherited from Alexander a new concept of the East. Through Alexander, the Hellenistic royalty had gained authority over the universe from the priesthood of Ra, and this in turn helped to legitimize Rome's domination of the entire world. The union of the master of this world with Cleopatra, the last descendant (however fictitiously) of the pharaohs, was effectively the marriage of Helios and Selene, finally consecrating the fusion between East and West. But the union was brief, and when Augustus arranged for the assassination of Caesarion (the son of Julius Caesar and Cleopatra) in 30 BC, after the capture of Alexandria, he must have felt that he was removing as great a threat to the nascent empire as the Bacchanalia had been to Cato's republic.

Egypt, now the personal property of the emperor, had become just another of Rome's vassal states. However, it still preserved its aura of wisdom and learning, which was revived and transmitted via the Mediterranean *koine* to the new Roman centre of the universe.

Two images of Egypt were then superimposed on one another. The first was that of the Hellenistic civilization of Egypt, which is recorded in the works of such writers as Theocritus. The cultures of the Greeks and the Egyptians were blended successfully both in the works of Apollonius of Rhodes and in the general currents of Alexandrian thought. The second image of Egypt was based on a tradition that can already be described as 'orientalizing', illustrated by the writings of Apuleius or Heliodorus of Emesa. The orientalizing tradition continued to emphasize the mysteries of the ancient civilization, while progressing along the same lines as the contemporary schools of philosophy. The appearance of Neoplatonism led to the Hermetic Corpus, a set of philosophical writings ascribed to Hermes Trismegistus (the Hellenistic version of the Egyptian god Thoth), which were compiled after the revival of Pythagorism, marking the beginning of the empire in the east. The Hermetic Corpus, like the cabbala, was later to be the main means of access to a civilization that had become incomprehensible to Christians. This movement towards esoterism was encouraged by the spread of Egyptian cults throughout the Roman Empire. Through the figures of Osiris, Isis and Anubis, the cults popularized the suffering of the archetypal Egyptian sovereign, perceived as one of the models for life after death.

Everything changed in AD 380 with the Emperor Theodosius' declaration that Christianity was the state religion and all pagan cults were forbidden. With this edict he effectively silenced Egyptian civilization. The closure of Egyptian temples, which Constantius II had begun in AD 356, culminated in 391 with the massacre of the Serapeum priests at Memphis. This was not merely the prohibition of a set of religious practices but the abandonment of the culture from which they had sprung, since both had been preserved from one generation to another through the language and writing system of the priests. The Christians gained revenge for their persecution at the hands of the 'idolaters' by destroying pagan temples and libraries and by massacring the intellectual elite of Alexandria, Memphis and the Theban region. The last survivors of this onslaught were the ancient centres of Lower Nubia and Upper Egypt, and they endured only because they lay on the frontier of the Roman Empire, where there was already a long tradition of resistance to colonists from the north. From the mid-sixth century AD onwards, after the final closure of the temple of Isis at Philae, a veil of silence was drawn over the necropolises and temples, which were now vulnerable to pillaging and reuse. Chapels were used as houses and stables or simply quarried for building materials, while many sanctuaries were converted into churches. For more than five hundred years Karnak was to accommodate convents and monasteries, while on the walls the eyes of the ancient gods, hidden by coats of rough plaster, still peered out at the rites of the new religion.

The pharaonic town sites were also doomed, for the annual Nile flood and the repeated exploitation of the same tracts of land meant that settlements continued to occupy the same locations, gradually covering most of the ancient towns. Modern Egyptian cities, mostly in the north but also in the south, represent only the final stage of a process of constant superimposition of settlements, often stretching back to the beginning of Egyptian history. Some of the ancient temples have managed to retain their reputations as sacred sites, as if the ancient peoples' deep sense of religious syncretism had survived in their modern descendants, resulting in the protection of temple precincts containing thousands of years of stratigraphy.

In the temple at Luxor, the layers that separate the level of the court of Ramesses II from the mosque of Abu Haggag cover a period of more than two thousand years. The site was subject to successive waves of Persian, Assyrian, Greek and Roman invasions. In the Roman period a military camp was established on it and the whole range of Roman imperial cults was celebrated, as well as Christianity and Islam. Abu Haggag, the holy man to whom the mosque is dedicated, is still the object of an annual religious procession, complete with sacred barques reminiscent of those which conveyed the image of the god Amon-Re from one temple to another.

Luxor is by no means unique: there are numerous sites preserved in this way throughout the Nile valley and the Delta, as well as more distant locations such as the Dakhla Oasis, where the mosque of the ancient Ayubbid capital of el-Qasr is founded on layers of stratigraphy reaching down to the Eighteenth Dynasty and possibly even to the Middle Kingdom. Archaeologists may delight in these accumulations of past debris, but it is clear that in the short term at least, the historian cannot find his answers there. The social and economic structures of the Egyptians were transformed and distorted when they became subject to the laws of the Roman Empire; they lost their language, their religion and their traditional values.

Egyptian Christianity, which justifiably claimed historical and religious primacy in the Near East, produced a civilization as rich and original in its art as in its intellectual achievements. Coptic Egypt made a fresh start, sweeping aside the old traditions and giving full rein instead to popular culture, which was a far cry from the religious canons of the period. The undeniable influence of the vernacular in art and architecture can be seen in the flourishing of figured tapestry and in the extraordinary funerary portraits popularized by the Faiyum schools of art. Coptic art also prefigured the Islamic revival of ornamental decoration and the introduction of the cupola in architecture. In the mid-third century AD the monastic movement was founded by Paul the Egyptian, and the continued vigour of this tradition even now is proof enough of its significance within Egypt's heritage.

The Islamic regime was relatively flexible and tolerant at the time of the Arab conquest, but gradually it grew more stringent in its demands on Egyptian society. New values developed, laying the foundations of contemporary Egyptian society and moving further away from those of the pharaonic period. The ancient religious tradition, acquiring new themes from such scholiasts as Pseudo-Berosus, survived the oppressors of the true faith: Ramesses II became first the adversary of Moses and then the personification of evil itself. It was not until the end of the nineteenth century and the creation of the Arab Republic of Egypt that Ramesses – re-established as a historical figure – could finally take his place amid the ups and downs of contemporary politics as a symbol of the united Arab nation and, more generally, of the past glory of Egypt.

The Egyptians' memory of the pharaohs began to fade from the fifth century AD onwards, and the gradual ascendancy of Arab over Copt eventually expunged the last links with the ancient world. Legend took over from history, just as when the pharaohs' subjects themselves had told tales of their rulers worthy of the *Arabian Nights*. All too soon the clandestine digging that was itself an intrinsic part of Egypt's past was beginning to provide glimpses of its great riches. Works such as the *Book of Buried Treasure* began to circulate, guiding treasure-hunters into a world peopled by such spirits as the gnome Aitallah (a version of the dwarf-god Bes), a terrible ogress modelled on the goddess Sekhmet, and the giantess Saranguma. The wise men of the time took pleasure in mocking the lunatics who pursued such delusions. The historian Ibn Khaldun castigated the madness of the treasure-hunters, but this did not prevent the Caliph al-Mamun, son of the famous Harun al-Raschid, from pillaging Cheops' pyramid. A process of pillaging and quarrying was inaugurated, which was to strip the Giza pyramids of their mystery as well as their outer casing of fine limestone blocks, which were reused to build the palaces of Mamluk and Ottoman Cairo.

The relics of the past, which were everywhere exposed to the ravages of treasure-hunters, quarriers and lime-burners, were also transformed by the country's new occupants. Some great achievements and deep beliefs survived almost unchanged through individuals such as Abu Haggag. But the general tendency when faced with the incomprehensible was to rely on the only approach that could be trusted: the sacred texts. Christians, like Muslims, carried out research into these sources. They saw Egypt as a Biblical land ranging from Babylon to the route of the Exodus, to which both Copts and western Christians made their way. Westerners discovered the country in the course of pilgrimages and crusades to the Holy Land, but their view was coloured by traditions inherited from the Greco-Byzantine civilization. The most famous example of such misinformation is the very word that they used to describe the great stone structures they passed on their way to the holy places: the word 'pyramid' is Greek in origin. It referred to a cake of wheat, and it may be that the shape of the pyramids reminded the first tourists of such delicacies. Subsequently, the term 'wheat cake' was used to support a belief that the pyramids were actually grain silos, for their true role had been forgotten. It would have seemed quite feasible to medieval pilgrims that the pyramids should have been the granaries in which Joseph stored grain for the years of famine, since Egypt was at that time still a great exporter of cereals.

These Biblical versions of history were tempered with hints of the lost wonders of pharaonic Egypt. Since the beginning of the fourth century AD the Roman emperors had been fascinated by these traces of Egypt's more distant past, and their great collections of obelisks and Egyptian art are now part of the riches of Rome and Istanbul. At the time of the European Renaissance there was a revival of exotic architecture, and Egyptianizing sphinxes jostled with stone or wooden pyramids in European gardens. However, it was not until after the Ottoman conquest, in the second half of the sixteenth century, that Egypt became enduringly fashionable; at this time the renewal of commercial activities allowed France to play an entrepreneurial role in the Middle East, like that played earlier by Venice.

The tales written by western travellers in Egypt, who were following in the footsteps of such Arab predecessors as Abu Salih, Ibn Battuta and Ibn Jobair, were mostly in the same romantic style. Noteworthy among these were the pilgrimage of the Dominican monk Felix Fabri or the journey of the botanist Pierre Belon du Mans in the entourage of the French ambassador sent to the Sublime Porte (the Ottoman government in Constantinople) just after the conquest. These tales are usually true to the rules of their genre, as with Jean Palerne, Joos van Ghistele (en route for the mysterious kingdom of Prester John), Michael Heberer von Bretten, Samuel Kiechel, Jan Sommer and many others. Perhaps it is precisely because they are written in so artificial a style that the accounts are so popular.

This brief summary of early travellers in Egypt should also include writers such as Ahmad ben Ali Maqrizi or, closer in time to the travellers mentioned above, Leo Africanus. Certain individuals, such as Christophe Harant, set out in the footsteps of the Classical authors (essentially Strabo and Diodorus Siculus), many of whose works were published for the first time at the end of the fifteenth century. Others attempted to pursue a more scientific path: the geographer André Thevet and the Italian physician Prospero Alpini. Alpini combined the results of four years' travel in Egypt with a deep knowledge of the work of his predecessors from Herodotus to Belon du Mans, and produced three books on the flora, fauna and medicine of Egypt which are still classics of their type.

Seventeenth-century travellers might be expected to have followed up this more scientific view of Egypt, or at least to have left better documented accounts of their experiences. But this is by no means the case, despite the growing fashion for orientalism and the appearance of such Turkish-influenced literary works as *Bourgeois Gentilhomme*, in which merchants, diplomats or tourists confined themselves to conventional and often inaccurate descriptions rarely covering anything more exotic than the area around Cairo. Items of useful information about Egypt appeared only rarely and were essentially pragmatic, intended more as practical travel-guides than as scientific or historical accounts. This was certainly the case with George Christoff von Neitzschitz, Don Aquilante Rocchetta and Johann Wild, whose adventures are worthy of a picaresque novel. Their concerns were very much with the contemporary East, and their accounts dealt with brief journeys or long stays in the bosom of the new 'French nation' of Egypt – Père Coppin is a good example of this type.

The seventeenth century was also the period when 'curiosity cabinets' became popular, reviving the fashion for antiquities and foreshadowing the great collections that were to form the basis of the major European museums. Travellers and scholars undertook the rediscovery of Egyptian civilization, which was marked primarily by chance finds of mummies. These were ground into a powder which was said to be able to regenerate the cultivable lands that the European powers had seized. In Britain, so-called 'mummy mills' were even constructed to satisfy the insatiable demand. Europeans read the works of the ancient writers voraciously, and before the nineteenth century Herodotus was still the most common guidebook to be taken on a journey to Egypt.

Some important figures stand out among these travellers, who had become more 'professional' since Thévenot: archaeologists and antiquaries such as Père Vansleb, Paul Lucas and Claude Fourmont, doctors such as Granger, and explorers such as Poncet and Marie-Alexandre Lenoir. Ancient Egypt was gradually becoming better known through the published descriptions of some of the principal sites. The existence of Karnak had been known since the end of the fifteenth century from the map of Ortelius and the description given by an anonymous Venetian, but in about 1668 the site itself was rediscovered, and almost a century later the city of Memphis was also revealed. In 1646 the first work devoted exclusively to the pyramids was published by the English mathematician John Greaves.

In the eighteenth century important scientific studies of Egypt began to be published by such scholars as Norden, Pococke, Donati, the relations of Père Sicard, Volney, Balthazar de Monconys (the friend of Athanasius Kircher, whose works inspired Champollion), Savary and many others, all variously preparing the ground for the Napoleonic expedition to Egypt, which represented a watershed in Egyptology. The conflicts between the European nations as the French Revolution drew to a close, led to great opportunities and an almost unlimited field of research to satisfy European scholars' thirst for knowledge. The young savants who travelled with Bonaparte's army embarked on a monumental *Description de l'Égypte*, which embraced not only flora and fauna but also the architecture and art which comprised the surviving evidence for each successive civilization in Egypt.

Over a period of months, the Napoleonic expedition painstakingly assembled a great mass of documents which not only provided the decipherers of hieroglyphs with the necessary corpus of written material but even laid the foundations for many modern syntheses. From then on orientalism was a genuine literary and artistic movement rather than a mere fad. The number of works dealing with Egypt multiplied, from Gerard de Nerval to Eugène Delacroix, as part of the 'Egyptian Revival' style. James Owen and David Roberts produced excellent paintings, combining orientalizing themes with an almost archaeological precision. There were also numerous nineteenth-century paintings associated not so much with Egypt specifically as with the birth of the colonial age, including the works of Gérôme (who visited the Sinai in the company of Paul Renoir and Bonnat on the occasion of the opening of the Suez Canal), Fromentin, Guillaumet and Belly (whose *Pilgrims to Mecca* caused a scandal at the Salon of 1861). During the same period, the work of Thomas Young in England and Jean-François Champollion in France laid the foundations of modern Egyptology.

Champollion was beset by numerous problems, firstly in the form of the political changes that propelled him from Grenoble to Paris and Figeac, and secondly in the scientific authorities' resistance to his methods. But in 1822, in the *Lettre à M. Dacier*, he revealed the basic elements of his method for deciphering hieroglyphs, which was further developed the following year in a *Précis du système hiéroglyphique*. While his detractors were still looking for a flaw in his system of decipherment, he buried himself in the growing collections of Egyptian antiquities brought to Europe by a new generation of adventurers. To nineteenth-century travellers Egypt must have held all the attractions of a new world, as they skimmed through the sites on behalf of their foreign consuls, deriving enormous profits from the exploitation of the country which was permitted during the time of Muhammad Ali and his successors. There was great rivalry between Giovanni Belzoni, who was acting on behalf of Henry Salt (the British consul in Cairo), and Bernardino Drovetti, who was sponsored by Jacques Rifaud of Marseilles, among others. These epic confrontations, closer to pillaging than archaeology, provided some of the first works in the collections of the British Museum, the Louvre and the Museo Egizio, Turin.

It was the collection at Turin, amassed by Drovetti and sold in 1824 to the King of Sardinia, which allowed Champollion to become the first Egyptologist to make full use of the ancient king lists. He also wrote a *Panthéon*, the first study of Egyptian religion, finally completing it in Egypt in 1823. He compiled an enormous mass of documents which would be published forty years after his death as *Monuments d'Égypte et de Nubie*. When he returned to Paris he barely had time to teach a few courses in the chair of Egyptology created for him at the Collège de France before he died on 4 March 1832, at the age of forty-two. He had by then firmly established the basic components of the Egyptian language in his *Grammaire égyptienne*, which was eventually published in 1835.

France was in the forefront of the new science of Egyptology, and this role was to be consolidated by the work of Champollion's successors, especially by the fieldwork of Auguste Mariette. The excavation methods which Mariette used at great sites such as Saqqara and Tanis are virtually indefensible compared with modern archaeology, but he was not content merely to be the fortunate excavator of sites such as the Serapeum, Karnak and Tanis: he also fully exploited his own discoveries and any other work of which he was aware. It was through his determination that the viceroy Said Pasha was persuaded to set up the National Antiquities Service, an organization with powers to end the massive drain of antiquities into European collections and to amass instead a collection of antiquities within Egypt.

From the Bulaq Museum to the modern Egyptian Museum in Cairo, the largest collection of material remains from ancient Egypt began to be gathered together. At the same time, the newly established Antiquities Service gradually began to safeguard sites for scientific excavation by clamping down on pillaging. The rivalries which divided the European nations for almost a century had no real effect on the work of their nationals in Egypt except during periods of actual war. The

Prussian expedition of 1842–5 and the *Denkmäler aus Ägypten und Äthiopien*, published ten years later by Richard Lepsius, provided the scientific community with a third corpus of inscriptions and monuments still used by modern scholars.

By the end of the nineteenth century Egyptology was definitely established as a field of research; it had also reached another turning point in its history, both in terms of discoveries in the field and in the creation of institutions capable of ensuring its continued development. Gaston Maspero was the most important of Mariette's successors: he discovered the *Pyramid Texts*, served as Director of the Antiquities Service, and managed to save most of the royal mummies at Thebes from pillagers. He was also the founder of the French *École*, succeeding de Rougé to occupy Champollion's chair. Henri Brugsch, Sir Flinders Petrie and Gaston Maspero are considered to have been the fathers of modern Egyptology, and it was Petrie who laid down the rules of scientific archaeology in Egypt with the establishment of the British School of Archaeology.

By the turn of the twentieth century the European museums and universities had created a number of organizations within which modern researchers still operate: the French Archaeological Mission (which was formed in 1880 and became the French Institute for Oriental Archaeology at Cairo in 1898), the Egypt Exploration Fund (which later became the Egypt Exploration Society) and the German Oriental Society. Improvements in communications with the media were then to provide maximum publicity for the ensuing discoveries, which included the capital city of Akhenaten at Tell el-Amarna before the First World War, the tomb of Tutankhamun in 1922, the necropolis of the Tanite kings in 1939, the great boat of Cheops in 1954, and the rescue campaign for the monuments of Nubia in the 1960s. It was the treasure of Tutankhamun which particularly popularized Egyptology, especially with the travelling exhibition that took place in the 1970s – the success of which was to lead to various others on similar themes.

But the mystery that seemed to surround the discovery of Tutankhamun's tomb also revived a mystical interest in Egypt, still more or less fuelled by the influences of Hermeticism and the cabbala, and marked by secret societies requiring elaborate initiation ceremonies. This mystical tendency led to the development of the theme of Isis-worship in such works as the *Magic Flute* and *Aida*, for which Mariette wrote the libretto; the celebration of the cult of Isis at Notre-Dame in Paris during the Revolution; and numerous esoteric interpretations of such aspects of Egyptian civilization as the pyramids and religion. Howard Carter's discovery provided the public with its classic image of Egyptology, more by the sheer quantity of precious objects than by the tomb's historical importance (which was not fully exploited until later). It was a mixture of mystery with treasures and curses – two words firmly linked with the pharaohs – that created a romantic aura around the Egyptologist.

The combined effect of all these elements and the rapid development of mass tourism have inevitably increased the gap between the public image and the reality of Egyptology as a field of research. The fact that Egyptology is still a relatively young subject tends to be minimized, as does the amount of ground still to be covered before a civilization as rich as that of Egypt can be understood in detail.

As a result of progress in the archaeology of Egypt 'before the pharaohs', the conventional chronological limits of Egyptian civilization have been called into question – the subject has now moved a long way from the 'forty centuries' which separated Napoleon from the time of the pyramids. Having freed the history of Egypt from the grip of Biblical chronology, the new knowledge and methodology acquired since the end of the nineteenth century have gradually clarified the chronology and pushed back the origins of the civilization.

The question of the true meaning of the term 'history' is perhaps more relevant to ancient Egyptian civilization than to any other culture. The exceptionally long duration of the pharaonic period with its rigid social system, tends to highlight the classic distinction between history and prehistory, in which the appearance of writing acts as an implicit barrier between the two. This change from prehistory to history is supposed to have taken place, in Egypt's case, in the fourth millennium BC. Until the 1970s this date was relatively well accepted, since it more or less corresponded with Biblical times in Mesopotamia, and was a sufficiently late date to give Lower Mesopotamian civilization a 'head start' on Egypt, thus ensuring that the place where writing first appeared was also the supposed location of the Garden of Eden. The fourth millennium also conveniently appeared to be a phase during which human evolution had reached a decisive stage, with the emergence of social structures suggesting man's final separation from the natural world, over which he gained control by becoming a sedentary cultivator in the Nile and Euphrates valleys.

The achievement of 'civilization' is indicated archaeologically by the introduction of writing, and this level of achievement is easy to distinguish from the preceding 'preparatory' phase. However, the length of the preparatory phase – which very much depends on when it is considered to have started – tends to be maximized by prehistorians and minimized by historians.

This problem, which until the 1930s was considered to be a kind of Darwinian quarrel, acquired a new dimension when the system of dating with reference to fluvial erosion was adopted. The system was created by Boucher de Perthes for the Somme valley, and applied to the Nile by K. S. Sandford and A. J. Arkell. The establishment of an association between traces of human activity and geological banding supplied a point of contact with the archaeological data which, although invariably unstratified, could nevertheless be arranged in a chronological order by the use of the 'sequence dating' system worked out by Petrie at the beginning of the century. Although more recent analyses of palaeoclimatology and geology (such as the work of Karl Butzer and Rushdi Said) have modified the scale of the dates, it has been clear since the Second World War not only that 'prehistory' before the pharaohs was expanding on a hitherto unsuspected scale, but also that it appeared to be so diverse and self-contained that it was difficult to regard it as simply a 'preparatory' stage for the dynastic period.

The state of knowledge of Egyptian prehistory in the late twentieth century is still fragmentary despite the basic fieldwork of Gertrude Caton-Thompson in the Faiyum region and the Kharga Oasis, and the work of J. Hester and P. Hoebler in the Dunqul Oasis. The information provided by the systematic exploration of Lower Nubia has not been completely published and other areas are still relatively unexplored, such as the Dakhla Oasis, Gebel Uweinat and, further to the west, Kufra and Darfur. Without even going so far in space or time, our knowledge of earliest Egypt is still very patchy. Studies since World War II, particularly in the Delta, have revealed further predynastic evidence, but it is significant that the prehistoric remains at Elkab were only discovered by the Belgian archaeologist Pierre Vermeersch as recently as 1968.

The true significance of prehistory as 'history without texts' has only reached its full extent since anthropologists and ethnologists began to reveal civilizations such as those in pre-Columbian America or black Africa, in which a high degree of sophistication was achieved without any written tradition. This has led to a revision of the criteria by which levels of social complexity are assessed. Such a change in perspective has, in its turn, led to the adoption of prehistorians' methods outside the field of prehistory itself, so that archaeologists in Egypt are more interested in the relative chronology of historical sites than was previously the case. After more than a century of fieldwork, Egyptologists – now faced with a relative dearth of sites containing inscribed blocks and papyri – have turned to the excavation of sites which had previously been neglected because of their lack of written evidence.

The exploitation of settlement sites undertaken over the last twenty years both within and outside the Nile valley has often taken the form of rescue excavations or surveys, carried out when sites are threatened by the rapid expansion of urban conglomerations. This development has rendered obsolete the old Egyptological distinction between philology and archaeology, whereby the former was the only means of interpreting the civilization and the latter was simply the ancillary discipline devoted to the basic task of acquiring documents.

The willingness of modern Egyptologists to absorb new points of view has tended to favour the adoption of newer and more accurate techniques of dating. All the methods based on measurements of radioactivity (including radiocarbon, thermoluminescence and potassium-argon dating), as well as such other techniques as dendrochronology and palynology, have thus become relatively common within the discipline. Research methods have also improved, with the increasing use of aerial photography, topographical and architectural surveys using stereophotogrammetry, computer analysis of data, and the development of methods of axonometric reconstruction using computer graphics.

Apart from the purely technical advances that have been made, these innovative methods have also changed the attitudes of Egyptological researchers: now potsherds, grains of pollen and fragments of papyrus are all treated as equally important aspects of the evidence. Faced with such a multiplicity of archaeological sources, the act of writing a history of Egypt necessarily incorporates the skills of many other disciplines.

Part I

The Formative Period

1

From Prehistory to History

The immediate impression of Egyptian civilization is of a coherent entity, the extraordinary duration of which has guaranteed it a special place in the history of mankind. The culture seems to have emerged, already fully formed, towards the middle of the fourth millennium BC, eventually vanishing at the end of the fourth century AD. For almost forty centuries Egypt possessed an air of unchanging stability and a political system that did not appear to be shaken by anything – even the occasional invasion.

The internal geographical unity of the country perhaps contributed to the apparent lack of change. Egypt is a long strip of cultivable land stretching for more than a thousand kilometres between the latitudes of 24 and 31 degrees north. It centres on the lower course of the Nile, carved out from Aswan to the Mediterranean and wedged between the Libyan plateau and the Eastern Desert (which is in fact only an extension of the Nubian desert). Although the width of the valley rarely exceeds 14 kilometres, the Nile valley has been one of the most in-habitable parts of eastern Africa for approximately a million years (from the Oldowan phase onwards), while the Sahel region, on the other hand, was transformed into an arid zone by radical climatic changes.

Nevertheless, the traditional image of the Nile valley – as an area that was always welcoming to man – needs to be modified to some extent, since the general overview of Egyptian prehistory has been altered by the results of recent geomorphological studies. New evidence has been made available through the prospection of desert zones and western subdeserts, firstly in connection with the Aswan High Dam project and secondly during the process of searching the Libyan Desert for new land capable of replacing the alluvial soil of the Nile valley, which is rapidly being exhausted. Through improved knowledge of the general mechanisms of soil formation, particularly in the work of Rushdi Said and the surveys of Romuald Schild and Fred Wendorf (the results of which have been published over the last few years), it is now possible to update the theories put forward at the beginning of this century, theories which are still frequently quoted in general books.

One recurrent question in Egyptian prehistory is the role played by the lacustrine depressions of the Libyan plateau, which were eventually to be transformed into the modern string of oases. Current excavations at the oases are producing a better appreciation of the role that these depressions played in the migration of civilized groups towards the Nile valley: certain qulifications have now been introduced into the theory of the 'Ur Nil' (a huge ancestral version of the Nile), which would have been created after the retreat of the Eocene sea between the Libyan dunes and the area of the modern Nile valley. A similar note of caution has also been sounded with regard to the concept of the Nile as a primeval valley of luxuriant fertility when it was first inhabited by man.

THE FORMATIVE PERIOD

The question of when the Nile valley was first occupied leads naturally to consideration of the age and geographical spread of Egyptian culture. How does one identify the factors which gave rise to the earliest Pharaonic civilization and at the same time pay due attention to the characteristics of the lengthy prehistoric phase that preceded it?

The evidence suggests a starting point for Egyptian prehistory at the end of the Abbassia Pluvial period in the Middle Palaeolithic (*c.*120,000–90,000 BC). In fact, a grossly oversimplified scenario might be that the desert was gradually being populated during the long Abbassia Pluvial period and that this zone was eventually opened up to the expansion of the Acheulean culture which was developing on the banks of the Nile. This was the last stage in a process of development that can be traced back to the remains discovered near the rock temple at Abu Simbel, the earliest of which probably date to the end of the Lower Pleistocene, about 700,000 BC. From the end of the Oldowan period onwards (i.e. throughout the Acheulean), there was a continuous human presence in the Egyptian and Nubian sections of the Nile valley, from Cairo to Thebes and Adaima.

This phase of the Lower Pleistocene was a long transitional period of hyperaridity lasting for about a million years between the Pliocene and Edfon Pluvials, both of which were characterized by regular and heavy rainfall. For about 100,000 years the Proto-Nile carved out its course to the west of the modern Nile valley, to be eventually replaced by the Pre-Nile, which was to endure for five times as long.

THE FIRST INHABITANTS

At the end of this long sequence came the Abbassia Pluvial, a period of almost 15,000 years during which the Acheulean culture was able to spread into the western regions. If this diffusion actually happened, it should certainly be regarded as the origin of the connections between the Nilotic and African civilizations. Traces of these connections are preserved in the later evolution of the two cultures without, however, indicating whether they reflect a change, or the way in which this change might have taken place. It is tempting to interpret the Nilotic and African civilizations as opposite sides of the same culture, which would have advanced along the obvious natural routes from the region that was to become the Sahara. Both the diffusion of the Nilo-Saharan languages from the high valley of the Nile into the eastern Sahara and the recent palynological analyses in the oases of the Libyan desert have made an important contribution to this assessment. Consequently, a set of flora corresponding to a common process of development has been identified.

This apparent link is particularly plausible in that it coincides with the change from *Homo erectus* to *Homo sapiens* around 100,000 BC, and with the establishment of a common culture represented by a dolichocephalic human type, the evolution of which has been compared to that of contemporaneous humans in North Africa and Europe. It is essential to remain cautious in this kind of assertion however, since the African side of the situation is still poorly known and the Egyptian evidence itself is far from complete.

The lacustrine depressions of the Eastern Desert provided the late Acheulean and Mousterian cultures (*c.*50,000–30,000 BC) with a distinctive habitat which is characterized by the presence in the archaeological record of ostrich eggs and possibly even the remains of an ancestor of the onager. The end of the Acheulean was marked by a sudden technological revolution – the change from bifacial to flake tools. This artefactual change was to be a longlasting feature of African cultures, corresponding well to the new social conditions. This period lasted until about 30,000 BC and can be correlated with the Mousterian and Aterian phases. It represented the end of the hunting economy that had evolved in the savannah, culminating in the Aterian culture with its use of the bow and arrow. The Aterian culture, which was widespread throughout the Maghreb and southern Sahara and survived for a

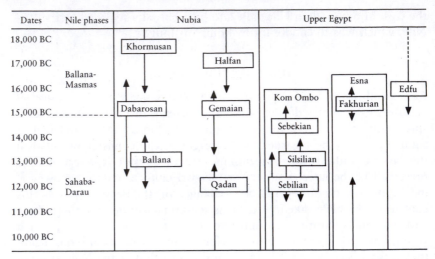

FIGURE 1   *Chronological table of the end of the Late Palaeolithic period.*

long time in Sudanese Nubia and the oases of the Libyan Desert, could well have been the last stage of an original common African culture.

HUNTERS AND AGRICULTURALISTS

The Khormusan culture was named after the site of Khor Musa, located some distance from Wadi Halfa, where traces were found of a civilization which began in the Middle Palaeolithic (*c.*45,000 BC) and had disappeared by the Late Palaeolithic (*c.*20,000 BC). Compared with the Aterian culture, the Khormusan was more reliant on the river valley, combining the subsistence of the savannah – exploiting wild cattle, antelopes and gazelles – with the products of fishing, thus demonstrating that the populations driven out of the Saharan zones by drought were adapting to the Nilotic environment. During this period – when the Subpluvial Makhadma was being replaced by the arid phase of the Neo-Nile, which has lasted until modern times – the Nile valley was a crucible in which the various elements of the future pharaonic civilization were blended together. The desertification of the Saharan zones seems to have driven even the inhabitants of the Libyan oases into the Nile valley. They made up separate groups, each developing a unique way of life which was nevertheless based on a common source, sometimes paralleled by local industries such as those found at Gebel Suhan.

The next turning point was between 15,000 and 10,000 BC, when in Nubia the Gemaian period replaced the Halfan; the Dabarosan succeeded the Khormusan; and the use of the microlith, which was already perceptible in the second half of the Halfan phase, had by the Ballana period definitely taken place.

The Qadan culture, represented at more than twenty sites from the Second Cataract to Toshka, constituted an important stage of development both in its stone tools, which were characteristically microlithic, and in its signs of economic development. Some Qadan tools show traces of 'sickle gloss', which is commonly interpreted as evidence for the beginnings of agriculture. Pollen analyses have confirmed the presence of *Gramineae* (a wheat-like grass) and – at Esna at least – wild barley. However, this agricultural experiment – if that is the right word for it – does not appear to have lasted beyond the turn of the tenth millennium.

It is perhaps too early to formulate large-scale theories, but it seems likely that the population explosion brought about by this Qadan agricultural development might have led to the rise of a more warlike culture, the growth of which would have been detrimental to agriculturalists. This earliest form of agriculture, although short-lived, appeared in the Nile valley at a time when cultivation was still unknown in the Near East; nevertheless, the evidence is insufficient either to support a truly Nilotic origin of agriculture or to call into question the Near Eastern roots of the type of agricultural society that developed in the Nile valley at the end of the Mesolithic. The archaeological material from the Qadan proto-agricultural sites – including evidence concerning the distribution of children's as opposed to adults' tombs (Hoffman 1979: 94) and details of the overall lifestyle of their occupants – bears many points of resemblance to that of Neolithic cultures.

Evidence for the period of transition from the Qadan phase to the Neolithic has been provided by the discoveries of Pierre Vermeersch at the site of Elkab. The earliest remains at Elkab were contemporary with the change from the Arkinian to the Sharmakian in the neighbourhood of Wadi Halfa and the end of the Qarunian phase in the Faiyum region, in which a hunting culture adapted to the Nilotic environment by becoming a community of fishers but not agriculturalists. The transition to agriculture took place in conditions that are still a little unclear, around the middle of the sixth millennium BC. The influence of the Near East is thought to have been involved, despite the earlier indigenous attempt at agriculture and notwithstanding the fact that the first domesticated animals were distinctly African types. The development of agriculture in Egypt clearly took place over a long period, and recent research such as the survey conducted in the Theban region by the University of Krakow and the German Archaeological Institute at Cairo

(Ginter, Kozlowski and Pawlikowski 1985: 40–1) shows that it was a process incorporating various separate phases.

THE EMERGENCE OF THE NEOLITHIC

The eventual break between prehistory and history took place at the end of the seventh millennium BC. This event, separating the Mesolithic from the Neolithic, is even more poorly known than earlier phases (Finkenstaedt 1985: 144ff.). Virtually all environmental and cultural factors seem to have contributed to a radical modification of the nature of Egyptian civilization, with the onset of a new subpluvial period that favoured animal domestication and the development of agriculture at the fringes of the Nile valley and in the area of the western oases. This environmental change accelerated the development of textile and ceramic production techniques, and during the two thousand years from the beginning of the Neolithic to the emergence of the predynastic period proper (from the mid-seventh to mid-fifth millennium BC) virtually all the essential characteristics of Egyptian civilization appeared. Despite the introduction of various metals, this Neolithic culture was to remain essentially stone-based throughout its existence.

Apart from the Nubian groups and the Elkab sequence described above, the last phase of Egyptian prehistory is particularly exemplified by a number of sites in the Faiyum (phase B then phase A in about the middle of the sixth millennium) and by various sites in the Nile valley itself, including el-Badari (Hemamia) and Deir Tasa at the southern end of Lower Egypt, and Merimda Beni Salama and el-Omari near Helwan (now a suburb of modern Cairo). These sites provide evidence of a mixture of hunting traditions and new developments (Huard and Leclant 1980). There was an improvement in weapons, with the introduction of sharp arrowheads worked from polished flint and the growing use of bone harpoons, part of the classic toolkit of the fisherman. It was in this early period that the archetypal cultural image of the Nilotic environment first developed. This image was perpetuated in scenes of hunting and fishing in the marshes which were later painted on tomb walls in the pharaonic period, recalling a time when agriculture was first establishing its grip over the untamed world. The development of organized society took place on an agricultural basis: settlements tended to consist of farms devoted to animal husbandry and the cultivation of crops. Granaries were used to preserve the products of the fields (mainly wheat and barley). In addition to the production of pottery and basketry, Egyptians of the Neolithic period were already weaving linen and processing animal skins, as well as rearing sheep, goats, pigs and cows. Such agricultural practices as these went through little subsequent change over the course of the following millennia.

Egyptian funerary practices experienced a change which paralleled the switch from hunting to agriculture. Graves were gradually placed further away from the settlements, eventually taking up a position outside the world of the living, at the edge of the cultivable land. The deceased was given provisions in the form of cereals and food offerings, but he also took hunting gear into the hereafter, as well as the necessary equipment, such as pottery, for a continued rural existence. Laid out on his side in a contracted position, he embarked on a journey that was already oriented towards the western horizon, bathed in sunlight every evening after the sun had left the land of the living.

Since the systematic study of the Neolithic sites in the Nile valley is still far from complete, it is too early to say whether the distribution of known sites is simply the result of chance discoveries or whether it reflects real differences between the south and north of the country. One clear impression is that the northern sites (between Cairo and the Faiyum) had a superior lithic industry, with fine flint weapons and stone vases; the southern sites were characterized by higher quality pottery, red with a black border and decorated with inlay, which was to become the hallmark of the predynastic period.

The implications of the real or perceived differences between north and south are far-reaching: they affect the interpretation of the whole process of the unification of Egypt's two lands, the duality of which continues to be stressed throughout the dynastic period. The process of unification took a little over a millennium, from about 4500 to 3150 BC, and throughout this period the differences between the two cultural groups appear quite distinct – in later times they became more vague, but total fusion seems never to have been achieved. The emergence of the dynastic period roughly coincided with the appearance of metal-working, but its impact was not as great as might be expected: for a long time copper was only used to a small degree, and the change in artefacts was far from abrupt. Four phases can now be distinguished between the beginning of the Chalcolithic period and the Thinite period.

THE 'PRIMITIVE' PREDYNASTIC (BADARIAN AND FAIYUM A)

The first Chalcolithic phase (the 'primitive' predynastic, lasting from the sixth to the fifth millennium) corresponds to the final stage in the development of the Faiyum A culture in the north and the Badarian culture in the south. The differences between north and south were still

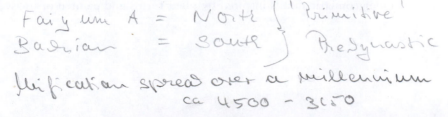

primarily in the areas of stone-working, pottery manufacture and the production of flint tools and weapons, which were perhaps more advanced in the north and had already begun to resemble the late Old Kingdom industries of the Libyan Desert oases. There are, for instance, the magnificent, skilfully retouched knives found by Gertrude Caton-Thompson, which recall those from Balat in the Dakhla Oasis. But it is advisable to remain cautious, since Badarian flint-working, particularly for arrowheads, could be equally sophisticated. The difference between the two groups (Faiyum A and Badarian) lay mainly in the relative proportions of their hunting and fishing activities, as opposed to agriculture; the population of the Faiyum, like the later peoples of the oases, certainly continued to obtain a greater percentage of their food by such non-agrarian means.

However, alongside more predictable advances in furniture and agricultural equipment there was also a perceptible development in funerary practices which involved both of these aspects of the 'primitive' predynastic culture. The deceased might still be buried under the simple protection of an animal skin, but the tomb began to take on a more solid architectural appearance. The plastic arts – destined for a long process of development in Egyptian civilization – also began to be practised: the production of black-topped pottery (described above) reached a sophisticated level; bone and ivory objects such as combs, cosmetic spoons and female figurines became particularly common (the latter had exaggerated sexual chacteristics, anticipating the later 'concubines' that were used to regenerate the sexual powers of the deceased). There were also items of jewellery and amulets in the form of human figures or animals, made of a substance that can already be correctly described as 'Egyptian faience' (Hoffman 1979: 138–9, figs 38–9).

THE 'OLD PREDYNASTIC' (NAQADA I OR AMRATIAN) PERIOD

The appearance of the 'Old Predynastic', in about 4500 BC, also took place amid a distinct lack of drastic cultural change. The cut-off point is relatively arbitrary in fact, corresponding to the first known phase at the site of el-Amra, about 120 kilometres south of el-Badari, in the very heart of the zone stretching from Asyut to Gebelein, the area which has yielded the richest deposits of Predynastic material. This phase also corresponds to the earliest occupation at Naqada, 150 kilometres further to the south, and it is found throughout the bend of the Nile between Gebel el-Arak and Gebelein. Ceramics went through a dual evolution in this phase, firstly in their decoration, which began to include geometric motifs inspired by plant forms and painted or incised

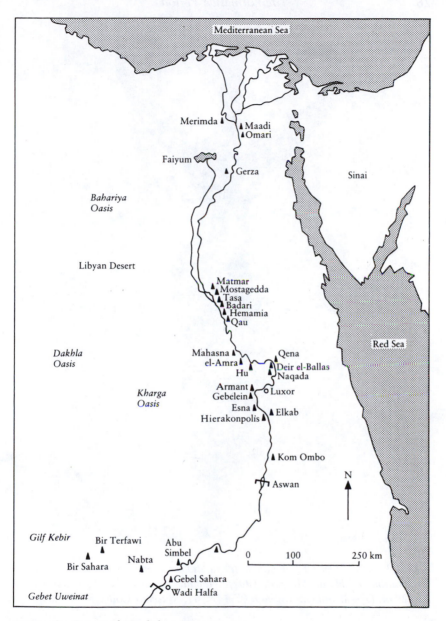

FIGURE 2   *Principal Neolithic sites in Egypt.*

PLATE 1 *The 'Dancer'. Painted terracotta statuette from Ma 'amariya (excavations of H. de Morgan, 1907). Naqada II period, c.3650–3300 BC, h. 0.29 m. (The Brooklyn Museum 07.447.505, Museum Collection Fund.)*

depictions of animals, and secondly in their shapes, with the appearance of theriomorphic vessels. The art of clay-working had already reached its peak, particularly in the painted terracotta female 'dancers' with raised arms. The most beautiful of these is in the Brooklyn Museum,

New York; the streamlined form of its body is reminiscent of a Cycladic figurine (Plate 1).

By the end of the Predynastic period the Nile valley was obliged to open itself up to the outside world, for it had very few natural resources. Metals such as copper were found in Nubia, to the south of the Wadi Allaqi and in the region of the Red Sea. Lead, tin, galena and a little gold were found in Sinai and the Eastern Desert and gold was also to be found in the area of the First Cataract. Nubia, however, was always the Egyptians' principal source of gold. Later, the distant kingdom of Meroe was one of the rare sources of iron, along with the Bahariya Oasis. As for precious stones, turquoise and malachite were to be found in the Sinai, jasper between the Wadi Gasus and the Wadi el-Qash in the Eastern Desert, emeralds on the southern shores of the Red Sea and amethysts in the area around Aswan.

Soft stones such as limestone were fairly widespread, particularly on the Libyan plateau. In the Nile valley limestone could be obtained from the northern site of Tura, one of Egypt's most well-used quarries from the Old Kingdom until modern times, as well as from Beni Hasan in the el-Amarna region of Middle Egypt, and from Abydos and Gebelein in Upper Egypt. Egyptian alabaster (travertine) was quarried at Wadi Gerrawi near Memphis and especially at Hatnub in Middle Egypt, while gypsum was obtained from sites in the Faiyum region. Sandstone was quarried at various locations to the south of Esna, particularly Gebel el-Silsila in Upper Egypt and Qertasi in Lower Nubia.

Hard stones, which were very highly valued in prehistoric times, were widely distributed across the country. Basalt was to be found in the north, dolerite in the Faiyum, porphyry, granite and dolerite in the Eastern Desert, and finally quartzite, diorite, steatite and granite in the zone around the First Cataract.

The only type of stone prevalent throughout the country was flint, deposits of which tend to follow limestone outcrops in the valley and on the Libyan plateau. Other stones had to be obtained through quarrying, generally on an *ad hoc* basis. The locations of the mineral deposits – usually in regions distant from cultivated lands and on the borders of the country – meant that the Egyptians were obliged to organize expeditions which relied for success on tight control over the place of extraction and the routes there and back. This necessity became an important factor in the pharaohs' foreign policy, the primary aim of which was to protect the areas near the Nile valley from foreign encroachment.

These growing external influences appeared in the pharaonic iconography in representations of bearded men similar to Libyans, and of products being brought from the south: obsidian and perhaps even copper, once thought to have been obtained only from the Sinai. Such contacts with the outside world, which grew more frequent in the period before the union of the two kingdoms, suggest that even at this early stage there were vigorous trading contacts as much with the south (presumably with caravans of traders) as with the west and the east via the oases, the Sinai and the coastal zone. Similar commerce was also taking place between the two Egyptian cultural groups of the north and the south, judging from the discovery at el-Amra of a stone vessel apparently imported from the north.

Even more important is the appearance of historical architectural forms, 'models' that the deceased took with him into the afterlife: these have revealed the existence of houses and mud-brick enclosure walls of the same type as those of the pre-Thinite period (Hoffman 1979: 147–8). This suggests that the concept of the Egyptian town and urban planning can be traced back as far as the Amratian (Naqada I) phase (*c.*4500–4000 BC).

THE GERZEAN PERIOD

The discovery of the culture of el-Gerza, several kilometres from Maidum, provided the evidence for a third Predynastic phase and a second stage of the Naqada period: the Gerzean (*c.*4000–3300 BC). The differences between the Amratian and Gerzean groups are so marked that it is possible to see in them the increasing influence of the northern peoples on those in the south, which was eventually to result in the appearance of a third, mixed, culture: the Naqada III or Late Predynastic period. This culture flourished from about 3500 to 3150 BC, a period of some three hundred years immediately before the unification of Egypt.

The major difference between the Amratian and the Gerzean lay in their ceramic production. Certainly the constituents of the pottery were not the same, although this was as much a matter of the specific site involved as a reflection of any technical advance. Gerzean pottery developed particularly in terms of decoration, with the use of stylized motifs including geometrical representations of flora and more naturalistic depictions of fauna and other aspects of their culture. There are few surprises among the birds and animals represented: ostriches, ibexes and deer confirm the existence of a Gerzean sub-desert hunting habitat. On the other hand, the decoration of these ceramics is also enlivened with human figures and boats carrying emblems that are clearly divine (Vandier 1952: 332–63; El-Yahky 1985: 187–95) and were perhaps the forerunners of the standards that, a few hundred years later, came to symbolize the different provinces of Egypt. These scenes seem to have been formally related to early pictograms, but were they historical documents or purely emblematic in function? Unfortunately, the material is primarily votive and mostly from funerary contexts. It is significant, however, that the pottery decoration is complemented by another type of representation dating back to the Badarian period: the carved schist palettes used to grind eye-paint, which were also frequently buried with the deceased; these palettes would soon acquire value as historical documents.

Compared with the pharaonic civilization, the Gerzean culture reached a stage of development that was already well advanced, especially in its funerary and religious aspects. Gerzean tombs had become virtual replicas of earthly dwellings; sometimes they comprised several profusely furnished rooms. There were also amulets, figurines and ceremonial objects decorated with thematic scenes of animals (lions, bulls, cattle, hippopotami and falcons) which are known to have represented various gods from a very early period in Egyptian history. Naturally, there is always a great deal of uncertainty in reconstructions based on a series of diverse elements. One cannot, for instance, take into account those elements that have not survived for posterity. But it is clear that the main constituents of the civilization of unified Egypt were gradually introduced during the Gerzean period.

Archaeological evidence shows that the change from prehistory to history was the result of a slow process of evolution and not, as was long imagined, a brutal revolution involving the simultaneous appearance of new technology (essentially metallurgy) and new social structures (organization into agriculturally-based cities and the pro-liferation of mud-brick buildings and writing). These elements of Egyptian civilization have often been traced back to Mesopotamia, partly because they are attested there at the same time and partly because it is simpler to envisage a common origin for the 'Asiatic mode of production'. But the presence in Egypt of Mesopotamian cylinder seals of the Jemdet Nasr period (*c*.mid-fourth millennium BC) is evidence, as Jean Vercoutter (1987: 101ff.) has pointed out, only of the existence of commercial links like those that were also clearly established with Syria-Palestine, Libya and the African regions to the south of Egypt. Such isolated pieces of evidence can no longer be considered sufficient basis for hypothesizing an invasion at the end of the Predynastic period. The knife found at Gebel el-Arak (Paris, Louvre) certainly bears Mesopotamian decorative motifs, but it is only one of a well-documented series of figuratively decorated ivories (Vandier 1952: 533–60). It is not sufficiently convincing that the same theme reappears in the 'Painted Tomb' at Hierakonpolis, where it is represented in a less typical style (Plate 2; Vandier 1952: 563). A

TABLE 1 *Chronological table of the end of the Neolithic period.*

Approximate dates	Phase	Nubia and Sudan	Nile Valley	Nile Delta	Faiyum
5540–4500 BC	Neolithic	Shaheinab Khartoum variant Shendi (el-Ghaba)	Badari A Hemamia	Merimda	Faiyum A Beni Salam
4500–4000 BC	Early Predynastic	Shamarkian Shendi (el-Kadada)	Amratian (Naqada I) Badari B (el-Khatara)	Omari A (Helwan)	
4000–3500 BC	Middle Predynastic	Group A (First through Third Cataracts)	Gerzean A (Naqada II)	Omari B	
3500–3300 BC	Late Predynastic		Gerzean B (Naqada III)	Maadi	
3300–3150 BC	Pre-Thinite				

Thinite-period gaming-piece (Paris, Louvre), found at Abu Roash, was sculpted to represent a house consisting of three buildings surmounted by a double-sloped roof (i.e. one designed to allow rain-water to drain off). This piece of evidence has often been cited as another instance of Mesopotamian influence, but it is hardly any more convincing than the Gebel el-Arak knife. Apart from the fact that the gaming-piece may simply have been an imported object, as exotic as the cylinder, it is also worth pointing out that rain was by no means unknown in Egypt itself.

As far as mud-brick architecture is concerned, the Egyptians had no need to look abroad for inspiration, since they had begun to use mud-bricks themselves as early as the fifth millennium BC. It might even be argued that clay was a building material as readily available in the Nile valley and the western oases as it was in Mesopotamia. If stone architecture did not appear until later in history, this was not so much because of the lack of metal tools – since quarry-workers had less frequent recourse to metal than might be expected – but because building in stone required a level of organization and degree of resources that were more suited to the pharaohs than to the provincial rulers of the late predynastic period.

WRITING

The question of whether writing was imported into Egypt or evolved there is easily answered by a consideration of the representations on Naqada-period pottery, which apparently chart the gradual stylization of the plants, animals and religious dances depicted, eventually resulting in a set of divine symbols that are virtually hieroglyphic signs (Vandier 1952: 264–96 [Amratian], 333–63 [Gerzean]). These Naqada pictures reflect a fundamental principle of hieroglyphic writing that was to remain unchanged throughout Egyptian history: the combination of pictograms and phonograms. It is difficult to determine the moment of change from one to the other or even to see whether it took place at all. The only argument in favour of a development from pictogram to phonogram is the brevity of the earliest inscriptions, which seem to have worked through direct pictographic representation, judging from the common use of single unique signs with none of the phonetic additions that regularly characterize later hieroglyphic writing. The phonetic notation was therefore perhaps a technical advance that tended to gather momentum over the course of time, eventually resulting in a kind of overloading of the written language and culminating in some form of proto-alphabetic writing. This is certainly the broad impression gained by comparing Old Kingdom texts with those of the first millennium BC.

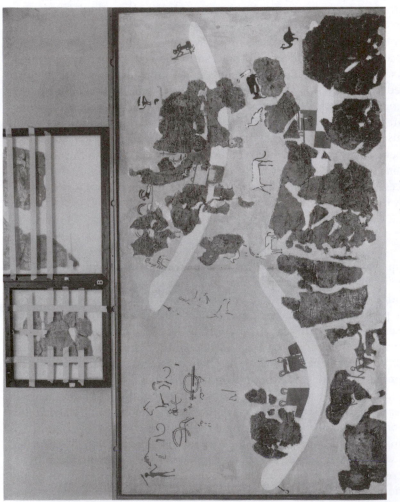

PLATE 2 *Copy of paintings in the predynastic 'painted tomb' at Hierakonpolis. (Photograph: John G. Ross.)*

Hieroglyphic writing brought together the pictogram, the ideogram and the phonogram. The pictogram is a direct representation: to draw a man, house or bird is equivalent to naming it. The basic concept is very easy to understand; like prehistoric mural paintings its limits coincide with those of the real world. The representation of concepts, however, is not so simple, even with the use of metonymic methods such as the effect equalling the cause (e.g. the representation of the wind by a boat's billowing sail) or the use of a container to denote the contents (e.g. the beer jar representing beer and the papyrus roll denoting writing). There is still the problem of homophones, such as *sa*, written in the form of a duck seen in profile, which means both 'duck' and 'son'. Consequently, certain signs had to be detached from their ideogrammatic meaning, retaining only their phonetic value, so that the duck hieroglyph could be used to transcribe the biliteral sound *sa*, meaning either son or bird. The difference between the two was then indicated by a generic determinative sign that was added to the phoneme: a man for the son and a bird for the duck. In the case of the latter, the bird determinative would actually be replaced by a single vertical stroke indicating that the sign was being used to signify its original meaning, since the depiction of two ducks in a row would have been confusing.

Although every phonogram theoretically retained its original ideogrammatic meaning, certain signs became specialized symbols of the more common phonemes. These were essentially uniliteral signs which comprised a kind of twenty-six-letter alphabet, with the aid of which it was theoretically possible to reproduce all of the sounds. In practice, however, the Egyptian language used a number of other signs to transcribe phonemes of two to six letters. Each of these phonemes could also retain their ideogrammatic values in other contexts. The writing system therefore relied on a collection of ideograms, phonograms and determinatives, using anything from one to several thousand signs, depending on the exuberance of the expression and the period.

Hieroglyphs were generally reserved for inscriptions carved on slabs of stone or, more frequently, incised and painted on walls. The basic forms did not change at all from the earliest inscriptions to those in temples of the Roman period. The only variations were palaeographic: degrees of stylization or elaboration, realism, archaizing or innovation, according to the varying aims of the writers.

For administrative, accounting and legal documents, as well as the archival notation of other texts (from literary compositions to religious or funerary rituals), a cursive method of writing was adopted at an early stage in Egyptian history. Greek tourists visiting Egypt in the Late Period called this cursive system 'hieratic', since from what they oberved they assumed that it was restricted to members of the priesthood; this contrasted with the 'demotic' script, which seemed to them to be used by the population at large. In fact, the demotic was only a later version of hieratic which had evolved by the seventh century BC. The basic principle of hieratic was simple: abbreviated hieroglyphic signs representing – individually or in groups – the most frequent groups of signs. From the Old Kingdom to the last centuries of the Egyptian civilization, this shorthand method of writing evolved towards increasing brevity. At the peak of its development, in about the middle of the first millennium BC, it appeared not only as demotic but also as 'abnormal hieratic', a form which evolved in the Theban region during the Kushite and Persian periods. As a result of increasing contacts with the Mediterranean and the effects of the Greek and Roman domination of Egypt, the writing evolved finally towards alphabetic notation in the form of Coptic, which was actually the Greek alphabet augmented by seven letters necessary for the reproduction of phonemes that did not exist in the Greek language. Coptic reproduced the stage reached by the Egyptian language around the third century AD. With the abandonment of polytheism, it became the writing of the Church in Egypt, although the official written language was Greek and later Arabic. Coptic was used by Egyptian Christians and today it is the liturgical language of the Copts. It was thanks to Champollion's knowledge of Coptic that he was able to recreate the phonetics of ancient Egyptian.

Since hieratic was the most practical version of the Egyptian writing system, it was used by scribal schools as the medium for learning the written language. It was in hieratic that the young pupil formed his first letters with the aid of a reed pen on an 'ostracon' (i.e. a potsherd or limestone chip). The ostracon was the humblest of writing materials, obtained from a broken vessel or quarry debris, and sometimes replaced by a clay tablet inscribed with a stylus. The more costly papyrus was reserved for more important documents, such as archival material, accounting inventories and religious, magic, scientific or literary texts, which might also be transcribed onto leather rolls or stucco tablets.

POLITICAL UNIFICATION

Discussions concerning the appearance of characteristic elements of pharaonic civilization lead naturally to the much-debated question of the events leading up to final unification – the two centuries that culminated in the union of two cultural groups. Egyptian sources represent the process as the triumph of the south over the north, but modern analysis of the earliest dynastic social system clearly shows the influence of the north rather than the conquered south. Kurt Sethe and Hermann Kees first embarked on the study of this process some time ago (Vandier 1949: 24ff.), when the reconstruction of the predynastic period was purely speculative. The results are still far from conclusive, although in future it should at least prove possible to clarify the historical events that led to the formation and confrontation of the two kingdoms. Kees's hypothesis was that the kingdom was first unified under the aegis of the north, but that this unification broke down for some reason and was reformed by the kings of the south, who were happy to retain the pre-existing northern system of government. This theory has now been discredited by recent archaeological information, which suggests that from the Tasian period onwards, Middle and Upper Egypt from el-Badari to Naqada were increasingly influenced by the culture of the north (Kaiser 1985).

The description that the Egyptians themselves have given of this period in their history is not sufficient to reach a definite decision one way or the other. The direct documentation consists mainly of palettes from the Badarian period onwards, artefacts which lie on the interface between myth and history. These objects, apparently all votive, comprise two basic types. The first consisted of a simple zoomorphic figuration, with the shape of the palette representing the body of an animal such as a tortoise, fish or hippopotamus. The second type was more complex, combining symbolic figurations with historical records involving human figures. The scenes depicted in this way commemorate specific events, the real significance of which is difficult to assess. The find-spots of these documents, mostly between the apex of the Delta and Hierakonpolis (the capital of the southern kings), confirm the possibility that the Gerzean culture was gradually spreading. The themes are similar to those that decorate ivory objects throughout the Gerzean phase until the beginning of the Thinite period. They display the characteristic fauna of the Nile valley as well as that of the subdesert regions – wading birds, lions, elephants, bulls, deer, serpents and hippopotamuses – either in the form of animal processions or in scenes that involve confrontations, often between herbivores and carnivores (Vandier 1952: 539ff.; 547), but also involving elephants and serpents or bulls between them.

THE PALETTES

These representations of animals on palettes occur with or without human figures. Among the palettes from Hierakonpolis are two of the animal type, one in the Louvre and the other in the Ashmolean Museum, Oxford. Both scenes are framed by opposing dogs with, between their bodies, an inextricable tangle of animals of the types listed above (Vandier 1952: 579ff.). The animal group on the Ashmolean palette includes a flute-playing fox – a theme which later appears frequently in Egyptian stories – and on the recto, two fantastic animals with necks stretched around in such a way as to encircle the central depression in which the cosmetics were ground. These two animals have numerous equivalents in the fabulous bestiary: already present on the Gebel Tarif knife-handle (Cairo, Egyptian Museum), they are also depicted on the Narmer Palette and resemble the opposing wild beasts on the Gebel el-Arak knife-handle.

Inevitably, there is some speculation as to whether these votive depictions of animals are anything more than prehistoric survivals comparable to the cave paintings of their distant forebears at the Spanish site of Altamira. The animals cannot be ascribed to particular species: each detail is superimposed on a different animal form, the overall effect of the composition being to imbue them with a monstrous appearance that is vaguely evocative of great beasts and reptiles. The elements of these compositions are not irrelevant: they are always impressive animals, wild and primeval, which form the characteristic parts of the objects – their grips, sockets and handles. In the real world these compositions became symbols of the power of wild animals, which man had to confront in his efforts to control the cosmos. The warrior depicted on the Gebel el-Arak knife-handle holds back two opposing wild animals with the sheer force of his hands, while the monsters on the Narmer Palette are held captive and bound together with collars to form the central depression for grinding cosmetics. Human intervention in the scenes on the palettes always aims at the ordering of the world, from the Ostrich Palette (Manchester Museum) to the Hunters' Palette (London, British Museum and Paris, Louvre). The Hunters' Palette is quite explicit, depicting an organized expedition to slaughter and capture wild animals: lions are pierced by arrows, while deer and goats are driven along by dogs and taken captive. Men armed with bows and arrows, spears, axes, throwsticks and pear-shaped maceheads are shown organized in a military fashion, under standards representing a falcon on a perch and a version of the hieroglyphic sign that would eventually stand for the east. There are also depictions of a holy shrine and a bull with two heads recalling the upper section of the Narmer Palette.

The Battlefield Palette (British Museum and Oxford, Ashmolean Museum) depicts a simple conflict between humans that is evidently full of symbolism. It shows warriors, probably of Libyan origin – long-haired, bearded and wearing the penis-sheath – being attacked by a lion and vultures, while two personifications of standards (identical to those in the Hunters' Palette) are leading prisoners with their hands tied behind their backs. In this instance the symbolism is clear: the lion (which, along with the bull, is one of the main images of royal power), assisted by the vulture (the tutelary deity of Hierakonpolis), is ensuring the domination of the southern kingdom of the falcon (not yet identified with Horus, the royal dynastic god) over the northern peoples.

Other stages in this conquest are documented elsewhere. The Bull Palette (Louvre) introduces the second image of royal power, the bull, in the process of goring a man of northern ethnic type; below, a long line of prisoners is tied together with a single cord held by the personified standards of five federated kingdoms. The verso bears a depiction of two crenellated town walls with the names of two conquered peoples written in the form of pictograms.

Two other pieces of evidence regarding the final phase of the conquest also derive from Hierakonpolis. The first is the Scorpion Macehead (Oxford, Ashmolean Museum) on which a king is depicted as a standing figure wearing the white crown of the south. Dressed in a kilt and a belted loincloth to which a bull's tail is attached, he is using a hoe to dig out a canal, while in front of him one man fills a basket with earth and below him others busy themselves around the water next to a pot containing a palm tree. The king, whose name is indicated by a pictogram representing a scorpion, is portrayed in heroic fashion, in characteristic royal postures and beneath a range of standards, among which the future provinces of Egypt can be discerned. From these standards hang lapwings, the *rekhyt* birds whom later texts identify as the inhabitants of Lower Egypt.

The Narmer Palette (Plate 3; Cairo, Egyptian Museum) may depict the final stage of unification. The verso bears the figure of the king, this time identified by two hieroglyphs – the *nar* (fish) and the *mer* (chisel); he is dressed in the same apparel as Scorpion but is also wearing the false beard. He holds a pear-shaped macehead in his right hand, to smash the head of a man clearly intended to represent a northerner, judging from the depiction above his head of a falcon (recognizable as the southern Horus) holding a head emerging from a papyrus thicket. The king is followed by a sandal-bearer and under his feet lie two dead foemen.

The recto of the Narmer Palette shows a scene of the same type as that on the Scorpion Macehead: above and below the central grinding depression two registers celebrate Narmer's triumph. In the lower section a bull destroys a city wall and tramples over a conquered enemy; in the upper section is the king, this time wearing the red crown of the north – although the name inscribed in front of him shows that he is the same person as on the verso. Here he is marching forward, still followed by his sandal-bearer but now preceded by the standards of victorious provinces and by another man who may be the first known

PLATE 3   *The Narmer palette from Hierakonpolis. Schist, h. 0.64 m, recto and verso. (Cairo, Egyptian Museum JE 32169. Photograph: Laurie Platt Winfrey, Inc.)*

vizier. In front of him, beneath the sign of a triumphant Horus making a pilgrimage to the sacred city of Buto, the decapitated dead are laid out with their heads between their legs. Another macehead belonging to the same Narmer (Oxford, Ashmolean Museum; Vandier 1952; 603, fig. 394) perhaps celebrates this victory, showing the king under a jubilee canopy, accompanied by the same courtiers, protected by the same emblems and receiving the homage of captives (and also of 'hundreds of thousands' of animals, if the accompanying caption is to be believed). More remarkable still is the fact that the animals, represented on earlier palettes as wild beasts, are now shown enclosed in pens.

These documents, reinforced by others such as the Libya Palette (British Museum), provide some support for the 'hydraulic' theory of the birth of Egyptian civilization, which argues that the control of irrigation played an essential role in the inauguration of an Early Dynastic state already comprising virtually all the elements of pharaonic power, from religion to writing, economic organization and the system of government (Butzer 1976).

2

Religion and History

The animal symbolism employed in the documents associated with the various stages of the conquest of Egypt is evidence of a direct integration of myth and history. The totemic origins of Egyptian religion can be deduced from the fact that there were emblems representing the various provinces of Egypt (Moret 1923) from the predynastic to the end of the dynastic period. Their symbolic nature is obvious: an oryx on a standard, for instance, represents the region of Beni Hasan; a hare represents the neighbouring province of Ashmunein and a dolphin that of Mendes. It is tempting to see here evidence for the creation of a confederation of geographical or tribal entities, either organized around a divinity whose symbol was reproduced in the local emblem (such as the arrows and shield for the goddess Neith at Sais, the *wasr*-sceptre for Thebes and the fetish of Osiris for Abydos) or crystallized in some symbolic entity (such as the White Walls, representing the city walls of Memphis, or the Land of the Bow, designating the region of Lower Nubia, which had been included within the boundaries of Egypt by conquest).

These divine standards must therefore have represented the earliest stages of Egypt's political development, since each group of people would have been identified by a totem representing the local deity. The existence of this formative totemic phase presupposes the existence of an Egyptian cosmology which was able to explain the way in which power was shared. In other words, each local religious grouping must have formed around a demiurge chosen from among the divine 'family' worshipped in each of the provincial capitals. Each geographical member of the federation comprised the region surrounding a sacred area characterized by the divine precinct, upon which was superimposed the power of such symbols as the White Walls (Memphis) or the Fetish of Osiris (Abydos).

This religious geography thus established the rules of Egyptian political organization since it precisely delimited each region's place in the hierarchy and identified in each locality a representative of the universal system into which they were all integrated. Each god, as the head of his own family, was able to take on the role played by the universal creator at the head of the Egyptian pantheon. There was therefore a great similarity between the cults and chapels of each of the local gods.

The totemic explanation of Egyptian religion is not completely satisfactory, principally because the Egyptian system does not include all the usual elements of totemism, and because the concept of totemism itself does not conform particularly well with the anthropomorphization of the Egyptian gods, the gradual move towards more abstract cosmologies in the dynastic period or the tricky problem of hypostasis, which lies at the heart of the Egyptian theocratic system (Assmann 1984). There are certain similarities with totemic concepts (which are essentially African in origin) but not to the extent of being able to speak of structural borrowings from these systems.

THE COSMOLOGIES

There are three Egyptian cosmologies, but they all represent political variations on a single theme: the sun's creation of the universe from a liquid element, the original archetype for which was supplied by the annual flooding of the Nile. The main system of cosmology was developed at Heliopolis, now a suburb of Cairo but once the ancient holy city where the pharaohs came to have their power consecrated. Not only was the Heliopolitan cosmology the earliest, but it also provided inspiration for Egyptian theologians throughout later periods of history.

The Heliopolitan cosmology described creation according to a scheme which is generally echoed by the other cosmologies. In the beginning was Nun, the uncontrolled liquid element, often translated as 'chaos'. Not a negative element in itself, Nun was simply an uncreated mass, without structure but containing within it the potential seeds of life. This chaotic element did not disappear after creation had taken place; it was held back at the edges of the organized world, occasionally threatening to invade at moments when the equilibrium of the universe was disturbed. It was the dwelling place of negative forces, always quick to interfere in the real world. It was also, in a more general sense, the abode of everything that lay outside the known categories of the

universe, from distressed souls who had not been given appropriate
funerary rites, to stillborn babies without sufficient strength to enter the
world of the living, all floating like drowned bodies.

It was from this chaos that the sun emerged. The origin of the sun
itself was not known, for it was said to have 'come into being out of
itself'. It appeared on a mound of earth covered in pure sand emerging
from water, taking the form of a standing stone, the *benben*. This
benben stone was the focus of a cult in the temple at Heliopolis, which
was considered to be the original site of creation. The mound of earth
clearly evokes the *tell* emerging from the waves at the very height of
the Nile's inundation, and the *benben* was the petrifaction of the sun's
rays, worshipped in the form of a truncated obelisk placed on a
platform. This god who created himself was referred to alternately as
Ra (the sun itself), Atum (the ultimate perfect being) or Khepri (in the
form of a scarab, the name of which signified 'transformation'); this last
was represented by the image of the beetle rolling its dung ball along
the roads.

The demiurge produced the whole of creation out of his own seed,
masturbating to create a pair of deities: Shu (god of dryness) and Tefnut
(goddess of humidity). The evocative meaning of Tefnut's name is 'spit',
which – if the legend of Isis and Ra is to be believed – was another way
of ejecting the divine substance. From the union of the Dry and the
Humid was born a second divine couple: the sky goddess Nut and the
earth god Geb, a woman and a man. The Sky and the Earth had four
children: Isis and Osiris, Seth and Nephthys. This divine ennead,
consisting of four generations, acted as a link between the process of
creation and the appearance of mankind. In fact, the final generation –
Isis, Osiris, Seth and Nephthys – introduced the era of mankind by
integrating the legend of Osiris into the Heliopolitan system. The myth
of Osiris was a model for the suffering that is the fate of all humans.
Seth and Nephthys were sterile, but the fertile Osiris and Isis were the
prototype for the Egyptian royal family: Osiris, king of Egypt, was
treacherously assassinated by his brother Seth, who represented the
negative and violent contradiction of the organizational force that was
symbolized by the pharaoh. After Osiris' death, Seth seized the throne.
Isis, the model wife and widow, helped by her sister Nephthys, pieced
together the dismembered body of her husband. Anubis, the jackal-god,
said to have been born of the illegitimate love between Osiris and
Nephthys, came to Isis' aid by embalming the dead king's body. Isis
then gave birth to Horus, a posthumously conceived son of Osiris
whose name was the same as that of the solar falcon-god at Edfu. Isis
hid Horus in the marshes of the Delta, near the sacred town of Buto,
with the help of the goddess Hathor, the wet-nurse in the form of a

cow. The child grew up and, after a long struggle against his uncle Seth, persuaded the court of the gods presided over by his grandfather Geb to restore to him the inheritance of his father Osiris, who was by then the ruler of the kingdom of the dead.

On to this picture of the realm of the gods were grafted numerous secondary or complementary legends, which were introduced by theologians in order to incorporate local deities, to elaborate the various gods' roles in the cosmology or to achieve the syncretic fusion of several groups. The result of this was a complex tangle of myths which dictate the actions of gods reigning over the world and effectively subject them to the whims of humans. With one exception, there is little discussion in all this of the actual creation of mankind, which seems to have been thought of as having taken place at the same time as the creation of the world. In this exception, the legend of 'the eye of Ra', the sun loses his eye; he sends his children Shu and Tefnut to seek out the fugitive, but time passes and they do not return. He then decides to replace the missing eye with a substitute. When the lost eye reappears and finds that it has been replaced it begins to weep with rage, and its tears (*remut*) give birth to people (*remet*). Ra then transforms the eye into a cobra and places it on his forehead – this is the uraeus, which is given the task of striking down the god's enemies. The anecdotal nature of this story of the creation of mankind is exceptional and its origins may well lie in the punning of the Egyptian words for 'tears' and 'people', which seems to have proved too tempting for the theologians to ignore.

The cosmological theme of the 'damaged' or 'replaced' eye went through several stages of development: it provided an explanation for the creation of the moon, the second eye of Ra that was entrusted to Thoth (the ibis-headed god of the scribes), and for the 'healthy' eye of Horus. It was Horus who lost his eye in the battle against Seth for control of the kingdom of Egypt; Thoth returned it to him and simultaneously transformed it into an archetypal symbol of physical well-being. This is why the eye of Horus was usually depicted on coffins, since it guaranteed that the dead person would have full use of his body.

Ra, the king of the gods, was constantly forced to fight to retain his position of power, since each night, as he journeyed through the afterworld, fierce enemies led by Apophis (personification of negative forces) attempted to carry him off. Horus, standing at the head of the harpooners in the divine barque, helped Ra to defeat the machinations of Apophis, thus legitimizing another contamination of the solar and Osirid myths. The attacks made on the king of the gods sometimes took a more unexpected turn: for example, it was Isis, the Great Magician, who attempted to seize power from Ra by causing him to be bitten by a serpent. This serpent had been fashioned from clay moistened with the saliva that fell from the mouth of the god (who had become a debilitated old man) as he left each morning to light up the universe. The divine king was overcome by this charm fashioned from his own vital energy, and in order to be saved had to reveal the names of his *ka*s to Isis. By finding out the names of his *ka*s, Isis hoped to acquire Ra's power. It is clear that the old god would eventually have defeated the sorceress's plan, but the text breaks off at this point, so the end of the story is unknown.

Egypt also has a myth telling of the rebellion of mankind against its creator, who then decides, on the advice of the assembly of gods, to destroy humanity. For this purpose he sends his eye to earth in the form of the goddess Hathor, the bearer of his messages. In one day she devours a large part of humanity and then goes to sleep. Ra, considering this punishment to be sufficient, pours out beer during the night. The beer mixes with the waters of the Nile, thus taking on the appearance of blood, so that when the goddess wakes up she laps up the drink and is struck down with drunkenness. Mankind is saved but Ra is disappointed with it and withdraws into the heavens on the back of the celestial cow, which is supported by the god Shu. He hands over the administration of the earth to Thoth and gives the serpents, signs of royalty, to Geb. This myth accounts for the separation between mankind and the gods, each being given their own place in the universe, which henceforth possesses space and time: *djt* and *nḥḥ* This legend of appeased wrath recalls the story of the Distant Goddess, a raging lioness which was terrorizing Nubia. A messenger from her father Ra eventually appeased her and escorted her back to Egypt, where she took on the appearance of a female cat guarded by the sun.

The Heliopolitan cosmology seems to have gained its popularity by assimilating the principal myths of Egypt, but it was not the only theological system to achieve this. The city of Hermopolis (now el-Ashmunein), about 300 kilometres south of Cairo, was the capital of the fifteenth nome of Upper Egypt. The system of cosmology that was developed at Hermopolis came to rival the Heliopolitan system. It approached the problem of creation in a different way, treating the sun as the last rather than the first link in the chain. The starting point, however, was the same: a liquid and uncreated chaos in which there were four pairs of frogs and serpents who combined their generative powers to create an egg, which they placed on a mound emerging from the water. These couples were each composed of a single element and its partner: Nun and Nunet, the primordial ocean that is included in the Heliopolitan system; Heh and Hehet, the water that seeks its way; Keku and Keket, darkness; and finally Amun, the hidden god, and his consort

Amaunet. Later, when the last element of the ogdoad, Amun, became the dynastic god *par excellence*, the Theban priesthood succeeded in reconstituting Amun's 'family' on a more human level; as at Heliopolis, this ensured the transition between creation and the human domination of the world.

The Heliopolitan and Hermopolitan systems, like such popular myths as the story of Osiris, present elements drawn from the deepest substratum of civilization, some having resonances in the African civilizations: Anubis recalls the incestuous jackal in a Promethean role which existed prior to the Nommos among the Dogon people of Mali, whose cosmology also depends on eight original gods. There are further African links with Egypt: Amun, for instance, resembles the golden heavenly ram whose brow is adorned with horns and a gourd reminiscent of the solar disc; Osiris recalls the Lebe, whose resurrection is announced by the regrowth of the millet; and finally, each individual was thought to be made up of a soul and a vital essence (Griaule 1966: 28–31, 113–20, 166, 194ff.), which the Egyptians called the *ba* and *ka*.

FROM MYTH TO HISTORY

The third major Egyptian system of cosmology was by far the most sophisticated, from a theological point of view. This system is known from a unique document in the British Museum, dating to the reign of the Kushite ruler Shabaka, at the end of the seventh century BC. It consists of a large granite slab from the temple of Ptah at Memphis, which bears an inscription claiming to be the copy of an old 'worm-eaten' papyrus; it combines the elements of the Heliopolitan and Hermopolitan systems in an attempt to establish the local god Ptah in the role of demiurge. The Heliopolitan and Osirid elements seem to dominate the text, but at the same time there is a clear movement towards greater abstraction in the description of the process of creation, which consists of the combined use of thought and word.

The original version of this text obviously dates to the Old Kingdom, during which Memphis played a primary national role. It can probably be traced back more specifically to the Fifth Dynasty, when the Heliopolitan doctrine was definitively introduced. Another document dating to the Fifth Dynasty is the first known attempt to explicitly describe the link between gods and men: the Palermo Stone.

The Palermo Stone belongs to the category of historical annals, which have survived in relatively large numbers in the form of lists of kings' names, sometimes annotated with commentaries. The most famous of these is the work of Manetho, a priest from Sebennytos (now Samanud on the western bank of the Damietta branch of the Nile Delta) who lived during the reigns of the first two Ptolemies (*c*.305–246 BC). Manetho was the first historian to split the chronology of Egypt into thirty dynasties, from the unification of the land by Menes (who had been assimilated with Narmer) to the Macedonian conquest. Unfortunately, his *Aegyptiaca* has survived only in very fragmentary form in later works (Helck 1956). The lists dating to periods earlier than Manetho are mainly from Ramessid times, the most important being a papyrus written in the reign of Ramesses II, now in the Museo Egizio, Turin. Champollion was the first to work on this document, which bears a dynastic king-list stretching back to the beginning of the New Kingdom. It is clear that a papyrus of this type was the inspiration for 'tablets' such as those in the Hall of Ancestors at Karnak (now in the Louvre), the temple of Sethos I at Abydos (still *in situ*), the neighbouring temple of Ramesses II (now in the British Museum), the Saqqara tomb of Tunroi, a contemporary of Ramesses II, and other lesser examples (Grimal 1986: 597ff.).

The Palermo Stone is a fragmentary slab of black stone bearing a list of kings extending from Aha, the first sovereign of the First Dynasty, until at least the third king of the Fifth Dynasty, Neferirkare. Unfortunately, the text is incomplete and the provenance of the object is unknown, but it is entered in the Palermo Museum as a legacy bequeathed in 1877. Since that date six other fragments have appeared in the antiquities market – these are now at the Egyptian Museum in Cairo and the Petrie Museum, University College, London. The authenticity of these other pieces has been questioned and their connection with the Palermo Stone doubted, resulting in a controversy which has raged for almost a century.

The fragments in Cairo list a number of kings who, in the initial stages of Egyptian history, alternately bear the crowns of Upper and Lower Egypt. Manetho and the Turin Canon have a basic annalistic structure but they include a cosmological narrative of the origins of Egypt. The integration of myth and history is achieved by the introduction of a mythical Golden Age, during which the gods reigned on earth. The royal lists reproduced the narratives of the cosmogonies, particularly that of Memphis, which describes the moment at the beginning of time when the divine potter Ptah (whose role here is close to that of the ram-god Khnum) created humanity on his potter's wheel and fashioned the receptacle of the divine spark of life from clay, a material that had been at the disposal of mankind since the beginning of time. Ra then succeeded Ptah on the throne. As the sun who creates life by dispelling the darkness, Ra is the prototype for kingship, which he then passes on to Shu, the god of the air and separator of heaven and earth.

In this myth the principal events of creation were recounted. The Greek compilers of Manetho's text made no mistake in this, identifying Ptah and Ra with the blacksmith-god Hephaistos and the sun-god Helios respectively. According to Diodorus Siculus, Shu and his successor Geb (the earth-god) play the roles of Kronos and Zeus, thus implying that Geb, like Zeus, was the father of humanity. History was therefore presented simply as a continuation of myth, and as far as the Egyptians were concerned there was no other solution to the transition from gods to men: Egyptian society was a daily re-enactment of creation and as such it was a reflection of the order of the cosmos on all its levels. Its system of organization therefore automatically followed that of the universe as a whole – a fact which cannot fail to influence contemporary social analysis.

Osiris succeeded Geb and, after the usurpation of Seth, Horus rose to the throne. The Turin Canon then presents a sequence of three gods: Thoth, whose role is described above, Maat and another Horus whose name is missing. Maat occupies a unique place in the Egyptian pantheon: she is not so much a goddess as an abstract entity. She represents the equilibrium which the universe has reached through the process of creation, enabling it to conform to its true nature. As such she is the moderator of all things, from justice to the integration of a dead man's soul into the universal order at the time of the final judgment. She therefore serves as the counterbalance when hearts are weighed on the scales of Thoth. Maat is also the food of the gods, whom she imbues with harmony. The reign of Maat was a Golden Age which each ruler undertook to recreate by confronting the traditional negative forces that each day attempted to obstruct the course of the sun across the sky – the time of Maat was the beginning of cyclical history.

Nine further gods, whom Eusebius identifies with the Greek heroes, then came to the throne. Like the heroes, these beings ensured the transition of power from the gods to the founders of human society; they were known as the 'spirits' (*akhw*) of Hierakonpolis, Buto and Heliopolis, and the last ones were described as the 'companions of Horus'. Clearly, this succsesion of gods from different localities, concluding with devotees of Horus, is a direct reflection of the struggles that led up to the unification of the country, and the Turin Canon identifies several local descendants of these figures. The first 'king of Upper and Lower Egypt' (*nsw bity*) is unequivocally named as Meni, his name actually being written twice, but with one important difference – the first time his name is written with a human determinative and the second time with a divine determinative (Gardiner 1959: pl. I; Málek 1982: 95). Is this Meni – or Menes according to Eratosthenes and Manetho – to be identified with Narmer, as is generally thought, or is it simply a literary method of designating 'someone' in general, whose name is lost? One possible contender might then be King Scorpion or perhaps even some earlier ruler whose name has not survived. It is difficult to see why Meni's name is repeated. Is it perhaps because he passed from being 'so-and-so' to being 'king so-and-so', changing his name at the same time as he changed his status, with the text regarding him as an incarnation of all of the local holders of power combined into one archetypal ruler of a united country? This would explain the fact that the Palermo Stone mentions only Aha as the first king, whose 'Horus name' might perhaps have been Narmer-Menes.

Palermo Stone
AHA — 1st King

'Horus name' might have been
Narmer — Menes

Twin Canon

meni —— 1st King upper/lower
/menes   Egypt

3

The Thinite Period

[handwritten: This = near ABYDOS]
[handwritten: AHA ~ 1st]
[handwritten: AHA = NARMER]

THE FIRST KINGS

Aha is the first known king of the First Dynasty. Manetho described the first two dynasties as 'Thinite', from the name of the kings' supposed city of origin: a place called This, near Abydos. The tombs of all of the First Dynasty kings have been found at Abydos, as well as those of some from the Second Dynasty. Most of the Thinite kings, however, had a second tomb in the region of Memphis. The state of these tombs has prevented confirmation of the theory that the early kings were actually buried near the new political capital of Egypt, but in order to respect the dual nature of the land were also provided with a cenotaph in Upper Egypt, from which their power was supposed to derive, at a site which would soon be known as the sacred city of Osiris.

These two dynasties formed a single entity, lasting from 3150 to 2700 BC – a period of almost five hundred years during which the Egyptian civilization developed its characteristic traits. The Thinite period is a poorly known phase, essentially because of a lack of surviving texts. The main source of evidence, apart from the Palermo Stone, is the funerary equipment from the tombs at Abydos and Saqqara.

As overall founder of the Thinite period, Aha is usually attributed with having achieved rather more perhaps than was actually the case. If he was the same person as Narmer then he was the inaugurator of the cult of the crocodile-god Sobek in the Faiyum region as well as the founder of Memphis. He would probably have established both his administration and the cult of the Apis-bull at Memphis. It is likely that he also organized the newly unified land by instigating a policy of conciliation with the north. Such a policy may be deduced from the fact that the name of his wife, Neithhotep ('may Neith be appeased') was formed from the name of the goddess Neith, originally worshipped at Sais in the Delta. The tomb of Neithhotep, excavated at Naqada, was provided with a large amount of equipment including a tablet bearing the name of Aha. It seems that Aha founded a temple of Neith at Sais and celebrated the festivals of Anubis and Sokar (the mummified falcon), as well as his own royal jubilee or *sed* festival. He appears to have enjoyed a peaceful reign, although this did not prevent him from initiating a long series of wars against the Nubians and Libyans – Egypt's southern and western neighbours – and establishing trading relations with Syria-Palestine (judging from the mention of boats on the Palermo Stone). These military and economic initiatives were carried on by his successors. The reign of Aha, which must have ended in about 3100 BC, was thus reasonably well documented on the whole. He had two tombs: one at Saqqara and the other at Abydos.

The choice of Aha's successor probably did not pass without problems. The Turin Canon leaves a blank space between Meni and his successor It(i), who was then followed by a second Iti, which was perhaps simply the Horus name of King Djer. This gap in the record may possibly reflect a court quarrel as to which concubine's son should inherit the throne. These questions of filiation, which are very difficult to solve given the scantiness of the documentation, are equally relevant for the succession of Djer. Djer's daughter would have been Queen Merneith ('beloved of Neith'), whose tomb has been excavated in the royal necropolis at Abydos. It has been possible to deduce that Merneith was the wife of his successor Wadjit, since texts in her tomb identify her as the mother of Den, the fourth king of the First Dynasty. The reign of Djer was characterized by further developments in foreign policy, including expeditions into Nubia (as far as Wadi Halfa), Libya and the Sinai (judging from the fact that his tomb contained jewellery made of turquoise, which was traditionally imported from Sinai). He also set about the economic and religious organization of the country, establishing a palace at Memphis and building a tomb for himself at Abydos, where he may even have been the historical prototype of Osiris. He was buried along with the rest of his court, although this does not necessarily mean, as was long thought, that his courtiers were obliged to die violently in order to accompany their sovereign into the grave (*LÄ* I, 1111, n. 9). This is, however, the first case of the pharaoh's recognition of the funerary needs of his subordinates, whose tombs were linked with his in much the same way as they were later to be associated with the great royal necropolises. Judging from the funerary furniture in the private tombs of his contemporaries, the reign of Djer was a time of great prosperity.

CALENDARS AND DATING

A single text from Djer's reign has affected the whole chronology of the First Dynasty by raising the question of the type of calendar being used. This text is an ivory tablet on which there is said to be a representation of the dog-star Sirius in the guise of the goddess Sothis, who was depicted in the form of a seated cow bearing between her horns a young plant symbolizing the year (Vandier 1952: 842–3; Drioton and Vandier 1962: 161). This simple sign would seem to indicate that from the reign of Djer onwards the Egyptians had established a link between the heliacal rising and the beginning of the year – in other words, they had invented the solar calendar.

It seems that at first they used a lunar calendar, many traces of which have survived. But when they realized the discrepancy between this lunar method of computation and the passage of real time, they changed to a calendar based on the most easily observed and regular phenomenon available to them: the flooding of the Nile. They therefore divided up the year into three seasons of four thirty-day months, with each season corresponding to the agricultural pattern determined by the rise and fall of the Nile. The first season was the inundation itself (Akhet), the second was the period of germination and growth (Peret) and the third was the time of harvest (Shemmu). It emerged, however, that the first flooding of the Nile, which was chosen as the beginning of each new year, was observable at the latitude of Memphis, which is considered to have been the centre of a united Egypt, at the same moment as the heliacal rising of Sirius. This phenomenon took place according to the Julian calendar on July 19th (or about a month earlier according to the Gregorian calendar), but not every July 19th. Since the real solar year is actually 365 days and six hours, the discrepancy of a quarter of a day per year gradually lengthened the gap between the two phenomena. This discrepancy could only be corrected after a complete cycle had elapsed over a period of 1460 years, which is now known as a 'Sothic period'. The syncronization of the first day of the solar year and the rising of Sirius was recorded at least once in Egyptian history, in AD 139. It is therefore possible, due to the various points in time recorded by the Egyptians themselves, to establish precise dates within these Sothic periods, the terminal points of which can be dated to 1317, 2773 and 4323 BC. The ninth year of the reign of Amenophis I, for example, corresponds to 1537 or 1517 BC, depending on the precise location at which the phenomena were observed, and the seventh year of Sesostris III corresponds to 1877 BC. The date of 4323 BC is thought unlikely to have been the first year of the Egyptian solar calendar, since the archaeological remains suggest that the civilization would not have been sufficiently developed at this period. The date 2773, on the other hand, is a good candidate for the beginning of the calendar, although it is later than the reign of Djer. It is arguable, anyway, that the presence of Sothis on the ivory tablet is not necessarily proof of the use of the solar calendar. The fact that the phenomenon of the Sothic rising was recognized does not automatically imply that a new calendar had been adopted. Just as the civil and religious calendars coexisted thoughout Egyptian history, so it seems reasonable to suppose that the lunar calendar was still flourishing in the time of Djer, and that it was not replaced by the solar calendar until the next Sothic period began, at the end of the Second Dynasty.

THE END OF THE FIRST DYNASTY

Very little is known about Djer's successor, Djet or Wadjit (or 'Serpent' if his name is taken as a pure pictogram), except that he led an expedition to the Red Sea, perhaps with the aim of exploiting the mines in the Eastern Desert. Djet's tomb at Abydos contained numerous stelae, including a magnificent limestone example inscribed with his name (Paris, Louvre).

The reign of Den (Udimu), the fourth king of the dynasty, appears to have been a glorious and prosperous one. He limited the power of the high court officials, which had previously been allowed to grow dangerously during Merneith's regency at the beginning of his reign. He pursued a vigorous foreign policy, rapidly turning his attention to the Near East with an 'Asiatic' campaign in the first year of his reign. He even brought back a harem of female prisoners, an act which was to be copied hundreds of years later by Amenophis III. This military activity, along with an expedition into the Sinai to deal with the bedouin, must have influenced his choice of 'Khasty' (meaning 'foreigner' or 'man of the desert') as his *nsw-bity* (King of Upper and Lower Egypt) name, which was changed to Usaphais in Manetho's Greek version. He was the first Egyptian king to add to his titulature this third name; the *nsw-bity* title was evidently intended to reflect his active internal policy, including the building of a fortress, celebration of religious ceremonies to the gods Atum and Apis, and a national census (if the Palermo Stone is to be believed).

Den also seems to have pursued a policy of conciliation with northern Egypt, which was expressed not only through the name of his wife, Merneith, but also by the creation of a post of 'chancellor of the King of Lower Egypt'. The tomb of Hemaka, a holder of this office, was discovered at Saqqara. It contained a quantity of rich funerary furniture as well as a wooden tablet bearing the name of Djer which may have been a record of Den's *sed* festival (Hornung and Staehelin 1974: 17). The inscription on this tablet includes the earliest depiction of a mummy, perhaps that of Djer (Vandier 1952: 845–8). This is surprising in view of the fact that there is no other evidence for the practice of mummification until some time later. In the tomb built by Den at Abydos a granite pavement was found, the first known example of stone-built architecture, which until then had been exclusively of mud brick.

Den's reign is estimated to have lasted for about fifty years, which helps to explain the comparative brevity of the reign of his successor, Anedjib (Andjyeb, Enezib), whose name means 'the man with the bold heart'. Anedjib's other name, as King of Upper and Lower Egypt, was Merpubia (or Miebis according to Manetho). He probably only came to the throne late in life – so late in fact that he very quickly celebrated his *sed* festival, or royal jubilee. This ceremony took its name from the word for a bull's tail, and perhaps also from the name of the canine deity Sed, who was associated with Wepwawet, the 'opener of the ways', the jackal to whom Anubis passed on his funerary attributes. The precise origin of the *sed* festival is obscure, but it was a ritual renewal of power which was intended to demonstrate the king's vigour, theoretically after thirty years of his reign. It was basically a re-enactment of the king's coronation ritual, with the presentation of the two crowns and the symbols of power over the two lands of Egypt in pavilions devoted to each kingdom. There was also a more practical aspect of the ritual, comprising a race and a processional visit to the national gods in their chapel. Finally, the king enacted various rites relating to birth and foundation. This ceremony was an occasion for the issue of commemorative objects, including – in the Thinite period – stone vases bearing the king's titulature. There are several surviving vases celebrating the jubilee of Anedjib in his new palace at Memphis with the significant additional name of 'protection surrounds Horus'.

It was in Anedjib's reign that the 'Two Lords' name (the name placed under the protection of Horus and Seth) was introduced; this title reunited the two divine antagonists of the north and the south in the person of the king. In other words, the king not only symbolized the duality of the nation but also wielded the power of Horus (which maintained the natural equilibrium of Egypt) and the destructive potential of Seth (which could be unleashed on the world outside Egypt).

The end of the First Dynasty is a problematic period, since it is clear that the unusually long duration of Den's reign had led to a struggle for succession to the throne after his death. The reign of Semerkhet certainly represented a distinct change from the rule of his predecessor. He evidently attempted to emphasize his legitimacy by having Anedjib's name erased from his jubilee vases. This very legitimacy was, however, called into question by the omission of Semerkhet's own name from the Saqqara king-list. His titulature certainly indicates a previous career, perhaps in a priestly role, before his rise to the throne. His Horus name was 'companion of the gods' and his *nebty* name was 'he whom the two mistresses guard' – the two mistresses being Nekhbet, the vulture-goddess of Nekheb (Elkab), and Wadjet, the serpent-goddess of Pe and Dep (Buto), who were the patron-goddesses of the south and north of Egypt respectively.

THE SECOND DYNASTY

Both Semerkhet and his successor Ka'a (who was probably also his son) had themselves buried at Abydos. Ka'a's reign was the last of the First Dynasty; this change of dynasty is reported by Manetho without explanation. The centre of power seems to have shifted to Memphis, judging from the fact that at least the first three kings of the Second Dynasty had themselves buried in the Saqqara necropolis. Another indication of this geographical shift of power was the name of the first ruler of the Second Dynasty: Hetepsekhemwy, 'the Two Powers are at peace'. The 'Two Powers' were clearly Horus and Seth, and this interpretation is confirmed by Hetepsekhemwy's *nebty* name: 'the Two Mistresses are at peace', which must be another allusion to the political opposition between north and south. This north–south confrontation was not necessarily an actual physical struggle – it more likely referred to the country's tendency to split into these two regions at any time of conflict. The royal family built up strong links with the eastern Delta, and particularly the region of Bubastis: they practised the cult of the cat-goddess Bastet (from which the name Bubastis derives) as well as the worship of Soped, a local falcon-god who was soon syncretized with Horus, son of Osiris. It was also during this period that the cult of the sun-god was established, although the name of Ra at this stage only appeared in the Horus name of Hetepsekhemwy's successor, Reneb (meaning either 'lord of the sun' or, more likely and with less hubris, 'Ra is (my) lord'). Ra completely took over the role of his progenitor, the 'god of the horizon'. This religious change is confirmed by the name of Reneb's successor, Nynetjer (Nutjeren), 'he who belongs to the god'.

Reneb and Nynetjer may have been buried in a pair of tombs under the causeway of the pyramid of Wenis at Saqqara, since clay cylinder sealings bearing their names were found there. This attribution, however, in the absence of any other written evidence, is far from certain; such seals are not exclusively found in the tombs of the kings whose names they bear. They have also occasionally been found in the tombs of private individuals or even in those of later kings: the tomb of Khasekhemwy at Abydos, for instance, contained a cylinder seal bearing the name of Nynetjer but this is not considered to cast any doubt on Khasekhemwy's ownership of the tomb.

Another set of documents, stone vases, are also often found out of their original historical context. The inscriptions on the vases are as crucial as the ivory tablets of the First Dynasty in terms of providing information about historical events and about the way in which the administration of the country was organized. Some very important caches of vases have survived, such as the group dating to the reign of Nynetjer that was found in the subterranean galleries of the Step Pyramid of Djoser, the second king of the Third Dynasty. This discovery confirmed the tendency of this type of historical evidence to remain in use, passed on from one generation to another, regardless of the fact that they might have already been used for some other purpose. In the case of Djoser's tomb, the vases remained in the same kind of context (a royal tomb), whereas the royal jubilee vases of the Second Dynasty often ended up in quite different contexts: they were originally handed out to dignitaries and were then carefully preserved by their families, eventually to appear among the funerary equipment of some distant descendant of the original recipient.

Since Weneg and Sened, the successors of Nynetjer, are known only from inscriptions on vases from Djoser's pyramid complex (apart from references to them in king-lists), it is possible that their power was limited to the Memphite area. Sened was a contemporary of King Peribsen, a statue of whom was most probably placed in Sened's tomb, especially considering that there was a Fourth Dynasty personage describing himself as 'chief of the *w'b*-priests of Peribsen in the necropolis of Sened, in the temple and the other places'. Peribsen's local successor Sekhemib, 'the man with the powerful heart' (one theory suggests that these two were actually the same man), built him a tomb at Abydos containing stone vases, copper objects and two stelae bearing the name of the king in a *serekh* (a representation of a palace ground-plan with its distinctive panelled façade depicted in elevation along the lower edge; the king's name was inscribed in the space delimited by the plan). The whole *serekh* ensemble constituted the normal method of writing the Horus name of kings; usually the palace façade was surmounted by the Horus falcon, but the Horus name of Peribsen was surmounted by a depiction of the god Seth.

These various factors suggest that relations between the northern and southern kingdoms had begun to deteriorate by the end of Nynetjer's reign, perhaps as a result of the new religious orientation adopted by Reneb, which would have been too favourable towards the north. The omission from both king-lists of Peribsen and his Abydene successor, combined with the choice of Seth as tutelary deity, would appear to indicate either that the south had reasserted its independence (Peribsen, for example, appointed a 'chancellor of the king of Upper Egypt') or that the southern kingdom no longer recognized the Memphite sovereigns, who were traditionally to be regarded as the legitimate holders of power according to the system that would eventually become the status quo. The power of Peribsen extended at least as far as Elephantine, where seal impressions bearing his name were found in 1985 (and where a temple of Seth is known to have existed in later times). The fact that Sened and Peribsen were eventually the focus of a joint funerary cult in the Fourth Dynasty suggests that this north-south conflict was not a violent one – or at least not during Peribsen's reign.

The situation changed considerably with the appearance of Khasekhem, 'The Powerful (Horus) is crowned', who was a native of Hierakonpolis. On the occasion of his coronation Khasekhem made a temple offering of several objects commemorating his victory over northern Egypt, comprising inscriptions on stone vases and two statues (one of schist and one of limestone) showing him seated on a low-backed chair. These statues, virtually the first of their type, already conform to the canon of royal Egyptian representations. In both works the king is enveloped in a *sed* festival robe and wears the white crown of Upper Egypt. This does not necessarily suggest that he considered Upper Egypt to be the source of his power: bearing in mind the clothes in which he is dressed it seems likely that these two statues formed part of a group, of a kind found elsewhere, showing the king at the time of his coronation rituals in the alternate guises of ruler of Upper and Lower Egypt, according to the different stages of the *sed* festival. The bases of both statues are decorated with figures of prisoners piled up in a tangle of dislocated bodies.

It is thought likely that the victory over the north was the reason why he later changed his name to Khasekhemwy: 'the Two Powers are crowned', placing both Horus and Seth over the *serekh*. At the same time he chose 'the Two Mistresses are at peace through him' for his name as King of Upper and Lower Egypt. His establishment of control over Egypt – and apparently the reunification of the country – was accompanied by an energetic building policy that led to technical advances in architecture. Khasekhemwy built in stone at Elkab, Hierakonpolis and Abydos, where his tomb is the largest of the Second Dynasty.

For no apparent reason, Manetho ends the Thinite period with the regin of Khasekhemwy. This cut-off point seems particularly surprising given the family links between Khasekhemwy and the Third Dynasty king Djoser: one of Khasekhemwy's wives was the princess Nimaatapis, who was eventually to be the mother of Djoser. It is clear, however, that the late Second Dynasty was already more of a 'Memphite' than a 'Thinite' monarchy. The reign of Khasekhemwy simply brought an end to the political opposition of north and south and established the basic economic, religious and political systems of the dynastic period. His reign was the beginning of a great epoch during which Egyptian civilization reached a level of artistic skill and perfection which is now regarded as archetypal.

THE THINITE MONARCHY

The Thinite monarchy was very similar to that of the Third Dynasty, and most of the major institutions were in place before the reign of Djoser. The principle of transmission of power through direct filial inheritance, on which the pharaonic tradition was based, had already been established, since the king was no longer described only as Horus. He now had three names, forming the basis of his titulature: the Horus name (which expressed his hypostatic role as divine heir to the throne), the name of King of Upper and Lower Egypt (*nsw-bity*) and, from the reign of Semerkhet onwards, a *nebty* name (which probably reflects the career of the crown prince before his anticipated coronation). The role of the king's wife in the transmission of power should also be noted: she was 'the one who unites the Two Lords', 'the one who sees Horus and Seth' and also 'the mother of the royal children'.

The organization of the royal household had already taken on the form that it would continue to assume throughout the pharaonic period. The royal palace, which was probably the mud-brick prototype for the funerary architecture of the time, accommodated both the harem (the king's private apartments) and the administration. The royal 'house' was effectively the infrastructure surrounding the king. Although it was the king who theoretically held all the reins of power, in practice he was helped by high officials. It is not always easy to untangle the purely honorific titles from those that indicate a genuine administrative post, but nevertheless it is possible to gain a general idea of the basic elements of the administration.

The king was surrounded by more or less specialized advisors, such as the 'controller of the Two Thrones', 'he who is placed at the head of the king' or the 'chief of the secrets of the decrees'. This latter title suggests that there was already an explicit legal system. As the heir of the gods, the king was holder of the theocratic power vested in him. He was, however, only the temporary holder of power: at the time of his coronation the title deeds of the country were handed over to him – in principle directly from the hands of the god (Grimal 1986: 441) – on condition that he governed with respect for the laws of the land, which were actually identical to the laws of the universe. In order to fulfil this role, the king issued decrees. In a sense every word uttered by the king constituted a decree with the full force of the law, whether it was fixed in writing or not – as in the Islamic system of *daher*. It seems that the interpretation of these decrees comprised, along with recourse to written laws and the consultation of jurisprudence, the basis of the Egyptian legal system.

As early as the Second Dynasty the circle of officials around the king included a *tjaty*, but it was not until the Fourth Dynasty that the office of *tjaty* seems to have acquired the enormous power that made it comparable to that of the Ottoman vizier. There was also a chancellory and a complete scribal hierarchy – the omnipresent linchpin of the system. The first known chancellor of the king of Lower Egypt was Hemaka, who held office during the reign of Den, and the first chancellor of Upper Egypt seems to have appeared in the reign of Peribsen. The two chancellors were responsible for the census, the organization of irrigation and everything relating to land registration. They dealt with the collection of taxes and the redistribution of the goods which were handed over to 'treasuries' and 'granaries', particularly grain, herds and food of all kinds. They then co-ordinated the redistribution of these goods among the great bodies of workers employed by the state both in the administration and in the temples.

These representatives of central power dealt with local areas split up into provinces, which the Greeks called 'nomes' and the Egyptians at first called *sepat* and then *qâh* from the Amarna period (*c*.1350 BC) onwards. Although the provinces were not actually identified as such until the time of Djoser, it has already been demonstrated in chapter 2 that the emblems representing each of the nomes date back to the period before the unification of Egypt. These were the territories of the ancient provincial dynasties, which managed to retain their individuality and independence in the traditional 'topographical lists'. These lists, attested from the reign of Neuserre onwards, divide the country into the twenty-two nomes of Upper Egypt and the twenty nomes of Lower Egypt.

There were federal authorities concerned with each of the two kingdoms, such as the 'Council of Ten of Upper Egypt' and the 'Official in charge of Nekhen', who must have played a role close to that of Viceroy of the South. They dealt with the local officials, the nomarchs (known as the *adj-mer*: 'administrators'), who were themselves assistants to an assembly, the *djadjat*.

Nothing is known about national military organization during the

Thinite period, and conscription is not attested until later, but it is usually assumed that the basic pharaonic military system was already in place. A good idea of military architecture at the time can be obtained from the representations of fortresses and the remains of the Archaic enclosure at Hierakonpolis.

Evidence for domestic architecture is restricted to gaming pieces in the form of houses and representations of 'palace façades' in tombs. Funerary decoration is the principal source of evidence for Thinite art, while the equipment from both royal tombs and the great private tombs, such as that of Hemaka, suggest that there was a flourishing artistic tradition. Ivory and bone objects were prominent in this tradition, as well as 'Egyptian faience', ceramics and stone vases. Small-scale statuary has been found in large numbers, incorporating a variety of human types: prisoners, children and numerous female figurines (which are not merely 'concubines of the dead', but also suggest the appearance of women in everyday life). Many animal figurines, carved in a number of different materials, have survived. Some popular themes of later times were already firmly established, as in the case of the female monkey cradling her young in her arms (cf. Vandier 1952: 976; Valloggia 1986: 80). Large-scale statuary – still a long way from the gracefulness of the Old Kingdom – was generally rough, and figures tended to be stiffly posed; there were some elegant exceptions however, such as the black granite figure of a man erroneously known as the 'Lady of Naples' (Naples, Museo Nazionale), the statue of Nedjemankh (Louvre) and an anonymous figure at the Ägyptisches Museum, Berlin.

Part II

The Classical Age

Part II

The Classical Age

4

The Old Kingdom

THE BEGINNING OF THE THIRD DYNASTY

Ironically, the Third Dynasty is less well known than the two earlier dynasties, and there is still no agreement on its origins, which were dominated by the personality of Djoser. King Djoser, however, was not the first ruler of the Third Dynasty; although the archaeological evidence and the king-lists tend to suggest that he was its founder, there are reasonable grounds for suggesting that the first Third Dynasty king would actually have been Nebka, who is mentioned in Papyrus Westcar. He was also known to Manetho, and a priest of Nebka's mortuary cult is known to have lived in the reign of Djoser. However, nothing is known of Nebka's reign since this section is missing from the Palermo Stone. He and Djoser would have reigned for about the same length of time. Their parentage is not documented; it is possible that Djoser may have been either the brother or son of Nebka.

The situation is even more complicated in the period after Djoser's reign: according to the Turin Canon he reigned for nineteen years and was succeeded by a man named Djoserti or Djoser(i)teti, who is not mentioned in any other records. As a result of Zakaria Goneim's discovery of an unfinished pyramid at Saqqara designed along the same lines as Djoser's, it is now known that his successor was called Sekhemkhet (Lauer 1988: 143ff.), but it is not clear whether Sekhemkhet was the same person as Djoserti. It is by no means easy to prove this identification, because the Third Dynasty was marked by a change in the royal titles whereby the king's 'first name', which was usually that given to a prince at the time of his birth, became the 'Golden Horus' name. In the Thinite period the king's first name had been the 'King of Upper and Lower Egypt' (*nsw-bity*) name, which he was given at the time of his coronation. The *nsw-bity* name instead became more closely associated with the Horus name.

The situation is further complicated by evidence of another Third Dynasty king called Sanakht, who is known from seals found at Elephantine. The German Archaeological Institute has revealed a town and enclosure of the Thinite period at Elephantine, which seems to have acted as the southern border post of Egypt in the First Dynasty. Evidence of Sanakht has also appeared at a tomb in the necropolis of Beit Khallaf, north of Abydos. It was once believed that this was the tomb of Sanakht himself, but it is now thought to be that of one of his officials. Sanakht's own tomb is therefore still undiscovered, although the most likely location would be at Saqqara, to the west of the funerary complex of Djoser, where seal impressions bearing the name of Sanakht have been found. It is not clear whether he was the first or second king of the Third Dynasty, or indeed whether he was the same person as Nebka, but his reign cannot have lasted any longer than six years according to Manetho. All that can be said of Sanakht is that like the equally obscure Sekhemkhet his name was recorded at the Wadi Maghara turquoise mines, in the western Sinai peninsula.

DJOSER AND IMHOTEP

Djoser, whose Horus name was Netjerykhet, owes his fame not only to his building works but also to Egyptian historiography itself. One of the major figures in the Egyptian annals, he is famed for having invented stone-built architecture with the help of his architect Imhotep (who was himself deified in the Late Period). Djoser's reign has tended to be associated with a particular view of the monarchy, which is perhaps best expressed in a well-known apocryphal Ptolemaic inscription on the island of Sehel near Elephantine. This inscription, engraved in the rock-face at Sehel by Ptolemy V Epiphanes over 2000 years after Djoser's time, describes the action taken by Djoser to deal with a famine during his reign. Djoser complains of the state of the country:

> My heart was in sore distress, for the Nile had not risen for seven years. The grain was not abundant, the seeds were dried up, everything that one had to eat was in pathetic quantities, each person was denied his harvest. Nobody could walk any more: the children were in tears; the young people were struck down; the old people's hearts were sad and their legs were bent when they sat on the ground, and their hands were hidden away. Even the courtiers were going without, the temples were closed and the sanctuaries were covered in dust. In short, everything in existence was afflicted.

The king looks back into the archives, attempting to find the origins of the Nile flood and to understand the role of Khnum, the ram-god of

Elephantine, in the rising of the waters. He then makes an offering to Khnum, and the god appears to him in a dream, promising: 'I will cause the Nile to rise up for you. There will be no more years when the inundation fails to cover any area of land. The flowers will sprout up, their stems bending with the weight of the pollen.'

Ptolemy V Epiphanes was no doubt actually referring to himself in the guise of Djoser, as he coped with the combined effects of famine and the revolt of the successors of the Meroitic king Ergamenes. But the effect of the text is to identify Djoser as the founder of the Memphite dynasty. Ptolemy V was thus able to associate himself with the origins of the Egyptian national tradition and the much-documented image of kingship, in which the literate and pious ruler did not hesitate to delve back into the theological and historical sources to rediscover the original cosmology and the fundamental patterns of the past. Djoser and Imhotep were both men of this type, but they are known more from legend than from historical fact.

It has only proved possible to identify Djoser with Netjerykhet because of ancient tourists' graffiti at his pyramid, or sources such as the *Famine Stele* that confirm the importance of Memphis during his reign. Strangely enough, Imhotep the courtier is now better known than Djoser the king, and it was Imhotep, rather than Djoser, who later became the object of a popular cult.

Imhotep is thought to have lived until the reign of Huni, in other words almost to the end of the Third Dynasty. His role never seems to have been that of a politician: the only offices he is known to have held are high priest of Heliopolis, lector-priest and chief architect. It was his post as architect that gave him such fame, but the legend that survived him shows that quite apart from his architectural work he quickly developed a reputation as the most striking personality of his time. The literature of the New Kingdom describes him as patron of scribes, not because of his qualities as a writer but because of his role as a personification of wisdom – and therefore also of education, the principal form taken by wisdom. His intellectual, rather than literary, abilities provide evidence of the offices that he probably held under Djoser. In fact it was in recognition of his achievements as a wise counsellor – which were identical to those that Egyptian religion recognized in Ptah, the creator-god of Memphis – that Imhotep was described in the Turin Canon as the son of Ptah. This was the first stage in a process of heroicization that led eventually to him becoming a local god of Memphis, served by his own priesthood and having his own mythology, in which he was considered to be an intermediary on behalf of men beset by the difficulties of daily life, specializing particularly in medical problems. The Greeks, who knew him as Imouthes, recognized this specialization by equating him with their own god of medicine, Asklepios. In fact, the cult of Imhotep was to spread from Alexandria to Meroe (via a temple of Imhotep at Philae), and even survived the pharaonic civilization itself by finding a place in Arab tradition, especially at Saqqara, where his tomb was supposed to be located. Djoser, on the other hand, was not deified, and he only achieved immortality through his pyramid – the first example of a new architectural form that was to be adopted by his successors until the end of the Middle Kingdom.

THE END OF THE THIRD DYNASTY

The end of the Third Dynasty was hardly any clearer than its beginning had been, and it has proved difficult to reconcile the documentary information provided by king-lists with the evidence supplied by archaeologists. In the absence of explicit historical texts, the archaeological data have supplied the basis for a succession of kings based on the development of the architectural form of royal tombs. At the site of Zawiyet el-Aryan, midway between Giza and Abusir, two pyramidal tombs have been excavated; the southernmost tomb (known as the 'Layer Pyramid') closely resembles the pyramid complexes of Djoser and Sekhemkhet at Saqqara.

The Layer Pyramid, which was probably unfinished, has been ascribed by means of inscriptions on vases to Horus Khaba, an otherwise unknown ruler. Khaba is perhaps to be linked with King Huni, who is himself cited by the Saqqara king-list and the Turin Canon, where he is credited with a twenty-four-year reign in the first quarter of the twenty-sixth century BC. Huni's position as last king in the dynasty is confirmed by a literary text composed, if the Ramessid miscellanies are to be believed, by the scribe Kaires. This text is an *Instruction*, said to be for the edification of Kagemni, a contemporary of King Teti. Kagemni was a vizier and was eventually buried near Teti's pyramid at Saqqara. Like Imhotep, he had become a legendary figure since the end of the Old Kingdom and his career was thought to have begun in Snofru's reign. Indeed, the text of the *Instruction* concludes in this way: 'Then the majesty of King Huni died; the majesty of King Sneferu was raised up as the beneficent king in this whole land. Then Kagemni was made mayor of the city and vizier' (Papyrus Prisse, 2, 7–9; Lichtheim 1973: 50).

If Huni was definitely the last Third Dynasty king, the other king who built at Zawiyet el-Aryan – whose Horus name, according to graffiti, was Nebka(re) or Neferka(re) – also has to be accommodated in the list of Third Dynasty rulers. The architecture of this king's pyramid dates stylistically to the Third Dynasty, or at least represents a revival of the style of that period. But it is doubtful whether architectural style should be considered sufficient reason for him to be identified either with the Saqqara king-list's Nebkare (Manetho's Mesochris) or with one of Huni's predecessors.

It is not yet possible to give a satisfactory account of the Third Dynasty, but archaeological research may yet provide the data for more sense to be made of it. The change to the Fourth Dynasty is equally difficult to understand, but the most concrete surviving evidence of change is the transferral of the royal necropolis southwards, from Zawiyet el-Aryan to Maidum and Dahshur, before returning north from Cheops' reign onwards.

SNOFRU

Snofru's mother Meresankh, the founder of the Fourth Dynasty, was not of royal blood – doubtless she was one of Huni's concubines. There is no definite proof of this, but if she was, her son would have married one of her half-sisters, Hetepheres I, (the mother of Cheops and another daughter of Huni) in order to confirm by blood the legitimacy of his rule. This relationship set the tone for the complex genealogies of the Fourth Dynasty – even the briefest study of the period shows that the royal family was deeply involved in the actual administration of the country.

Like his Third Dynasty predecessors, Djoser and Nebka, Snofru soon became a legendary figure, and literature in later periods credited him with a genial personality. He was even deified in the Middle Kingdom, becoming the ideal king whom later Egyptian rulers such as Ammenemes I sought to emulate when they were attempting to legitimize their power. Snofru's enviable reputation with later rulers, which according to the onomastica was increased by his great popularity with the people, even led to the later restoration of Snofru's mortuary temple at Dahshur. There is no lack of literary references to his reign, which appears to have been both glorious and long-lasting (perhaps as much as forty years).

The Palermo Stone suggests that Snofru was a warlike king. He is said to have led an expedition into Nubia to crush a 'revolt' in the Dodekaschoenos region, and to have captured 7000 prisoners in the campaign. This is a huge number considering that the population of the Dodekaschoenos, effectively corresponding to Egyptian-dominated Nubia, was thought to be about 50,000 only in the 1950s. The account of this campaign also mentions the even higher number of 200,000 head of cattle, as well as 13,100 cattle which, according to the same

TABLE 2   *Family tree of the Fourth and Fifth Dynasties (generations 1–6).*

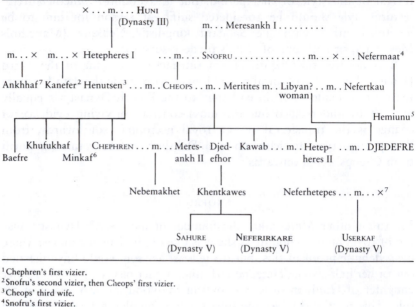

[1] Chephren's first vizier.
[2] Snofru's second vizier, then Cheops' first vizier.
[3] Cheops' third wife.
[4] Snofru's first vizier.
[5] Cheops' second vizier.
[6] Chephren's second vizier.
[7] Priest of Heliopolis in Papyrus Westcar.

source, were obtained in a campaign against the Libyans; 11,000 of them are said to have been taken prisoner. These military campaigns were not merely isolated raids against rebellious peoples: from the beginning of the Archaic period Nubia had provided Egypt with a source of manpower both for major building works and for the maintenance of order. The desert peoples – the Medjay and later the Blemmyes – provided the core of the troops that policed Egypt itself. The domination of Nubia was also useful in terms of guarding the trade routes for such African trade goods as ebony, ivory, incense, exotic animals (including giraffes and monkeys, which were particularly popular throughout the Old Kingdom), ostrich eggs and panther skins. The domination of Nubia also enabled Egypt to control the sources of certain raw materials, such as the gold mines located throughout the desert in Nubia from Wadi Allaqi to the Nile and the diorite quarries to the west of Abu Simbel.

It was this desire for raw materials that led to the campaigns into the Sinai which were launched by virtually all Old Kingdom rulers from Sanakht onwards. Their aim was not to contend with possible invaders from Syria-Palestine but to exploit the copper, turquoise and malachite mines in the western part of the Sinai peninsula at Wadi Nasb and Wadi Maghara. Snofru was no exception: he led an expedition against the bedouin, recapturing those areas of the Sinai that the Egyptians were only able to exploit temporarily. He must certainly have done much to establish Egyptian mines in the region, judging from the popularity of his cult among Middle Kingdom miners in the Sinai. At the same time, the continual state of war with the nomadic peoples appears to have presented no hindrance to Egypt's commercial links with Lebanon and Syria via the Phoenician seaboard. Snofru even sent a fleet of about forty vessels to bring back quantities of timber, which was always in short supply in Egypt.

Not only is Snofru credited with the construction of ships, fortresses, palaces and temples but he is the only ruler to whom three pyramids are ascribed. Initially he built a tomb at Maidum, some distance to the south of his predecessors' pyramids at Saqqara. This first tomb, modelled closely on Djoser's Step Pyramid, was barely finished when he abandoned it, in the thirteenth year of his reign, to undertake two new buildings at Dahshur, both of which were intended to be perfect pyramids. It is difficult to understand why the royal necropolis was moved south to Maidum and then back north again. The choice of Maidum must have been a deliberate attempt to break with the previous dynasty, and therefore clearly belonged to the first half of Snofru's reign. The royal family seems to have developed links with the Maidum area, since members of the elder branch of the family were buried there, notably Nefermaat, who was Snofru's vizier and the architect of King Huni's tomb. Nefermaat's son, Hemiunu, became Cheops' vizier, and following the tradition set by Nefermaat was also the builder of Cheops' Great Pyramid at Giza. Hemiunu was rewarded by being allowed to site his own tomb nearby at Giza, placing inside it a statue of himself. Another illustrious tomb-owner at Maidum was Rahotep, whose statue, showing him alongside his wife Nofret, is one of the masterpieces of the Egyptian Museum in Cairo (Plate 6).

CHEOPS

The Fourth Dynasty necropolis *par excellence* was undoubtedly the Giza plateau, dominated by the pyramids of Cheops and his successors. The Giza pyramids were surrounded by streets of *mastaba* tombs belonging to the officers and dignitaries who continued to attend their masters' courts in the hereafter. A curious fate awaited Cheops, whose name in Egyptian was Khufu, an abbreviated version of *Khnum-khuefui* ('Khnum is protecting me'). His pyramid transformed him into the very symbol of absolute rule, and Herodotus' version of events chose to emphasise his cruelty:

> Cheops ... drove them into the extremity of misery. For first he shut up all the temples, to debar them from sacrificing in them, and thereafter he ordered all Egyptians to work for himself. To some was assigned the dragging of great stones from the stone quarries in the Arabian mountains as far as the Nile; to others he gave orders, when these stones had been taken across the river in boats, to drag them, again, as far as the Libyan hills. The people worked in gangs of one hundred thousand for each period of three months. The people were afflicted for ten years of time in building the road along which they dragged the stones ... The pyramid itself took twenty years in the building ... But to such a pitch of wickedness did Cheops come that, when in need of money, he sent his own daughter to take her place in a brothel, instructing her to charge a certain sum – the amount they did not mention. The girl did what her father told her, but she also got the idea of leaving some memorial of her own; and so she asked each man that came at her to make her a present of one stone in the works, and from these stones, they say, a pyramid was built midmost of the three, in front of the great pyramid. Each side of it measures one hundred and fifty feet. (*Histories* II, 124–6; trans. Grene 1987: 185–7)

Cheops was not remembered as fondly as Snofru, although his funerary cult was still attested in the Saite (Twenty-Sixth) Dynasty and he was increasingly popular during the Roman period. According to Papyrus Westcar, Cheops liked to listen to fantastic stories of the reigns of his predecessors. He is portrayed in this text as the traditional legendary oriental monarch, good-natured and eager to be shown magical things, amiable towards his inferiors and interested in the nature of human existence. The construction of his tomb was one of his main concerns, and the fourth tale in Papyrus Westcar describes his quest for 'the secret chambers of the sanctuary of Thoth', which he wanted to reproduce in his own mortuary temple. It was on this occasion that he made the acquaintance of a magician from Maidum, a certain Djedi, 'a man aged 110 who eats 500 loaves of bread and a side of beef for his meat, and still drinks 100 jugs of beer to this very day'. The sorcerer revealed to him that the secret he desired would be passed on to him by the first king of the next dynasty, Userkaf, the eldest son of Ra and the wife of a Heliopolitan priest. The rest of the papyrus describes the marvellous birth of the three first rulers of the Fifth Dynasty. The text breaks off before the end of the story, but it is already clear that Cheops has given a poor impression, caught between the wisdom of his predecessors and the virtue of his successors. His behaviour even shocks the magician Djedi, who urges him to retract his command that a prisoner should be decapitated so that he can have the pleasure of watching Djedi replace the head, telling him, 'No, not a human being, oh sovereign master! It is forbidden to commit such an act on the divine herd.' It is no coincidence that this magician, who was so respectful of the divine wish, was a man from Maidum, as Snofru probably had been.

These texts that describe the Fourth Dynasty kings were all written after the image of the Old Kingdom ruler had been remodelled during the First Intermediate Period. It was therefore quite logical for the Egyptians of the Middle Kingdom and later to link those past rulers represented primarily by their buildings with the greatest tendencies towards immoderation, thus distorting the real situation (Posener 1969a: 13). However, it is difficult to accommodate within this theory the fact that Snofru's reputation remained untarnished when he built more pyramids than any of his successors.

Apart from Cheops' place in the literary tradition, not much is known about him. Considering that his tomb was the largest monument in Egypt and one of the Seven Wonders of the World, it is ironic that the only surviving sculpture of Cheops is a tiny ivory statuette (9 cm high), which shows him seated on a cubic throne, dressed in a *shendyt*-kilt and wearing the Red Crown of Lower Egypt. The broken fragments of this unique portrait were found at Abydos by Flinders Petrie and the reconstructed statuette is now in the Egyptian Museum, Cairo. Only a few texts provide information concerning his reign: a graffito in Wadi Maghara shows that he continued his father's work in the Sinai peninsula, while a stele in the diorite quarries of the Nubian Desert to the west of Abu Simbel testifies to his activity south of the First Cataract. It is not even known whether Cheops' reign lasted for twenty-three years, as the Turin Canon suggests, or sixty-three years, which is the length ascribed to him by Manetho.

CHEOPS' HEIRS

Cheops' two sons, each born of a different mother, both succeeded him on the throne. The first was Djedefre (Didufri or Radjedef), who ascended the throne at the death of his father. His personality and his reign are still obscure; it is not even possible to say whether he reigned for only eight years, as the Turin Canon indicates, or a longer period (without going as far as the sixty-three years suggested by Manetho). Nevertheless, his rise to power marks an indisputable turning-point, a forewarning of the changes at the end of the Fourth Dynasty. He was the first Egyptian ruler to include among his titles the name 'son of Ra', and he chose to locate his tomb not in Giza but in Abu Roash, about 10 kilometres to the north.

The choice of Abu Roash for the site of the new necropolis was not arbitrary, and the change should doubtless be regarded as a return to the values of the period before Cheops. Indeed, this part of the plateau had already been used for burial in the Third Dynasty. Djedefre also returned to the north-south orientation of the pyramid and an overall rectangular ground plan for the complex which was probably inspired by the Saqqara pyramids. This complex, including a mortuary temple, a huge sloping causeway and a still-unexcavated valley temple, was ultimately left unfinished, leading to speculation that Djedefre's reign was comparatively short. The complex has also been widely pillaged, though this is probably not an indication of immediate dynastic feuds: it was constructed of valuable materials such as syenite and red quartzite from Gebel el-Ahmar, which would have been much sought after. In 1901 Emile Chassinat discovered in the area around the pyramid a large number of quartzite fragments (now in the Louvre) which originally made up a set of about twenty statues representing the king. The best examples of these royal statues from Abu Roash are among the masterpieces of Old Kingdom royal sculpture.

The place of Djedefre in the royal family, particularly his relationship with his half-brother Chephren who succeeded him on the throne, is unclear. His mother's name is unknown, but he is thought to have married his half-sister, Hetepheres II, who was also the wife of Kawab, Cheops' crown prince, who died before his father without having assumed the role of vizier. The tomb of Kawab, one of the earliest in the Giza necropolis, lies to the east of Cheops' pyramid, and it is clear that his memory was still maintained up to the time of Ramesses II at least, for Ramesses' son Khaemwaset is known to have restored a statue of Kawab in the temple at Memphis. Meresankh III, the daughter of Kawab and Hetepheres II, married Chephren, while Neferhetepes, the daughter of Djedefre and Hetepheres II, is one of the possible candidates for the mother of Userkaf.

After the death of Kawab, Djedefre's only rival for the throne would have been his other half-brother, Djedefhor, whose unfinished and deliberately damaged *mastaba* has been discovered near that of Kawab. It is difficult to tell whether this damage is an indication of a struggle for the succession between Djedefhor and Djedefre. Such a struggle may well have occurred, given that Djedefhor was the father of Queen Khentkawes, the mother of Neferirkare and Sahure. Khentkawes was probably the historical model for the woman Redjedet in Papyrus Westcar, who according to the magician Djedi was destined to give birth to the children of Ra, the first kings of the Fifth Dynasty. There might therefore have been a struggle between two rival branches of the royal family. Djedefre might have gained the upper hand over

Djedefhor temporarily, but power would have been restored to the elder branch of the family (Djedefhor's) with the reign of Chephren.

This view of Djedefre's reign as the temporary ascendancy of the younger branch of the royal family is perhaps supported by later references to Cheops' sons. A Twelfth Dynasty graffito found in the Wadi Hammamat includes Djedefhor and his other half-brother Baefre in the succession of Cheops after Chephren. Furthermore, the 'legitimist' tradition has transformed Djedefhor into a figure who, in some regards, was almost equal to Imhotep: he was considered to have been a man of letters and even the writer of an *Instruction* from which scribal students were taught. A number of passages from his *Instruction* were quoted by the best authors, from Ptahhotep to the Roman period. Djedefhor was thought to have been well-versed in funerary texts, and it was said that in the sanctuary of Hermopolis 'on a block of quartzite in Upper Egypt, under the feet of the majesty of the god', he had discovered four of the most important chapters of the *Book of the Dead*. These four chapters were the formula of chapter 30b, which was intended to prevent the heart from giving evidence against its owner, the formula of chapter 64, which was an important text since it brought about the transfiguration of the deceased, the formula of the 'four torches' (chapter 137a), and finally the formula that ensured the deceased's glory in the afterworld (chapter 148). A precursor of Satni Kamois, Djedefhor was also the person who was said to have introduced the magician Djedi in Papyrus Westcar. Because of this semi-mythical dimension, Djedefhor's true historical role cannot be properly assessed. If the texts are to be believed, he was already a wise counsellor during the reign of Cheops and still alive even in Mycerinus' time.

The beginning of Chephren's twenty-five-year reign represents the restoration of power to the elder branch of the family and the return to the tradition of Cheops. Chephren moved the royal necropolis back to Giza, building his own pyramid and a valley temple of limestone and granite to the south of his father's tomb. Auguste Mariette cleared the main hall of the temple in 1860, and among several fragments that had fallen into a shaft he discovered a statue which is now one of the most magnificent objects in the collection of the Egyptian Museum, Cairo: a representation of Chephren seated on the royal throne, protected by the dynastic god Horus who wraps his wings around the nape of Chephren's neck. A parallel example of this statue type from the reign of Chepren has also recently been found (Vandersleyen 1987).

The rift between the reigns of Djedefre and Chephren was probably not as great as scholars have often suggested, and there was in fact no real ideological contrast between the two kings. On the contrary, Chephren seems to have pursued the same theological course as his predecessor: he continued to bear the title of 'son of Ra' and also developed, in a masterly fashion, the theological statement of Atum's importance *vis-à-vis* Ra, which had already been emphasized by Djedefre. The reign of Djedefre had already produced the first surviving example of a royal sphinx, excavated at Abu Roash; it is thought likely that a magnificent head of Djedefre, among the statues discovered by Chassinat, was originally part of a sphinx. But it was Chephren who created the Great Sphinx, ordering his craftsmen to sculpt a colossal statue out of the rough monumental block of stone left behind by the quarrying of the Giza plateau during the reign of Cheops. He gave the monument the form of a seated lion and its head reproduced the image of his own face wearing a *nemes*-wig. This pyramid-sized sphinx was to be associated in the New Kingdom with Harmachis, who represented the king in his role as Atum. The position of the Great Sphinx at the foot of the necropolis, alongside the valley temple of Chepren's pyramid, demonstrated the king's double significance as the *shesep ankh* of Atum, both in his living form and in the afterworld when his trans-figuration had been accomplished. The Egyptian term *shesep ankh*, meaning 'living image' was written with the help of a hieroglyph representing a reclining sphinx.

Chephren's immediate successor was his son by his wife Khamerernebti, who was called Menkaure ('Stable are the *kau* of Ra') or, to take Herodotus' transcription, Mycerinus. Between Chephren and Mycerinus, Manetho adds another ruler called Bicheris or Baefre ('Ra is his *ba*'), who is described in the Twelfth Dynasty as being at the side of Djedefhor. Baefre is probably also the same person as Nebka, whose unfinished pyramid was found at Zawyet el-Aryan. Mycerinus lost one son and when his second son, Shepseskaf, rose to the throne, it was he who completed Mycerinus' mortuary temple and perhaps even his pyramid. Mycerinus' pyramid was the third and smallest of those at Giza but it was also the only one to be faced with granite in its lower section and fine limestone above. Manetho is uncertain about the length of this reign, which was probably eighteen years rather than twenty-eight.

Shepseskaf was the last king of the Fourth Dynasty. He clearly sought to reunite the two sides of the family when he married Khentkawes, Djedefhor's daughter, who is described in her Giza tomb as 'mother of the two kings of Upper and Lower Egypt'. This inscription is no doubt a reference to Sahure and Neferirkare, for she was considered by the Egyptians to have been the ancestress of the Fifth Dynasty. Shepseskaf does not seem to have produced an heir by Khentkawes, unless one counts the ephemeral Thamptis (Djedefptah) mentioned by Manetho, to whom the Turin Canon ascribes a reign of two years. He chose a different religious policy to that of his predecessors, issuing a decree — the earliest known edict — which safeguarded the funerary estates of the earlier kings, but he himself broke with tradition by having his tomb at southern Saqqara built in the form of a giant sarcophagus. His wife Khentkawes also seems to have been pulled in two directions: she had two tombs, one at Giza and the other at Abusir, near her son's pyramid but built in a style that indicated a return to the architectural tradition of the Third Dynasty. This apparent move away from the Heliopolitan tradition was also expressed in Shepseskaf's choice of Ptahshepses, the chief priest of Memphis, as the husband of his daughter Khamaat.

USERKAF AND THE FIRST PART OF THE FIFTH DYNASTY

The beginning of the reign of Userkaf ('Powerful is his *ka*') does not appear to have triggered off any changes in the country as a whole or in the administration — there are some instances of Fourth Dynasty officials who remained in office, such as Nykaankh at Tihna in Middle Egypt. Moreover, it is only Papyrus Westcar that suggests that Userkaf was the son of Redjedet (Khentkawes), whereas there is a strong tradition for seeing him as a son of the princess Neferhetepes, an extraordinary limestone bust of whom is in the collection of the Louvre (Vandier 1958: 48–9). This would make him the grandson of Djedefre and Queen Hetepheres II and therefore a descendant of the younger side of the family. Everything depends on the identity of Neferhetepes' husband, who it is suggested may have been the 'priest of Ra, lord of Sakhebu' mentioned in Papyrus Westcar.

Userkaf ordered a pyramid of modest dimensions (now much ruined) to be constructed at northern Saqqara, some distance from Djoser's complex. At the same time he also built a sun temple at Abusir which seems to have been a replica of the one at Heliopolis (the city to which the new dynasty particularly traced back its origins), thus inaugurating a tradition that was to be carried on by his successors. His choice of Abusir as the location of his sun temple is doubtless connected with the closeness of this site to the home of the father of the new dynasty, Neferhetepes' husband. This was the town of Sakhebu, generally thought to have been located at Zat el-Kom about 10 kilometres north of Abu Roash, almost at the point where the Nile splits into two branches: the Damietta and the Rosetta. It was at Abusir that Sahure, Neferirkare and Neuserre were to be buried.

The new order was also expressed through the Horus name chosen by Userkaf, which was Iry-maat ('He who puts Maat into practice'), Maat being the universal harmony that the creator had to maintain. By this means Userkaf was deliberately claiming responsibility for the maintenance of the whole of creation. His reign was probably brief, nearer to the Turin Canon's seven years than Manetho's twenty-eight, and the early abandonment of his mortuary cult at the end of the Fifth Dynasty is a clear enough indication of his relative importance. Nevertheless, his reign was characterized by a certain amount of building activity, particularly in Upper Egypt, where he enlarged the temple at Tod dedicated to Monthu, the local god of the Theban region and later also the national god of war. The first known contacts – probably commercial – between Egypt and the Aegean world can also be dated to Userkaf's reign, since an inscribed stone vessel from his mortuary temple was found on Kythera. The continuation of trading links with the northern Mediterranean throughout the Fifth Dynasty is indicated by the discovery, at Dorak, of a chair stamped with the name of Sahure and, in the surrounding area, various objects bearing the names of Menkauhor and Djedkare-Isesi.

THE HELIOPOLITAN SUPREMACY

During the Fifth Dynasty Egypt seems to have been opened up to the outside world, both northwards and southwards. The reliefs in the mortuary temple built at Abusir by Userkaf's successor, Sahure, include the usual representations of conquered countries (belonging more to rhetoric than to historical evidence), but they also show the return of a maritime trading expedition probably from Byblos, as well as forays into the Syrian hinterland, if the references to bears in these regions are to be believed. A campaign against the Libyans has also been dated to Sahure's reign, although there is some doubt surrounding this. It seems that relations with foreign countries during Sahure's time, just as in Userkaf's, were primarily economic: the exploitation of mines in the Sinai, diorite quarrying to the west of Aswan and an expedition to Punt, which is mentioned on the Palermo Stone and perhaps also depicted on the reliefs in Sahure's mortuary temple.

The Egyptians described the location of Punt as 'the land of the god', a term that they used to refer to eastern countries from the beginning of the Middle Kingdom. The land of Punt is thought to have been situated somewhere between eastern Sudan and northern Eritrea; it was a country from which Egypt imported mainly myrrh and later incense, as well as such exotic goods as electrum, gold, ivory, ebony, resins, gums and leopard skins, all of which are products of tropical Africa. There is evidence for commercial links with Punt throughout the Fifth and Sixth Dynasties and especially during the Middle Kingdom, when expeditions were led by Heneni on behalf of Mentuhotpe III. The expeditions sent by Sesostris I and Ammenemes II have left valuable indications of the route followed by the traders. These expeditions evidently travelled through the Wadi Hammamat from the Theban region to Mersa Gawasis, a site on the Red Sea coast where the joint excavations of the University of Alexandria and the Egyptian Antiquities Organization have revealed the remains of a Middle Kingdom port (Sayed 1977; 1983). After a voyage through the Red Sea (reconstructed from the Eighteenth Dynasty reliefs of Hatshepsut at Deir el-Bahri, which depict an expedition to Punt), the boats must have landed near the modern Port Sudan; the traders would then have penetrated inland to the west, eventually reaching a point to the south of the Fifth Cataract. These links with Punt were continued throughout the New Kingdom, in the reigns of Tuthmosis III, Amenophis III, Horemheb, Sethos I, Ramesses II and especially Ramesses III, but then the trade died out and by the end of the pharaonic period journeys to Punt had become mythical events.

The reigns of Sahure's immediate successors are poorly documented. Little is known of the policies of Neferirkare-Kakai (who was Sahure's brother according to Papyrus Westcar), except that the Palermo Stone was probably carved during his reign. A very important archive of papyri, spanning a period from the reign of Isesi to that of Pepy II, was preserved in Neferirkare-Kakai's mortuary temple at Abusir and excavated between 1893 and 1907. This was the most important known collection of papyri from the Old Kingdom until the 1982 expedition of the Egyptological Institute of the University of Prague discovered an even richer cache in a storeroom of the nearby mortuary temple of Neferefre. The finds at Abusir, supplemented by the documents from the mortuary temple of Neferefre, form the basis of current knowledge of royal estates in the Old Kingdom.

Between Neferirkare and Neferefre came Shepseskare, an ephemeral ruler whose reign must have lasted for only a matter of months; the only surviving evidence of it, apart from Manetho, is a seal impression found at Abusir. The reign of Neferefre, on the other hand, is quite well known, especially since the Prague expedition has undertaken the excavation of his mortuary temple. The discoveries made between 1980 and 1986 have to some extent modified the general perception of this king, who had previously been regarded as second-rate on the grounds that his pyramid was unfinished. Quite apart from the great find of the cache of papyri and inscribed plaques, the grandeur of this previously unrecognized ruler is indicated by finds of wooden boats, statues of prisoners and sculptures of the king himself, which were excavated in 1985.

Neuserre reigned for about twenty-five years. He may have been the son of Neferirkare, for he constructed his valley temple using fragments from Neferirkare's unfinished constructions at Abusir. He is remembered mainly for his sun temple at Abu Ghurob, which is the only extant structure of its type to be built entirely of stone; it has survived virtually intact and its architectural style and reliefs help to give an idea of the appearance of the original Heliopolitan sun temple on which it must have been modelled. Because of his sun temple, Neuserre's reign is considered to have been the peak of the solar cult – but this is doubtless an exaggeration. Nevertheless, a definite process of change seems to have ensued after Neuserre's reign. The reign of his successor, Menkauhor, is poorly known, except that like Neuserre he sent expeditions to the Sinai mines, and he did not have himself buried at Abusir.

Menkauhor's pyramid has not yet been identified, and it is difficult to decide whether it is more likely to have been at Dahshur or at northern Saqqara, where a personal cult was dedicated to him in the New Kingdom (Berlandini 1979). However, the argument that he was the owner of the ruined pyramid to the east of Teti's at northern Saqqara is flawed by the existence of the remains of a Third Dynasty *mastaba* in its southern corner (*LÄ* IV, 1219). It is not known whether his sun temple, known only through inscriptions, was indeed located at Abusir, but if so he would have been the last to use the site, since his successors moved the royal necropolis back to Saqqara.

It was during this period that the provincial governors and court officials gained greater power and independence, creating an unstoppable movement which eventually threatened the central authority. The effect of this gradual devolution of power is clear from the wealth of the Fifth Dynasty *mastaba* of Ti at Saqqara. Ti was an official who married the princess Neferhetepes, pursued his career during the reign of Neferirkare Kakai and died in the time of Neuserre. He was 'chief barber of the royal household' and steward of the funerary complexes of Neferirkare and Neferefre. He was also the controller of the lakes, farms and cultivated land. The size of the tomb he had built for himself and his family, and the quality of its decoration, would have been beyond the means of a private individual in the previous dynasty.

ISESI AND WENIS

Isesi's new policy established a certain amount of distance between himself and his predecessor, without however moving away from the Heliopolitan dogma. He chose the name Djedkare – 'The *ka* of Ra is stable' – as his *nsw-bity* (King of Upper and Lower Egypt) title, thus placing himself under the protection of Ra; but he did not build a sun temple and he had himself buried at southern Saqqara, nearer to

Memphis and in the vicinity of the modern village of Saqqara. His reign was long: Manetho suggests that it lasted for about forty years, but this figure is not confirmed by the Turin Canon, which suggests a reign of only twenty-eight years. At any rate, either figure would have been high enough for him to have celebrated his *sed* festival (jubilee), the evidence for which is an inscribed vase in the collection of the Louvre. Like Sahure, he pursued a vigorous foreign policy that led him in similar directions: to the Sinai, where two expeditions at ten-year intervals are recorded at Wadi Maghara; to the diorite quarries west of Abu Simbel; and further afield to Byblos and the land of Punt. Isesi's expedition to Punt, mentioned in a graffito found at the Lower Nubian site of Tomas, was evidently still remembered in the time of Merenre.

The acquisition of greater powers by officials continued during Isesi's reign, leading to the development of a virtual feudal system. The viziers who took office during this period of a third of a century had tombs built for themselves at Saqqara which bear witness to their great opulence; one of these was Rashepses, the first governor of Upper Egypt. But the most famous noble of Isesi's reign was Ptahhotep, who was traditionally considered to have been the author of an *Instruction* often quoted by philosophical and royal texts until the Kushite period.

In reality it is necessary to speak of more than one Ptahhotep, since two people of this name possessed tombs at Saqqara, in the area to the north of Djoser's pyramid. Djedkare Isesi's vizier is the Ptahhotep who is buried alone (*PM* III/2, 596ff.). His grandson, Ptahhotep Tshefi, who lived in the reign of Wenis, was buried nearby in an annexe of the *mastaba* of Akhethotep, who was son of the first Ptahhotep and also a vizier himself (*PM* III/2, 599). It is to the second, younger Ptahhotep that the *Maxims* are usually ascribed. These texts have survived in the form of about ten different manuscripts, four of which – a papyrus and three ostraca – derive from the Workmen's Village at Deir el-Medina. The Deir el-Medina *Maxims* provide some indication of the intended audience for such texts in the Ramessid period, when they were still being used as teaching material for the scribal schools.

The attribution of the *Maxims* to Ptahhotep does not necessarily mean that he was the actual author: the oldest versions date to the Middle Kingdom, and there is no proof that they were originally composed in the Old Kingdom or, more specifically, at the end of the Fifth Dynasty. The question, moreover, is of no great importance. The conformist contents of these *Maxims* define general rules for life, and they are attributed to Ptahhotep in all likelihood because he symbolized those high officials who guaranteed the maintenance of the status quo.

The political and administrative personnel of the late Fifth Dynasty displayed a remarkable continuity, in contrast with the royal family. This seems to have faded out with Wenis, who is thought (without any real proof) to have been the son of Isesi. Manetho claims that Wenis was the last ruler of the Fifth Dynasty, and his reign is generally thought to have been the end of the Classic phase of the Old Kingdom, whereas the Sixth Dynasty represents the beginning of a period of decline that stretches on into the First Intermediate Period until the reunification of the Two Lands by Nebhepetre Mentuhotpe II. This sharp distinction between the Fifth and Sixth Dynasties is illusory in two basic ways. Firstly, it is only an extension of Manetho's artificial division, and secondly, it disrupts the natural flow of history by creating a distinction that is not apparent in the historiography of the Egyptians themselves. Apart from the fact that there were a good number of officials who served under Djedkare and Wenis as well as Teti, the first Sixth Dynasty ruler, it is also clear that Wenis' reign was by no means a time of decadence. During his reign, the length of which is set at about thirty years by both Manetho and the Turin Canon, Egypt pursued a policy of diplomatic contact with Byblos and Nubia, and building activity took place at Elephantine and especially at northern Saqqara, where the Wenis funerary complex (restored by Prince Khaemwaset in the reign of Ramesses II) displays a grandeur that was later to elevate him to the level of a local god.

THE BEGINNING OF THE SIXTH DYNASTY

Although the Old Kingdom seemed to have reached its peak and there is no surviving evidence of civil warfare, the feudal local governors throughout the country were probably already posing a threat to central authority by the end of the Fifth Dynasty. The problem of growing provincial power was compounded at this time by the lack of a male heir. It seems that Teti's rise to the throne provided a solution to this double crisis. His adoption of the Horus name Sehetep-tawy ('He who pacifies the Two Lands') was an indication of the political programme upon which he embarked. Indeed, this Horus name was to reappear in royal titulatures throughout subsequent Egyptian history, always in connection with such kings as Ammenemes I, Apophis, Pedubastis II and Pi(ankh)y, who were attempting to re-establish the unity of the country after serious political troubles. Teti, however, seems to have made no conscious break with the preceding dynasty; in fact, he married a daughter of Wenis, Iput, who was to be the mother of Pepy I. Thus ensconced in the legitimate royal line, he pursued a policy of co-operation with the nobles by marrying his eldest daughter, Sesheshet, to his vizier Mereruka. Mereruka later also became the chief priest of Teti's pyramid complex, and had himself buried close to Teti's pyramid in one of the finest *mastabas* of northern Saqqara.

The pyramid that Teti ordered to be constructed, which was the second one – after Wenis' – to be inscribed with Pyramid Texts, represented a return to certain Fourth Dynasty traditions. He reintroduced the construction of queens' pyramids, whereas Wenis had been content to provide *mastabas* for his wives. The pyramid of Queen Khuit has disappeared, but the remains of Iput were found in a small pyramid built about 100 metres north-west of her husband's tomb.

Clearly, Teti's policy of pacifying the nobles bore fruit. There is evidence at Abydos of his activity as a legislator, in the form of a decree exempting the temple from tax; he was also the first ruler to be particularly associated with the cult of Hathor at Dendera. The overall stability of his administration within Egypt itself is suggested by the fact that he was able to continue many of the international links of the Fifth Dynasty: he maintained relations with Byblos and perhaps also with Punt and Nubia, at least as far as the site of Tomas in northern Nubia.

The various sources are not in agreement on the length of Teti's reign. The Turin Canon gives an unlikely estimate of less than seven months while Manetho suggests a long period of thirty to thirty-three years, improbable considering that there is no evidence for him having celebrated a jubilee festival. The latest known date from Teti's reign is that of 'the sixth census', an operation that took place on average every two years or every year and a half. Manetho says that Teti was assassinated, and it is this claim that has led to the idea of growing civil disorder, a second similarity with the reign of Ammenemes I. Teti's violent death would also explain the short reign of his successor Userkare, whose name – 'The *ka* of Ra is powerful' – has such strong resonances of the Fifth Dynasty that he has often been seen as one of the leaders of opposition to the legitimate rulers and therefore, according to Manetho, perhaps even the person who assassinated Teti. But contrary to popular opinion, Userkare is not a completely unknown figure; he is not only mentioned in the Turin Canon and the Abydos king-list, but various other documents bearing his name have survived. One such text mentions a team of salaried workers from the nome of Qau el-Kebir, south of Asyut, who were engaged on a large-scale project – no doubt the construction of his tomb. The subsequent rise to power of Pepy I appears to have taken place without impedence, and perhaps Userkare should in fact be regarded as a stopgap ruler who would have overseen the regency of Queen Iput, Teti's widow, while her son was still too young to come to the throne.

PEPY I

The length of Pepy I's reign was about fifty years according to both Manetho and the Turin Canon (despite a copying error), and in reality it must have been at least forty years, which suggests that he was very young when he came to the throne at the end of his mother's regency. His Horus name was Mery-tawy ('He who is loved by the Two Lands'), which at least indicates his desire for political appeasement. But two events provide grounds for thinking that the difficulties described above must have assumed an increasing prominence. The first is difficult to date precisely within Pepy I's reign and only one piece of direct evidence has survived. There seems to have been a conspiracy against the king in his harem, ending in the punishment of the guilty wife and also, apparently, of the son for whom she committed the crime.

The evidence in question is provided by an official called Weni, in the form of an autobiography which he had inscribed in his funerary chapel at Abydos. The autobiography is the oldest and best-documented literary genre in Egypt. In the time of Pepy I there was a type of text, written exclusively in the funerary chapel, that fulfilled the same function as the various representations of the deceased, building up a picture of his character by describing him at the important stages of his life, thus showing him worthy of enjoying funerary offerings. In other words, this text acted as a kind of justification of a man's life. But apart from their function as traditional panegyrics, tending to present the subject as an ideal man in harmony with the universal order, these texts also include a purely descriptive element, recounting the career of the deceased.

In later periods such biographies were no longer found in funerary chapels, being engraved instead on the backs of statues or on stelae that were not necessarily associated with necropolises. They reflect the development of society: in the Old Kingdom they evoke a form of 'humanistic' loyalty, then there was the rise of local power expressed in the form of individualism, and finally, in the Middle Kingdom, there was a return to a loyalty which had become more intertwined with personal bonds. The Middle Kingdom form of loyalty could sometimes be expressed in rather sentimentalized forms, such as the tale of *Sinuhe*. With the arrival of the New Kingdom, the texts' historical interest increased, so that, although they continued to adhere to the rules of the genre, they tended to free themselves from the constraints of phraseology in order to leave more space for the individual. This process of change was accentuated in the first millennium BC, resulting in compositions, such as those in the tomb of Petosiris at Tuna el-Gebel, that have become philosophical works or didactic treatises.

Weni served under the three first pharaohs of the Sixth Dynasty, and his progression through life is an ideal noble's career path with all the stereotypes that this implies: he passed from the administration to the army, then, after a royal funerary endowment, he embarked on a series of great works, from the exploitation of quarries to the cutting of a canal at the First Cataract. All this is expressed in a perfect literary form, from which the underlying reality of the events is not always clear:

> When there was a secret charge in the royal harem against Queen Weretyamtes, his majesty made me go in to hear (it) alone. No chief judge and vizier, no official was there, only I alone; because I was worthy, because I was rooted in his majesty's heart; because his majesty had filled his heart with me. Only I put (it) in writing together with one other senior warden of Nekhen, while my rank was (only) that of overseer of royal tenants. Never before had one like me heard a secret of the king's harem; but his majesty made me hear it, because I was worthy in his majesty's heart beyond any official of his, beyond any noble of his, beyond any servant of his. (Lichtheim 1973: 19)

This same conspiracy seems to have found an echo in the last third of the reign: in the year of the twenty-first census, the king married, one after the other, two daughters of Khui, a noble from Abydos. These two queens, both renamed Ankhenesmerire ('Merire lives for her') after their marriages, were each to give him children. Ankhenesmerire I was the mother of Merenre and the princess Neith, who later married her half-brother Pepy II, the son of Ankhenesmerire II. It is tempting to link Pepy I's late remarriage to the two daughters of Khui with the harem conspiracy, in view of the fact that it was these wives who gave birth to his successors, and that the remarriage itself was evidently accompanied by a change in policy. The alliance with Khui's family was advantageous to the nobility at Abydos beyond even the effect of the marriage itself, since Khui's son, Djau, was to be vizier under both Merenre and Pepy II; it is also thought that Djau acted as Pepy II's tutor at the beginning of his reign. The choice of an Abydene family was undoubtedly an attempt to renew the weakening links between the central power and Middle and Upper Egypt, since these connections played a key role in transport from north to south at that time, both by caravan and by river. This situation partly explains the power of the provinces such as Herakleopolis during the First and Second Intermediate Periods.

Pepy I also pursued a policy of involvement in Upper Egypt by ordering building-works in the main southern sanctuaries: Dendera, Abydos, Elephantine and Hierakonpolis. It was at Hierakonpolis that

Frederick Green and James Quibell discovered two copper statues, now in the Egyptian Museum at Cairo, the larger of which is a life-size representation of Pepy I, while the other is a much smaller representation probably of Merenre, who was no doubt thus established as the heir to the throne. Both are trampling underfoot the Nine Bows, a stylized representation of the people traditionally conquered by Egypt. The Nine Bows played a role within pharaonic cosmology that was equivalent to that played by barbarians in the Greeks' view of the world. This reaffirmation of royal power, which was also expressed in Lower Egypt through the work undertaken in the temple at Bubastis, was accompanied by an unmistakable return to ancient values: Pepy I changed his coronation name from Neferdjahor to Merire ('The devotee of Ra'). He also issued, in the twenty-first year of his reign, a charter awarding tax immunity to the town that had grown up around Snofru's funerary domain at Dahshur. His own 'pyramid town', established near the temple of Ptah in the capital, was called Mennefer-Pepy, which eventually became the name of the whole city of Memphis from the Eighteenth Dynasty onwards.

THE EXPANSION SOUTHWARDS

Pepy I's son, Merenre I ('Beloved of Ra'), clearly advertised his links with Upper Egypt by adopting Antiemdjaf ('Anti is his protection') as his coronation name: Anti was a falcon-god of war worshipped in the region stretching from the Twelfth to the Eighteenth Nome of Upper Egypt, and particularly at Deir el-Gebrawi. The fact that Merenre rose to the throne at an early age is probably confirmation of the late date of Pepy I's second marriage, which would have left his two wives with very young heirs. Merenre died young, after a reign of only about nine years, and his half-brother Pepy II was only about ten when he succeeded him on the throne. The unfinished state of Merenre's pyramid, which he had built close to that of his father at southern Saqqara, confirms that the death of Merenre was premature, but it is still difficult to guess his precise age at death. Within the tomb chamber the body of a young man was discovered, but this was probably a later reuse of the tomb, since the unfinished chamber would have been easily entered by robbers and eventually reused for a new burial.

Merenre followed policies similar to those of his father. In the economic sphere he continued to exploit the mines in the Sinai and, to provide materials for the construction of his pyramid, the quarries in Nubia, at Aswan and at Hatnub, where a graffiti confirms the expeditions recounted by Weni in his autobiography. He also steered a political course similar to that of Pepy I, maintaining control of Upper

Egypt and delegating its administration to Weni. Merenre's activities outside Egypt constituted a high point in the Sixth Dynasty. The expeditions that were launched into Syria-Palestine were led by Weni, who was rewarded with the governorship of Upper Egypt:

> When his majesty took action against the Asiatic Sand-dwellers, his majesty made an army of many tens of thousands from all of Upper Egypt: from Yebu in the south to Medenyt in the north; from Lower Egypt: from all of the Two-Sides-of-the-House ... His majesty sent me at the head of this army, there being counts, royal seal-bearers, sole companions of the palace, chieftains and mayors of towns of Upper and Lower Egypt, companions, scout-leaders, chief priests of Upper and Lower Egypt, from the villages and towns that they governed and from the Nubians of those foreign lands. I was the one who commanded them ... This army has returned in safety; it had flattened the Sand-dwellers' land. This army returned in safety; it had sacked its strongholds. This army returned in safety; it had cut down its figs, its vines. This army returned in safety; it had thrown fire in all its (mansions). This army returned in safety; it had slain its troops by many ten-thousands. This army returned in safety; (it had carried) off many (troops) as captives. His majesty praised me for it beyond anything. His majesty sent me to lead this army five times, to attack the land of the Sand-dwellers as often as they rebelled, with these troops ... I crossed in ships with these troops. I made a landing in the back of the height of the mountain range, to the north of the land of the Sand-dwellers, while half of this army was on the road. I came and caught them all and slew every marauder among them. (Lichtheim 1973: 19–20)

During Merenre's reign the policy of Egyptian expansion into Nubia bore fruit, judging from the inscriptions left by successive expeditions to Tomas. It was via Tomas that the expeditions travelled between the Nile and the caravan routes, so that the First Cataract was negotiated by way of Dunqul Oasis, thus providing access to the land of Wawat. There is evidence that Merenre was not only active in these places, like Pepy I before him, but also sent officials to maintain Egyptian rule over Nubia, from the northern border to the area south of the Third Cataract. Lower Nubia was above all a fertile land – it was here that the Kerma culture and the Kingdom of Kush were later to develop. This was the land that would supply the Egyptians with many of those exotic foodstuffs which were also imported from the land of Punt, to the east of the Nile. Lower Nubia provided access to sub-equatorial Africa via Darfur and Kordofan. If three graffiti in the Aswan region are to be believed, Merenre had achieved the subjugation of the chiefs of Lower Nubia (i.e. Wawat) by the tenth year of his reign.

The conquest of Nubia was achieved through control of the caravan

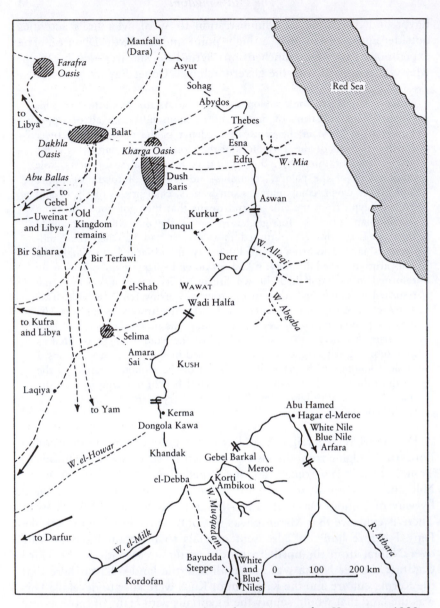

FIGURE 3 *Egyptian routes of southward expansion (after Vercoutter 1980a, 167).*

trails and domination of the oases in the Western Desert that relied on such trade routes. Harkhuf, a governor of Aswan buried at Qubbet el-Hawa, opposite the town of Aswan, undertook three missions of this type. He tells in his autobiography, inscribed on the façade of his tomb, how he twice reached the land of Yam 'by the Elephantine route', but the third time went by another way:

> Then his majesty sent me a third time to Yam. I went up from This upon the Oasis road. I found that the ruler of Yam had gone off to Tjemeh-land, to smite the Tjemeh to the western corner of heaven. I went up after him to Tjemeh-land and satisfied him, so that he praised all the gods for the sovereign ... [I came down through Imaau?] south of Irtjet and north of Setju. I found the ruler of [the confederacy of] Irtjet, Setju and Wawat. I came down with three hundred donkeys laden with incense, ebony, *ḥknw*-oil, *sat*-grain, panther skins, elephants' tusks, throw sticks and all sorts of good products. Now when the ruler of Irtjet, Setju and Wawat saw how strong and numerous the troop from Yam was which came down with me to the residence together with the army that had been sent with me ... (Lichtheim 1973: 25–6)

The 'Oases route' led from the Thinite nome to Kharga, and from there it passed along the Darb el-Arbain ('forty-day trail') to Selima. To the north of Kharga it also joined the trail that led through the Dakhla and Farafra Oases towards the territories of the Tjemehu to the west. The recent excavations of the French Institute of Oriental Archaeology and the Royal Ontario Museum have provided general confirmation of the Egyptian colonization of Dakhla Oasis by the beginning of the Sixth Dynasty, if not earlier. The inhabitants of the Nile valley travelled to the Balat region, at the entrance to the oasis, via the Darb el-Tawil which stretched from Dakhla to the area of the modern town of Manfalut. This process of colonization was designed both to facilitate the exploitation of the extensive agricultural resources of the oasis and to control travel from the south to the north and west (Giddy 1987: 206–12). Evidence of the oasis' role as a frontier may also be provided by the text on an 'execration figurine' excavated in the town of Balat, which lays a curse on the people of Yam (Grimal 1985). Nevertheless, Egypt continued to develop its links with Africa as well as with the countries around the upper reaches of the Nile during the lengthy reign of Pepy II, which was a period of great prosperity at Dakhla. Only a year after the young Pepy II had succeeded his half-brother on the throne, he became so fascinated by the travels of Harkhuf that he sent him a letter. This royal letter was eventually incorporated into Harkhuf's funerary autobiography:

> You have said ... that you have brought a pygmy of the god's dances from the land of the horizon-dwellers, like the pygmy whom the god's

seal-bearer Bawerded brought from Punt in the time of King Isesi. You
have said to my majesty that his like has never been brought by anyone
who went to Yam previously... Come north to the residence at once!
Hurry and bring with you this pygmy whom you brought from the land
of the horizon-dwellers live, hail and healthy, for the dances of the god, to
gladden the heart, to delight the heart of King Neferkare who lives
forever! When he goes down with you into the ship, get worthy men to be
around him on deck, lest he fall into the water! When he lies down at
night, get worthy men to lie around him in his tent. Inspect ten times at
night! My majesty desires to see this pygmy more than the gifts of the
mine-land and of Punt! When you arrive at the residence and this pygmy
is with you live, hale and healthy, my majesty will do great things for you,
more than was done for the god's seal-bearer Bawerded in the time of
King Isesi... (Lichtheim 1973: 26–7)

Perhaps remembering his childhood preoccupations, Pepy II later
pursued a policy of pacification in Nubia; he had the help of
Pepynakht, nicknamed Heqaib ('He who is master of his heart'), who
was Harkhuf's successor and was also buried in a tomb at Qubbet
el-Hawa. Heqaib led a campaign to bring back the body of an official
killed on a mission in the area of Byblos where he had been sent 'to
build a 'Byblos' (sea-going?) fleet in order to sail to Punt'. He also led
two expeditions into Nubia. It was perhaps these foreign campaigns, as
much as his energetic administration, that led to Heqaib's deification
very soon after his death. On the island of Elephantine he received his
own cult centre, which continued in use from the First to the Second
Intermediate Period. The deifications of such local heroes as Heqaib at
Elephantine and the vizier Isi at Edfu were probably a reflection of the
great increase in the power of local administrators that was to mark the
end of the dynasty. The evidence of this provincial power can be traced
at Elephantine itself, where the noble Mekhu, his son Sabni, and his
grandson Mekhu II were able to maintain Egyptian control over Nubia
long after the end of the reign of Pepy II.

THE APPROACH OF THE END OF THE OLD KINGDOM

The growing power of local officials was a major factor in the decline of
the Egyptian state; as Pepy II's reign dragged on, these officials were
gradually becoming local rulers in their own right. At the same time
foreign policy was becoming a heavier burden. The maintenance of
order in Nubia had been difficult during the time of Heqaib, but it
became even more troublesome for his successors, particularly as the
Kerma civilization, flourishing to the south of the Third Cataract, was
beginning to combine with the C-Group, its northern neighbour in

Lower Nubia, in an attempt to resist Egyptian efforts at colonization up to the beginning of the second millennium BC (Gratien 1978: 307–8).

Pepy II is traditionally thought to have governed the country for ninety-four years, but the latest known regnal date is that of the thirty-third census, which would suggest a definite length of about fifty to seventy years. At any rate, his reign was certainly very long – indeed, too long with regard to the increasing power of the local fiefdoms, which had become mainly hereditary. The wealth of the local rulers is apparent in the provincial necropolises at Cusae, Akhmim, Abydos, Edfu and Elephantine. The exceptional longevity of Pepy II resulted not only in the gradual fossilization of the administrative system but also in a succession crisis. The Abydos king-list mentions a Merenre II (also called Antiemdjaf), who seems to have been the son of Pepy II and Queen Neith. This very ephemeral ruler, who reigned for only a single year, would have been married to Queen Nitocris, who according to Manetho was the last Sixth Dynasty ruler. The Turin Canon lists Nitocris immediately after Merenre II, describing her as the 'King of Upper and Lower Egypt'. This woman, whose fame grew in the Ptolemaic period in the guise of the legendary Rhodopis, courtesan and mythical builder of the third pyramid at Giza (*LÄ* IV: 513–14), was the first known queen to exercise political power over Egypt (Beckerath 1984a: 58, n. 11). Unfortunately, no archaeological evidence has survived either from her reign or from the time of her possible successor, Neferkare, the son of Ankhesenpepy and Pepy II.

SOCIETY AND POWER

The Old Kingdom ended with a period of great confusion. Central authority was in rapid decline and the situation outside Egypt's borders became more and more threatening as the country's power diminished. The growing power of local individuals led to rivalry for the throne characterized by repeated confrontations between the controllers of different geographical blocs, each claiming to be the only legitimate ruler. Although the nature of the kingship itself does not seem to have changed, the throne now seems to have become more accessible to members of society who would have had no chance of claiming absolute power in earlier times. At the beginning of the Third Dynasty the Egyptian monarchy had developed a theological dimension, with the adoption of two new names among the king's titles: that of the 'Golden Horus', which first appeared with Djoser, and especially that of 'Son of Ra', the use of which was systematized from the reign of Neferirkare onwards. The rise to power of the Fifth Dynasty shows that the theocratic foundation had gained the upper hand over all other sectors of society, and the kings were closely linked with a specific priesthood. This dependence on the priesthood, which was to be exemplified by events over the succeeding centuries, served to reinforce the centralization of power, creating an extremely hierarchical society based on the king and the royal family. The concrete expression of this hierarchy is to be found in the organization of the necropolises of private tombs around the king's pyramid. The provincial powers, whose power increased as the generations went by, were increasingly feudalized by the concession of more and more privileges, and their local authority was enhanced by granting them places in the national hierarchy.

This policy was transformed by a growth in purely courtly titles, which were often the remnants of ancient offices that had fallen into disuse but were maintained for their honorific value. This process, which Louis XIV of France was later to demonstrate to perfection, was accentuated by increases in the size of the administration both in terms of its departments and the numbers of its officials. As the various elements of the bureaucracy increased, so did the workload of the scribes, on whom such a system of government fundamentally relied. A whole series of leading officials' titles were created, although it is some-times difficult to determine the degree to which any of the titles were genuine offices, as in the case of the title, 'chief of secrets' (*ḥri sšta*). It seems to have been possible to qualify this title in various ways such as 'chief of secrets of secret missions', 'of all of the king's orders', 'of judicial decisions', 'of the palace', 'of things that only one man can see', 'of things that only one man can hear', 'of the house of worship', 'of divine sayings', 'of the king, everywhere', 'of the court of justice' and 'of the mysteries of the heavens'.

The purely honorific titles are easier to identify, since they often relate to roles that are known to have no correspondence with reality, such as 'unique friend', which was once the role of the king's sole counsellor but developed into a generic title for courtiers, as well as 'chief of the ten in Upper Egypt', 'mouth of Pe' and 'warden of Nekhen', all of which appear to have been purely symbolic offices. To these titles should also be added others that were directly linked with the king's person – the 'barbers', 'sandal-bearers', 'doctors', 'stewards of the crowns' and 'other launderers' – as well as the sacerdotal roles linked with a local deity or a funerary cult.

The general structure of the administration took the form of a pyramid with the king at its apex. The king was theoretically in charge of everything, but in practice only dealt directly with military and religious affairs. Most of the time he acted through the vizier (*tjaty*), who appears to have first emerged in the Second Dynasty. The title was given by Snofru to various royal princes: Nefermaat, his son Hemiunu, Kawab and others. The vizier was in a sense the chief executive, with authority in practically all areas of government; his titles included 'chief of all royal works', 'chief of the house of weaponry', 'chief of the chambers of the king's adornment', 'royal chancellor of Lower Egypt'. He was also the chief judge – as Weni's intervention in the harem affair of Pepy I demonstrates – but he did not necessarily deal with all legal matters.

The emergence of the office of vizier coincided with the appearance of the 'chancellor of the god', a trusted person chosen directly by the king to undertake a specific task: an expedition to the mines or quarries, trading trips to foreign lands, or management of a particular royal monopoly. In order to fulfil his task the 'chancellor' was provided with a troop or fleet of which he was the general or admiral.

It was no doubt a sign of the weakening of central power and the increasing demands of the administration that Pepy II split the role of vizier into two separate offices dealing with Upper and Lower Egypt. The vizier controlled the four main parts of the central administration, as well as the provincial administration (which was linked with the central authority by means of the 'chiefs of missions'). The first department of the central administration was the 'Treasury', or more correctly the 'Double Granary' (a term alluding to the original two halves of the country), which was overseen by a 'chief of the Double Granary' who operated under orders from the vizier. The Treasury was in charge of the economy was a whole, but it was particularly concerned with the collection of taxes, which derived essentially from the second major department: Agriculture. The department of Agriculture was subdivided into two sections. The first was concerned with the breeding and fattening of livestock, and was further subdivided into two 'houses', each delegated to a sub-director and scribal assistants. The second section of Agriculture was concerned with actual cultivation and lands recovered from the inundation (*khentyw-she*), and consisted of the 'care of the fields', over which the 'chief of fields' presided, assisted by 'scribes of the fields'.

The third major department of state, the Royal Archives, looked after the deeds for land-ownership. This department also held copies of documents recording civil actions, consisting essentially of contracts and testaments as well as the texts of royal decrees. Such documents provided the statutory basis of the fourth major department, that of Justice, which was concerned with the application of laws (*hepw*). The importance of each vizier was in direct proportion to his role within the theocratic system. This situation was demonstrated by the titles 'the greatest of the Five of the House of Thoth' and 'priest of

Maat', which were given to viziers in the Fourth and Fifth Dynasties respectively.

The central government was backed up by a system of provincial administration that relied on the division of the country into 'nomes'. The local administration of the Delta is badly documented owing to the continuing dearth of archaeological information from that part of the country. The great mass of available data derives from Middle and Upper Egypt, but the picture that can be constructed for the south of the country was no doubt equally applicable to the north.

Local administration appears to have undergone considerable development during the Old Kingdom. The basic trend was towards a modification of the statute covering the appointment of nomarchs so that the office became to all intents and purposes hereditary, even though it was still non-hereditary in legal terms. Lists of titles in the necropolises of provincial capitals indicate that the office of provincial governor began to be passed on from father to son in just the same way that the role of funerary priest was traditionally inherited, although there had previously been no such tradition for governors. This feudal system rested mainly on the economic exploitation of each individual region, which was one of the nomarch's principal tasks. The nomarch was above all the administrator entrusted with the maintenance of irrigation (*adj-mer*) and warden of the estates (*ḥeka-ḥwt*).

Originally this transfer of power from the king to the provincial governors would have been unthinkable, since the whole country theoretically belonged to the king, in his role as the personification of the creator. The officials were therefore each obliged to work for the king in return for the guarantee of their own continued existence. This situation was expressed by the Egyptian word *imakhw*, which is an almost untranslatable term describing the relationship between subject and king. The pharaoh rewarded, protected and nourished his subjects both on earth and in the afterworld, and it was he who provided his servants with their funerary concessions and those aspects of their tombs that they could not obtain through their own resources: the sarcophagus, the false door, the offering table and even the statues that sustained their spirits after death. The king was especially responsible for the provision of offerings by a funerary endowment, which was confirmed through a charter of immunity freeing the deceased's funerary estate from the obligation to pay tax. But this principle (which was essentially the same as the tax-exemption of temple estates) contained the seeds of the state's destruction, in that it favoured the dissemination of wealth and the gradual – and ultimately irreversable – impoverishment of the king. The profits enjoyed by the recipients of these concessions acted as a drain on the economy, since they effectively lay outside the redistribution network provided by the state. But even this was not the most important effect. The most serious problem was the social mechanism that was created by these concessions: the private funerary estates became the basis of a feudal system and the recipients attempted to acquire not only wealth but also the prerogatives associated with royal property.

The system of government established in the late Old Kingdom remained in place throughout the dynastic period, alongside the other basic elements of society. This does not mean, however, that the system did not evolve over time: this development principally took place in terms of the relationship between central authority and the local power bases, as in the reinforcement of the power of the viziers, the remodelling of the administrative districts and the creation of new governorates. The structure that this system imposed on the life of the country was to remain virtually unchanged until modern times. The social hierarchy continued to be based on the same values, and the nature of daily life evolved only to a minimal degree, especially in the less favoured strata of the population. There was hardly any difference between the farmers of the Old and Middle Kingdoms – between the Eloquent Peasant whose tale is related below, and the *fellahin* who supplied Rome with its wheat.

EGYPTIAN SCULPTURE

The art of the Old Kingdom is a faithful reflection of the social development of the period. During the 500 years that separated the reign of Djoser from that of Nitocris, the officials gradually usurped certain attributes and modes of representation that had initially been reserved for kings and members of the royal family. This was the first stage of a process of change that cannot be strictly characterized as democratization, but rather a progressive growth in political ideals. This change took place through the same mechanism as the nobles' acquisition of property. The means of production of works of art were beyond the capabilities of private individuals. It would have been unthinkable, at least in the Old Kingdom, for a noble – however powerful he might have been – to mount his own quarrying expedition to provide the material for the sarcophagus, door-jambs or statues that he would have needed for his tomb. It was the state that was responsible for these things, and the workshops in which statues were sculpted or reliefs engraved depended on the central power: art was the business of state employees. This principle meant that Egyptian art excluded practically all non-functional pursuits, and 'art for art's sake' is hardly ever encountered. Egyptian statues, paintings and relief sculpture have only two purposes: politico-religious or funerary. The first category was concerned only with the king, while the second was gradually taken over by private individuals. Thus Egyptian art was dominated by the tendency of individuals to adopt the style defined by the king, simply omitting those aspects that were impossible to translate into the private realm.

The whole of Egyptian art remained firmly fixed within a system which aimed at the creation of the most explicit possible representation of an individual or office. It was primarily concerned with stereotypes, but from time to time an astonishing harmony developed between 'Egyptian-style' realism and the individual sensitivity of the artist. This preoccupation with reproducing the deepest level of reality tended to expunge virtually all traces of subjectivity. The Egyptians were therefore able to avoid the potential pitfalls of human perspective by using their writing, reliefs and paintings to reduce people or objects to their most characteristic elements. This principle of 'combining different points of view' sometimes led to strange results. The basic idea was that each element of the representation should be unambiguously recognizable. The human eye, for example, is only recognizable when represented frontally, whereas the nose, like the ear, chin or head, is best represented in profile. The shoulders and hands are also shown frontally, whereas the arms are shown in profile and the pelvis in semi-profile. The torso is therefore subject to strange distortions, which can appear disconcerting at first sight. Traditional perspective is not used, although a few not very accomplished representations show that the Egyptians had some acquaintance with the concept. An army on the march is represented with each row of soldiers walking one in front of the other. Two simultaneous events are portrayed by placing them on separate registers, one above the other. A house and its garden were often shown in a combination of elevation and plan, even to the extent of adding on sections of walls at the sides and tacking elevations of trees onto the sides of a stretch of water shown in plan.

The same rules applied to statuary. Since the aim was to supply an 'inhabitable' body for all eternity, it was essential for it to be as perfect as possible. This is not to say that the artists always refused to depict physical deformity, but in most cases the body was idealized to a greater extent than the face, which was intended to preserve individual characteristics. The poses of the statues were restricted in the same way – they represented an office or a state and were therefore stereotyped images. Everything contributed to a rather uniform effect, characterized by a tremendous preoccupation with detail and such negligible variations in style that it is difficult to distinguish individual artists' personalities. The artists never attempted to draw attention to themselves, for their work was, by definition, anonymous. Collective creation continued to be the rule for the rest of the pharaonic period, as much in the plastic arts as in literature, with the individual always aiming to melt into the community as a whole.

STATUARY

The sculptural techniques of the Egyptians are known not only from scenes of craftwork that decorate the walls of *mastabas*, but also from an actual sculptors' workshop discovered by George Reisner in the funerary complex of Mycerinus at Giza. There he found a number of unfinished works, some at the rough outline stage and others in a state of near completion, allowing the various stages and methods of sculpting to be deduced. First the stone block was removed from the quarry, using techniques which varied according to the hardness of the stone: for soft rocks, direct blows with the chisel were employed; for harder rock, wooden wedges might have been driven gradually into cracks in the surface and soaked with water so as to split the block along a straight line. (This method of splitting blocks is refuted by Arnold 1991: 39.) Once extracted, the block was roughed out *in situ* then transported to the workshop. It was initially shaped by marking out the basic form of the future statue, after which its outlines – particularly the shape of the head – were gradually picked out. This was the beginning of a slow process of refinement which culminated in the creation of a definitive image. The sculptor delineated the arms and legs as much as possible by paying attention to every detail, and finally the statue was polished and engraved.

The tools used by the artists were essentially lithic, consisting of flint drills, rubbing stones, borers, grinding pastes, hammers and burins, and occasionally copper saws. The statues themselves were usually of limestone or sandstone (and these materials were most frequently painted), but also occasionally of granite, quartzite or schist. Egyptian alabaster (travertine) was used more for vases than for statues. Wood was used for statues, but it became genuinely widespread only later in the dynastic period. Copper was also used, the most famous examples being the figures of Pepy I and his son Merenre (Cairo, Egyptian Museum JE 33034 and 33035).

The various types of statuary were determined by a man's position in life. From the earliest times the king was shown seated on a solid cubiform throne the sides of which were decorated with the *sema-tawy* motif, consisting of the interlaced plants symbolic of Upper and Lower Egypt, joined together by a windpipe (Plate 4). The king was dressed in a *shendyt* kilt and wore the insignia of power on his head: one of the

PLATE 4 *Chephren protected by Horus. Seated statue from the valley temple of Chephren's funerary complex at Giza. Fourth Dynasty, diorite, h. 1.68 m. (Cairo, Egyptian Museum CG 14. Photograph: Laurie Platt Winfrey, Inc.)*

PLATE 5 *Djoser. Painted statue from the* serdab *of his mortuary temple at Saqqara. Third Dynasty, limestone, h. 1.35 m. (Cairo, Egyptian Museum JE 49158. Photograph:* © *John P. Stevens/Ancient Art & Architecture Collection.)*

crowns or the *nemes* wig and the false beard (Plate 5). In this type of statue the king was usually alone; if his wife accompanied him she was normally seated at his feet, as in the case of Hetepheres II(?) shown at the feet of Djedefre in the fragment of a statue found at Abu Roash (Louvre E 12627; Vandier 1958: pl. II, 1). Group statues are less common, although those of Mycerinus with his wife (Boston, Museum of Fine Arts 11.738) and in the centre of a number of triads from Giza (Vandier 1958: pl. IV–V) are particularly well known. There is a clear development in types of statuary after the Fourth Dynasty, perhaps as a means of linking the ideology of the theocracy and the actual reality of

political power. It is a little difficult to prove, but it is likely that the
king is shown in the process of celebrating various religious cults. The
Brooklyn Museum (39.121) has in its collection a schist statue of Pepy I
kneeling with two vessels of wine held in his hands. Another novel type,
also introduced in the Sixth Dynasty, were the statues representing the
king as a child, such as the alabaster statue of Pepy II (Cairo, Egyptian
Museum JE 50616). In this particular instance the innovation was
probably intended to draw attention to the young age at which that
particular king had risen to the throne. This shows how the official
phraseology of kingship could be adapted visually to the political
reality, as in the case of the group statues showing Pepy II seated on his
mother's lap, one example of which is in the Brooklyn Museum
(39.119). These statues of the royal mother and son are all carved from
alabaster, perhaps because their association with early childhood and
breast-feeding was deliberately being expressed in the milky appearance
of this stone. The association of Ankhenesmerire II with her son Pepy II
– represented not as a child but as a scaled-down figure of the adult
pharaoh – acts as a statement of the transmission of power from the
Queen as Regent to Pepy II as King.

These new types of statuary, particularly those that evoked family
relationships, were returning to themes that had already been addressed
by private statues. Statues of men with their wives and children drew to
some extent on the royal repertoire, but nevertheless worked effectively
on their own level. Like royal statuary, private statuary also went
through a process of change after the Fourth Dynasty: the style to some
extent moved away from the perfection that had characterized the
statues of Rahotep and Nofret (Plate 6) or the family of Hemiunu.
The statues of private individuals, which already outnumbered royal
statuary, became even more numerous in the Fifth and Sixth Dynasties
and tended to move away from the classic canons, although as the
example of the Louvre *Scribe* (N 2290) clearly demonstrates, this
did not affect their quality. Conventional types of private statuary,
consisting of standing and seated individuals shown with the symbols of
their position in life, continued to be produced alongside the family
groups and other new varieties. But there was a much greater freedom
to express individual taste as well as a growing concern with realism,
similar to that which is observable in royal statuary of the same period.
The works of the Sixth Dynasty acquired a certain degree of sensitivity
which was already evident in some statues of the preceding dynasty,
contributing enormously to the move towards greater realism; examples
of this increasing realism include the representation of the dwarf Seneb
and his family (Plate 7), or the magnificent statue of Nyankhre (Cairo,
Egyptian Museum).

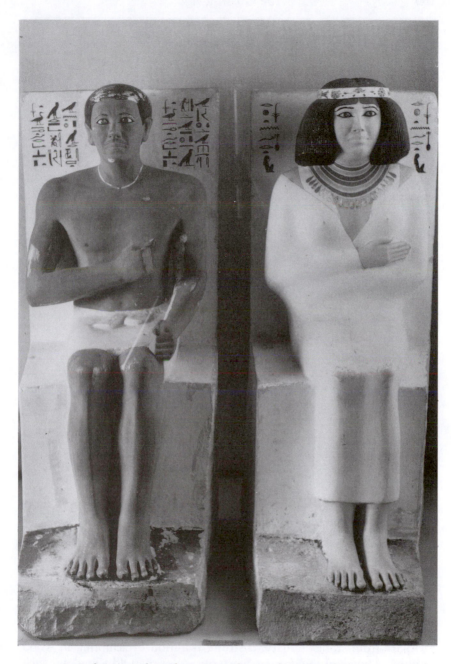

PLATE 6 *Rahotep and Nofret. Painted, seated statues from their tomb at Maidum. Fourth Dynasty, limestone, h. 1.2 m. (Cairo, Egyptian Museum CG 3 and 4. Photograph: John G. Ross.)*

PLATE 7   *The dwarf Seneb, with his wife and children. Painted group statue from Giza. Sixth Dynasty, limestone, h. 0.33 m. (Cairo, Egyptian Museum JE 51281. Photograph: Photographie Giraudon, Paris.)*

Apart from stone statuary, a strong tradition of sculpting in wood resulted in some of the greatest masterpieces of the Old Kingdom, such as a Memphite official and his wife (Louvre) and the statue of Kaaper (Cairo, Egyptian Museum). The figure of Kaaper is so realistic in its

appearance that Auguste Mariette's workmen, who discovered it in a
mastaba at Saqqara, saw a striking resemblance to the mayor of their
village – it was therefore given the nickname *Sheikh el-Beled*. This
development of wooden statuary prepared the way for the introduction
of another new form during the First Intermediate Period: the painted
stone and wooden 'models' which are essentially three-dimensional
versions of the scenes carved on the tomb walls. The earliest examples,
made of clay or painted stone, have a striking air of realism.

RELIEFS AND PAINTINGS

The procedure for the creation of reliefs and paintings was similar to
that used for statuary. Representations were carved directly onto the
fine limestone wall of the *mastaba*, the surface of which had been
previously cleaned and smoothed. A preliminary team of workmen
marked out a grid of lines on the tomb wall that was intended to bear
the reliefs. The scenes were sketched out with line drawings down to the
smallest detail, including their accompanying hieroglyphic descriptions.
The next stage was the creation of the bas-relief itself: the main subjects
of the reliefs were not carved until the whole of the surrounding area
had been cut back. This method of working evolved gradually from the
time of Cheops onwards, until a stage was reached at which, instead of
carving out the whole background, the artists simply made a deep
enough incision around the edges of the figures to create an illusion of
'raised relief'; they then engraved the details both within the figures and
in the background area of the relief. True raised relief, which involved
engraving into a protruding surface, was in practice used only for the
hieroglyphic mural inscriptions, as well as the inscriptions on monuments, statues or stelae.

New techniques also emerged when subterranean rock-cut tombs
began to replace the earlier *mastaba*s. The artists were obliged to
modify the surface of the wall itself in rock-tombs, as the irregular
expanse of natural rock was far less homogeneous than the fine limestone masonry of the *mastaba* tombs had been. The wall had to be
flattened and smoothed with a layer of plaster or, in less sophisticated
examples, with a coat of *muna* – a mixture of clay and straw or
sand which is still used by modern Egyptian potters and builders. The
paintings were then applied directly onto this artificial surface using
lamp-black, red and yellow ochre, and azurite and malachite mixed in
different quantities for blue and green. The subjects of the paintings
brought together a repertoire of scenes representing daily life and
funeral ceremonies.

5

Funerary Ideas

The pyramid, introduced by Djoser and reaching its most definitive form with the Great Pyramid of Cheops, is without a doubt the perfect image of the Old Kingdom. During the Thinite period at Abydos and Saqqara, the tombs of the élite had the appearance of great brick-built slabs, hence the term *mastaba* (Arabic for 'bench') which was given to them by Auguste Mariette's workmen. This architectural form continued to be employed for private tombs throughout the Old Kingdom in the Memphite region and for a slightly longer period in the area to the west of the Nile valley. The *mastaba* tomb was intended to reproduce the earthly environment of the deceased, or at least to preserve its outward appearance. It took the form of a massif, usually enclosing rooms intended as chapels and magazines. The outer surface of the tomb was faced with mud-brick walls decorated with pilasters and recesses giving the impression of a 'palace façade' in false perspective. The structure as a whole was often surrounded by an enclosure-wall marking out the territory of the dead.

The *mastaba* was the culmination of an architectural development that had begun with the predynastic tumulus covering the pit in which the deceased was buried. This tumulus was more or less derived from the idea of the original mound on which the solar creator had first appeared according to the Heliopolitan theologians. The tumulus must have been composed originally of sand supported by piles of stones or a framework of wooden planking. The deceased was placed below the tumulus in an oval or rectangular pit which gradually evolved during the prehistoric period, although its purpose always remained fundamentally the same: a place in which the owner of the tomb was deposited, together with the means to reach the afterworld and survive there. The body was most often laid in a contracted position on its side, sometimes on a reed mat or wrapped in a shroud. In the tomb chamber several objects were spread around the body, including varying amounts of pottery; these ceramic vessels were the main components of the tomb equipment, holding the food offerings placed at the disposal of the deceased. To this minimal set of grave goods were added various other items, depending on the period and wealth of the tomb's owner: a stone vase, provisions stored in jars, chests containing precious objects (essentially flint knives and arrows), jewels and gaming objects.

During the first two dynasties, the infrastructure and superstructure of the tomb developed into the classic *mastaba* type, which acted both as a centre of cult and as a representation of a man's earthly domain. Inside the *mastaba* the various means of subsistence and symbols of life were constantly repeated. The cultic aspect of the tomb took the form of niches containing stelae which served as a basic record of the name of the deceased from the tombs of the Thinite kings onwards. From an early date the high court officials appropriated this practice, which was originally reserved only for the king in the classic form of *mastaba* described above. The royal funerary prerogatives passed gradually down to common individuals, with the exception of the actual symbols and attributes of royalty. In the course of its development, the funerary stele also went through a process of elaboration: beyond simply naming the tomb's owner, it actually described the offerings which had to be brought to the deceased.

By this time the stele incorporated a virtual 'menu' offered to the beneficiary. Plate 8 shows a stele dedicated to the princess Nefertiabet, a contemporary of Cheops who was buried in a *mastaba* at the Giza necropolis. Everything in this document is arranged for maximum efficiency, starting with the identification of the recipient, which was achieved by means of a pictorial representation accompanied by her name and her principal title. Next the offerings are depicted, placed on a table with each individual item separated from the rest by simple horizontal or vertical spacing, so that they are all visible. They are also described in a list above the table, and this description is accompanied by a chart, on the right-hand side of the stele, giving details of the quantities of offerings provided.

The representations on the funerary stele mark a point of transition between the realms of the dead and the living. Theoretically, the stele continued to indicate the correct place for the deposit of offerings, as it must have done in earliest times. But it was soon incorporated into the architectural feature known as the 'false door', which was a representation in false perspective of the same type as the 'palace façade': a doorway surmounted by a rolled mat. The false door had developed

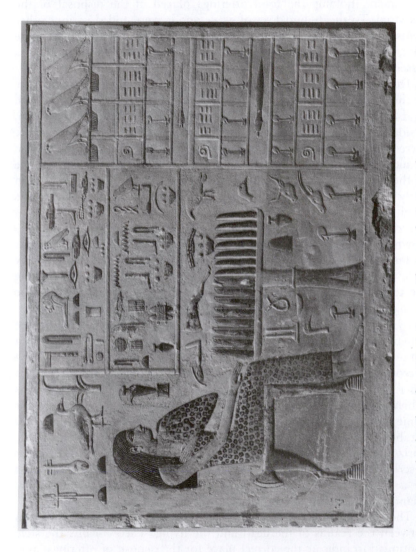

PLATE 8 Stele of Nefertiabet. (Musée Louvre. Photograph: Reunion des musées nationaux.)

out of a niche, a simple recess in the superstructure of the primitive *mastaba*, which was supposed to provide a means for the energy of the deceased, his *ka*, to enter the world of the living in order to obtain the provisions necessary for his survival.

THE ELEMENTS OF SURVIVAL

To the Egyptians, each human individual was made up of five elements: the shadow (the non-corporeal double of each of the forms assumed in a lifetime), the *akh*, the *ka*, the *ba* and the name.

The *akh* was an aspect of the sun, the luminous element that permitted the dead to join the stars when they passed into the hereafter; it was the form in which the power – the spirit – of the gods or the dead manifested itself.

The *ka* was the vital force possessed by every being; it multiplied according to the power of the being in question – Ra, for example, had fourteen *ka*s – and it had to be provided with food supplies in order to maintain its efficiency. Once the body had been suitably prepared for its triumph over death, it was the *ka* that allowed it to resume a life similar to the one it had enjoyed on earth. The *ka* not only needed nutrition in order to exist, it also needed a medium. From an early date therefore the Egyptians provided substitutes for the body, which was prone to decay, in the form of effigies of the deceased. They adopted the custom of incorporating a special chamber in the royal tomb: the *serdab*. This was a subterranean gallery inside the *mastaba* or the funerary infrastructure in general, which was connected with the cult rooms by means of an eye-level slit so that the statues placed there could gain access to the offerings. This practice was at first restricted to the king, but before very long it began to be adopted by private individuals. A deliberate gap left at the side of the tomb chamber played the role of the *serdab*, thus allowing the dead person to gain access to offerings left at the bottom of the shaft during the funeral.

The *ba* was also a non-corporeal entity which possessed the power of its owner, whether a god, corpse or living being. It was a kind of double of the deceased, existing independently of the body. The *ba* (usually incorrectly translated as 'spirit') was represented in the form of a bird with a human head which left the mortal remains at the moment of death, only returning after the process of mummification had taken place. It was an *alter ego* which could actually converse with its owner (Goedicke 1970).

Finally, the Egyptians believed that the process of naming an individual was an act of creation, not only when the baby was named at the moment of birth – when the mother gave it a name which described its appearance and predicted its fate in life – but also on every occasion that the name was uttered. This belief in the creative power of the word determined all behaviour regarding death: the act of naming a person or thing corresponded to the act of endowing it with life even after it had physically disappeared. It was therefore essential to provide numerous different means of recognizing the individual. This was why the funerary chapel, or the general cult-place, brought together as many explicit references as possible to the means by which the *ka* could enjoy the offerings due to it.

The combination of the stele and false door (the 'false-door stele') was a response to the *ka*'s needs, and during the Old Kingdom it went through a long process of development. The stele was the focal point of the tomb chapel, and the mural decorations were arranged so as to converge on it. The door itself varied in the degree to which it was decorated. It often included the *kheker* frieze, a decorative strip carved at the top of ordinary doors and walls which represented the tops of palm-trees, the trunks of which were tied together to serve as the walls of the earliest dwellings. This has survived into modern times in the form of the tops of *muna* walls that enclose country gardens, modelled around a core of *gerid* stalks.

The stele was placed between the upper and lower lintels of the door. The lower lintel listed the titles of the deceased, which were repeated and augmented on the jambs at either side of the door; occasionally these also bore a raised relief representation of the *ka* of the deceased. The first was generally inscribed with the beginning of the 'offering formula', by which the king dedicated offerings to a divinity who would, in his turn, supply benefits to the deceased. This principle theoretically ensured the continued observance of the funerary cult, even after the disappearance of the estate normally intended for the maintenance of the concession and the supplying of provisions for the tomb, which was entrusted to a specialized priesthood. It was sufficient, in fact, that the formula describing the offerings was still able to be read – at least by the deceased or by one of the images representing and standing in for him – for them to become a reality. The continued flow of offerings was guaranteed by the perpetuation of the cult of the god which then passed on some of its offerings to the deceased. This 'transferral' of offerings was a means of keeping the dead within the fabric of the universe. By ensuring that the deceased remained united with the organized world, his survival was rendered as certain as that of the rest of the cosmos.

THE FIRST PYRAMIDS

It was Djoser who brought about the evolution from *mastaba* to pyramid. Thanks to the work of the French archaeologist Jean-Philippe Lauer, the gradual stages of the change to the pyramidal form can now be traced. At first Djoser undertook the construction of a traditional *mastaba* tomb. A large shaft, 28 metres in length, which could be blocked after the funeral with a granite stopper, led to a granite-lined chamber with adjoining galleries which served as storerooms, containing vases carved out of hard stone. These subterranean rooms were completed by the construction of funerary apartments, many of the walls of which were decorated with blue faience tiles. One of these tiled rooms was evidently intended to reproduce the wood and reed mats of the building in which the king's double, or *ka*, was supposed to live, while another room reproduced the granaries of the royal residence. One of the panels of faience tiles, discovered in 1938 by Lauer, has been transferred to the Egyptian Museum at Cairo.

The whole substructure was initially covered by a massive square *mastaba*-like superstructure, measuring about 60 metres along each side and 8 metres in height. Since all the rooms were incorporated into the substructure, this massif consisted of a solid pile of blocks strengthened by a double casing of limestone. In the next stage of construction, new shafts were excavated along the eastern side of the structure, providing access to further subterranean funerary installations evidently intended for members of the royal family who had already died during Djoser's lifetime. In order to cover the entrances to these shafts, the initial *mastaba* was extended to the east.

It was at this stage in the construction that the builders embarked on a radical modification of the external appearance, which Lauer has interpreted as an attempt to make the tomb more visible: the original 8-metre high superstructure would have been rendered invisible to the distant spectator by the high enclosure wall surrounding the complex. Imhotep first enclosed the initial *mastaba* in a four-stepped pyramid; he then heightened the monument still further by transforming it into a larger pyramid of six steps, reaching a height of about 60 metres (Plate 9).

This type of step pyramid structure was reproduced by Sekhemkhet in his own funerary complex at Saqqara, before the Zawiyet el-Aryan pyramids introduced a new architectural style, culminating eventually in Snofru's pyramid at Maidum. The first stage of the Maidum pyramid was probably a *mastaba* surmounted by a small step pyramid, but this was the only link with the Third Dynasty monuments: the square plan, the entrance built into the masonry of the north face, and the location

PLATE 9   *View of the Saqqara Step Pyramid. (Photograph: © E. Hobson/Ancient Art & Architecture Collection.)*

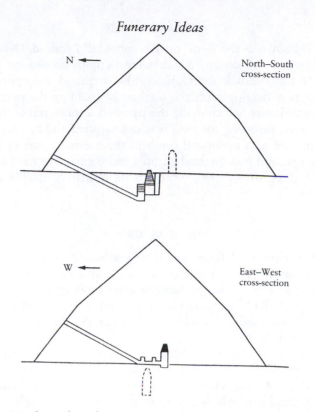

FIGURE 4   *North-south and east-west cross-sections of Snofru's 'Rhomboidal Pyramid' at Dahshur.*

of the internal rooms, partly in the substructure and partly in the upper part of the monument, were all closer to the appearance of the classic Fourth Dynasty pyramid. The basic nucleus was augmented by six vertical layers of local limestone, each sloping at an angle of 75° to form a seven-stepped pyramid. The architect then added a final outer layer and cased the eight steps with fine Tura limestone. Later the gaps between the steps were filled in and encased with another layer of limestone, finally giving the monument the appearance of a 'true' pyramid with a slope of 51° 52′, sides of 144.32 metres each and a height of 92 metres.

Snofru was evidently not satisfied with this tomb, for he made a second attempt with the 'southern' pyramid at Dahshur, the construction of which was clearly beset with problems. The internal rooms were constantly altered and modified, and the external slope of the pyramid was changed halfway up, from 54° 31′ to 43° 21′. This change of angle gave the whole monument its characteristic appearance, as a result of which it is known as the 'Bent' or 'Rhomboidal' Pyramid. Despite these imperfections in its design, which were perhaps caused by the poor quality of the bedrock foundations, this pyramid incorporated one important new development: the method of building the outer surface in horizontal layers, which made the pyramid a more stable structure.

Once more, however, the king was not satisfied and he embarked on a third attempt at a pyramidal tomb in the northern part of Dahshur. This new pyramid was established on a more extensive base and had a consistent slope of 43° 36′, although its mortuary temple remained incomplete.

THE GIZA GROUP

The perfect pyramidal form was finally achieved by Cheops at Giza, where the natural plateau offered a more stable base for construction than that at Dahshur. Cheops' tomb was the most spectacular and well-constructed of all of the pyramids, and hardly a generation has gone by without the formulation of some new theory explaining its method of construction or its use.

The internal structures of Cheops' pyramid are a convenient guide to the basic principles of pyramid building. At first a tomb chamber was incorporated into the substructure, in the style of the Maidum and Saqqara pyramids in which a long shaft sloped at an angle of 26° 31′ down from an entrance way in the northern face of the pyramid. But this earlier part of the pyramid was abandoned for unknown reasons and instead a room, now incorrectly described as the 'queen's chamber', was left in the superstructure, reached by a passage leading off from the original descending shaft. This chamber, the roof of which was made up of stone blocks forming an inverted V-shape, was also abandoned in its turn, before the completion of the air-vents leading towards the north and south outer faces. The final stage of the pyramid included a 48-metre-long sloping corridor (the 'grand gallery') 5.4 metres wide and 8.5 metres high, topped with a vaulted ceiling usually described as 'corbelled' (whereas in fact it has no corbels and would be better described as a *tas-de-charge* vault). The grand gallery emerged out of the passageway leading to the 'queen's chamber' and led to the actual tomb-chamber of the pyramid. The so-called 'king's chamber' measured 10.5 metres east-west and 5.25 metres north-south; its ceiling, consisting of nine stone blocks with a total weight of about 400 tonnes, was 5.8 metres above the floor of the chamber. This ceiling was surmounted by five successive compartments intended to relieve the weight and disperse the pressure of the superstructure, and the topmost of these rooms had a ceiling of heavy stone blocks forming an inverted V-shape.

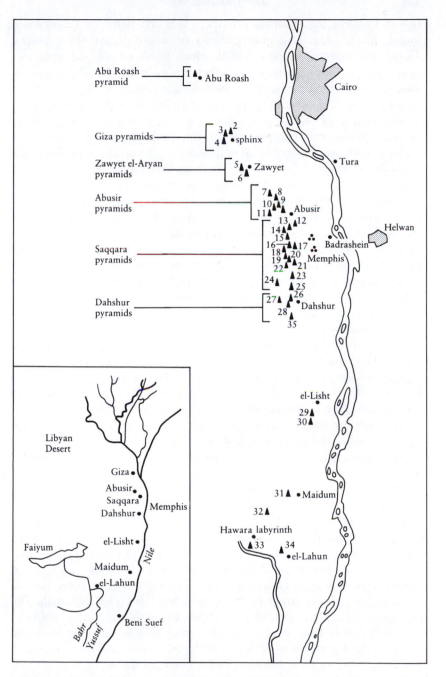

FIGURE 5 *Map of Egypt, showing locations of pyramid towns (numbers refer to Table 2).*

It was in these load-bearing chambers that the name of Cheops was found, inscribed among quarry-marks on some of the stone blocks. Throughout the rest of the pyramid, which has been pillaged repeatedly since earliest times, there is no other evidence of the identity of its builder. The 'king's chamber', which contained a broken granite sarcophagus, was linked with the grand gallery by a direct passageway in the course of which were three granite portcullises intended to prevent anyone from gaining entry to the tomb.

An endless succession of descriptions, analyses and soundings has made the structure of the Great Pyramid well known: the sides of its square base each measure 230 metres, to an accuracy of 25 centimetres, and each side is orientated to a cardinal point. It has a slope of 51° 52' and a height of 146.59 metres, to which the estimated height of a pyramidion (probably of granite) should also be added. The Egyptians themselves have left little evidence of their methods of construction but it is possible nevertheless to gain some idea of the way in which the pyramids were built from a few representations, archaeological remains, and the analysis of the monuments themselves. Even modern geophysical investigations using sophisticated techniques are no substitute for simple logic.

The site of the pyramids was chosen so as to be convenient both for the capital city and the river. It needed a platform of bedrock capable of supporting the tremendous mass of the proposed buildings, and it had to be on the west bank of the Nile, which was the traditional location for the kingdom of the dead: as the sun set each day it bathed the western skyline with its rays before embarking on its journey through the night. The necropolis also had to be above the level of the annual flood waters, which would have been able to come within at least 300 metres of the plateau.

Once the site had been chosen, it then had to be levelled out – in the case of Cheops' pyramid the ground surface was all within 18 millimetres of the same level – leaving only a central mass of bedrock to be incorporated into the masonry, both to economize on materials and to perpetuate the idea of the primeval mound covering the burial chamber. The orientation of the pyramid was related to its sides, which pointed towards the cardinal points. This would have been easy to calculate for the western and eastern sides but less so for the north. The possibility of a fixed measurement from the pole-star seems unlikely, since this would have led to a greater error than is perceptible on the ground. The Egyptians must have employed a relatively simple method involving the use of a *merkhet* ('instrument of knowing'), a kind of astronomical device consisting of a plumb-line attached to a wooden handle. The *merkhet* could be used to sight on the two points along an artificial horizon where a fixed star – perhaps part of the Great Bear constellation – rose and set. The bisection of the angle between these two points would have then given the direction of true north (Edwards 1985: 243–7).

Once correctly orientated, construction of the base of the pyramid could then commence. Local quarries provided the rough material used for the internal fill of the pyramid: at the northern corner of Chephren's pyramid are traces of quarrying into the bedrock, as well as the remains of buildings a little further to the west which might have housed about 5500 of the workers, quarriers or craftsmen of the necropolis. Similar workmen's barrack-blocks were later constructed at Kahun and Deir el-Medina. The fine limestone necessary for the outer casing was brought from the nearby quarries at Tura, and Aswan granite was used for the lining of corridors and internal rooms as well as for the cult buildings. Other types of stone, used for the manufacture of such items as sarcophagi, paving stones, statues and architraves, must have sometimes been brought from a great distance, as in the case of the diorite transported from quarries in the desert west of Aswan. Once extracted from the quarries, the blocks were usually worked *in situ*, then conveyed by foot onto Nile barges. The transportation took place at the time of the inundation, so that the harbour would be as close as possible to the blocks. This explains some of the details of Weni's account of his final mission as governor of Upper Egypt for King Merenre. He had been sent to obtain the materials necessary for the pharaoh's pyramid, including granite from Aswan, alabaster from Hatnub and basalt from Nubia:

> His majesty sent me to Ibhat to bring the sarcophagus 'chest of the living' together with its lid, and the costly august pyramidion for the pyramid 'Merenre appears in splendour', my mistress. His majesty sent me to Yebu [Elephantine] to bring a granite false door and its libation stone and granite lintels, and to bring granite portals and libation stones for the upper chamber of the pyramid 'Merenre appears in splendour', my mistress. I travelled north with them to the pyramid 'Merenre appears in splendour' in six barges and three tow-boats of eight ribs in a single expedition . . . His majesty sent me to Hatnub to bring a great altar of alabaster of Hatnub. I brought this altar down for him in seventeen days. After it was quarried at Hatnub, I had it go downstream in this barge I had built for it, a barge of acacia wood of sixty cubits in length and thirty cubits in width. Assembled in seventeen days, in the third month of summer, when there was no water on the sandbanks, it landed at the pyramid 'Merenre appears in splendour' in safety . . . His majesty sent me to dig five canals in Upper Egypt, and to build three barges and four tow-boats of acacia wood of Wawat . . . I did it all in one year. Floated, they were loaded with very large granite blocks for the pyramid 'Merenre

appears in splendour'. (*The Autobiography of Weni*, Lichtheim 1973: 21–2)

The period of inundation was also the season when the work-force, essentially consisting of peasants, were available for the corvée-work that they were obliged to undertake for the king. In these conditions of seasonal work, Herodotus' estimate of twenty years for the construction of a pyramid does not seem unreasonable, although some of the monuments, such as Snofru's pyramids, must have taken less time. However, Herodotus' description of the techniques of building up the blocks of the pyramid (Edwards 1985: 257) is hardly credible, and the theory proposed by Jean-Philippe Lauer, based on the use of one or more ramps of varying slope, is much more plausible. According to Lauer, the construction ramp would have been perpendicular to the face of the pyramid. Its width would have been greatest at ground-level but it would have gradually narrowed and lengthened as the pyramid grew in height, in such a way that the slope of the ramp would always have been about 1:12, making it sufficiently gentle to allow sledges to be used to drag the blocks up. This theory, which has the advantage of simplicity, seems to be confirmed by the survival of remains of mud-brick ramps at the First Pylon of the temple of Amon-Re at Karnak and at Maidum and el-Lisht. The fine outer casing, set in layers like the internal rooms, would have been fixed in place from the top downwards, once the pyramidion had been placed on the apex of the monument.

No other pyramid has equalled the scale or the perfection of the Great Pyramid of Cheops. The pyramid of Djedefre, who preferred to locate his tomb at Abu Roash rather than Giza, has not survived in sufficiently good condition to allow a proper comparison to be made. That of Chephren, on the other hand, follows Cheops' model quite closely, as does Mycerinus' pyramid, which is only half the size (although the internal arrangements of Mycerinus' tomb are quite different, incorporated into the substructure and of a different design).

The Fifth and Sixth Dynasty pyramids reproduced the external appearance of the archetypal Great Pyramid but on a smaller scale. The only differences related to the development of the internal chambers (the plan of which was virtually fixed in the reign of Wenis) and the various non-pyramidal elements of the funerary complex. The only exception was the tomb of Shepseskaf, in southern Saqqara, which was not a pyramid but a huge *mastaba*, now known as the Mastabat el-Fara'un. This monument was a masonry sarcophagus almost 100 metres in length, 75 metres wide and about 19 metres high. It is difficult to find an explanation for Shepseskaf's apparent return to previous funerary traditions, especially as this was only a partial reversion to the Early Dynastic *mastaba* style of tomb: the *mastaba* was surrounded by a double enclosure wall but it also had a causeway leading up to it, like those introduced in the Fourth Dynasty. The arrangement of the funerary apartments chosen by Shepseskaf was retained by the kings of the Sixth Dynasty, who also located their tombs close to that of Shepseskaf, perhaps regarding him as their precursor.

Shepseskaf's apparent 'revival' of Early Dynastic architecture is an indication of the difficult transition from the Fourth Dynasty to the Fifth. After Shepseskaf's death, Khentkawes, the mother of Sahure and Neferirkare and probably Shepseskaf's second wife, built a tomb for herself at Giza (between the causeways of Chephren and Mycerinus) that was also *mastaba*-like in appearance. It was half *mastaba* and half pyramid, consisting of two steps reaching a height of 18 metres above the ground. But Khentkawes also had a second tomb in the form of a pyramid, excavated at Abusir, to the south of Neferirkare's pyramid, which must have been almost as high as her tomb at Giza. In the mortuary temple of her Abusir pyramid she was the object of a personal cult in which she was revered, long after she had died, as the ancestor of the Fifth Dynasty.

THE FUNERARY COMPLEX

The general organization of the funerary complex changed in the Fourth Dynasty, at much the same time as the introduction of such new components as the queens' pyramids (which had only their own cult temples, otherwise being dependent on the king's own funerary installations). Three queens' pyramids were built to the east of Cheops' pyramid; the southernmost was for Queen Henutsen. Mycerinus also had three of these small pyramids to the south of his tomb, the largest of which (also the easternmost) played the same role as that which flanked the southern face of Chepren's pyramid: both were 'satellite' pyramids serving the king's double. The satellite pyramid first appeared at Maidum; it contained neither sarcophagus nor cult installation, but it did have its own entrance and tomb chamber. It is reminiscent of the building against the southern enclosure wall of Djoser's complex, which was intended for the king's *ka* and included a traditional Thinite cenotaph and a cult chapel. Djoser's enclosure wall was intended to reproduce the one that enclosed the royal domain during his lifetime. This type of palace façade had been represented since earliest times in the form of the *serekh*.

The entrance to Djoser's Step Pyramid is near the south-east corner of the enclosure, via the only real doorway out of fourteen apparent

TABLE 3 *Table of major pyramids of the Old and Middle Kingdoms*

Dynasty	Ruler	Ancient name	Location
III	Djoser		North Saqqara
	Sekhemkhet		North Saqqara
	Khaba (?)		Zawyet el-Aryan (south)
IV	Snofru	Snofru is stable	Maidum
	Snofru	Snofru of the south appears in glory	South Dahshur
	Snofru	Snofru appears in glory	North Dahshur
	Cheops	The horizon of Cheops	Giza
	Djedefre	Djedefre is the dispensor of light	Abu Roash
	Chephren	Chephren is great	Giza
	Mycerinus	Mycerinus is divine	Giza
	Shepseskaf	Shepseskaf's place of libation	South Saqqara
	Khentkawes		Giza
	Khentkawes		Abusir
V	Userkaf	Pure are the places of Userkaf	North Saqqara
	Userkaf	Ra is in the precinct	Abusir
	Sahure	The *ba* of Sahure appears in glory	Abusir
	Neferirkare	Neferirkare is a *ba*	Abusir
	Neferefre	The *bas* of Neferefre are divine	Abusir
	Neuserre	Established are the places of Neuserre	Abusir
	Neuserre	Place agreeable to Ra	Abu Ghurob

No. on Figure 5	Modern name	Base (m)	Principal excavators
14	Step Pyramid	123.3 × 107.4	Brugsch, Firth, Quibell, Lauer
16	Step Pyramid	118.50	Goneim
6	Layer Pyramid	83.80	Barsanti, Reisner, Dunham
31	'Southern' Pyramid	144.32	Lepsius, Maspero, Petrie, Rowe, Stadelmann
27	'Bent' or 'Rhomboidal' Pyramid	188.60	Perring, Vyse, Jéquier, De Morgan, Husein, Varille, Fakhry, Stadelmann
24	'Red' Pyramid	219.28	Perring, Vyse, De Morgan, Stadelmann
2	Great Pyramid	230.30	Vyse, Borchardt, Petrie, Reisner, Junker, Lauer
1		105	Vyse, Lepsius, Chassinat
3		215.25	Belzoni, Vyse, Mariette, Maspero, Petrie, Borchardt, Junker, Baraize, S. Hassan
4		104.60	Vyse, Perring, Borchardt, Reisner
22	'Mastabat Faraʿun'	99.60 × 74.40	Mariette, Jéquier
–	Step Pyramid cenotaph	43.70 × 45.80	Junker, S. Hassan
–			Verner
13		73.30	Perring, Vyse, Firth, Lauer
8	sun temple		Perring, Vyse, Borchardt, Ricke
9		78.50	Perring, Vyse, Borchardt
10	unfinished	108	Perring, Vyse, Borchardt, Verner
11			Borchardt, Verner
10A		78.80	Perring, Vyse, Borchardt
7	sun temple		Borchardt, Schäfer, von Bissing

TABLE 3 *Continued*

Dynasty	Ruler	Ancient name	Location
	Menkauhor	Divine are the places of Ra	Dahshur
	Menkauhor	The horizon of Ra	Abusir (?)
	Djedkare-Isesi	Isesi is beautiful	South Saqqara
	Wenis	Beautiful are the places of Wenis	North Saqqara
VI	Teti	Enduring are the places of Teti	North Saqqara
	Ipuit		North Saqqara
	Khuit		North Saqqara
	Pepy I	Established and beautiful is Pepy	South Saqqara
	Merenre	Merenre appears in glory and is beautiful	South Saqqara
	Pepy II	Pepy is established and living	South Saqqara
	Neith		South Saqqara
	Ipuit		South Saqqara
	Wedjebten		South Saqqara
VIII	Qakare Iby		South Saqqara
XI	Nebhepetre Mentuhotpe	Glorious are the places of Mentuhotpe	Deir el-Bahri
XII	Ammenemes I	Ammenemes is risen and beautiful	el-Lisht
	Sesostris I	He who is associated with the places of Sesostris	el-Lisht
	Ammenemes II	The *ba* of Ammenemes	Dahshur
	Sesostris II	Sesostris is brave	Lahun
	Sesostris III	Sesostris appears in glory	Dahshur
	Ammenemes III	Ammenemes is beautiful (?)	Dahshur
	Ammenemes III	Ammenemes lives	Hawara
	Sobkneferu (?)		Mazghuna
XIII	Khendjer		South Saqqara

No. on Figure 5	Modern name	Base (m)	Principal excavators
–	undiscovered		
–	undiscovered		
19		78.50	Vyse, A. Husein, Varille
15	pyramid 'with texts'	57.75	Vyse, Barsanti, Maspero, Firth, S. Hassan, A. Husein, Piankoff
12	pyramid 'with texts'	78.75	Vyse, Perring, Maspero, Loret, Lauer, Leclant
–		15.50	Loret, Firth
–	disappeared		Loret
17	pyramid 'with texts'	78.75	Vyse, Mariette, Maspero, Lauer, Leclant
18	pyramid 'with texts'	78.75	Mariette, Maspero, Jéquier, Lauer, Leclant
20	pyramid 'with texts'	78.75	Maspero, Bouriant, Jéquier, Lauer, Leclant
–	pyramid 'with texts'	24	Jéquier
–	pyramid 'with texts'	24	Jéquier
–	pyramid 'with texts'	24	Jéquier
21	pyramid 'with texts'	30.60	Jéquier
hp	mortuary temple		Naville, Hall, Winlock
29		84	Maspero, Gautier, Jéquier
30		105	Lansing, Lythgoe, Mace, Winlock, Arnold
26			De Morgan, Arnold
34		104.20	Petrie, Brunton
25		105	Petrie, De Morgan, Arnold
28	cenotaph	102.60	Petrie, De Morgan, Arnold
33		100.20	Petrie, Fakhry
35			Petrie, Mackay
23			Jéquier

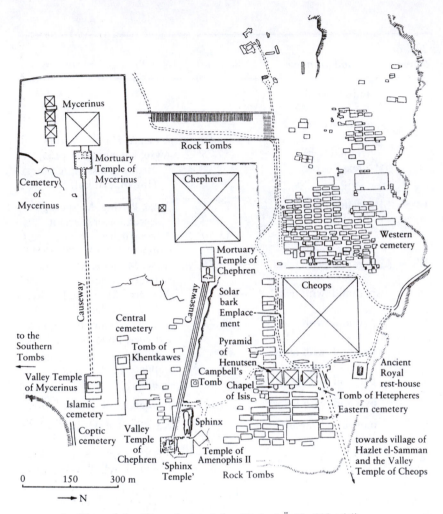

Labels on figure:

Mycerinus

Mortuary Temple of Mycerinus

Cemetery of Mycerinus

Rock Tombs

Chephren

Western cemetery

Mortuary Temple of Chephren

Solar bark Emplacement

Causeway

Causeway

Central cemetery

Cheops

to the Southern Tombs

Tomb of Khentkawes

Pyramid of Henutsen

Valley Temple of Mycerinus

Campbell's Tomb

Chapel of Isis

Ancient Royal rest-house

Islamic cemetery

Sphinx

Tomb of Hetepheres

Eastern cemetery

Coptic cemetery

Valley Temple of Chephren

'Sphinx Temple'

Temple of Amenophis II

towards village of Hazlet el-Samman and the Valley Temple of Cheops

Rock Tombs

0   150   300 m

→ N

FIGURE 6   *Plan of the Giza plateau (after Zivie, LÄ II, 613–14).*

entrances spread at intervals along the edge of the enclosure wall. The doorway opens on to a passage with a row of twenty fluted columns on either side, leading first to a small hypostyle hall and then into a huge north-south orientated courtyard, separating the Step Pyramid from the southern cenotaph. In the area to the south of the courtyard and the pyramid is a complex of buildings designed for the celebration of the *sed* festival. One first approached a T-shaped temple, which must have been a type of pavilion in which the king waited at various points in the ceremony, then a court surrounded by chapels, which included a

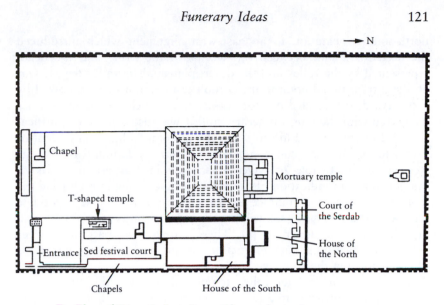

FIGURE 7 *Plan of Djoser's Step Pyramid complex at Saqqara.*

platform. In this court the deceased king was supposed to be able
to enact the different phases of the jubilee festival by moving from
one building to another through doors along the walls which are
represented as being eternally open (Lauer 1988: 208ff.). When the king
had accomplished the rites in the jubilee complex, he went to the 'house
of the south' and the 'house of the north' where he was enthroned as
King of Upper and Lower Egypt respectively.

The northern part of the Step Pyramid complex comprises the actual
installations of the funerary cult, including the *serdab*, which contained
a statue of Djoser (Plate 5; now in the Egyptian Museum, Cairo).
Through two eye-level holes carved in the *serdab* wall Djoser was
able to watch the presentation of funerary offerings in the adjoining
mortuary temple.

This physical grouping of all of the elements of the funerary complex
inside a single enclosure wall was to disappear in the Fourth Dynasty,
when it was replaced by a looser arrangement articulated around the
three major elements of the complex: the pyramid and its annexes, the
valley temple and the causeway. The valley temple, located at the edge
of the cultivated land, was where the dead king was brought for his
funerary rites; it theoretically represented the quay on which the king
embarked on a voyage that corresponded to the god's journey through
the oceans of the sky. The first valley temple appeared in the funerary
complex of Snofru at Maidum, coinciding with the change from a

north-south orientation to an east-west alignment which introduced
the need for a link between the worlds of the living and the dead,
represented by the valley and the desert plateau. The valley temple was
at first a transitional point in the complex: an entranceway followed by
a courtyard, surrounded by storerooms and chapels containing statues
connected with the king's funerary cult. It was also a place of purification and reception, and in this sense it was comparable to any point of
access to an Egyptian cult complex. The four triads found by George
Reisner in the temple of Mycerinus (now in Cairo and Brooklyn
museums) are an indication of the valley temple's role: in each triad the
king is shown in the embrace of the goddess Hathor and a goddess
representing a nome (respectively the Eighteenth, Fifteenth, Seventh and
Fourth Nomes of Upper Egypt). These statues were part of a larger
collection which must have originally incorporated the personifications
of every nome in the country.

The decoration in later valley temples shows that this function of
reception was entrusted to a female divinity such as the lioness-goddess
Sekhmet, who is shown suckling the king in Neuserre's funerary complex at Abusir. This must also have been the role of Hathor with regard
to Mycerinus; indeed, the inscriptions on the triads describe her as the
'Lady of the Sycamore', who was clearly – whether in the guise of
Isis or Hathor – identifiable with the mother-goddess of the Theban
necropolis, later depicted as a tree suckling Tuthmosis III in his tomb at
the Valley of the Kings (Mekhitarian 1978). If this interpretation is
correct, it seems likely that the valley temple should be interpreted not
merely as a place of purification and reception but also as a place of
rebirth. After the funeral ceremonies the king's statues eternally relived
the ritual practised at the moment of embalmment (the valley temple in
this way foreshadows the role of the *mammisi*, or 'birth-house', in later
temples) and at the moment of the passage from life to death. The
arrangement of the buildings does not indicate if the valley temple was
used for the practice of mummification, which according to Herodotus
lasted for seventy days. Parts of the temple even suggest that there were
a number of external architectural elements, probably only temporary
installation. Ultimately, it was the transition point through which the
deceased had to pass in order to reach the pyramid.

The causeway led from the valley temple to the mortuary temple, the
final point of contact between the worlds of the living and dead; it was
often roofed and decorated, like that of Wenis at Saqqara, which
stretched for 700 metres. The decorative themes in the causeway were
similar to those which adorned the walls of private tombs, but with an
additional pharaonic dimension: processions of servants bringing the
products of the royal estates, scenes from the economic life of the

country, episodes of animal husbandry, hunting, fishing, and other aspects of daily life, as well as scenes of the building of the temple and the supplying of offerings. There was also a tradition of including a number of scenes depicting important events of the reign of the king in question. The practice is thought to date back as early as the Fourth Dynasty, although there is no surviving evidence of such scenes until the Fifth Dynasty. Events depicted on Wenis' causeway include the transportation of granite columns from the quarries at Aswan to the temple, a procession of representatives from the various nomes, a fleet returning from Byblos, battles against bedouin tribes, and representations – unique to this period – of starving desert peoples, which perhaps constitutes evidence of the kind of famine conditions that were to affect the whole country four centuries later.

The mortuary temple, which was placed against the northern face of the pyramid throughout the Third Dynasty, was moved in the Fourth Dynasty in response to the change in the orientation of the complex that began with the Maidum pyramid. In order to correspond to the daily course of the sun, the mortuary temple was positioned against the east face of the pyramid. The temple consisted of two distinct parts: first, a vestibule leading to a court (which was a peristyle court from the time of Cheops onwards), together constituting the cult temple itself; and second, the inner sanctum, where offerings could be placed by the false door. Statues of the king, shown eventually in the company of his family, as in the case of those depicting Djedefre (Louvre), were placed in the chapels of the mortuary temple to take advantage of the offerings and act as the focus of the cult. These two functions – the funerary offerings and the cult of the royal statues – made up the core of the temple's activities.

From the reign of Sahure onwards there was an increase in the number of annexes, such as magazines, attached to the mortuary temple, and there was a more definite distinction between the cult temple and the inner sanctum. In the latter, the king's cult was centred around the *sed* festival and the rituals associated with the regeneration of the king, particularly through divine suckling. The decoration of the mortuary temple focused on scenes of hunting and warfare, including the ritual massacre of enemies. It also stressed the close relationship between the king and the gods and gave greatest prominence to the cult of the royal statues.

Another element of the funerary cult in the immediate vicinity of the pyramid was the pits which held wooden barques. Known since the Thinite period, these sacred barques allowed the deceased to travel through the afterworld by the side of Ra. There are five known boat pits at the foot of the eastern and southern faces of Cheops' pyramid.

One of those in the southern group was excavated in 1954, and the fragments of the boat found inside it have now been rebuilt and are exhibited in a museum beside the pyramid. These boats were not necessarily made of wood, however; Wenis, for example, had two stone-built boats to the south of his causeway.

Sacred barques have also been found in another type of religious building peculiar to the Fifth Dynasty: the sun temple. Although the sun temple was functionally different from the pyramid complex – being a temple rather than a tomb – it was structurally very similar. The surviving examples are at Abusir and Abu Ghurob, that of Neuserre at Abu Ghurob being the best preserved. It was doubtless modelled on the original sun temple at Heliopolis, which has now vanished for ever under the urban expansion of Cairo.

The sun temple is composed of the same basic elements as the pyramid complex. The valley temple, on the walls of which were reproduced the decrees announcing the supply of offerings, communicates with the upper temple by means of a sloping causeway. The upper temple consists essentially of a courtyard open to the sky, in the middle of which is an altar. In Neuserre's temple four interlinked altars – each pointing to one of the cardinal points and each carved from the same block of alabaster – faced the representation of the *benben* stone. The *benben*, the incarnation of the sun as creator according to Heliopolitan theology, was a truncated obelisk placed on a large podium. The cult was celebrated in the open air, as in all known sun temples, including those later integrated with the New Kingdom mortuary temples or the Amarna sanctuaries in which Akhenaten adored the sun-disc. Like these New Kingdom temples, Neuserre's sun temple included a slaughter-yard for the sacrifice of animals. Among the surviving reliefs are representations of the sun cult and the *sed* festival, and also, in the Neuserre temple, an original set of representations known as the 'Seasons', decorating the ascending passageway which surrounds the *benben*'s platform. This theme was partially reproduced on Wenis' causeway, and found another distant echo much later in the 'Botanical Garden' that decorated the solar rooms to the east of the festival hall of Tuthmosis III in the temple of Amon-Re at Karnak; it also occurs in the Great Hymn to the Aten of Akhenaten.

Each of these works, from Neuserre's 'Seasons' to Akhenaten's hymns, is in its own way a description of creation as well as a hymn to the creator, describing the whole of the fauna and flora nourished by the rays of the sun. Another type of representation was subsequently to

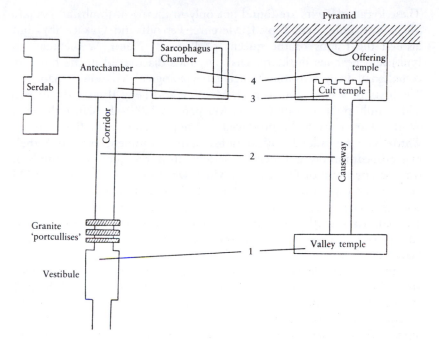

FIGURE 8 *Comparison between plans of (a) the tomb chambers of a pyramid and (b) the pyramid complex as a whole.*

become more common: the processions of nomes bringing the king the products of the land. This theme recurs not only in Wenis' complex but also, in a systematic way, in the later temples.

THE PYRAMID TEXTS

Wenis established the typical plan of the internal chambers of the pyramid according to a scheme that was to remain in use until the end of the Old Kingdom. The entrance was in the north, leading down first to a vestibule and then, past three granite portcullises such as those already described in Cheops' pyramid, to an antechamber. This antechamber was served by a *serdab* to the east (the side of the living) where the statues of the deceased were placed. To the west of the antechamber (towards the world of the dead) was the room containing the sarcophagus. This design was abandoned in the Twelfth Dynasty, when attempts were made to resist the onslaughts of tomb-robbers.

The pyramid of Wenis is also important for another reason: it is the first in which the internal corridors were decorated with funerary texts.

These Pyramid Texts are found not only in the royal tombs at Saqqara (those of Wenis, Teti, Pepy I, Merenre, Pepy II and Qakare Iby) but also in the tombs of the queens of Pepy II (Neith, Wedjebten and Ipuit) and perhaps in the queens' pyramids discovered in the funerary complex of Pepy I by the French Archaeological Mission at Saqqara. The texts of Wenis, Teti, Pepy I, Merenre and Pepy II were discovered and rapidly published by Gaston Maspero in 1880–1. Before the First World War, Kurt Sethe produced a synoptic edition of the texts, to which he later added critical notes and a commentary. But Sethe's masterly edition did not include the texts from the queens' pyramids or from the pyramid of Qakare Iby, which were discovered between 1925 and 1935 by Gustave Jéquier. Since Sethe's edition of the texts was also too early to include the new fragments discovered by French archaeologists in the pyramids of Teti, Pepy I and Merenre, a new edition of the corpus is being prepared under the direction of Jean Leclant.

The texts consist of a succession of formulae, some of which only appear in Wenis' tomb, while the majority were passed on until the time of Qakare Iby. These formulae also appear in another aspect of the funerary corpus: the *Coffin Texts*, the earliest examples of which have been found on Sixth Dynasty sarcophagi at the Dakhla Oasis. The Coffin Texts were not restricted to kings' tombs, and they superseded the Pyramid Texts in the Middle Kingdom. In the mortuary temple of Pepy I traces have even been found of the literary transition from the Pyramid Texts to the Coffin Texts. Later, the Coffin Texts in their turn provided the basis for the *Book of the Dead* of the New Kingdom and the Late Period.

These funerary formulae recount a ritual which was intended to ensure that the deceased passed through into the afterworld and an existence among the blessed. They describe his ascension into the sky, his establishment among the stars, his transformation into the sun and his metamorphosis into Osiris. They also provided him with the necessary texts for his purification and the magic incantations that enabled him to overcome the obstacles blocking his path. The formulae probably derived from a set of archaic rituals that have not survived, either because the documents themselves have been destroyed or more probably because they were at first oral traditions.

The Pyramid Texts supply certain pieces of information that allow the development of the royal tomb in the Old Kingdom to be better understood. The *mastaba* reproduced, within the home of the dead, the primeval mound from which Atum created the world – and so stood as a symbol of creation. The texts also suggest why Imhotep decided to turn the *mastaba* into a square and to cover it with a pyramid. According to the Pyramid Texts the aim of the king was to rise up to the sky, where he would undergo transformation into both the sun and a star. To achieve this aim, he had several means at his disposal: the desert whirlwinds (which still retain their supernatural connotations in the modern term *afrit*), the assistance of the god Shu who could lift him up in his arms, transformation into a bird (most often the falcon, which flew highest) or, most poetically, he could drift up into the sky with the smoke from the censers. On the other hand, the king could choose the more prosaic method of ascending a stairway or a ladder formed by the rays of the sun. This stairway was provided by the step pyramid, the hierogyphic symbol for which was also the determinative sign of the word ʿr ('to climb'). The step pyramid method of ascension was, however, superseded after just over a century by the smooth-sided pyramid of the Fourth Dynasty. From the Fourth Dynasty onwards the pyramid, like the *benben* stone, appears to have symbolized the petrified rays of the sun by means of which the king could climb up to heaven. The pyramid was therefore a prototypical image, like the solar barque which accompanied it. The change to the smooth-sided pyramid and then the introduction of the *benben* stone were intended to reconcile the conflict between Atum and Ra. After the first attempts at such a theological reconciliation by Djedefre and Chephren, a solution was finally found in the Fifth Dynasty, whereby the two gods were assimilated with one another.

Thus Wenis was assimilated with Atum in the Dwat, the underworld. Dwat was presented as an equivalent of Nun, the first waters from which the creator had evolved. Wenis was then lifted up in the solar form of Atum in order to enter Dwat, the horizon. It was this passage from one state to another, doubtless already expressed in the form of the Great Sphinx at Giza, that the texts describe. The texts can therefore be read in an order corresponding to their position in the tomb, linked first with the enactment of the funeral ceremony and secondly with the process of the king's resurrection.

The texts first describe the march to the tomb: the entrance hall of the pyramid corresponds to the valley temple, the corridor is the equivalent of the causeway and the antechamber is the mortuary temple. The chamber containing the sarcophagus serves as the inner sanctum, and the *serdab* – both here and in the mortuary temple itself – contains the images of the king. This sense of being able to read the texts from the entrance of the tomb to the sarcophagus is clearly apparent in Pepy I's pyramid. Once the deceased has been placed in his sarcophagus the texts can be read again but in the opposite direction, from the tomb chamber towards the extrance; this time the meaning relates to resurrection, in the course of which the rooms acquire symbolic roles. When the king leaves the sarcophagus, he is leaving Dwat, the underworld. When he finds himself in the antechamber – the horizon – he is Atum. From there he embarks on his ascension by climbing back up the corridor to the granite portcullises, which now symbolize the gates of heaven closed by a bolt in the form of the god Bebon's phallus. Once the doors have been broken, the king finds himself back in the tomb, which has become Dwat, night, domain of the stars in the midst of which he achieves immortality.

PRIVATE TOMBS

At the time of his ascension to the heavens, the king was not content with gaining eternal life only for himself. He himself became one of the companions of Ra, but he was also responsible for his subjects, whom he took with him into the hereafter. For their part, his subjects welcomed his guardianship as they sought to ensure their own survival. They obtained life after death not by being buried in the same tomb as the king, as they had been in earlier times, but by placing their tombs in close proximity to his. Complete cities of the dead grew up in this way, with tombs arranged like houses into roads and quarters, and the hierarchical position of each occupant was measured by his distance from the pyramid. In this way the social hierarchy was perpetuated after death, with the nobles, courtiers and officials guaranteed their eternal reward alongside the king.

The tombs of private individuals were built in the form of *mastabas* until the end of the Old Kingdom. The term 'private individuals' is here understood to cover the whole of the population except the king, including members of the royal family. Princes tended to assume political roles and therefore saw themselves primarily as officials, even though their titles stressed their royal origins or connections with the ruling family. It is more difficult to make this kind of distinction between the tombs of kings and queens, for not all queens had a small pyramid attached to their husbands' tombs. In general, queens' tombs are treated as private monuments which are more or less similar to the king's, depending on their importance and the role they had played as a wife or mother of a ruler. The two most illustrious queens are Hetepheres, the mother of Cheops, and Khentkawes, who was presented as the 'mother of two kings' in her tomb at Giza and worshipped as the founder of the Fifth Dynasty at Abusir. Nitocris is the only genuine instance of a female ruler in the Old Kingdom, but unfortunately the pyramid that she must surely have been entitled to build has not yet been discovered.

The development of the *mastaba* gradually caught up with the

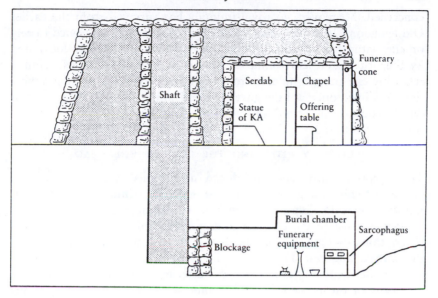

FIGURE 9   *Cross-section of a typical* mastaba *(after Desroches-Noblecourt 1946, 54).*

pyramid, changing at the end of the Third Dynasty from mud-brick to marly limestone, and then, in the Fourth Dynasty, to siliceous lime-stone, which was particularly impressive when furnished with an outer casing of fine limestone. It was the superstructure rather than the substructure that underwent the most development. The tomb chamber itself went through hardly any process of evolution; it was essentially the container for the corpse, sometimes square, sometimes rectangular and sometimes even circular. In the Fourth Dynasty tombs were still most frequently built of mud-brick with a stone roof in the form of a 'corbelled' vault. Each contained a rectangular sarcophagus made of either limestone or granite according to the generosity of the king who granted it to the official, since the man himself would have been unable to afford the expense of a quarrying expedition to Tura, Hatnub or Aswan.

It is difficult to be sure whether bodies were mummified at this date. Theoretically, there is evidence for mummification as early as the First Dynasty and remains of a mummy were found in the tomb of Djoser. The remains of the dead buried in the great necropolises of the Old Kingdom are very poorly preserved however, and there is no scene in any of the chapels to confirm the practise of mummification, which is only described in later periods, at least as far as private individuals are concerned. Moreover, no royal mummy has survived from the earlier Old Kingdom. It is likely that most of the population continued to rely on the natural dessication of the body, which was greatly facilitated by the arid desert environment. This was probably the case until a relatively late period, judging from the lack of evidence of mummification in the necropolis of the governors of Dakhla Oasis at Balat, part of which dates to the second half of the Sixth Dynasty.

FUNERARY RITES AND THE CULT OF THE DEAD

The Egyptians themselves produced no detailed description of the process of embalming, or at any rate no such document has survived. Existing pictorial representations of embalming are never totally explicit, consisting more of religious than technical allusions. Written descriptions of Egyptian mummification therefore derive mainly from the Greek authors: Herodotus, Diodorus, Plutarch or Porphyrus. From these sources it is possible to reconstruct the principal methods and aims of the process and the symbolic value which the Egyptians ascribed to mummification. But sometimes it is only the 'unwrapping' of mummies and their analysis with modern technology that can definitively refute the received ideas on mummification. Mummies have been scientifically examined in many museums throughout the world: in the mid-1970s the remains of Ramesses II had to be taken to Paris for emergency treatment when they were found to be infested with beetles. And in 1985 a multidisciplinary team of researchers examined an anonymous Late Period mummy at Lyons Museum (Goyon and Josset-Goyon 1988). The main stages of mummification, in the New Kingdom at least, are described below.

After death the body was taken to a special 'house of purification', where the treatment began. It was stretched out on a table and the brains were removed. One of the dissectors – the surgically-trained priests who specialized in the preparation of cadavers – made an incision in the left side, using a knife which, for ritual purposes, was made of flint. Through the wound the priest broke through the diaphragm and eviscerated the corpse. The internal organs were removed and treated separately; once they had been embalmed and wrapped in bandages they were usually placed in vessels, a practice continued until the beginning of the Third Intermediate Period. The first known jars for viscera were found among the funerary furniture of Queen Hetepheres, the mother of Cheops. On the basis of Athanasius Kircher's false interpretation of their symbolism and purpose these vessels became known erroneously as 'canopic jars'. The jars were placed alongside the sarcophagus in the tomb chamber, under the protection of the Four

Sons of Horus – Imsety, Hapy, Duamutef and Qebehsenuef – who looked after the liver, the lungs, the stomach and the intestines respectively. In later times the viscera were simply placed in their correct place on the body in the form of 'canopic packets' which had been properly treated. Only the heart and kidneys were left in the body, since their location made them difficult to extract.

Once the corpse had been emptied of its internal organs, the embalmer began the task of 'salting' the body by placing it in natron for about thirty-five days. Since this treatment had the side-effect of darkening the flesh, some of the limbs were died with henna or coated with ochre (red for the men and yellow for the women, as in the painting of statues and reliefs) in an attempt to counteract this process. Then the abdomen and chest were stuffed with pieces of material usually provided by the family of the deceased; the wads of material were soaked in gums, herbs and various unguents so that the body could be preserved and restored to its original shape. The opening made by the surgeon in the abdomen was covered up with a plaque which was also placed under the protection of the four sons of Horus.

The body, having been restored in this way, was cleaned and purified. It was then wrapped in bandages, in a process consisting of several stages. First of all, linen strips were used to wrap each individual part of the body, including the fingers and the phallus; then the body was covered with a large piece of material acting as a shroud and the whole of the torso was bandaged. This process was carried out according to a very precise ritual, which took the same form whether the body was that of a king or a private individual. The only difference was in the value of the amulets which were slid under certain parts of the body and among the bandages. From the New Kingdom onwards funerary texts were also included in the bandages, fulfilling the same purpose as the amulets and jewels; a *Book of the Dead*, for instance, was often inserted between the legs of the mummy. Finally, the face was covered with a mask. This was usually of cartonnage, but in the case of important persons it could be made of gold and lapis-lazuli, the flesh and hair of the gods. The mask gradually developed from the New Kingdom onwards until it became a 'board' covering the whole of the body and reproducing the appearance of a coffin lid. The final stage in its development was reached with the Faiyum 'mummy portraits' painted on wood in encaustic (a mixture of pigment and wax).

The coffin in which the mummy was placed also went through a long process of evolution. At first it acted primarily as a kind of house for the deceased, judging from its rectangular appearance and 'palace façade' decoration. But from the Sixth Dynasty onwards, although it still maintained its role as a false door, the coffin began to be decorated with texts. The painted hieroglyphs on the coffin consisted of offering formulae and friezes of objects acting as substitute offerings, but also chapters from the Coffin Texts (Valloggia 1986: 74–8), the surviving examples of which date mainly to the Middle Kingdom. The material and shape of the coffin also evolved, and a distinction is usually made between the sarcophagus, often made of stone or carved out of the rock surface, and the actual coffin, which tended to mould to the shape of the body from the Middle Kingdom onwards.

The funerary furniture continued to be made up of the same basic elements: headrests, pottery vessels, toiletries and the remains of the funeral feast. The entrance to the tomb chamber was at first blocked by a stone slab as in the royal tombs, and the shaft, which might include a stairway or a corridor emerging into the courtyard in front of the superstructure, was blocked at the time of the funeral ceremony.

It was the chapel, always located in the superstructure of the monument, which went through the most complicated process of development. The chapel was at first cruciform and located in the eastern part of the *mastaba*; at this stage it was simply the logical development of the original niche acting as a false door. But after the reign of Snofru the plan of the chapel changed and a complex typology began to evolve, varying in such aspects as the general plan, the presence of niches and the number of rooms. The most radical developments took place at Giza, where more systematic use of stone brought about a drastic change in the appearance of private funerary monuments: stone chapels could be built with a more accentuated batter than mud-brick, and they tended to have more extensive surfaces available for internal decoration. The development of the chapel in the Fifth and Sixth Dynasties involved the addition of more and more rooms, which gradually altered the general layout and produced the richest and most beautiful examples of this type of tomb, which was barely to outlast the Old Kingdom itself.

The career of Ti, whose tomb was discovered by Auguste Mariette in 1865, has already been described above (p. 78). Both in terms of architecture and quality of reliefs, the *mastaba* of Ti is one of the masterpieces of funerary art in the Old Kingdom. The vestibule is decorated with the procession of the thirty-six estates of the deceased and the presentation of his farms and poultry on each side of the door; this bears the 'call to the living', an address to the visitor asking him to pronounce the offering formula for the benefit of the deceased. When this formula is spoken by a living person, the offerings come into being and ensure the subsistence of the tomb's owner. Beyond the doorway is a pillared court, its walls decorated with scenes relating to daily life on Ti's estates (aviaries, bird-keeping and the collection of taxes) and the preparation for the funeral ceremony (including the transport of the funerary equipment, while Ti is carried to the tomb in a palanquin, along with the family dog). The first *serdab*, which was found to contain a statue of Ti (Cairo, Egyptian Museum CG 95), adjoins this court, which also contains a false door bearing the name of Ti's son Demedj, who was a courtier like his father.

A little further into the chapel, in the first corridor; another false door is dedicated to his wife Neferhetepes. The reliefs show Ti acting out his priestly roles, and there are scenes of music-making and dancing, as well as a sailing trip made by Ti and his wife. The second corridor is decorated with a depiction of Ti visiting his Delta estates, his return to Memphis afterwards, the transport of statues and scenes of offerings. This corridor leads to a storeroom, the walls of which show scenes of potters, brewers and bakers at work, as well as the presentation of offerings which must, in practice, have been stored in a niche.

Finally, at the far end of the tomb is the main chapel, which is connected to the second *serdab* by three entrances. This room is decorated with themes intended to encompass all the elements of Ti's life in the hereafter. Opposite the *serdab* are depicted a procession of estates, hunting and fishing in the marshes, animal husbandry and agricultural and Nilotic scenes incorporating Ti, his family and their pets. On the eastern and southern walls are scenes of the harvesting of flax and corn, the presentation of livestock, the assessment of taxes and craftsmen at work. Scenes of craftsmen were an indispensable part of private tomb chapel decoration until the end of the Old Kingdom, when they were transformed into three-dimensional 'models'. On either side of the two false door stelae embedded in the western wall – at the transitional point between the kingdoms of the living and the dead – were scenes of slaughter and offering.

The basic scheme of decoration in the tomb chapel was virtually always identical. The deceased welcomed the visitor at the doorway to the tomb, which was decorated with his own image and titles. Inside the chapel, on the western wall opposite the entrance door, were one or more false doors which allowed the deceased and his family to enjoy their offerings. The northern false door was usually reserved for the owner of the tomb and the southern one was usually his wife's, while the wall between tended to be decorated with plant forms or imitation tapestries. On the wall opposite the false doors were scenes of the funerary pilgrimage by boat to the holy cities of Busiris and Abydos, at the northern and southern ends of the wall respectively (corresponding to their geographical locations). The northern and southern walls were decorated with scenes of daily life on the estates: agriculture, animal husbandry, games, arts and crafts. The southern wall usually bore depictions of the censing of the statues which were placed in the *serdab* behind it.

This decorative system was also used, for the most part, in a new type of tomb that appeared in the Fourth Dynasty: the rock-cut tomb. The earliest known rock-tombs were carved out of the Giza plateau. The layout of the rooms was the same as that of the *mastaba*, consisting of antechamber, chapel and *serdab*. The shaft leading down to the tomb chamber began either in the chapel or in a special room. The only significant difference, naturally enough, was the external appearance of the tomb, the outer façade usually being carved with niches in order to simulate the entrance to a *mastaba*. The rock-cut tomb usually served as a substitute for a *mastaba* tomb when the nature of the terrain rendered the construction of a *mastaba* superstructure impossible. The inhabitants of provincial towns adopted the same type of tomb as those in the capital, but they did not always have suitable locations for such necropolises, particularly in Middle Egypt where the cemeteries were usually clustered in the cliff-face at the edge of the valley. This led to the construction of rock-cut *mastabas*, such as those found at the Tihna necropolis from the Fourth Dynasty onwards – this architectural type rapidly developed into the full-blown rock-cut tomb. The nomarchs of the Hare province (the Sixth Dynasty chiefs of the palace – Meru, Wau and Ankhteti) had rock-cut tombs at Sheikh Said, south of the modern town of Mallawi. There were also rock-tombs at Deir el-Gebrawi and especially at Aswan, where the Qubbet el-Hawa necropolis included about thirty tombs of this type.

The undecorated façade of the tomb of Sabni at Aswan is entered through a doorway flanked by two stone stelae resembling the large slabs adorning the entrances to the contemporaneous *mastabas* of the governors of Dakhla Oasis at Balat. The chapel itself, wider than it is deep, is divided by three rows of six pillars. In the central aisle an offering table is placed in front of the cult chapel, which consists basically of a false door carved into the western wall. The tomb communicates with that of Sabni's father, Mekhu. Both are decorated with a selection of typical subject matter.

With this type of Aswan tomb it was not merely a question of adapting to the local terrain. When the environment was not suitable either for a traditional *mastaba* or a rock-cut tomb – as in Dakhla Oasis where the clayey ground prevented building in stone – the architects tended to adopt a mixed strategy, combining a subterranean tomb-chamber of stone masonry, built inside a pit excavated into the clay, with a mud-brick superstructure resting on its foundations and a layer of mud-brick fill (Valloggia 1986: 43–8). When the rock-tomb eventually superseded the *mastaba*, it was primarily because the political centre moved to the south and necropolises were no longer situated on the plateau but in the cliff-face itself.

The scenes in Old Kingdom tombs are a crucial source of information on the economic and, to some extent, the social aspects of life during this period. They also provide information on funerary traditions and practices themselves. It is apparent above all, that whereas the king was thought to ascend to the heavens, the deceased private individual remained in his tomb, where he enjoyed a continued existence based on his earthly life. It was the proximity of the god, and therefore of the king (expressed in the layout of the necropolis), that guaranteed the incorporation of the deceased into the divine world. This explains the omnipresence of the king inside private tombs: first, through the actual patch of land allotted to a private funerary monument; second, through the concession of key architectonic elements such as the sarcophagus, the false door and the offering table; and third, in the autobiography of the tomb's owner. The deceased was totally dependent on the king, of whom he was an *imakhu*. The imprisonment of the deceased in the interior of his tomb, accompanied by an extraordinary wealth of precautions taken to multiply the chances of the soul's survival (including statues and simple 'reserve heads' placed in the *serdab* with texts and representations), reduced the image of the universe to a set of earthly realities.

Decorative themes developed in detail as time went by, but continued to focus on the essential realities of the life of the deceased. All the various phases of human existence can be followed in these themes: from life itself, through the scenes of daily activities, to the final acts in which the deceased was conveyed from the funereal house to eternity. The mourners are shown gathered around the corpse, making the typical gestures of those who weep over the dead, just as Isis and Nephthys mourned the death of Osiris, continually sighing and moaning as they watched the passing of their loved one. The body – still watched over by the mourners – was then carried in a canopied barque to the house of embalmment, dedicated to Anubis. There the corpse received the various attentions described above, and the dead man was then supposed to travel in a boat to the Delta town of Sais. This ritual was a kind of first pilgrimage to a place where, according to Herodotus, the Osirian Passion was later enacted. On this journey to Sais the deceased received offerings in the 'pure place' (*wabet*). These offerings consisted mainly of items of food, and the act of offering included slaughtering rituals involving the embalming priests and the ritualist as well as the mourners. The dead man then embarked on a second journey, this time to the holy city of Buto. Neither of these journeys physically took place, since the whole ceremony was enacted within the necropolis, where two locations were simply nominated as 'Sais' and 'Buto'. After visiting the Heliopolitan sanctuaries, the dead man was brought back to the area in front of the necropolis, and there the last rites were administered, marking his final departure from the world of the living. The corpse was then purified again with libations and incense while the mourners continued to weep around it.

This ritual is followed by a number of linked episodes. Two priests act as if they are arguing over who will take the sarcophagus: one is the embalmer trying to drag him towards the living, while the other is the funerary priest, whom the deceased must ultimately follow. Next the *tekenu* appears – a human form wrapped in an animal skin and carried on a sledge. It is usually given the name 'neighbour', which suggests that it may have been a kind of protective force in the necropolis, helping the dead man to triumph over his enemies as he entered the tomb. The sarcophagus was dragged towards the west, while behind it a group of men carry the canopic jars. The procession arrives at the entrance to the tomb, and in front of the false door the funeral feast – the prototype for the offerings that must continue to be brought to the tomb throughout eternity – is laid out. Next the funerary furniture is taken into the tomb-chamber, followed by the sarcophagus and a statue of the deceased in the act of making his pilgrimage to Abydos, the holy city of Osiris. After the enactment of the rites of protection, the chamber is sealed for ever: the scenes on the walls of the tomb can then spring to life, providing the dead with eternal enjoyment of his earthly possessions.

6

The Struggle for Power

The 150-year period between the Old and Middle Kingdoms is known as the First Intermediate Period – a term which is arguably almost meaningless. The 'intermediate' period is not an acceptable historical concept, since every period is in a sense intermediate between two other phases of a civilization. It is also clear that the Egyptians themselves did not consider the First Intermediate Period a major disruption in the flow of their history. Not only was there no apparent break in the continuity of pharaonic rule, but the archetypal institutional form of government was still claimed by the local dynasties, each desiring to establish its own grip on the reins of power that had slipped from the hands of the Memphite rulers.

The chronological span of the First Intermediate Period is also a problem. There is general agreement that it ended with the reign of Nebhepetre Mentuhotpe II, a Theban prince who saw himself and his forbears as the legitimate rulers of Egypt rather than mere provincial governors. He reunited the two kingdoms, which are said to have once more separated into autonomous regions as they had been in the predynastic period. This disintegration into two separate regions may be presented as an indisputable political feature of the First Intermediate Period, but it is actually incompatible with Egyptian historiography – both the accounts of the Theban princes and Manetho's history suggest that the succession of rulers in the First Intermediate Period continued to be split up into dynasties. The end of the Old Kingdom is an equally problematic issue: was it gradually extinguished by a period of slow decline in royal authority (which can be traced back to the reign of Pepy II and the collapse of the Sixth Dynasty at the time of the difficult succession to Nitocris) or was it ended by the crisis that engulfed Egypt at that time?

Manetho's description of the Seventh Dynasty betrays the confused nature of his sources: 'seventy kings in seventy days'. This formulation may have been a pun on the number of the dynasty, emphasizing its ephemeral character (Helck 1956b: 32), or it may have been a metaphor for the seventy creative forces in the Heliopolitan cosmology. The Egyptian sources themselves are relatively quiet about this shadowy period. The only known written evidence is a literary work, of a somewhat apocryphal nature, which has survived in the form of a single manuscript. This text, said to have been written by a man called Ipuwer, is an apocalyptic evocation of the crimes committed in his lifetime. The general tone and the choice of facts in the 'prophetic' *Admonitions* suggest that the aims of the work were political. Ipuwer longs for the order that prevailed in the past as he describes the state of the country in his own time, listing the disasters brought on by the decline of central power and the lack of a strong king. The arrival of a powerful ruler appears to have been announced in the closing section of the prophecy, but unfortunately this has not been preserved:

> See now, things are done that never were done before,
> The King has been robbed by beggars.
> See, one buried as a hawk is . . .
> What the pyramid hid is empty.
> See now, the land is deprived of kingship
> By a few people who ignore custom.
>   (*Admonitions* 7, 1–4)

This was a double sacrilege, for not only had the country been deprived of its ruler, and therefore its guarantee of the continuity of established order, but the preceding generations had also been stripped of their means of survival by the destruction of the king's body. It was the collapse of the whole of society, and Egypt itself had become a world in turmoil, exposed to the horrors of chaos which was always waiting for the moment when the personification of the divine being – the pharaoh – neglected his duties or simply disappeared. Behind the phraseology of the *Admonitions* there was a context of real events, the evidence for which has survived in more indirect ways. Some attempt has been made to interpret these events as a social revolution, but this is unlikely, considering that no new form of government subsequently emerged; the ancient method of rule was maintained, as it would be after the next two Intermediate Periods.

The events described by Ipuwer were probably the revolt of the most disinherited strata of society, provoked not by a feeling of social injustice –' which would have been totally alien to Egyptian society – but by forces outside Egypt itself, which found fertile ground in the weakened country. The end of the third millennium BC was characterized by the onset of a Sahelian climate, particularly in eastern Africa (Bell 1971: 1–8). The resultant shortage of food in Egypt was exacerbated by the decline in central administration, doubtless no longer able to restrain the power of the nomarchs, who had become more or less independent rulers within their provinces. The nomarchs would have kept their irrigation canals in a good state of repair in order to ensure the most economical use of the annual inundation, assuming that the floods had already become less and less adequate over a period of several years. This theory is supported by evidence which also illustrates the fragility of the concept of an 'intermediate period': it would seem that the famine, or at any rate the troubles that accompanied it, were limited to the Nile valley. The agricultural town of Balat in the Dakhla Oasis, for example, and its adjacent necropolis, show no signs of destruction or disruption at the end of the Sixth Dynasty (Giddy 1987: 206ff.).

This critical phase lasted no longer than one or two generations, but the violence that it engendered did not immediately die down. In fact, the climate of violence may have persisted for quite some time, judging from the regrets expressed by the king of Herakleopolis (probably Khety III) in the *Instruction* that he passed on to his son almost a century later:

> I attacked This straight to its southern border at Taut,
> I engulfed it like a flood . . .
> Lo, a shameful deed occurred in my time:
> The nome of This was ravaged;
> Though it happened through my doing,
> I learned it after it was done.
> (*The Instruction addressed to King Merikare*;
> Lichtheim 1973, 102, 105)

Khety III's protestations of innocence show that long after the troubles recounted in the *Admonitions*, he himself was still unable to control his troops properly. The famine had not disappeared in a single year, and it seems that these generations of starvation and violence had left an enduring mark on the Egyptians (Vandier 1936).

Another difficulty began to undermine the state of the country – the situation outside Egypt. No evidence has survived of the maintenance of links with the outside world that had been established in the Old Kingdom: the trade through Syria-Palestine with Byblos and the Eastern Mediterranean seems to have stopped, and the exploitation of mines in the Sinai peninsula also seems to have been abandoned. Worse still, the bedouin (the 'sand-dwellers' against whom Weni had campaigned not so long before) invaded the Delta region towards the end of the Eighth Dynasty. Events in the south were hardly any better, as the commercial and military forays into Nubia temporarily ceased, leaving the indigenous C-group culture free to develop without Egyptian interference.

THE HEIRS

There is more evidence of the Eighth Dynasty than of the Seventh. Of the seventeen kings that can be assigned to the former (von Beckerath 1984a: 58–60), at least five of the names cited in the king-lists incorporate the coronation name of Pepy II: Neferkare. It has therefore been suggested that these may actually have been his sons or grandsons, and this may well be the case with Nebi, Khendu and Pepyseneb. A little is known concerning the final kings of the Eighth Dynasty from copies of decrees issued to the family of the vizier Shemay at Koptos, but the only Eighth Dynasty king who can be precisely indentified is Qakare Iby, the fourteenth in the succession, whose reign lasted for two years according to the Turin Canon. Qakare Iby's pyramid has been discovered in southern Saqqara, close to that of Pepy II. Despite its smaller dimensions, it continued the Memphite tradition in being inscribed with Pyramid Texts on the inside walls.

During this period (*c*.2160–2150 BC) the situation in Egypt was far from satisfactory, for the Delta had been seized by invaders from the east, whom the Egyptians described as 'Asiatics'. Virtually the whole of the country lay outside the authority of the Eighth Dynasty kings, whose power seems to have been restricted to the area around Memphis. In Upper Egypt, Thebes was no longer the capital of the fourth nome, and its princes – the successors of Ikni – were laying the foundations for their future kingdom. Meanwhile the control of Middle Egypt had passed to the princes of Herakleopolis, the capital of the rich and fertile twentieth nome of Upper Egypt, Nennesut (the 'royal child'), now known as Ahnas el-Medina.

Herakleopolis was situated in an important strategic position, acting as the gateway from north to south along the Bahr Yussuf, a little to the south of the entrance to the Faiyum region. The Herakleopolitan province, protected from northern invaders by its geographical position, had derived great benefit from the increase in trade as a result of the colonization of Nubia. The power acquired by the prince of Herakleopolis, Meribre Khety I, does not appear to have been contested by the other nomarchs, for his name is found as far south as Aswan. The dynasty that he founded – Manetho's Ninth – only lasted for about thirty years (*c*.2160–2130 BC), but it had the effect of bestowing a certain legitimacy on the Tenth Dynasty, which was also Herakleopolitan. The coronation titles chosen by the kings of Herakleopolis – such as Meribre, Neferkare and Nebkaure – were intended to suggest that they were the successors of the Memphite royal line. The Herakleopolitan kings may even have retained Memphis as an administrative seat (Vercoutter 1987: 147), judging from the location of Qakare Iby's tomb at Saqqara. The excavations of archaeologists from Hanover and Berlin have revealed a Ninth Dynasty private necropolis at Saqqara, which suggests that the city of Memphis must have still been active at this time (Leclant and Clerc 1986: 256–7). If the tradition that Merikare was buried near Teti is correct, then Saqqara may still have been the royal necropolis during the Tenth Dynasty. But ultimately these are nothing more than suppositions, for nothing is known of most of the Ninth Dynasty kings apart from their names, and it is difficult to interpret the rare information that archaeology has provided concerning their time. At Dara, for example, near the modern town of Manfalut (at the entrance to the Darb el-Tawil that leads to Dakhla Oasis), an entire royal necropolis has been found. In the centre of the Dara cemetery is a pyramid belonging to King Khuy, whose reign has been dated, without any great certainty, to the middle of the Eighth Dynasty (von Beckerath 1984a: 60). The resumption of excavation at Dara by the French Institute for Oriental Archaeology at Cairo may shed light on this phase of the history of Middle Egypt.

HERAKLEOPOLITANS AND THEBANS

The Tenth Dynasty, which lasted for almost a century, was both longer and better-documented than its predecessors. Its founder, another Neferkare, would have been the seventh ruler to bear this name. In a graffito at Hatnub he is called either Mery-Hathor – 'beloved of Hathor' (Vercoutter 1987: 143) – or perhaps more plausibly, Meribre (*LÄ* VI, 1441 n. 5), which would have given him a secure link with the Memphite tradition on which he based his claim to the throne. His successor, Wahkare Khety III, initiated a feud with his southern neighbours the Thebans, who were attempting to conquer the Herakleopolitan kingdom. After the collapse of the Memphite government, the provinces had at first played a game of alternate alliances with or against the legitimate power. Later, however, they chose to take their own chances, or at least to bolster their own positions. It is no longer believed that there were actual kingdoms ruled from Abydos or even from Koptos (although the slightly unusual location of Koptos at the entrance to the Wadi Hammamat would perhaps have given it some influence). The family of the vizier Shemay at Koptos, mentioned above, were quick to ally themselves with their Theban neighbours during the period of confrontation between Thebans and Herakleopolitans. This conflict is described in the autobiography of a certain Ankhtifi, the governor of the third nome of Upper Egypt, Hefat (now el-Moalla), which was about 40 kilometres south of Luxor:

> The Prince, Count, Royal Seal-bearer, Sole Companion, Lector-priest, General, Chief of scouts, Chief of foreign regions, Great Chief of the nomes of Edfu and Hierakonpolis, Ankhtifi, says: Horus brought me to the nome of Edfu for life, prosperity, health, to re-establish it, and I did (it) . . . I found the House of Khuy inundated like a marsh, abandoned by him who belonged to it, in the grip of a rebel, under the control of a wretch. I made a man embrace the slayer of his father, the slayer of his brother, so as to re-establish the nome of Edfu (. . .)
>
> I was as concerned for the lowest of men as for the highest. I was the man who found the solution when it was lacking in the country thanks to poor decisions, and my speech was clever and my bravery won the day when it was necessary to join the three provinces together. I am an honest man who has no equal, a man who can talk freely when others are obliged to be silent. At a time when it was necessary to shake off fear, Upper Egypt was silent (. . .)
>
> The general of Armant said to me: 'Come, oh honest man. Sail with the current down to the fortresses of Armant!' I then went down to the country to the west of Armant and I found that all the forces of Thebes and Koptos had attacked the fortresses of Armant (. . .) I reached the west bank of the Theban province (. . .) Then my courageous crack troops, yes my bold crack troops, ventured to the west and the east of the Theban nome, looking for an open battle. But no one dared to come out from Thebes because they were afraid of my troops (. . .)
>
> The whole of Upper Egypt died of hunger and each individual had reached such a state of hunger that he ate his own children. But I refused to see anyone die of hunger in this province. I arranged for grain to be loaned to Upper Egypt and gave to the north grain of Upper Egypt. And I do not think that anything like this has been done by the provincial governors who came before me (. . .)
>
> I brought life to the provinces of Hierakonpolis and Edfu, Elephantine and Ombos! (Inscriptions 1–3, 6–7, 10 and 12; Vandier 1950, 161–242)

Ankhtifi was therefore nomarch of Hierakonpolis and faithful follower of the overall ruler of the Herakleopolitan kingdom, who must at that time have been Neferkare VII. It is significant that Anktifi's titles are deeply rooted in the Memphite tradition and completely out of proportion to the actual size of his province. That the prince of Hierakonpolis should simultaneously have filled the roles of generalissimo, chief of prophets, interpreters and 'mountainous regions' (i.e. foreign affairs) as well as chancellor of the King of Lower Egypt is perhaps an indication of the degree to which the Herakleopolitan kingdom must have diminished. There is another striking aspect of Ankhtifi's account: Weni had listed his national offices first, whereas Ankhtifi describes himself first of all as the chief of his province; he is not governor of a region but simply the chief of three nomes. Furthermore, he only became the nomarch of Edfu after having wrested it from Khuy, who was allied with Thebes. There is a large gap between the terms used in Ankhtifi's titulature, which are drawn from royal phraseology, and the reality of the historical events of the time, which are more indicative of diplomatic machinations than the maintenance of order.

Most of the conflicts took place in the area around Armant, the town of the god Monthu, which was in the heart of Theban territory. This gives some indication of the power of the people of Thebes, who had formed an alliance with Koptos: even when they were pressed on their own territory by the troops of the three first nomes of Upper Egypt, they refused to come out and fight. The text does not describe the outcome of these battles, which were doubtless interrupted by famine, but Ankhtifi, who would not have been interested in recounting his failures, devotes the rest of his autobiography to a description of his peaceful activities. It is likely that he was involved in some kind of military reversal, even if the completion of his tomb suggests that he was not personally defeated.

Ankhtifi's main enemy was the founder of the Theban dynasty, prince Inyotef I, who proclaimed himself king with the Horus name of Seherutawy ('He who has brought calm to the Two Lands'). This was a name that would be adopted again half a millennium later by Kamose, the next Theban unifier. Inyotef I was not the founder of the Theban line, for there had been two princes before him. The dynasty began with an earlier Inyotef, who – like his successor Mentuhotpe – was named as a nomarch in the royal list of the 'Hall of Ancestors' at Karnak. This first Inyotef must have held office at the end of the Eighth Dynasty, to which he paid allegiance, perhaps already expressing his opposition to the rising power of Herakleopolis. As the original founder of the dynasty he became the object of a religious cult in the reign of Sesostris I. Mentuhotpe I, also the object of a cult and recipient of a new fictitious Horus name, Tepy-aa ('The ancestor'), was the father of Inyotef I, who proclaimed himself first 'supreme chief of Upper Egypt' and then king of all Egypt.

Having apparently scored a victory over Ankhtifi, Inyotef gained control of southern Egypt by taking Koptos, Dendera and the three nomes ruled by Hierakonpolis. His successor, Inyotef II Waḥankh, renewed the conflict with Herakleopolis, where Khety III had now risen to the throne. This time the theatre of war was Middle Egypt, which the

Thebans were attempting to snatch from the grasp of the northern kings.

The history of Middle Egypt throughout the period of these conflicts is derived from information provided by the necropolises of three key provinces: the thirteenth, fifteenth and sixteenth nomes of Upper Egypt. The capital of the fifteenth nome was Hermopolis Magna, where the god Shu was supposed to have raised the sky up above the earth. The princes of Hermopolis were buried at Deir el-Bersha, a few kilometres north of the modern town of Mallawi. Their ten tombs at Deir el-Bersha have provided the basis for the reconstruction of a royal dynasty that claimed descent from the Memphite kings. This dynasty can be traced from Aha II, a contemporary of King Khety II, to Thutnakht I, II and III, then to Ahanakht (who came to power during the reign of King Neferkare) and Thutnakht IV (who assisted in the struggle between Khety III and Waḥankh Inyotef II, although he did not participate in it himself). The full military commitment of the Hare nome does not appear to have been rendered to the Thebans until Mentuhotpe II's final conquest of Egypt. Neheri, who was the nomarch of Hermopolis at that time as well as being vizier and commander of one of the two Herakleopolitan divisions, simply protected his province with the help of his son Kay and the future Thutnakht V, who was to remain on such peaceful terms with Thebes that his descendants were still governing Hermopolis in the reign of Sesostris III.

The situation was almost the same in the neighbouring Oryx nome, the sixteenth and northernmost province of Upper Egypt, which had its necropolis at Beni Hasan, opposite the modern town of el-Minya. The princes of the Oryx nome, whose ruling family was related to that of the fifteenth nome, remained neutral for a long time; eventually, however, Baket III formed an alliance with the Thebans in the time of Mentuhotpe II. This pro-Theban attitude seems to have worked to their advantage in that power over the Oryx nome continued to be wielded by the same family after the Theban conquest.

The province of Asyut was more closely involved in the struggle – its history can be followed from around 2130 BC, with the prince Khety I, whose name alone is evidence of this dynasty's loyalty to the Herakleopolitan cause. He claimed credit both for having saved his nome from famine by distributing supplies, and for having obtained cultivable land by a policy of judicious irrigation. His successor, Tefibi, followed a similar policy while waging war against Thebes on the side of the Herakleopolitan ruler Waḥankh Khety III. The province of Asyut achieved a high level of prosperity during the reign of Merikare, who installed the prince Khety II as governor of the nome. He became commander of a large army and was responsible for the restoration of the temple at Asyut.

The conflict between the north and the south was by no means uninterrupted, but each camp used the periods of uneasy peace to consolidate their positions. The days of famine and social discontent were long past, so that the eventual victor was able to reunify a country which had already regained its strength.

Khety III of the Herakleopolitan dynasty described his struggles for the possession of This in the *Instruction* (quoted above) that he gave to his son Merikare; but his real preoccupation was with northern Egypt, which he succeeded in liberating from the occupying populations of Bedouin and Asiatics. He reintroduced the division of Egypt into nomes under the control of the ancient capital, whereas previously 'the power that had been wielded by one ruler alone was in the hands of ten'. He also reconstructed the irrigation canals and colonized the eastern Delta. He advised his son to show caution with regard to southern Egypt and to content himself with simply being a good administrator who looked after the prosperity of his subjects: 'He who has wealth in his home will not cause trouble, for the rich man cannot want for anything'. He encouraged his son both to rebuild the strength of his kingdom and to maintain a powerful army, in anticipation of a probable confrontation with Thebes.

Khety III was the last great king of Herakleopolis, and his wise policies within his kingdom appear to have had little success outside his borders. In 1860 Auguste Mariette was excavating the funerary chapel of Inyotef II in the Theban necropolis at el-Tarif, when he discovered a stele on which the king of Thebes had inscribed an account of his conquest of Upper Egypt:

> I have extended the southern borders [of my kingdom] up to the nome of Wadjet [the Tenth Nome of Upper Egypt] . . . I have captured Abydos and the whole surrounding region. I have broken into all of the fortresses of the nome of Wadjet and I have made them into the gateway [of my kingdom]. (*Catalogue Génerale du Caire* 20512)

The discovery in the sanctuary of Heqaib at Elephantine of a statue of Inyotef II, wrapped in a *sed* festival robe, suggests that his authority must also have extended over the region of the First Cataract and perhaps over part of Lower Nubia. This would appear to be confirmed by the expedition led by Djemi from Gebelein to the land of Wawat. By the time that this territory was bequeathed to Inyotef III, Thebes had gained undisputed control of the whole of Upper Egypt with a northern border just to the south of Asyut. This northern frontier was to be

the scene of the final battles that culminated in the reunification of
the country by the son of Inyotef III, Nebhepetre Mentuhotpe II, the
founder of the Middle Kingdom.

The First Intermediate Period might have been expected to have been a
period of obscurity and intellectual decline, but in fact these troubled
times had the opposite effect, forcing the Egyptians – faced with the
collapse of some of the principal values on which their society had been
based – to reasess their place in the universe. The decline of royal power
and rivalry for the throne served to weaken still further the image of
Egyptian royalty, which had already been crumbling in the late Sixth
Dynasty. Since the State had ceased to be a confident and unyielding
hierarchy, the individual was left unprotected and exposed to the violence of the law of the jungle, and the resulting anguish was expressed
in literary works which, although of several different genres, are all
marked by the same air of pessimism.

The *Instruction addressed to King Merikare* is dated to the
Herakleopolitan period since its author was probably Khety III; he is
not actually named, but he is known to have been the predecessor of
Merikare, for whom the advice was intended. The text is known from
three incomplete copies made in the Eighteenth Dynasty, reproducing
an original of the Middle Kingdom which may itself have been only a
copy. The repeated copying of this original text well after the events it
describes, shows the high literary esteem in which it was held. There is
also another *Instruction*, traditionally ascribed to Ammenemes I but
probably more a work of propaganda than a historical record. The
common ground between the themes of the two works is clear (Volten
1945): both are full of literary quotes and composed with a skill that
implies the vast literary heritage at the disposal of their authors. The
suggestion that Merikare may have composed the text himself to justify
his own policy, is of no great importance. The words of Khety III are in
fact simply the transposal into the king's mouth of the Old Kingdom
Maxims. Like Ptahhotep and Kagemni, whose thoughts were collected
(or perhaps even first composed) during the First Intermediate Period
and Middle Kingdom, Khety III was passing on to his son the secrets of
success in life and work. The son represented the inheritor of any role
or office, who was obliged to ensure the continuation of the order that
his father had managed to maintain by perfecting the technique that he
himself had received from his predecessor. Only this method of passing on knowledge from generation to generation could guarantee the
preservation of order.

Apart from reproducing the stereotypes of didactic literature, the *Instruction addressed to King Merikare* is characterized by a remarkable lucidity concerning the role of the king. Khety III does not hesitate to acknowledge his own errors and encourages his son to learn from them. He also encourages him to look after his nobles and officials, in order to avoid future confrontations – this is all a long way from the monolithic monarchy of the Fourth Dynasty. Khety even alludes to a concept that would previously have been totally unthinkable: retribution exacted from a sovereign after his death:

> The Court that judges the wretch,
> You know they are not lenient,
> On the day of judging the miserable,
> In the hour of doing their task.
> It is painful when the accuser has knowledge,
> Do not trust in length of years,
> They view a lifetime in an hour!
> When a man remains over after death,
> His deeds are set beside him as treasure,
> And being yonder lasts for ever.
> (*The Instruction addressed to King Merikare*;
> Lichtheim 1973: 101)

This preoccupation with the afterlife also appears in a work of the same period but a different genre, consisting of a dialogue between a despairing man and his *ba* or 'essence'. The text of the dialogue, a unique work in Egyptian literature, has survived in the form of a Twelfth Dynasty papyrus at Berlin (P. Berlin 3024). It bears on its verso the fragments of another unparalleled composition describing an encounter between a shepherd, worried about his sheep because of the Nile flood, and a goddess. *The Shepherd and the Goddess* may be only a story, but the political metaphor is clear, and it may be worth looking for a parallel in the *Epic of Gilgamesh*: the troubles brought about by famine would appear to be sufficient basis for this parable. *The Dispute of a Man with his Ba* has a different tone – it is a disenchanted tale told by a man whose life is dominated by the violence of wicked men:

> To whom shall I speak today?
> Brothers are mean,
> The friends of today do not love.
> To whom shall I speak today?
> Hearts are greedy,
> Everyone robs his comrade's goods.
> ⟨To whom shall I speak today?⟩
> Kindness has perished,
> Insolence assaults everyone.

To whom shall I speak today?
One is content with evil,
Goodness is cast to the ground everywhere.
(*The Dispute of a Man with his Ba*;
                    Lichtheim 1973: 166–7)

The man feels helpless to resist the forces of evil and calls on death to come to his aid:

Death is before me today
⟨Like⟩ a sick man's recovery,
Like going outdoors after confinement.
Death is before me today
Like the fragrance of myrrh,
Like sitting under sail on breeze day.
Death is before me today
Like the fragrance of lotus,
Like sitting on the shore of drunkenness.
Death is before me today
Like a well-trodden way,
Like a man's coming home from warfare.
Death is before me today
Like the clearing of the sky,
As when a man discovers what he ignored.
Death is before me today
Like a man's longing to see his home
When he has spent many years in captivity.
(*The Dispute of a Man with his Ba*;
                    Lichtheim 1973: 168)

The Tale of the Eloquent Peasant, a work from another genre, provides further precious clues as to the nature of society and morals in the First Intermediate Period. This text is preserved only in the form of four papyrus copies dating to the end of the Twelfth Dynasty and the Thirteenth Dynasty, and the apparent lack of any surviving post-Middle Kingdom copy suggests that it did not form part of the classic scribal education. It is the story of a peasant, an inhabitant of Wadi Natrun, who lives by selling oasis products in the Nile valley during the reign of Nebkaure Khety II. While travelling to the capital through the region of the Dahshur heights, he falls into a trap set for him by a greedy steward called Nemtynakht. The trap is simple: the steward has placed across the peasant's path a piece of material, which has the effect of forcing one of his donkeys to trample on the edge of the steward's field, eating a clump of barley as it passes through. Nemtynakht is then legally empowered to seize the donkey and all of the goods that it is carrying. The peasant goes to Rensi, son of Meru, the governor of the region appointed by the king, and catches him just as he is leaving his house to set off in a boat:

> Oh high steward, my lord, greatest of the great, leader of all! When you go down to the sea of justice and sail on it with a fair wind, no squall shall strip away your sail, nor will your boat be idle. No accident will affect your mast, your yards will not break. You will not founder when you touch land, no flood will carry you away. You will not taste the river's evils, you will not see a frightened face. Fish will come darting to you, fattened fowl surround you. For you are father to the orphan, husband to the widow, brother to the rejected woman, apron to the motherless. Let me make your name in this land according to all the good rules. Leader free of greed, great man free of baseness, destroyer of falsehood, creator of rightness, who comes at the voice of the caller! When I speak, may you hear! Do justice, oh praised one, who is praised by the praised; remove my grief, I am burdened. Examine me, I am in need. (*The Tale of the Eloquent Peasant*; Lichtheim 1973: 172)

The peasant then wonders whether Rensi is perhaps in league with the man who has robbed him, for Rensi does not reply to this first appeal but passes it on to the king, the great lover of judicial eloquence. Rensi then leaves the peasant to make his appeal nine times, while secretly making sure that his family are looked after. The unfortunate peasant endures alternate moments of hope and anguish – he imagines that he has succeeded, but he is too quick to congratulate himself and he is given a beating. At the end of his ninth plea he considers that his cause is lost and, ready for death, puts himself in the hands of Anubis. It is then, however, that he triumphs: the justice of his cause is recognized by the king, who recompenses him with the goods of the dishonest steward.

The flowery eloquence of the peasant is not simply an entertaining composition: each of his speeches is designed to express metaphorically the conflict between negative and positive forces that was tearing apart Egyptian society. The optimistic ending to the story is also its basic message: royal power is capable of restoring harmony by punishing the evildoer. It is perhaps possible, moreover, to argue that the piece was originally composed before the Middle Kingdom. But the final argument presented by the peasant is the recourse to Anubis, whose influence is already suggested by the peasant's own name: Khuy-n-inpw ('one protected by Anubis'). Does this mean that justice on earth is maintained only because the tribunal of the gods fills humans with fear for their lives? Without going quite this far, it is nevertheless arguable that the Egyptians no longer relied on the king's decision alone, but looked towards an afterlife in which everyone would be required to account for their own actions during life.

THE INDIVIDUAL FACED WITH DEATH

The theme of the individual confronting his death was new to the Egyptians, and it was linked with the development of the funerary role of Osiris. In the *mastaba* chapels the deceased is identified with Osiris by means of his pilgrimage to Abydos, where the bodily remains of the god were thought to have been reassembled. In the same way, the king is described in the Pyramid Texts as an Osiris, without calling into question his solar identity in the afterlife: Osiris was an integral part of the great Egyptian cosmologies but he was above all a link in the chain that connected the creator-god with mankind. In the Coffin Texts, the first examples of which date to the end of the Old Kingdom, the dead are all judged before the court of Osiris.

This was not the result of a revolution in Egyptian society, but simply the combined effect of two developments. The first of these was the disintegration of Memphite domination, while the second is often described as the 'democratization' of royal privileges; this process has already been mentioned in terms of post-Fourth-Dynasty art. The increasing power of the local dynasties also resulted in a certain degree of funerary independence. Local rulers ensured their own continued existence in the afterlife: rather than relying on the demiurge (of whom the king was still the only representative) they instead appealed directly to their local gods, whose importance grew in direct relation to the normarchs' own powers. It was for this reason that some of the secondary divinities of the Old Kingdom were able to rise to higher positions in the divine hierarchy, as in the case of Wepwawet of Asyut, Khnum of Elephantine and Monthu of Thebes, for whom there were already shrines at Armant and el-Tod. Amun was initially one of the Hermopolitan gods before associating himself with Min at Koptos and eventually, playing down his previous role as the protector of those who died of suffocation, becoming the syncretic national god Amon-Re, king of all of the gods. Osiris undoubtedly gained great benefit from this development, which increased his popularity. This, however, does not explain everything that took place during the First Intermediate Period.

When the king died, he was able to assume a place alongside Ra providing that he had correctly accomplished his earthly mission, which was to ensure that the equilibrium of creation was maintained during his lifetime. It is clear that private individuals would have been unable to use the same argument to ensure their own admission into the company of the blessed. Their legitimacy in the afterlife was therefore broadly similar but transferred to a different level: it was simply necessary for each individual to have accomplished his or her specific role on earth without having disrupted society in any way. On this basis was created a system of morals, first expressed in the *Maxims of*

Ptahhotep. Unless this kind of text is interpreted purely as a reflection of social problems, it would appear that it was the Fifth Dynasty explanation of the individual's method of dealing with death. Anyone who did not fulfil his allotted role was a criminal in the eyes of the creator, who would then be obliged to exclude him from the cosmos after his death since he had refused to play his proper part during his lifetime. This same sense of self-justification was later to be found in the *Autobiographies* of the New Kingdom and in the 'negative confession' that the deceased had to make in front of the court of Osiris, transferring to the afterlife the fundamental aspects of his conduct on earth:

I have not done falsehood against men,
I have not impoverished my associates,
I have done no wrong in the Place of Truth,
I have not learnt that which is not,
I have done no evil,
I have not daily made labour in excess of what was due to be done for
      me, my name has not reached the offices of those who control slaves,
I have not deprived the orphan of his property,
I have not done what the gods detest,
I have not calumniated a servant to his master,
I have not caused pain,
I have not made hungry,
I have not made to weep,
I have not killed,
I have not commanded to kill,
I have not made suffering for anyone,
I have not lessened the food-offerings in the temples,
I have not destroyed the loaves of the gods,
I have not taken away the food of the spirits,
I have not copulated,
I have not misbehaved,
I have not lessened food-supplies,
I have not diminished the aroura,
I have not encroached upon fields,
I have not taken anything from the plummet of the standing scales,
I have not taken milk from the mouths of children,
I have not deprived the herds of their pastures,
I have not trapped the birds from the preserves of the gods,
I have not caught the fish of their marshlands,
I have not diverted water at its season,
I have not built a dam on flowing water,
I have not quenched the fire when it is burning,
I have not neglected the dates for offering choice meats,
I have not withheld cattle from the god's-offerings,
I have not opposed a god in his procession.
                    (*Book of the Dead*, Chapter 125; Faulkner 1985: 29–31)

PLATE 10 Model of a group of archers from the tomb of Mesehti at Assyut. Tenth Dynasty, wood, h. 1.93 m. (Cairo, Egyptian Museum CG 257. Photograph: John G. Ross.)

But the deceased has still not been completely transformed into a subject of Osiris. If he appears before Osiris' court, he does so in order to achieve a continued existence copied from that of the king:

> Oh Thoth, vindicate Osiris against his foes in the tribunal of: Heliopolis, on that day of the inheriting of the thrones of the Two Banks for the son of the lord thereof; Busiris, on that day when the Sacred Eye was given to its lord; Pe and Dep, on that day of the shaving of the female mourners; Letopolis, on that day of the night offerings in Letopolis; Rostau, on that day of counting the multitudes and of erecting the two flag-poles; Abydos, on that day of the *ḥakr* festival in the pool(?) of numbering the dead and at the reckoning of him who is nothing; Herakleopolis, on that day of ploughing the earth and of making secret the land in Naref.
>
> See, Horus is vindicated, the Two Conclaves are pleased at it, and Osiris is glad. It is indeed Thoth who will vindicate me against my foes in the tribunal of Osiris.
>
> As for him who knows this, he will transform himself into a falcon, the son of Ra. [As for] whoever [knows] this [...], neither he nor his soul will ever be destroyed. It means that his foe will be destroyed and that he will eat bread in the house of Osiris; he will enter into the temple of [every] potent [god(?)], [...] gifts [...] He will never eat faeces [...]. (Coffin Texts, Spell 339; Faulkner 1973–8: 274–5).

Whether in 'wisdom texts' or funerary spells, the basis of Egyptian morality was a respect for universal equilibrium, personified by the goddess Maat, against whom human conduct always had to be measured. The Egyptians took this image literally, envisaging the judgement of the deceased by a court consisting of forty-two gods (one for each nome), over which Osiris presided. The deceased was brought before them and placed in front of a large set of scales, beside which stood Thoth and a mythical animal, part lion, part crocodile, whose role is explained by his name: 'the Great Devourer'. On one of the scale pans was placed a small vessel representing the heart of the dead person, and on the other there was an image of the goddess Maat seated on a basket. As the beam tilted to one side or the other of the knife's edge, it might condemn the unfortunate owner of the heart to be handed over to the Great Devourer. But if the deceased emerged victorious from this 'weighing of the soul', he was brought into the presence of Osiris, who welcomed him into the company of the blessed.

PROVINCIAL ART

The greater awareness of the individual also emerged in the art of the First Intermediate Period, and this change can also be traced back to the weakening of central power. It is not possible to reconstruct the full history of the artistic school at Memphis, but it presumably declined at roughly the same rate as the central government. A good number of works were certainly made by Memphite artists for Herakleopolitan rulers, but in general each region began to develop its own style. The basic canons remained the same. What the works lost in academicism they gained in spontaneity, although at the price of a certain amount of clumsiness. Because great expeditions to the quarries were no longer sent from the capital, there was a dearth of fine stone and consequently new materials began to be used by sculptors. Wood was among the best of these new materials; it was used to create models which sometimes take liberties with realism. The necropolis of the princes of Asyut has produced many wooden sculptures, such as the statue of the Tenth Dynasty chancellor Nakht (Louvre E 11937), which is a masterpiece of its type.

These tombs have provided some of the most beautiful examples of 'models', the rendering in three dimensions of the scenes that previously decorated the walls of the funerary chapel (Plate 10). Since the walls of rock-cut tombs were often unsuitable for decoration, artists were obliged to resort to these 'minor arts', which tended to be closer to feelings of the people both in terms of the subject matter and the techniques employed. This type of artistic production, like that of statuary in general, was clearly very different from that of the Old Kingdom, and already more similarities with the art of the Middle Kingdom, which began with the conquests of Mentuhotpe II. This was also the case with the literature of the First Intermediate Period, which had already attained the state of classic perfection from which it was to deviate only slightly for a millennium. Funerary architecture was also to remain unchanged in the Middle Kingdom, at least as far as private individuals were concerned, and the great provincial necropolises such as those at Asyut, Aswan, Gebelein, Beni Hasan, Meir, Deir el-Bersha and Qau el-Kebir show no break in continuity between the First Intermediate Period and the Middle Kingdom. Eventually, however, the *mastaba* was to reappear when the Twelfth Dynasty rulers reintroduced the pyramid in an attempt to imitate the Memphite model of kingship, which was the sole means of legitimizing their rule.

7

The Middle Kingdom

THE FIRST PERIOD OF UNITY

Mentuhotpe II (Plate II) succeeded Inyotef III in about 2061 BC. When he came to the Theban throne under the name S'ankhibtawy ('He who breathes life into the heart of the Two Lands'), his domain stretched from the First Cataract to the tenth nome of Upper Egypt; in other words, it was still curtailed to the north by the territory of the princes of Asyut. A hostile peace was maintained between the two kingdoms, but this was disrupted when the Thinite nome, suffering grievously from famine, revolted against the Herakleopolitan clan. Mentuhotpe captured Asyut and passed through the fifteenth nome without encountering resistance – this was effectively the fall of the Herakleopolitan dynasty.

Proclaimed king of Egypt with the new title of 'Nebhepetre, the Son of Ra', Mentuhotpe declared his southern origins by taking the Horus name Netjerihedjet ('Divine is the White Crown'). He had not yet stamped his authority over the whole country however, and the process of pacification was to last for several more years. At this time Dakhla Oasis, in the Western Desert, acted as a temporary place of refuge for the political opponents of the Theban regime until they were hunted down by the followers of Mentuhotpe. He rewarded the loyal princes of the Oryx and Hare nomes by allowing them to continue to rule their provinces, and with the exception of those at Asyut, he also reinstalled the other local rulers in Upper Egypt. He controlled the rest of the country through Theban administrators, particularly watching over the provinces of Herakleopolis (now once more simply a nome) and Heliopolis. Mentuhotpe moved the capital to Thebes, created the new office of 'governor of the North' and re-established the old chancellories and the post of vizier. Three of the viziers who held office during his reign are known: Dagi, Bebi and Ipy.

PLATE 11 *Head of Mentuhotpe II. Eleventh Dynasty, painted sandstone, h. 0.38 m. (Reproduced courtesy of the Trustees of the British Museum, London.*

These political changes were probably accomplished by about the thirtieth year of Mentuhotpe's reign. Having thus achieved the reunification of the country, he took a new Horus name: Sematawy ('He who unifies the Two Lands') in the thirty-ninth year of his reign. He was a prolific builder: while continuing the work of restoration undertaken by Inyotef III in the temples of Heqaib and Satis at Elephantine, he also carried out further construction in Deir el-Ballas, Dendera, Elkab, the temple of Hathor at Gebelein (where his artists depicted the submission of the North) and Abydos (where he made additions to the Osireion). He added to the decoration of the sanctuaries of Monthu at el-Tod and Armant and in the cliffs of Deir el-Bahri he built himself a funerary monument modelled on the pyramid complexes of the Old Kingdom.

He also revived the foreign policy of the Old Kingdom by leading an expedition to the west against the Tjemehu and Tjehenu Libyans and into the Sinai peninsula against the Mentjiu nomads. In this way he protected the country's boundaries from the threat of the Asiatics, whom he succeeded in pushing back as far as the River Litani. In Nubia, he attempted to attain the level of domination that had been achieved by the end of the Sixth Dynasty, at least as far as mining and trading were concerned. The capture of Kurkur was particularly crucial in safeguarding the ancient caravan trading routes. But Nubia itself still remained independent, despite the fact that such areas as Abu Ballas were reconquered and various expeditions were sent under the command of the chancellor Khety, who had been entrusted with the rule of all the countries of the south. Two of Khety's forays are known to have taken place in the twenty-ninth and thirty-first years of Mentuhotpe II's reign, extending Egyptian influence as far as the land of Wawat. The result was not so much the control of Nubia as the *de facto* occupation of the northern part of the country as far as the area of the Second Cataract.

Mentuhotpe II died around 2010 BC, after a reign of fifty-one years; he left his second son, Mentuhotpe III S'ankhtawyef ('He who breathes new life into the Two Lands'), the throne of a prosperous and very organized country. Since Mentuhotpe III was already fairly advanced in years when he came to power, his reign was only to last for about twelve years. During this time he continued to pursue the construction programmes begun by his father at Abydos, Elkab, Armant, el-Tod, Elephantine and western Thebes, where he built a chapel to Thoth. His own tomb, near Deir el-Bahri, was never completed.

Following the example of the Herakleopolitan rulers, Mentuhotpe III consolidated Egyptian control over the eastern Delta, building fortresses along its borders in order to protect the area from the incursions of 'Asiatics'. This defence system was to be maintained for the whole of the Middle Kingdom, although later Egyptians tended to credit Khety III with being the founder of the Delta defences, and a religious cult was dedicated to both Khety III and Mentuhotpe III at el-Khatana in the eastern Delta.

Now that his father had reconquered Nubia, Mentuhotpe III was also able to revive the practice of sending expeditions to Punt. In the eighth year of his reign, an expedition of 3000 men under the command of Henenu were sent from Koptos to Wadi Gasus, digging twelve new wells along the route in order to provide water for future expeditions between the Nile valley and the Red Sea. The expedition acquired numerous products from Punt, including quantities of 'gum Arabic'. On their return journey the same expedition also quarried stone in Wadi Hammamat.

A particularly interesting piece of evidence has survived from the end of Mentuhotpe III's seemingly prosperous reign. This takes the form of the correspondence of a man named Hekanakht, who was funerary priest of the vizier Ipy at Thebes (James 1962). Detained far from his estates, he sent a whole series of letters to his family, who were looking after his lands while he was absent. These documents were discovered at Deir el-Bahri in the tomb of a certain Meseh, who was also connected in some way with Ipy. The letters include all kinds of information concerning the distribution of the properties of Ipy, farming, taxes, and an inventory of goods dated to the eighth year of Mentuhotpe III – all precious sources of information for the economic and legal systems of the period. Hekanakht also described the problems of his time, including the onset of famine in the Theban region.

After the death of Mentuhotpe III in about 1998/7, the country was evidently left in a confused state. At this point the Turin Canon mentions 'seven empty years' which correspond to the reign of Mentuhotpe IV, whose coronation name, Nebtawyre ('Ra is the lord of the Two Lands') perhaps represents a return to the values of the Old Kingdom. A graffito in Wadi Hammamat, in which he is simply named as Nebtawy, announces the sending of an expedition of 1000 men in the second year of his reign to bring back stone sarcophagi, find new wells in the Eastern Desert and locate a more favourable port on the Red Sea. This port, Mersa Gawasis, was to be established during the reign of Ammenemes II as the embarkation point for expeditions to Punt.

AMMENEMES I

Mentuhotpe IV's expedition to the Red Sea was led by his vizier, Ammenemes, who is generally identified with Ammenemes I, his successor. Only one inscription unequivocally links the two kings in such a way as to suggest that there was a (probably fictitious) co-regency (Murnane 1977: 227–8). Mentuhotpe IV was the last representative of the family of Theban princes, and Ammenemes I was the first ruler of a new dynasty. This is confirmed by his choice of Horus name: Wehem-meswt ('He who repeats births'), which suggests that he was the first of a new line. Despite this definite dynastic change, there does not seem to have been any major political disruption in Egypt. This is not to say, however, that the transition from Eleventh to Twelfth Dynasty was a totally smooth one, since it appears that there were at least two other claimants to the throne: a man called Inyotef and another, in Nubia, called Segerseni, with whom Ammenemes I was probably still battling in the first few years of his reign. The links with the Eleventh Dynasty had not after all been broken: the officials, like the new rulers themselves, continued to trace their power back to the previous regime. Even the rise to power of Ammenemes I may not have been a shock to the system, for at this time the royal succession perhaps depended as much on the choice expressed by the Theban princes as on the king's familial connections with his predecessor.

Ammenemes I continued the new ideological stance taken up by Mentuhotpe IV by adopting Sehetepibre ('He who appeases the heart of Ra') as his coronation name. His own name, Ammenemes ('Amun is at the head'), served to announce a political programme that was to combine the primacy of Amun with a return to Heliopolitan theology, thus creating the syncretic god Amon-Re, on whom the new pharaohs were to base their authority. Ammenemes himself was not a Theban but the son of a woman from Elephantine called Nofret and a priest called Sesostris ('The man of the Great Goddess'). In the Eighteenth Dynasty it was Sesostris, Ammenemes' father, who was considered the actual founder of the Twelfth Dynasty.

Like his predecessors in the Fifth Dynasty, the new ruler used literature to publicize the proofs of his legitimacy. He turned to the genre of prophecy: a premonitory recital placed in the mouth of Neferti, a Heliopolitan sage who bears certain similarities to the magician Djedi in Papyrus Westcar. Like Djedi, Neferti is summoned to the court of King Snofru, in whose reign the story is supposed to have taken place. But the reason for the choice of Snofru is not the same in both cases: at the beginning of the Twelfth Dynasty he had become the model of good-natured kingship to whom the new kings traced their origins. Neferti conjures up a sombre scenario in the closing stages of the Eleventh Dynasty, which curiously concerns the eastern Delta particularly, finally announcing the appearance of Ammenemes under the name of Ameny:

> Gone from the earth is the nome of On,
> The birthplace of every god.
> Then a king will come from the South,
> Ameny, the justified, by name,
> Son of a woman of Ta-Seti, child of Upper Egypt.
> He will take the white crown,
> He will wear the red crown;
> He will join the Two Mighty Ones,

He will please the Two Lords with what they wish.
(The Prophecies of Neferti; Lichtheim 1973: 143)

This text thus legitimized the passing of power from Heliopolis, cradle of the Old Kingdom monarchy, to Thebes. The prophecy's expressed desire to reconcile the eastern Delta is probably based on reality to some extent: Ammenemes I is known to have built at Bubastis (where Neferti is said to have served as a priest), el-Khatana and Tanis (Posener 1969a: 39). Even if the administration accepted the change, the new king must have sent an expedition to Elephantine soon after his accession to the throne. He placed Khnemhotpe I, governor of the Oryx nome, in charge of this expedition; it travelled up the Nile in twenty boats, possibly reaching Lower Nubia, where it would have encountered the supporters of Segerseni. Ammenemes I also undertook a tour of inspection in Wadi Tumilat, where he ordered the construction of the fortifications known as the 'Walls of the Prince'. He undertook important building works at Karnak, from which a few statues and a granite naos (which must have contained a cult statue) have survived. It is even possible that it was Ammenemes I who established the original temple of Mut to the south of the precinct of Amon-Re. Traces of his building work have also survived at Koptos, where he partly decorated the temple of Min; at Abydos, where he dedicated a granite altar to Osiris; at Dendera, where he consecrated a gateway, also in granite, to Hathor; and at Memphis, where he built the temple of Ptah. He also had a pyramid built for himself at el-Lisht, about fifty kilometres south of Memphis.

Ammenemes I was especially responsible for the reorganization of the administration. He transferred the capital from Thebes to Middle Egypt by founding a new city near el-Lisht, which was to serve as its necropolis. He named it Ammenemes-itj-tawy ('It is Ammenemes who has conquered the Two Lands'), later abbreviated to Itj-tawy. Like Mentuhotpe II before him, he allowed those nomarchs who had supported his cause (including the rulers of the Oryx nome) to retain their power. On the one hand he reinforced their authority by reviving ancient titles; on the other hand he restricted their power in practice by appointing completely new governors (as at Elephantine, Asyut and Cusae) or by new measures of land registration. Khnemhotpe II of Beni Hasan records that Ammenemes I divided the nomes into a different set of towns (*Urk.* VII, 27, 13). He also redistributed the territories by reference to the Nile flood and reintroduced military conscription.

The twentieth year of Ammenemes' reign was an important turning point, for it was then that he began a co-regency with his eldest son Sesostris, thus inaugurating a practice that was systematically followed throughout the Twelfth Dynasty. This association with his son coincided with the introduction of a new phase of foreign policy: the heir apparent acted as the king's deputy and was entrusted with the control of the army, probably in order to introduce the prince to the foreign nations with whom he would eventually have to deal. This strategy was to assume great importance in the Ramessid period, when Egypt was fighting for overall control of the Near East. In Ammenemes' time however, the king's main efforts were still directed towards Nubia. In the twenty-third year of his reign he undertook the first recorded Twelfth Dynasty campaign into Nubia, capturing Gerf Hussein and the ancient diorite quarries at Wadi Toshka. A second campaign in the twenty-ninth year resulted in a much deeper incursion into Nubian territory, reaching as far as Korosko and beyond, which culminated in the foundation of a frontier fort at Semna on the Second Cataract. A statue of Djefaihapy, the nomarch of Asyut in Ammenemes I's reign, has been found at Kerma, suggesting that the Egyptians were at least present in Upper Nubia in the early Twelfth Dynasty. The suggestion that Djefaihapy was the governor of Kerma seems unlikely (Vercoutter 1987: 158); more probably the statue was taken there at a later period, perhaps during the reign of Sesostris I.

On the Near Eastern front, the general Nysumontu reported a victory over the Bedouin in the twenty-fourth year of Ammenemes I's reign – this would have safeguarded the turquoise-mining operations at Serabit el-Khadim in the Sinai. At the same time diplomatic relations resumed with Byblos and the Aegean world.

LITERATURE AND POLITICS

Just as the prince Sesostris was returning from a campaign beyond the Wadi Natrun, waged against opponents seeking refuge with Libyans, a crisis broke out: Ammenemes I was assassinated in about mid-February 1962 BC after a secret conspiracy in his harem. The royal succession was certainly not as smooth as the documents simultaneously dated to both rulers suggest (Murnane 1977: 2ff.). Sesostris I undoubtedly succeeded to the throne, but the repercussions of the conspiracy were sufficiently worrying for the official literature to deal with the problem in no less than two new compositions. In the New Kingdom these two works, like the *Prophecies of Neferti*, became the most common classic school texts of the royal ideology.

The first text is a story recounting the tribulations of a harem official named Sinuhe, who was among Sesostris' retinue when he returned from his campaign in Libya. Sinuhe chanced to overhear the announcement made to the young prince concerning his father's assassination. He

took fright, either because he had heard something that he shouldn't or
for some other unknown reason. He passed through the Delta to the
east, crossing the Suez isthmus and finally reaching Syria. There, one of
the Bedouin recently conquered by Egypt welcomed and adopted him.
The years passed by, and after various adventures Sinuhe became a
respected and powerful tribal chieftain. But he was filled with nostalgia
for Egypt. In response to his pleas, Sesostris agreed to give him a royal
pardon. He returned to his own country, met the royal children once
more and died among his own people. These picaresque adventures
serve as a context for the expression of loyalty by a wayward servant
who eventually returns to the fold. In this respect, the two key moments
in the *Story of Sinuhe* are his speech to the Syrian prince praising the
new king and the reply that he sends to the pharaoh after having
received permission to return home:

> The servant of the Palace, Sinuhe, says: In very good peace! Regarding the
> matter of this flight which this servant did in his ignorance. It is your
> *ka*, oh good god, lord of the Two Lands, which Ra loves and which
> Monthu lord of Thebes favours; and Amun lord of Thrones-of-the-Two-
> Lands, and Sobek-Re lord of Sumenu, and Horus, Hathor, Atum with his
> Ennead, and Sopdu-Neferbau-Semseru the Eastern Horus, and the Lady
> of Yemet – may she enfold your head – and the conclave upon the flood,
> and Min-Horus of the hill-countries, and Wereret lady of Punt, Nut,
> Haroeris-Re, and all the gods of Egypt and the isles of the sea – may they
> give life and joy to your nostrils, may they endue you with their bounty,
> may they give you eternity without limit, infinity without bounds! May
> the fear of you resound in lowlands and highlands, for you have subdued
> all that the sun encircles! This is the prayer of this servant for his lord
> who saves from the West.
>
> The lord of knowledge who knows people knew in the majesty of the
> palace that this servant was afraid to say it. It is like a thing too great to
> repeat. The great god, the peer of Ra, knows the heart of one who has
> served him willingly. This servant is in the hand of one who thinks about
> him. He is placed under his care. Your Majesty is the conquering Horus;
> your arms vanquish all lands (...)
>
> Lo, this flight which the servant made – I did not plan it. It was not in
> my heart; I did not devise it. I do not know what removed me from my
> place. It was like a dream. As if a Delta-man saw himself in Elephantine,
> a marsh-man in Nubia. I was not afraid; no one ran after me. I had not
> heard a reproach; my name was not heard in the mouth of the herald. Yet
> my flesh crept, my feet hurried, my heart drove me; the god who had
> willed this flight dragged me away. Nor am I a haughty man. He who
> knows his land respects men. Ra has set his fear of you throughout the
> land, the dread of you in every foreign country. Whether I am at the
> residence, whether I am in this place, it is you who covers this horizon.
> The sun rises at your pleasure. The water in the river is drunk when you

wish. The air of heaven is breathed at your bidding... Your majesty will do as he wishes! One lives by the breath which you give. As Ra, Horus and Hathor love your august nose, may Monthu lord of Thebes wish it to live forever! (*Story of Sinuhe*; Lichtheim 1973: 230–1)

A moral tale of a repentant official who is pardoned because he has remained loyal, the *Story of Sinuhe* was one of the most popular works in Egyptian literature, and several hundred copies have survived. Equally large numbers of copies were made of the *Instruction of Ammenemes I*, a text modelled on the earlier *Instruction for Merikare*, the aim of which was less to explain the assassination of Ammenemes I than to confirm the legitimacy of his successor.

In contrast to the *Story of Sinuhe*, even the oldest surviving versions of the *Instruction* were not written any earlier than the first half of the Eighteenth Dynasty: Senenmut, Queen Hatshepsut's steward, evidently enjoyed this story. The lack of early copies of the work does not exclude the possibility that it was composed at some time in the reign of Sesostris I with the aim of justifying his rule. But the way in which the facts are related, with a general insistence on the co-regency and the principles of government, transforms the text into a political blueprint; this would explain why it became so popular from the reign of Tuthmosis III onwards. Before describing his own death, the king – like Khety III before him – passes on wise advice to his successor:

> Beware of subjects who are nobodies,
> Of whose plotting one is not aware.
> Trust not a brother, know not a friend,
> Make no intimates, it is worthless.
> When you lie down, guard your heart yourself,
> For no man has adherents on the day of woe.
> I gave to the beggar, I raised the orphan,
> I gave success to the poor as to the wealthy;
> But he who ate my food raised opposition,
> He whom I gave my trust used it to plot.
> Wearers of my fine linen looked at me as if they were needy,
> Those perfumed with my myrrh poured water while wearing it.
> You my living peers, my partners among men,
> Make for me mourning such as has not been heard,
> For so great a combat had not yet been seen.
> (*The Instruction of Ammenemes I*; Lichtheim 1973: 136)

The theme of human ingratitude is not in this case a memory of the First Intermediate Period but rather a recollection of the revolt of humans ('my living peers, my partners among men') against their creator. The king, who was by this means assimilated with Ra, passed on his authority to his successor, just as in the past the demiurge had passed on its power when it withdrew into the heavens, appalled by its own creations:

> Thus bloodshed occurred while I was without you; before the courtiers had heard I would hand over to you; before I had sat with you so as to advise you. For I had not prepared for it, had not expected it, had not foreseen the failing of the servants. Had women ever marshalled troops? Are rebels nurtured in the palace? (*Instruction of Ammenemes I*; Lichtheim 1973: 137)

The rest of the text is very clear, leading to some doubts as to whether there was a genuine co-regency of Ammenemes I and Sesostris I (Helck 1983b: 43–6). However, other evidence suggests that Sesostris' rise to power took place with no problems and that his long reign of forty-five years was a peaceful one. On the other hand, this does not mean that Sesostris himself was the direct beneficiary of the harem conspiracy against his father.

Like Ammenemes I, Sesostris was a prolific builder, and there is surviving evidence of his activity at thirty-five sites (including the Faiyum region, which he was the first to exploit), as well as his pyramid at el-Lisht, to the south of his father's. Having revived the Heliopolitan tradition by taking Neferkare as his coronation name, he rebuilt the temple of Re-Atum at Heliopolis in the third year of his reign. On the occasion of his first *sed* festival, in the thirtieth year of his reign, he erected two obelisks in front of the temple pylon at Heliopolis. His activities also extended to the temple of Amon-Re at Karnak, where Henri Chevrier has reconstructed a *sed* festival kiosk of Sesostris I, using blocks that had been reused by Amenophis III in the building of the Third Pylon. This kiosk (the 'White Chapel') is now exhibited in the open-air museum at Karnak.

THE OUTSIDE WORLD

In the sphere of foreign policy, Sesostris I continued the work of the last ten years of his father's reign. He conquered Lower Nubia and in the eighteenth year of his reign established a garrison at Buhen in the area of the Second Cataract. He also exercised control over the land of Kush, from the Second to the Third Cataract, including the island of Saï, and he maintained commercial links with the kingdom of Kerma. The southernmost inscription containing Sesostris I's name has been found on the island of Argo, north of modern Dongola. In the Eastern Desert, exploitation of the gold mines to the east of Koptos and quarrying in Wadi Hammamat both continued: Sesostris appears to have extracted sufficient stone blocks for sixty sphinxes and 150 statues, numbers that correspond well with his activities as a builder. He also obtained alabaster from the quarries at Hatnub, sending at least two expeditions in the twenty-third and thirty-first years of his reign. In the west he consolidated his hold over the oases in the Libyan Desert, and particularly maintained the links between Abydos and Kharga Oasis. He continued to bolster the country's north-eastern frontiers, thus protecting the mining work at Serabit el-Khadim in the Sinai. Commercial links with Syria-Palestine extended as far north as Ugarit during this period.

These policies began to pay real dividends in the reign of Ammenemes II, who ruled for almost thirty years after a brief two-year co-regency. The conquest of Nubia had, for the time being at least, been accomplished, and while Ammenemes was still prince regent he took part in a peaceful expedition led by Ameny, nomarch of the Oryx region. The reigns of Ammenemes II and his successor, Sesostris II, were very peaceful. Ammenemes exploited the gold and turquoise mines through local princes who were subject to Egyptian control, and the only military event recorded during his reign was the inspection of a fortress in Wawat conducted by one of his officials. At the end of his reign he also organized an expedition to Punt.

During this phase Egypt began to play a more important role in the Near East as a whole. In 1936 the remains of a foundation deposit were found in the temple of Monthu at el-Tod; these consisted of four chests filled with Syrian 'tribute' in the form of silverware, including a certain number of Aegean-style vessels and lapis lazuli amulets from Mesopotamia. Although the Egyptians usually applied the term 'tribute' even to goods that were the result of commercial exchange, this el-Tod foundation deposit is evidence of the importance of relations with the outside world during the reign of Ammenemes II. There are also clear traces of Egyptian activity at Ras-Shamra, where a statuette of one of Ammenemes II's daughters was found, as well as at Mishrife and Megiddo, where four statues of the Memphite nomarch Djehutihotpe were discovered. There is even evidence of a Twelfth Dynasty cult of Snofru in the region of modern Ankara. It was during the reign of Sesostris II that Khnemhotpe, the governor of the Oryx nome, received the Abisha 'Hyksos' and their tribute, which he displays in a wall-painting in his tomb at Beni Hasan. This is an important event, for it shows that the relations were not one-way: the Egyptians themselves were exposed to eastern influences, which began to have more and more impact on their civilization and art. Minoan ceramics have been found both at el-Lahun and in a tomb at Abydos, while at the same time Egyptian objects were being taken to Crete. Foreign workers were also flowing into Egypt, bringing with them new techniques and preparing the way for a slow infiltration that would eventually result in 'Asiatics' gaining temporary control over the country. Egypt exerted particularly strong influence over Byblos, where the chiefs gave themselves Egyptian titles, wrote hieroglyphs and used artefacts originally made on the banks of the Nile.

THE HEIGHT OF THE MIDDLE KINGDOM

After a co-regency of almost five years, Sesostris II succeeded his father on the throne. His reign of about fifteen years was to be eclipsed by that of his own successor, Sesostris III, the main prototype for the later mythical figure of Sesostris. It was, however, Sesostris II who first undertook the extensive exploitation of the Faiyum area (only a marshy zone during the Old Kingdom) for hunting and fishing, with Crocodilopolis as its regional centre. This project was not to mature fully until the reign of his grandson, Ammenemes III. The Faiyum was a huge oasis, about 80 kilometres south-west of Memphis, which offered the prospect of a completely new area of cultivable land. Sesostris II embarked on the construction of an irrigation system emanating from the Bahr Yussuf and flowing into the future Lake Qarun. He achieved this by building a dyke at el-Lahun and adding to it a network of drainage canals. Although the project was not finished until the time of Ammenemes III, the presence of these great building works in the Faiyum was no doubt the reason why the royal necropolis was moved first to Dahshur, in the reign of Ammenemes II, and next to el-Lahun. To the east of his funerary complex at el-Lahun, Sesostris II established a community of workers engaged on these important building projects. The site of this community, now known as Kahun, was the first 'artificial' town to be discovered in Egypt; another, better preserved, example of this type of settlement is the workmen's village of Deir el-Medina, which dates mainly to the Ramessid period. For a long time Kahun was the only relatively complete example of an Egyptian settlement, but the excavations at various other sites, such as el-Amarna, Balat and Elephantine, have begun to shed further light on domestic architecture.

The characteristic aspect of the so-called workmen's villages at Kahun, el-Amarna and Deir el-Medina was their relative isolation from the main area of settlement by a distance of some 350–440 metres. Each was surrounded by a mud-brick enclosure wall with two gateways, one for each half of the village. The western half of Kahun must have been the most prosperous, for the houses there are more spacious and better constructed. In the eastern half there are more than two hundred houses, always with only three rooms or less.

The town of Kahun has survived only in plan, but a large number of papyri have been discovered in the houses as well as in the temple of Anubis, which was located in the southern part of the settlement. These texts are extremely diverse, providing evidence of artistic, economic and administrative activity. There are a number of different literary genres, including royal hymns, the *Story of Hay*, episodes from the *Tale of Horus and Seth*, a gynaecological treatise, a veterinary work, a fragment of a mathematical calculation, some judicial documents, some accounting texts, and fragments from temple archives covering the whole period of the Twelfth Dynasty. This does not mean that Kahun was Sesostris II's capital, since the Deir el-Medina settlement supplied an even larger number of texts but played no significant political role.

When Sesostris III rose to the throne he had to deal with a political problem which his great-grandfather, Sesostris I, had already attempted to address by his division of the vizier's office into two posts. The basic problem was that the families of local rulers had once more become almost as powerful as the king himself, judging from the wealth of the tombs at Beni Hasan and the quarrying activity at Hatnub conducted by the family of Djehutyhotpe. Sesostris III curtailed the authority of these local rulers, who had been gradually transforming themselves into local dynasties with traditions that were sometimes more ancient than the origins of the Twelfth Dynasty rulers themselves. He reduced the importance of all of the nomarchs except for Wahka II of Antaeopolis, who was to remain in place until the reign of Ammenemes III. In this new system of government, the country was under the direct control of the viziers of three ministries (*waret*): one for the north, another for the south, and the third for the 'head of the south', namely Elephantine and Lower Nubia. Each ministry was headed by one official with the help of an assistant and a council (*djadjat*). Orders were passed on to various officials who had them carried out by scribes. There were two main consequences of this reform: the loss of the nobles' influence and the rise of the middle classes, which can be observed in the increasing frequency of ex-votos dedicated to Osiris at Abydos. The king himself raised the status of his own home province by undertaking the construction of a temple of Monthu at Medamud.

Provincialism had appeared initially in the First Intermediate Period but it reached its peak in the Middle Kingdom, and the history of the country can be traced through the necropolises of the nome capitals. At Asyut, for example, was built the tomb of Tefibi, the nomarch mentioned above who fought for the Herakleopolitans against the Thebans, as well as the tombs of his son, who was appointed by Merikare, and the nomarch Khety I. This list should also include two important Asyut-based officials of the Middle Kingdom: Mesehti and

Djefaihapy. Mesehti's career spanned both the Eleventh and Twelfth Dynasties and his coffins are decorated with one of the most important surviving sections of the Coffin Texts. Djefaihapy was a contemporary of Sesostris I whose activities have been traced as far south as Kerma. He revived the fortunes of the thirteenth nome, which had been ruined by the war against Thebes, and he left behind him ten funerary contracts which have provided important evidence concerning the Egyptian legal system.

The necropolis at Aswan, already flourishing in the Sixth Dynasty, continued to prosper: the tomb of Sarenput I was built in the reign of Ammenemes I, and that of Sarenput II in the reign of Ammenemes II. Various other areas were also important, such as Gebelein, Deir el-Bersha (which included the tomb of Djehutyhotpe, whose career lasted into the reign of Sesostris III), Qau el-Kebir, Beni Hasan (which reached a high point with the line of Khnemhotpe in the Twelfth Dynasty), and Meir, the necropolis of Cusae, where the last known nomarch is Khakheperreseneb, a contemporary of Sesostris II.

The long period of military inactivity in Nubia during the two preceding reigns had encouraged the Sudanese tribes to move gradually north of the Third Cataract. Sesostris III therefore took urgent steps to deal with this threat. He began by enlarging the canal that Merenre had built near Shellal to allow boats to pass through the rapids at Aswan. Then, in the eighth, tenth and sixteenth years of his reign, he sent military expeditions against Kush. In the nineteenth year of his reign the Egyptians were able to travel by boat up to the Second Cataract, for the campaigns of the eighth and sixteenth regnal years had allowed the southern border to be established at Semna. This frontier was reinforced by a chain of eight mud-brick fortresses between Semna and Buhen. Sesostris III built (or perhaps simply rebuilt: the commemorative inscriptions make no distinction between the two acts) the fortresses at Semna West, Kumma and Uronarti, which are the best examples of Egyptian military architecture.

Sesostris III is only known to have sent one military expedition into Syria-Palestine: this was a campaign against the Mentjiu, involving the defeat of the people of Shechem and the Litani region. Nevertheless, a good insight into Egypt's foreign adversaries at this time is provided by the survival of numerous 'Execration Texts' in Nubia and in Egypt itself. These texts, inscribed either on magical figurines or on pottery sherds, consisted of the names of enemies whom the Egyptians wished to defeat. The enchantments were performed in an official manner, at the time of a building's foundation, with the ritual breaking of figurines and sherds. They were then either buried under the building – and thus smothered by it just as the the Nine Bows (which symbolized Egypt's

PLATE 12 *Head from a statuette of Ammenemes III. Twelfth Dynasty, lime-stone, h. 0.12 m. (Cambridge, Fitzwilliam Museum E.2.1946. Reproduced by kind permission.)*

neighbours) were crushed under the king's feet as he sat on the throne – or nailed at the edge of the area that they were intended to protect. These lists are precious sources, but their role as historical evidence is not very reliable, since it is more ritualistically useful to mix contemporary adversaries with past enemies in order to ensure the greatest possible universality and power of the enchantment. On the other hand, the Execration Texts have certainly helped to confirm the names mentioned in more directly factual sources, as in the case of Nubia, the Kushites, Medjay, inhabitants of Wawat, Nehesyw or Iwntiw. For Palestine the picture is less clear, despite a great abundance of place-names such as Byblos, Jerusalem, Shechem and Ashkelon.

Sesostris III's foreign policy was to reaffirm Egypt's influence over the Near East and Nubia, while Ammenemes III strengthened the frontier at Semna. Ammenemes III (Plate 12) was honoured and respected from Kerma to Byblos and during his reign numerous eastern workers, from peasants to soldiers and craftsmen, came to Egypt. This influx of foreign workers resulted both from the growth in Egyptian influence abroad and from the need for extra workmen to help exploit the valuable resources of Egypt itself. For forty-five years Ammenemes III ruled a country that had reached a peak of prosperity – peace reigned both at home and abroad, and the exploitation of the Faiyum went hand-in-hand with the development of irrigation and an enormous growth in mining and quarrying activities. In the Sinai region the exploitation of the turquoise and copper mines reached unprecedented heights: between the ninth and forty-fifth years of his reign no less than forty-nine texts were inscribed at Serabit el-Khadim, as well as ten at Wadi Maghara and Wadi Nasb. The seasonal encampments of the miners were transformed into virtually permanent settlements, with houses, fortifications, wells or cisterns, and even cemeteries. The temple of Hathor at Serabit el-Khadim was enlarged and the mines were given defences against bedouin attacks. This construction programme in the Sinai was continued by Ammenemes IV. The expeditions to quarries elsewhere in Egypt also proliferated, whether to Tura, Wadi Hammamat, Aswan or the area around Toshka.

This economic activity formed the basis for the numerous building works that make the reign of Ammenemes III one of the summits of state absolutism. Apart from the fortifying of Semna and the construction of the temple at Quban in Nubia, he dedicated himself to the development of the Faiyum; his name became closely associated with the area in the Greco-Roman period, when he was worshipped under the name of Lamares. Excavations at Biahmu revealed two colossal granite statues of the seated figure of Ammenemes III resting on a limestone base. He also decorated the temple of Sobek at Kiman Fares and built a chapel of Renenutet, goddess of the harvest, at Medinet Maadi. Above all, he built himself two pyramids, one at Dahshur and the other at Hawara. Beside the Hawara pyramid were found the remains of his mortuary temple, which Strabo described as the Labyrinth.

When Ammenemes IV succeeded his father in 1798 BC, after a brief co-regency, he continued to treat the Faiyum region as a high priority. It was perhaps Ammenemes IV who built the temple of Qasr el-Sagha, 8 kilometres north of Lake Qarun. He finished the construction of the temple that his father had begun at Medinet Maadi, then known as Dja (the Narmouthis of the Greco-Roman period). The sanctuary, dedicated to 'the living Renenutet of Dja' and Sobek of Shedit, consisted at that time of a pronaos in the form of a hypostyle hall leading to three chapels which associated the two deities with Ammenemes III and IV. The sanctuary was later enlarged, and then redecorated much later, during the reign of the Emperor Hadrian.

THE END OF THE TWELFTH DYNASTY

Ammenemes IV reigned for a little less than ten years and by the time he died the country was once more moving into a decline. The reasons were similar to those that conspired to end the Old Kingdom. The excessive length of the reigns of Sesostris III and Ammenemes III (about fifty years each) had led to various successional problems. This situation perhaps explains why, just as in the late Sixth Dynasty, another queen rose to power: Sobkneferu ('The beauty of Sobek'), a sister (and possibly also a wife) of Ammenemes IV. She was described in her titulature, for the first time in Egyptian history, as a woman-pharaoh. The northern pyramid at Mazghuna, in the southern part of Dahshur, has been ascribed to her, while the southern pyramid probably belonged to Ammenemes IV. If this attribution is correct, Sobkneferu did not actually use the pyramid, which perhaps indicates that her short reign (lasting only three years according to the king-lists) ended in violence. There is, however, no proof for this: the Thirteenth Dynasty, which began the Second Intermediate Period, appears to have been the legitimate successor – whether by blood or marriage – to the Twelfth Dynasty, at least as far as the first Thirteenth Dynasty ruler, Sekhemre-Khutawy, is concerned. Moreover, there is nothing to support the suggestion of an outbreak of violence like that at the end of the Old Kingdom: during the century and a half leading up to the appearance of the Hyksos rulers in Egypt, the country does not seem to have collapsed in any way, either within or outside its frontiers. There is instead a feeling that it was only the central power that was subject to crises, whereas the stability of the civilization as a whole remained constant.

CLASSICISM

Several literary works have already been described. The Middle Kingdom, in the larger sense of the phase of Egyptian history from the First Intermediate Period to the Thirteenth Dynasty, is the time when Egyptian language and literature reached their most perfect forms. All the different genres, as far as genres can be said to exist, are represented. Didactic writings had already been encountered in the form of *Instructions* (*sebayt*), such as the *Maxims of Ptahhotep*, *Instructions for Kagemni*, *Maxims of Djedefhor*, *Admonitions* and *Instructions for Merikare* – all of which were actually political works, despite the fact that they appear to be mainly apocryphal compositions. The *Kemyt*, one of the most popular *Instructions*, was also composed in the Middle Kingdom. *Kemyt* was the perfect 'sum' of instructions, and its perfection mirrored that of Egypt – the ancient name for which was Kemet, 'black (land)' – the ultimate image of the universe. Another important text, the *Satire of Trades*, is known from over a hundred surviving manuscripts; it was composed at the beginning of the Twelfth Dynasty by the scribe Khety, son of Duauf. As far as the political genre is concerned, there are the *Instruction of Ammenemes I* and the *Prophecy of Neferti*, as well as the *Loyalist Instruction*, the *Instructions of a Man to his Son* or the *Instructions to the Vizier*, which appeared in the reign of Ammenemes III.

The Twelfth Dynasty was also the heyday of the narrative tale such as *The Eloquent Peasant* and *Sinuhe* (both of which had similarities with the loyalist Papyrus Westcar), of which the earliest versions date to the reign of Ammenemes III. The *Tale of the Shipwrecked Sailor*, which is known only from a single manuscript, seems to have arisen out of commercial links with the land of Punt. These important works were being composed from the Eleventh Dynasty onwards.

Part exotic story and part mythological account, the *Tale of the Shipwrecked Sailor* is the narrative recounted by an attendant to an official who has just failed in his mission because of a shipwreck that is thought to have occurred in the Red Sea. The attendant describes how he himself had once been shipwrecked and found himself on a marvellous island, cared for by a serpent. This serpent, endowed with supernatural powers, was the only survivor of a catastrophic descent from the heavens (perhaps the fall of a meteorite) and the owner of a cache of valuable products from the land of Punt. The serpent predicted that the unfortunate Egyptian would be rescued from the island and then loaded him down with gifts. The extraordinary thematic richness of this text, despite its brevity, has made it one of the most frequently translated and studied works in Egyptian literature.

Many of the great mythological accounts, often resembling epics with their picaresque elements, were originally composed in the Middle Kingdom, although they are generally known from later versions such as the legend of the *Destruction of Humanity*, which also has political resonances, the *Tale of Isis and Ra*, and the *Tale of Horus and Seth*. Middle Kingdom origins can also be assumed for the important sacred dramas, such as the *Drama of the Coronation* or the *Memphite Drama*, which is known from a version dating to the reign of the Twenty-fifth Dynasty king Shabaka.

The pessimistic tone set by the *Dispute of a Man with his Ba* is picked up again in the *Collection of Sayings of Khakheperreseneb*. Another popular Middle Kingdom genre, particularly among the texts from Kahun, is the royal hymn. Large numbers of diplomatic documents, autobiographical and historical accounts, letters and administrative texts have also been found, as well as more specialized types of text such as medical and mathematical treatises (also known from later copies), gynaecological and veterinary fragments from Kahun, Theban medico-magic fragments and, at the Ramesseum, the first known discovery of *onomastica*: catalogues of words listing the different entities within society and the universe (occupations, birds, animals, plants, toponyms etc.). The *onomastica* were used to train pupils in the scribal schools.

The literary works of the period suggest a series of refinements that combined the Old Kingdom tradition with a more humanitarian sobriety. These developments were also apparent in the artistic, architectural and decorative works of the period. The 'White Chapel', built by Sesostris I at Karnak, has a remarkable purity of form which is echoed in the austerity of the temple at Qasr el-Sagha and the simple arrangement of the temple at Medinet Maadi.

Unfortunately, only a few of the religious buildings of the Middle Kingdom rulers have survived. The quality of the Middle Kingdom cult temples, however, can be judged from the royal funerary complexes, particularly that of Mentuhotpe II at Deir el-Bahri. In this bay in the cliffs on the west bank at Thebes – beneath the shadow of the great pyramidal peak that hides the tombs of the kings and nobles – Mentuhotpe II ordered the construction of a funerary complex modelled on the Old Kingdom royal tombs, with its valley temple, causeway and mortuary temple. The only difference was in the tomb itself, which was no longer housed in a separate pyramid but enclosed within the temple complex. The remains of the building are difficult to interpret, but it is likely that the idea of representing the primeval mound with a pyramidal shape was still maintained, resulting in the overall appearance described below.

Beneath the main section of the complex, which consisted of a colonnade surmounted by a pyramid or a simple mound of masonry, were foundation deposits referring to Monthu-Re; the complex can therefore be seen as a Theban counterpart to the Heliopolitan establishments dedicated to Ra-Horakhty. The section nearest the cliff-face consists of the tomb and the installations concerned with the royal cult associating Mentuhotpe II with Amon-Re, thus foreshadowing the 'Mansions of Millions of Years': the mortuary temples of the New Kingdom.

The sanctuary and the tomb of Tem, the king's wife, were discovered by Lord Dufferin in the mid-nineteenth century. But the site was not properly excavated until Howard Carter's discovery of the cenotaph of Bab el-Hosan in 1900–1, followed by the work of Edouard Naville and Henry Hall on behalf of the Egypt Exploration Society from 1903 to 1907. Excavations were resumed from 1921 to 1924 by H. E. Winlock

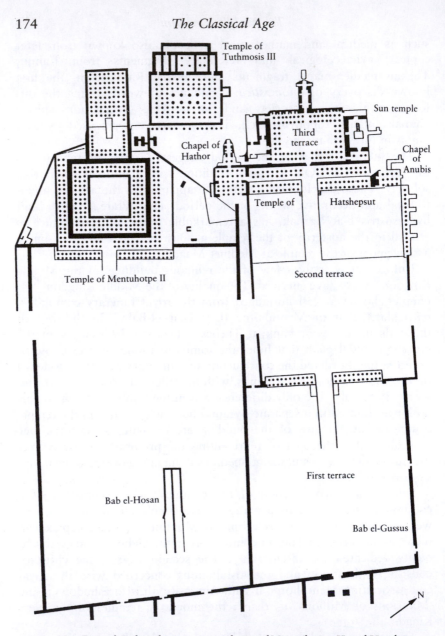

FIGURE 10   *Deir el-Bahri: funerary complexes of Mentuhotpe II and Hatshepsut.*

of the Metropolitan Museum of Art, and by Dieter Arnold of the German Institute since 1967.

These investigations have enabled four stages of construction to be identified, beginning with an enclosure wall of dressed stone running

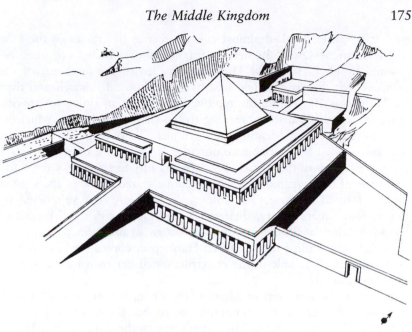

FIGURE 11 *Reconstruction drawing of the mortuary temple of Mentuhotpe II at Deir el-Bahri.*

outside and at an oblique angle to the eastern wall of the forecourt, the purpose of which is not known. Then between about the twentieth to thirtieth years of Mentuhotpe II's reign (judging from the use of the Horus name Netjerihedjet in his titulary) the main enclosure wall was built, following the natural curve of the rock-face in such a way as to enclose the tomb of Bab el-Hosan and the tombs of the queens who died before the king. The main phase was constructed between the thirtieth and thirty-ninth years of the king's reign, to judge by the use of the Horus name Sematawy. This was a terrace structure consisting of a central core and an ambulatory leading further back to a peristyle court, a hypostyle hall, a chapel and the royal tomb. The fourth stage of construction, which began before the third stage had finished, involved the construction of a causeway, the building and alignment of the inner wall of the forecourt, and the construction of the gateways to the forecourt, the courts surrounding the ambulatory and the sanctuary of Amon-Re.

The valley temple, hidden under the cultivated land of the Kom el-Fessad, has not yet been excavated, but the causeway leading from it has been cleared. Paved with mud-bricks and walled in limestone on either side, it stretched up to the funerary complex for a distance of

over 950 metres, flanked almost every 9 metres by statues of the king
in the form of Osiris, numerous fragments of which have been recovered by H. E. Winlock. The causeway led to the forecourt of the
complex, which was modified first by Mentuhotpe II himself and then
by Tuthmosis III. Tuthmosis removed part of it in order to provide
space for another causeway leading to the chapel of Hathor, which he
built to the north of Mentuhotpe's temple. The back of the forecourt
was surrounded by a double colonnade, at the centre of which was a
ramp leading up to the terrace, bordered by fifty-five tamarisk trees and
two rows of four sycamores, each shading a seated statue of the king in
his *sed* festival costume. The colonnade, with its roof supported by
twenty-four square pillars, sheltered a wall faced with small limestone
blocks bearing reliefs depicting a campaign against the Asiatics and
scenes of cultic sailing boats. Queen Hatshepsut copied the basic details
of Mentuhotpe's temple in the construction of her own funerary complex alongside it.

It was in the forecourt of Mentuhotpe's temple that Howard Carter
literally stumbled on the cenotaph, when his horse tripped over a
hollow in the ground; hence the name given to the tomb, Bab el-Hosan
('entrance way of the horse'). The entrance was still sealed; it led to a
long rock-cut corridor which stretched for 150 metres to the west,
eventually reaching a vaulted chamber under the pyramid. In this
chamber Carter found an uninscribed royal statue of painted sandstone
representing the king in the *sed* festival costume, and a sarcophagus,
also anonymous, accompanied by several offerings. From this chamber
a vertical shaft led to another room, 30 metres deeper, containing vases
and three boat models. The name of Mentuhotpe appears only on a
wooden chest found in another shaft in the middle of the first corridor.

Underneath the terrace structure was an earlier stage of the complex,
incorporating six chapels and tombs of the queen-priestesses of Hathor,
the patroness of this sacred site. These chapels were included in the
second stage of the eastern wall of the ambulatory. They were decorated with extremely interesting scenes showing the queens at their
toilet, visiting farms, feasting, and drinking cows' milk. The funerary
theme of suckling, the Hathoric source of rebirth, was later to be
magisterially recaptured by Tuthmosis III in the rock sanctuary to the
north of Mentuhotpe's temple. In the centre of this sanctuary stood an
impressive statue (now in the Egyptian Museum, Cairo) representing
Tuthmosis being suckled and protected by the goddess in the form of a
cow standing at the opening to the marshland that constituted the final
stage before the kingdom of the blessed. Behind each of the queens'
chapels was a shaft leading down to a tomb chamber; four of the six
tombs had been pillaged only once, and from these have come the

sarcophagi of Henhenet, Kawit and Ashayt, and another that belonged to a child called Mayt.

The second stage of the terrace also included an ambulatory with mural decoration consisting of cultic and administrative scenes; this was separated from the nucleus of the structure by a covered court. The hypostyle hall, the most secret part of the temple, was then reached via a peristyle court. The walls of the hypostyle hall were decorated with offering scenes; in the centre of the western wall was a niche designed to hold a statue of the king, and in front of it was a small sanctuary dedicated to Amon-Re and Mentuhotpe and decorated with cultic representations. In the south-west corner of the corridor of the hypostyle hall was the tomb of the royal wife Tem.

The real tomb of the king was to the west of the sanctuary; it was entered via a long passageway leading from the peristyle court, under the hypostyle hall and into the cliff-face. The tomb was cased in granite and had remained unpillaged as late as the reign of Ramesses XI, when a written account was compiled concerning the inspection of the Theban royal necropolis, which had become prey to numerous tomb-robbers. When the tomb chamber was excavated, a granite and alabaster naos was discovered, as well as model boats, ceremonial canes and sceptres.

The originality of the architectural achievement of Mentuhotpe II remained a purely Theban phenomenon, for his successors, having moved the capital back to the Memphite region, returned to the Memphite system for their funerary complexes. They chose sites to the south of Saqqara and the plans of their funerary installations drew on the architectural forms of the end of the Sixth Dynasty. The first site to be used was el-Lisht, almost exactly midway between Dahshur and Maidum, where Ammenemes I and Sesostris I were buried.

In the northern part of el-Lisht Ammenemes I built a pyramid that was very much modelled on those of the Sixth Dynasty, both in its slope of 54° and in its dimensions – 84 metres along each side and 70 metres in height. He reused stone blocks from the Abusir and Giza necropolises, and added an outer casing of fine Tura limestone that has now disappeared. The entrance was in the northern face, hidden beyond a granite false door inside an offering chapel, and the tomb chamber itself is now inaccessible because it lies below the modern water level. The mortuary temple was built during Ammenemes I's 'co-regency' with Sesostris I. The ramp and the surrounding complex were an enlarged version of Pepy II's. Against the western face of the pyramid were the tombs of royal princesses and to the south-west was a necropolis of the courtiers of his reign, including the cenotaph of Antefoqer, who was a vizier during the reigns of Ammenemes I and Sesostris I. Antefoqer was actually buried in the Theban necropolis at Sheikh Abd el-Qurna (TT60) but by having an additional tomb at el-Lisht he was evidently going through the motions of following his master into the afterlife.

Sesostris I built his pyramid in the southern part of el-Lisht. His complex, like Ammenemes I's, was enclosed by two walls, one in stone and the other in mud-brick; his pyramid was larger than that of his predecessor, however, measuring about 105 metres along each side and only 60 metres high, giving it a smaller slope of 49°. The construction technique used by Sesostris I was less costly than that of Ammenemes, since it consisted of a central framework of stone walls radiating out from the centre, with the gaps filled by rough blocks of Tura limestone, some traces of which have survived. Apart from the pyramid for the king's *ka*, there were also nine satellite pyramids. The rest of the complex was against modelled on that of Pepy II. When J.-E. Gautier excavated it in 1894 he found a group of ten statues of Sesostris I seated on cubic thrones, each throne decorated on its short back with a different variation on the theme of *sema-tawy*, the heraldic emblem of the unification of the Two Lands. These statues, which had been hastily concealed in a pit undoubtedly as a means of preventing their theft, have now been brought back together in the Egyptian Museum, Cairo.

Ammenemes II had himself buried further to the north, at Dahshur, and his grandson Sesostris III was buried at the same site, although his great-grandson Ammenemes III only had a cenotaph there.

The pyramid of Ammenemes II seems to have been built in a similar way to that of Sesostris I, but it is now in such a ruined state that it is not possible to describe it in any detail. To the west of his enclosure are the tombs of the princesses Ita, Itaweret and Khnemt, whose jewels are now in the collection of the Egyptian Museum, Cairo.

Sesostris III followed the technique adopted by his father, Sesostris II, at el-Lahun: a framework of stone retaining walls resting on a core of natural rock, the spaces being filled with mud-bricks, with an outer layer of fine Tura limestone. The entrance passage consisted of a shaft leading from the western part of the enclosure to a funerary chamber lined with red granite. To the south and east of the complex, inside a mud-brick enclosure wall, were the *mastaba*-tombs of his nobles. To the north were the tombs of the princesses Nofret-henut, Mereret and Senet-senebtisi, consisting of rock-cut galleries which contained not only the sarcophagi and canopic chests but also magnificent pectorals bearing the names of Sesostris II and III (now in the Egyptian Museum, Cairo).

Ammenemes III built a mud-brick cenotaph at Dahshur: this was once faced with limestone but as a result of its current denuded appearance it is now known as the 'black pyramid'. The structure was of enormous size (sides of 100 metres and a slope of 57° 20′) and was surmounted by a pyramidion. Its entrance and its mortuary temple were on the eastern side of the cenotaph. The complex infrastructure contained a granite sarcophagus which was decorated with a replica of the enclosure wall of the Step Pyramid complex of Djoser at Saqqara. (Edwards 1985: 211–12)

The site of Dahshur was also used as a necropolis by the Thirteenth Dynasty rulers, particularly Hor I Awibre, whose wooden *ka* statue is in the Egyptian Museum, Cairo. But el-Lisht and Dahshur are not the only royal cemeteries of the Twelfth Dynasty: the two kings who were most associated with the exploitation of the Faiyum, Sesostris II and Ammenemes III, seem to have been anxious to maintain their links with the region, for they had themselves buried at el-Lahun and Hawara.

The pyramid of el-Lahun was built to the north of the dyke raised by Sesostris II at the edge of the cultivated land. It had a square base of 107 metres along each side, with a slope of 42° 35′ and a probable original height of 48 metres. The entrance, to the south of the pyramid, consisted of a shaft descending vertically to a complex set of corridors which surrounded the funerary chamber in the same way that the streams had flowed around the island on which the tomb of Osiris at Abydos was supposed to have been built. Inside the tomb chamber of Sesostris II a red granite sarcophagus was discovered, as well as a golden uraeus lying nearby. An important collection of jewellery (now in Cairo, Egyptian Museum and New York, Metropolitan Museum) was found in the tomb of Sithathoriunet, one of the princesses.

The pyramid built by Ammenemes III at Hawara, 9 kilometres south-east of Medinet el-Faiyum, had numerous similarities with that of Sesostris II. The tomb chamber contained two sarcophagi: one enormous quartzite sarcophagus and another smaller one intended for his daughter, Neferuptah (who was actually buried 2 kilometres to the south, while the other princesses were buried at Dahshur). The mortuary temple, also located to the south, is probably the building that Strabo calls the Labyrinth; it consists of three rows of separate blocks covering an area of 200 × 300 metres, in which a magnificent seated figure of Ammenemes III (Cairo, Egyptian Museum, CG 385) was discovered. This was clearly a *sed* festival installation, comparable to the jubilee complex of Djoser at Saqqara, with which Ammenemes' structure has several similarities. The temple appears to have been completed by Queen Sobkneferu, but it is not possible to determine whether this later work was intended to complete the original building or to install a cult of the deified Ammenemes III.

The traditions of the Old Kingdom continued to influence Middle Kingdom royal statuary, despite the fact that the ruler was no longer considered to be an unapproachable god. Royal statuary was at this time going through a more significant process of development than private sculpture. There was very little innovation in private statuary not based on royal prototypes. One new form introduced during the Middle Kingdom was mummiform figurines placed in niches and based on the Osirid royal colossi. Other private statues shown in an attitude of prayer or enveloped in cloaks were also based on types of royal statuary. The only real innovation in private statuary during the Middle Kingdom was the block statue: a seated figure whose legs were bent up towards his chin, forming a cube shape from which only the head emerged. This form, which resulted from the geometric experimentation of the First Intermediate Period, provided a large amount of space for inscriptions, which became particularly prolific on block statues of the Late Period.

The Theban style of sculpture was initially quite crude, judging from the statue of Inyotef II enveloped in a *sed* festival cloak that was discovered in the sanctuary of Heqaib at Elephantine. The same might be said of the statues from the sanctuary of Mentuhotpe II at Deir el-Bahri which are now spread among the museum collections of Cairo, Boston, New York and London. From the reign of Ammenemes I onwards, the crudity of the Theban artistic style was somewhat tempered by contact with northern sculptural schools, demonstrated by examples from Mendes and Tanis (Cairo, Egyptian Museum JE 60520 and 37470 respectively). But there was still a marked difference between the art of the north and south, just as the kings themselves were torn between their southern homeland and Middle Egypt. In the prolific artistic production of the reign of Sesostris I several different sculptural styles are apparent: that of Thebes, exemplified by two standing colossi from Karnak temple (Cairo, Egyptian Museum JE 38286–7); that of the Faiyum, including the cache of ten statues from el-Lisht, the Osirid pillars and the wooden statues from the temple of Imhotep (Cairo, Egyptian Museum JE 44951 and New York, Metropolitan Museum 14.3.17); and that of Memphis, represented in works found at Memphis and elsewhere in the north. This diversity of styles was accompanied by a general return to the royal tradition, which was expressed in the form of a variety of statues representing kings from past times, such as those of Sahure, Neuserre, Inyotef and Djoser created during the reign of Sesostris II.

The classical style was maintained during the reigns of Ammenemes II and Sesostris II, particularly in the statues that were later reused at Tanis. The reigns of their two successors were extremely rich in high quality works. The series of 'portraits' of Sesostris III from the temple at Medamud represent him as alternatively young and aged, thus suggesting the essential humanity of the Middle Kingdom rulers, which had emerged during the First Intermediate Period. A comparable set of statues represents Ammenemes III (Cairo, Egyptian Museum CG 385 from Hawara), as well as several sphinxes and cult figures showing the king kneeling to present wine vessels, a type previously encountered at the end of the Old Kingdom (Cairo, Egyptian Museum CG 42013 from Karnak; Khartoum, Sudan National Museum 448 from Semna). A complete set of statues from the end of Ammenemes III's reign – the sphinxes from Tanis, Bubastis and Elkab, and statues of the king offering fish (Cairo, Egyptian Museum CG 392) – were at first assigned to the Hyksos period because of their unusual style; they are in fact simply products of a more northern school, traces of whose style occur again in later periods.

The Middle Kingdom is considered to have been the classical period *par excellence* of Egyptian civilization, although it was neither the longest nor the best documented. Indeed, its architecture is not at all well-known, since important temples such as those of Amon-Re at Karnak and Tanis have been preserved only in the form of reused blocks. Aesthetic judgement can therefore be applied only to the small number of surviving works, all of which are characterized by a certain degree of moderation which can appear more human in scale after the grandeur of the pyramids. The importance of these provincial centres should also be taken into account: the whole country seems to have allowed itself to be united in a style that had previously been restricted to a minority, without descending into excessive extravagance. The Middle Kingdom has a certain air of peacefulness, as if it were virtually the reign of the goddess Maat. This appears at least to be the message given by the only source that evolved more rapidly in the Middle Kingdom than in other periods: literature. A considerable proportion of the literary works that form the basis of Egyptian civilization were written in the Middle Kingdom, and they express a particular idea of the nature of civilization that was later to be adopted as the perfect model. From this point of view the time of Ammenemes and Sesostris was certainly the classical period of Egypt's history.

8

The Invasion

As far as international affairs were concerned, Nubia had been re-conquered and the Egyptians had once more reached a position of supremacy in the Near East. The influx of Asiatic workers, which had peaked during the reign of Ammenemes III, developed into a peaceful but persistent migration from the east. These peoples – who were themselves pressurized by large-scale population movements further to the east – gradually settled in northern Egypt. By the end of the Middle Kingdom the immigrant communities were starting to unite and gain control over the territories available to them. The mechanism that had brought about the fall of the Old Kingdom was therefore being re-enacted: the weakening of the state leading to political fragmentation, with native Egyptian power retreating southwards.

The Second Intermediate Period did not begin abruptly at the end of the Twelfth Dynasty. Like the First Intermediate Period it is not a true historical phase in itself but simply a convenient label for a chronological gap, since only the dates of its beginning and end are definitely known: it began with the death of Queen Sobkneferu (c.1785) and lasted until the rise to power of Ahmose (c.1560), which initiated the New Kingdom. Between these two dates was a period of about two hundred years, the first half of which is so poorly documented that knowledge of it hardly extends further than the names of rulers in the king-lists. At first the Thirteenth Dynasty was the only power in the land, but then it encountered opposition from the princes of Xois and Avaris in the Delta; these Fifteenth and Sixteenth Dynasties (the two Hyksos dynasties), running concurrently with the Seventeenth, were eventually expelled by Ahmose.

The lists enumerate more than fifty kings for the Thirteenth Dynasty, and there is not yet any general agreement on the order of their succession. The first ruler may have been Sekhemre-Khutawy (*CAH* II, 3rd edn., 13, 42ff.) or Ugaf (von Beckerath 1984a: 67). In fact any of the known rulers at this time might have been first, for they came and went at such a rapid pace that they may even have been elected into office (rather than inheriting the throne) as in the early Theban dynasty. This is a seductive theory: the activities of these 'straw-men' rulers took place mainly in the Theban region, although the capital was to remain at Itj-tawy until about 1674 BC, and during this period Egypt retained sufficient force to be respected abroad and powerful at home. In this situation it is tempting to suggest that the real power resided in the administration, controlled by a vizierate that was virtually separate from the royal court.

THE HISTORICAL CONTINUITY

The first impression to be gained from the few surviving texts is one of great continuity from the Twelfth Dynasty to the Second Intermediate Period. Sekhemre-Khutawy built at Deir el-Bahri and Medamud, and his successor Ammenemes V is named on the monuments of Upper and Lower Egypt as Hornedjheritef ('Horus avenger of his father'); the name might be more precisely interpreted at 'the "curator" of his father's interests', just as the god Horus had looked after the interests of his father Osiris. Ammenemes V also built at el-Khatana. Later in the dynasty, Sobkemsaf I was named in architectural inscriptions at Medamud, and he was also responsible for building activity at Abydos, Karnak, el-Tod and Elephantine. Sobkhotep III built a colonnade and gateways in the temple of Monthu at Medamud; he was also present at Elkab and two particularly important administrative documents have survived from this reign: one at the Brooklyn Museum, New York, which provides a list of officials, and another in the Egyptian Museum, Cairo (Papyrus Bulaq 18) which consists of tables listing the income and expenditure of the royal court during a month in residence at Thebes. The latter text names three 'ministries' (*waret*), at least one of which – that of the Head of the South – had been originally founded by Sesostris III, the two others being the Treasury and the Ministry of Works. Sobkhotep III is also known to have been not of royal blood but the son of Mentuhotpe, a Theban prince.

All these kings had themselves buried with the trappings of Middle Kingdom tradition, and a few of their pyramids have survived. At Dahshur a pyramid belonging to 'Ameny the Asiatic' (probably to be identified with Ammenemes VI) was discovered in 1957. Khendjer was buried in southern Saqqara, in a mud-brick pyramid faced with limestone and furnished with a quartzite tomb chamber. Near Khendjer's pyramid a larger, unidentified pyramid was also discovered. Finally, Neferhotep I was perhaps buried in a pyramid at el-Lisht, some distance from Sesostris I.

Without a doubt the most astonishing aspect of the Thirteenth and Fourteenth Dynasties was the apparent maintenance of Egyptian influence over neighbouring countries. In Nubia there are surviving records of Nile floods in Semna, at the level of the Second Cataract, in the first four years of the reign of Sekhemre-Khutawy. These records are not available for the reign of Ammenemes V, but the Egyptian grip on Lower Nubia remained firm during this period, at least until the reign of Ugaf, a statue of whom has been found at Semna. A graffito at Shatt el-Rigal provides evidence of an expedition sent into Nubia by Sobkemsaf, and the authority of Neferhotep I is known to have stretched as far as the First Cataract.

In the Egyptian-dominated areas of the Near East there seems to have been little change under Ammenemes V and Sehetepibre II; Byblos, for example, was still paying tribute to Egypt. Hornedjheritef is even described as 'the Asiatic', doubtless indicating that he pursued an energetic foreign policy, details of which have unfortunately not survived except for a scarab bearing his name found at Jericho. However, scarabs and other such small mobile objects are too widely distributed for them to act as any kind of proof of Egyptian dominance (or even presence) at a site. On the other hand, one stele found at Byblos indicates that it was still a vassal of Egypt in the time of Neferhotep I.

NEFERHOTEP I AND SOBKHOTEP IV

The reign of Neferhotep I was a significant period in the history of Egypt. He reigned for eleven years and his titulature is an indication of the efforts he made to reorganize the country. His Horus name was Gereg-tawy ('He who has founded the Two Lands') and his Two Ladies name was Up-Maat ('He who separates the good (from the bad)'). In practice he must have controlled not only southern Egypt but also the whole of the Delta, with the exception of the Sixth Nome of Lower Egypt. According to Manetho, Xois (Qedem, near Qafr el-Sheikh), the principal town in the Sixth Nome, was also the capital of the Fourteenth Dynasty, which was concurrent both with the Thirteenth Dynasty and with the Hyksos Dynasty that was to be established at Avaris.

It was during the eight-year reign of Neferhotep's brother, Sobkhotep IV, that the town of Avaris (Hwt-weret, 'the great mansion') passed into Hyksos control. Avaris was the capital from which their influence

was to spread across the Delta. The excavations of Manfred Bietak at
el-Khatana and Tell el-Dab'a (about 7 kilometres north of Faqus),
which was once identified as Tanis, have succeeded in demonstrating
that it was actually the site of Avaris, and later also Piramesse. The
Hyksos seizure of Avaris took place around 1730–1720 BC, according
to a stele which was set up at the site by Ramesses II and later moved to
Tanis, where it was discovered by Auguste Mariette in 1863 (Paris
1976: 33–8). This stele, which commemorated the foundation of the
temple of Seth at Avaris, is dated to 'year 400, fourth day of the fourth
month of the inundation season of the King of Upper and Lower Egypt
Seth, great of courage, son of Ra, chosen one, beloved of Ra-Horakhty'.
If this is not the date of the stele's erection but the date of the original
text, of which this is only a copy, then the text probably dates to the
reign of Horemheb while the actual event described (the foundation of
the temple) would have taken place around 1720 BC.

THE HYKSOS

Hyksos control over northern Egypt evolved in a number of stages.
Starting from Avaris they gradually moved towards Memphis, following the eastern edge of the Delta. They established centres at Farasha,
Tell el-Sahaba (at the mouth of the Wadi Tumilat), Bubastis, Inshas
and Tell el-Yahudiya (about 20 kilometres north of Heliopolis). This
progression took place over a period of almost half a century, until
about 1675 BC. The Thirteenth Dynasty had by then reached its thirty-
third or thirty-fourth king, Dedumesiu I. If this king is to be identified
with Manetho's Tutimaius, then it would have been during his reign
that the Hyksos became rulers of Egypt. This identification would
appear to be confirmed by the fact that Dedumesiu is the last known
king of the Thirteenth Dynasty in the inscriptions on Theban monuments at Thebes, Deir el-Bahri and Gebelein. The Thirteenth Dynasty
was by no means totally extinguished at this point, but henceforth it
was to wield only local power and eventually, after 1633 BC, it disappeared altogether from the written records.

The founder of the first Hyksos dynasty, Manetho's Fifteenth
Dynasty, was a man called Salitis, who was probably the same person
as the Sheshi mentioned on several seals found at Kerma, suggesting
perhaps that the Nubians allied themselves with the Hyksos against
the Thebans from the very beginning of the Hyksos period. Salitis is
probably also to be identified with a ruler called Sharek whose name
appears at this time in Memphis. But who were the Hyksos? Their
name is the debased Greek version of the Egyptian term: *ḥekaw-khasut*
('the chiefs of foreign lands'). This name gives no indication of race or

any clearly defined homeland: it was a term applied to all foreigners in Nubia and Syria-Palestine during the Old and Middle Kingdoms. The Hyksos seem to have approximated the 'Asiatic' peoples whom the Egyptians had previously fought: the Aamu, Setjetiu and Mentjiu of Asia or Retjenu. The final stage of the Hyksos rise to power may have been violent, but their gradual infiltration seems to have been much more widely accepted by the Egyptian population at the time than the later nationalistic texts of the New Kingdom suggest. The aforementioned Brooklyn Papyrus' list of officials shows that Egyptians and Asiatics were apparently able to live together without difficulty. The Hyksos Kings themselves were great builders and artisans, leaving behind them temples, statues, reliefs and scarabs, and even encouraging the continued dissemination of Egyptian literature. The Rhind Mathematical Papyrus for example (now in the British Museum), is dated to the thirty-third year of the reign of Apophis I, father of the rival of the Seventeenth Dynasty king Kamose. Although it is actually a copy of a Theban original, it is nevertheless evidence of the Hyksos rulers' respect for Egyptian culture.

The Hyksos introduced a method of government which was to prove equally successful for all the later invaders who applied it to Egypt: instead of attempting to impose their own governmental structures on the country, they immersed themselves in the existing Egyptian political system. Although this did not prevent them from expressing their own cultural identity, which is perceptible in architectural styles (such as the 'Hyksos forts') and the pottery at Tell el-Yahudiya, nevertheless they transcribed their names in the hieroglyphic system of writing, adopted the traditional royal titulature, and copied Middle Kingdom sculptural styles. In the sphere of religion, as in the political arena, they instituted an official Egyptian-style cult based on Seth of Avaris, the enemy of Osiris; contenting themselves with the introduction of more Semitic features into his iconography; it was at this time that Seth was assimilated with Baal-Reshef and with the Hittite god Teshub. The Hyksos also continued to worship the Syro-Palestinian goddess Anat-Astarte, but they nevertheless showed no signs of neglecting the traditional Egyptian gods, and kings continued to hold the title 'son of Ra'.

The Hyksos presence in Egypt was evidently less damaging than later Egyptian sources tend to suggest. It must, however, have made its mark on Egyptian civilization, which from then on was far less insular. In terms of religion, culture and philosophy, the Hyksos rulers created a legacy from which the New Kingdom pharaohs would eventually draw inspiration. The technological innovations of the Hyksos period were innumerable, particularly in the field of warfare, which was revolutionized by the introduction of the harnessed horse (even though the horse was already known and reared in the Nile valley). The Egyptians were also introduced to innovative items of armour created with new techniques of bronze-working, which would eventually allow the New Kingdom pharaohs to expand eastwards. For twenty years Salitis/ Sheshi/Sharek, probably based at Memphis, ruled a kingdom comprising both the Delta and the Nile valley down to Gebelein, as well as the desert trade routes that allowed the Hyksos to make contact with their Nubian allies. This state of affairs lasted until the reign of Apophis I, who delegated part of his authority to another Hyksos family of vassal princes, which Manetho incorrectly describes as the Sixteenth Dynasty.

THE THEBANS

A new dynasty emerged in Thebes out of a local branch of the Thirteenth Dynasty. It was founded by Rahotep, who took Wahankh as his 'Horus' name. According to the Turin Canon there were fifteen kings in the Seventeenth Dynasty, but according to the Karnak Table of Kings (now in the Louvre) there were nine. The Theban monuments bear the names of ten Seventeenth Dynasty kings, and the tombs of seven of the listed kings have also been found at Thebes, as well as an eighth tomb of a king whose name does not appear in either of the lists. For about seventy-five years these kings ruled over the first eight nomes of Upper Egypt, from Elephantine to Abydos – roughly the same area as the Theban rulers had controlled in the late First Intermediate Period. Their economic resources were meagre, and they were particularly lacking in access to mines or quarries. However, subject to these limitations they managed to maintain the civilization of the Middle Kingdom. Rahotep, for example, restored the temples of Min and Osiris at Koptos and Abydos respectively. In the cemetery of Dra Abu el-Naga, each Seventeenth Dynasty ruler had himself buried under a mud-brick pyramid (which was to provide the immediate prototype for the pyramidia surmounting New Kingdom private tomb chapels). Traditional Egyptian education continued in the form of constant recopying of literary and technical texts. Papyrus Prisse, containing a version of the *Maxims of Ptahhotep* and the *Instructions for Kagemni*, dates to this period, while the New Kingdom versions of the *Songs of the Harpist* claim to be copies of a text originally inscribed in front of a figure of a harpist in the wall decoration of Inyotef VII's tomb.

At the time of Rahotep's reign, the Hyksos king was Yaqub-Har (or Yaqub-Baal), Salitis' successor. Yaqub-Har reigned for eighteen years and seals bearing his name have been found from Gaza to Kerma. He remained on good terms with the three Theban kings who succeeded

Rahotep. The first was Inyotef 'the Old', who by choosing Up-Maat as his Horus name implied that his claim to the throne went back to Neferhotep I. He reigned for three years and was buried by his young brother and short-lived successor Inyotef VI at Dra Abu el-Naga. Papyrus Abbott, which describes the inspection of the royal Theban tombs after their pillaging during the reign of Ramesses IX, reports that the tomb of Inyotef the Old was still intact in the Twentieth Dynasty. The tomb itself has not yet been discovered, but it appears to have been robbed in modern times judging from the mysterious appearance of the pyramidion, canopic chest and a small anthropoid coffin (which must have contained Papyrus Prisse). The sarcophagus of Inyotef VI, who reigned for only a few months, is in the Louvre. His successor, Sobkemsaf II, is one of the better known Seventeenth Dynasty rulers: his sixteen-year reign was a prosperous one. He built at Karnak and Abydos, and his tomb is also mentioned by the Papyri Abbott, Ambras and Amherst-Leopold II, all of which describe him as a great king provided with rich funerary equipment.

In about 1635/1633 BC, during the reign of Sobkemsaf II, the Thirteenth Dynasty came to an end, and the Fourteenth Dynasty managed to survive for only two or three generations at Xois. As for the Hyksos, Yaqub-Har's successor Khyan cannot be said to have ruled an actual empire, although his name appears frequently – not only in Egypt, on an architectural fragment at Gebelein and at Bubastis, but also in foreign countries, on a stone vessel in the palace at Knossos, scarabs and seal impressions in Palestine and a granite lion at Baghdad. These objects show that commercial relations had been restored to at least the level attained in the Middle Kingdom. With regard to Nubia, there is no surviving indication that it was an Egyptian vassal; on the contrary, a king named Nedja took power in Kush with the help of Egyptian officials. He established his capital at Buhen and ruled an area from Elephantine to the Second Cataract, and certainly as far south as Kerma. The kingdom of Kerma, which was allied with the Hyksos according to texts describing the final confrontation between them and Thebes, was to last until the Theban King Kamose recaptured Buhen. Like the later kingdom of Napata, the Upper Nubian court of Kerma in the Second Intermediate Period appears to have had all the trappings of Egyptianization in its officials' titles, building types and religious cults. The Lower Nubian region between Toshka and Dakka was inhabited by the C-Group. During the same period cemeteries of oval-shaped graves were established both in Nubia and in Upper Egypt, from Deir Rifa to el-Moalla. These tombs, rich in military equipment, belonged to the 'pan grave' people, a group of nomadic immigrants whom the Egyptians and Nubians recruited as elite troops.

The Theban contemporaries of Khyan are obscure. There is one Theban ruler named Djehuty who reigned for only one year, but nothing more than a canopic chest bearing his name (later reused) has survived. Mentuhotpe VII, whose reign was also short, left a pair of limestone sphinxes at Edfu. The name of Nebiryaw I appears on a stele at Karnak bearing a legal text which describes an agreement made between the *waret* of the north and the office of the vizier.

Two great figures emerge next: Inyotef VII of Thebes and Apophis I of the Hyksos. Inyotef VII is the first king of the Seventeenth Dynasty for whom there is evidence of military and administrative activities. He built at Koptos, Abydos, Elkab and Karnak, and in the eighth year of his reign issued a decree concerning the temple of Min at Koptos that gives some indication of the autocratic nature of Theban power. Among his constructions in the temple of Min there is a block which – like a plinth also bearing his name found at Karnak – is decorated with depictions of Asiatic and Nubian conquered enemies. It might be argued that both items were simply decorated with the typical royal phraseology, but it is perhaps significant that Inyotef VII had himself buried with military regalia: two bows and six arrows were found in his coffin (now in the British Museum). It is no doubt significant that he placed his tomb to the north of his predecessors at Dra Abu el-Naga, thus inaugurating a new group of royal tombs. This apparent fresh start is perhaps confirmed by a later tradition that his wife Sobkemsaf, who was buried at Edfu, was an ancestor of the Eighteenth Dynasty.

During Inyotef VII's reign Thebes was at peace with the Hyksos king Apophis I, who ruled for forty years according to the Turin Canon. There were numerous contacts between the two kingdoms. The Rhind Mathematical Papyrus, mentioned above, was evidently a Hyksos copy of a Theban original, which could be interpreted as proof of peaceful relations between the two kingdoms or even as an indication of the Thebans' allegiance to the northern kingdom. This second possibility should not be discarded, for not only is there evidence for the presence of Apophis I as far south as Gebelein, but he may even have been related by marriage to the Theban royal family: the tomb of Amenophis I contained a vase bearing the name of Apophis I's daughter Herit. This object was probably passed on through successive generations, commemorating a marriage that would have made her one of the ancestors of the Eighteenth Dynasty. This is clearly a long way from the mutual hatred described in later texts. In addition, Apophis I is called the 'King of Upper and Lower Egypt' on a scribe's palette from the Faiyum and on several scarabs.

Towards the end of Apophis I's reign the open conflict with Thebes began, when Ta'a I ('the Old') succeeded Inyotef VII. His wife

TABLE 4   *Family tree of the early Eighteenth Dynasty (generations 1–4).*

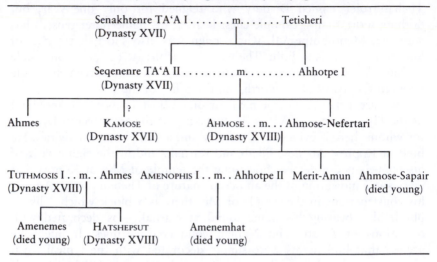

Tetisheri, who lived on until the beginning of the Eighteenth Dynasty, was revered after her death as the grandmother of the great liberator Ahmose. Taʿa I was succeeded by Seqenenre Taʿa II ('the Brave'), who married Queen Ahhotpe I, the mother of Ahmose.

The mummy of Seqenenre Taʿa II was saved from pillaging in the time of Ramesses IX and was placed, along with other threatened royal remains, in the cachette discovered in 1881 by Gaston Maspero: the body bears the marks of a violent death, providing evidence of the hostility between north and south. There are two surviving records of the conflict, one much more valuable than the other. The first, the *Quarrel of Apophis and Seqenenre*, is a fantastic tale of which only the beginning has survived, in the form of a copy made by the scribe Pentawer in the reign of Merneptah. The other, more historical source is an official description of the conflict, dated to the third year of the reign of Kamose and preserved in two different media: first, two fragmentary stelae which complement one another, having been set up by the king at Karnak; and second, a tablet which was part of the collection of Lord Carnarvon. The first text transforms the conflict into a game of riddles played by the two kings, presented as follows:

> Now it so happened that the land of Egypt was in distress. There was no Lord – life, prosperity, health! – or King of the time. However, it happened that, as for King Seqenenre – life, prosperity, health! – he was Ruler – life, prosperity, health! – of the Southern City. Distress was in the town of the Asiatics, for Prince Apophis – life, prosperity, health! – was

in Avaris, and the entire land was subject to him with their dues, the north as well, with all the good produce of the Delta.

Then King Apophis – life, prosperity, health! – made him Seth as Lord, and he would not serve any god who was in the land except Seth. And he built a temple of good and eternal work beside the House of King Apophis – life, prosperity, health! – and he appeared every day to have sacrifices made . . . daily to Seth. And the officials of the King – life, prosperity, health! – carried wreaths, just exactly as it is done in the temple of Re-Harakhty. (Pritchard 1955: 231)

Seqenenre waged war with the Hyksos as far north as Cusae. When he died, his son Kamose rose to the throne. He adopted a titulature which was at least as bellicose in his three Horus names, Khay-her-nesetef ('He who has been crowned on his throne'), Hornefer-khab-tawy ('The perfect Horus who curbs the Two Lands') and Sedjefa-tawy ('He who nourishes the Two Lands'), as in his Two Ladies name, Wehem-menu ('He who renews the fortifications'). The text of the two stelae and the tablet describe the resumption of hostilities against the Hyksos:

His Majesty spoke in his palace to the council of grandees who were in his suite: 'I should like to know what serves this strength of mine, when a chieftain is in Avaris, and another in Kush, and I sit united with an Asiatic and a Nubian . . .' (Gardiner 1961: 166)

The king rejected the advice of his courtiers, who preferred to preserve the peace between Elephantine and Cusae rather than risk the loss of their cattle and possessions in the north (which suggests that the Thebans had previously been at peace with the Delta Kingdom). Kamose marched his Medjay troops north to Nefrusy, in the region of Beni Hasan, and there he defeated the army of a man called Teti son of Pepi, who is said to have transformed Nefrusy into a 'nest of the Asiatics':

I spent the night in my ship, my heart happy. When the earth became light, I was upon him as it were a hawk. The time of perfuming the mouth [i.e. the midday meal] came, and I overthrew him, I razed his wall, I slew his people . . . (Gardiner 1961: 167)

Unfortunately, the text of the first Kamose stele breaks off at this point, and that of the tablet peters out soon afterwards. When the account is taken up again, in the surviving section of the second stele, Kamose is hurling insults at his rival in accordance with the tradition of the 'royal annals'. Finally he sent a naval expedition against the Hyksos possessions in Middle Egypt, which perhaps advanced as far as the borders of the Fourteenth Nome of Lower Egypt, in other words the region around Avaris itself. Kamose gained control of the river trade,

captured at least the towns of Gebelein and Hermopolis and intercepted
a message from Apophis to the king of Kush:

> I captured a messenger of his high up over the oasis travelling southward
> to Kush for the sake of a written dispatch, and I found upon it this
> message in writing from the chieftain of Avaris: 'I, ʿAwoserreʿ, the son
> of Ra, Apophis, greet my son the chieftain of Kush. Why have you arisen
> as chieftain without letting me know? Have you (not) beheld what Egypt
> has done against me, the chieftain who is in it, Kamose the Mighty,
> ousting me from my soil and I have not reached him – after the manner of
> all that he has done against you, he choosing the two lands to devastate
> them, my land and yours, and he has destroyed them. Come, fare north at
> once, do not be timid. See, he is here with me ... I will not let him go
> until you have arrived.' (Gardiner 1961: 167–8)

At this juncture the military activity seems to have stopped, and
Kamose returned to Thebes, where he had the account of his exploits
inscribed on the temple wall. There was no question of an outright
victory, but he had at least secured the trade routes, thus effectively
cutting off northern Egypt from Kush. It is not clear whether Apophis'
allusions should be interpreted as evidence that Kamose had already
reconquered Nubia. He had certainly begun to move southwards, and
this expansion into Nubia was to be continued by Ahmose, judging
from a graffito found at Toshka which gives the names of both rulers
together. A scarab bearing Kamose's name was found at Faras but this
could well have been taken there after Kamose's reign.

Somewhere between Thebes and Dendera, Kamose founded a new
estate, calling it Sedjefa-tawy, his Horus name. He also set up a naos
and stelae at Karnak. His tomb at Dra Abu el-Naga was still intact
when the pillaging of the necropolis took place during the reign of
Ramesses IX. His coffin, however, was transferred for the sake of
security into the Deir el-Bahri cachette, where it was one of the first to
be stripped by modern pillagers. In 1857 a non-royal anthropomorphic
sarcophagus was discovered – this must have been Kamose's, but it
contained only a mummy crumbled to dust and a few precious objects.

THE RECONQUEST

At the death of Kamose, both sides in the conflict seem to have stood
their ground. The stele explicitly identifies Kamose's adversary as
Apophis I ʿAwoserreʿ. After his struggles with Kamose he was probably succeeded by Apophis II ʿAqenienre, whose name is not recorded
on any monuments or objects found south of Bubastis, except for a
dagger bought on the antiquities market in Luxor but not necessarily
excavated from that area. The authority of the Hyksos king seems to

have been drastically reduced: he conducted a building programme at Bubastis and simply usurped the statues of his predecessors: two granite sphinxes of Ammenemes II, which were later moved to Tanis (Louvre A 23 and Cairo, Egyptian Museum JE 37478), and two colossal statues of the Thirteenth Dynasty king Smenkhkare. Various chronological problems have not been clarified. The last known date for Kamose is the third year of his reign, the date of the stele. The fact that he bore three Horus names, without the least indication of a *sed* festival having taken place, is also worrying. Finally, the question should perhaps be posed as to whether the poverty of his coffin is an indication of an accidental – or at least inpromptu – death.

The dates of Ahmose's reign are understandably obscure: he must have come to the throne in about 1570, 1560 or 1551 BC according to the astronomical calculation, and his reign must have ended in 1546, 1537 or 1527 BC. The physical examination of his mummy, which was among those rescued by Ramesses IX, suggests that he lived until the age of about thirty-five, with a reign of just over twenty-five years according to Manetho. He must have resumed the struggle against the Hyksos in about the eleventh year of his reign, and this conflict would have lasted for several years in the Delta, leading eventually to the capture of Memphis and then Avaris. Hyksos domination within Egypt itself had already been overwhelmed when, a short time later, Egyptian troops captured the fortified town of Sharuhen in south-western Palestine, which was the last bastion of the 'Asiatics'. This final stage of the reconquest took place before the sixteenth year of Ahmose's reign. The most detailed surviving account of these campaigns is that left by an official at Elkab, Ahmose son of Ibana, in the autobiography decorating his tomb:

> Now when I had established a household, I was taken to the ship 'Northern', because I was brave. I followed the sovereign on foot when he rode about in his chariot. When the town of Avaris was besieged, I fought bravely on foot in his majesty's presence. Thereupon I was appointed to the ship 'Rising in Memphis'. Then there was fighting on the water in 'Pjedku' of Avaris. I made a seizure and carried off a hand. When it was reported to the royal herald the gold of valour was given to me. Then they fought again in this place; I again made a seizure there and carried off a hand. Then I was given the gold of valour once again. Then there was fighting in Egypt to the south of this town, and I carried off a man as a living captive. I went down into the water – for he was captured on the city side – and crossed the water carrying him. When it was reported to the royal herald I was rewarded with gold once more. Then Avaris was despoiled, and I brought spoil from there: one man, three women: total four persons. His Majesty gave them to me as slaves. Then Sharuhen was besieged for three years. His Majesty despoiled it and I brought spoil

from it: two women and a hand. Then the gold of valour was given to
me, and my captives were given to me as slaves. (Lichtheim 1976: 12–13)

The chronology of the last two Hyksos kings is somewhat confused.
They ruled between the tenth and fifteenth years of Ahmose's reign. The
name of one of them, Aazehre, the last king of the Fifteenth Dynasty,
appears on an obelisk at Tanis – he probably corresponds to Manetho's
Asseth and the Turin Canon's Khamudy. The other, Apophis III, was
the last of the Sixteenth Dynasty Hyksos vassal kings, and his name
appears on several monuments, including a dagger from Saqqara. No
textual source can supply the least detail on the final phase of Hyksos
rule. They were obviously no longer posing a real threat to the Thebans
when Ahmose undertook a campaign in the twenty-second year of his
reign, in which he advanced at least into the Djahy region of Syria-
Palestine and perhaps even up to the Euphrates. This would have
made him the first pharaoh to have extended the frontiers this far into
Western Asia.

After routing the Hyksos, Ahmose undertook the reconquest of
Nubia, and Ahmose son of Ibana also describes this campaign:

> Now when His Majesty had slain the nomads of Asia, he sailed south to
> Khent-hen-nefer, to destroy the Nubian Bowmen. His Majesty made a
> great slaughter among them, and I brought spoil from there: two living
> men and three hands. Then I was rewarded with gold once again, and
> two female slaves were given to me. His Majesty journeyed north, his
> heart rejoicing in valour and victory. He had conquered southerners,
> northerners. (Lichtheim 1976: 13)

But this campaign was not decisive, and a man called Aata, who was
perhaps Nedjeh's successor as king of Kerma, went into revolt:

> Then Aata came to the South. His fate brought on his doom. The gods of
> Upper Egypt grasped him. He was found by his majesty at Tent-aa. His
> Majesty carried him off as a living captive, and all his people as booty. I
> brought two young warriors as captives from the ship of Aata. Then I
> was given five persons and portions of land amounting to five arourae in
> my town. The same was done for the whole crew. Then came that foe
> named Tetian. He had gathered the malcontents to himself. His Majesty
> slew him; his troop was wiped out. Then I was given three persons and
> five arourae of land in my town. (Lichtheim 1976: 13)

Tetian must have been an Egyptian opposed to the new Theban
power, but Ahmose succeeded in restoring Egyptian control over
Nubia. He may also have founded the first New Kingdom temple there,
on the island of Saï to the south of Buhen; at any rate, he established
Buhen as the administrative centre of the province. He appointed a
man called Turi as commander at Buhen, and under his successor

Amenophis I, Turi was to become the first clearly attested viceroy of Kush, although his father Zatayt may have already performed this administrative role without holding the specific title.

When Ahmose died, he left the throne to Amenophis I, his son by Ahmose-Nefertari. In his twenty-five-year reign he had achieved the liberation of Egypt and restored Egyptian links with the rest of the world, at least bringing them back to the level that had been achieved at the end of the Middle Kingdom. It was on this firm foundation, supplemented by a steady flow of precious Asiatic imports, that his successors were able to build a power that dominated the Near East for half a millennium.

Part III

The Empire

9

The Tuthmosids

Once Ahmose had reconquered the country he reorganized its system of government. It appears that the administrative infrastructure of the Second Intermediate Period continued to function along lines established in the Middle Kingdom and was locally maintained by the nomarchs. Ahmose at first reassured himself of the loyalty of these nomarchs, but he did not restore power to the ancient families who had been supplanted in the late Twelfth Dynasty. The only regions which he could definitely trust were Thebes (his own province) and Elkab. Nothing is known about the process of reorganization itself, but it is clear that some kind of change took place, judging from the state of the administration in the rest of the Eighteenth Dynasty. Undoubtedly, Ahmose promoted the local governors who had supported the Theban cause in the Seventeenth Dynasty. There is some debate as to whether he shared out the conquered lands, but it is unlikely that any rewards would have exceeded the simple recompense given to a veteran in his home town, as was the case with the veteran soldier Ahmose son of Ibana. The new administration probably took control of irrigation and therefore also of the fiscal system, though it is equally possible that it simply took over the fiscal system left behind by the Hyksos. The country had become prosperous again, and the fact that the Thebans were renting out pastures in the Delta, the territory of the 'Asiatics', is an indication of the efficiency of their regime.

In the economic and artistic spheres, the process of opening up contacts with the Near East – already well advanced during and after the Twelfth Dynasty – was maintained. The resulting influx of raw materials led to a resumption of artistic production. The evidence for this is contained in a text on a stele that Ahmose set up in the temple

of Amon-Re at Karnak (Cairo, Egyptian Museum CG 34001) to commemorate his own exploits as well as the achievements of his mother,
Queen Ahhotpe. The precious offerings made to Amon-Re consisted of
the imported materials that were once more flowing into Egypt: silver
and gold from Asia and Nubia, lapis-lazuli from central Asia, turquoise
from the Sinai. There is renewed evidence of activities at the Serabit
el-Khadim turquoise mines, in the form of votive offerings bearing the
name of Ahmose-Nefertari that were placed in the temple of Hathor.
Turquoise was used in some of Ahhotpe's jewels inscribed with the
name of Ahmose; others of silver and lapis lazuli were decorated
with Minoan motifs. This does not definitely prove the existence of
commerce with Crete, but it suggests that there was at least some
Minoan influence on Egypt, perhaps via Byblos. Commercial relations
with Byblos itself are indicated by the existence of a reference, on the
Karnak stele mentioned above, to a cedar bark dedicated to Amon-Re.
According to this same stele, the Aegean world had finally become part
of the Egyptian 'Empire', alongside Nubia and Phoenicia, but this was
perhaps only a rhetorical expression.

The reign of Ahmose was characterized by the resumption of major
religious and funerary architectural projects, and the technical standard
of the work seems to have been very high, judging from the funerary
equipment of Queen Ahhotpe. The fine engraving on the royal stelae of
Ahmose at Abydos and Karnak compares well with that of the Middle
Kingdom. There is, however, no evidence of any artistic tradition in the
Delta at this time: Hyksos art seems to have dried up with the expulsion
of the Asiatics.

Few temples built during the reign of Ahmose have survived, perhaps
because they were built of mud-brick. Ahmose is known to have built at
Buhen, where some fragments of a doorway bearing his name have
been found. He also built additions to the temple of Amon-Re in
Karnak and the temple of Monthu at Armant. At Abydos he had two
brick cenotaphs erected in the southern part of the necropolis: one
for himself and the other for Queen Tetisheri, his grandmother. In
the twenty-second year of his reign he reopened the Tura limestone
quarries, perhaps to provide stone for the construction of a temple of
Ptah at Memphis and another temple – the 'southern harem' of Amun –
at Luxor. These projects were not accomplished in his lifetime; nevertheless it is clear that he favoured the Theban god Amun rather than the
cults of Middle and Lower Egypt. This is certainly the reason why
Hatshepsut later presented herself as the renewer of the temples destroyed by the Hyksos in Middle Egypt.

Buried at Dra Abu el-Naga, Ahmose was the object of a posthumous
funerary cult in his cenotaph at Abydos – a cult that he shared with

Tetisheri, who was the owner of the neighbouring cenotaph at Abydos. Tetisheri is one of three women who dominated the early development of the New Kingdom. Although of humble origins, she was considered to be the ancestor of the royal line and was venerated as such in the Eighteenth Dynasty. She was still alive in the time of her grandson, with whom she is associated on a stele now in the Petrie Museum, University College London. Ahmose offered her a cult on a stele dedicated to her in his funerary chapel at Abydos; she herself possessed cenotaphs and funerary estates both at Abydos and Memphis.

The second woman to become the object of a posthumous cult was Ahmose's mother, Ahhotpe I, who died in the first or second years of her son's reign. In his stele at Karnak Ahmose says of her:

> She is the one who has accomplished the rites and taken care of Egypt. She has watched over her troops and protected them. She has brought back her fugitives and rallied her deserters. She has pacified Upper Egypt and hunted down the rebels. (*Urk.* IV 21, 9–16)

This is a clear allusion to the role of the queen mother as regent for her son, who was too young to rule alone in the first years of his reign. Although this period was never actually described as a co-regency, there is an inscription on the doorway set up by Ahmose at Buhen in which the names of Ahhotpe I and her son are linked.

Ahmose Nefertari, the wife of Ahmose, was the last queen to be the recipient of a Theban cult until the custom was revived in the time of Herihor (*c.*1080 BC). She evidently outlived her husband, since she is mentioned in an inscription of the first year of Tuthmosis I. She was a key figure at the beginning of the New Kingdom. In the eighteenth or twenty-second year of the reign of Ahmose she renounced the title of Second Prophet of Amun and received instead an endowment maintaining the estate of the 'Domain of the God's Wife' (*pr ḥmt ntr*), an office which she was the first to hold. On the stele recording this event (the so-called Stele of Donations) she is shown with the crown prince Ahmose Sapair, who was to die before becoming king. On the death of her husband, Ahmose Nefertari became regent on behalf of her son Amenophis I, who was too young to rule. Meanwhile, she was regularly associated with important royal occasions and her name appears on inscriptions from Saï to Tura. When she died she became the object of a very popular religious cult, sometimes in association with her son Amenophis I, and her name appears in the litany of Amenophis I's own cult. She is mentioned in at least fifty private tombs and on more than eighty monuments, from Tuthmosis III to the end of the Ramessid period (the turn of the 1st millennium BC), both in eastern and western Thebes. The centre of her personal cult was at Deir el-Medina.

THE ORIGINS OF THE EIGHTEENTH DYNASTY

Because of problems with the chronology of the time of Ahmose, estimates of the date of accession of Amenophis I vary by almost a quarter of a century. At one stage the date was thought to be 1557 BC (Drioton and Vandier 1962), but now it appears that the heliacal rising of Sirius was observed during the reign of Amenophis I, thus allowing the calculation of the beginning of a Sothic period. The phenomenon is mentioned in Papyrus Ebers, which contains the following very precise statement:

> Ninth year of the reign of his majesty the king of Upper and Lower Egypt, Djeserkare – may he live for ever! Festival of the New Year: third month of summer, ninth day – rising of Sirius. (*Urk.* IV 44, 5–6)

If this is evidence for a heliacal rising of Sirius (Helck 1983b: 47–9), the astronomical calculation gives the date 1537 BC for the rising, and therefore 1546 BC for the beginning of Amenophis' reign (*CAH* I:1, chapter VI; II, 308), but only if the astronomical observation was made at Memphis. If, however, the observation was made at Thebes – which would logically have been the reference point if it was the capital – twenty years have to be deducted from the figure, giving the date of 1517 BC for the astronomical event and 1526 BC for the coronation of Amenophis I (*LÄ* I, 969).

Amenophis probably became king in the summer or autumn of 1526 BC. His political programme evidently stressed foreign policy, for his 'Horus' name was Ka-waf-taw ('Bull who conquers the lands') and his 'Two Ladies' name was Aa-nerw ('He who inspires great terror'). Ramesses II later evoked these two titles in his own 'Horus' name (Grimal 1986: 694). Amenophis I's twenty-one-year rule was, however, harmonious both at home and abroad. Nubia had clearly been pacified, for Ahmose son of Ibana describes a campaign against the Iwntyw which seems to have been scarcely more than a raid. Another soldier of the time, Ahmose Pennekhbet (a compatriot of Ahmose son of Ibana who was eventually to become the tutor of the daughter of Hatshepsut), left an account of his life in his tomb at Elkab in which he mentions a campaign against Kush which may perhaps be the same as the one described by Ahmose son of Ibana. Amenophis I appointed a man called Turi as Viceroy of Kush and established a temple marking the southern frontier of Egyptian territory at the Nubian town of Saï. There is no evidence of war in Western Asia, although Mitanni is listed among

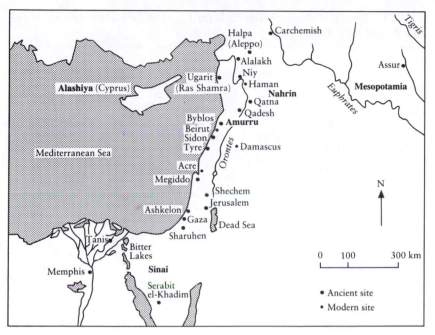

FIGURE 12   *Map of Egypt and the Near East at the beginning of the New Kingdom.*

the enemies of Egypt. It was still too early for conflict between the two great powers, but that did not prevent Mitanni from once more contesting Egypt's control of the area around the Euphrates. Closer to home, the oases had been totally reconquered, judging from the use of the title 'prince-governor (*ḥaty-ʿ*) of the oases' (Louvre, Stele C47). At the same time the Serabit el-Khadim mining installations were restored.

Egypt continued to make advances, both in economic and artistic terms. Unfortunately this progress is difficult to deduce from the sculptural products of artists' studios, since few royal statues are datable to Amenophis I's lifetime. Most are associated with his posthumous cult and therefore the work of his successors. It is possible, however, to gain some idea of the level of his achievements through the fragments of his monuments that were recycled in later constructions. Some of his works at Karnak were reused by Amenophis III as part of the fill of the Third Pylon, including a sacred bark chapel of the finest alabaster (on which his name is associated with that of Tuthmosis I) and a limestone copy of the White Chapel of Sesostris I. The Third Pylon also contained several fragments from rooms originally built by

TABLE 5 *Simplified chronological table for Egypt and the ancient world in the Middle and Late Bronze Ages.*

Dates BC	Egypt	Anatolia		
		Western	*Central*	*Southern*
c.1800	Second Intermediate Period – Hyksos (Dynasties XIII–XVII)	Troy V 1900–1800 Troy VI 1800–1300	End of Boğazköy IV Pitkhana of Kussara Anitta Kussara	Kingdom of Aleppo 1800–1650
			Old Hittite Empire 1680–1500	
			Labarnas I 1680–1650	
1600			Hattusilis I 1650–1620	
	New Kingdom		Mursilis I 1620–1590	
1552–1069	(Dynasty XVIII) Ahmose		Telepinus 1525–1500	
1526	Amenophis I			
1506	Tuthmosis I			Idrimi of Alalakh
1493	Tuthmosis II		New Hittite Empire	
1479	Hatshepsut		1460–1180	
1458	Tuthmosis III		Tudhaliyas I 1460–1440	Peak of Ugarit
1425	Amenophis II		Arnuwandas I 1440–1420	1400–1250
1401	Tuthmosis IV		Hattusilis II 1420	
1390	Amenophis III		Tudhaliyas III 1400	
1352	Amenophis IV		Arnuwandas II 1385	
1336	Tutankhamun		Suppiluliumas I 1375	
1327	Ay		Arnuwandas III 1335	
1323	Horemheb		Mursilis II 1334	
	(Dynasty XIX)	Troy VIIa		
1295	Ramesses I	1300–1260		
1294	Sethos I		Muwatallis 1306	
1279	Ramesses II		Urhi-Teshub 1282	Battle of Qadesh
		Troy VIIb	Hattusilis III 1275	
1212	Merneptah	1260–1100	Tudhaliyas IV 1250	
1202	Amenmesse			
1202	Sethos II		Arnuwandas IV 1220	Neo-Hittite
1196	Siptah			principalities
	Twosre			1200–700
1188	Sethnakhte		Suppiluliumas II 1190	
1186	Ramesses III			
1154	" IV			
1148	" V			
1144	" VI			
1136	" VII			
1128	" VIII			
1125	" IX			
1107	" X			
1098	" XI			
1050		Beginning of Greek colonization		

| Palestine | Mesopotamia | | Iran | Crete | Greece |
	North	South			
Middle Canaanite Hyksos	Old Assyrian Period Shamsi-Adad Zimri-Lim of Mari	First Dynasty of Babylon 1894–1596 Hammurapi 1792–1750	Old Elamite Period 2000–1500	Middle Minoan II 1850–1700 Middle Minoan III 1700–1550	Middle Helladic 1850–1580
		Kassite Period 1595–1155		Late Minoan I 1550–1450	Mycenaean I 1580–1450
	Mitannian Empire 1500–1360		Middle Elamite Period 1500–1000		
Late Canaanite Late Bronze Age 1500–1100	Sansatar Artatama I Sutarna II Artassumara Tushratta Mattiwaza	Karaïndash 1445–1427	Glyan 1A	Late Minoan II 1450–1400 Late Minoan III 1400–1180	Mycenaean II 1450–1400 Mycenaean III 1400–1100
	Middle Assyrian Period: 1360–900 Assuruballit I 1360 Adad-Nirari I 1300 Shalmaneser I 1273 Tukulti Ninurta 1244	Melishipak II 1202–1188	Chogha-Zambil Glyan 1B Luristan bronzes 1200–750	Subminoan 1180–1060	
	Tiglath-Pileser I 1112–1074	Nebuchadrezzar 1136		Protogeometric	Submycenaean

Amenophis I and later reconstructed by Tuthmosis III. Nothing has
survived of the mud-brick sanctuary of Hathor which Amenophis I set
up at Deir el-Bahri, since this was demolished by Hatshepsut during
the construction of her mortuary temple. There are a few remaining
traces of Amenophis' constructions in Upper Egyptian sites such as
Elephantine, Kom Ombo, Abydos and the temple of Nekhbet, but
following the policy of his father, he seems to have undertaken no
building in Lower Egypt.

The earliest surviving water-clock (Cairo, Egyptian Museum JE
37525) dates to the reign of Amenophis III, but it was one of Amenophis
I's subjects, a man called Amenemhat, who invented it (Helck 1975b:
111–12). Papyrus Ebers also dates to the reign of Amenophis I: discovered at Luxor and now in the Leipzig Museum, this document is one
of the main sources of evidence for ancient Egyptian medicine. It
was probably around the same time that the definitive version of the
principal royal funerary text, the *Book of What is in the Underworld*
(*Am Dwat*), was composed, for it makes its first appearance on the
walls of the burial chamber of Tuthmosis I. This text is now thought to
have originated in the Middle Kingdom or even as early as the Old
Kingdom.

The *Book of What is in the Underworld* is a generic term for a
collection of royal funerary texts. To a certain extent it was intended as
a replacement for the earlier great funerary compositions. Its function
was both to describe the nature of the Underworld – as its name
suggests – and to provide the deceased with the ritual keys which would
actually allow him to reach the Underworld. It therefore consists of a
descriptive composition, divided into twelve hours and focusing on the
nocturnal journey of the sun. Apart from a short period of neglect
during the Amarna period it retained its popularity in royal tombs until
the end of the Twentieth Dynasty. From the Twenty-first Dynasty until
the time of Alexander the Great it was used in the tombs of private
individuals.

The burial place of Amenophis I is not known. He may have been
interred at Dra Abu el-Naga – if so, he would have been the last of his
line to be buried there, for his successor Tuthmosis I inaugurated the
tradition of burial in the Valley of the Kings. The tomb of Amenophis I
was at the top of the list in an inspection report recorded on Papyrus
Abbot of the sixteenth regnal year of Ramesses IX, but its geographical
location cannot be precisely deduced from the description provided (*PM*
I, 599). The only sure fact concerning his tomb is the introduction of a
radical change in the structure of the royal funerary complex, since the
tomb was separate from the mortuary temple for the first time. This
change was emulated by all of his successors, each of whom constructed

their 'Mansions of Millions of Years' (mortuary temples) along the Theban west bank.

HATSHEPSUT

As a result of the premature death of Amenophis I's son Amenemhat, it was the descendant of a collateral branch of the family who succeeded him. This man, Tuthmosis I, bolstered his claim to the throne by marrying Ahmes, the sister of Amenophis I. From this union came a daughter, Hatshepsut, and a son, Amenemes. The latter did not reach the throne, but Hatshepsut married her half-brother, the son of Tuthmosis I by a concubine called Mutnofret. Hatshepsut's half-brother and husband eventually became king under the name of Tuthmosis II. The marriage of Tuthmosis II and Hatshepsut failed to produce a male heir; instead they produced another daughter, Neferure. Hatshepsut probably married Neferure to her stepson, Tuthmosis III, who was the son of Tuthmosis II and a royal concubine called Isis.

These, broadly speaking, were the successional problems of the descendants of Ahmose. The principle of marriage to a half-sister took place twice to general satisfaction. But in 1479 BC Tuthmosis II died – probably through some illness – after only fourteen years on the throne. His son, the future Tuthmosis III, was too young to rule in his own right, therefore Hatshepsut, stepmother of the young Tuthmosis, became regent. The evidence for this regency takes the form of an inscription on a stele in the rock tomb of Inene (Steward of the Granaries of Amun from the reign of Amenophis I to Tuthmosis III) at Sheikh Abd el-Qurna (TT 81), on the west bank at Thebes:

> [The King] went up to heaven and was united with the gods. His son took his place as King of the Two Lands and he was the sovereign on the throne of his father. His sister, the God's Wife Hatshepsut, dealt with the affairs of the state: the Two Lands were under her government and taxes were paid to her. (*Urk.* IV 59, 13–60, 3)

In the second or third year of her regency Hatshepsut abandoned the pretext and had herself crowned as king, with complete titulature: Maatkare ('Maat is the *ka* of Ra'), Khnemet-Amun-Hatshepsut ('She who embraces Amun, the foremost of women'). Officially Tuthmosis III was no longer her co-regent. In order to justify this usurpation she effectively ignored Tuthmosis II by inventing a co-regency with her father, Tuthmosis I. She incorporated this fabrication into a group of texts and representations with which she decorated her mortuary temple in the bay of the cliffs at Deir el-Bahri, close to the mortuary temple of the Eleventh Dynasty king Nebhepetre Mentuhotpe II. This

PLATE 13 *Sphinx of Hatshepsut. Eighteenth Dynasty, red granite, h. 1.64 m, front view. (The Metropolitan Museum of Art, Rogers Fund, 1931. [31.3.166]).*

'Text of the youth of Hatshepsut', the fundamentals of which were reproduced by Tuthmosis III at Karnak, is both a mythological and a political narrative.

> In the first scene Amun announces to the Ennead his intention to present Egypt with a new king. Thoth recommends to him Ahmose, the wife of Tuthmosis I. Amun visits her and announces to her that she will give birth to a daughter by him whom she will call 'She who embraces Amun, the foremost of women'. Then, at Ahmose's request, Khnum the potter-god fashions on his wheel the child and her double. Ahmose gives birth to her daughter and presents her to Amun. Amun arranges the education of the child with the help of Thoth and the divine nurse Hathor.
>
> This is followed by scenes of Hatshepsut's coronation. After she has been purified, Amun presents her to the gods of the Ennead. In their company she travels to the north. She is then enthroned by Atum and receives the crowns and royal titles. After being proclaimed king by the gods, she must still be crowned by mankind. Her human father, Tuthmosis I, introduces her to the royal court, nominates her and has her acclaimed as heir. As soon as her titulature has been announced she undergoes a further rite of purification. (*Urk.* IV 216, 1-265-5)

Hatshepsut associated her father with her own funerary cult by dedicating a chapel to him in her temple at Deir el-Bahri. A sarcophagus of Tuthmosis I was found in her tomb (QV 20), despite the fact that one had already been found in Tuthmosis I's own tomb (KV 38). It is unfortunately not possible to ascertain whether Hatshepsut took her concern for the legitimacy of her rule to the extent of transferring the body of her predecessor into her own tomb, for the mummy of Tuthmosis I eventually became part of the Deir el-Bahri cache and was reinterred in a third sarcophagus (Cairo, Egyptian Museum CG 61025) which was to be usurped by Pinudjem 400 years later.

Hatshepsut (Plate 13) reigned until 1458 BC, the twenty-second year of the reign of Tuthmosis III, who then regained the throne. It seems that during her lifetime she faced less opposition than might have been expected, considering the fury with which her stepson later set out to erase her memory after her death. During her reign she relied on a certain number of prominent figures of whom the foremost was a man called Senenmut (Plate 14). Born of a humble family at Armant, he pursued during Hatshepsut's reign one of the most amazing careers in ancient Egypt. He was 'spokesman' for the queen as well as steward of the royal family and superintendent of the buildings of the god Amun. It was in the latter role that he supervised the transport and erection of the obelisks that the queen installed in the Temple of Amon-Re at Karnak, as well as the construction of her mortuary temple at Deir el-Bahri; in front of this he had a second tomb (TT 353) dug for

PLATE 14 *Statue of Senenmut nursing Neferure. Eighteenth Dynasty, black granite, h. 0.76 m. (Reproduced courtesy of the Trustees of the British Museum, London.)*

himself in addition to the one that he already owned at Sheikh Abd el-Qurna (TT 71).

Even in Senenmut's time there was spiteful gossip suggesting that he owed his good fortune to intimate relations with the queen. In fact it appears that his close connections arose from the role he played in the education of her only daughter Neferure, for whom one of his brothers, Senimen, acted as nurse and steward. Many statues associate the princess with Senenmut, who was a cultured man. His constructions show that he was an architect, but other dimensions of his career are suggested by the presence of an astronomical ceiling in his tomb at Deir el-Bahri and about 150 ostraca in his tomb at Qurna, including several drawings (notably two plans of the tomb itself), as well as lists, calculations, various reports and some copies of religious, funerary and literary texts including *The Satire of the Trades*, *The Tale of Sinuhe* and *The Instruction of Ammenemes I* (Hayes 1942). Senenmut was a ubiquitous figure throughout the first three-quarters of Hatshepsut's reign, but he subsequently seems to have fallen into disgrace for reasons which are not precisely known. It is thought that after the death of Neferure, which perhaps occurred in the eleventh year of Hatshepsut's reign, he may have embarked upon an alliance with Tuthmosis III which led Hatshepsut to discard him in the nineteenth year of her reign, three years before the disappearance of the queen herself.

At Deir el-Bahri Senenmut recreated the basic plan of the temple of Mentuhotpe II and positioned it in relation to the northern enclosure wall of Mentuhotpe's temple. The great originality of Hatshepsut's complex lay in its organization into a succession of terraces in which the changes in plan enabled the monument to harmonize with the natural amphitheatre of the cliffs. The lower (first) terrace was entered through a pylon probably flanked by trees; an axial ramp with colonnades on either side led up to the middle (second) terrace, raised above the lower one by the height of the colonnades. These colonnades themselves were flanked at their northern and southern ends by colossal Osirid statues. The decoration in the south colonnade showed the erection of the Karnak obelisks, while that in the north showed scenes of hunting and fishing.

The middle terrace had the same plan as the lower: the south colonnade contained the account of the expedition to the land of Punt, while the northern colonnade bore scenes of the divine birth and acted as a type of *mammisi* (or divine birth-house). The northern part of the middle terrace provided access to a sanctuary of Anubis with a chapel cut into the cliff. The southern end was bordered by a stepped retaining wall. Between the retaining wall and the enclosure wall a passage, accessible from the lower terrace, led up to a chapel dedicated to

Hathor. The second hypostyle hall of this Hathor chapel could be reached directly by way of the colonnade on the uppermost (third) terrace, which was fronted by a peristyle hall. To the north of the peristyle hall was a solar temple consisting of an altar in an open court and a rock-cut chapel in which Tuthmosis I was shown worshipping Anubis. The main sanctuary of the whole temple – cut into the cliff face and flanked by niches containing statues of the queen – consisted of three chapels, the most important of which was the resting place of the sacred bark.

The royal entourage still included a High Priest of Amun, a man called Hapuseneb who was related to the royal family through his mother Ahhotep. He was descended from an important family: although his father, Hapu, was only a lector-priest of Amun, his grandfather, Imhotep, had been Tuthmosis I's vizier. Hapuseneb carried out the construction of the temple at Deir el-Bahri and was then awarded the office of High Priest of Amun. He later installed his son as Scribe of the Treasury of Amun.

Another important member of Hatshepsut's court was the Chancellor Nehsy who, in the ninth year of her reign, led an expedition to Punt in a revival of a Middle Kingdom tradition. This expedition, recounted in great detail on the walls of Hatshepsut's mortuary temple, represented the high point of a foreign policy that was limited to the exploitation of the Wadi Maghara mines in Sinai and the despatch of one military expedition into Nubia. The queen appointed a new Viceroy of Kush called Inebni to replace Seni, who had held the post in the reign of Tuthmosis II. She was also assisted by various other officials, including the Treasurer Thutmose, who was buried in a tomb on the west bank at Thebes (TT 110); the Chief Steward and veteran Amenhotep (buried in TT 73), who carried out the erection of the two obelisks at Karnak; and Useramun, who was her vizier from the fifth year of her reign onwards.

When Tuthmosis III finally regained the throne in about 1458 BC he still had thirty-three years of rule ahead of him, in which he was to carry out a political programme that established Egypt as the undisputed master of Asia Minor and Nubia. During the reign of Hatshepsut the only military actions were to consolidate the achievements of Tuthmosis I, whose preventive raid into Retjenu and Nahrin had enabled him to set up a boundary stele on the bank of the Euphrates. In Nubia Tuthmosis I had extended Egyptian control to the Island of Argo at the Third Cataract, where he built the fortress of Tombos. He was able to leave an inscription at Argo on what is known as the Tombos Stele (*Urk.* IV 85, 13–14), describing an empire that extended from the Third Cataract to the Euphrates. Tuthmosis II had preserved his father's empire with two campaigns: one crushing a revolt in Nubia, in the first year of his reign, and the other directed against the Shosu Bedouin of southern Palestine, which took him to Niy (later called Apamea and now Qalat el-Mudikh) in the region of Nahrin.

THE GLORIOUS REIGN OF TUTHMOSIS III

Immediately after the death of Hatshepsut, Tuthmosis III found himself confronted by a revolt of the main Asiatic peoples, united around the prince of Qadesh with the support of Mitanni; he had to undertake no less than seventeen campaigns before the situation was finally under control. Mitanni is the name of the Hurrian civilization which was contemporary with the Kassites in Babylon. Its empire, made up of the remains of the domain of the Babylonian king Hammurapi, reached its peak in the fifteenth century BC. The nucleus of Mitanni was located between the Tigris and the Euphrates, to the south of the Taurus, and its empire stretched across Syria and Kurdistan as far as the Palestinian region. This was the geographical area of their conflict with Egypt from the time of Ahmose onwards, because the Egyptians' aim was to push back as far as possible the 'Asiatics' who threatened their borders. Mitanni, on the other hand, attempted to embroil its Egyptian rivals in local struggles among the Syrian city-states, thus ensuring that the Mitannian empire itself was not directly threatened. The Mitannians achieved this aim by exacerbating the constant rivalries between each of the small city-states through a subtle game of switching alliances.

The conflict between Egypt and Mitanni proceeded in five stages, which can be followed in the *Annals* which Tuthmosis III had inscribed in the Temple of Amon-Re at Karnak, near the sanctuary of the sacred bark. The function of these texts was both commemorative and practical. They presented the facts in a dramatic style that was suitable for the traditional royal account, accompanied by a description, campaign by campaign, of the booty obtained by the Egyptian armies and dedicated to Amon-Re.

Tuthmosis III dealt with his most urgent problems first: in the twenty-second to twenty-third years of his reign he launched a campaign to reconquer Retjenu. He set out from the eastern Delta and went up, via Gaza, towards Yehem (modern Yemma, south-west of Mount Carmel), reaching the plain of Megiddo by way of a narrow pass. For seven months he laid siege to the town of Megiddo, which eventually fell into his hands. He was then able to move up towards Tyre, capturing en route the towns of Yanoam, Nuges (Nuhasse, to the south of Aleppo) and Herenkeru. In this way he crushed the western branch of the coalition and moved towards the traditional port of Egypt on the Mediterranean.

TABLE 6   *Family tree of the late Eighteenth Dynasty (generations 9–11).*

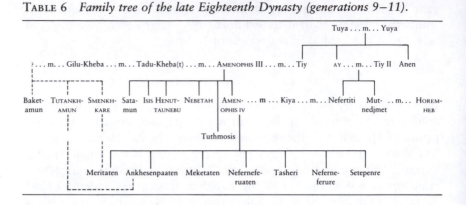

Tuthmosis organized this conquest in a series of three campaigns, from the twenty-second to the twenty-fourth years of his reign, and each year he conducted a tour of inspection which allowed him to ensure the collection of tribute due from the conquered, including the princes of Assur and Retjenu. He also seized the wheat harvest of the plain of Megiddo and had it transported to Egypt, along with numerous examples of the flora and fauna of Syria. He commemorated this aspect of the campaign held in the twenty-fifth year of his reign by ordering the depiction of a 'botanical garden' on the walls of one of the rooms he had built to the east of his Festival Hall at Karnak temple. This was, in a sense, a sequel to the description of the flora and fauna of Punt in the temple of Hatshepsut at Deir el-Bahri. Like the 'Scenes of the Seasons' in the sun temple of the Fifth Dynasty king Neuserre at Abu Ghurob, both probably expressed the universality of the solar cult to which they were dedicated.

From his twenty-ninth to his thirty-second regnal years, Tuthmosis III dealt with Djahy (the coastal plain of Palestine) and the city of Qadesh. He first made sure of the maritime front by taking Ullaza, a town at the mouth of the river Nahr el-Barid which was held by the prince of Tunip and his allies from Qadesh and Nahrin; then he captured Ardata, a city several kilometres south-west of Tripoli. After pillaging the region of Ardata, destroying the wheat fields and orchards, the Egyptian troops occupied Djahi, which the texts describe as a Syrian version of Capua:

> His majesty then discovered the trees of the land of Djahi, all groaning under the weight of their fruit. This was the discovery of the delicious wines that they make in their wine-presses. Their wheat too, piled up in

heaps on the ground, was more abundant than the sand on the sea-shore. The army took their fill of it. (*Urk.* IV 687, 9–688, 1)

At the time of the sixth campaign in the following year, the Egyptians arrived in Syria from the sea. They went up as far as Qadesh, where they devastated the surrounding area, then they turned once more towards the coast, marching on Simyra to the north of the Nahr el-Kebir and finally subduing Ardata which had probably rebelled again by then. In an attempt to avert any further rebellions, Tuthmosis III resorted to a policy that the Romans were later to adopt: he brought back to the Egyptian court thirty-six sons of chiefs. These princes were kept as hostages and educated in Egyptian ways before being sent back to their homelands to succeed to their fathers' thrones.

But this was still not sufficient to bring about the pacification of Syria-Palestine. The next year Tuthmosis waged a second campaign against Ullaza, which had rejoined the anti-Egyptian coalition. The fall of Ullaza led to the subjugation of the Phoenician ports, through which the king could then ensure the provision of supplies from the hinterland and therefore avoid a further reversal of the situation there. Upon his return to Egypt he received an ambassador from an unidentified Asiatic land who came to pay him homage.

Up to this point the *Annals* only mention military action in Syria-Palestine. In Tuthmosis' thirty-first regnal year there is for the first time mention of tribute paid by the Nubian lands of Kush and Wawat. These appear until the thirty-eighth year of his reign, then less regularly afterwards except when there are real problems. Tuthmosis III launched only one Nubian campaign near the end of his reign, in his fiftieth year as king. This campaign, moreover, was aimed only at the expansion of the empire as far as the Fourth Cataract, where Egyptian influence had already spread: the oldest known text from Gebel Barkal dates in fact from the forty-seventh year of Tuthmosis III.

In the thirty-third year of Tuthmosis III's reign a new phase of the Asian wars commenced: direct confrontation with Mitanni. In order to reach Mitanni it was essential to find a reliable method of crossing the natural barrier that protected it: the Euphrates. For this purpose Tuthmosis III's army hauled specially constructed river boats across Syria. Having reached and occupied Qatna (modern Mishrife), on the east side of the river Orontes, they turned towards the Euphrates. Tuthmosis III crossed the river and set up a stele alongside the one erected by his grandfather. He then headed north, pillaged the land south of Carchemish, defeated a party of the enemy and passed back over to the west. He returned via the Orontes to the heights of Niy, which from then on would be the northern limit of Egyptian influence, while Aleppo was the outermost of the major cities in the Mitannian empire. At Niy Tuthmosis III indulged in an elephant hunt, as Tuthmosis I had done before him. Before returning to Egypt from this and each subsequent campaign, he made sure of the supplies for the Phoenician ports. In the thirty-third year of his reign he received tribute from Retjenu, as well as from Babylon, Assur and the Hittites: all areas that had been theoretically incorporated into the Egyptian empire by crossing the Euphrates.

The next nine campaigns were devoted to an attempt at reducing the Mitannian military presence in Nahrin. In the thirty-fourth regnal year, at the time of his ninth campaign, Tuthmosis III suppressed a rebellion at Djahy and captured Nuges. He was forced to come back the following year to deal with a new Mitannian coalition to the north-west of Aleppo. This tenth campaign was perhaps a little more successful than that of the previous year, since victory was followed by the arrival of tribute from the Hittites. The account of the campaigns of the next two years is lost. Doubtless they were not much more decisive than those before them: the Egyptian army was obliged to raid the region of Nuges once more. On this occasion the people of Alalakh were among those paying tribute – the prince of Aleppo had evidently been pushed back into his own domain. The following year Tuthmosis was content to suppress a revolt of the bedouin Shosu people. It was not until the forty-second year of his rule that he undertook a sixteenth and final campaign in Djahi, where the Phoenician principalities had once more gone over to Mitanni. He seized the port of Arqata near Tripoli, sacked Tunip and moved on to the region of Qadesh, where he took three cities and wiped out a large force of Mitannians. This victory, which brought about a twelve-year gap in the conflict between Egypt and Mitanni, must have had quite an impact, for the next tribute lists include Adana, a Cilician city.

The last years of Tuthmosis III's reign were more peaceful: Egyptian supremacy was, for the time being, recognized in the Near East and relations with the Aegean region were cordial. But Tuthmosis III was not merely a great soldier. He pursued the building programmes undertaken since the time of Tuthmosis I, whose architect, Inene, had initiated the transformation of the temple of Amon-Re at Karnak. He also embarked on buildings at Deir el-Bahri and Medinet Habu, to which we will return later. His activity as a builder emerged particularly towards the end of his reign, rivalling that of Hatshepsut. He attempted to hammer out Hatshepsut's name on all of her monuments, thus condemning her to oblivion – a fate worse than death for an Egyptian. But her name is still to be found at Armant, in the temple of Monthu that was enlarged by Tuthmosis III, and in the area of Beni Hasan, where she had dedicated a rock temple to the goddess Pakhet (which the Greeks – equating Pakhet with their goddess of war, Artemis – later called Speos Artemidos). Tuthmosis III finished off the decoration at Speos Artemidos and the sanctuary was later completed by Sethos I. In the entrance way of Speos Artemidos Hatshepsut listed the buildings that she had dedicated to the gods in Middle Egypt, including the restoration of the temples of Cusae, Antinoe and Hermopolis (*Urk.* IV 386, 4–389, 17). She had also had other rock temples constructed: a chapel dedicated to Hathor at Faras, to the north of Wadi Halfa, and two others at Qasr Ibrim and Gebel el-Silsila. The temple at Buhen dated from the early years of her reign, as did the temples of Satis and Khnum at Elephantine and Kumma respectively. Tuthmosis III built with the same energy as he had fought against Mitanni. In Nubia he built at Buhen, Saï, Faras, Dakka, Argo, Kubban, Semna and Gebel Barkal; in Egypt he built at Thebes, Kom Ombo, Armant, el-Tod, Medamud, Esna, Dendera, Heliopolis and also at numerous sites in the Delta where the physical traces of his activity have not survived.

AMENOPHIS II AND TUTHMOSIS IV

Two years before he died Tuthmosis appointed as his heir Amenophis II, his son by his second wife, Hatshepsut II Merire. It was Amenophis II who as his successor took care of Tuthmosis' funerary cult, burying him in the the Valley of the Kings (KV 34). Tuthmosis left behind him the memory of a great king who was rapidly to become legendary. His crossing of the Euphrates, especially, was to endure for ever in the Egyptians' memories. His Syrian campaigns even served as a backdrop to the story of the taking of Joppa by the famous general Djehuty.

This story, recorded on Papyrus Harris 500, describes the way in which the general Djehuty took the port of Joppa (modern Jaffa) using the kind of plan which is a common element in stories all over the world, from the taking of Babylon by Darius to the Trojan Horse in the *Iliad* and the jars of Ali Baba and the Forty Thieves in the *Arabian Nights*. Having killed the Prince of Joppa while he was on a diplomatic mission, Djehuty then captured the city by smuggling in 200 soldiers hidden in baskets.

Tuthmosis III's great deeds and numerous buildings have ensured his immortality, but he is also remembered for his creativity, described by the scribes as more durable than monuments. His enthusiasm for botany has already been noted, but he also practised the art of pottery and was apparently able to compose literary works himself. His vizier, Rekhmire – one of the great intellects of his time – combined literature with the decorative arts in his tomb at Sheikh Abd el-Qurna, which was one of the most remarkable creations of the New Kingdom. Tuthmosis III, a well-educated man who enthusiastically threw himself into the reading of ancient texts, revived the tradition of piety to ancestors. The list of his ancestors which he set up at Karnak and the care that he took with their monuments certainly show deep piety, but they also suggest an acute sense of history appropriate to a great king.

His successor, Aakheperure Amenophis II, is remembered as a far less intellectual ruler, but he was still able to preserve the prosperity and power of Egypt. His main claim to fame was his unusual physical strength. In the third year of his reign, during his first Syrian campaign, he is supposed to have singlehandedly killed seven princes at Qadesh. He clearly combined his strength with a cruelty intended to demoralize enemies, for he is then said to have had the bodies of the Qadesh princes publicly displayed on the walls of Thebes and Napata. His prowess has emerged both from the practice of military sports, which he considered an honourable activity, and the pursuit of various activities derived originally from western Asia. This Asiatic influence was equally apparent in religion, with the rise of the cults of Astarte, the goddess of horse-riders, and Reshef. The infiltration of Syro-Palestinian culture into Egypt had begun in the Middle Kingdom; it was subsequently exacerbated by the growing need to import those raw materials (Syrian tin, Cypriot copper and Cilician silver) that had become essential to an Egyptian economy dependent on bronze-based technology. From the same lands came specialized craftwork, while the ranks of foreign artisans were swollen by prisoners installed in workmen's communities of the type that had already developed at Deir el-Medina.

Sport was also incorporated into royal tradition in a fashion that was widely copied by his successors (Decker 1971). The importance of the lion hunt – which Amenophis II undertook on foot – and the hunting of wild animals in general went back to the dawn of Egyptian history and played a part in the very ordering of creation. This taste for strength is apparent in Amenophis' titulary: his Horus name was 'Powerful bull with great strength' or 'with sharp horns' and his Golden Horus name was 'He who siezes all the lands by strength'.

Amenophis tested his strength in three Syrian campaigns. The first, in the third year of his reign (already been mentioned above), was necesitated by the rebellion of Nahrin as a result of the change of pharaoh. The fall of Qadesh, with which this campaign ended, did not, however, solve the problem: two further expeditions were required, directed specifically against Mitanni. These campaigns took place in regnal years seven and nine as a result of a revolt in Syria instigated by Carchemish. The conflict took place on the heights of Niy and resulted in Egypt's loss of the whole area between the rivers Orontes and Euphrates, despite the Egyptian texts' description of abundant booty from their pillages in Retjenu. Among the prisoners of war were said to be 3600 Apiru, an ethnic group clearly distinct from the Shosu Bedouin, who are enumerated separately. There are reports of Apiru in Cappadocia in the nineteenth century BC and in Mari and Alalakh in the eighteenth century BC. They are synonymous with the Hebrews mentioned in the Amarna correspondence; by Amenophis II's time they seem to have become integrated into the societies to which they had emigrated, playing marginal roles as mercenaries or servants, as in the events described in *The Taking of Joppa*. In Egypt they appear during the reign of Tuthmosis III as wine-makers in the Theban tombs of the Second Prophet of Amun Puyemre (TT 39) and the herald Intef (TT 155).

These two campaigns were the last to pit Egypt against Mitanni. Indeed, in the reign of Tuthmosis IV relations between the two countries changed completely when Mitanni – now threatened by the Hittite empire of Tudhaliyas II – attempted to forge an alliance with its erstwhile foes. The city-state of Aleppo had already changed sides and only the Hittites' involvement in conflicts within Anatolia itself was preventing them from becoming even more of a threat. It is also likely that the Mitannians and Egyptians made terms that were acceptable to both parties, in that Mitanni allowed Egypt to keep Palestine and part of the Mediterranean coast in exchange for Mitannian control of northern Syria. Tuthmosis IV's tour of Nahrin seems to confirm this division of Syria-Palestine, in that he had evidently abandoned Alalakh to Mitanni. The Egyptian king then took the alliance to its logical conclusion by asking for the hand in marriage of the daughter of the Mitannian king, Artatama I. The very fact that such a union was even envisaged is a clear indication of the new state of relations between the two old enemies.

In Nubia the inheritance of Tuthmosis III was easy to look after: peace reigned there in the time of Amenophis II, who appointed Usertatet, his old companion in arms, to the post of Viceroy of Nubia. Usertatet pursued building programmes at Qasr Ibrim and Semna. Various troubles seem to have erupted in Nubia after the end of Amenophis II's reign. As a result, in the eighth year of Tuthmosis IV's reign an expedition was sent against the tribes that had infiltrated the land of Wawat, judging from the account given on a stele set up on the island of Konosso, near the First Cataract in Nubia (*Urk.* IV, 1545ff.). This, however, did not affect the progress of commercial activities in Nubia or the construction of sanctuaries there: Amenophis II ordered the decoration of part of the temple at Kalabsha and continued the

construction begun by Tuthmosis III at Amada, while Tuthmosis IV
built a columned court at Amada on the occasion of his second jubilee.

Amenophis II also constructed a number of shrines and temples in
the Theban area, at Karnak, Medamud, el-Tod and Armant. He had a
mortuary temple built for himself, but this has not survived. His tomb
in the Valley of the Kings (KV 35) is only partially decorated, with a
few divine scenes and a complete version of the *Book of What is in the
Underworld*. His tomb, however, is interesting for another reason:
when it was excavated in 1898, Victor Loret found not only the
mummy of the tomb's owner but also those of Tuthmosis III (KV 43),
Merenptah-Siptah (KV 47), Sethos II (KV 15), Setnakht (KV 14),
Ramesses III (TT 11) and Ramesses IV (TT 2), all of which had been
placed there by the Twenty-first Dynasty High Priest Pinudjem in order
to protect them from tomb robbers.

When Amenophis II died, it was Tuthmosis IV who succeeded to the
throne – the crown probably passed to him because of the premature
death of his elder brother who had been the real heir. Tuthmosis IV had
a stele set up between the paws of the Great Sphinx at Giza to commemorate an unusual act of piety on his part. The Sphinx was then, as
it is today, regularly covered in sand from the desert, which the wind
blew up against its body day after day. It happened that the young
prince loved to go hunting on the Giza plateau and one day he was
enjoying a siesta in the shadow of the Sphinx:

> One day it happened that the royal son Tuthmosis went for a walk at
> midday. He sat down in the shadow of this great god; sleep and dreaming
> came upon him when the sun was at its height. He discovered the majesty
> of this venerable god who spoke to him as a father speaks to his son:
> 'Look at me, gaze upon me, Tuthmosis my son. It is I, your father
> Harmachis-Khepri-Ra-Atum. I will give you my kingdom on earth at the
> head of all that live; you will wear the white crown and the red crown on
> the throne of Geb as heir; the country will belong to you in its length and
> breadth, as well as everything that is lit by the eye of the universe (...)
> See, my condition is that of a sick man, for my body is totally ravaged.
> The desert sand on which I stand is engulfing me (...)' (C. Zivie 1976:
> 130–1)

Tuthmosis cleared the sand away from the god and in return the
Sphinx granted him the throne that he had not expected – but his reign
was to last for only nine years, since he died at the age of about thirty.
The old yarn of the prince and the Sphinx actually conceals a difficult
political situation which had already become apparent in the reign
of Amenophis II. That the young prince should have been active at
Memphis is no surprise, for it was there that all young heirs to the
throne had been brought up since the time of Tuthmosis I. What is

more remarkable is the diligence with which Tuthmosis IV venerated the Memphite gods. He continued the construction of a temple dedicated by Amenophis II in the vicinity of the Sphinx, and he also left a foundation deposit containing his cartouche in the temple of Ptah at Memphis. Perhaps this activity was the result of a desire to counterbalance the power of Thebes, where the nobles enjoyed great luxury judging from the splendour of the tombs of the most important national figures, including the vizier Amenemope (TT 29) and his brother Sennefer (TT 96), the Mayor of Thebes; Qenamun, the Steward of the Royal Palace at Memphis, and his brother Kaemheryibsen, the Third Prophet of Amun (TT 98); the Chief Priests of Amun, Meri and Amenemhat (TT 97); the Chief of the Granaries, Menkheperraseneb (TT 79); the Royal Scribe and Tutor, Userhat (TT 56) and Kha (TT 8), whose 'treasure' is preserved in the Museo Egizio, Turin.

AMENOPHIS III AND THE HEIGHT OF THE EIGHTEENTH DYNASTY

Theban painting may have reached its peak under Tuthmosis IV, but the reign of Amenophis III, when Egypt was further exposed to eastern influences, was characterized by a new sense of refinement which was to remain unequalled even in later times when the precious products of Asia and Nubia were once more supplying the royal ateliers. Amenophis III was the son of a concubine of Tuthmosis IV called Mutemwia, once wrongly identified as the daughter of Artatama I. He was born in Thebes and when he reached the throne, with his mother as regent, he was only twelve years old. He married – in the second year of his reign at the latest – a woman of non-royal origins who was to have a decisive impact on the rest of the dynasty: Queen Tiy. She was the daughter of Yuya, a man of distinction at Akhmim, who along with his wife Tuya would also play an important political role. Between them, Yuya and Tuya assisted the cause of one of their sons, the divine father Ay, who was eventually to rise to the throne after Tutankhamun, at a difficult time in Egyptian history. Tiy bore six children to Amenophis III: the first, perhaps called Tuthmosis, died without reigning; then came the future Amenophis IV as well as four daughters, two of whom (Satamun and Isis) were given the title of queen.

In the Eighteenth Dynasty, just as much as in the Fifth Dynasty, family ties dominated the national political scene. The main government posts were shared out among the members of the royal family and marriage into that family came to be a way of officially recognizing the influence of a non-royal official who had become too important to be ignored. This was the case with Tuthmosis I and later with Ay and Horemheb. The marriage of Amenophis III to the commoner Tiy was,

from this point of view, by no means the passionate romance that it is
sometimes claimed to have been. Yuya was an officer in the Chariotry
and Master of the Stud Farms. It is thought that he was also the father
of the queen-mother Mutemwia, which would make him Amenophis
III's uncle. He installed his son Ay as Master of the Stud Farms during
the reign of his grandson Amenophis IV, having already made his other
son, Inen, the Second Prophet of Amun at Thebes and the 'Chief of
Seers' in the Temple of Ra at Karnak.

Queen Tiy was an important influence on the late Eighteenth
Dynasty not only because of her strong personality but also through
her longevity: she evidently outlived her husband and did not die until
the eighth year of the reign of her son Amenophis IV, having been
closely linked with the policies of both kings, both as wife and mother.
In fact, she was the first person to exploit the role of royal wife (the
'King's Great Wife': *ḥmt nsw wrt*) which thereafter supplanted that of
the queen mother (*mwt nsw*) as the traditional image of matriarchy.
Tiy was associated with her husband in a complementary rather than
dependent fashion. She stood alongside him as the personification of
Maat and therefore received certain royal privileges such as partici-
pation in the great religious festivals, including the *sed* festival. Not
only was she allowed to have herself represented in the form of a sphinx
but a temple was dedicated to her at the Nubian site of Sedeinga
(between the Second and Third Cataracts). She played an important
role in Egypt's foreign policy and looked after the country in the early
years of the reign of her son, acting as regent for him after having
perhaps instilled in him the basics of the new religious dogma that he
was to propagate. Finally, she followed him to el-Amarna and insisted
that when she died she should be buried there. Her mummy, however,
was later 'repatriated' in the reign of Tutankhamun and placed with
that of Smenkhkare in Tomb 55 of the Valley of the Kings.

The rule of Amenophis III was marked by peace: the only act of war
was a preventive campaign waged in the fifth year of his reign. Apart
from this, the relations with the Near East during his reign bear witness
to the burgeoning influence of Egypt in Asia and the Mediterranean
region. This is clear from the appearance of the name of Amenophis III
in such diverse locations as Crete, Mycenae, Aetolia, Anatolia, Yemen,
Babylon and Assur. Another source of information concerning the
foreign policy of the time is a collection of 379 clay tablets discovered
by an Egyptian peasant in 1887 near the royal palace at el-Amarna.
These texts, written in cuneiform (the diplomatic lingua franca of the
period), included the correspondence of Amenophis III and IV with the
kings of the Near East. The information that they contain, combined
with the archives of Boğazköy (the Hittite capital) and the Assyro-

Babylonian chronicles, presents a picture of the changing relations between Egypt and the Hittites, as well as the vicissitudes of the kingdom of Mitanni, which was continuing to lose control of its territory to the Hittites. The Egyptian-Mitanni alliance was consummated by Amenophis III's marriage, in his eleventh regnal year, to Gilu-Kheba, daughter of Suttarna II of Mitanni. During the last third of Amenophis' reign, the prince of Amurru, Abdi-Ashirta, formed a coalition with the Hittites in order to cast off the Egyptian yoke.

In the Mitannian capital the situation was deteriorating: Artashumara, the eldest son of Sutarna II, was assassinated by a pro-Hittite group led by Tuhe, who then proclaimed himself regent of the kingdom. Eventually, however, the son of Artashumara, Tushratta, avenged the death of his father and regained power. Tushratta re-established the alliance with Egypt by giving Amenophis III the hand of his daughter Tadu-Kheba(t). Babylonia, always worried by the proximity of Mitanni, followed suit, and Amenophis III married first the sister then the daughter of Kadashman-Enlil. These matrimonial networks were not totally solid guarantees in the face of the territorial appetites of the various parties. Assyria, although theoretically the vassal of Mitanni, was coveted by Babylonia, and the Assyrian king Assur-Uballit I was faced with great problems in maintaining a balance between the two. He was only able to preserve a modicum of independence for Assyria through a skilful policy of conspicuously displayed friendship towards Egypt.

Meanwhile, the fastest growing power in the region was that of the Hittites, who were eventually to reach a decisive position of dominance at the time of the transmission of power from Amenophis III to Amenophis IV (*c*.1375 BC). Prince Suppiluliumas rose to the throne in Hatti, and spent the first ten years of his reign pacifying Anatolia. He then turned towards northern Syria, capturing Aleppo and extending the Hittites' southern border as far as the Lebanon. When Amenophis IV came to the throne he sent no armies to the aid of his Mitannian allies and they were consequently obliged to accept defeat by the Hittites.

During the fifty years which preceded these events, Egypt was at the peak of its power and influence. Amenophis III was one of the greatest builders the country had ever seen. He covered Nubia with monuments, including a small temple with a colonnade (dedicated to Tuthmosis III) at Elephantine, a rock temple dedicated to Amun 'Lord of the Ways' at Wadi es-Sebua, and the temple of Horus of Miam at Aniba. He founded additional temples at Kawa and Sesebi (to which Amenophis IV added the Gem-Aten, a shrine to the Aten), while at Soleb he dedicated a temple to the cult of himself and his wife, in association with Amun.

With this sanctuary at Soleb Amenophis III established a tradition that was to be widely followed by the kings of the Nineteenth Dynasty. As well as the temple at Sedeinga he set up various buildings at Mirgissa, Quban and the islands of Saï and Argo.

In Lower Egypt Amenophis III built at Athribis and Bubastis and continued his predecessors' programmes of construction at Heliopolis with the building of a temple to Horus. He also began work on the Serapeum (the gallery of the sacred Apis bulls) at Saqqara. In the Nile valley he built at Elkab, at Sumenu near Gebelein, at Abydos and Hermopolis Magna (where he set up the colossal statues of baboons, still *in situ*). At Thebes he ordered the construction of the Luxor temple which was supposed to be the 'southern harem' of Amon-Re, while in the temple of Mut of Asheru, to the south of the Karnak precinct of Amun, he set up 600 statues of the goddess Sekhmet, some of which are now on display in the Luxor Museum, the British Museum and the Louvre. On the West Bank he built a palace at Malkata as well as an enormous mortuary temple which was later dismantled by Merneptah to provide stone for his own temple. The only substantial remains *in situ* of Amenophis III's mortuary temple are the two colossal statues, which originally stood in front of the pylon: the Colossi of Memnon.

There was evidently a phonetic similarity between the prenomen of Amenophis III, Nebmaatre (which probably sounded like 'Mimmuria' to visiting Greeks), and the name of the hero Memnon, son of Aurora (the Dawn) and mythical commander of the Ethiopian troops in the Trojan War, who was killed by Achilles. It was said that Memnon himself was buried at the feet of the Colossi. An earthquake in 27 BC served to reinforce this legend, shaking apart the blocks of the statue and creating a fissure which made a noise at daybreak when the sun's rays caused the evaporation of the moisture that had built up during the night. It was thought that this was the sound of Memnon moaning out a greeting to his mother each morning. Unfortunately, the piety of the Roman emperor Septimius Severus led him to have the monument repaired, and since then the Colossi have been struck dumb.

Both the public and private monuments of Amenophis III's reign are imbued with a finesse and delicacy that indicate an unquestionably high degree of technical ability. The influence of the Near East can be perceived in the appearance of greater sculptural freedom, which contrasts with the rigour of early Eighteenth Dynasty sculpture and anticipates the sensitivity of the works of the Amarna period. Consider, for instance, the technique of 'clinging drapery' apparent in statues at the end of Amenophis III's reign. These are traits which foreshadow the art of the Amarna period and they have frequently been cited as indications that Akhenaten's mystical preoccupations did not come out of the blue but were gradually elaborated in a royal court where a spirit of Eastern intellectualism seems to have been steadily growing.

Amenophis III's preoccupation with Heliopolitan theology suggests that the growth of the cult of the Aten was a logical consequence of the restoration of the sanctuaries at the ancient religious capital of Heliopolis. This does not necessarily mean, however, that Atenism was the only rising cult at the time: the construction of the Serapeum, which was intended to hold the remains of the Apis bulls, indicates that the king was equally keen to encourage the official cult of animal worship. In neither case, however, were Theban cults involved: the excessive political influence of the Theban priesthood was doubtless one of the things that forced Amenophis IV to sever his links with Amon-Re. The power of the priesthood of Amon-Re had been strengthened by the buildings that Amenophis III set up at Karnak, as he struggled to enlist divine aid in his fight against the illness that had dogged him since his first *sed* festival in the thirty-fourth year of his reign. The scenes on the walls of the temple at Soleb and those in the Theban tomb of Kheruef, Steward of the King's Great Wife (TT 192), show Amenophis III as a weak and visibly sick figure. It was because of poor health that he dedicated 600 statues to Sekhmet, Lady of Asheru, the ultimate female warrior. His father-in-law, the Mitannian king Tushratta, even sent him a statue of Ishtar, another goddess of war. But nothing would work and the gods could not alter Amenophis' fate.

Just before his marriage to Tadu-Kheba(t), Amenophis III celebrated his second *sed* festival in regnal year thirty-seven; if we take into account the duration of thirty years before his first *sed* festival, it is clear that the period between his first and second jubilees was cut down to a tenth of the usual length. He died in the thirty-ninth year of his reign, having perhaps shared the throne with his son during the final phase of his life. His tomb (KV 22), decorated with a version of the *Book of What is in the Underworld*, was robbed in the Twenty-first Dynasty, but his mummy survived along with the other royal bodies bundled together into Amenophis II's tomb. His was the body of a fifty-year-old man who had died of some sickness.

When Amenophis III died he took with him an Egypt of political and religious certainties, a state that had regained strength and respect both at home and abroad. The upheavals of his son's short reign were to drastically change the balance of power by forcing the pharaohs to ask a single, straightforward question which lies at the root of the concept of theocracy: what is the relationship between the temporal and spiritual worlds?

10

Akhenaten

Amenophis IV was sole ruler from 1378/1352 BC onwards. His coronation name was Neferkheperura ('The transformations of Ra are perfect'), to which he added the epithet *wa-n-ra* ('unique one of Ra'). The rest of his titulary associated him with Thebes, although his Golden Horus name described Thebes as 'the Heliopolis of the South'. The importance of Heliopolis was, as we have seen, linked with the princes' education at Memphis, and was therefore not automatically a sign of opposition to the cult of Amun.

Amenophis IV's co-regency with his father is a matter of some debate. Even if a co-regency took place we cannot be sure of its length: some argue that it would have begun in the twenty-eighth or twenty-ninth year of Amenophis III's reign, while others suggest the thirty-seventh or thirty-ninth year. In both cases it seems clear that the ideas which led to the Amarna 'revolution' developed sufficiently early to affect the later public works of Amenophis III's reign. Furthermore, the fact that Amenophis IV had himself crowned at Karnak suggests that he was not at that stage in open conflict with the priesthood of Amon-Re.

The continuity between the mid-Eighteenth Dynasty and the Amarna period was also familial, as far as it is possible to tell in the labyrinthine network of the Amarna royal family. Amenophis IV married his cousin Nefertiti, who was the daughter of Ay and Tiy II and therefore the granddaughter of Yuya and Tuya. This family from Akhmim were evidently always at the centre of the Amarna drama, as they would continue to be in the time of Horemheb through Mutnodjmet, the sister of Nefertiti. Perhaps this Akhmim connection even played a part in the choice of a site in Middle Egypt for the new capital. The marriage of Amenophis IV and Nefertiti was certainly more politically orientated than that of Amenophis III and Tiy. The wife of Amenophis IV accompanied him in religious ceremonies, just as Tiy had accompanied her husband, but a new factor now arose: from the very beginning the official artists also depicted the royal pair in the midst of family scenes that would previously have been considered far too intimate to be shown. Their roles were not always equivalent: in the Great Hymn to the Aten, for instance, only the king could know the god.

It was only in the second year of his reign that Amenophis IV replaced Amon-Re with the Aten. Until then he had undertaken a traditional programme of construction. When he opened the sandstone quarries at Gebel el-Silsila, for instance, he had himself portrayed in the act of making offerings to Amun (*Urk.* IV, 1962), while at Soleb he completed the decoration of Amenophis III's temple. But early in his reign there was already a feeling of novelty (and a certain hastiness) in the constructions that he made for the Aten at Karnak. He ordered the extraction of blocks of sandstone – both easier to work and unusually small in size – which were more suitable for the purposes of an unspecialized workforce operating in large groups. These so-called *talatat* (the local Arabic soubriquet for the blocks that was adopted by the Egyptologist H. Chevrier) were decorated with a technique that was often crude but characterized by a consistently realistic and lively style. This style reflected a new ideology that was actually taught to the artists by the king himself, if a graffiti at Aswan of his chief sculptor, Bek, is to be believed. It was probably the extremely small size of the blocks that saved them from destruction when Egypt returned to the orthodox worship of Amun and the buildings set up to the east of Karnak by the heretic pharaoh were razed to the ground. King Horemheb used most of them to fill the Ninth Pylon at Karnak. The 12,000 *talatat* blocks that the Franco-Egyptian Centre for the Karnak Temples have extracted from the demolished pylon over the last ten years are still being studied; they represent a priceless source of evidence for the history of the cult of the Aten.

In the fourth year of Amenophis IV's reign, the king and queen visited the site of the future capital, which had been 'revealed by the Aten himself' and was to be called Akhetaten ('Horizon of the Sundisc'). The following year Amenophis founded his new domain there. The site of Akhetaten is a vast natural bay of cliffs stretching for 25 kilometres on the east bank of the Nile (from Sheikh Said in the north to Sheikh Abd el-Hamid in the south), about 10 kilometres to the south of modern Mallawi. It was virgin territory, like the mound of sand at Heliopolis from which the universe was said to have been created. The king marked out the site with fourteen 'boundary stelae': eleven on the east bank and three on the west. The city was to have been the equivalent of Thebes, judging from the names and the reconstructed appearance of its monuments. Its royal and private necropolis, as well as a cemetery of Mnevis bulls, were also intended to turn it into a new Heliopolis.

RELIGIOUS REFORM

The new titulature of the king, which revealed to the nation the Atenist dogma, was first proclaimed in the inscriptions of the boundary stelae on the east bank at el-Amarna. He changed his Horus name from 'Mighty bull, tall of feathers' – which was too closely linked with Thebes – to 'Mighty bull beloved of the Aten'. His Two Ladies name 'Great of kingship on Karnak' became 'Great of kingship in Akhetaten' and his Golden Horus name was changed from 'He who uplifts his diadems in Southern Heliopolis' to 'He who uplifts the name of the Aten'. He kept the same coronation name but changed Amenophis to Akhenaten ('Agreeable to Aten'), thus comprehensively replacing Amun with Aten.

The change was not in itself revolutionary and was far from being the revelatory religion that scholars have occasionally claimed it to be. It has been suggested that Atenism lies at the roots of Christianity, when in fact it does nothing more than reflect the common ground of Semitic civilizations. The whole of the Eighteenth Dynasty was marked by the rise of the Heliopolitan cults, which were themselves only the continuation of a movement that had begun in the Middle Kingdom: the 'solarization' of the principal gods, as in the transformation of Amun into the syncretic Amon-Re. This religious tendency takes up the theme that had appeared in the funerary texts, the *Book of What is in the Underworld*, the solar litanies and the *Book of Gates*, constituting a return to the view that the creation and preservation of life were centred around Ra. It is certainly excessive to speak of monotheism (Assmann 1984: 235ff.) since this concentration on Ra does not preclude any other god. However, the sun – the ultimate creator – was evidently a fusion of numerous different divine attributes. Amenophis IV chose to worship the visible aspect of the sun – its Disc – the role of which had been clearly defined in Heliopolitan theology since the Old Kingdom. The result suggests a universalist tone which has all the trappings of monotheism. The Great Hymn to the Aten, inscribed on the west wall of the tomb of Ay at el-Amarna, has often been compared to Psalm 104:

> When you set in western lightland,
> Earth is in darkness as if in death;
> One sleeps in chambers, heads covered,

One eye does not see another.
Were they robbed of their goods,
That are under their heads,
People would not remark it.
Every lion comes from its den,
All the serpents bite;
Darkness hovers, earth is silent,
As their maker rests in lightland.
Earth brightens when you dawn in lightland,
When you shine as Aten of daytime;
As you dispel the dark,
As you cast your rays,
The Two Lands are in festivity.
Awake they stand on their feet,
You have roused them;
Bodies cleansed, clothed,
Their arms adore your appearance.
The entire land sets out to work,
All beasts browse on their herbs;
Trees, herbs are sprouting,
Birds fly from their nests,
Their wings greeting your *ka*.
All flocks frisk on their feet,
All that fly up and alight,
They live when you dawn for them.
Ships fare north, fare south as well,
Roads lie open when you rise;
The fish in the river dart before you,
Your rays are in the midst of the sea.
Who makes seed grow in women,
Who creates people from sperm;
Who feeds the son in his mother's womb,
Who soothes him to still his tears.
Nurse in the womb,
Giver of breath,
To nourish all that he made,
When he comes from the womb to breathe,
On the day of his birth,
You open wide his mouth,
You supply his needs.
When the chick in the egg speaks in the shell,
You give him breath within to sustain him;
When you have made him complete,
To break out from the egg,
He comes out from the egg,
To announce his completion,
Walking on his legs he comes from it.

                                      (Lichtheim 1976: 97–8)

This religious device was later to be revived in the Nineteenth Dynasty by gathering all aspects of the creator into the person of the king himself. The originality of Akhenaten was to turn the rays of the Disc into a physical reality, the tangible manifestation of the creator within the range of the common man. He therein provided an image that was easy to understand and avoided the need to rely on a specialized clergy as sole intermediaries between men and an impenetrable god. The Aten literally provided mortals with immediate perception of the divine, in complete contrast to Amun, who was the 'hidden' god.

All that remained was to establish the personal connection with the Aten that would endow the king with the role of creator. Akhenaten transformed the Disc itself into a celestial pharaoh by writing its name in a cartouche like his own. The 'titulature' of the Aten is very explicit: 'Ra-Horakhty appearing on the horizon in his name of Shu who is in the Disc'. In other words, the Disc, like the king, is an aspect of the creator: his earthly representative. This is a return to the traditional Egyptian system of hypostasis in a virtually unmodified form. It was also logical that the Aten took care of the dead since he had taken on the various roles of the solar creator, although judging from the Osirid royal colossal statues of the Amarna period (Plate 15), Osiris continued to be honoured by the royal family. The traditional funerary cult, however, was generally discouraged.

This programme of religious reform seems to have had virtually no effect on the population, for two basic reasons. First, the royal court very quickly confined itself to Akhetaten, so that apart from the buildings at Karnak, the population had virtually no chance to assess the new cult. Second, and more significantly, the new cult had nothing to do with the traditional structure of Egyptian society – people therefore continued to live according to the old religious customs, and prayers to Amun have even been found in the Workmen's Village at el-Amarna itself. It is no longer considered necessary to suggest that at the humblest level of society there was any great knowledge of religion and the mysteries of power, which were in fact usually hidden within the walls of the temples and the palaces.

The rise of popular religion in the New Kingdom shows that among the common people religious preoccupations were fairly basic and metaphysical concerns rare. Moreover, the image that Akhenaten presented was less original than modern tradition would like to imagine, for he maintained all the ceremonial phraseology of his predecessors. Some have called him a pacifist because he did not take part in any conflicts in the Near East during his reign, but the evidence shows that he had himself represented in the act of massacring his conquered enemies: not only in such traditional depictions as the relief on the

PLATE 15   *Akhenaten. Osirid colossal statue from Karnak East. Eighteenth Dynasty, sandstone, h. 3.10 m. (Cairo, Egyptian Museum JE 49528. Photograph: Laurie Platt Winfrey, Inc.)*

façade of the Third Pylon at Karnak, but also on the *talatat* blocks, where even Nefertiti was to be seen brandishing the White Mace over the heads of vanquished foes (Hall 1986: figs 36–40). Nor did his 'revolution' significantly affect the administration, which remained essentially unchanged, often with the same officials in control. On a political level the Amarna ideology reinforced theocratic absolutism: the king, 'the beautiful child of the Aten', was the essential intermediary between mankind and the Disc. As such he was depicted as the object of worship at the entrances to the tombs of his high officials. This divine cult of the king had a tendency to marginalize the other divinities, but the act of linking the funerary development of the courtiers with that of the king is in one sense a return to basics. This apparent regression is linked with the tendency for inquiring into the past that was already apparent in the reigns of Amenophis III and his predecessors: the search for ancient annals, the Tomb of Osiris at Abydos and so on.

The reform particularly affected two areas of life: economics and art. Akhenaten closed down certain temples, or at least limited their activities, and confiscated priestly goods for the state. The first consequence of this act was an increase in centralization of both the administration and its executive arm, the army. The neglect of local government increased the problems of maintaining an effective administration and introduced a whole new system characterized by corruption and arbitrariness, which Horemheb was later obliged to reform. The construction of the new capital and new temples was to the detriment of the economy in general and the temple-based economy in particular: the system of divine estates was, from a centralizing viewpoint, harmful, but its abandonment in the Amarna period led to the ruination of a whole system of production and redistribution without providing any new structure to replace it.

The consequences of Atenism in the arts and literature were even more spectacular and, to a certain extent, more lasting. Literature was by no means thrown into disarray: works in traditional genres continued to be produced and schoolboys still learned the story of Sinuhe. But the influence of the new ideology led to greater freedom in contemporary literary works. This freedom was particularly expressed in poetic compositions such as divine and royal hymns and litanies, in which creativity could be given full rein. Such unusual creativity appeared again in the historical works of the Ramessid period. The most striking aspect of this literary reform was the introduction of the spoken language into official texts. The conservatism of the state schools had artificially preserved the 'classical' language, i.e. that of the Middle Kingdom, in literary works. Akhenaten caused everyday language, including idiomatic phrases and foreign loan-words, to be introduced into the great literary works, producing a written language that was closer to Coptic than to the Pyramid Texts.

The new literary open-mindedness proceeded in the same spirit as that of art but it never reached the same excesses. Since the reign of Ammenemes III official idealism had tended to give way to a more sensual realism, boldly emphasizing the outlines of the body by means of techniques such as 'clinging drapery'. This more generous treatment of volumes affected the drawing, where the use of line became less rigorous and the employment of colours more flexible. There was also a development in fashion, with a greater 'modernity' being translated into new hairstyles and costumes as well as simple stylistic details, such as the restriction of the eye to the area of the socket and the stretching of lines which was to produce the famous 'almond' eyes of Akhenaten. Such features as folds on the neck and pierced ears are also readily apparent. These changes, however, were not universally accepted: the vizier Ramose, for instance, whose tomb (TT 55) is one of the most beautiful in the Sheikh Abd el-Qurna necropolis, held on to a classicism of unusual refinement.

Akhenaten exaggerated this new tendency in depictions of himself and his family from the second year of his reign onwards, moving from realism to the realms of caricature. The accentuation of his facial features and the deliberate sagging of his torso produce such a disease-ridden appearance in the colossal Osirid statues (executed by the sculptor Bek) that their bloated stomachs might even be interpreted in terms of bodily fluids inflating the decomposed corpse of Osiris.

With the passage of time this exaggerated aspect of Amarna art was gradually softened, but the style was still excessive compared to traditional methods of representation, the canons of which were nevertheless preserved. New themes appeared: the image of the family dominated all kinds of scenes, especially those relating to the cult of the Aten. This familial theme was by no means new, but the use of scenes taken from daily life introduced a more 'human' element into the representations. Individuals were presented in poses and contexts that aimed at naturalism, giving a distinctly intimate impression. The technique was essentially the same as the introduction of the vernacular into literature: it was a trivialization of form that blurred the artistic structure. The artists' drawings placed less emphasis on outlines; the symmetry was more discreet; false perspective was introduced and there were new opportunities for the expression of the artists' feelings, which were now more at home amid the less rigorous guidelines. Scenes from daily life and naturalistic themes took over from traditional representations, so that the depictions gained in naïvety and freshness what they lost in terms of technique. Towards the end of the reign studies of nature, with their more harmonious styles, became more popular.

At the el-Amarna workshop of the sculptor Thutmose have been found several trial drawings, plaster casts and portraits of the royal family, including the famous head of Nefertiti (Plate 16; W. Berlin, Ägyptische Museum). The mastery and sensitivity of these portraits is far removed from the excesses of the beginning of the reign. Something of this final state of the Amarna style was to be maintained in post-Amarna works of art; produced during the transition from the Eighteenth to the Nineteenth Dynasties, this art preserved its sensuality of volume and finesse of line, particularly in the constructions of the reign of Sethos I.

THE ROYAL FAMILY

The construction and earliest occupation of the city of Akhetaten took place at the site of el-Amarna between the fifth and sixth years of Akhenaten's reign. The inscriptions on the fourteen boundary stelae in the cliffs surrounding the site give the precise dimensions of the domain of Akhetaten and also contain an oath never to overstep the boundaries of the city. This promise, which only defines the limits of the domain, has sometimes been wrongly interpreted as the expression of the royal wish never to leave the Horizon of the Aten. In the eighth year of his reign the king inscribed a second group of stelae. In the twelfth year he organized great festivals along traditional lines, with their supply of tribute from conquered lands, festivals which are represented in the tombs of Merire II and Huya in the Amarna necropolis. In the same year Queen Tiy, accompanied by the princess Baketaten, paid a visit to the Amarna court and settled there. The festivals and the presence of the queen-mother at her son's side have been interpreted as evidence that Akhenaten did not become sole ruler until after this date, but this hypothesis is difficult to prove conclusively. The twelfth year of Akhenaten's reign was also marked by the death of Meketaten, one of the royal couple's six daughters.

After the twelfth regnal year Nefertiti seems to have played a lesser role than before – she may even have been separated from her husband, judging from the fact that one of her daughters, Meritaten, appears to have taken her place alongside the king in ceremonies. The reason for this separation has been the source of much debate, since the motives may have been political. Nefertiti did not leave the city, where a place had already been set aside for her in the necropolis. She simply seems to have faded into the background, and she definitely died in the fourteenth year of Akhenaten's reign. The three final years of his reign

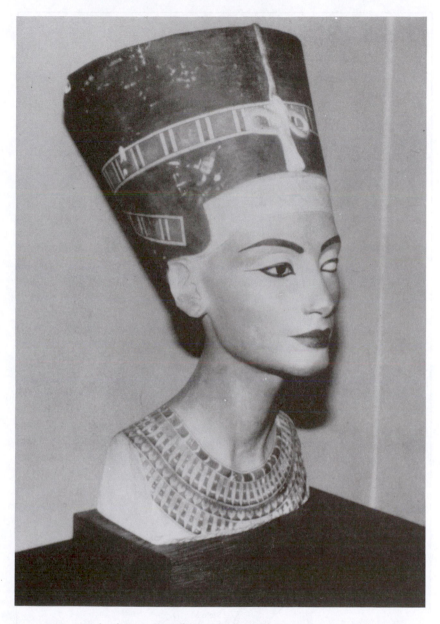

PLATE 16 *Head of Queen Nefertiti. Eighteenth Dynasty, painted limestone, h. 0.50 m. Ägyptisches Museum, Berlin. (Photograph: © John P. Stevens/ Ancient Art & Architecture Collection.)*

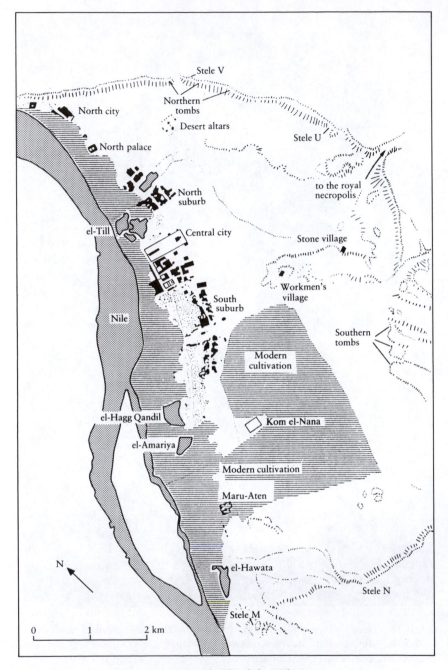

FIGURE 13 *Site of el-Amarna, east bank of the Nile.*

were troubled: the land became prey to anti-Amun persecutions that involved hammering out the names of the god on monuments – the very same fate that awaited Akhenaten and the Aten some years later.

It is apparent from a scene in the el-Amarna tomb of Merire, dated to Akhenaten's twelfth year and showing the king face to face with Smenkhkare and Meritaten, that there was a co-regency between Akhenaten and Smenkhkare. Although unproven, this association between the two kings is considered likely: Neferneferuaten Smenkhkare is indeed eventually attested as king and his reign – possibly lasting only two years – must have intervened between those of Akhenaten and Tutankhaten. It is not clear whether this was a simple co-regency or whether Smenkhkare in fact became sole ruler of the country for a few months. The problem is at present insoluble, since Smenkhkare himself is a poorly-known figure and a great deal of the data concerning him are contradictory. The abandonment of the site of el-Amarna in the first years of the reign of his successor Tutankhaten, has totally confused the evidence. Akhenaten himself was apparently buried, in theory at least, at el-Amarna. The body of Smenkhkare, who died at the age of twenty, was found in a tomb assigned to him in the Valley of the Kings (KV 55). But everything in the tomb – from his funerary equipment to the bandages wrapped around his body – suggests that this was a hasty reburial, probably following upon his transfer from el-Amarna to Thebes. Moreover, Smenkhkare was not the only occupant of the tomb: other remains have been found there which may belong to Queen Tiy. It is therefore generally assumed that the bodies of the whole royal family were transferred there during the reign of Tutankhamun, and only the stone sarcophagi were left in the necropolis of Akhetaten (until they were destroyed by the quarrymen of the Ramessid period).

There are no certainties concerning the succession at the end of the Amarna period – especially regarding the relationship between Akhenaten and his immediate successors. It is likely that the only male heirs were Smenkhkare and Tutankhaten, who may have been cousins or nephews of Akhenaten. Each seems to have legitimized his claim to the throne by marrying one of the king's daughters.

When Tutankhaten inherited the throne from Smenkhkare, at the age of about nine, he married the princess Ankhesenpaaten and lived at first in the 'north city' at Akhetaten. Very soon afterwards, however, Tutankhaten left el-Amarna, although the precise date of his departure is not known; he moved the royal residence back to Memphis, using the palace of Malkata as his temporary residence in Thebes. The city of Akhetaten continued in existence only for those members of the court who remained there – otherwise it was almost entirely abandoned, having only been occupied for about thirty years in all. The only things left at el-Amarna were objects considered valueless or not worth the cost of transporting, such as the remains of craftsmen's activities (as in the studio of the sculptor Thutmose) and copies of diplomatic correspondence (the Amarna tablets). The complete abandonment of the site by the beginning of the Ramessid period, worked to the ultimate advantage of Hermopolis Magna, a city on the opposite bank of the river where the *talatat* blocks from the dismantled temples and palaces of Akhetaten were reused to build new temples. The site of Akhetaten returned to the desert, condemned to oblivion until the middle of the nineteenth century AD. Sir John Gardner Wilkinson and Karl Richard Lepsius explored some of the rock-tombs at el-Amarna in the early nineteenth century, but it was the discovery of the Amarna Letters in 1887 that eventually focused attention on the city once more.

THE HORIZON OF THE ATEN

Flinders Petrie embarked on the first scientific excavations at el-Amarna in 1891, uncovering the royal palace and making a survey of the site with the assistance of the young Howard Carter. The finds from this season were packed into 132 boxes which were eventually taken to the Ashmolean Museum, Oxford. In 1902 the Egypt Exploration Fund began an epigraphic study of the rock-tombs which Petrie had cleared in 1893. From 1904 to 1914 the German Oriental Society gained the concession, under the direction of Ludwig von Borchardt; they began the clearance of the eastern residential part of the city, uncovering the studio of Thutmose and the numerous royal busts, models and masks that it contained – including the head of Nefertiti, which was quickly spirited away to Berlin.

After the First World War the Egypt Exploration Society regained the concession between 1921 and 1937. They set out to complete the clearance of the main city; their discovery of the Workmen's Village and their studies of the surviving paintings and tombs became a race against the plunderers. The whole 'north suburb' was excavated. Since 1977 the Egypt Exploration Society has resumed systematic investigation of the site, undertaking a new survey, new excavation and interpretation of the Workmen's Village, and further study of various other remains.

The city centre, focusing on the Great Temple and the adjacent King's House, was in the northern part of the site. The north suburb separated the central city from the North Palace, while the south suburb separated it from the Maru-Aten, a set of gardens devoted to pleasure and prayer. The Workmen's Village was an outlying part of the site, hidden in the cliffs midway between the city and the necropolis.

The monuments of Akhetaten extended for a length of about 9 kilometres and a width of up to a kilometre. The most important influence on the city plan was the desire for proximity to the royal palace. There was no social distinction between the rich and poor quarters of the town: the population was simply distributed according to their particular needs. The city was intersected by three great arteries running north-south, joined together by streets crossing from east to west. The heart of the city was split by a great avenue that divided the Great Palace from the two temples of the Aten, which lay on either side of the King's House. It was possible to cross over the avenue by a bridge leading from the Palace to the King's House.

The Palace was stretched out along the side of the avenue, comprising, from north to south, outbuildings, the harem opposite the bridge across the avenue, the Palace proper, then storerooms and the Coronation Hall. The outbuildings consisted of servants' dwellings, entrance courtyards and stores linked by a corridor that led to two harems. The harems were set on either side (i.e. to north and south) of a courtyard that could be entered both from the street and from a great inner courtyard, lined with colossal statues of the king and queen, that gave access to the interior of the palace itself.

The North Harem was laid out in similar fashion to a traditional private house, centring on a garden furnished with a pool and bordered by two rows of fifteen rooms; these were decorated with painted river scenes depicting the flora and fauna of the Delta marshes. A courtyard separated the harem from the servants' housing to the north. To the south, small apartments surrounded a central hall which was reached from the garden via a hypostyle hall. On the other side of the passageway the South Harem was set out similarly but orientated at right angles to the other harem. Each of these two harem arrangements was typical of the private house, inward-looking and set apart from the passageways in order to preserve the privacy of their occupants. The southernmost section of the Palace was made up of several hypostyle halls, the largest of which led into the throne room.

The core of the Palace was set at right angles to this series of buildings and on the same axis as the bridge that spanned the avenue. The bridge was effectively part of the processional way from the Great Court to the throne room and from the river to the King's House on the other side of the street.

A court in the centre of the Palace also assisted the flow of people through the complex by means of an entrance pavilion to the north and three ramps on the other sides of the court. These ramps led from the central court to two symmetrical courts at the riverbank and, on the residential (southern) side of the palace, to a central hall. This hall provided access to two rooms with parallel colonnades in the courts, in the centre of which must have been statues of the king or altars. The hall also provides access to the throne room at the south. When the king crossed the bridge he would have been able to enter the King's House by passing in front of the caretaker's living quarters.

The layout of the King's House was similar to that of the harems. In the centre a garden provided access to storerooms (to the east) and the main body of the house (to the south). The servants' quarters were separated from their masters' and the only communication between the two was via a service door. The royal apartments did not communicate with the reception rooms, which consisted of a vestibule and a large columned room leading to the family shrine and the private apartments. The princesses' rooms were separate.

There were numerous royal residences at el-Amarna. The residence in the North Palace was organized around a pool and furnished with aviaries and animal pens in an arrangement which has been described as an 'architectonic transposition of the Hymn to the Aten' (Michalowski 1968: 521). They all offered the same comfortable luxury, in contrast to the severe organization of the Workmen's Village.

The houses of the Workmen's Village were arranged in strict rows and served by five streets orientated north-south. The village was completely walled, so that it could only be entered by a single guarded gate. Immediately to the right of the entrance was a larger house which probably belonged to the head of the community. The typical Village house consisted of four rooms: an antechamber, followed by a reception room, a kitchen and a bedroom, as well as a set of stairs leading up to the roof.

The Great Temple to the Aten was more closely related to the solar temples of the Fifty Dynasty than the classic Egyptian temple. Its entrance – a pylon made up of two piers of masonry representing the horizon from which the sun rises – was ostensibly traditional in form, except that the lintel, which would usually have united these two piers into a gateway, was broken in the middle. Similarly, the temple itself, far from being the traditional steady progression from daylight to the mystery of the sanctuary, was simply a succession of open courtyards.

The Great Temple was razed to the ground after the desertion of the site but it is possible to reconstruct the original plan thanks to the foundation trenches which still bear the remains of the original black architects' lines drawn on the plaster. The 'broken' pylon served as the entrance to a pavilion called the Per-hai, which led on to the first of a series of six courts. The two final courts were effectively the sanctuary of the temple, known as the Gem-Aten, while the first four were each occupied by two sets of altars lined up along either side of an axial ramp rising from west to east. The fifth court, surrounded by small chapels, probably contained the main altar.

THE VENGEANCE OF AMUN

The return to the orthodox state worship of Amun probably took place under the influence of the Divine Father Ay who guided the steps of the young Tutankhaten. He issued an edict restoring the traditional cults and describing at great length the wretched state to which the nation had been reduced by the mistakes of Amenophis IV. This edict was set up at the foot of the Third Pylon of the temple of Amon-Re at Karnak (*Urk*. IV, 2025–32). The measures that Tutankhaten announced amounted to a return to the situation before Amenophis IV's rise to the throne. He himself began the process by changing his name from Tutankhaten ('Living image of the Aten') to Tutankhamun ('Living image of Amun'). He had a tomb built for himself near that of Amenophis III and he began the construction of his mortuary temple at Medinet Habu, from which only one colossal statue (later usurped by Horemheb) now survives. Tutankhamun also continued the construction of the Karnak temple and finished the second of a pair of granite lions of Amenophis III at Soleb (both now in the British Museum). He evidently had no time to set the lion up at Soleb, for it was around then that he died, aged nineteen, after a reign of only nine years. The examination of his mummy has revealed a wound in the region of his left ear suggesting that he may have died from a cerebral haemorrhage. Whatever the cause of his death, it was certainly premature and his wife, Ankhesenamun (formerly Ankhesenpaaten), had not yet produced any heirs. It is possible that the two foetuses found in his tomb were stillborn babies accompanying their father into the beyond.

The wildest theories have been proposed concerning this young king, and the unusual condition of his tomb (KV 62) provides some confirmation of the tragic circumstances surrounding his reign. The sensational discovery of his tomb by Howard Carter fired the popular imagination, especially when Egyptologists realized that this magnificent funerary treasure was only a collection of comparative bric-à-brac hastily thrown together (and consisting partly of the funerary equipment of his two predecessors) for the burial of a powerless kinglet who was characteristically depicted promenading in fantastic gardens with his young wife.

Tutankhamun was the last of Ahmose's line. His wife begged the Hittite king Suppiluliumas to send her one of his sons to marry her and become pharaoh of Egypt. Suppiluliumas agreed, but the son he sent, Prince Zennanza, failed to survive the journey. The unification of the Egyptian and Hittite empires was never to happen. Perhaps Ankhesenamun then married Ay, the vizier of her dead husband; he can be seen on the wall of Tutankhamun's tomb administering the rite of the Opening of the Mouth to the king's mummy – a rite traditionally performed by a son and heir. This marriage between Ay and Ankhesenamun remains only hypothetical, since there is no further evidence of Ankhesenamun after the death of Tutankhamun and Ay has himself depicted in his tomb in the company of his wife Tiy II. Ay's reign lasted for only four years, giving him time enough only to contribute to the temples at Karnak and Luxor and dedicate a rock-temple to Min at Akhmim. He also constructed a mortuary temple for himself at Medinet Habu, including a palace which was to be taken over and expanded by Horemheb. Ay was buried near Amenophis III in the Valley of the Kings, in a tomb (KV 23) that had originally been intended for someone else.

The vilification of the memory of the heretic pharaoh perhaps began as soon as the worship of Amun had been restored, but the Amarna period does not seem to have finally ended with the beginning of the reign of Ay. Certainly the old Master of the Stud Farms was not one of the direct descendants of Ahmose, but his family was too closely linked with the Tuthmosids for his reign to be seen as a true break with the past. A new man was needed if a new start was to be made. As is often the case in such circumstances, it was a military man – the commander-in-chief of the army – who took charge. The general Horemheb – who was apparently not the same person as Paatenemheb, the commander-in-chief of Amenophis IV's army – began his political career under Tutankhamun and is depicted at this king's side in his own tomb chapel at Memphis. At that stage he was the royal spokesman for foreign affairs and it was he who led the diplomatic mission to the Nubian governors that was to result in the visit of the Prince of Miam (Aniba) to the court of Tutankhamun, an event depicted in the tomb of the viceroy Huy.

It was also Horemheb who undertook a 'flag-flying' campaign in Palestine at Tutankhamun's side. It is known from cuneiform sources that the Hittites had made a raid on the cities of Amki, in the Beqaʻa Valley area of the Lebanon; this was interpreted as an invasion of Egyptian territory. In reprisal the Egyptians seized Qadesh and attacked Nuges, thus regaining control of the region for several years. This Egyptian dominance was eventually curtailed when the Hittites recaptured Qadesh and Amki after the assassination of Zennanza (the prince sent in answer to Ankhesenamun's request for a Hittite husband). At the time of this attack Suppiluliumas imprisoned the Egyptians who were in Amki. Unfortunately for him these prisoners were carrying a plague which some years later was to become endemic in the Hittite kingdom, an occurrence that was probably interpreted as a sign of the gods' wrath against those who had dared to break the peace. When Mursilis II came to power after the events described above, he handed Amki back to the Egyptians in atonement for the sacrilege. Throughout the reign of Horemheb the frontier remained fixed in the approximate region of the Lebanon.

Horemheb was above all the restorer of established order, as his royal titulature indicates. His Horus name is 'Powerful bull with wise decisions'. The verb employed here is *seped*, a technical term describing the process of putting things in order that recurred in the inscriptions of other legislators such as the Twenty-sixth Dynasty ruler Amasis. Horemheb's Golden Horus name was along the same lines: 'He who is satisfied with Truth and who causes the Two Lands to increase'. Here again the verb *herw*, translated here as 'satisfy', has a precise judicial sense linked to the enforcement of law. The restoration of order was closely connected with the process of physical reconstruction, which was evoked in his Two Ladies name: 'With countless miracles in Karnak'.

Horemheb was certainly a prolific builder: at Medinet Habu he enlarged the mortuary temple of Ay for his own use and at Gebel el-Silsila he dedicated a rock temple to Amun and Thoth. He also confirmed the importance of Memphis by setting up buildings in the precint of the temple of Ptah and the sun temple at Heliopolis. But it was to Karnak that he devoted most of his energies, as his choice of Two Ladies name suggests. He began work on the Great Hypostyle Hall at Karnak and set up three pylons, the Second (which closed off the hypostyle hall on the west), Ninth and Tenth (on the north-south axis of the temple), filling them with the *talatat* blocks from the destruction of the Aten temple to the east of Karnak. At the foot of the Tenth Pylon, which he linked with the temple of Mut by a processional way of criosphinxes, he erected a stele bearing the text of a decree issued specifically to restore order to the nation. He set out in this edict the measures with which he was addressing the abuses that had taken place due to over-centralization in Amenophis IV's reign. Tutankhamun's earlier edict had been unable to remedy this situation, for there had been many injustices and corrupt practices inherent in the Amarna system. To this end Horemheb appointed judges and regional tribunes and reintroduced local religious authorities. Legal power was split between Upper and Lower Egypt, shared between the viziers of Thebes and Memphis respectively. The idea of the Two Lands was also revived in the organization of the national army, which was divided into two geographical entities, the north and the south.

Horemheb was buried not in his earlier tomb at Memphis (which he had built during Tutankhamun's residence in the north) but at the Valley of the Kings in western Thebes. His tomb (KV 57) preserved the memory of the Amarna period in the depiction of clothing and in its unusual artistic style, but it was innovative on a technical level in the use of sunk relief instead of painting on plaster or a coat of gypsum. He also introduced new subject matter to the tomb, including the first example of the *Book of Gates*, which was to become one of the great royal funerary texts of the Ramessid period. The decoration, however, is unfinished, perhaps because work on the tomb only began late in his reign. Since Horemheb had no male heir, or at any rate none that survived him, he passed on the crown to another military figure, a Delta-born general who was to found a new dynasty: the Ramessids.

11

The Ramessid Period

Ramesses I was not of royal blood. He came from a long line of soldiers whose homeland was in the eastern Delta, probably in the region of Qantir. He began his career as an army officer and subsequently became vizier under the name of Pramesse or Ramessu. The fact that he already held political power in the reign of his predecessor suggests that Horemheb may even have appointed him as heir before he died. Ramesses married the daughter of another soldier, Satre, who gave him a son, the future Sethos I.

Through his Golden Horus name of 'He who confirms Maat throughout the Two Lands', Ramesses I indicated his desire to carry on the work of Horemheb. Nevertheless, he also established the new political orientation of the country, in that his coronation name, Menpehtyre ('Stable is the power of Ra'), like his prenomen, Ramessu ('Ra has brought him into the world'), stressed the privileged nature of his relationship with Ra. He went further than this by declaring the primacy of the Heliopolitan theology, through the invocation of Atum in his Two Ladies name, 'He who has been crowned king, chosen by Atum'. In fact, the most important after-effects of the Amarna revolution seem to have been the shifting of power from Thebes back to Memphis, the rediscovery of the theocracy and the prevention of the Theban priesthood from regaining a degree of influence that would only have led to further conflict. This determination, however, did not prevent Ramesses I from spending the two short years of his reign in a programme of decoration at Karnak, although he devoted most of his efforts to the construction of a chapel and a temple (which was to be finished by his son) at Abydos.

The brevity of Ramesses I's reign precludes a proper evaluation of the immediate consequences of his policies, but the contents of his tomb in the Valley of the Kings (KV 16) suggest that his inspiration came primarily from the past. The only decoration in his tomb is from the *Book of Gates*, modelled on that of Horemheb, but the funerary equipment (London, British Museum 854 and 882–3) is closer in style to the beginning of the Eighteenth Dynasty than the reign of his son Sethos.

When Sethos I succeeded to the throne he had already been closely linked with the kingship, probably from the very beginning of Ramesses I's reign; he held an office similar to that of vizier and also acted as the general in charge of foreign policy. Sethos I's early association with the throne probably resulted from Ramesses I's concern (shared by later Ramessid rulers) that there should be no repetition of the successional problems that had brought about the ruin of the Eighteenth Dynasty. Sethos I stressed this prior association with the throne by describing the rites of filial piety that he established for his father at Abydos (*KRI* I, 110–115). He also pursued a policy of restoration in home affairs and thus effectively rewrote history so as to legitimize his own dynasty. He depicted himself and his son and successor (Ramesses II) adoring the cartouches of previous pharaohs. The list of sixty-seven names begins with Menes and ends with Sethos I; it establishes the canon of official historiography for the Eighteenth and early Nineteenth Dynasties, arranging the names in the following order: Ahmose, Amenophis I, Tuthmosis I, Tuthmosis II, Tuthmosis III, Amenophis II, Tuthmosis IV, Amenophis III, Horemheb and Ramesses I. All of the Amarna kings had been removed from the record, just as their names were erased from the monuments. Also absent is Hatshepsut, who despite all her efforts was still considered a usurper. This same list of kings was to be repeated, with the gradual addition of new rulers' names, until the reign of Ramesses III.

Sethos I also laid stress on his family's links with the north: the decree for the Buhen temple, in the first year of his reign, was issued from Memphis. He also had a palace at Qantir, in the eastern Delta, but Thebes was still the capital and he took care to maintain it. This desire to uphold the power of Thebes was apparent in his titulature: his Horus name was 'Powerful bull who gives life to the Two Lands after having been crowned at Thebes'. He also attempted to reconcile the two principal religious centres by referring to them both in the epithets following his coronation name, Menmaatre: 'Sovereign of Thebes' and 'Sovereign of Heliopolis'; in the same way, his prenomen, Sethos, was followed either by 'Beloved of Amun' or 'Beloved of Ptah'.

This balanced policy was completely transformed by the encouragement given to the god Seth of Avaris and the reconstruction of the sanctuary of Ra at Heliopolis. The reconstruction is probably indicated by a votive model discovered at Tell el-Yahudiya, dedicated by Sethos I and probably representing the temple. Sethos also undertook the construction of part of the great hypostyle hall at Karnak temple (completed by Ramesses II) as well as another hypostyle hall in the temple at the Nubian site of Gebel Barkal, which was dedicated in the eleventh year of his reign.

The greatest achievement of his fourteen-year reign was his foreign policy. He chose as his Two Ladies name, 'The strong-armed one who renews births and recaptures the Nine Bows'; but the legacy of the Amarna period still represented a heavy burden. Activities in Asia had been resumed under Horemheb and Ramesses I, judging from a foundation deposit placed under a temple constructed near Beth Shan, in Jordan, after Sethos' first military campaign. But the whole of Palestine was still hostile to Egypt and only the fortresses of Beth Shan, Reheb and Megiddo were in Egyptian hands.

Sethos I embarked on the trail to Asia within the first year of his reign, departing from the border fortress of Tjel (el-Qantara) and heading initially for Raphia. En route to Raphia he had to do battle with the Shasu bedouin (who were probably based at Raphia) in order to gain possession of the nine wells that lined the route through the Sinai. He captured Raphia and Gaza in Canaan and from there sent a column of men towards Beth Shan and Reheb, both of which were being attacked by the allied cities of Hamath and Pella, assisted by bands of Apiru in the highlands. While the army of Ra marched on Beth Shan, the armies of Amun and Seth headed for Hamath and Yenoam respectively. Marching north, they took Acre and Tyre and advanced on the Lebanon. On their return journey they also captured Pella.

Sethos I drew on the experience of this campaign to organize the second one in the following year, which took him to the city of Qadesh. The temporary pacification of the country of Amurru then enabled him to organize a third campaign, this time against the Libyans. It was only after his fourth expedition into Asia that Egypt was respected again in the Near East. There are few details known about this fourth expedition, which was waged against the Hittites. After it the Egyptians felt assured that they had full control of Syria – their influence ended just south of Qadesh, which had resumed its traditional role of frontier town. The Hittite king Muwatallis made peace with Sethos, but the treaty simply gave both sides time to regain their strength.

Nearer home, the Egyptian turquoise mines in the Sinai had already been reopened under Ramesses I, and their exploitation continued under Sethos I. He also facilitated access to the gold mines in the desert to the east of Edfu, constructing the wells of Wadi Mia and Wadi

Abbad in the ninth year of his reign. In Nubia he exploited the gold mines of Wadi Allaqi without encountering any problems, only launching a campaign to pacify Irem (attested by an inscription at Qasr Ibrim).

Sethos' tomb (KV 17) has some of the most complete funerary texts and decoration in the Valley of the Kings, and its astronomical ceiling is particularly splendid. Its very characteristic style was still close – in its finesse and aesthetic sensibility – to the art of the Amarna period. These two qualities are also to be found in his royal mortuary temple at Qurna in western Thebes, but the subtlety and elegance of the art of Sethos' reign are best appreciated in his other mortuary temple at Abydos and in the 'Osireion', a temple to Osiris that he built nearby.

The history of the site of Abydos goes back at least to the Naqada period (*c.*4500–3300 BC), for it was always one of the great holy cities of Egypt. Sethos I placed his mortuary temple in the same enclosure as the so-called 'Osireion', which he had rebuilt at the edge of the cultivated land and to the south-east of the town.

Sethos' mortuary temple is L-shaped, the actual sanctuary being at right angles to the preceding succession of courts and hypostyle halls. It is built of fine limestone on sandstone foundations. A sandstone pylon built by Ramesses II provided access to the first court. Both pylon and first court are now destroyed. A ramp runs along the axis of the temple, through a portico to the second court, which constitutes the present entrance to the temple. The decoration of the portico at the back of the second court dates to the time of Ramesses II, who is shown offering an image of Maat (the goddess of Truth) to Osiris and Isis, the local gods with whom Sethos I was associated. A long dedicatory inscription (*KRI*, II, 323–36) tells how Ramesses II finished the construction of his father's temple and describes the occasion when he was appointed co-regent.

Beyond the portico there are two successive hypostyle halls, and then seven parallel corridors leading to seven sanctuaries, each in the form of a cavern with false barrel vaulting on the ceiling, similar to that in the 'grand gallery' of the Great Pyramid at Giza. Except for the one in the centre, each of these sanctuaries ends in a false door combined with a stele. Each is divided into two equal parts by pilasters, and their walls are decorated with thirty-six scenes apparently showing the enactment of the daily religious ritual in the temple (David 1981) and the use of cultic equipment, including the barques of each of the gods. The names of the deities are written over the entrance of each sanctuary. The first sanctuary from the left is dedicated to the cult of Sethos I himself, with depictions of a *sem* priest bringing offerings; the second is dedicated to Ptah, the third to Ra-Horakhty, the fourth to Amun, the fifth to Osiris,

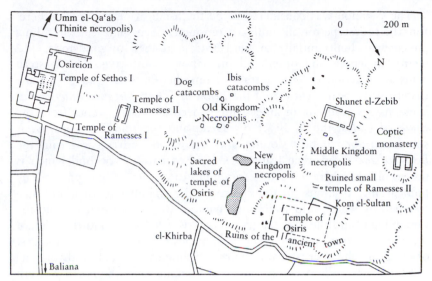

FIGURE 14   *General plan of Abydos.*

the sixth to Isis and the seventh to Horus. The fifth sanctuary leads to a
set of three chapels dedicated to Isis, the king (in the form of Osiris) and
Horus.

To the south of the second hypostyle hall are two rooms dedicated to
Ptah-Sokar and Nefertum as well as the corridor of the King List. The
walls of the corridor are decorated with the reliefs described above
showing Sethos I and his son adoring the cartouches of the kings of
Egypt. At right angles to this another corridor provides access to a set
of steps leading up to the temple roof. The southern end of the temple
also includes a room dedicated to the solar barques, and a sacrificial
chamber.

Apart from the unusually high aesthetic standards of its reliefs, the
temple of Sethos I at Abydos provides evidence for the basic nature of
the royal mortuary temple, which was designed to associate the cult of
the dead king with that of the family of local deities. This was intended
to have the effect of sharing offerings between the king and the gods
and assimilating the ruler with the god of the city. The choice of
Abydos was particularly significant in that the local god was Osiris: by
associating himself with Osiris' cult, Sethos I was assuring the continuation of the dynasty that he himself had founded, just as Osiris had
been the original progenitor of the descendants of Horus. For this
reason Sethos ordered the rebuilding of the Osireion, which lay to the
west of his temple.

The Osireion was considered to be the tomb of Osiris: it was there-fore the prototype for all tombs. A ten-metre-deep shaft leads to a long passageway built initially of mud-brick and then of sandstone, 112 metres in length and orientated on a north-south axis. The western walls are decorated with extracts from the *Book of Gates* and the eastern walls bear scenes from the *Book of What is in the Underworld*. This passage leads to an antechamber decorated with scenes from the *Book of Gates*, the *Book of the Dead* and the *Book of Caverns*. A short corridor, slightly sloping and decorated with scenes from the *Book of the Dead*, then leads to a kind of narthex, beyond which is the tomb chamber itself: a rectangular room, its roof supported by pink granite columns. In the centre of the chamber is an island sur-rounded by water, into which two cavities were excavated to hold the sarcophagus and the canopic jars. There is a ledge around the edge of the chamber, from which seventeenth niches radiate. Finally, to the east of the tomb chamber is a room with a ceiling of sculpted sandstone, its south-eastern walls decorated with a dramatic text; the north-western walls bear representations of the goddess Nut held up by the god Shu, the decans, the nocturnal journey of the sun, the construction of a sundial and a scene depicting the resurrection of Sethos I.

The tomb was clearly intended to commemorate the funerary rites of Osiris, in which his body – swollen with fluids – was restored to life in the water by Isis. This rebirth through fermentation was still remembered in the form of the 'Osiris bed': a receptacle in the shape of the body of Osiris, in which cereal grains were sown. But the tomb chamber of the Osireion, like Sethos' temple, was also a model of the universe; it represented the primeval mound emerging from chaos, on which the first creator breathed life into the universe.

RAMESSES II AND THE CONFRONTATION WITH THE HITTITES

Ramesses II succeeded his father on the throne in 1304 or 1279–8, depending on how the Sothic date in Papyrus Ebers is interpreted. Ramesses (Plate 17) is undoubtedly the best-known pharaoh in Egyptian history and, like the pyramids, has become a symbol of Egyptian civil-ization. His reign was by far the most glorious and also the best known: over the course of sixty-seven years he covered the Nile Valley with monuments and left an ineradicable mark on ancient Near Eastern history. His extraordinary personality was the primary influence on a period of memorable confrontations between the great Near Eastern empires.

In the second year of his reign, Ramesses II – who had not yet come into direct conflict with the Hittites – had to deal with a raid by the

PLATE 17 *Ramesses II holding the ḥeḳa sceptre, with his wife (not visible here)*
and Prince Amonhirkhepeshef at his feet. Granite statue from Karnak, h. 1.90 m.
(Turin, Museo delle Antichità Egizie. Photograph: Chomon s.n.c.)

PLATE 18 *Scenes from the battle of Qadesh, temple of Ramesses II at Abu Simbel. (Photograph: © E. Hobson/Ancient Art & Architecture Collection.)*

Sherden pirates, whom he defeated in a sea battle and subsequently incorporated into his own army. His real offensive only began in the fourth year of his reign, with the first campaign into Syria. This campaign took the Egyptian army from Tjel to the lands of Canaan, Tyre and Byblos. From there they advanced eastwards into Amurru and surprised Prince Benteshina, a Hittite ally, who surrendered to them. They then returned to Egypt via Phoenicia.

The next year the Egyptian army set out again from the city of Piramesse, the new capital in the eastern Delta. They passed through Canaan and Galilee, reaching the springs of the River Jordan beyond Lake Hulah and marching up towards Kummidi, via the Beqa'a Valley between the Lebanon and the Anti-Lebanon. Finally they reached Qadesh, which had once more become the focus of conflict between the two empires. It was there that one of the most famous battles in the history of the ancient Near East took place.

Ramesses II considered this battle the military high point of his reign, and had it documented on the walls of many of his temples: at Abydos on the external wall, in three different parts of the temple of Amon-Re at Karnak (the north-east corner of the Cachette Court, the eastern face of the west wall of the court of the Ninth Pylon, and the 'palimpsest version' on the external south wall of the Great Hypostyle Hall), twice at Luxor (on the north pier of the pylon and the walls of the first court), at the Ramesseum (on the two pylons), and finally at Abu Simbel, on the north wall of the Great Temple (Plate 18). There are also several surviving accounts of the battle written on papyrus (Raife, Sallier II, Chester Beatty III verso). Altogether there are at least thirteen versions, in three different literary styles ('poem', 'bulletin' and 'representational'), making this conflict the best documented event in Egyptian military history. This epic was to become a kind of archetype of Egyptian victory over foreign countries, repeatedly asserting the pharaoh's control of the universe. The phraseology of this collection of texts can be tempered thanks to a unique Akkadian version of the battle. The following extracts are taken from the 'poem':

> Now His Majesty had made ready his infantry and his chariotry, and the Sherden in his majesty's captivity whom he had brought back in the victories of his strong arm. They had been supplied with all their weapons, and battle orders had been given to them. His Majesty journeyed northward, his infantry and his chariotry with him, having made a good start with the march in year five, second month of summer, day nine. His Majesty passed the fortress of Sile, being mighty like Monthu in his going forth, all foreign lands trembling before him, their chiefs bringing their gifts, and all rebels coming bowed down through fear of his majesty's might. His Majesty's army travelled on the narrow paths as if on the roads of Egypt ... (Lichtheim, 1976: 63)

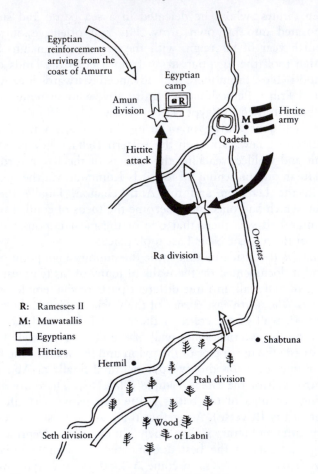

FIGURE 15   *Troop movements in the battle of Qadesh.*

The Egyptians arrived in the vicinity of Qadesh:

> Now the vile foe from Hatti had come and brought together all the
> foreign lands as far as the end of the sea. The entire land of Hatti
> had come, that of Naharin also, that of Arzawa and Dardany, that of
> Keshkesh, those of Masa, those of Pidasa, that of Irun, that of Karkisha,
> that of Luka, Kizzuwadna, Carchemish, Ugarit, Kedy, the entire land of
> Nuges, Mushanet and Qadesh... They covered the mountains and the
> valleys and were like locusts in their multitude. He had left no silver in his
> land. He had stripped it of all its possessions and had given them to all
> the foreign countries in order to bring them with him to fight. (Lichtheim
> 1976: 64)

The Hittite army, lying in ambush behind Qadesh, allowed the first Egyptian division to pass by, then swooped down on the second division while the third was still crossing the ford of Shabtuna:

> Then they came forth from the south side of Qadesh and attacked the army of Pre in its middle, as they were marching unaware and not prepared to fight. Then the infantry and chariotry of his majesty weakened before them, while His Majesty was stationed to the north of the town of Qadesh, on the west bank of the Orontes. They came to tell it to His Majesty, and His Majesty rose like his father Monthu. He seized his weapons of war; he girded his coat of mail; he was like Baal in his hour. The great horse that bore His Majesty was 'Victory-in-Thebes' of the great stable of Usermaatra-setepenra, beloved of Amun. Then His Majesty drove at a gallop and charged the forces of the Foe from Hatti, being alone by himself, none other with him. His Majesty proceeded to look about him and found 2500 chariots ringing him on his way out, of all the fast troops of the Foe from Hatti and the many countries with him...
> (Lichtheim 1976: 64)

Deserted by his men, the king turned to Amun for help:

> I call to you my father Amun,
> I am among a host of strangers;
> All countries are arrayed against me,
> I am alone, there's none with me.
> My numerous troops have deserted me,
> Not one of my chariotry looks for me;
> I keep on shouting for them,
> But none of them heeds my call.
> I know Amun helps me more than a million troops,
> More than a hundred thousand charioteers,
> More than ten thousand brothers and sons
> Who are united as one heart (...)
> Now though I prayed in the distant land,
> My voice resounded in Southern On.
> I found Amun came when I called to him,
> He gave me his hand and I rejoiced.
> He called from behind as if nearby:
> 'Forward, I am with you,
> I, your father, my hand is with you,
> I prevail over a hundred thousand men,
> I am lord of victory, lover of valour!'
> (Lichtheim 1976: 65–6)

Galvanized by the presence of the god, the king hacked the enemy to pieces and castigated the cowardice of his troops. The following day Muwatallis sent his envoy to Ramesses, asking for a truce:

Your servant speaks to let it be known that you are the Son of Ra that comes from his body. He has given you all the lands together. As for the land of Egypt and the land of Hatti, they are your servants, under your feet. Ra, your august father, has given them to you. Do not overwhelm us. Lo, your might is great, your strength is heavy upon the land of Hatti. Is it good that you slay your servants, your face savage toward them and without pity? Look, you spent yesterday killing a hundred thousand, and today you came back and left no heirs. Be not hard in your dealings, victorious king! Peace is better than fighting. Give us breath. (Lichtheim 1976: 71)

Ramesses II retreated after achieving what he described as a victory, which was actually nothing of the sort: he had simply managed to rescue his army. Barely was his back turned when Muwatallis deposed Benteshina, the Prince of Amurru, and replaced him with Shapilis, thus putting an end to the Egyptian province of Upi and effectively creating an anti-Egyptian buffer zone in Syria. Meanwhile the Hittites were faced by a new threat from Adad-Nirari I of Assyria, who had conquered Hanigalbat, the heartland of Mitanni between the Tigris and the Euphrates, which was allied to Muwatallis. But Egypt also had a 'second front': Ramesses II was forced to turn west to deal with the incursions of the Libyans. He therefore built a chain of fortresses from Rakotis to Mersa Matruh in order to control the movements of the nomads.

When Ramesses once more turned towards Syria, in the seventh year of his reign, he had to cope with new kingdoms that had been allowed to develop under the protection of the Hittites, such as Moab and Edom-Seir, as well as groups of Shosu bedouin who made frequent raids into Canaan. In order to resolve this situation he adopted a pincer movement, splitting his army into two sections. One section, led by his son Amonhirkhepeshef, pursued the Shosu across the Negev to the Dead Sea, captured Edom-Seir and marched on Moab as far as Raba Batora. Meanwhile, Ramesses II advanced with the rest of the army on Jerusalem and Jericho. He entered the territory of Moab from the north, took Dibon and joined up with Amonhirkhepeshef. The two armies then marched together on Hesbon and Damascus via Ammon, capturing Kumidi and completely regaining the province of Upi.

In the eighth and ninth years of Ramesses II's reign, the Egyptians bolstered their position with a fresh campaign into Syria. They crossed the Galilean hills and occupied Acre. From this position they headed north along the coastal strip, securing the passage from Tyre, Sidon, Byblos, Irqata and Simyra, to the north of Nahr el-Kelb (Dog River). They pushed on as far as Dapur, where a statue of Ramesses II was erected, and reached the city of Tunip, where no Egyptian had been seen for 120 years.

Thus Ramesses II recaptured Qadesh and northern Amurru, profiting from increasing difficulties which were causing the Hittites to lose territory both in Syria – where Benteshina seized power again thanks to the Egyptian advance – and in Nahrin. Shalmaneser I rose to the throne of Assyria and once and for all curtailed the power of the Mitannian heartland, Hanigalbat. The Hittite empire, menaced from the outside, was no less troubled on the home front. A dynastic crisis had just begun, a result of the death of Muwatallis: his illegitimate son, Urhi-Teshub, had succeeded him under the name of Mursilis III, usurping his uncle Hattusilis who was exiled to Hakpis, leaving the king of Carchemish with the task of confronting the Egyptians. Mursilis III attempted to recapture Hakpis from his uncle, but was defeated. Hattusilis III then regained his throne and exiled his nephew to northern Syria; here Mursilis tried to initiate contacts with Babylonia, which was then in open conflict with Assyria and Elam. Hattusilis III once more fended off his troublesome nephew, perhaps exiling him to Cyprus, and in his turn attempted to make terms with Babylonia by seeking peace with Shalmaneser.

This was a turning point in Egypto-Hittite relations. In the eighteenth year of the reign of Ramesses II, Urhi-Teshub took refuge in Egypt and Hattusilis demanded his extradition. Ramesses II placed his army on alert and launched a campaign to Edom and Moab to suppress the rebellion of the local princes, returning to Egypt via Canaan. Three years later he signed with Hattusilis the first state-to-state treaty in history, a copy of which was kept in both capitals, transcribed into the language of each of the empires. By chance, different parts of these parallel versions have been preserved. The Egyptian version was a copy of the original text engraved on a silver tablet. This version is reported on two stelae, one at the Karnak temple of Amun and the other at the Ramesseum (*KRI* II, 225–32). This treaty, which included extradition clauses for political opponents, provided the basis for a lasting peace, since throughout the rest of Ramesses' reign the two countries had no further conflict with one another. Personal links were forged between the two royal families, which can be traced through twenty-six letters addressed to Hattusilis III and thirteen sent to his wife, Pudukhepa. The members of each family exchanged letters and presents, and Ramesses II even married two Hittite princesses: the first after his second *sed* festival (royal jubilee), in the thirty-third year of his reign. He set off for the marriage with a large and peaceful retinue and met his Hittite bride at Damascus, where the two armies fraternized. The occasion was commemorated by the carving of a stele, copies of which were placed at Abu Simbel, Elephantine, Karnak, Amara-West and Aksha. The Hittite crown prince – the future Tudhaliyas IV – visited Egypt in the thirty-sixth year of Ramesses' reign, followed perhaps by his father in the

fortieth year. Four years later, Ramesses II married his second Hittite
princess and the peaceful relations continued throughout the reigns of
Tudhaliyas IV and Arnuwandas III. Moreover, tradition preserved the
memory of these friendly exchanges between the two countries in the
form of an apocryphal text of the Ptolemaic period, describing the
sending of a 'healing statue' of the god Khonsu from the Egyptian king
to the princess of Bakhtan (Paris, Louvre C 284).

THE EXODUS

It is considered possible that the Jewish Exodus may have taken place
during the reign of Ramesses II. Mention has already been made of the
appearance of the people known as 'Apiru' in the Egyptian records at
the time of Tuthmosis III. Their presence in Egypt is well-attested under
Ramesses II: they were employed in the transport of stone for a temple
listed in Leiden Papyrus 348; they are also mentioned in Papyrus Harris
I and it is known that some of them (800 according to one inscription)
worked in the quarries of Wadi Hammamat in the time of Ramesses IV.
In the reign of Ramesses II the Apiru were also brick-makers, and some
are mentioned in the neighbourhood of the royal harem at Mi-wer
(Medinet el-Ghurob) in the Faiyum. Nowhere is any revolt mentioned;
on the contrary, the principal known foreign community of the time –
the workmen of the land of Midian (modern Eilath) – were clearly a
free group trading with Egypt. Excavations at Eilath have revealed a
local temple dedicated to Hathor alongside indigenous cults.

There is no surviving Egyptian source describing the Exodus. This is
not in itself surprising, given that the Egyptians had no reason to attach
any importance to the Hebrews. The only document providing evidence
of a newly formed kingdom of Israel is a stele, dated to the fifth year of
the reign of Merneptah, on which the name of Israel appears (*KRI* IV,
12–19). There are two further historical landmarks: the sojourn of the
Chosen People in the desert, which lasted for forty years – at least a
generation – and the capture of Jericho, which took place after the
death of Moses. The fall of Jericho supplies a date of 1250 BC as the
terminus ante quem, so that the Exodus must have taken place at
around the beginning of the thirteenth century BC.

Theoretically, it should be possible to reconstruct the course of
events leading up to the Exodus, as in the exhibition catalogue of the
Ramesses the Great exhibition (Desroches-Noblecourt 1985). Moses
would have received the Egyptian education described in the Bible
(*Acts* 7: 22) in order to represent his community to the administration.
The description of his education 'at the court' (*Exodus* 2: 10–11) may
be interpreted not so much as a familiarity with the entourage of the

pharaoh of the time (Horemheb) but a simple reference to the fact that he benefited from the official education provided for future state employees. He would have been back among his own people by the reign of Sethos I, when a set of fortifications was established in the eastern Delta and the foundations of the future city of Piramesse were laid. Moses' murder of the guard, his flight to the land of Midian, his marriage, his acceptance of God's revelation and the encounter with the Burning Bush, and finally his return to Egypt take the date to the first years of Ramesses II's reign. The king's refusal to allow the Hebrews to depart into the desert is understandable, since this territory, particularly between years two and eight of his reign, was a constant threat. Other factors also suggest that the Exodus took place in the reign of Ramesses II, such as the location of the capital and the death of the heirs to the throne. Nevertheless, many modern scholars would place the Exodus somewhat later, in the reign of Merneptah, who according to some, actually died in pursuit of the Hebrews (Bucaille 1987: 147–51).

THE EMPIRE

In the south of Egypt, nothing had happened to interrupt the peace except a revolt of the Irem in the twentieth year of Ramesses II's reign (which was evidently fiercely crushed, since the king is said to have brought back 7000 prisoners) and a raid that the viceroy Setau must have led against the southern Libyans in the forty-fourth year. The Egyptian empire encompassed the whole of Nubia, and Nubian gold mines supplied the Egyptian Treasury. Ramesses II reinforced his power in Nubia by extending the existing religious installations and having more than seven new temples built between the First and Second Cataracts. These temples have been rescued from the waters of Lake Nasser through the efforts of the international community.

At Beit el-Wali, 50 kilometres south of Aswan, Ramesses II set up a speos at the beginning of his reign. This consisted of a vestibule, a room with two columns, and a sanctuary dedicated to Amon-Re and the local gods. The Beit el-Wali temple, now reconstructed beside Kalabsha temple, contains a large number of military scenes.

In the thirtieth year of his reign the king had another speos built at Derr, on the eastern bank of the river. This temple, 'The House of Ramesses-Meryamun in the House of Ra', was dedicated to Ra 'Lord of the Sky' and Amon-Re of Karnak. More elaborate than the speos at Beit el-Wali, it consisted of a sequence of two hypostyle halls (probably preceded by a forecourt and a pylon) leading to a triple sanctuary where a cult of the statues of Ramesses II, Amon-Re, Ra-Horakhty and Ptah was celebrated.

Fifteen years later Ramesses established another temple at Gerf Hussein, on the west bank; this 'House of Ptah' was built by the viceroy Setau. It was a 'hemi-speos', dedicated to the worship of Ptah, Ptah-Tatenen and Hathor, and associated with Ramesses, 'the Great God'. An avenue of criocephalous sphinxes led up to a pylon serving as the entrance to a peristyle court decorated with colossal Osirid statues. The eastern side of this court took the form of a second pylon carved into the mountain-face, which was the entrance to a hall with Osirid colossi, followed by the actual sanctuary. The temples at Abu Simbel, built between the twenty-fourth and thirty-first years of Ramesses' reign, had the same plan as the Gerf Hussein temple. The Great Temple at Abu Simbel was dedicated to the king (associated with Amon-Re, Ptah and Ra-Horakhty), while the Small Temple was dedicated to Nefertari (associated with Hathor).

At Wadi es-Sebua, Ramesses II restored the temple built by Amenophis III which had been damaged by Atenists during the Amarna period, and also constructed a new temple there, dedicated to Ra and his deified self. The cult of the king's 'living image in Nubia' was also celebrated at Aksha, along with the cult of Amun and Ra. This cult was paralleled in Egypt by the worship of the statues of the king placed in front of the temples, which were the object of adoration according to particular rites and religious institutions. The cult was centred not on the worship of the deified king, but on the adoration of him in his role as divine hypostasis; it was therefore not devoted to any individual king but to the manifestation of the godhead that he represented. The basic principle behind the cult was related to the concept of the royal mortuary temple (or 'House of Millions of Years'), which created strong links between the god and the king, thus re-emphasizing their interdependence.

Ramesses II also built at Amara-West, a strategically important site at the end of the route from Selima joining the Sudan with the Dunqul oasis. He completed the construction of the town founded by Sethos I, the 'House of Ramesses-Meryamun', which was later to be the Twentieth Dynasty seat of government for the province of Kush. To the north-east of the town he ordered the building of a temple with a north-south orientation, dedicated to Amon-Re and the gods of the cataract (with whom Amon-Re was regularly associated). On the walls of the hypostyle hall, among the traditional representations of countries vanquished by Egypt, was a list of conquered nations copied from that in the temple of Amenophis III at Soleb. By the time of Ramesses II a good number of the names in the list were of purely ritual significance, no longer corresponding with the situation in the real world. In this temple the king was therefore announcing in an archetypal fashion, as in the Execration

Texts on figurines in the Old and Middle Kingdom, that his power was not limited by temporal constraints. This may suggest that Amara-West was by then effectively the southern limit of the Egyptian 'empire', which might anachronistically be termed its African *limes*.

The expansion of the Egyptian empire, which now extended from the Fifth Cataract to Syria, was certainly one of the main reasons for the abandonment of Thebes as capital, since it had become too far away from the geographical centre of Egyptian territory. The new capital was a site in the eastern Delta, nearer both to the Asiatic lands and to the roots of the Ramessid royal family. The location of this capital was unknown until as late as the 1980s. Sites such as Tanis, Pelusium and Sile had been suggested until the 1930s, when Mahmud Hamza discovered a Ramessid palace at Qantir; Labib Habachi then proposed that Qantir was the site of Ramesses' capital. During the 1980s, however, new excavations in the eastern Delta, directed by Manfred Bietak, have shown that the true site of Piramesse was actually at Tell el-Dabaʿa, near Faqus – also the site of ancient Avaris. In addition, Bietak has shown that the Stele of Year 400 already mentioned (p. 185) commemorated the re-establishment of the city at Tell el-Dabaʿa, probably at the end of the reign of Horemheb, whose cartouche has been found on the remains of certain buildings at the site.

Sethos I built a palace at Avaris, of which a few fragments have survived, but it was Ramesses II who turned it into his capital and undertook the construction of the actual town of Piramesse. The international role of Piramesse was confirmed by the reception of the Hittite peace envoy there in the twentieth year of Ramesses' reign. There were more than purely diplomatic reasons for the choice of Piramesse as capital: it also allowed the king to distance himself from Thebes and to reinforce the links between the royal family and the cities of Heliopolis and Memphis. Piramesse was to remain the capital until the end of the Ramessid era, and almost all of the pharaohs during this time undertook further construction there, doubtless in imitation of Ramesses II himself. Piramesse was abandoned in the Twenty-second Dynasty, probably because of the movement of the Pelusiac branch of the Nile, and the site was subsequently used as a stone quarry for the construction of the new capital at Tanis.

THE TEMPLES IN EGYPT

Ramesses II removed the last surviving traces of the Amarna period by demolishing the temples at Akhetaten (el-Amarna) and reusing the stone blocks to enlarge the city of Hermopolis Magna on the opposite bank. He also built the Ramesseum on the west bank at Thebes. This was a

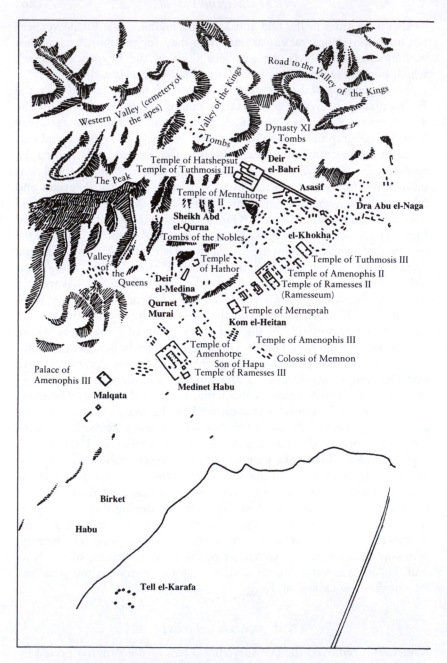

FIGURE 16 *General plan of Thebes.*

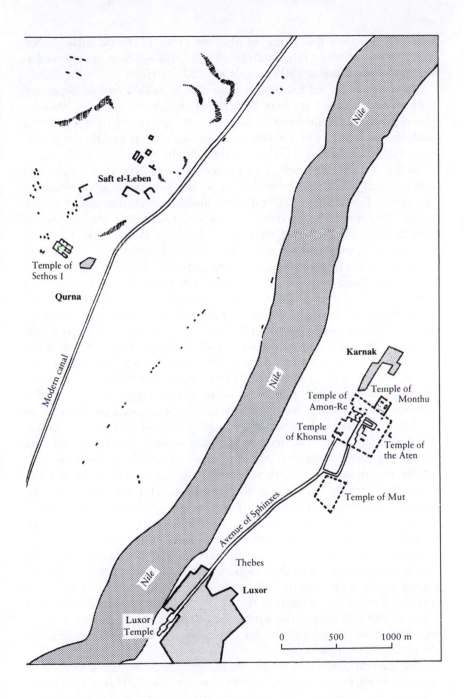

Saft el-Leben

Temple of
Sethos I

Qurna

Modern canal

Nile

Nile

Nile

Karnak

Temple of
Monthu

Temple of
Amon-Re

Temple
of Khonsu

Temple of
the Aten

Temple of Mut

Avenue of Sphinxes

Thebes

Luxor

Luxor
Temple

0   500   1000 m

mortuary temple – the 'House of Millions of Years United with Thebes' and also the 'tomb of Osymandyas' of Diodorus – which later served as the model for Ramesses III's temple at Medinet Habu.

Ramesses II placed his temple immediately beside and in alignment with an earlier sanctuary built by Sethos I, which provided the basis for the plan of the Ramesseum. The sanctuary consisted of a courtyard leading, via a ramp and a portico, to a peristyle court and then a pair of hypostyle halls, behind which were the cult chambers.

In the Ramesseum itself, a pylon served as the entrance to the first court, which could also be entered from the palace via a colonnade to the south. The palace consisted of an audience chamber and a throne room. Behind the throne room were a series of apartments where the king could stay, for short intervals at least. A ramp flanked by two royal colossi, only one of which has survived, led through a second pylon to a second (peristyle) court. The eastern and western sides of this court were lined with Osirid colossi representing the king. Following this, the central axis of the temple was supplemented by two parallel secondary axes, as in the temple of Sethos I at Abydos. All three axes led through a great hypostyle hall to the sanctuaries. The central axis continued through three successive small hypostyle halls, of which the first had an astronomical ceiling. The main sanctuary was in the centre, and the sanctuary of the barques was to the north of the small hypostyle halls; to the south was a miniature temple consisting of a vestibule, a hypostyle and a triple sanctuary dedicated to the Theban triad and Sethos I. Immediately to the south of this was a temple dedicated to Osiris. The temple was surrounded by storerooms and administrative buildings, all within a large mud-brick enclosure wall.

The principle of association between the king and the local gods, which had already occurred in the temples of Hatshepsut (at Deir el-Bahri) and Sethos I (at Abydos), is clearly apparent in the Ramesseum. The Ramesseum also gives an idea of the traditional plan of the Egyptian temple, orientated in line with the east–west course of the sun: the entrance faces the east so that the rays of Ra, passing through the double-mountain form of the pylon at sunrise, can reach the cult statue, placed at the westernmost end of the temple's axis. The temple itself was not a place of meditation for the faithful but simply the home of the god. For this reason the temple was designed to be a replica of the universe at the moment of the act of creation, which was re-enacted by the god at every new dawn.

The general pattern of temple buildings was consistent with an axis running from the main extrance to the sanctuary. This arrangement ensured that a gradual approach was made to the divine being, thus allowing time for the successive stages of purity necessary to approach the god. The approach consisted of a gradual movement from light to shadow, reaching total darkness in the holy of holies where the god dwelt. At the same time the ground slowly rose, achieving its highest point under the naos, which was thus located on the primeval mound emerging from Nun, the lake of chaos. Out of this aqueous environment rose the stems of the papyrus columns, their architraves holding up the sky which was usually represented on the ceiling. In order to achieve this effect, the temple had to consist of at least three elements: a courtyard, a colonnade and a pylon entrance. The courtyard, usually open to the sky, could be either empty or bordered by a colonnade, but had to be closed off by a pylon made up of two trapezoidal masses representing the horizon. At el-Amarna this barrier was symbolically broken by a gap in the centre of the entrance lintel, whereas in conventional Egyptian temples it was the entrance where the divinity made ritual appearances. The court usually led to a hypostyle hall in which the central row of columns were raised above the rest in such a way as to create three naves. The difference in height between the ceiling of the central nave and the two lower ceilings at the sides created clerestory windows, allowing a softened light to percolate into the hall. This section of the temple, with its atmosphere of half-light, served as the place of purification for the sole officiant admitted into the presence of the god in order to attend to his toilet and provide for his daily needs. The officiant was supposed to be the king, but in practice he was invariably represented by a chief priest. After being purified in the *per-dwat*, the officiant moved on to the naos (also known as the *adyton*, or 'inaccessible place'), which was sometimes preceded by an offering chamber. Finally, there was a quay in front of the temple, providing a reception point for the divine bark during processions.

This temple plan was the minimum scheme to which all Egyptian cultic buildings conformed. It was not prescriptive and there were as many possible additional features as the needs or wealth of the god allowed. Such additions ranged from the development of side chapels or processional ways to the various extensions of the temple axis that succeed one another throughout the ages. Luxor temple is a striking example of the use of such extensions, which could double the size of the complex, virtually transforming it into a city.

Luxor temple owes its name to the Arabic term *el-uqsur*, which refers to the military camps (*castra*) of the Roman period. The temple has survived because, like many other Egyptian sites, it was gradually covered by the expanding city, of which the mosque of Abu el-Haggag is the only remainder. The temple was discovered in the course of a general drainage of the area, and archaeological clearance began in 1883.

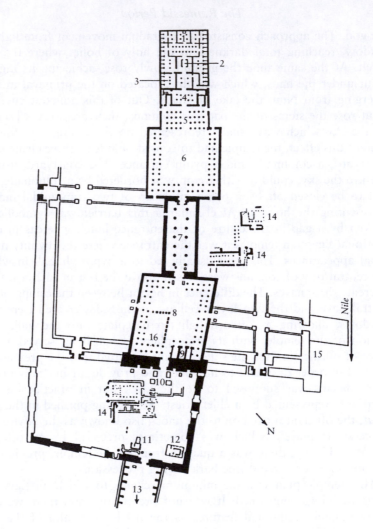

1 Temple of Amenophis III
2 Chapel of Alexander the Great
3 *Mammisi*
4 Roman Temple
5 Hypostyle hall
6 Forecourt of Amenophis III
7 Processional colonnade of Amenophis III
8 Court of Ramesses II

9 Niches for the Theban Triad
10 Obelisk *in situ*
11 Temple of Hathor
12 Roman chapel to Zeus-Helios-Serapis
13 Causeway
14 Churches
15 Quay and Nilometer
16 Mosque of Abu el-Haggag

FIGURE 17 *Plan of Luxor Temple.*

Amenophis III's temple at Luxor (Figure 17) was partly constructed from elements of earlier buildings, some dating back to the Thirteenth Dynasty. This first stage of the temple conformed closely to the classical norms, with a pylon, a peristyle court (6) and a hypostyle hall (5). The hall led to two successive columned antechambers, the second of which was adjoined by a *mammisi* to the east. Beyond the second antechamber was a resting place for the sacred barks consisting of a dais originally of wood, which was rebuilt in stone by Alexander the Great. This bark sanctuary was followed by a transverse columned offering chamber leading to the holy of holies. The whole temple acted as the 'southern harem' for the temple of Amon-Re at Karnak.

During the reign of Tutankhamun work began on the depiction of the annual Opet Festival (celebrating Amun's journey to Luxor) on the walls enclosing the colonnade (7). Ay, Horemheb and Sethos I each continued this decoration on the walls and the columns. Ramesses II enlarged the temple by developing the sections in front of the sanctuary. Amenophis III had treated the processional colonnade as the termination of an avenue of sphinxes stretching from Luxor to Karnak, but Ramesses II simply used it as a link between Amenophis III's court and a new peristyle forecourt (8). He also built a main pylon flanked by two obelisks (one of which is now in the Place de la Concorde, Paris) and six colossal statues.

The change in the temple's axis arose from a reorientation at the time of Ramesses II's enlargement of the complex. The difference between the new axis and that of Amenophis III appears to correspond to the difference in angle between the points of observation of the heliacal rising of Sirius (by which the temple was traditionally orientated to the east) in the two different reigns. The temple subsequently underwent further additions: by the reign of Diocletian the first antechamber (4) had been converted into a chapel dedicated to the cult of the Emperor.

THE DIFFICULT SUCCESSION OF RAMESSES II

Ramesses II died after one of the longest reigns ever known in Egypt. He left the country at the peak of its strength and international influence, but his own family was wracked by successional problems, despite the fact that tradition credits him with about a hundred children. By the time he had celebrated fourteen jubilee festivals, he had outlived many of his sons: Sethirkhepeshef, who became crown prince in the nineteenth year of his reign; Ramesses, who became heir in the twenty-fifth year; and Khaemwaset, the prince-archaeologist and restorer of the Memphite monuments. The cultured Khaemwaset had been linked with the worship of Ptah since the fifteenth year of his father's reign, first as a *sem* priest then as Chief Priest, and it was in this office that he celebrated the first nine jubilees of his father. Khaemwaset died in the fifty-fifth year of Ramesses' reign, leaving his brother Merneptah as the new heir. The mummy of Ramesses II was buried in the Valley of the Kings (KV7) and eventually came to light in the Deir el-Bahri cache.

The Nineteeth Dynasty survived for only a generation after Ramesses II's death. Merneptah's rise to the throne does not seem to have posed any problems, in that he had been appointed as heir during the lifetime of his father. He was the thirteenth son of Ramesses, born of Queen Isisnofret, who had already given birth to three sons. Merneptah reigned for just under a decade, bearing a son by another woman called Isisnofret. The son's name was Sethos-Merneptah: the future Sethos II.

Merneptah retained Piramesse as the capital but he increased the importance of Memphis, where he constructed a palace, worked on the Temple of Ptah and built himself a temple intended to serve his own funerary cult. There are also traces of his activity at the port of Heliopolis and at Hermopolis, where he may have completed the temple begun by Ramesses II. At el-Sirirya, to the north of el-Minya, he dedicated a speos to Hathor 'Lady of the two infernos' and built another rock-temple at Gebel el-Silsila. He may also have established a temple at Deir el-Medina. At Abydos he usurped the Osireion, and at Dendera he took over the sanctuary that Nebhepetre Mentuhotpe II had dedicated to Hathor. He built his mortuary temple on the west bank at Thebes, using stone plundered from the mortuary temple of Amenophis III. Finally he was buried in the Valley of the Kings (KV8).

The most important event of Merneptah's reign came from outside Egypt. In Western Asia, the Egyptians were still benefiting from the treaty made with the Hittites in the twenty-first year of Ramesses II's reign. Merneptah is even known to have supplied grain to the Hittites when they were stricken by a famine. The border between the two empires was still in the neighbourhood of the Damascus-Byblos line and Egypt had managed to retain its garrisons in Syria-Palestine. Merneptah was, however, obliged to mount one campaign into Syria-Palestine in order to suppress the forces of Ashkelon, Gezer and Israel. He also had to put down a rebellion in Kush, which was apparently instigated by the southern Libyans.

Libya itself was beginning to play an increasingly important role in the Mediterranean. Ramesses II had earlier been forced to defend himself against attempts by the Sherden to establish a chain of forts to the west of Egypt. These peoples had arrived in the territory of the Tjehenu from the Mediterranean almost a century earlier, pushed southwards by waves of Indo-European migrants. They included the

Libu, who eventually gave their name to the land of Libya itself, as well as the Meshwesh, reinforced by certain Indo-European peoples in search of new territories: the Ekwesh, Shekelesh and Teresh, all of whom came from the coasts of Anatolia and the Aegean isles. The Egyptians gave them the generic name of 'Sea Peoples' (Sandars 1985). A federation of these peoples attempted a raid on Egypt at the end of the fifth year of Merneptah's reign. The foreigners' attack took the Egyptians so much by surprise that they did not retaliate until a month later. They succeeded in forcing the Sea Peoples back, killing 6000 soldiers and taking 9000 prisoners. These high numbers indicate the importance of the offensive, which was only a first attempt. The second wave of Sea Peoples came twenty years later, in the reign of Ramesses III.

The remaining fifteen years of the Nineteenth Dynasty were very confused and the account which was given afterwards, in the reigns of the Twentieth Dynasty pharaohs Sethnakhte and Ramesses IV, simply evokes a gloomy scenario and hardly clarifies the situation. The death of Merneptah was followed by the onset of the succession crisis that had always been predictable after the excessively long reign of Ramesses II: the disappearance of his heirs, one after the other, and the passing of power to Merneptah, who was the thirteenth in line, led to conflicts between rivals for the throne. It was one of these who next took power, a man called Amenmesse, the son of an otherwise unknown daughter of Ramesses II called Takhat. He married Queen Tiaa, who bore him a son, the future Siptah. According to Papyrus Salt 124, Amenmesse reigned for five years, but since he was later considered a usurper it is somewhat difficult to trace his career on the surviving monuments. Although he attempted to credit himself with some of the buildings of his predecessors, his name was later removed by his own successor. His tomb in the Valley of the Kings (KV 10) was unfinished and deliberately destroyed. There is one relatively reliable source of information for this period: the archives of the workmen's community at Deir el-Medina. The supplying of government rations to the workmen was erratic at this time and there was general unrest in the Theban region.

THE USURPERS

Amenmesse was replaced after five years by Sethos II, Merneptah's rightful heir; he reigned for six years and seems to have kept the land in a state of relative peace. There is no evidence of foreign policy during this period, but it is no doubt significant that the Serabit el-Khadim mines were in use. Sethos II claims to have undertaken an extensive building programme, but there is little indication that his words were transformed into actions. There are surviving traces of his work at Hermopolis, where he finished the decoration of Ramesses II's temple, and at Karnak, where he was responsible for a new way-station of the sacred barks in the First Court of the temple of Amon-Re and various additions to the temple of Mut.

Sethos II's own succession was complicated by the fact that he married three queens. The first was Takhat II, who does not seem to have provided him with an heir. The second, Twosre, gave him a son named Sethos Merneptah (like his father), but unfortunately he died young; it was the son of his third queen, prince Ramesses Siptah, who finally ascended the throne. Because he was too young to exercise power, his stepmother, Twosre, became regent of the country. The legitimacy of the young king does not seem to have been doubted by the administration: graffiti left by Egyptian officers in Nubia are attributed to his reign. He ruled under the double supervision of his stepmother and the chancellor Bay, 'who established the king on the throne of his father'. Both Bay and Twosre had evil reputations. Bay, originally royal scribe to Sethos II, is said to have seduced the pharaoh's widow, who then – if tradition is to be believed – gave him total control of the Treasury. His position at court was high enough to enable him to own a tomb in the Valley of the Kings (KV 13). He is generally thought to have been of foreign origin and may therefore have been the person to whom Papyrus Harris I refers, in far from flattering terms, when it describes the anarchy of the period.

> The land of Egypt was overthrown from without and every man was thrown out of his right; they had no chief for many years formerly until other times. The land of Egypt was in the hands of chiefs and of rulers of towns; one slew his neighbour great and small. Other times having come after it, with empty years, Iarsu, a certain Syrian was with them as chief. He set the whole land tributary before him together; he united his companions and plundered their possessions. They made the gods like men and no offerings were presented in the temples (Papyrus Harris I, 75: 2–6; Breasted 1906: IV, 198–9).

The name of Iarsu, which can be interpreted in Egyptian as 'the one who has made himself', the 'self-made man', would have been a derogatory way of referring to Bay. The use of this name would also have had the effect of denying him the immortality that he might have gained simply through the utterance of his real name. The political texts convey a similar picture, as in the time of the conspiracy against Ramesses III. A number of 'empty' years designate a period when the throne was effectively considered to be vacant because it was occupied by a usurping line.

After three years Siptah changed his name from the one that he had held on ascending the throne, Ramesses Siptah, to Merneptah Siptah (Drenkhahn 1980: 15). He died three years later and was buried in the Valley of the Kings (KV 47), where his cartouche was first removed then replaced. His mortuary temple, probably unfinished, is now lost. After his death Twosre reigned for perhaps two years, and although her reign was probably less glorious than Théophile Gautier has suggested, she was nevertheless active in the Sinai and Palestine and there is evidence of building work at Heliopolis as well as Thebes, where she constructed a mortuary temple to the south of the Ramesseum and a tomb in the Valley of the Kings (KV 14).

Twosre's tomb was usurped and completed by her successor Sethnakhte after workers excavating his own tomb (KV 11) accidentally broke through into the adjacent tomb of Amenmesse (KV 10). Sethnakhte announced that he had 'driven out the usurper' (*KRI* V, 671–2) and Papyrus Harris I cites him as the reorganizer of the country. The change of dynasty seems to have been relatively peaceful, given that Sethnakhte kept Hori son of Kama in office as Viceroy of Kush, although it is true that he had been appointed by Merneptah Siptah rather than Twosre. His namesake, the vizier Hori, was also allowed to remain in power.

Sethnakhte reigned for only two years, and was succeeded by the last great ruler of the New Kingdom: Ramesses III, his son by Queen Tiymerenaset ('Tiy beloved of Isis').

RAMESSES III

From the very outset Ramesses III's role-model was Ramesses II. His successors also modelled themselves on the earlier Ramesses, but it was Ramesses III who went to the greatest lengths, from the choice of his titulature to the construction of a mortuary temple copying the plan of the Ramesseum. Although he failed to equal his glorious predecessor, it was under his rule that Egypt regained – for the last time – a certain influence in the Near East. Like Ramesses II, he had to deal with a very delicate state of affairs in his foreign policy. The Libyans, driven back by Merneptah, had returned to the fray in the western Delta, though Ramesses managed to defeat this new onslaught and was even able to incorporate a number of the Libyan captives into the Egyptian army. This victory was only temporary, however, and a new wave of Libyan invaders were unleashed on Egypt six years later, in the eleventh year of his reign. Once more, however, he emerged victorious, and the prisoners were taken to work as mercenaries in the Faiyum and the Delta. These mercenaries, marked with a branding iron as a sign of their servitude, were taken into captivity along with their wives and children; their goods, particularly their herds, were confiscated and transferred to the estate of Amun. The captured Libyans were given the opportunity to establish themselves in the population, thus reviving the same mechanism that had encouraged the invasions at the end of the Middle Kingdom: little by little, Libyan communities began to accumulate in Egypt. Made up partly of the descendants of the defeated troops and partly of colonists who entered the country more or less peacefully through the western Delta, these communities gathered together in Egyptianized chiefdoms and eventually seized power when the state had once more collapsed into anarchy.

In the eighth year of Ramesses III, in the period between the two Libyan wars, the King was forced to deal with a new invasion by an alliance of the Sea Peoples and the Philistines. The Egyptian garrisons in Palestine held them back by land, but they managed to enter the Delta through the eastern mouths of the Nile. Ramesses III eventually repelled them in a naval battle which was recorded, along with his two other campaigns, on the walls of his mortuary temple at Medinet Habu. The walls of Medinet Habu were also decorated with 'genre' scenes copied from the walls of the Ramesseum, in which Egyptians are shown engaged in fictional battles with Hittites, Syrians and Nubians.

Ramesses III chose to locate his mortuary temple at a site about one kilometre south of the Ramesseum. The modern name of the site, Medinet Habu ('town of Habu'), refers to the Christian community which was later established within the precincts of the temple, before finally moving to Esna at the time of the Arab conquest. In the Eighteenth Dynasty the site was dependent on Luxor temple, in relation to which it was 'the mound of the west'. That the memory of this connection with Luxor lasted into the Late Period is indicated by the tomb of Amun Kematef and the celebration of the procession of Amenemopet. In the Twenty-first Dynasty the area within the temple enclosure became a place of refuge for the surrounding population, as they gradually evolved into a city. This community was a bishopric in the Christian period and its name, Iat-tjamet, shortened to Djeme, was rendered by the Greeks as Thebes.

A continuous stratigrapic record from the Twenty-first Dynasty to the Arab conquest has survived at Medinet Habu, but unfortunately this part of the site has been poorly excavated. Abandoned after the conquest, it was still virtually intact when Auguste Mariette arrived at the site in about 1860. Mariette's preliminary clearance (later to be continued by Eugène Grébaut and Georges Daressy) consisted of the rapid removal of mud-brick urban remains, with the sole intention of gaining access to the underlying dynastic levels. In 1912 Theodore

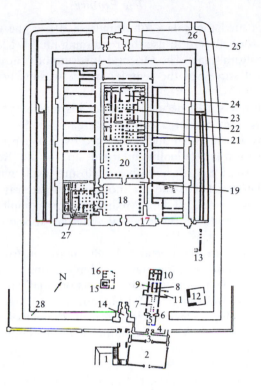

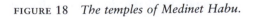

1   Quay

Dynasty XVIII Temple

2   Roman court
3   Ptolemaic gateway
4   First Pylon (Ptolemaic)
5   First court (Nectanebo I)
6   Second court (Shabaka, usurped by Taharqa)
7   Colonnaded court (Saite period)
8   Bask shrine
9   Peristyle
10 Western rooms
11 Chamber of Achoris
12 Sacred Lake
13 Nilometer
14 Gate

Chapels of the Divine Adoratrices

15 Chapel of Amenirdis 'the Elder'
16 Chapels of Nitocris, Shepenwepet II
    and Queen Mehytenwaskhet

Mortuary Temple of Ramesses III

17 First Pylon
18 First court
19 Second Pylon
20 Second court
21 First hypostyle hall
22 Second hypostyle hall
23 Third hypostyle hall
24 Bark shrine
25 Fortified West Gate
26 Gate of Ramesses III
27 Palace
28 Enclosure wall

FIGURE 18   *The temples of Medinet Habu.*

Davis excavated the palace of Ramesses III; at the end of 1913 the *sebakhin* were allowed to use the remaining mud-brick debris to enrich their agricultural land. The Oriental Institute of Chicago undertook an architectural survey of the temples in six seasons between 1927 and 1933.

When Ramesses III decided to place his mortuary temple there, the site already consisted of a complex (Figure 18, 9–11) that had been founded by Amenophis I and completed by Hatshepsut and Tuthmosis III. The site was gradually enlarged up to the Roman period. It was surrounded by an extensive enclosure wall, with an esplanade between the First Pylon and the monumental gateway which led down to a landing stage (1). The Medinet Habu complex now provides a striking example of the original external appearance of Egyptian temples.

The eastern entrance portal (14), 80 metres in front of the temple, was actually a double-storey pavilion, built in imitation of a *migdol*, or Syrian fortress. Its two crenellated towers originally reached a height of 22 metres. The western gate (25) has now disappeared.

Surrounded by its own enclosure wall, the actual mortuary temple copied the plan of the Ramesseum, with its cultic installations in the centre and the storerooms and outbuildings spread over the surrounding area. Two successive pylons (17 and 19) provided access to each of the two main courts, followed by three hypostyle halls leading gradually towards the sanctuary. The first court (18) gave access to the palace (27), which consisted of both ceremonial apartments and private chambers, including a bathroom.

The battles of Ramesses III were depicted on the inside walls of the temple and on the outside of the enclosure wall. The southern section of the outer face of the First Pylon (17) was decorated with scenes of the dedication of spoils of war to Amun while the northern section displayed an account of the second Libyan war. The enclosure wall related, year by year, the King's campaigns, with particular emphasis on the naval battle against the Sea Peoples.

These reliefs were intended to be viewed by the faithful who had no access to the interior: the temple therefore served as a place of display. At the same time, however, it was a representation of the universe, centred around the figure of the god to whom the king rendered service. It was therefore the place where the king provided evidence of his activities activities on behalf of the god in all the domains under his sway. The texts and military representations were a monument – in the true sense of the word – to the fact that Ramesses III's exploits could transform him into an archetypal figure, removed from his own specific place in time: the king was represented as eternally victorious not only over the Libyan confederations and the Sea Peoples, but also over the enemies conquered by Ramesses II and the whole of Egypt's foes since the beginning of time. History combined with myth, transposing real events into components of the religious cult. For this reason the wars of Ramesses III were also depicted on the inner walls of the temple in the first and second courts. They stood alongside the commemoration of purely religious events, such as the procession of Min, as well as more political representations, such as the list of Ramesses III's sons on the west portico of the second court, in imitation of the list of the sons of Ramesses II in the Ramesseum.

The temple of Medinet Habu was probably completed in the twelfth year of Ramesses III's reign. Although he did not build as prolifically as Ramesses II, he was still responsible for a major construction programme, especially at the Luxor and Karnak temples. At Karnak he began the construction of the temple of Khonsu, the divine son of the Theban triad, as well as building a shrine for the sacred barks in the area that would later be the first court. According to Papyrus Harris I, which includes a chronological account of his reign in its historical section, he also built at Piramesse, Heliopolis, Memphis, Athribis, Hermopolis, Asyut, This, Abydos, Ombos, Koptos, Elkab and various other sites in Nubia and Syria. He sent trading expeditions to Punt and exploited the copper mines at Atika (Timna).

Ramesses III's reign, however, was not without its troubles. After its twelfth year, he was beset by both political and economic problems. He dismissed his vizier at Athribis and seems to have taken personal control of the regulating of rations to the temples. The same problem was once more apparent towards the end of his reign, when the payment of wages to the community of Deir el-Medina was two months in arrears; this provoked the first known strike, when the artisans stopped work and took their complaints to the vizier Ta at the Ramesseum. These problems must certainly have arisen through economic crises, but they also suggest the weakening of the power of the State compared with the priesthood and the temple estates, both of which had become excessively strong.

The dynastic problems that had brought about the demise of the Nineteenth Dynasty were still not solved. Ramesses married a woman named Isis, daughter of Habadjilat, who was probably of Syrian origin. This fact is not in itself overly surprising, but his children turned out to resemble Rammesses II's not only in their names but also in their early deaths. Those who died before the king himself included Parahirwenemef (QV 42), Sethhirkhepeshef (QV 43), Khaemwaset II (QV 44), Ramesses and Amonhirkhepeshef (QV 55). Since there was apparently no officially recognized Great Royal Wife, the reign ended

with a conspiracy hatched in the harem by a second wife, Tiy, who
was attempting to secure the throne for her son, Pentaweret. Several
surviving papyri have recorded the proceedings of the court which was
held in the reign of Ramesses IV to prosecute the conspirators, but the
principal account is on a papyrus in the Museo Egizio, Turin.

Tiy had won over to her cause several women of the harem, a
majordomo and a butler. One of the women had even sent a message to
her son, who was commanding the troops in Kush. There was also a
general involved in the affair. Twenty-eight defendants appeared, all
named by insulting pseudonyms such as 'Evil in Thebes' and 'Ra detests
him', in an effort to stigmatize their crime for ever. The plan was as
simple as it was diabolical: the criminals had decided to strike at the
same time as the Festival of the Valley at Medinet Habu, using, among
other methods, sorcery with magic figurines. They failed however, and
found themselves in front of a tribunal made up of twelve high-ranking
civil and military officials. Seventeen of the conspirators were executed,
and seven of them – including Pentaweret – were ordered to commit
suicide. The affair had such wide implications that the judges themselves were not safe from accusations. Five judges were arrested for
collusion or even for relationships with the accused women; one was
condemned to commit suicide, three had their noses and ears amputated
and the fifth was let off with a reprimand.

Ramesses III died after a reign of thirty-three years, leaving behind
a somewhat less glorious reputation than his great predecessor. Even
the excavation of his tomb proved to be problematic. The workers
abandoned it (KV 3) in the middle of construction, transferring to
another tomb which had been begun by Sethnakhte and is now known
as 'Bruce's Tomb' or the 'Harpers' Tomb' (KV 11). Just after the
excavation of the third corridor, Sethnakhte's tomb-workers had broken
through into the tomb of Amenmesse (KV 10), making it necessary to
change the axis of Ramesses' tomb so that it ran parallel to its neighbour. The king's mummy, rediscovered in the Deir el-Bahri cache, is
that of a sixty-five-year-old man who seems to have died of natural
causes.

The reign of Ramesses III was followed by a rapid succession of eight
kings covering a period of less than a century. All of them bore the
name Ramesses and all claimed varying degrees of blood-link with
Ramesses II, who had become the archetype of Egypt's glorious past.
Ramesses IV, who succeeded his father on the throne, was at least
fourteen years old when he became king. Papyrus Harris I states that
he faithfully handed over endowments to the temples. He considered
himself to be a temple-builder of such stature that he asked the gods to
grant him a reign longer than Ramesses II's in exchange for everything

that he had done for them during the first five years of his reign. But the gods were evidently deaf to his prayers, for he died two years afterwards, leaving unfinished a construction programme that was still far below his ambitions. He was forced to abandon the construction of a gigantic mortuary temple in the vicinity of the causeway of the temple of Deir el-Bahri and instead had to content himself with a small establishment between the temple of Amenhotpe son of Hapu and Deir el-Medina. Nevertheless, he also built at Abydos, Heliopolis and Karnak, where he dedicated statues and decorated part of the Temple of Khonsu. He left his name in the Great Hypostyle Hall at Karnak, as well as at Luxor, Deir el-Bahri, the Ramesseum, Memphis, Koptos, Medamud, Armant, Esna, el-Tod, Edfu, Elkab, Buhen, Gerf Hussein and Aniba, while scarabs bearing his cartouche have been found as far afield as Palestine. He sent expeditions to the Wadi Hammamat quarries and the Sinai, and the village at Deir el-Medina was at its peak in the Twentieth Dynasty, when the size of its work teams doubled to a total of 120 workmen.

THE WORKMEN OF DEIR EL-MEDINA

The community of workmen at Deir el-Medina constitutes a documentary source of the highest importance for the Ramessid period. Since it was an isolated, relatively self-contained society made up of 120 workers and their families, it has made a major contribution not only to the study of urbanism, funerary apparel and literature (in the form of the thousands of texts on ostraca and some 200 papyri found there), but also to the knowledge of developments in daily life, which can be traced through generation after generation over a period of more than 300 years.

The village was located in the bed of an ancient wadi with a north-south orientation, between the Qurnet Murai and the western cliffs of Thebes. The modern name, 'the monastery of the village', derives from a monastery that was built inside the temple of the ancient village by a group of monks associated with Djeme in the fifth century AD. Under the patronage of Saint Isidore, the monastery revived the ancient name of the site, Pahebimen, which became Phoebamon. The name of the village and its cemetery, which was spread over the western hillside, was known in the Ramessid period as Set-Maat, the 'Place of Truth'.

The history of the site began in the Eleventh Dynasty, when it was an extension of the necropolis of Dra Abu el-Naga and Deir el-Bahri. The workmen's village appeared only after the Valley of the Kings came into use. It was founded by Tuthmosis I and initially consisted of about sixty houses placed in the bottom of the valley and surrounded by a wall;

several chapels dedicated to the community cults appeared on the hillside. No traces have been found of the Amarna period. The workers may have followed Amenophis IV to Akhetaten, but this is difficult to ascertain: there are, understandably, no records from this period, and information concerning the Amarna artists is not sufficiently detailed. All that can be said for certain is that activities at Deir el-Medina resumed in the reign of Horemheb, at which time the village was enlarged and took on a more definitely urban plan. The small individual tombs of the early community were replaced by family vaults on the western hillside; from then on this area was totally given over to tombs.

The heyday of Deir el-Medina was in the Nineteenth and Twentieth Dynasties. The total number of workmen had reached 120, meaning that the community as a whole must have numbered about 1200. The population clearly reached its maximum during the reigns of the Nineteenth Dynasty, when the royal cemeteries where they worked were very active. At the end of the Nineteenth Dynasty the village was beset by troubles caused as much by economic problems as by the corruption among officials charged with the supply of provisions to the village. At the beginning of the Twentieth Dynasty the rhythm of village life improved, only to be disturbed again with the onset of strikes at the end of Ramesses III's reign. After an abortive attempt to expand the community under Ramesses IV, the number of workmen was reduced to sixty in the reign of Ramesses VI, after which the community fell into gradual decline. The troubled times of Ramesses IX's reign were followed by bouts of looting that ravaged the whole Theban area. The community was disbanded in the Twenty-first Dynasty, after just under 500 years of occupation. Many of the villagers eventually sought refuge, along with the peasants of the region, behind the walls of Medinet Habu.

However, the site of Deir el-Medina had not yet been abandoned. In the Twenty-fifth Dynasty King Taharqa built a chapel to Osiris there, and soon afterwards – in the Saite period – the blocks from this building were reused to construct the tomb of the divine adoratrice Ankhnesneferibre, with the team of workmen assigned to this task temporarily housed in the abandoned village. In the Ptolemaic period Thebes was no longer the capital of the province, having been eclipsed by Ptolemais Hermiou, in the region of Sohag. But the town of Djeme underwent such a period of growth that new buildings were constructed, extending as far as Deir el-Medina. The small Ptolemaic temple dedicated to Hathor and Maat was built and decorated over a period of about 150 years, during which time the builders stayed in the neighbouring houses. They reused the cemetery on a commercial scale, emptying the tombs and selling off the furniture and the cleared spaces.

This was the first looting of the site. Christian hermits contributed further to its decline by taking up residence in the open tombs, until the site was finally deserted at the time of the Arab conquest.

It was not until the nineteenth century that life returned to Deir el-Medina again, when Jean François Champollion arrived to make copies of the decoration in some of the tombs. The collectors Henry Salt and Bernardino Drovetti were lured there by the unusually high quality of the first discoveries at the site. In 1885 the tomb of Sennedjem was discovered, but the site was then abandoned to looters for about fifty years. Consequently, many objects from Deir el-Medina are now in the great museum collections, such as the Museo Egizio, Turin (which supplemented its collection through the excavations of Schiaparelli in 1906), the British Museum, the Louvre and the Ägyptische Museum in Berlin (which, through Karl Richard Lepsius, obtained complete tomb walls). By the beginning of the twentieth century the site was being thoroughly pillaged and left to the mercy of collectors, and there was a pressing need for proper scientific excavation. Gaston Maspero undertook the restoration of the Ptolemaic Temple of Hathor, then a German team excavated a few sondages across the site before the First World War.

Finally, in 1914, the French Institute of Oriental Archaeology took over the concession. From 1922 to 1940 and from 1945 to 1951 the village and the necropolis were cleared by Bernard Bruyère. These excavations produced a greater understanding of funerary architecture and techniques of construction. The tombs built by the workers outside their official working hours were created with a great deal of ingenuity, and despite their very modest materials they achieved a final effect that bears comparison with the tombs of the nobles. This effect was the product of the art of imitation: painted and decorated mud-plaster, for instance, took on the appearance of stone, and the pylons that marked the entrances to the chapels were often filled with rubble. The same ability to make the most of what was available dominated the construction of the village houses, which were made of a mixture of stone blocks and mud-brick, erected around a core of wood. These building techniques – very similar to those still used today in rural Egypt – provide a more realistic view of daily life than the tombs of the nobles. At the same time, the population density of the community and its sense of continuity, which can be followed in the family tombs, provide a better indication of the social framework.

The village of Deir el-Medina is the best surviving example of an artificial settlement of the New Kingdom. It is not very extensive, the enclosure as a whole measuring 131×50 m and comprising seventy houses, as well as an extra-mural settlement of fifty buildings. The main constraint on the community was the fact that these workmen were employed to excavate, fit out and decorate the royal tombs. This role meant that they must be isolated, since they knew the locations and contents of the tombs. It is nevertheless remarkable that none of the workers at Deir el-Medina was implicated in the pillaging of the necropolis that took place in the reign of Ramesses IX; unfortunately, the same cannot be said for the looting that took place in the last years of the community. The villagers were not treated as servants, except in the case of foreigners recruited for their particular skills; nevertheless, their situation must actually have amounted to a form of slavery. It is therefore not possible to deduce from this village any laws concerning urbanism that would apply overall to urban or rural conditions.

The organization of the village is a reflection of a very specific type of social arrangement modelled on that of the expeditions sent by the kings of the mines and quarries, which was in turn based on the system used in the Egyptian navy. Like a boat, the village was divided along its north-south axis, creating two sectors to east and west (port and starboard), each accommodating a team; this 'team of the right' and 'team of the left' worked alternate shifts. At either end of the street were gates, both guarded and closed at night. At the time of the village's period of expansion (its third phase) the south gate was dismantled and a new one was built to the west, as well as transverse streets providing access to the new quarter.

The village houses must have been very much the same as elsewhere. They opened on to alleys which were probably covered to protect the inhabitants from the sun, as is still the case, for example, in the villages of the oases in the Libyan Desert. The walls of the houses were painted white, and their red-painted doorways were inscribed with the names of the occupants. They were built without foundations, using undressed stone up to a height of about 1.5 m, then unbaked mud-bricks. The roofs were made of mud modelled around a wooden framework. The houses had neither courtyards nor gardens, and draught animals used for official work and odd jobs were kept outside the village.

The first room of the house, entered from the street, contained an altar inside a type of canopied closet separated from the floor by two or three steps. The walls of the closet were decorated with such domestic motifs as scenes of childbirth and representations of the god Bes. At these altars the women practised a domestic cult dedicated both to the household gods and to their ancestors, and the room was filled with offering tables, lamps, vases and all kinds of objects relating to the cult. This first room was intended for the reception of visitors and the purification of the family.

The Workmen's Village: second and third stages

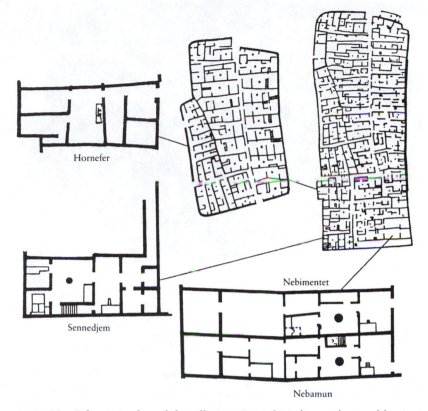

Hornefer

Nebimentet

Sennedjem

Nebamun

FIGURE 19 *Schematic plan of the village at Deir el-Medina and several houses.*

The second room was larger and better decorated. Its ceiling was higher than that of the other rooms so that the interior was lit by a clerestory window. The roof was generally supported by a column, sometimes two, on the base of which the house-owner's name was sometimes inscribed. The main item of furniture was a couch which, as in modern times, served for the reception of guests. A staircase led down to a subterranean room used as a storage area for the family's treasures. Behind the second room were the living rooms. This distinction between the two reception rooms and the private rooms corresponded to the idea of a harem, as at el-Amarna. At the rear of the house, the kitchen provided access to a cellar, which was sometimes reused as a tomb; it also led up to the roof terrace, which was used for

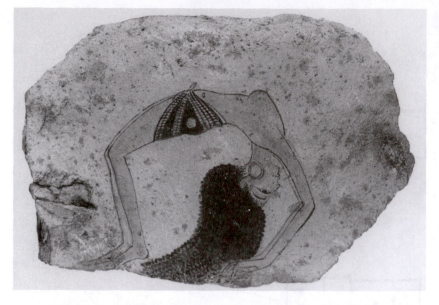

PLATE 19 *Nineteenth Dynasty ostracon showing a female acrobat. (Turin, Museo delle Antichità Egizie. Photograph: Chomon s.n.c.)*

relaxation and discussion in the cool of the evening. As in modern Egyptian houses, the roof was also used for the disposal of rubbish. The kitchen contained all the essential items for the cooking of bread and other food: grindstones, mortars, kneading-troughs, water jars and ovens. It was partly covered by a trellis of branches, providing protection from the sun.

The village also contained the usual debris of urban life, consisting mainly of worn-out and broken domestic objects and potsherds: in other words, those artefacts that were neither removed at the time of the village's abandonment nor salvaged at a later date (as in the case of the wooden lintels). Not unexpectedly, the most interesting finds were made among the rubbish: the first set of ostraca were found in the house ruins during the 1934–5 excavation season. Perhaps the most important discovery was a well in the northern part of the site; it had been filled with rubbish in the Ptolemaic period, when the area was being cleared to make room for the temple. By 1948 the excavation of this well had yielded 5000 inscribed and decorated ostraca (Plate 19), the publication of which began in 1934 and is still in progress. The study of the Deir el-Medina ostraca, as well as some 200 literary and documentary papyri associated with the village, provides a detailed view of the intellectual life of the community and of the transmission of traditional culture through the centuries.

The acquisition of water was one of the workmen's major pre-occupations. Since the nearest major wells were at the Ramesseum and Medinet Habu, there was a constant toing and froing of trains of donkeys passing under the gaze of the Nubian policemen responsible for guarding the village. Another path led away from Deir el-Medina, cutting across the mountainside towards the villagers' work-place, the Valley of the Kings. Along the way, temporary shelter was supplied by a resting place consisting of a group of dry-stone huts and a chapel.

Clustered at the north end of Deir el-Medina were cult buildings constructed in the form of provincial private chapels which included a room (either roofed or open-air) in which groups could meet. The room was furnished with two benches stretching along the walls, the curved backs of which have been found, along with the names of the occupants of the seats – five on the left and seven on the right. Amphorae contained the lustral water, while in the walls there were stelae and ex-votos. A pronaos, or ceremonial porch, was separated from this room by low walls on either side of the entrance so that spectators could follow the ceremonies. The pronaos led through to the naos, which re-sembled a sentry-box and contained the divine statue. The complex was rounded off with a sacristy. The best surviving cult buildings of this type are the temple itself and the chapels to the north of the village enclosure. The better preserved examples were dedicated to Amun by Ramesses II and to Hathor by Sethos I; the latter was adjacent to a chapel dedi-cated to Amenophis I and Ahmose-Nefertari. Hardly anything has sur-vived of the cult statues from these chapels, apart from one stone statue of Amenophis I, a wooden relief of the local snake-goddess Meretseger and a wooden statue of Ahmose-Nefertari (Turin, Museo Egizio).

The workmen used a system of rotation to practise, one after the other, the cults of Amun of Luxor and Karnak, Min, Ptah, Sobek, Harmachis of Armant, the hippopotamus goddess Thoeris, Mut, Renenut and the New Kingdom pharaohs who were buried in the Valley of the Kings. For the sake of completeness the small speos-temple of 'Ptah of the Valley of the Queens' and Meretseger should also be mentioned; this was located about a hundred metres along the road leading from Deir el-Medina to the Valley of the Queens.

The temple of Hathor was the largest and most revered of the chapels of the Deir el-Medina community. Initially it was only a simple chapel, built by Tuthmosis I and maintained until the reign of Amenophis III. Several humbler sanctuaries grew up around it, and immediately to the north Sethos I placed a sanctuary complete with forecourt, steps, paving, pylon, hypostyle hall and naos. On the site of the ruined Eighteenth Dynasty temple, Ramesses II erected a new

building that was eventually abandoned at the end of the Twentieth
Dynasty. In the Ptolemaic period, Ramesses II's sanctuary was demolished by Ptolemy IV Philopator to make way for a new sandstone building. The decoration of the new building was begun by Ptolemy IV and
completed by Ptolemy XII Neos Dionysos. The last ruler to build at Deir
el-Medina was Julius Caesar, who ordered the construction of the
Iseion.

The workmen's cemetery, like their village, went through two
distinct phases. In its first phase the tombs were built without an overall
plan; then, at the end of the Nineteenth Dynasty, they began to spread
out over the north-western hillside in chronologically arranged groups.
They adopted a composite architectural form, blending a superstructure
in the shape of the traditional Heliopolitan pyramid with a new type of
substructure introduced by Libyan migrant workers. Naturally, they
were also influenced by the rock-cut tombs in the Valley of the Kings.
As a result of demographic pressure, the workmen soon began to build
family tombs. The characteristics of each tomb varied according to
social rank and chronological phase, but the basic structure remained
the same: a court, a chapel, a tomb shaft and associated subterranean
chambers. Each family was grouped around one important workman –
perhaps the foreman of a gang – and an attempt was made to align the
tomb's axis as closely as possible with the mortuary temple of the king
whom the deceased had served.

Initially the Deir el-Medina tombs corresponded to the so-called
'Nubian' type, which consisted of a simple mud-brick vaulted chamber.
This arrangement, the oldest known example of its type, was not a true
vault, since it consisted simply of layers of bricks, slanting up from the
tops of two parallel vertical walls and resting on a third wall which was
at right angles to them, forming arches. The layers of bricks in the arch
were held in place by their own weight. This Nubian type of tomb was
soon superseded by a superstructure decorated with a pyramid, the last
stage in a process of funerary democratization by which New Kingdom
private individuals adopted the Heliopolitan symbol that had been
restricted to the royal family during the Old Kingdom. The pyramid
was of relatively modest size and was either located over the chapel or
built around it. The pyramids over the vaulted chapels were hollow
mud-brick structures, whereas those placed over the roof of the façade
were built of bricks or stones and filled with rubble. Orientated towards
the rising sun, they were as high as 2–3 metres, and their bases were
2–5 metres in width. Each pyramid was plastered, painted white and
surmounted by a stone pyramidion decorated with bas-reliefs.

Each tomb was approached by a monumental set of steps, equipped
with a central ramp so that the sarcophagus could be dragged up. The

entrance consisted of a pylon leading to a court surrounded by high whitewashed walls. At the far end of the court was the chapel façade, preceded by a peristyle and dominated by the pyramid. It was there, in the forecourt, that the funeral ceremonies and festive rites of the dead were performed. The rites were celebrated in a special kiosk covered with an awning and furnished with a basin, as well as with the essential items necessary for a banquet. At each festival the *ushabtis* (which at this period should more correctly be described as *shawabtis*) were renewed – the small funerary figures that accomplished the work owed to Osiris in the afterlife. Offerings, were made and incense burned before the stelae attached to the walls, as well as under the canopy roof at the rear of the court, which protected the large stelae and statues of the tomb-owner. Behind these was the chapel, decorated with painted portraits and scenes of the family and their immediate relations. At the back of the chapel, facing the entrance, a naos was carved into the rock face. This usually contained a statue of the deceased or a tutelary divinity such as Amenophis I or Hathor in the form of a cow.

The tomb shaft was cut into the floor of the forecourt or chapel. By simply lifting a paving stone it was possible to descend to a wooden door which was resealed after each new burial. The tomb itself was virtually a subterranean house, comprising passages, staircases and rooms. The chambers were usually vaulted, painted white and decorated. A set of model furniture was packed into the tomb alongside the belongings of the deceased. A single tomb might accommodate as many as several dozen burials: Sennedjem's, for instance, contained twenty coffins.

The subject matter of the tomb decoration was at first very traditional, but in the Nineteenth Dynasty it became more spiritually orientated under the influence of the royal tombs, with a number of religious images (derived from the *Book of the Dead* papyri) that were comparable with mythological themes decorating the walls of the village houses. The technique involved painting on the wet surface of *pisé* or stucco. The *pisé*, a coating of sand mixed with clay and lime (the ingredients of the traditional *muna*), was applied directly to the mud-brick wall. It received a first outline drawing in red paint, which was corrected in white then repainted in black; this process is still visible through the layer of yellow ochre that was next applied. The scenes were then coloured with flat tints: the men's skin in red ochre, the women's in yellow, and the linen drapery in white with the edges picked out in black or red. Details were added in green and blue. This assortment of colours on a yellow background was more characteristic of the Nineteenth Dynasty, in the tombs of such men as Sennedjem (TT 1) and Pashed (TT 3). Later, perhaps because of the growing impoverishment of the villagers, the decoration was purely monochromatic on a white background, as in the case of Nebenmaat (TT 219) and Irynefer (TT 290). The scenes reproduced vignettes from the *Book of the Dead* bordered with texts arranged in panels or, as on a papyrus, according to the order of the funerary procession (as in TT 290). The tomb thus acted as an extension of the coffin; the ceiling, like the coffin lid, was often decorated with geometrical motifs. Few Eighteenth Dynasty tombs have survived at Deir el-Medina, but several of the Ramessid period are well preserved, with such fine examples as the tomb of Sennedjem (TT 1), discovered intact; Peshedu (TT 3), another 'Servant in the Place of Truth'; Ipy (TT 217), a sculptor contemporary with Ramesses II; Amenennakht and his family (TT 218–20); and Anherkhe (TT 359), chief workman under Ramesses III and IV.

Only a small amount of precious jewellery has been found in the tombs: the raw materials would have been beyond the financial means of the workers, and they used a great deal of faience (glazed composition) and glass paste instead. The pottery included the complete set of local types, as well as a number of vessels made with imported techniques or Mediterranean styles of decoration. There were also many small finds, including various figurines and items of joinery and basketry, all contributing to an appreciation of life in a community which numbered over a thousand inhabitants when a census was taken in the Twentieth Dynasty. The community included a complete range of non-Egyptian groups, from Nubians to Syrians and Libyans, but the Egyptians were always in a majority. Continually under surveillance by the state, Deir el-Medina was under the direct authority of the vizier of western Thebes.

This virtual microcosm of Egyptian society incorporated the whole range of occupations, from building to decorative arts. At their height, the two gangs of workmen each consisted of sixty men commanded by an architect or government agent. The gang typically included one or two scribes, as well as draughtsmen, painters, wood-carvers, sculptors, stucco-workers, plasterers, masons, quarry-workers, miners, unskilled labourers, assistants and various apprentices. A royal scribe usually acted as the intermediary between the workmen and the administration, noting down in his *Diary* the tasks accomplished, materials used, daily wages, absentees and any incidents that occurred. The royal scribe also headed a special workmen's tribunal made up of eleven members of the gang. The work was organized in terms of ten-day shifts, during which the workmen remained at the work place, living at the temporary resting place by the side of the track to the Valley of the Kings. At the end of their shift they had one day of leave, which allowed them to take care of their personal affairs.

The government was responsible for supplying the village with provisions from the storerooms of the neighbouring temples – a duty that was not always reliably carried out, judging from the problems encountered during the reign of Ramesses III. The families of workmen lived in an inward-looking society, and the combination of generations of polygamy and inbreeding effectively produced dynasties in each profession or craft, which formed the basis of the social hierarchy. Village life was extremely eventful, full of thefts, adultery, revenge, crimes and robberies, which give the tiny community a definite air of claustrophobia. In the time of Ramesses II, for instance, an unwholesome individual called Paneb indulged in the distinctly anti-social pastime of throwing stones at passers-by. Not content with this, he also stole some stone sculptures from the nearby temple of Sethos I to decorate his own tomb. Having already passed from assaults to theft, he one day embarked on the murder of his gang foreman, Neferhotep (TT 216), after an argument, his intention being to take over Neferhotep's position. He was arrested by the authorities, but by exerting a certain amount of influence managed to gain not only his freedom but also the position of foreman. He subsequently built himself a beautiful tomb (TT 211). At Deir el-Medina, crime apparently paid: there was another instance of an unpunished misdemeanour in the case of Amenwah, a man accused of robbing the tomb of Ramesses III; he was discharged through lack of proof. The modern excavators of his tomb found that he was guilty after all, for he had kept the stolen object hidden in his burial chamber.

There were other, more public distractions in the village, such as religious festivals, among which the Festival of the Valley took pride of place. This festival was held on the occasion of the burial of kings and village gatherings. The workers took turns to play the role of *wab*-priest ('purified priest') in the processions, preparing for this role by retiring into the desert and fasting; women participated in the processions as well. There was also the burial of the villagers themselves, whose final resting places had been gradually embellished over the years.

The whole *raison d'être* of the Deir el-Medina community may have been death, but the atmosphere of the village appears, paradoxically, to have been characterized by a sense of life in all its intensity, complete with all of the familiar joys and pains of humanity.

KINGS AND PRIESTS

Ramesses V Amonhirkhepeshef succeeded to his father's throne in 1148. He died four years later (probably from smallpox), having had insufficient time to see through his ambitious programme, beginning with the reopening of the Gebel el-Silsila sandstone quarries and the Sinai mines. Apart from his tomb in the Valley of the Kings (KV 9) and his mortuary temple, which was modelled on that of Ramesses IV, he also built at Heliopolis and Buhen. Among the documents dating to his reign is a great fiscal text called the Wilbour Papyrus (New York, Brooklyn Museum), as well as the first of a series of royal hymns, later versions of which appeared in the reign of Ramesses VII (Condon 1978). Another document from this reign, of a quite different genre, is Papyus Turin 1887, which describes a financial scandal involving the priests of Elephantine (Sauneron 1988). This text is a useful indication of the corruption that had evidently become rife in the administration.

The situation did not improve with the reign of Ramesses VI Amonhirkhepeshef II who, unlike his predecessor, was actually a son of Ramesses III. The two branches of the royal family – those claiming direct descent from Ramesses III and those descended from his sons and nephews – fought for power among themselves until the end of the Twentieth Dynasty. It was during the reign of Ramesses VI that the size of the Deir el-Medina work gangs was restored to sixty men. Although the country was not actually in a state of civil war, numerous records of acts of banditry indicate the government's increasing weakness.

Ramesses VI inscribed his cartouche at Karnak and a number of other temples, but he also took care to add his name in one other place: the list of sons of Ramesses III in the portico at Medinet Habu, where his name had not originally appeared, any more than his father's had (for all the names of the figures had been left blank, including that of the king himself). Was this perhaps a sign of the war of succession that was raging among members of the royal family? Certainly Ramesses VI is known to have usurped and enlarged the tomb begun by Ramesses V in the Valley of the Kings (KV 9), taking it for his own use only two years after his predecessor's death.

The signs of decay were increasing. Egyptian domination beyond the Nile valley had become more and more limited: Ramesses VI was the last ruler of the New Kingdom whose name is attested in the Sinai. At Thebes and throughout the kingdom, the power of the chief priests of Amun was growing, despite the fact that Isis, daughter of Ramesses VI, maintained a link with the priesthood in her role of God's Wife of Amun, or Divine Adoratrice. In the reign of his son Ramesses VII, who succeeded to the throne in 1136, the country's misery increased. Deir el-Medina sources show that there was a rise in prices, and in the course of seven years the king left his name at only a small number of sites: Tell el-Yahudiya, Memphis, Karnak and Elkab. Ramesses VIII

Sutekhherkhepeshef, one of the last surviving sons of Ramesses III, came to the throne in 1128 but reigned for only one year.

Ramesses IX ruled for eighteen years and achieved a great deal more than his predecessors: in the sixth year of his reign he inscribed his titulature at Amara West, and his name has also been found at Gezer in Palestine, the Dakhla Oasis and Antinoe. He undertook construction at Heliopolis, where the most important architectural works of his reign are situated, confirming the royal family's growing identification with the northern part of the country. This did not prevent him, however, from decorating the wall to the north of the Seventh Pylon in the Temple of Amon-Re at Karnak, where the office of chief priest was held first by Ramsesnakht then, in the tenth year of the reign, by his sons Nesamon and Amenhotep. Ramsesnakht had exploited a series of alliances and marriages to transform his family into a power base which included the second, third and fourth prophets of Amun, the mayor of the city of Thebes and various other notable figures. This control over the main priestly posts allowed him to buttress the power of the chief priests of Amun.

The end of the reign of Ramesses IX was marked by a scandal that was to be repeated under Ramesses XI and Herihor: the pillaging of the royal necropolis, including Ramesses IX's own tomb (KV 6) and that of his son, Monthuhirkhepeshef (KV 19), as well as the looting of certain private cemeteries. The robberies took place in the sixteenth year of Ramesses IX's reign. They are mentioned in the *Diary* of Deir el-Medina (Valbelle 1985a: 42) and have also been reported in fourteen other textual sources on papyri (Peet 1930), which allow the facts to be very faithfully pieced together.

The authorities looking after the Theban necropolis in the reign of Ramesses IX were represented by the vizier Khaemwaset, governor of Thebes, and Paser III, the mayor of Thebes (the highest civil office). Under Paser III's command was Paweraa, mayor of western Thebes, who was directly responsible for the necropolis.

Some time before the ninth regnal year of Ramesses IX, a band of five robbers plundered an unnamed tomb. They then argued about the division of the copper and silver loot and one of them threatened to tell all to the authorities. In an attempt to resolve this problem by acquiring more treasure they then spent a further four days digging into the tomb of Ramesses VI, who had been buried there only fifteen years earlier. The papyrus recording the robbers' eventual trial does not specify their fate, but in Ramesses IX's ninth regnal year a commission was sent to reseal the tomb of Ramesses VI.

Subsequently, another gang of thieves raided the Valley of the Queens as well as the royal Seventeenth Dynasty tombs, which were isolated, neglected and less strictly guarded. Doubtless these robbers were from the ranks of the Libyan bandits who infested the region, but they also appear to have made use of local accomplices, among whom was perhaps the mayor of western Thebes himself, if the documents of the Deir el-Medina workmen are to be believed. Paser III, the mayor of Thebes, was informed of the robbery and of the rumours that hung over the head of Paweraa. He made a report to Khaemwaset, who then ordered an inquest, which took place in the sixteenth regnal year of Ramesses IX. Ten tombs were examined and found to be either intact, like that of Amenophis I, or only partially robbed, as in the case of the tombs of Inyotef V and VI. But the tomb of Sobkemsaf II had been entered and robbed by way of one of the adjacent private tombs, all of which had been totally devastated.

Several arrests were then made. One suspect confessed to having raided the tomb of Queen Isis, wife of Ramesses III. The court transferred to the scene of the crime, where the suspect turned out to be mistaken, unable to recognize the places in question. The investigation was held behind closed doors, to the scandalized horror of the people of Deir el-Medina, who declared it corrupt. Eventually the affair was taken to the vizier himself, in the form of a criminal trial. The accused were brought before a tribunal in eastern Thebes, in the temple of Maat (the goddess of truth), which was in the precinct of Monthu at Karnak. The stone-carver Amenpanefer confessed to having participated in the looting of Sobkemsaf II's tomb. He revealed everything: how the eight robbers had entered the tomb by digging a tunnel, broken into the sarcophagus, stolen the jewels by setting fire to the mummy (to save time), and how they had used the same strategy on the tomb of Queen Nubkhas. The scandal was all the greater because the robbers belonged to the personnel of the nearby temples. The Deir el-Medina workmen, however, heaved sighs of relief – there were no black sheep in their midst. Most of the seventeen guilty persons were sentenced to be impaled.

A further series of robberies later took place in the Valleys of the Queens and the Kings, but this time with help from Deir el-Medina. In the time of Ramesses XI it was the tomb of Ramesses VI that was devastated. The authorities attempted at least to save the royal mummies by successive transferrals, little by little, whenever necessary. The movements of the mummy of Ramesses II, for instance, can be followed thanks to the inscription on the lid of the last coffin in which it was placed. Evidently the chief priest Herihor placed it in the tomb of Sethos I in the sixth year of the Renaissance (i.e. the twenty-fifth year of Ramesses XI). Later, in the Twenty-first Dynasty under Siamun, the chief priest Pinudjem had it transported into the cache at Deir el-Bahri along with the body of Sethos I.

The Deir el-Bahri cachette was gathered together by Pinudjem II in the tomb of Inhapy, the wife of Amosis, which had to be enlarged for the purpose. He brought there some forty coffins of kings and chief priests of the Seventeenth to Twenty-first Dynasties, including Seqenenre Taʿa II, Amenophis I, Ahmose, Tuthmosis I, II and III, Sethos I, Ramesses I, II and IX, the mother of Pinudjem I and the daughter of the chief priest Menkheperra. Pinudjem II himself and his wife were eventually buried there as well. It was this cachette that Gaston Maspero investigated in 1881. Another cachette, discovered by Victor Loret in 1898, shows that the Theban necropolis had also been pillaged a little earlier, in the reign of Pinudjem I, who had evidently moved various royal bodies into the burial chamber of Amenophis II. Among those whom Pinudjem I reinterred alongside Amenophis II were Tuthmosis IV, Amenophis III, Merneptah, Siptah, Sethos II and Ramesses IV, V and VI.

Another cachette containing sixty mummies was found by Galli Maunier in the Asasif in 1850. There were also two others discovered at Deir el-Bahri: one, containing seventy-one sarcophagi of priests of Monthu, was excavated by Auguste Mariette during his clearance of the temple in 1858; the other, containing 153 sarcophagi and 200 statues of chief priests of Amun after the end of the Twenty-first Dynasty, was discovered by Georges Daressy in 1891, at the entrance to the Bab el-Gasus.

These robberies indicate the level of insecurity that had prevailed in Upper Egypt since the reign of Ramesses IX and would increase under the last two kings of the dynasty. Even the length of the reign of Ramesses X Amonhirkhepeshef III is uncertain, possibly being three or nine years. He is the last Egyptian king whose rule over Nubia is attested, at least at Aniba. Nubia was then the only territory outside Egypt which was still subject to Egyptian domination; Egypt's influence in Syria-Palestine had been negligible for some time.

After his burial in the Valley of the Kings (KV 18) Ramesses X was succeeded by Ramesses XI; he reigned for twenty-seven years, of which only the first nineteen were to any extent effective. Troubles in the Theban region increased: apart from the robberies and the atmosphere of insecurity that have already been described, it appears that Upper Egypt was in the grip of famine, and each of these problems exacerbated the other. Moreover, the fighting of great battles fell increasingly within the domain of the chief priests, who usurped the royal prerogatives so that they were virtually equal to the pharaohs. The chief priest Amenhotep had himself depicted at Karnak at the same scale as the king, thus demonstrating his low regard for the power of the pharaoh. It seems, however, that Amenhotep may have gone a little too far, for he was sent into exile in the first part of the reign of Ramesses XI. A kind of civil war broke out, causing Panehsy, the viceroy of Kush, to intervene at Thebes and as far north as Hardai. A second Ramsesnakht may then have succeeded as chief priest.

A little before the nineteenth year of Ramesses XI there appeared a new chief priest of Amun with a strong personality: Herihor. His origins are not properly known, but he was probably descended from a Libyan family. Through his decoration of the Temple of Khonsu at Karnak it is possible to follow the progressive growth in Herihor's powers until his assumption of a quasi-royal titualture which may not have completely transformed him into a pharaoh, but certainly suggests that he had acquired complete control over Upper Egypt. This was the beginning of the 'Renaissance', in which the term previously used by the founders of new dynasties, *wehem meswt* ('he who repeats births'), was revived. This phrase sanctioned a kind of equilibrium between three powerful men: Ramesses XI, Smendes and Herihor.

The first of these was the king, who remained in principle the most powerful of the three, but in practice no longer wielded any power: when Ramesses XI died around 1069 BC, the tomb that was being prepared for him in the Valley of the Kings (KV 4) was not even finished. The second personality was an administrator named Smendes, who was theoretically subservient to the Amun priesthood but in fact appears to have controlled the northern part of the kingdom from the royal residence of Piramesse. This city was then going through the final years of its existence, for it was soon to be dismantled to provide stone for the construction of Tanis. Herihor, the third member of this poorly balanced triumvirate, fulfilled both the secular and spiritual roles of a ruler. It was he who controlled the armies of Upper Egypt and Nubia, a situation which led eventually to the secession of Nubia. From that point onwards, the territory of Egypt was reduced to the Nile Valley between Aswan and the Mediterranean.

The triumvirate failed to survive beyond the death of Ramesses XI and power was eventually divided between Upper and Lower Egypt, the two kingdoms as usual reverting to their natural boundaries at a time of crisis. In the north, Smendes founded a new royal dynasty and established a new capital, Tanis. In the south, the chief priests of Amun had returned to the roots of Egyptian theocracy, blending myth and history even more inextricably than in the earliest times. The cornerstone of their regime was the temple estate of Amun, which was ultimately the only true beneficiary of the immense empire created by the Ramessid kings. By the end of the Twentieth Dynasty the temple of Amun had unquestionably become wealthier and more powerful than pharaoh himself.

12

The Domain of Amun

All the rulers of the New Kingdom made some impact on the temple of Amon-Re at Karnak (Plate 20), if only in the form of an inscribed cartouche. The modern visitor to Karnak cannot fail to be impressed by the complexity and wealth of a temple complex that was a perpetual building site for almost 3000 years.

Karnak was rediscovered in the early eighteenth century by Captain Frederik L. Norden, who made the first drawings of the temple, and the Reverend Richard Pococke, who created the first plan of the site. However, Napoleon's expedition was the first real stage in the scientific exploration of Karnak, beginning with the *Description de l'Égypte*, then the visit by Jean-François Champollion in 1828. The temple became better known in the West after the sketches made by B. Constrand, David Roberts, Nestor L'Hôte and Hector Horeau. But when Muhammad Ali opened Egypt to Europeans he attracted entrepreneurs as well as archaeologists. The modernization of the economy and the provision of stone for the construction of sugar factories meant that the ancient temples were once more used as quarries. It was through quarrying that the Middle Kingdom temple of Amun at Karnak had already disappeared. For their part, the fellahin used *sebakh* (mud-brick and lime) as fertilizer on their lands, destroying the monuments and archaeological evidence in the process. Faced with this pillaging – in which numerous self-appointed 'excavators' participated – Champollion, Rifaud and L'Hôte were the first to raise the alarm, but compared with the scale of the economic interests at stake, their efforts were completely derisory. In 1835 Muhammad Ali issued a decree protecting the ancient monuments of Egypt but five years later the pylons in the processional way were still being used as

PLATE 20   *The Sacred Lake and the Temple of Amon-Re at Karnak. (Photograph: © Ronald Sheridan/Ancient Art & Architecture Collection.)*

stone quarries. The Luxor obelisk was carried off to Paris, and then in 1843 the Hall of the Ancestors at Karnak was transported to the Louvre by Achille Prisse d'Avennes. It was not until 1858 that the Egyptian Antiquities Service was founded and Auguste Mariette began the clearance of the temples.

After an initial period of excavation between 1858 and 1860 Mariette published two volumes entitled *Karnak: étude topographique et archéologique* (1875), which presented the first historical outline of the development of Karnak temple. Next, Georges Legrain directed a series of excavations from 1895 to 1917; he carried out the restoration and anastylosis of the Great Hypostyle Hall, cleared the court of the First

Pylon and the shrines of Ramesses III and Sethos II, and discovered the cachette of sculpture in the court of the Seventh Pylon. Legrain published his excavation reports in the journal of the Antiquities Service, the *Annales du Service des Antiquités de l'Égypte*, and in one of the two great French Egyptological journals of the time, the *Receuils de Travaux*. In 1929 Capart's *Karnak* appeared; he had worked on it until his death in 1917.

Between 1921 and 1926 Maurice Pillet worked at Karnak, emptying the Third Pylon (built by Amenophis III) and revealing the remains of sixteen previous monuments that had been reused in its fill. Pillet also cleared the southern processional way, the chapels of North Karnak and the temple of Mut, consolidated the Tenth Pylon and discovered the first Osirid colossi of Akhenaten to the east of the precinct of Amon-Re. He published the results of his work in *Thebes* (1928). The third architect to take charge of the excavations at Karnak was Henri Chévrier, who directed the excavations from 1926 to 1954 (apart from a break during the Second World War). He finished emptying the rubble from the Third Pylon and cleared and began restoration on the Second. He also excavated a trench through the Middle Kingdom Court and rebuilt the older monuments that had been dismantled for reuse in the New Kingdom, such as the alabaster bark shrine of Amenophis I, the White Chapel of Sesostris I and the shrine of Hatshepsut (which he prepared for publication).

From 1931 the French Institute of Oriental Archaeology at Cairo was based at North Karnak in the Temple of Monthu, which was excavated first by C. Robichon and Alexandre Varille and subsequently – up to the present – by French Institute excavators. In 1936 the temple of Amon-Re Kamutef and the entrance to the temple of Mut were uncovered. In 1950 Varille cleared and published the Eastern Sanctuary of Tuthmosis III and Paul Barguet supervised the clearance of the only obelisk of Tuthmosis III. Some years later Barguet published a study entitled *Le Temple d'Amon-Rê à Karnak*, which is still the best reference work on the site. In 1967 Egypt and France finally combined their efforts to ensure the preservation and scientific examination of the temples of Karnak; they established a Franco-Egyptian Centre which in twenty years, has succeeded in emptying, dismantling and partially rebuilding the Ninth Pylon, as well as producing various studies on the deterioration of the monuments, discovering the priests' houses around the sacred lake, reconstructing Tuthmosis III's Hall of the Ancestors and the chapel of Achoris in front of the First Pylon, and studying the blocks reused by Akhenaten. Apart from these specific achievements, the Franco-Egyptian Centre has succeeded in maintaining, exhibiting and protecting the most visited site in Egypt. A Canadian expedition

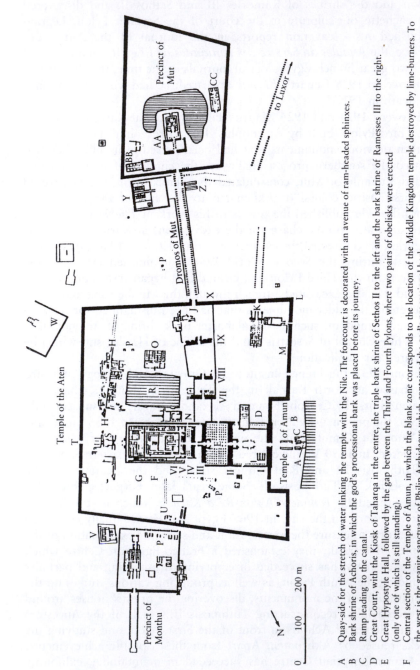

Temple of the Aten

Precinct of Mut

to Luxor

Dromos of Mut

Precinct of Monthu

Temple of Amun

N

0   100   200 m

A   Quay-side for the stretch of water linking the temple with the Nile. The forecourt is decorated with an avenue of ram-headed sphinxes.
B   Bark shrine of Achoris, in which the god's processional bark was placed before its journey.
C   Ramp leading to the canal.
D   Great Court, with the Kiosk of Taharqa in the centre, the triple bark shrine of Sethos II to the left and the bark shrine of Ramesses III to the right.
E   Great Hypostyle Hall, followed by the gap between the Third and Fourth Pylons, where two pairs of obelisks were erected (only one of which is still standing).
F   Central section of the Temple of Amun, in which the blank zone corresponds to the location of the Middle Kingdom temple destroyed by lime-burners. To the west is the granite sanctuary of Philip Arrhidaeus which contained the god's processional bark.
G   The Akh-menu, Jubilee temple of Tuthmosis III.

H   Tuthmosis III's enclosure wall, with priests' houses overlooking the Sacred Lake.

I   Roman ramp used to remove the obelisk now in Istanbul.

J   Court of the Tenth Pylon with a building constructed by Amenophis II, a kind of bark shrine.

K   Gate of Ptolemy III Euergetes I.

L   Chapel of Nectanebo.

M   Section of the Temple of Khonsu, the moon-god and son of Amun, and the Temple of Opet, the place of the mythical birth of Osiris.

N   Temple of divine regeneration, built by Taharqa.

O   Storerooms.

P   Late Period chapels of Osiris

R   The Sacred Lake: setting for sacred boat trips.

S   Eastern sanctuary of Amon-Re 'the hearer of prayers' (location of the 'Lateran obelisk').

T   Great eastern gate.

U   Temple of Ptah, the great god of Memphis.

V   Treasury of Tuthmosis I.

W   Temple of Khonsu 'who governs in Thebes'.

Y   Temple of Amon-Re Kamutef, the procreative aspect of Amun.

Z   Bark shrine of Amun built by Queen Hatshepsut.

AA   Temple of Mut, wife of Amun and mistress of calamities.

BB   Temple of Khonsu the child.

CC   Bark shrine of Ramesses III.

Pylons labelled I–X.

FIGURE 20   *General plan of the Karnak temples (after Traunecker and Golvin, 1984, 20–1).*

has been working on the Amarna-period buildings in East Karnak (Redford 1984a; 1986b) and an American team has studied the temple of Mut.

The temple of Karnak dates back to the Third Dynasty if the list in the Hall of the Ancestors is to be believed, but there is little likelihood that this textual evidence will be backed up by archaeological finds, since the oldest part of the temple has been pillaged. Karnak was the site of a cult of the local god Monthu, probably from the Old Kingdom onwards; there is certainly evidence for the existence of the Karnak temple in the reign of Inyotef II, when it was called 'the abode of Amun'. Its classic name of Iput-isut, ('The most esteemed of places'), originally referred only to that part of the temple between the Fourth Pylon and the Festival Hall of Tuthmosis III, and this is the name used on the White Chapel of Sesostris I.

The ancient site covered by the group of Karnak temples was therefore in use from the Eleventh Dynasty until the end of the Roman period and it would almost be possible to write a history of Egypt based on the evidence at Karnak alone. The site consists of three complexes: the temple of Amon-Re Monthu (North Karnak), the temple of Amon-Re itself and the temple of Mut (South Karnak). To these three should also be added the Luxor temple, which was Amun's 'southern harem'.

The enclosure wall of the precinct of Monthu, built of Thirtieth Dynasty mud-bricks as was the wall around the temple of Amon-Re, contained a sacred lake and a sanctuary dedicated to Monthu-Re, from which a dromos leads north to its own quay. The Monthu complex was originally the work of Amenophis III, who reused a building erected by Amenophis II; like most of the Karnak monuments it was enlarged and modified during the Ramessid period. The propylons were added by Taharqa, along with the colonnade, which was rebuilt during the Ptolemaic period. Immediately to the south of the colonnade were two temples, one dedicated to Maat, dating back at least as far as the Eighteenth Dynasty, the other to Harpre, dating to the Kushite period. Near the southern enclosure wall were six chapels of Osiris set up by the Divine Adoratrices.

To the east of the enclosure wall of the precinct of Amon-Re, in line with the east-west axis of the main temple, is the Gempaaten of Akhenaten. This has been totally destroyed and the 'Temple of the *benben* in the Gempaaten' still shows traces of fire. A little to the south of Akhenaten's temple is the temple of 'Khonsu who governs in Thebes', the foundation of which has proved difficult to date. The Berlin Museum possesses blocks of Tuthmosis III that derive from this temple of Khonsu, but the whole monument was extensively restored during the Ptolemaic period. It was there that Champollion found the

Stele of Bakhtan (Louvre, C 284) mentioned above (p. 257). This might confirm the attribution of the original temple to the reign of Tuthmosis III, for Tuthmosis – like the hero of the stele, Ramesses II – was the pioneer of diplomatic links between Egypt and the nations of Asia Minor.

To the south of the precinct of Amon-Re was that of Mut (the second member of the Theban triad), rebuilt under the Emperor Tiberius and extending over an area of some 10 hectares; the precincts of Amon-Re and Mut were linked by a processional way leading from the Tenth Pylon. The main building in the precinct of Mut was the temple, which was surrounded on three sides by the horseshoe-shaped lake of Asheru. The forecourt of the temple contains two statues dedicated to the lioness-goddess Sekhmet by Amenophis III, who founded the temple. The site was originally occupied by a structure attributed to Hatshepsut, from which only a chapel of Amon-Re Kamutef ('Amon-Re bull of his mother') and a bark shrine have survived. The shrine was enlarged and decorated by Sethos II, Taharqa (one of the greatest rebuilders of Karnak) and the Ptolemies. The main temple was devoted to the cult of Mut in her role as mother of Khonsu, the third member of the Theban triad, who had his own temple inside the precinct of Amon-Re. Tuthmosis IV founded a second temple in the precinct of Mut which was not completed until the Kushite period. Judging from depictions of the royal birth in the main court, this sanctuary of 'Khonsu the child' seems to have played a role similar to that of a *mammisi*.

Finally, to the west of the precinct of Amon-Re the only extensions were bark chapels, including one dating to the Greco-Roman period and another belonging to Achoris, which was begun in the reign of Nepherites I.

This rapid overview of the precincts shows how the Karnak complex developed over the centuries, with virtually every ruler contributing some modification or addition to the works of his predecessors until the whole area became a chaotic accumulation of buildings. Modern visitors, entering via the landing stage and the First Pylon, actually move back through time, passing from the later structures towards the most ancient section of the site as they follow the traditional order of the monuments from the First to Sixth Pylons along the east-west axis and the Seventh to Tenth Pylons from north to south. The original sanctuary was located in the area of the 'Middle Kingdom Court' and the temple expanded away from the sanctuary towards the west (i.e. in the direction of the exit) and towards the east, where a solar 'counter-temple' grew up, orientated towards the rising sun. At the same time the north-south processional way was also extended, linking the precincts of Monthu, Amon-Re and Mut. From the reign of Amenophis III onwards, the north-south axis marked out the western edge of the sanctuary and separated it from the new constructions which, generally speaking, were only additions to the approach route of the sacred bark.

Originally the entire temple of Amon-Re was contained within the area between the site of the future Festival Hall of Tuthmosis III and the sanctuary of the sacred bark. It must have included, in addition to the sanctuary itself, two rooms in succession: the minimal components of a temple. This plan does not seem to have evolved properly until the reign of Tuthmosis I who, helped by his architect Inene, began its transformation into a true temple. On the other hand, the temple's appearance in the period before Tuthmosis I is still poorly known. The early bark shrines, reused in the construction of later buildings, suggest that the Middle Kingdom and early New Kingdom complex consisted of a long processional way leading to a landing stage, punctuated by a few way-stations for the bark.

In Inene's Theban tomb at Sheikh Abd el-Qurna (TT 81) there are depictions of the buildings that the architect constructed for his king. According to these paintings Ineni surrounded the Karnak sanctuary with an enclosure wall entered through the Fifth Pylon. The court bounded by this wall was surrounded by a colonnade that may have incorporated Osirid colossal statues. Built of sandstone and embellished with limestone, the Fifth Pylon provided access, via a gate flanked by two flag-poles, to a vast chamber which Ineni himself describes as 'a magnificent hypostyle hall with papyriform columns'. This hypostyle hall between the Fourth and Fifth Pylons had a timber roof and walls lined with royal colossi alternately wearing the crowns of Upper and Lower Egypt. The whole temple was surrounded by a second enclosure wall entered through the Fourth Pylon, of which the base at least was sandstone. In front of the western façade – at that time the main entrance to the temple, decorated with four flag-poles – Tuthmosis I set up two obelisks; only the southern one still stands today. The whole complex constituted the Iput-isut proper, and it may have been the inspiration for the temple of the Aten at el-Amarna.

The second major stage of development at Karnak corresponds to the reigns of Hatshepsut and Tuthmosis III, with the latter defacing or modifying the monuments set up by his step-mother.

Hatshepsut installed offering chambers against the western façade of the sanctuary, preceding them with a resting place for the sacred bark, now known as the Red Chapel. In the sixteenth year of her reign she set up two obelisks of pink Aswan granite coated in electrum, of which only the northern one is still *in situ*. These obelisks stood in front of the Fifth Pylon, in the very midst of Tuthmosis I's hypostyle hall. She placed a sanctuary dedicated to the rising sun and furnished with two

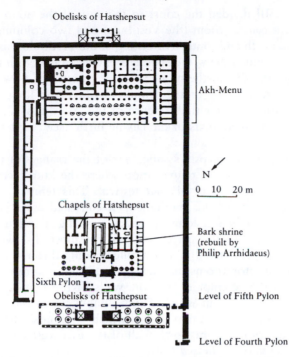

FIGURE 21   *The constructions of Hatshepsut and Tuthmosis III at Karnak.*

obelisks beside Tuthmosis I's eastern enclosure wall, but this was soon replaced by Tuthmosis III's Festival Hall. She probably also undertook the construction of the temple of Mut Lady of Asheru and rebuilt the Eighth Pylon (on the north-south axis) in stone instead of mud-brick.

Tuthmosis III greatly modified the Iput-isut. He enclosed Hatshepsut's two obelisks inside a kind of sandstone coffer, leaving only the points of the obelisks visible, and he linked this structure with the Fifth Pylon in such a way as to create an antechamber between it and the Fourth Pylon. He tripled the size of Tuthmosis I's colonnade and replaced the wooden roof of the hypostyle hall with one of stone.

To the east of the Fifth Pylon he set up a new one, the Sixth, bearing depictions of his triumph at Megiddo. The Sixth Pylon divided the court between the Fifth Pylon and Hatshepsut's chapels, between which he placed a pink granite bark shrine. Although this shrine was later destroyed, Philip Arrhidaeus replaced it with an exact copy that has survived *in situ*. The southern exterior wall of this shrine is decorated with scenes of the dedication of the sanctuary and the procession of the sacred bark.

Tuthmosis III divided the court to the east of the Sixth Pylon into three parts: a central room (the Vestibule) and two colonnaded courts flanking it to north and south. The ceiling of the Vestibule was supported by two pink granite pillars, the southern one decorated with the lotus of Upper Egypt and the northern one with the papyrus of Lower Egypt. It was in this crucial part of the temple – where the king was finally purified in order to enter the presence of the god – that Tuthmosis III inscribed the so-called 'texts of the Divine Birth' (see chapter 9) and his *Annals*.

On the site of Hatshepsut's sanctuary of the rising sun he built his Festival Hall, a temple of rejuvenation where the king received divine power on the occasion of his *sed* festival. This temple, called Akh-menu ('Blessed through his monuments'), consisted essentially of four sections. The first was a long approach, passing along the northern side of the temple in the space between Tuthmosis I's two enclosure walls. The approach ended in a vestibule, leading through an east-west corridor to nine storerooms intended to hold the ornaments and ritual items used in the ceremonies. On the walls of the first six magazines runs a long dedication in which Thoth announces to the assembly of the gods the decree of Amon-Re by which Tuthmosis III was made pharaoh. Depictions on the north wall of the east-west corridor record several moments from the *sed* festival.

The western entrance of the vestibule leads to the second part of the Akh-menu, the actual festival hall; this was a hypostyle hall with thirty-two square pillars along its sides. The architraves of the ceiling in the central 'nave' of the hall, painted blue and sprinkled with golden stars, are supported by two rows of ten columns with '*sed* festival' capitals. These architraves bear the titulature of Tuthmosis III, who is represented on the pillars wearing the crowns of either the North or the South, depending on the pillars' orientation. The southern half of the eastern wall depicts the enthronement of the king. In the south-west corner of the festival hall Tuthmosis III is shown making offerings to his deceased predecessors, in the same way as Sethos I in his temple at Abydos. This is the Hall of the Ancestors – the stele listing previous kings is now in the Louvre and a cast has been put in its place.

In the south-eastern part of the hall, the third section of the Akh-menu was dedicated to the cult of Sokar, including a sanctuary, a bark shrine, a shrine dedicated to Sokar's physical manifestation in the form of a mummified falcon, another shrine for the cult statue and a set of storerooms. Finally, the fourth part of the Akh-menu consisted of two sanctuaries in the north-east corner, one of which was later rebuilt by Alexander; there were also particular rooms dedicated to Amun, including the 'Botanical Garden', the function of which has been described above (p. 214).

Tuthmosis III surrounded these buildings with an enclosure wall that extended Tuthmosis I's wall in the east and duplicated it as far as the Fifth Pylon in the north. They were closed off completely by a second enclosure wall that started at the Fourth Pylon in the south and encircled the temple to join up with the Fifth Pylon in the north, leaving an ambulatory corridor between the two walls. To the east of the outer enclosure wall Tuthmosis III erected on the occasion of his royal jubilee a peripteral counter-temple containing a naos in which Amun was depicted sitting at the king's side and holding him by the shoulder. He created the sacred lake and constructed on the north-south axis the Seventh Pylon, which was also connected with his jubilee. The two faces of the pylon were decorated with traditional scenes of the massacre of enemies from the south and east. Colossi were placed on both sides of the gateway and the two in front of the southern face were preceded by two obelisks, of which only the base of the eastern one has survived. The western obelisk was transported to Constantinople in the reign of Theodosius I, where Proclus erected it in the Hippodrome in AD 390.

Amenophis II also built at Karnak, but it was not until the reigns of Tuthmosis IV and Amenophis III that significant modifications were made to the temple. The late Eighteenth Dynasty rulers did not make any further alterations to the general appearance of the Iput-isut, but each ruler gradually added new buildings to the complex. Most of the later construction work took place in the areas in front of the temple, to the west, on the processional way or in buildings outside the sanctuary itself.

It was Tuthmosis IV who erected the eastern obelisk of Tuthmosis III's counter-temple, calling it the *tekhen waty* ('unique obelisk'). This obelisk finally stood at the heart of the temple in the reign of Ptolemy VIII Euergetes II. At more than 33 metres high, it is the tallest known obelisk, which doubtless explains why Constantius II transported it to the Circus Maximus at Rome in AD 357. It was eventually excavated from the ruins of the Circus Maximus and re-erected by Pope Sixtus V in 1588 at the Piazza San Giovanni in Laterano, and it is now known as the 'Lateran obelisk'.

Tuthmosis IV was the first to build to the west of the Fourth Pylon. In front of the pylon he set up a pillared monument, part of which was later reused by Amenophis III for the construction of the Third Pylon, along with materials from a dozen other monuments. Preceded by a vestibule, this pylon acted as the entrance to the whole temple, judging from its decoration with scenes of the procession of the divine bark. It continued to perform this function until after the Amarna period. Amenophis III closed off the processional way to the temple of Mut by instructing his architect Amenhotpe son of Hapu to build a mud-brick pylon, which Horemheb was later to rebuild in stone.

During the Amarna period the only construction work that took place at Karnak was the building of the temple of the Aten in the eastern part of the site. Activity in the temple of Amon-Re resumed on a small scale during the reign of Tutankhamun, who dedicated the two statues of Amun and Amaunet in the court of the Sixth Pylon and perhaps several of the criosphinxes along the processional entrance-way. Horemheb, however, made some important changes, building three of the ten pylons and lining the avenue between the Tenth Pylon and the temple of Mut with criosphinxes.

On the north-south axis Horemheb closed off the court to the south of the Eighth Pylon with two sandstone walls and a new pylon (the Ninth). He replaced the mud-brick pylon to the south with the Tenth Pylon, and at its foot he erected the so-called 'Restoration Stele', which was inscribed with a decree intended to restore order to the country after the Amarna period.

The construction of the Second Pylon was begun by Horemheb and finished by Ramesses I; the decoration of its gateway did not take place until the reign of Ptolemy VIII Euergetes II. Horemheb placed this pylon at the end of a double row of seven campaniform columns, each reaching a height of more than 22 metres. The first twelve of these would form the central aisle of the future Great Hypostyle Hall (E). The two remaining columns, furthest to the west, were incorporated into the Second Pylon.

Horemheb's pylons gave the temple a general appearance that was already close to its present arrangement. Above all, the construction of the new pylons led directly to the disappearance of most of Amenophis IV's monuments, for the *talatat* blocks were reused as rubble to fill the Second and Ninth Pylons. The constructions of the heretic pharaoh may no longer have been a visible part of the monument but they were no more effectively destroyed than the other monuments that were reused as building materials – by their recycling as rubble the reliefs and decorations on the blocks were preserved even if they could no longer be seen. The *damnatio memoriae* was directed at the buildings set up by Akhenaten – who had been found guilty of blasphemy against Amun and the established order – rather than at the god Aten himself.

Sethos I provided the temple with one of its most spectacular components: the Hypostyle Hall, known as 'The temple of Sethos-Merneptah is shining in the Abode of Amun', the decoration of which was completed by Ramesses II.

Twice as wide as it is high, the Hypostyle Hall (Plate 21) consists of two sets of sixty-one columns, each split into seven rows on either side of the central aisle of twelve campaniform columns. The crucial difference in height of almost six metres between the central aisle

PLATE 21 *Detail of the Hypostyle Hall at the Temple of Amun, Karnak.*
(Photograph: © John Stevens/Ancient Art & Architecture Collection.)

and the rest of the columns meant that clerestory windows could be incorporated, thus allowing a dim light to diffuse over both sides of the aisle. The hall has two axes: the main temple axis and another at right angles to it leading to gates in the north and the south walls. It was built on top of a mound left by Amenophis III; the columns of the side aisles were raised on piles arranged under thick paving and built on top of a two-metre-high heap of *talatat* blocks, separated by a layer of beaten earth and marl.

The southern part of the hall, which Ramesses II decorated with sunken reliefs, functioned as a court in which the king was prepared for his purification. In the northern part (the *per-dwat*), he put on

the sacerdotal ornaments and received final purification before entering
the main temple. This ritual transition was reflected in the internal
decoration of the hall: in the first section were scenes of the temple
foundation, processions and the introduction of the king to the god,
while in the second section there were offering scenes. The outer faces
of the walls – those which would have been visible to the 'faithful' –
were decorated, as at Medinet Habu, with scenes from military campaigns. Those of Sethos I against Syria-Palestine adorned the eastern
part of the northern wall, while those against the Libyans and Hittites
covered the west; the battles of Ramesses II decorated the southern
wall, with Palestine at the west and Qadesh to the east. Each campaign
ended with the presentation of spoils to the Theban triad near the
northern and southern gates, which acted as pylons.

The construction of the Hypostyle Hall shows the particular stage
that had been reached in the development of the temple: the point of
contace with the outside world had been moved further to the west so
as to provide access to all of the buildings surrounded by the enclosure
wall of Tuthmosis III – which might be described as the 'extended' Iput-
isut – as well as everything beyond the Third Pylon, i.e. the processional
way and the eastern sanctuaries. The next stage in the temple's history
consisted of no more than the building of the entrance-way in front of
the Second Pylon; in the reign of Ramesses II this comprised a *dromos*
of criosphinxes known as 'the way of the rams', leading down to the
quay at which the divine bark landed, via a canal from the Nile. Sethos
II placed two obelisks on either side of the quay and set up a bark
shrine in front of the Second Pylon to serve the members of the Theban
triad. Ramesses III built another such shrine further to the east and on
the other side of the east-west axis; this was a scaled-down version
of a temple, including its own pylon preceded by royal colossi, a
peristyle court, a hypostyle hall and a sanctuary. The exterior walls
were decorated with scenes of the procession of divine barks towards
Luxor in the Festival of Opet.

Shoshenq I built two porticoes along the northern and southern sides
of the open area, which would eventually be the court of the First
Pylon (D), and also closed off the western side of the area with a portal
that was replaced by that pylon. At the same time he repositioned the
avenue of criosphinxes along the northern and southern sides of the
new court, in front of the porticoes. In the Twenty-fifth Dynasty Taharqa
built a kiosk in front of the vestibule of the Second Pylon, thus reviving the idea of the colonnade of Amenophis III; but the columns of
Taharqa's kiosk were eventually joined together by stone screens in the
reign of Ptolemy IV Philopator.

The main enclosure walls were restored by Mentuemhet in Taharqa's reign but the present walls, as well as the First Pylon (which is still unfinished), date to the Thirtieth Dynasty. The enclosure walls, about 12 metres thick and 25 metres high, make up a perimeter of 480 × 550 metres. They are built of mud-bricks which are alternatively convex and concave, imitating the undulations of the waters of Nun at the edges of the universe. The temple itself represents the universe and the original place of creation. The five gates piercing the enclosure walls each mark a point of contact with the waves of Nun. The gates allowed the rising sun to pass through to his temple, Monthu to reach his temple in the north, Mut to reach hers in the south and Amon-Re to pass through on his way to the Luxor temple.

The development of the Karnak temple complex was not limited to the magnificent lines of the east-west axis. There was also the temple of Ptah 'to the south of his wall', against the inner face of the northern enclosure wall (U). Built by Tuthmosis III on the site of an earlier mud-brick sanctuary, it was reconstructed during the Ptolemaic period. There were the eastern sanctuaries of Amon-Re Horakhty, which were given their final definitive appearance by Ramesses II, as well as the area of the sacred lake (R), beside the crossing of the two temple axes; here Taharqa set up a monument dedicated to the cult of Khepri, the sacred scarab, alongside a colossal statue of the scarab.

The temple of Khonsu was reconstructed by Ramesses III on top of an earlier installation of Amenophis III. This temple was extended by subsequent kings from Ramesses IV to Ramesses XII and was partly decorated by Herihor at his peak. During the first millennium BC the temple of Khonsu continued to grow: another kiosk of Taharqa was built in front of the pylon decorated by Pinudjem; then there was a monumental gateway, Bab el-Amara (K), decorated by Ptolemy III Euergetes I and standing at the end of an avenue of criosphinxes dating to the reign of Amenophis III.

A chapel dedicated to Opet, immediately to the west of the temple of Khonsu, was transformed into a temple in the Kushite period but its decoration was not completed until the reign of the Emperor Augustus. It was originally devoted solely to the cult of Opet but it gradually became the palace of Osiris as well; this change in use is indicative of the rise of the cult of Osiris from the Twenty-second Dynasty onwards. The northern sector of the precinct of Amun was full of chapels to Osiris from the time of the priest-kings (*c.*1080-945 BC) to the reign of Tiberius (AD 14–37).

In practice, the great building works at Karnak ended with the rulers of the Thirtieth Dynasty, but there was no subsequent king who did not in some way contribute to the embellishment or maintenance of one monument or another. These contributions included not only construction and decoration but also dismantling. By sheer weight of accumulated builings the complex must have become almost unusable in certain areas, particularly in the processional ways. It was therefore decided, during the Ptolemaic period, to bury under the court of the Eighth Pylon some of the sculptural pieces that had become either troublesome bric-à-brac or tempting prey for robbers. Georges Legrain was fortunate enough to rediscover this 'cachette', and between 1903 and 1905 he uncovered more than 800 statues, monuments and stelae, as well as 17,000 bronzes spread around the court. These precious objects included sphinxes (one of Amenophis I), statues of Senenmut, a *clepsydra* (water-clock) of Amenophis III, some pillars of Sesostris I, blocks from a jubilee chapel of Amenophis I as well as a limestone gateway bearing his name and some blocks from shrines. It is possible to deduce from the places where these items were buried at least the rough area in which they must originally have stood (Barguet 1962: 277ff.). In 1989 a much smaller cachette of sculpture was found under the peristyle court of the Luxor temple. Sixteen of the twenty-six Luxor sculptures, including a magnificent quartzite statue of Amenophis III, are now displayed in the Luxor Museum.

These cachettes provide a strong impression of the enormous wealth possessed by the estates of Amun and the power of the priests who were eventually to seize control from Ramesses XI. Compared with the pharaohs, the priests themselves made very little contribution to the building and decoration of the temple, but they are nevertheless very much in evidence. The excavation of the houses they occupied to the east of the sacred lake should provide valuable information concerning the poorly documented Third Intermediate Period (Anus and Saad 1971).

Part IV

The Final Phase

13

The Third Intermediate Period

SMENDES AND PINUDJEM

Smendes proclaimed himself king after the death of Ramesses XI. He effectively declared himself the heir of the Ramessid line through the set of titles that he adopted: his Horus name was 'Powerful bull beloved by Ra, whose arm is strengthened by Amun so that he may exalt Maat'. His origins are unknown and the familial links which he claimed to have with Herihor seem unlikely – it is more probable that he legitimized his power by marrying a daughter of Ramesses XI.

His coronation marked the final demise of the 'Renaissance' and – strange though it may seem, given his apparent lack of royal blood – his authority was openly acknowledged in Thebes. It was Smendes who reconstructed part of the enclosure wall of the Karnak temple, which had been damaged by a Nile flood. He transferred the capital from Piramesse to Tanis, where the excavations of Philippe Brissaud during the 1980s suggest a Ramessid community had already been established, probably as a result of the movement of the Pelusiac branch of the Nile (Yoyotte 1987: 56). Smendes also resided at Memphis, and it was from there that he odered a new programme of building activity in the Luxor temple. It is possible that he was consciously reinstating Memphis as primary political centre and royal residence, but it is actually more likely that he was simply based there while the buildings at Tanis were being constructed, since it was at Tanis that he was buried after a reign of just over twenty-five years.

At the same time as Smendes was proclaimed king, the office of high priest of Amun changed hands for the second time since Herihor. By the twenty-fifth year of the reign of Ramesses XI (c.1074 BC) Piankh had taken over from Herihor. His origins were as obscure as those of his predecessor, who may have been his father-in-law (Kitchen 1986: 536)

TABLE 7   *The royal family tree of the Twenty-first Dynasty.*

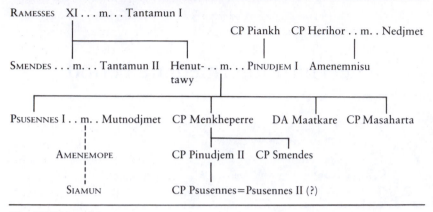

CP – Chief Priest of Amun
DA – Divine Adoratrice

and from whom he inherited the command of the armies of Upper
Egypt. His subsequent attempt to gain control of Nubia was apparently
unsuccessful, since he was still engaged in war against Panehsy's 'rebels'
in the twenty-eighth year of Ramesses XI's reign. Unlike Herihor,
Piankh managed to leave behind an heir: in 1070 BC his son Pinudjem
succeeded him as high priest of Amun and commander-in-chief of the
armies of Upper Egypt. These offices remained in Pinudjem I's titulature
throughout the reign of Smendes, whose authority he recognized, since
he did not assume the royal right of dating events with reference to his
own years of office any more than Herihor had. When he supervised
the reburial of the royal mummies, for instance, he dated the affair to
the years six through fifteen of Smendes' reign. During this period the
domain of the high priest included Medinet Habu, Karnak and Luxor
and the limits of his power extended as far as el-Hiba and Aswan.

In the sixteenth year of the reign of Smendes, Pinudjem adopted a set
of royal titles that clearly spelled out the Theban origins of his power:
his Horus name was 'Powerful bull, crowned in Thebes and beloved of
Amun'. From this point on his name was written in a cartouche and is
found in inscriptions at Thebes, Koptos, Abydos and even Tanis. He
still did not date events according to the years of his own reign,
however, even though he had now passed on the office of high priest
firstly to his son Masaharta and then, in 1045 BC, to another son,
Menkheperre. What then was the basis of Pinudjem's power, with
which he blatantly usurped the authority of the pharaoh and established

his own independent rule? The underlying reason for his assumption of royal prerogatives lay in the long history of interaction between the secular and religious spheres: in return for providing political support to the pharaohs, the Theban priesthood had grown in power during the Eighteenth Dynasty, benefiting particularly from the spoils of Egypt's imperial conquests. Hatshepsut traced her legitimacy, as did Tuthmosis III and Tuthmosis IV, back to the god Amun himself, who supported the pharaohs with appearances or oracles proclaiming their right to rule.

It was this religious ascendancy that Amenophis IV had sought to contest, although he had not actually changed the theocratic basis of his power, contenting himself with the subversion of Amun. The main outcome of Akhenaten's 'heresy', however, was the gradual evolution of a theological response to the problem during the Ramessid period. This response particularly centred on the role of the God's Wife of Amun, which was played by a royal princess from the time of Ahmose-Nefertari onwards. This role served to reinforce, to some degree, the link between the king and the god who appointed him. As the incestuous wife of the god and perhaps also of the king, the God's Wife was the king's representative in the performance of the god's cult. This association was a feature of royal couples from Amenophis III onwards, with the establishment of a strict correspondence between the royal and divine family in the reign of Akhenaten. Ramesses II systematized this procedure by ensuring that his wife received a parallel cult alongside his own at Abu Simbel. When Herihor inaugurated the 'Rennaissance' the main unresolved question was: who was to be the earthly counterpart of the divine family? This role could only be performed by the royal family, who were the only legitimate heirs of the god. It was therefore necessary to separate the temporal power of Amun, which the high priest claimed for himself, from the power of the pharaoh, which was accorded by Amun but quite distinct from that of the high priest. This division of power conveniently served to obscure the reality that the priesthood of Amun had gained a grip over Upper Egypt which the pharaoh was no longer able to control. The policy of the high priests of Amun appeared to be aimed at the maintenance of the pharaoh's power by subjecting him to the will of Amun, which was expressed in the form of oracles. Tanis was therefore built in the image of Thebes, in order to establish an exact correspondence between the Theban and Tanite aspects of Amun.

These parallels were further developed in the Kushite period (the Twenty-fifth Dynasty), with the correlation between the Theban and Napatan aspects of Amun. It is therefore perfectly logical that Pinudjem I should be attested at Tanis. On the other hand, Pinudjem married

Henuttawy, who was of royal blood, with the aim of preserving the practical reality of his power. By her he had four children: the next pharaoh Psusennes I, Masaharta and Menkheperre, the successive high priests of Amun, and a daughter called Maatkare, who combined the roles of God's Wife and chief of the priestesses of Amun in one title: 'Divine Adoratrice', sole wife of the god. She was allowed to choose her successor by adoption, thus avoiding the the inherent difficulties of passing on the office (Gitton 1984: 113–14). As divine mother she was doubly incarnate: both in the form of the Divine Adoratrice, incestuous mother of the god-child, and in the person of the king's wife and therefore the natural mother of his successor.

This system of secular and religious power was not officially introduced until the death of Smendes. In the brief period between his death and the coronation of Psusennes I the country was effectively split into two parts, ruled by the high priest and the pharaoh respectively, with the former expressing the will of Amun that enabled the latter to exercise royal power. This new political situation formed the background to the *Tale of Wenamun* (Papylus Moscow 120, Pushkin Museum of Fine Arts), which relates the story of an ambassador sent to Phoenicia to bring back a consignment of wood for the construction of the sacred bark of the Theban Amun. The story is set at the end of the reign of Ramesses XI, but Smendes is not mentioned as regent. The time when Egypt was a respected force in the Near East was long past: not only did Wenamun have to pay for the wood but he was robbed en route to Byblos and it was only after a certain amount of sordid haggling that the prince of Byblos agreed to supply the wood. Even then the wood was only obtained at a considerable price (Leclant 1987: 77ff.). Until the reign of Siamun, Egypt does not seem to have played any role in the regions which had once been traditionally subject to its influence. The chief political role had been bequeathed to Israel, ruled first by Saul and then, from 1010 to 970 BC, by David, who established Jerusalem as the capital. It seems likely that Egypt simply maintained adequate policing of its eastern frontier during the reign of Psusennes I (Kitchen 1986: 267).

When Smendes died, power was split between two co-regents: Neferkare Amenemnisu ('Amun is the king'), who was probably a son of Herihor (Kitchen 1986: 540), and Psusennes I, who reigned until his death in 993 BC. Amenemnisu was already on the political scene in the early years of the Theban pontificate of Menkheperre. He faced the final after-effects of the civil war, which had engulfed Thebes as a result of the growing power of the chief priests. Amenemnisu exiled his opponents to the oases of the Western Desert, which must then have been more or less under the control of the Libyan chiefs, then he pardoned them under an oracular decree of Amun, recorded on a stele (Louvre C 256). This pardon marked the beginning of concessions made by the kings to the great families of the Theban priesthood; these families would have been shocked to see their privileges usurped by the descendants of Herihor, who – to make matters worse – were only Libyan immigrants. This wish for appeasement is clear from the fact that during the rule of Pinudjem II, the chief priest's family no longer fulfilled priestly duties as they had in the time of Pinudjem I. Nevertheless, their women were awarded powers which, when combined with the territory already held by their parents, must have represented control of about a third of the land in Upper Egypt (Kitchen 1986: 275–7). The large degree of appeasement for which Menkheperre (1045–992 BC) was responsible seems to have resulted in a restoration of the peace, indicated by the fact that items of royal funerary equipment (salvaged from the pillaging of royal tombs in the Theban region) were sent to Tanis for the use of the Twenty-first Dynasty pharaohs.

THEBES AND TANIS

Between 1040 and 1039 BC, Psusennes I (whose name means 'The star appearing in the city') succeeded in securing in his own person the religious and political synthesis of the country. He clearly emphasized his Theban heritage: his Horus name was 'Powerful bull crowned at Thebes' and his Two Ladies name was 'Great builder in Karnak'. It is known that in the fortieth year of Psusennes I's reign the chief priest Menkheperre inspected the temples at Karnak, and that an enclosure wall was built to the north of the Temple of Amun eight years later in order to protect them from the encroachment of private housing. The same measure was probably taken at Luxor at about the same time. Psusennes I also strengthened his links with the priesthood of Amun by marrying his daughter Istemkheb to the chief priest Menkheperre. Like his successors, Psusennes himself was chief priest of Amun at Tanis, but he also traced his succession back to Ramesses XI by renaming himself 'Ramesses-Psusennes'.

At Tanis, Psusennes I built a new enclosure around the temple dedicated to the triad of Amun, Mut and Khonsu. If the few traces of reuse of earlier monuments are to be believed, he made many other contributions to the temple, but because of the current condition of the site little is known concerning this work. Neither is there much indication of the part played by Psusennes in the construction of the town of Tanis, which has still not been properly excavated.

The site of Tanis was discovered by Flinders Petrie at the end of the nineteenth century. Since then it has been connected not only with

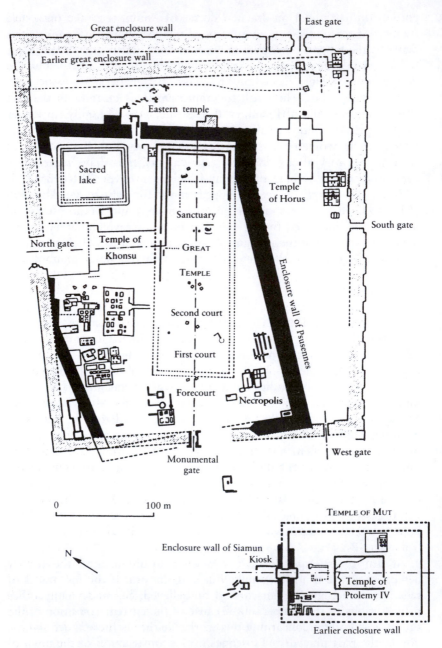

Great enclosure wall

East gate

Earlier great enclosure wall

Eastern temple

Sacred lake

Temple of Horus

South gate

Sanctuary

GREAT

Temple of

TEMPLE

North gate

Khonsu

Second court

Enclosure wall of Psusennes

First court

Forecourt

Necropolis

West gate

Monumental gate

0   100 m

N

TEMPLE OF MUT

Enclosure wall of Siamun

Kiosk

Temple of Ptolemy IV

Earlier enclosure wall

FIGURE 22   *General plan of Tanis (after plan by A. Lezine, 1951).*

Avaris, the capital of the Hyksos kings (on the basis of the numerous surviving monuments of that period), but also with Piramesse, since Ramesses II is frequently represented at the site. The principal excavator of Tanis was Pierre Montet, who worked there from 1929 to 1940 and from 1946 to 1951. He was a keen advocate of the city's association with both Avaris and Piramesse, despite the fact that his discoveries essentially derived from later periods. The current Tanis excavations, which have been directed since the late 1960s by Jean Yoyotte and since the 1980s by Philippe Brissaud, have concentrated mainly on stratigraphic analysis of the tell on which the site was built, revealing evidence of occupation in the Ramessid period (Yoyotte 1987: 25–49).

The historical interpretation of Tanis is by no means simple. Although Hyksos and Ramessid monuments have certainly survived, virtually all limestone buildings at the site have been destroyed by lime-burners. However, the discovery of foundation deposits proves that Psusennes I built the enclosure wall and the central part of the Great Temple. The monumental eastern gate and the main parts of the buildings dedicated to Amun have been dated to the Twenty-second Dynasty. The same date applies to the temple of Khonsu, which was located to the north of the temple of Amun and at right angles to it. Nothing remains of the actual buildings of Psusennes I – only a few blocks from additions made by Shoshenq V, which were later reused in the masonry of the nearby sacred lake. Also lost is the temple of Mut, established in the south of the site probably in the time of Psusennes I, who would have been attempting in this way to increase Tanis' parallels with Karnak. No more than a few traces of the original phase of the temple have been preserved, though there are some traces of its rebuilt phase.

The works of the Thirtieth Dynasty pharaohs (who were important builders both at Karnak and Tanis) as well as the achievements of the Ptolemaic period all contributed to the obfuscation of the buildings erected by the original founders of the temples at Tanis. The site was completely transformed by the rebuilding of the three temples and the temple of Horus of Mesen (to which Siamun made additions).

Psusennes I built a tomb for himself to the south-west of the enclosure wall, and it was there that Montet found the mummies and funerary equipment of both Psusennes and his wife Mutnedjmet. A tomb had also been prepared for the crown prince Ankhefenmut and for a high official called Wen-djeba-en-Djed, who was appointed both to high religious offices and to the post of commander-in-chief of the armies. For some obscure reason, Psusennes I's successor, Amenemope, was buried in the tomb intended for Mutnodjmet rather than in the one prepared for himself. Osorkon I later buried Hekakheperre Shoshenq II in this same tomb. Nearby, Montet found the tombs of Osorkon II and his son Hornakht, as well as that of Shoshenq III (which also contained the remains of Shoshenq I). These partly-pillaged tombs have helped to shed new light on the history of the Tanite kings.

The transferral of power took place at about the same time in both Thebes and Tanis. It is clear that Smendes II succeeded his father Menkheperre as Theban chief priest before the death of Psusennes I, since Smendes II sent a pair of bracelets to Psusennes on the occasion of his father's death, and these were eventually discovered by Montet among Psusennes' funerary equipment. Smendes II was probably already quite old when he assumed the office of chief priest of Amun at Thebes, for he passed on the post to his young son Pinudjem II after a period of only two years. At Tanis Amenemope succeeded Psusennes I, who may have been his father. Amenemope reigned for almost ten years, and the fact that his tomb was not as rich as that of his predecessor may be an indication that he was less powerful, although his reign was still uncontested at Thebes. His successor, Aakheperre Setepenre, who was probably the first Osorkon (Manetho's Osochor, now usually known as 'Osorkon the Elder'), is poorly known, but the next king, Siamun, is one of the most well-known figures of the Twenty-first Dynasty. This is despite the fact that Siamun's reign was marked by the last great phase of looting in the Theban necropolis, which led the chief priest of Amun to reinter the royal mummies in the tomb of Inhapy. Siamun built extensively at Tanis, doubling the size of the temple of Amun and undertaking various works in the temple of Horus of Mesen; he also transferred the remains of Amenemope to the tomb of Mutnedjmet. He built at Heliopolis and perhaps also at Piramesse (now Qantir), where a surviving block bears his name. More interestingly, a temple dedicated to a secondary aspect of Amun was built during his reign at Memphis. This temple was an example of the same kind of classic craftsmanship as the small bronze sphinx inlaid with gold, which bears the features of Siamun (Louvre E 3914; Yoyotte et al. 1987: 164–5). He also bestowed favours on the Memphite priesthood of Ptah, but his activities were limited to Lower Egypt and he appeared only eponymously on a few Theban monuments.

During the reign of Siamun, Egypt reverted to a more dynamic foreign policy. Indeed, there is no surviving Egyptian evidence for the foreign policy of the earlier Twenty-first Dynasty kings, presumably because they had none – there had evidently been no improvement on the situation described in the *Tale of Wenamun*. The main non-Egyptian source available is the Bible. The period from the end of the reign of Psusennes I to the middle of the reign of Siamun corresponds with the time of David's uniting of the tribes of Israel around the kingdom of Jerusalem and their war with the Philistines. The Egyptians only became involved in a very indirect way at the beginning of these struggles, when they provided sanctuary for Hadad, the crown prince of Edom, whose kingdom had been conquered by David (Schulman 1986). Hadad married an Egyptian princess and his son Genubath was brought up at the Egyptian royal court. When David died, Hadad returned to his kingdom. It can therefore at most be deduced that Egypt maintained certain historic links with her old vassals.

When Solomon succeeded David on the throne, Egypt intervened against the Philistines by capturing and laying waste the city of Gezer. This campaign is recorded in the Old Testament (*I Kings* 9: 16) and was perhaps also illustrated by a relief found at Tanis, showing a scene of ritual massacre of enemies (Kitchen 1986: 281). The reason for this interference was probably commercial in nature: the Philistines were endangering the Egyptians' trade with Phoenicia. Siamun was clearly taking immediate advantage of the Philistines' relative weakness after the wars waged against them by David and the period of uncertainty occasioned by the accession of Solomon in Israel. He therefore made his move before the awesome military strength of the troops gathered together by David could crush the Philistines themselves, thus imposing their own conditions on the Egyptian merchants. This new alliance between Egypt and Israel, by which Egypt safeguarded its commercial outlet and Israel ensured the security of its southern border, was consecrated by a marriage. It was a sign of the times, however, that the union this time took a form new to the Egyptians – it was Solomon who married an Egyptian princess, thus inaugurating a tradition of non-royal marriages for the princesses of the Nile valley.

The family relationships between Siamun, Amenemope and Osorkon the Elder are not clearly known. Nor is there definite evidence concerning the links between Siamun and his successor Psusennes II; it is not even possible to determine whether Psusennes II is the same person as the Theban chief priest Psusennes, who succeeded Pinudjem II in this office. If this were indeed the case, it would be necessary to argue that Siamun had died without issue. Probably related by marriage to the royal family, Psusennes II was the last ruler of the Twenty-first Dynasty, which may eventually have been reduced to destitution at Tanis (Yoyotte 1987: 64; but see also Dodson 1987d: 54). With his death the throne passed to the line of Great Chiefs of the Meshwesh, whose period of ascendancy began with the reign of Shoshenq the Elder. This was the beginning of the Libyan domination.

THE LIBYANS

When Shoshenq I came to the throne he was already the most powerful figure in the land, being commander-in-chief of all the armies and advisor to king Psusennes II (who was also his father-in-law, since he

Dates BC	Egypt	Palestine		Phoenicia
1098–1069	Ramesses XI	Gideon		
1069–1043	Smendes	Jephtha		
		Samson		
1043–1039	Amenemnisu			
1039–993	Psusennes I	Samuel		
		Saul		
		David		
				Ahiram
993–984	Amenemope			
984–978	Osorkon the Elder			Itobaal
978–959	Siamun	Solomon		
959–945	Psusennes II			
945–924	Shoshenq I	*Judah*	*Israel*	Abibaal
		Rehoboam	Jeroboam I	
924–889	Osorkon I	Abijah	Nadab	Yehimilk
		Asa	Baasa	
890–889	Shoshenq II			Elibaal
889–874	Takelot I		Ela	Shipitbaal
			Zimri Omri	
874–850	Osorkon II	Jehoshaphat	Ahab	
			Ochosias	Battle of Qasqar
850–825	Takelot II	Joram	Joram	
		Ochosias	Jehu	
		Athalie		
		Joash		
825–773	Shoshenq III			
	Pedubastis I		Joachaz	
	Osorkon III			
		Amasias	Joash	
773–767	Pimay	Osias	Jeroboam II	
	Takelot III			
767–730	Shoshenq V			
	Rudamon			

Syria	Assyria	Babylonia	Anatolia
	Tiglath-Pileser I	Enlil-nadin-apli	Beginning of the
		Marduk-nadin-ahhe	colonization
		Marduk-shapik-zeri	of Anatolia by
Neo-Hittite	Asharid-apal-Ekur	Adad-apla-iddina	Dorians,
Kingdoms	Assur-bel-kala		Ionians and
	Shamsi-Adad IV		Aeolians
Aramaeans	Ashurnasirpal I	Marduk-zer-X	
	Shalmaneser II	Nabu-shum-libur	
	Assur-Nirari IV	Simbar-shipak	
	Assur-Rabi II		
Hadadezer		Eulma-shakin-shumi	
		Mar-biti-apla-usur	
Hiram	Assur-Resh-ishi II	Nabu-mukin-apli	
	Tiglath-Pileser II		
		Ninurta-kudurri-usur	
		Mar-biti-ahhe-iddina	
	Assur-dan II		
	Adad-Nirari II	Shamash-mudammiq	
	Tukulti-Ninurta II	Nabu-shuma-ukin	
	Ashurnasirpal II	Nabu-apla-iddina	
Ben-Hadad I			
	Shalmaneser III	Marduk-zakir-Shumi I	*Urartu*
			Arame
Hazael			
			Sardur I
	Shamsi-Adad V	Marduk-balassu-iqbi	Ishpuini
		Baba-aha-iddina	
Ben-Hadad II	Adad-Nirari III	Ninurta-apla-X	Menua
		Marduk-bel-zeri	Argishti I
	Shalmaneser IV	Marduk-apla-usur	
	Assur-dan III	Eriba-Marduk	Sardur II
	Assur-Nirari V	Nabu-shuma-ishkun	

had married his daughter Maatkare). He inaugurated the new era of the Libyan chiefs, who were to restore Egypt to a position of power unknown since the time of Ramesses III. This situation was to last for several generations, until the dynasty wiped itself out with a succession of internal struggles that beset the country from the beginning of the reign of Shoshenq III. Shoshenq I immediately sought to prove that his claim to the throne went back to the preceding dynasty, and did so by adopting a set of titles based on those of Smendes I. Shoshenq was actually a native of a Libyan chiefdom based at Bubastis – a fact which the Theban annals of the priests of Amun point out, describing him as 'Great Chief of the Ma (Meshwesh)', and thereby showing an evident reluctance to recognize his authority.

Shoshenq I maintained the same policy as Pinudjem I, by appointing his son Iuput simultaneously to the offices of chief priest of Amun, commander-in-chief of the armies and governor of Upper Egypt; the combination of the three roles provided the essential link between the temporal and spiritual worlds. He was assisted by at least one other son(?), Djedptahefankh, acting in the role of third prophet of Amun, and Nesy, the chief of an allied Libyan tribe, as fourth prophet of Amun. He also established a policy of alliances through marriage, giving one of his daughters to Djedthutefankh, the successor of Djedptahefankh. This and other marriages strengthened relations between the two powers, although they did not prevent the prudent Shoshenq I from cultivating an alternative power base in Middle Egypt: he appointed his other son, Nimlot, as military commander of Herakleopolis, which was more than ever fulfilling its strategic role of controlling exchanges between the northern and southern kingdoms.

After his return from a victorious campaign into Palestine in 925 BC, the king undertook an ambitious building programme in the temple of Amon-Re at Karnak. He recounted the details of this programme on a stele set up on the occasion of the reopening of the Gebel el-Silsila quarries in 924 BC. His son, the chief priest Iuput, was in charge of the building works – he constructed the court in front of the Second Pylon at Karnak (see chapter 12 above). On the outer wall of the gateway to the south of the new court he depicted Egypt's victory over the two Jewish kingdoms of Judah and Israel; the same event was also described on a triumphal stele displayed in the Iput-isut, near Tuthmosis III's *Annals*. This apparent re-establishment of Egyptian pre-eminence was not mere boastfulness: the 'festival hall' built by Shoshenq I for Amun is an indication of a spectacular revival of Egypt's influence within the Near East as a whole.

Shoshenq I continued to follow the spirit of Siamun's foreign policy by renewing links with Byblos, the traditional commercial outlet for

Egyptian trade; a statue of Shoshenq I set up by King Abibaal in the sanctuary of the goddess Baalat-Gebal is perhaps an indication of economic rather than military ties. On the other hand, relations with the kingdom of Jerusalem went into decline, and the two states became open rivals at about the time when Solomon's power was weakened by the rebellion of Jeroboam (to whom the prophet Ahiyya had promised the kingdom of Israel). Shoshenq I provided a safe haven for Jeroboam until the death of Solomon (*I Kings* 14: 25) in about 930 BC. Jeroboam then reassembled his followers and established the independent kingdom of Israel. The kingdom of Judah – the other half of Solomon's domain – was ruled by Rehoboam, Solomon's heir. In 925 BC, with Hebrew military strength thus divided between Samaria and Jerusalem, Shoshenq I seized the opportunity (under the pretext of dealing with the bedouin in the region of the Bitter Lakes) to launch an attack on Jerusalem. Setting out from Gaza, he penetrated some distance into the Negev, capturing the principal towns of Judah and drawing up his forces opposite Jerusalem; at this point Rehoboam surrendered and handed over all of Solomon's treasure except for the Ark of the Covenant (Yoyotte 1987: 66). From there Shoshenq I moved on to Israel, by which time Jeroboam, belatedly recognizing the political ambitions of his former protector, had fled over the River Jordan. A military patrol captured him and carried on the campaign as far as Be(th)-shan. The Egyptian advance finally came to a halt at Megiddo, where Shoshenq set up a commemorative stele. He then marched south-wards over Mount Carmel and returned via Ashkelon and Gaza – Egypt had once more regained the suzerainty of Syria-Palestine.

In the twenty-eighth year of the reign of Osorkon I (*c*.897 BC), a Kushite general named Zerah led a campaign against the kingdom of Judah (*II Chronicles* 14: 8–15). The date of this expedition has been deduced from the known synchronization between Osorkon's reign and that of Asa, the king of Judah, in the fourteenth year of whose reign the invading Egyptians were defeated and driven out of Judah. If Zerah is to be identified with an otherwise unknown general sent by Osorkon I (Kitchen 1986: 309), then this ill-fated expedition would indicate the demise of an ambitious Egyptian foreign policy that was only to reappear briefly under Osorkon II. The situation probably did not amount to anything more than a loss of suzerainty over Judah, since Elibaal, the prince of Byblos, is known to have dedicated a statue to Osorkon I in the sanctuary of Baalat-Gebal (Yoyotte et al. 1987: 166).

In the early years of his reign, Osorkon I retained his father's policy with regard to the priesthood. He displayed great largesse towards the chief priests at Memphis, Heliopolis, Hermopolis and Karnak, as well as his native town of Bubastis, where he built – or perhaps rebuilt – the temples of Atum and Bastet (the town's own goddess). He also ensured that his father's control over Herakleopolis was maintained by resuming work on the temple of el-Hiba and on the temple of Isis at Atfih. He founded a military camp to control traffic into the Faiyum, and there is also evidence of his activities at Koptos and Abydos.

At Karnak, Osorkon I took the post of chief priest of Amun away from his brother Iuput, giving it instead to one of his own sons, Shoshenq, whom he appointed as co-regent in about 890 BC. This act reinforced the legitimacy of his new royal line, since the future Shoshenq II was also a grandson of Psusennes II through his mother Maatkare. Unfortunately, although Shoshenq II pursued a brilliant career as a chief priest he was denied the chance to rule in his own right, since he died before his father at the age of about fifty while still only co-regent. Having buried his son at Tanis, Osorkon I outlived him by only a few months, leaving the throne to Takelot I, his son by a secondary wife. Although Takelot reigned from 889 to 874 BC, not a single monument can be attributed to him. His authority does not seem to have been respected by his own son, Iuwelot, who took over the post of chief priest at Thebes. Takelot I's name does not even seem to have been recorded in Theban documents and it appears that the northward spread of Iuwelot's domain was impeded only by the military garrison that had been established by Osorkon I in the vicinity of Herakleopolis.

Gradually, the state of relative equilibrium established by the first Tanite kings (the Twenty-first Dynasty) and continued by the Bubastite kings (the Twenty-second Dynasty), was beginning to deteriorate. The system of prerogatives and marriage-alliances, specifically designed to unite the rulers of the north and the south, was beginning to break up; the establishment of local 'prebends' allowed the provincial regimes to become more and more independent, reviving the old separatist tendencies. The game of alliances and unification seems to have become increasingly difficult to maintain by the time that two grandsons of Osorkon I, the cousins Osorkon II and Harsiese, reigned simultaneously.

Osorkon II's principal mistake was to cede to Harsiese – however indirectly – the right to succeed his father (Shoshenq II) as the chief priest of Amun: he thus created a dangerous precedent of hereditary transmission of power, the greatest risk to which the long-observed policy of equilibrium could be exposed. Thanks to him, Harsiese was led to expect a career comparable to that of his father, with the result that he declared himself king after the fourth year of his cousin's reign. He adopted a set of titles that established him as a new Pinudjem I, with a Horus name describing himself as 'Powerful bull crowned at Thebes'. Meanwhile, Osorkon II's titles harked back instead to Shoshenq I and his Horus name incorporated an epithet of Ramesses II: 'He whom Ra has crowned king of the Two Lands' (Grimal 1986: 600–1). This war of the titles did not bestow on Harsiese any more power than he possessed as chief priest, but Osorkon II's power was undoubtedly limited by Harsiese's claims. Consequently, when Harsiese died Osorkon installed one of his sons, Nimlot (who had until then been commander of the Herakleopolis garrison and chief priest of Arsaphes), as chief priest of Amun. Osorkon II also enforced the same policy at Memphis, where he deposed the local line of priests by appointing another of his sons, prince Shoshenq, as chief priest of Ptah. He also nominated his young son Hornakht – who died before his tenth birthday – as chief priest of Amun at Tanis. Hornakht's youth is a clear indication of the purely political nature of the appointment, which must have been intended simply to unite all of the local dynasties of Egypt under the control of the royal family.

Osorkon II's reign was the last flourish of the Twenty-second Dynasty. The king embellished the temple of Bastet in his home-city of Bubastis, decorating the hypostyle hall and adding a new court for the celebration of the *sed* festival (royal jubilee). On the gateway of the new festival court he depicted his own jubilee, which he had celebrated in the twenty-second year of his reign (*c.*853 BC). The celebration of this jubilee seems all the more remarkable since it was undoubtedly unusual, in these troubled times, to reach such a late stage in a reign. The accompanying text on the gateway shows that during the ceremony Osorkon II reintroduced an Eighteenth Dynasty policy of fiscal exemption for the temples of Egypt, which had once been announced by Amenophis III at Soleb. Whether this decree was actually enacted or not, it shows that Osorkon's jubilee rites were based on the original classic Theban *sed* festival (Kitchen 1986: 320–2). In turn, this indicates not only that there were still clear links between Tanis and Thebes but also that there was a strong sense of continuity in the institutions of Egypt, despite the political conflicts that had torn the country apart for two centuries.

There is also evidence of the presence of Osorkon II at Leontopolis, Memphis and Tanis. At Tanis he built a court in front of the temple of Amun, in which was found a stelophorous statue of the king. The stele bears the text of a prayer to Amun, asking the god to provide an oracle demonstrating his approval of the policy that Osorkon was then pursuing (Yoyotte et al. 1987: 108). At Thebes he built a chapel and re-established the special privileges of the priesthood of Amun.

In the world outside Egypt, however, the balance of power was changing. Osorkon II followed the same policy of alliance with Byblos as his predecessors, but he was soon forced to deal with the growing power of Assyria. Ashurnasirpal II, whose name means 'the god Assur is the guardian of the first-born child', had risen to the throne in 883 BC. The prototypical conqueror, he unceasingly expanded his empire, and in his palace of Nimrud (near modern Mosul) he described the booty won from his enemies and his rivals with incredible cruelty:

> I built a pillar over against the city gate, and I flayed all the chief men who had revolted, and I covered the pillar with their skins; some I walled up within the pillar, some I impaled upon the pillar on stakes, and others I bound to stakes round about the pillar; many within the border of my own land I flayed, and I spread their skins upon the walls (...) Many captives from among them I burned with fire, and many I took as living captives. From some I cut off their hands and their fingers, and from others I cut off their noses, their ears and their fingers(?), of many I put out the eyes. I made one pillar of the living and another of heads, and I bound their heads to tree trunks round about the city ... (*Annals*; Luckenbill 1926: 145, 147)

By this means Ashurnasirpal conquered northern Mesopotamia and the Middle Euphrates, then Syria, the Orontes valley and the coast of Amurru. His son Shalmaneser III ('The god Sulmanu is pre-eminent'), succeeded him in 858 BC and reigned until 828 BC – he was therefore contemporary with Osorkon II and Takelot II. For thirty-one years he continued to launch campaigns into foreign territories, just as his father had, in a vain attempt to gain complete control of northern Syria. In fact, his aggressive policy succeeded in achieving something which Egyptian diplomacy had been unable to bring about: the kingdoms of Hamath, Damascus and Israel allied themselves together in 853 BC in order to present a united front to the invader. Byblos and Egypt each sent a contingent according to their respective means: 500 and 1000 soldiers respectively. The battle took place at Qarqar on the River Orontes, and although Shalmaneser III may have been the victor, his advance westwards was nevertheless effectively halted.

Egyptian foreign policy entered a new phase in which it was dedicated to the support of the Syro-Palestinian kingdoms, which now functioned as the last bastion between the Nile valley and the growing imperial appetite of Assyria. It was less than twenty years before these kingdoms finally surrendered to Shalmaneser III. Jehu, who reached the throne of Israel in 841 BC, paid tribute to Assyria from that date onwards. The Assyrians were then determined to conquer Egypt too. But Shalmaneser III did not succeed in consolidating his position, and the troubles that broke out at the end of his reign, resulting in a civil war within the Assyrian empire, kept the Assyrians out of Syria-Palestine for almost a century.

THE LIBYAN ANARCHY

The succession of Osorkon II was by no means straightforward: by the time Osorkon died, the crown prince Shoshenq was already dead and it was his younger brother, Takelot II, who rose to the throne at Tanis. Few traces of Takelot II's reign have survived anywhere in the country, although he ruled for almost as long as his father. The same does not apply, however, to the contemporaneous chief priests of Amun. Nimlot, Takelot II's half-brother, had made good progress since his appointment to that office by Osorkon II. In particular, he reunited Herakleopolis and Thebes under his sole authority by delegating the administration of Herakleopolis to his son Ptahwedjankhef. He also married his daughter, Karomama Merytmut II, to Takelot II, so that he became the father-in-law of his half-brother and, more importantly, grandfather of the new crown prince, who was called Osorkon in memory of his grandfather. A state of relative peace prevailed between Tanis and Thebes for the first ten years of Takelot II's reign. The pharaoh even arranged several marriages between Tanite princesses and various Theban dignitaries of old stock, who were less and less inclined to accept the authority of the Tanite family over the Amun priesthood.

When the chief priest of Amun died, in the eleventh year of Takelot II, hostilities broke out. Who would be chosen to succeed Nimlot? Was it to be one of Nimlot's sons (Ptahwedjankhef of Herakleopolis and another called Takelot), or was it to be the local pretender, a man named Harsiese, grandson of the chief priest (i.e. the original 'King' Harsiese)? Takelot II chose the crown prince Osorkon, but the Thebans – already disappointed once before by the appointment of the king's son Djedptahefankh as fourth prophet of Amun – were unable to ratify this decision. Harsiese then forced Thebes into revolt. Ptahwedjankhef had accepted Takelot II's choice, and prince Osorkon consequently reconfirmed him in his post of commander of Herakleopolis. Then Prince Osorkon left his fortress of el-Hiba and set off upriver to Thebes, passing safely through the Hermopolitan region. He arrived at Karnak and dealt out justice in accordance with the 'complaint' of the priesthood against the rebels. Not only did he execute the insurgents, but he had their bodies burnt, thus denying them eternal life. The revolt was totally crushed.

In the four years that followed, Prince Osorkon sought to ingratiate himself with the priesthood by gifts and promises of allowances: order had apparently been restored. Then in the fifteenth year of Takelot II's reign, civil war broke out – Osorkon's attempt to describe it in his *Chronicle* on the Bubastite Portal at Karnak (Caminos 1958) employs terms that recall the worst phase of the First Intermediate Period, although this text is beset by dating problems that are still far from being solved (Kitchen 1986: 546ff.). The conflict appears to have lasted for about a decade, ending with a period of general reconciliation at Thebes in the twenty-fourth year of Takelot II's reign. This was not, however, a lasting truce, and less than two years later the Thebans resumed the struggle, causing Prince Osorkon to lose his foothold in Upper Egypt. It was at this time that Takelot II died and was buried in a reused coffin in the antechamber of Osorkon II's tomb. Before Prince Osorkon could return to Tanis to claim the throne, his younger brother Shoshenq III had seized power.

Shoshenq III's rise to the throne was a disruption to the expected order of succession and it triggered off a new dynastic feud. During the early years of his reign Shoshenq seems to have been accepted by the Thebans, presumably because he had prevented Prince Osorkon from gaining the throne, which would have dangerously increased his power. He clearly allowed the priesthood of Karnak to make their own choice for the office of chief priest of Amun, and Harsiese reappeared as chief priest in the sixth year of Shoshenq III's reign. A new power struggle now ensued, but this time it came from within the royal family itself rather than from Thebes. In the eighth year of Shoshenq III's reign Prince Pedubastis proclaimed himself king and established a new royal dynasty – Manetho's Twenty-third – at Leontopolis in the Delta, giving himself a set of titles that harked back to Twenty-second Dynasty kings. The two pharaohs (Pedubastis and Shoshenq III) then reigned simultaneously, each with his own regnal dates; this time the break was not between north and south but between different parts of the Delta. The priests of Amun were quick to recognize the new pharaoh, from the twelfth year of Shoshenq III's reign at least, and they welcomed two of his sons into their ranks.

Prince Osorkon, who despite having been usurped by his brother, seems to have been the only person still referring to Shoshenq III at that time, had a further role to play in history: in the same year that Pedubastis appointed his son(?) Iuput I as co-regent, Shoshenq III reappointed Prince Osorkon as chief priest of Amun. The co-regency between Pedubastis and Iuput I probably did not last longer than two years, for Iuput seems to have died at the same time as his father, in the fifteenth year of Pedubastis' reign (804 BC, the twenty-second year of Shoshenq III's reign). Harsiese reappeared in the twenty-fifth year of Shoshenq's reign, only to disappear completely in the twenty-ninth year, leaving Prince Osorkon in control of Upper Egypt for about a decade. Meanwhile, similar disturbances were taking place at Herakleopolis, where Ptahwedjankhef had died, perhaps by the thirty-ninth year

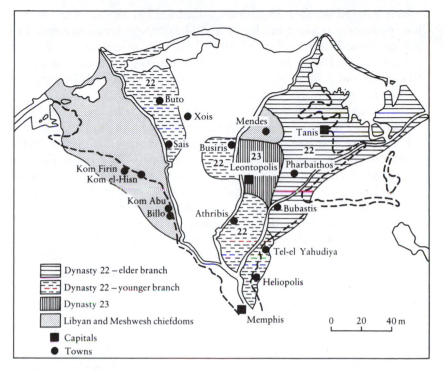

FIGURE 23   *Political map of the Delta c.800 BC (after Kitchen 1986, 346).*

of Shoshenq III's reign, and the power had passed to the general Bakenptah, a younger brother of the indefatigable Prince Osorkon. In the Delta, Shoshenq III – no doubt assisted by his Memphite lineage – continued to wield more power than his counterpart at Leontopolis, if the works he accomplished at Tanis are any indication. The reliefs on the monumental gateway of the temple of Amun at Tanis are perhaps records of Shoshenq III's *sed* festival, although there is no definite textual confirmation of this. He also had his tomb built in the Tanite royal necropolis, and undertook building programmes at Mendes, Mostai and Memphis.

Shoshenq III's authority seems to have extended little further than the Damietta branch of the Nile, even if the autonomous region of Athribis is considered part of his territory. In the central Delta the princedoms of Busiris, Sais and Buto were all subject to his hegemony. The land to the west of the Rosetta branch of the Nile was held by the Libyans. When Shoshenq III died in 773 BC, after a reign of fifty-three years, the whole Delta region was thrown into confusion.

Leontopolis was ruled by the Twenty-third Dynasty kings, the first of whom was Pedubastis I. Shoshenq IV succeeded Pedubastis I in 793 BC, but his reign was short-lived and in 787 BC Osorkon III succeeded to the Leontopolis throne. Osorkon III was thus in power for the last thirteen years of Shoshenq III's reign. His rule continued after Shoshenq III's death until 759 BC, and his authority was recognized by his immediate neighbours, the Chiefs of Ma at Mendes.

There is also evidence of Osorkon III's activity at Memphis, and he is attested more often in Middle Egypt than Shoshenq III. At Herakleopolis the closely related line of the Tanite dynasty was still in power in the early years of the reign of Shoshenq V (*c.*766 BC). This Tanite line was supplanted by Osorkon III, however, who installed his son Takelot there. He may also have managed to install a 'king' at Hermopolis in the form of a man called Nimlot, who was to surrender to the Kushite king Piankhy more than thirty years later.

The role of the Twenty-second Dynasty in the Theban region had become greatly reduced when Osorkon III allowed his son Takelot to combine the role of chief priest with the rule of Herakleopolis. The Twenty-third Dynasty seemed to have re-established the traditional alliance between Thebes and the political capital, but the priesthood of Amun (with the exception of the chief priest) appears to have been very much in the hands of the Thebans themselves.

In 765/764 BC Osorkon III nominated his son Takelot, the chief priest, as heir to the throne. Six years later Osorkon died and his co-regent Takelot III was sole ruler for only a very short time – one or two years at most, with his eighth and most recent regnal year being around 757 BC. His contemporary at Tanis was Shoshenq V, who had inherited the throne in 767 BC from his father Pimay, an ephemeral figure. Shoshenq V ruled until 730 BC, but his authority stretched no further than Tell el-Yahudiya. At Tanis he built a temple to the triad of Amun in the north-east corner of the precinct of Amun, on the site that was later occupied by a sacred lake. He also built a jubilee chapel there, dated to the thirtieth year of his reign. In the time of Shoshenq V the situation in the eastern Delta underwent a certain amount of change. In about 767 BC there was a chiefdom of Ma at Sais led by a man named Osorkon, who extended his control westwards at the expense of the Libyan territories, northwards to encompass Buto and southwards in the direction of Memphis.

At the end of Shoshenq V's reign and the beginning of the reign of his successor, Osorkon IV (*c.*730 BC), Sais was ruled by Tefnakht, the self-proclaimed 'Great chief of the Libu and great prince of the west', whose authority stretched across the western Delta and half of the central Delta. When Shoshenq V died, his son Osorkon IV, the last representative of the Twenty-second Dynasty, governed only his own city (Tanis) and Bubastis; his 'kingdom' was split in two by the chiefdom of Ma, ruled from Pharbaithos, although the latter was theoretically subject to his authority.

The Twenty-third Dynasty ruler Takelot III rose to the throne, and his sister Shepenwepet I was appointed as Divine Adoratrice of Amun, sharing with him the privileges of rule over the Theban region. She even seems to have taken over the role of chief priest, which Takelot III himself had given up in order to become pharaoh. This situation can be deduced from the fact that they are portrayed together (along with Osorkon III) in the construction and decoration of the chapel of Osiris *ḥeḳa-djet* ('lord of eternity') at Karnak. Shepenwepet I was the last Libyan Divine Adoratrice, for the next incumbent was to be Nubian. In Middle Egypt, Takelot's role as commander of Herakleopolis was given to a man called Peftjauawybastet, who married a daughter of Rudamon (Takelot's brother). Rudamon succeeded Takelot III on the throne in 757 BC, but his reign was particularly brief. It was during the reign of Iuput II (Rudamon's successor) that both Peftjauawybastet and Nimlot, the contemporaneous governor of Hermopolis, adopted royal titles. These three 'kings' were therefore among those conquered by the Kushite king Piankhy, who put an end to the period of so-called 'Libyan anarchy'. During the final phase of the Twenty-third Dynasty, from 757 to 729 BC, the power of Rudamon and his successor Iuput II was restricted to the kingdom of Leontopolis. At Thebes, Rudamon undertook several building projects in the chapel of Osiris *ḥeḳa-djet* at Karnak and in the temple of Medinet Habu.

When Piankhy, the king of Napata, embarked on the conquest of the Nile valley, the political situation was roughly as follows. Most of the military power of the Delta was in the hands of Tefnakht of Sais, who united under his command the four great Chiefs of Ma, comprising Sebennytos and Busiris (west of the Damietta branch of the Nile), Mendes (east of the Damietta) and Pi-Sopd (south-east of the Pelusiac branch). His allies included Osorkon IV, ruler of the kingdoms of Athribis and Tanis, as well as Iuput II of Leontopolis, who was supported by the rulers of Thebes, Herakleopolis and Hermopolis. This apparent political unity only obtained because of the Kushite threat emerging from the south, but it had the effect of bolstering the growing power of the Saite kings, who would eventually be the Kushite rulers' only rivals.

THE ARTISTIC TRADITION

The conquest of Piankhy brought an end to one of the most confused periods in Egyptian history, a period which historians have still not been able to disentangle satisfactorily from the fragments of evidence (James 1991). Academic disputes over the number of regnal years attributed to different rulers have further complicated the refinement of the chronology of the period, since scholars are forced to undertake meticulous studies of the prosopography of the leading state officials, using incomplete sources of funerary and juridical documentation. The chaotic chronology of these three centuries therefore appears to be a faithful reflection of the political disorder in Egypt at the time.

Throughout the country, the level of artistic achievement was no longer equal to the magnificence of the Ramessid period, but it was nevertheless of very high quality. During the first millennium BC the art of metalworking flourished as never before in the Near East, particularly in Egypt. The statue of the Divine Adoratrice Karomama, granddaughter of Osorkon I, and the small triad of Osorkon II representing the king as Osiris, protected by Isis and Horus, constitute two of the greatest masterpieces of Egyptian art. But although the kings continued to be great builders – at such times as their power and wealth allowed – the gap between them and private individuals was much reduced throughout the kingdom. Just as individuals had begun to usurp royal privileges, they had also begun to adopt royal artistic genres – the style adopted by the chief priests of Amun at Karnak, for example, was firmly in the Ramessid mould.

Conversely, the pharaohs of the Third Intermediate Period began to move away from the Nineteenth Dynasty model of kingship. Only the Tanite rulers remained faithful to it – first ideologically, in order to legitimize their rule (as the study of their titles has demonstrated), but secondly by necessity, as their resources gradually diminished. It was certainly easier to reuse and reinscribe the sculptures of the Ramessid city of Piramesse than to create new statues of themselves. This association with the Ramessid period was to be abandoned by the Saites and the Kushites. The Saites could not trace their claim to power back to their 'predecessors' at Tanis and Leontopolis. Like the founders of the Nineteenth Dynasty, they had to find their legitimacy in the fountain-head of Egyptian power: the Heliopolitan tradition, which they rendered in a more austere and less 'sententious' style than the Ramessids. The Kushites saw themselves as the true inheritors of this tradition, the essence of which they believed to have been debased.

The return to the past, which marks the end of the Third Intermediate Period, was accompanied by a new phenomenon: the rise of popular religion. This development had already become apparent in the Ramessid period, after the introduction of a new definition of the relationship between the god and the king in the post-Amarna period. The new religious relationship was systematized over a period of almost

300 years of oracular government, manifesting itself in the form of numerous ex-votos which – regardless of whether the subject was the king or a simple private individual – always represented the figure in exactly the same range of attitudes of worship. Private autobiographical texts adopted a tone more similar to that of hymns, while for their part the kings related the great events of their reigns in a style which was closer than before to the funerary autobiographies of private individuals.

14

Nubians and Saites

When Nubia split away from Egypt at the time of the disintegration of the empire of Ramesses II, the independent kingdom of Napata was already emerging in the region of the Fourth Cataract. Its existence is not properly attested until the beginning of the eighth century BC, due to a lack of information concerning the state of Nubia in the period immediately before this time. It is likely, however, that the expedition led by Shoshenq I to the south of Aswan almost a century after the rebellion of the viceroy Panehsy (Kitchen 1986: 293) was either the last instance of Egyptian influence over Lower Nubia or a final attempt to reconquer it. Whichever it was, it is clear that Nubia – heavily Egyptianized by the New Kingdom pharaohs – henceforth passed through its own stages of development, far removed from its old colonial condition. The temple of Amun at Gebel Barkal became an important religious focus from which there emerged a local dynasty, whose chiefs were buried in the neighbouring necropolis of el-Kurru. Over the course of generations the local priests of Amun acquired a high degree of influence, which must have contributed to the gradual process of Egyptianization of the Napatan culture. By the time these Kushite priests of Amun developed into a royal dynasty, they had taken on the accoutrements of pharaonic power and even adopted an orthodox cult of Amun based entirely on that established in Nubia by Tuthmosis III.

The first named Kushite ruler is Alara, who was actually the seventh king of the Napatan dynasty; his brother Kashta ('the Kushite') is the first to be directly attested. Since the length of Alara's reign is estimated at about twenty years and his accession dated to about 780 BC, it would seem that the dynasty first emerged around the late tenth or early ninth centuries BC, after Sheshonq I's invasion. Nothing is known of events during Alara's reign, but that of Kashta is comparatively well known. He came to the Napatan throne in 760 BC and probably succeeded in conquering Lower Nubia, if Alara had not already done so. His authority clearly extended at least as far as Aswan, since he dedicated a stele to Khnum at Elephantine, giving himself a pharaonic titulature with Maatre as his coronation name. He may even have pushed as far north as the Theban region (Kendall 1982: 9), but direct contact with the Thebans was not established until the following generation.

Kashta had several children, two of whom succeeded to the throne: first Piankhy and then Shabaka. Piankhy married the daughter of Alara, thus confirming the transmission of power from one generation to another, and came to power in 747 BC, continuing the northward expansion of Nubia during the first ten years of his reign. He took Thebes under his protection and ensured that his sister Amenirdis I was adopted by Shepenwepet I as Divine Adoratrice. Amenirdis I established the power of the Nubians over Karnak by inheriting the territory ruled by Osorkon III. An inscription in the Wadi Gasus shows that the succession was effective at Thebes 'in the nineteenth year of the king's reign', which would probably correspond to the twelfth year of Piankhy's reign; a correlation can therefore be made with the nineteenth year of the reign of Iuput II (the king recognized at that time in Thebes), which was 736 BC. At this date it seems that the Nubians were in control of the whole of Upper Egypt at least as far as Thebes and probably even further north, since at the time of his conquest of Egypt Piankhy reproached the kings of Hermopolis and Herakleopolis for having betrayed him.

Faced with growing Nubian power in the Theban region, Tefnakht, the enterprising king of Sais, reunited the kingdoms of northern Egypt and persuaded the kings of Hermopolis and Herakleopolis to join his cause. Strengthened by these alliances, he set out to conquer the south. Piankhy, however, launched his own invasion and defeated the northern coalition, describing this victory on a monumental stele which he set up in the temple of Amun at Gebel Barkal (discovered by Said Pasha in 1862). This text was not a military account of the campaign but a decree confirming Piankhy's dominion over Upper and Lower Egypt; his conquest is therefore described as if it were a crusade led by a pharaoh who was already in control of the country, fighting against the rebels on behalf of Amun. In other words, this stele is not a historical record but a work belonging to the classic tradition of the 'royal recitation', full of phrases directly inspired by literary sources in the library of the temple at Gebel Barkal. Piankhy had copies of this text placed in the great sanctuaries of the Egyptians at Karnak and probably also at Memphis, but only the Gebel Barkal text has survived.

In the twenty-first year of his reign, Piankhy learnt of Tefnakht's activities. An initial report from his troops stationed in Egypt, probably some time after 760 BC, informed him of the establishment of a confederation of northern kings and princes under Tefnakht's command. Piankhy did not react at first, but allowed the confederation to head south as far as Herakleopolis. Then he ordered the Nubian contingent in the Theban region to block their advance in the fifteenth nome and sent an expeditionary force to support them:

> His Majesty wrote to the counts and generals who were in Egypt, the commander Purem, and the commander Lemersekny, and every commander of His Majesty who was in Egypt: 'Enter combat, engage in battle; surround it, lay siege to it, capture its people, its cattle, its ships on the river! Let not the farmers go to the field, let not the ploughmen plough. Beset the Hare nome; fight against it daily!' Then they did so.
>
> Then His Majesty sent an army to Egypt and charged them strictly: 'Do not attack by night in the manner of draughts-playing; fight when one can see. Challenge him to battle from afar. If he proposes to await the infantry and chariotry of another town, then sit still until his troops come. Fight when he proposes. Also if he has allies in another town, let them be awaited. The counts whom he brings to help him, and any trusted Libyan troops, let them be challenged to battle in advance, saying: "You whose name we do not know, who musters the troops! Harness the best steeds of your stable, form your battle line, and know that Amun is the god who sent us!"'
>
> 'When you have reached Thebes at Iput-isut, go into the water. Cleanse yourselves in the river; wear the best linen. Rest the bow; loosen the arrow. Boast not to the lord of might, for the brave has no might without him. He makes the weak-armed strong-armed, so that the many flee before the few, and a single one conquers a thousand men! Sprinkle yourself with water of his altars; kiss the earth before his face. Say to him:
>
>> "Give us the way,
>> May we fight in the shade of your arm!
>> The troop you sent, when it charges,
>> May the many tremble before it!"'
>> (*Victory Stele*: 8–14; trans. Lichtheim 1980a: 69)

The Nubian troops blocked the advance of the allies at Herakleopolis and forced them into battle. Once defeated, the army of Tefnakht sought refuge in Hermopolis, which the Nubians then besieged. Piankhy decided that the time had come to take personal control of the military operations. While passing through Thebes, he seized the opportunity to celebrate the festival of the New Year and the Festival of Opet at Karnak, thus enlisting the support of Amun in order to weaken the morale of the besieged forces. During this period his troops pillaged Middle Egypt. When the arrived at Hermopolis the king surrendered, handing over his town to the conqueror. Peftjauawybastet of Herakleopolis then also surrendered without waiting for Piankhy to capture his town – he accepted the Nubian king's suzerainty in a speech which is laced with literary references:

> Hail to you, Horus, mighty king,
> Bull attacking bulls!
> The netherworld seized me,
> I foundered in darkness,
> Oh you who give me the rays of his face!
> I could find no friend on the day of distress,
> Who would stand up on battle day,
> Except you, oh mighty king,
> You drove the darkness from me!
> I shall serve with my property,
> Hnes owes to your dwelling;
> You are Horakhty above the immortal stars!
> As he is king so are you,
> As he is immortal you are immortal,
> King of Upper and Lower Egypt, Piankhy ever living!
> (*Victory Stele*: 71–6; trans. Lichtheim 1980a: 73)

Piankhy then marched northwards, first taking the fortress that Osorkon I had built to control access to the Faiyum, and then receiving the surrender of Maidum and el-Lisht. He eventually arrived at Memphis, where the forces of the Egyptian coalition had reassembled. He besieged the city with siege-towers, and once Memphis had fallen, the rest of the coalition also surrendered. Piankhy then set off for Heliopolis, where he celebrated the cult of Ra according to the traditional rituals, thus re-enacting the rites of his own coronation:

His Majesty went to the camp on the west of Iti. His purification was done: he was cleansed in the pool of Kebeh; his face was bathed in the river of Nun, in which Ra bathes his face. He proceeded to the High Sand in Heliopolis. A great oblation was made on the High Sand in Heliopolis before the face of Ra at his rising, consisting of white oxen, milk, myrrh, incense, and all kinds of sweet-smelling plants.

Going in procession to the temple of Ra. Entering the temple with adorations. The chief lector-priest's praising god and repulsing the rebels from the king. Performing the ritual of the robing room; putting on the *sdb* garment; cleansing him with incense and cold water; presenting him the garlands of the Pyramidion House; bringing him the amulets.

Mounting the stairs to the great window to view Ra in the Pyramidion House. The king stood by himself alone. Breaking the seals of the bolts, opening the doors; viewing his father Ra in the holy Pyramidion House; adorning the morning bark of Ra and the evening bark of Atum. Closing the doors, applying the clay, sealing with the king's own seal, and instructing the priests: 'I have inspected the seal. No other king who may arise shall enter here.' They placed themselves on their bellies before his majesty, saying: 'Abide forever without end, Horus beloved of Heliopolis!'

Entering the temple of Atum. Worshipping the image of his father Atum-Khepri, Great One of Heliopolis. (*Victory Stele*: 101–6; trans. Lichtheim 1980a: 77)

When the jubilee section of the ceremony was finished, Osorkon IV of Tanis came to adore the king. Prince Pediese of Athribis then brought all his possessions as tribute to Piankhy, as did the principal members of the coalition, all but one of whom are listed on the Victory Stele. The missing name is that of Tefnakht, who fled from Memphis before the city was captured and was exiled in the northern regions of the Delta. While regrouping his forces, Tefnakht sent to Piankhy a skilfully-worded message, full of traditional phraseology, seeking to negotiate a truce:

'Is Your Majesty's heart not cooled by the things you did to me? While I am under a just reproach, you did not smite me in accordance with (my) crime. Weigh in the balance, count by weight, and multiply it against me threefold! (But) leave the seed, that you may gather it in time. Do not cut down the grove to its roots! Have mercy! Dread of you is in my body: fear of you is in my bones!

'I sit not at the beer feast; the harp is not brought for me. I eat the bread of the hungry; I drink the water of the thirsty, since the day you heard my name! Illness is in my bones, my head is bald, my clothes are rags, till Neith is appeased toward me! Long is the course you led against me, and your face is against me yet! It is a year that has purged my *ka* and cleansed your servant of his fault! Let my goods be received into the treasury: gold and all precious stones, the best of the horses, and payment of every kind. Send me a messenger quickly, to drive the fear from my heart! Let me go to the temple in his presence, to cleanse myself by a divine oath!'

His Majesty sent the chief lector-priest Pediamen-nest-tawy and the commander Purem. He [Tefnakht] presented him with silver and gold, clothing and all precious stones. He went to the temple; he praised god; he cleansed himself by a divine oath, saying: 'I will not disobey the King's command. I will not thrust aside His Majesty's words. I will not do wrong to a count without your knowledge. I will only do what the King said. I will not disobey what he has commanded.' Then His Majesty's heart was satisfied with it.' (*Victory Stele*: 130–40; trans. Lichtheim 1980a: 79–80)

Strengthened by this virtual surrender, Piankhy reappointed the four kings as governors over their towns: Iuput II of Leontopolis, Peftjauawybastet of Herakleopolis, Osorkon IV of Tanis and Nimlot of Hermopolis. But no doubt wishing to avoid making too many concessions to the Libyan descendants of the pharaohs, he appointed Nimlot as the representative of the four, and it was with Nimlot alone that he was actually prepared to discuss terms:

> At dawn of the next day there came the two rulers of Upper Egypt and the two rulers of Lower Egypt, the uraeus wearers, to kiss the ground to the might of His Majesty. Now the kings and counts of Lower Egypt who came to see His Majesty's beauty, their legs were the legs of women. They could not enter the palace because they were uncircumcised and were eaters of fish, which is an abomination to the palace. But King Nimlot entered the palace because he was clean and did not eat fish. The three stood there while the one entered the palace.
>
> Then the ships were loaded with silver, gold, copper and clothing; everything of Lower Egypt, every product of Syria, and all plants of god's land [Punt]. His Majesty sailed south, his heart joyful, and all those near him shouting. West and East took up the announcement, shouting around his majesty. This was their song of jubilation:
>
> > Oh mighty ruler, oh mighty ruler,
> > Piankhy, mighty ruler!
> > You return having taken Lower Egypt,
> > You made bulls into women!
> > Joyful is the mother who bore you,
> > The man who begot you!
> > The valley dwellers worship her,
> > The cow that bore the bull!
> > You are eternal,
> > Your might abides,
> > Oh ruler loved of Thebes!
> > (*Victory Stele*: 147–59; Lichtheim 1980a: 80)

When Piankhy returned to Napata he added more buildings to the capital and enlarged the temple at Gebel Barkal. This sanctuary had originally been dedicated to Amun of the 'Pure Mountain' by Tuthmosis III, and the latest stage of Egyptian building has been dated to the reign of Ramesses II (B 500). Piankhy restored the sanctuary, rebuilding the enclosure wall around it. He then built in front of it a hypostyle hall and a second pylon, and finally a new peristyle court fronted by another pylon and an avenue of criosphinxes brought from the temple of Amenophis III at Soleb. The Gebel Barkal temple was therefore a replica of the temple of Amun at Karnak, and each of the Nubian rulers made a point of enlarging and embellishing both temples.

Piankhy erected a pyramid in the necropolis at el-Kurru, and his queens and two of his daughters were buried nearby. The revival of the pyramid-style royal tomb was part of the Kushite kings' general tendency towards ideological conservatism, although the Napatan pyramids were far removed from their Memphite originals.

It is interesting to speculate on the reasons for Piankhy's return to Napata. If the Victory Stele is to be believed then he had already gained complete control over Egypt. He may have preferred not to govern the country himself or he may have felt that the country's true capital was Napata. In fact, it is more likely that he deliberately maintained a policy of 'divide and rule', contenting himself with efficient control of the Theban region and the western trade routes at least as far as the Dakhla Oasis, where he is attested in the twenty-fourth year of his reign. This strategy seems to have been successful in Middle Egypt, both at Hermopolis and Herakleopolis. Piankhy himself sketched out the broad lines of his policy on another stele found in the Gebel Barkal temple:

> Amun of Napata has appointed me governor of the country, in the same way as I may say to someone: 'Be king' and he is it, or 'You will not be king', and he is not. Amun of Thebes has appointed me governor of Egypt, in the same way that I may say to someone: 'Be crowned' and he is crowned, or 'Do not be crowned' and he is not. Whoever is protected by me does not risk seeing his town captured, at any rate not if I can help it. The gods can make a king; even men can make a king; but I am made king by Amun! (Grimal 1986: 217–18)

This did not prevent Piankhy from using the monuments that he had built and decorated to emphasize his role as unifier of Egypt. His titles included the Horus name of Sematawy: 'He who has unified the two lands' or 'He who has pacified his two lands', as well as 'Bull of his two lands', and 'He who was crowned in Thebes'. He identified himself with the two great rulers who were most represented in the Nubian monuments, Tuthmosis III and Ramesses II, and adopted each of their coronation names: Menkheperre and Usermaatra respectively. His rule seems to have been recognized at Thebes, where Shepenwepet I and Amenirdis I jointly controlled the priesthood.

In the north, on the other hand, the limitations of this policy were clearly apparent. Tefnakht had lost virtually none of his power, which once more extended across the western Delta and as far south as Memphis. He declared himself King of Egypt around 720 or 719 BC, thus establishing himself as the first ruler of Manetho's Twenty-fourth

Dynasty, which was based at Sais. Tefnakht's reign lasted for no more than eight years, during which he consolidated his position in relation to his two neighbours at Leontopolis and Tanis. His son Bakenrenef (Manetho's Bocchoris) succeeded him and proclaimed his authority over the whole of northern Egypt. Not enough evidence has survived to allow a proper assessment of this short-lived dynasty, which was eventually to give way to Shabaka in 715 BC. It appears that the kings of Tanis and Bubastis, like those of Leontopolis and the chiefdoms of Ma, accepted the suzerainty of the kings of Sais, which would in fact have been no great concession. Bakenrenef is attested at Memphis, which may even have been his seat of power.

THE RISE OF ASSYRIA

Osorkon IV of Tanis, the last king of the Twenty-second Dynasty, had long since lost full control over Egypt itself; but paradoxically it was he who was to undertake the considerable task of re-establishing an Egyptian presence in Syria-Palestine, where events had taken a turn for the worse. Assyria was emerging from a long period of internal struggles, with Tiglath-Pileser III wresting the throne from Assur-Nirari V in 745 BC. However, the Assyrians then found themselves threatened by a restless neighbour in the form of the kingdom of Urartu, which occupied the area of modern Armenia. The two powers were rivals in a race to conquer northern Syria. Using the same method that he had employed in reorganizing his own country, Tiglath-Pileser III annexed north-western Syria and took over Phoenicia in 742 BC. He particularly forbade all commerce with the Philistines and Egyptians. As a result of this intervention the princes of the fertile crescent were persuaded to make terms with Assyria: Carchemish, Damascus and Israel recognized Tiglath-Pileser III's suzerainty and paid him tribute, as did various other peoples, including the Arabs, who are mentioned here for the first time.

Believing that he had thus secured his frontier in the direction of the Mediterranean, Tiglath-Pileser III made a deep incursion into Iran and turned to face Urartu. But Tyre and Sidon, who had been deprived of their commercial traffic with Egypt, stirred up resistance behind his back. The cities of Gaza and Ashkelon, probably motivated by similar commercial imperatives, organized a coalition in Palestine and Transjordania, but this was crushed by the Assyrians in 734 BC. Two years later Tiglath Pileser III took advantage of the conflict between Judah and Israel (allied with Damascus) to intervene again in the region, annexing Damascus and launching a raid into Israel.

Hosea, who had just assumed the throne of Samaria, then appears to have surrendered to Assyria, but according to the Biblical account he sent a message for help to 'So, the King of Egypt' (*II Kings* 17: 4). This short phrase has been interpreted in two different ways. Some scholars have treated it as a mistaken Hebrew spelling of the city of Sais, in which case – by a process of metonymy – Hosea would have been appealing to King Tefnakht. The dates agree with this interpretation in that the revolt of Hosea against Assyria must have taken place in 727/726 BC. Eventually the king of Assyria captured Hosea, thus putting an end to his nine-year reign. After a siege lasting another three years, Samaria itself was occupied by the Assyrians. The capture of Hosea took place in 724 BC at the latest, while the seizure of Samaria would have occurred in about 722/721 BC. By then the Assyrian king would have been Shalmaneser V, who had succeeded to his father's throne in 726 BC. However, if this chronology is correct, it is unlikely that the pharaoh to whom Hosea appealed could have been Tefnakht, since nothing suggests that the court of Israel would have regarded him as the main representative of Egypt. As far as Israel was concerned the traditional representative at that time was Tanis, which was often mentioned in other texts. The location of Tanis in the eastern Delta was naturally convenient for relations with Syria-Palestine. This interpretation is further strengthened by the possibility that there may have been a superfluous correction of the text, so that 'So' might actually be interpreted as Osorkon IV (Kitchen 1986: 551).

As a result of the capture of Samaria the Transjordanian alliances were thrown into disarray. In the years that followed, the Egyptians took up with their erstwhile enemies, the Philistines, who seemed to be the group most likely to hold back the Assyrian threat which was drawing closer to their own borders. Assyria itself was still beset by internal problems: Shalmaneser V was overthrown by the representative of another branch of the royal family who took the name of Sargon ('The legitimate king'). Sargon II must then have faced another coalition on his southern border reuniting two enemies, Elam and Babylon, whose mutual – and to some extent atavistic – hostility was founded on 3000 years of hatred. Having temporarily buried their differences, they succeeded in shaking off the Assyrian yoke in 720 BC. This year was not a good one for Sargon II, for it was then that the Prince of Hamath led Damascus into revolt. Meanwhile Hanuna, the king of Gaza, also took arms against the Assyrians, reinforced by an Egyptian expeditionary force under the command of a general called Raia. Nevertheless, the Assyrians succeeded in retaining their overall grip on the empire: Hamath was thoroughly absorbed into the Assyrian empire, Gaza and Raphia were pillaged, and Hanuna himself was burnt alive.

In about 716 BC the Assyrians resumed their intervention in Transjordania; this time they reached the Wadi el-Arish, and only the town of Sile was left between them and the eastern Delta frontier. On this occasion, Osorkon IV chose to employ diplomatic methods, presenting Sargon II with gifts in the form of 'twelve great horses from Egypt, which are unrivalled in the whole country'.

The year 716 BC was also a crucial transitional phase in the internal politics of Egypt. Piankhy died after a long reign of thirty-one years and was buried at Napata along with two of the famous Egyptian chargers he had loved so much – the same horses which had aroused the admiration of Sargon II. His brother Shabaka then rose to the throne and set out to take personal control of the whole Nile valley. In 715 BC, the second year of his reign, he was residing at Memphis, where he undertook the restoration of the Serapeum. He brought an end to the reign of Bakenrenef, strengthened his control over the oases and the Western Desert, and perhaps installed an Ethiopian governor in Sais, thus effectively taking over the whole of northern Egypt.

Direct confirmation of this achievement is provided by a new turn of events in Transjordania. Iamani had come to power in the Philistine city of Ashdod, to the north of Ashkelon, and had led a revolt against Assyria. Sargon II sent an army to recapture Ashdod, but Iamani managed to escape, taking refuge with the Egyptians whom he assumed to be his allies. In fact, Assyrian sources report that 'the pharaoh of Egypt – a land which henceforth belonged to Kush' extradited the rebel to Assyria, 'loading him down with chains, fetters and iron bands'. This pharaoh can only have been Shabaka, who was thus evidently avoiding a direct confrontation with Sargon II, even though he must have been reluctant to see the demise of the last obstacle between Egypt and the Assyrian Empire. He may have been preparing the ground for some kind of diplomatic agreement – perhaps even a treaty – with Assyria (Kitchen 1986: 380).

Shabaka continued with Piankhy's policy of a return to traditional Egyptian values. Not content with simply adopting Neferkare as his coronation name, he set out to draw directly upon the original sources of Old Kingdom theology. To his reign dates the *Memphite Drama* or *Memphite Theology*, a stone-carved text (now in the British Museum, London) which claims to have been copied from a 'worm-eaten' papyrus. This text, like others issued throughout the Kushite period by the temples of Gebel Barkal and Kawa, shows the depth of study undertaken by priests in the service of the Twenty-fifth Dynasty kings. They had no hesitation in reaching as far back as the reign of the Fifth Dynasty King Wenis in their pursuit of inspiration for the decorative themes covering the walls of their temples, hoping, no doubt, to rediscover the very roots of the power that they had inherited. As usual, it is in their religious monuments that the main evidence of this policy

TABLE 9 *Table of Near Eastern powers from the Kushite conquest to the end of the Saite period.*

Dates BC	Egypt	Judah	Israel	Phoenicia	Syria	Assyria
714–716	Pi(ankh)y	Jotham	Menahem		Razin	Tiglath-Pileser
		Achaz	Peqah			III
					Capture	
			Hosea		of	
	Tefnakht		Capture of		Damas-	Shalmaneser V
	Bocchoris	Hezekiah	Samaria		cus	Sargon II
716–702	Shabaka		(722)		(732)	
702–690	Shebitku			Lule		Sennacherib
690–664	Taharqa	Manasseh				
				Abdi-Milkuti		Esarhaddon
	Necho I					Ashurbanipal
664–656	Psammetichus					
	I					
	Tantamani					
		Amon				Assur-etil-ilani
		Josiah				Sin-shumu-lishir
610–595	Necho II	Jehoahaz				Nebuchadrezzar
		Jehoiakim		Battle of		II
		Jehoiachin		Carchemish		
595–589	Psammétichus	Zedekiah		(605)		
	II	Capture of				
		Jerusalem				
589–570	Apries	(587)		Capture of		
				Tyre		
570–526	Amasis					Evil-Merodach
						Neriglissar
						Nabonidus
						Capture of
						Baylon (539)
526–525	Psammetichus					
	III					

has survived. Shabaka demonstrated his enthusiasm for the Egyptian pantheon by building at Athribis, Memphis, Abydos, Dendera, Esna, Edfu and above all, Thebes. He was the first for many years to build on both sides of the river at Thebes: at Medinet Habu he enlarged the Eighteenth Dynasty temple, while his sister, the Divine Adoratrice Amenirdis I, built a mortuary chapel and tomb for herself within the temple enclosure; on the east bank, Shabaka worked both at Luxor and Karnak. At Karnak he constructed the building known as the 'Treasury of Shabaka', between the Akh-menu and the northern enclosure wall of

Babylonia	Medes	Persia	Elam	Urartu	Phrygia
Nabonassar			Humbash-tahrah	Sardur II	
Nabu-mukin-zeri			Humban-nikash I		Midas
	Deioces			Rusa I	
Merodach-Beladan II			Shutruk-nahhunte II	Argishti	
Assur-nadin-shumi			Hallutush-Inshushinak		
			Humban-nimena		
			Humban-haltash I		Gyges
	Phraortes	Teispes	Urtaki	Rusa II	
Shamashshumukin			Tempt-Humban-Inshushinak		
	Cyaxares		Tammaritu I		
			Humban-Haltash III		Ardys
		Cyrus I		Sardur III	
			Capture of Susa		
Nabopolassar					Sadyatte
					Alyatte
	Astyages				
					Croesus
		Cyrus II			

the Iput-isut, as well as enlarging the entrance-way to the temple of 'Ptah to the south of his wall'. It was also probably Shabaka who directed building work near the future kiosk of Taharqa, beside the sacred lake and in the precinct of Monthu. Not content with the mere construction of monuments at Thebes, Shabaka also revived the defunct office of chief priest of Amun, bestowing it on his son Horemakhet. However, the chief priest at Thebes now possessed only spiritual power, for secular power rested in the hands of the Divine Adoratrice.

Shabaka died in 702 BC after a reign of fifteen years. Like his brother, he was buried with his horses at el-Kurru and the throne then passed to Piankhy's sons, Shebitku and Taharqa. Djedkare Shebitku came to power first, having held a co-regency of perhaps two years alongside Shabaka (Kitchen 1986: 554–7), which would bring the total length of his reign to twelve years. He continued the building works begun by his uncle at Memphis, Luxor and Karnak, where he built a chapel (now in Berlin) to the south-east of the sacred lake and with his wife, the Divine Adoratrice Amenirdis I, enlarged the chapel of Osiris *ḥeka-djet*. It was doubtless during Shebitku's reign that their daughter, Shepenwepet II, was adopted as the next Divine Adoratrice after the death of Shepenwepet I, Amenirdis' predecessor.

The political programme expressed in the titulature of Shebitku was different from that of his uncle. He revived the great Ramessid themes, adopting Khaemwaset ('Crowned in Thebes') as his Horus name; 'In great authority over all countries' as his Two Ladies name; and 'With strong arm whenever he strikes the Nine Bows' as his Golden Horus name. This apparent return to the imperial values of the Ramessid period can doubtless be explained by a renewed desire to affirm royal power both inside and outside Egypt. At Sais, however, events were taking a new turn. Ammeris, the 'governor' installed by the Nubians, died around 695 BC; Stephinates, also known as Tefnakht II, reigned from 695 to 688 BC, maintaining the tradition inaugurated by Bakenrenef and foreshadowing the rise of the future Twenty-sixth 'Saite' Dynasty.

In his foreign policy Shebitku adopted a considerably more aggressive stance than his predecessors. The concessions made by Shabaka to Sargon II had provided Egypt with about fifteen years of respite. This breathing space also owed much to the fact that Palestine was temporarily too weak to rebel, even though Assyria was once more embroiled in conflicts with Urartu in the heart of Zagros. But in 704 BC, when Sennacherib succeeded Sargon II, Phoenicia and Palestine seized the chance to rise up in revolt. Sidon was led by King Lule, Ashkelon by Sidka, and Judah by Hezekiah. Shebitku responded quickly to Hezekiah's request for assistance, sending an expeditionary force led by his son Taharqa, while Sennacherib was advancing on Ashkelon, having routed Lule of Sidon.

Ashkelon fell and Sidka was carried off in exile to Assyria. The allies engaged the Assyrian troops to the north of Ashdod at Elteqa. Sennacherib then made a foray towards Lachish and sent the main body of his troops to lay siege to Jerusalem. Hezekiah surrendered in order to preserve his city. In Sennacherib's harangue of Hezekiah, demanding his surrender, he painted a portrait of the strength of his Egyptian ally which, though unflattering, was undeniably close to the truth:

What confidence is this wherein you trust? You say (but they are but vain words), 'I have counsel and strength for the war'. Now in whom do you trust, that you rebel against me? Now behold, you trust in the staff of this bruised reed, even in Egypt, on which if a man lean, it will go into his hand, and pierce it: so is pharaoh king of Egypt unto all that trust in him. (*II Kings* 18: 19–21)

While this was taking place, the 'bruised reed' was making a move towards Lachish. The Assyrians attacked the Egyptian troops and Taharqa chose to withdraw to Egypt. Sennacherib also retreated – without invading Egypt – in order to face a renewed threat from Babylonia. Towards the end of his reign Sennacherib was more occupied with the thorny problem of the Elamites than with Syria-Palestine. In 689 BC, pushed to the limit of endurance by the revolt of both Elam and Babylonia, he cast the city of Babylon into the waters of the Euphrates and was able to turn once more towards the Mediterranean. In 681 BC, however, Sennacherib was assassinated at Nineveh. His son, Esarhaddon, successfully fought his brothers for the throne and undertook the reconstruction of Babylonia. Hostilities between the Assyrians and Egyptians were then finally resumed in 677/676 BC.

Taharqa (Plate 22) had reigned over Egypt since the death of Shebitku in 690 BC. Unlike Shebitku, he had not been linked with the throne during his predecessor's lifetime. His twenty-six-year reign was without a doubt the most glorious phase of the Kushite period. The annals of his reign record a Nile inundation in the sixth year, which might have led to disaster if divine assistance had not been forthcoming. The king commemorated this divine aid with inscriptions at Koptos, Matana, Tanis and the temple of Kawa in Nubia:

My father Amon-Re', Lord of the Thrones of the Two Lands, has wrought for me these four goodly wonders within a single year, even the sixth year of my reign. The like [has not been seen] since those that were aforetime. For the inundation came as a cattle-thief, it inundated this entire land, the like of it was not found in writing in the time of the ancestors . . . It caused the cultivation to be good throughout for my sake; it slew the rats and snakes that were in the midst of it; it kept away from it the devouring of the locusts. It prevented the south winds from reaping it, but I reaped the harvest into barns, incalculable, even Upper Egyptian barley and Lower Egyptian barley and every seed that grows upon the surface of the earth. (Macadam 1949: 27)

In the same year Taharqa began construction in the temple of Kawa, another Nubian sanctuary originally established by Amenophis III in the Eighteenth Dynasty, located opposite Dongola in the heartland of the kingdom of Kerma. Shabaka and Shebitku reoccupied the site,

PLATE 22 *Sphinx of Taharqa. Twenty-fifth Dynasty, granite, h. 0.42 m. (Reproduced courtesy of the Trustees of the British Museum, London.)*

which had been abandoned since the time of Ramesses VII, but it was Taharqa who restored its lost grandeur. Perhaps he was taking the opportunity to secretly resettle his opponents from the north, who had become more agressive since Tefnakht II of Sais was succeeded by Nekawab (Nechepsos). Taharqa certainly seems to have moved Memphite craftsmen south to the restored temple of Amun of Gem-Aten, in order to reproduce various reliefs from the large Old Kingdom mortuary temples – mainly those of Sahure, Neuserre and Pepy II. His motivation for this work derived primarily from the archaizing influences described above.

This reconstruction at Kawa, which was commemorated by a stele (still *in situ*) dating to the sixth year of Taharqa's reign, transformed the temple of Amun into the second great sanctuary of the Napatan kings. Kawa henceforth came to be regarded as one of the main places at which the Kushite kings' power had to be ritually consecrated. Taharqa

PLATE 23 *Mentuemhet, Prince of the City. End of the Twenty-fifth Dynasty, grey granite, h. 1.35 m. (Cairo, Egyptian Museum CG 647. Photograph: John G. Ross.)*

built at most Nubian sites, including Sanam and Napata, where he constructed a new temple (B 300) and enlarged that of Amon-Re (B 500). At Abu Dom (not far from Napata) he constructed an entire temple with the same plan as those at Kawa, Meroe, Semna, Qasr Ibrim and Buhen. He undertook an equal amount of construction work at Thebes, where he built at Medinet Habu and particularly at Karnak (where he was one of the greatest restorers). The construction of the sacred lake and the kiosk in the first court at Karnak have already been described above. Taharqa also completed the embellishment of the temple entrance, constructing colonnades similar to those in the first court in front of the gateway of Monthu to the north, and to those of the eastern gateway and the temple of Khonsu. Along with Shepenwepet II, he also consecrated an Osirid chapel. These works were directed by a remarkable individual called Mentuemhet, who held the offices of 'Prince of the City' and fourth prophet of Amun (Plate 23). He and his brothers, whom Taharqa had appointed to the major priestly posts, shared power over the Theban region with the local nobility, with whom the Nubians had reached an agreement.

Events in Palestine finally conspired to call all these achievements into question. Sidon had rebelled once more, with the result that

Esarhaddon intervened in 677/676 BC and captured the king of Sidon, Abdi-Milkuti, deporting the inhabitants to Assyria and making the kingdom an Assyrian province, with a new capital: Kar-Esarhaddon. From 676 to 674 BC, the Assyrian king remained south of the Taurus because of Scythian and Cimmerian invasions. He was still obliged to guard against the Medes and his southern neighbours who were intent on shaking off his rule. However, once he had established a relative state of peace on all of these fronts, he was able to renew his efforts against Egypt. He knew that the Egyptians had been inciting hostility in the Levantine coastal ports because their commercial routes had been disturbed by the Assyrian control over the region. After a first attack on the Wadi el-Arish in about 677 BC, Esarhaddon assured himself of the neutrality of the Arab tribes around the Dead Sea. The next confrontation with Egypt took place around 674 BC, in the seventeenth year of Taharqa's reign, when Esarhaddon marched on Ashkelon, which was rebelling against him. On this occasion the Assyrians were obliged to retreat in the face of an Egyptian military response, but three years later, in 671 BC, a second battle went in Esarhaddon's favour. He defeated Taharqa and seized Memphis, capturing the crown prince and various members of the royal family:

> I laid siege to Memphis, his royal residence, and conquered it in half a day by means of mines, breaches and assault ladders. His queen, the women of his palace, Ushanahuru his 'heir apparent', his other children, his possessions, horses, large and small cattle beyond counting I carried away as booty to Assyria. All Ethiopians I deported from Egypt – leaving not even one to do homage (to me). Everywhere in Egypt, I appointed new (local) kings, governors, officers, harbour overseers, officials and administrative personnel. (Pritchard 1955: 293)

Taharqa retreated to the south, the control of which he was still apparently able to maintain. But the Assyrians then lent their support to Taharqa's rivals in the north, foremost among whom were the Saites. Once the Assyrians had gone, the Nubians incited rebellion in the north, eventually causing Esarhaddon to intervene again in 669 BC. He died while still *en route* for Egypt, however, leaving the throne at Nineveh to one son Ashurbanipal ('The god Ashur is the creator of the son') and the throne at Babylon to another, Shamashshumukin ('The god Shamash has established a legitimate line'). Despite the agreement achieved between these two kingdoms, Ashurbanipal did not immediately set out in his father's footsteps to Egypt. He preferred to remain in his capital, merely sending an expeditionary force that conquered Taharqa in front of the walls of Memphis. The pharaoh fled in defeat to Thebes, and Ashurbanipal decided to run him to ground.

He combined his troops with auxiliaries from Phoenicia, Cyprus and Syria, as well as contingents drawn from the Delta kingdoms who had chosen to join forces with the Assyrians against the Nubians. The Assyrians advanced deep into the south, as far as the Theban region, but they were unable to lay hands on Taharqa himself, who had returned to his distant kingdom of Napata. Nevertheless, they received the surrender of Kushite officials in Upper Egypt, such as Mentuemhet, and extended their control probably as far as Aswan.

The Assyrians did not stay very long in a country where they could not themselves directly control the administration, obliged as they were to leave this task to their local collaborators. But hardly had they turned their backs on Egypt than the northern kings changed sides again and began to make new overtures to Taharqa. Ashurbanipal's response was immediate: he seized and executed the ruling élite of Sais, Mendes and Pelusium, deporting the rest to Nineveh (where the same fate awaited them). Only one of them was spared: Necho I, king of Sais, who had succeeded Nekawab in 672 BC. Ashurbanipal not only allowed Necho I to remain as the ruler of Sais but also placed Necho's son Psammetichus (the future Psammetichus I) on the throne of the ancient kingdom of Athribis. It was by this means that the Saite dynasty was able to assume overall control of the north with the full knowledge and acquiescence of the Assyrian invaders.

In the same year, 665 BC, Taharqa appointed his cousin Tantamani as heir, and in the following year he died at Napata. Tantamani was then crowned king at Napata and resolved to reconquer Egypt. He described this conquest on a stele in the temple of Gebel Barkal, just as his grandfather Piankhy had done before him, and he obviously used Piankhy's text as his model. The inscription renews the tradition of the prophetic dream which was described above (p. 220) in relation to Tuthmosis IV:

> In the year 1, of his coronation as king...his majesty saw a dream by night: two serpents, one upon his right, the other upon his left. Then His Majesty awoke, and he found them not. His Majesty said 'Wherefore has this come to me?' Then they answered him saying: 'Thine is the Southland; take for thyself also the Northland.' The Two Goddesses shine upon thy brow, the land is given to thee, in its length and breadth. No other divides it with thee. (*Dream Stele*: 3–6; Breasted 1906: IV, 469)

The dream became a reality: Tantamani was crowned at Napata and his right to rule was acknowledged by Amun; he then embarked on a crusade which clearly echoed that of Piankhy. He travelled downstream to Elephantine, where he sacrificed to Khnum, and then to Thebes, where he sacrificed to Amon-Re. Finally he sailed to Memphis, taking it

by direct assault and crushing the northern 'rebels'. He paid homage to
Ptah, Ptah-Sokar and Sekhmet at Memphis, and celebrated his victory
at Napata by undertaking a number of restorations and dedicating gifts
in the temple of Gebel Barkal (*Dream Stele*: 18–24). It was only then
that he 'returned to take arms against the chiefs of the north'. His
campaign seems to have been successful in that Necho I was killed
in battle. The chiefs of the Delta sent a mission to announce their
surrender, which was presented by Prince Pekrur of Pi-Soped (Saft el-
Hinna):

> Then the hereditary prince of Pi-Sopd, Pekrur, arose to speak, saying
> 'Thou slayest whom thou wilt; and lettest live whom thou wilt.' They
> answered with one accord, saying: 'Give to us breath, oh lord of life,
> without whom there is no life. Let us serve thee like the serfs who are
> subject to thee, as thou saidest at the first on the day when thou wert
> crowned as king.' (*Dream Stele*: 36–8; Breasted 1906: IV, 472–3)

But Tantamani's triumph was short-lived, for in 664/663 BC
Ashurbanipal once more unleashed his armies on Egypt. Memphis was
recaptured and Tantamani could only withdraw to Thebes, closely
followed by the Assyrians. When they invaded the very capital of
Amun, Tantamani fled down to Napata. What then took place was
an event that had been totally inconceivable for over 1500 years –
Thebes was sacked by invaders, burnt, ravaged and all its temple
treasures pillaged. The sacking of Thebes marked the end of the period
of Kushite domination, during the last phase of which the Nubian
pharaohs had evidently been only theoretically in control; for the earlier
Assyrian incursion had shown that Mentuemhet and Shepenwepet II
were governing the Theban region in their own right, without any overt
dependence on Napata. Time was also running out for the whole of
Egyptian civilization now that the myth of the inviolability of pharaoh's
sanctuaries had been destroyed by the barbarous forces of the East, who
from then on struck terror into all peoples, from Asia Minor to the
banks of the Nile.

From the pillaging of Thebes until the end of the reign of Tantamani
(664–656 BC), the situation remained uncertain, reflecting the pro-
found political disorganization of the country; this in turn had the
effect of masking the fictitious nature of the power of the Nubians,
dependent on only three centres: Napata, Thebes and Memphis.
Tantamani retreated to Napata, the one place where his rule was
entirely undisputed. The Assyrians did not dare to venture south of
Aswan into regions which were still more alien to them than Egypt itself, since even the language and customs of the Nubians were unknown
to them. The surviving traces of Tantamani in Nubia are minimal, but
all private and public events in Thebes continued to be dated in terms of

the years of his reign. At Thebes itself, power was still in the hands of Mentuemhet, whose authority extended – at its greatest – from Aswan in the south to the kingdom of Hermopolis in the north. Hermopolis was ruled by a certain Nimlot, descendant of the earlier Nimlot whose power had been bolstered by Piankhy. Meanwhile, the Assyrians were clearly attempting to restore the political situation that had prevailed before the Kushite conquest, if necessary by changing the present rulers. This was certainly the case at Herakleopolis, where Assyrian sources refer to another king called Pediese, supposedly the 'legitimate' descendant of Peftjauawybastet.

The pre-eminent Delta kingdom was that of Sais, which had now been enlarged to incorporate the kingdom of Athribis, formerly held by Tefnakht but given by Ashurbanipal to the future Psammetichus I of Sais after the revolt of 666–665 BC. The ancient Libyan chiefdoms, from Sebennytos to Pi-Soped, were still held by the descendants of Piankhy's old enemies. The kingdom of Tanis remained in existence, initially under the rule of a figure who was to become legendary: Pedubastis II, probably one of the kings executed by Ashurbanipal. In the Greco-Roman period he became the protagonist of the epic *Pedubastis Cycle*, which has been preserved in the form of several demotic papyri. This collection of tales is couched in a curious mixture of genres, all hinging on a theme similar to that of the *Iliad*; it also recounts the struggle for the possession of heroic spoils. The tales describe historical events of the period (including the phases of Libyan anarchy and the Persian domination, in which the main protagonists are clearly recognizable) but transpose them into the mythical sphere, adding traditional themes from Greek writings.

The *Pedubastis Cycle* centres on Inaros, the legendary opponent of the domination of Artaxerxes I, who sought to kill the satrap Achaemenes before being executed in 454 BC. The first tale describes Inaros' combat with a griffin from the Red Sea. The second tale describes the struggle between the son of Pedubastis and the Chief Priest of Amun, as they both sought to gain the support of Amun. The third tale recounts a political conflict that took place soon after the end of the Kushite period. Inaros died, and his son, Pemu of Heliopolis, fought a rival at Mendes for the possession of Inaros' breastplate. This battle was supposed to have taken place during the reign of Pedubastis II and involved important figures of the time, such as Pekrur of Pi-Soped. A variety of other tales bring the cycle to a close. The most famous of these is the conflict that pits Pedikhons, another son of Inaros, against the Queen of the Amazons in Assyria. Pedikhons is eventually supposed to have allied himself with the Queen in order to conquer India before returning to Egypt.

PSAMMETICHUS I AND THE 'SAITE RENAISSANCE'

After the death of Necho I, Assyria recognized Psammetichus I as the sole king of Egypt, entrusting him with the administration of the country on condition that he refrain from any rebellion against them. This task was not an easy one. Although he maintained control of the western Delta and the kingdoms of Athribis and Heliopolis, his authority was not acknowledged by the Ma chiefdoms of the east – Sebennytos and Busiris – during the early years of his reign (from 664 BC onwards). However, these chieftains were too close to Psammetichus' kingdom to resist him for long. The definitive submission of the other northern princes took place in about 657 BC, in the eighth year of Psammetichus I's reign. Samtutefnakht, the prince of Herakleopolis who had succeeded Pediese in the fourth year of Psammetichus I's reign, was already subject to Psammetichus' authority. This support was essential, since it ensured that the king of Sais retained control over the riverine traffic along the Nile valley as well as the caravan links with the Western Desert oases and further afield with Nubia and Libya. It was, moreover, Samtutefnakht who helped Psammetichus to gain control of the Theban region without meeting any resistance.

In March of 656 BC he sent a powerful fleet down to Thebes as escort to Nitocris, his daughter by Mehytemwaskhet, who was herself the daughter of the chief priest of Heliopolis. Psammetichus I had Nitocris adopted by the Divine Adoratrices of the time, Shepenwepet II and Amenirdis II, who endowed her with properties in Upper Egypt, thus *de facto* accepting Thebes' domination by the north. When Mentuemhet – officially still only the fourth prophet of Amun, but in reality the most powerful figure in Thebes – accepted the suzerainty of Psammetichus I, the Kushite domination of Thebes was over, for they had shown themselves incapable of resisting the Assyrian invaders. On the other hand, it was paradoxical that Psammetichus I himself – who had been given power by the Assyrians and whose influence was primarily dependent on an élite corps of Greek mercenaries – was now setting himself up as the national champion and reunifier of the country.

The adoption of Nitocris, celebrated by great festivals at Thebes, may have constituted the symbolic reunification of Egypt, but this did not mean that Psammetichus I had eradicated all opposition to his rule. There were certain kinglets and princes in the Delta who steadfastly refused to surrender, and instead adopted the policy that northern opponents had employed since the Middle Kingdom: alliance with Libya. Psammetichus I then levied troops by conscription throughout the reunified provinces – which was a remarkable feat in itself – and marched his armies westwards; his victorious expedition is recorded on several stelae along the route from Dahshur. In the aftermath of this campaign the new pharaoh installed garrisons on the western and eastern frontiers and in Elephantine, which henceforth was to mark the border between Egypt and the Kingdom of Napata. The evidence that foreign troops manned these garrisons not only shows that Psammetichus was partly reliant on non-Egyptian support, but also hints at the growing complexity of international relations in the Mediterranean region, through which hordes of different peoples had recently passed. As well as the traditional mercenaries drawn from Nubia and Libya, the garrisons also included Greeks and Carians (who hawked their soldiering talents throughout the divided Near East) and many others – Phoenicians, Syrians, Jews – who had been driven out of their lands by the Assyrian conquests. A Jewish military colony was based at Elephantine during the Late Period.

The commanding officers of the border garrisons were still the Ma chiefs in the king's entourage, but the new troops succeeded in diluting the old Libyan stock, who were simply forced to share power with them. Moreover, Psammetichus further reduced the influence of the northern chiefdoms by allowing the Greeks and Carians who had helped him gain control of Egypt to establish colonies in the Delta region.

Egypt opened up increasingly to the outside world during the fifty-four years of Psammetichus' reign. Foreign merchants arrived on the heels of foreign soldiers, and diplomatic relations between Egypt and Greece evolved on a distinctly economic basis: Egypt exported such commodities as grain and papyrus and in return allowed the first Milesian trading posts to be established at the mouth of the Bolbitinic (Rosetta) branch of the Nile. This period also saw the appearance of a professional body of Egyptian interpreters who guided Greek intellectuals around the great shrines, particularly those in the Delta, foremost among which was the sanctuary of the goddess Neith at Sais. The Greeks were thus provided with a set of variously distorted facts, allowing them to trace their own history back to the ancient semi-mythical power by which they had become so fascinated. Gradually, almost unavoidably, Egypt became involved in the massive Mediterranean trade network that was developing from Asia Minor to the Aegean region.

The Egyptians were now exposed to foreign artistic influences and technological developments, but there was no question of surrendering the traditional Egyptian strengths. On the contrary, Psammetichus I continued, like the Kushite kings, to emphasize more 'nationalistic' art by returning to Old Kingdom and Middle Kingdom artistic sources. He thus counteracted the effect of the Assyrian invasion, and was also perhaps reacting against the presence of growing numbers of foreigners within Egypt, relations with whom were occasionally problematic during the Saite period. Psammetichus also radicalized religious thought by encouraging the restoration of original religious purity, or at least a return to the state of affairs before the onset of Asiatic influence. This tendency is evident from his proscriptions against non-Egyptian cults, including that of Seth, who was no longer considered patron of the conquering Nineteenth Dynasty kings but simply the god of the Hyksos. These foreign cults were often accompanied by the kind of rituals that the Bible describes (*Genesis* 43: 32).

During Psammetichus' reign − as throughout the Saite and Persian periods − the cults of divine animals underwent a considerable degree of development. In the fifty-second year of his reign Psammetichus enlarged the Serapeum at Saqqara, the necropolis of the Apis bulls (supposedly the incarnations of Ptah). The Serapeum is thought to have been founded by Amenophis III, but it may date further back than this; the subterranean galleries of Saqqara have clearly not yet given up all their secrets, judging from the rediscovery of the Lesser Vaults created at the time of Ramesses II by Prince Khaemwaset. Psammetichus I enlarged this necropolis by adding what is known as the Greater Vaults thus creating one of the most imposing monuments in Egypt.

In the Greater Vaults each bull was buried in its own tomb, linked together by a gallery 3 metres wide, 5.5 metres high and about 350 metres in length. The tombs, carved out below the gallery, were excavated for a depth of 8 metres from floor to ceiling. In the centre of each tomb was set an enormous granite sarcophagus tailored to the size of the Apis bull and weighing on average more than sixty tonnes. The tomb chamber was sealed at the time of the burial and outside it was placed a stele describing the existence of the living god. The Apis cult was not the only example of this type of animal worship: the nearby necropolises of cats or ibises also bear witness to the development of this particular religious trend in the Late Period.

The surviving evidence of the cult of Apis not only sheds fascinating light on the development of animal worship (which clearly made a strong impression on Greek travellers of the time), but also provides a vital means of establishing a precise chronology for the period. Each divine Apis bull had his own set of names and titles, which were equivalent to those of the pharaoh. Stelae at the Serapeum have provided dates for the coronation and death of the Apis that allow links to be made with the pharaoh's regnal dates. The stelae can then confirm the lengths of individual reigns by their connections with preserved items of local prosopography, dated both in terms of the Apis' age and the year of the king's reign. Only the Apis burial chambers have escaped destruction; there has been poor preservation of the cultic installations which must have occupied a large area above the galleries, in the midst of which Prince Khaemwaset was buried. Such installations have similarly not been preserved in the nearby Anubieion and Ibieion. Only the contemporary documentary sources allow an assessment of the importance and wealth of the priesthood entrusted with the care of the cult.

The specific influence of the Saite rulers is indicated by the fact that Thebes no longer set the tone in terms of theology and art, whereas the Memphite tradition had been revived. This archaizing renaissance reached a peak in the tombs of certain high officials such as Ibi (TT 36), the first known steward of the Divine Adoratrice Nitocris. Such archaism is also apparent in the literature of the time, both in the systematization of the 'royal recitation' in the style of the *Victory Stele* of Piankhy and in the continued use of traditional language in official texts. During the Twenty-sixth Dynasty the demotic script became the principal medium for vernacular writing, whereas the 'abnormal hieratic' script of Upper Egypt gradually fell out of use. Demotic was at this time used only for non-literary writings; it was not until the Persian period that the demotic script and language were accepted as a literary medium.

The new political and economic order was achieved by means of administrative reorganization. Initially Psammetichus did not interfere with the government of Upper Egypt; eventually, however, he took various measures to install personnel who could be relied upon to defend the interests of Sais, such as Ibi, the steward of Nitocris, who would have been entrusted with the management of her estates at Thebes. Ibi's successors must have also come from the north, as did the new governor of Edfu and Elkab. The Saite kings did not disturb the old feudal systems such as that at Herakleopolis (which was to last until the Greek period), for they relied on them to provide local support for the rule of the central government. Psammetichus continued to use Sais as the site of the royal residence and necropolis, but he moved the political capital back to Memphis. The city of Memphis, which had managed to preserve a certain theological pre-eminence over the centuries, now also regained its role as administrative centre.

Under Saite rule Egypt entered a period of unquestionable artistic brilliance and prosperity, the evidence for which has survived in the form of the rich tombs of the Saite nobles at Thebes and Memphis. As far as the Mediterranean countries were concerned, Egypt was still a powerful state and a force to be reckoned with. This renewed strength and prosperity arose not merely from Egypt's own means but also from the decline of Assyria. The Egyptians were thus able to dominate the Near East until such time as a new power came along to sweep aside their ambitions. From the moment that Ashurbanipal's troops returned from their conquest of Egypt, the Assyrians had been beset by serious difficulties. Their eastern borders were threatened by the Elamites and the Mannai, while their northern frontier was under attack from the Cimmerians. It was at this time that Gyges, king of Lydia and an ally of Psammetichus I, launched a desperate campaign against the Cimmerians. In 653 BC Psammetichus I took advantage of the conflict between Elam and Assyria to throw off Ashurbanipal's rule and drive out the Assyrian garrisons, pushing them back as far as Ashdod in Palestine.

Meanwhile, Ashurbanipal was still reaping the consequences of the confused succession to Esarhaddon. King Teumman had seized power at the Elamite capital of Susa, expelling the legitimate heirs to the throne who took refuge with the Assyrians. Teumman then attacked Akkad, but Ashurbanipal defeated him and handed over his domains to the exiled princes. These princes, however, subsequently betrayed Ashurbanipal by throwing in their lot with his brother, Shamashshumukin, who had begun to claim that Ashurbanipal had obtained too large a share of their father's domains. Shamashshumukin had also gained the support of most of the Syrians and Arabs. Ashurbanipal therefore blockaded his brother in Babylon, dividing his forces between the Elamite front and the rebellions in the west. His policy of exploiting the divisions between the two Elamite princes (who had not reached an equitable agreement on sharing their inheritance) paid off: in 648 BC Shamashshumukin died during the sack of Babylon, and two years later Susa also fell. At this stage Ashurbanipal, who had meanwhile subdued the Nabataeans and managed to bring Phoenicia to heel, was at the height of his powers; but only a generation later the Assyrian capital of Nineveh itself was to be put to the torch.

The rest of the Assyrian empire seems to have declined equally rapidly: Egypt had regained its independence. Phoenicia – now deprived of its maritime trade by the Greeks – was no longer as lucrative an outlet onto the Mediterranean as before, and the Nabataeans posed as great a threat as their hostile desert terrain. The ravaged land of Elam could provide no assistance, and it is said that Cyrus I of Persia rejoiced at the fall of Susa. Babylon dreamed only of vengeance, while beyond the Zagros the Scythians and the Medes were simply waiting for the first sign of weakness that would allow them to destroy Nineveh.

The death of Ashurbanipal in 627 BC set in motion the last stages of the Assyrian collapse, for his sons were still fighting among themselves for power as late as 612 BC. In 626 BC King Nabopolassar of Chaldaea, capitalizing on the fact that Assyria was weakened by internal struggles, captured first Uruk, then Sippar and Babylon. Nabopolassar then had himself proclaimed King of Babylonia, which he controlled completely by 616 BC. Meanwhile, the Scythians attacked the Assyrian Empire in the years 629–627 BC, and advanced through Asia Minor as far as southern Palestine; according to Herodotus they were halted by Psammetichus I in the area of Ashdod. This was probably not a full-scale Scythian invasion but simply a number of separate advances. These, however, had the effect of alerting Psammetichus to the danger that would be presented by the total collapse of Assyria, which was threatened by both the Chaldaeans and the Medes. He therefore decided in 616 BC to intervene for the first time on the side of the Assyrians against Nabopolassar. The Egyptian reinforcements, how-ever, were insufficient to prevent the Assyrians from being defeated twice over. In 625 BC Cyaxares united the Scythian and Persian armies and embarked on the conquest of Assyria, invading it in 615 BC. The following year he made an unsuccessful attempt to capture Nineveh, but Assur still slipped through his fingers. Nabopolassar then returned to the fray, and the two kings reached an agreement over the remains of the defeated Assyrian territories. Strengthened by their new alliance, they both returned in 612 BC and laid siege to Nineveh for three months. Finally they captured the city and destroyed it, executing the heir to the Assyrian throne. One military leader escaped, however, and claimed authority under the name of Assur-Uballit II. This man fled to the distant western fringes of the kingdom as far as Harran, near the border between modern Syria and Turkey, where he was given succour by Egyptian troops.

THE NEAR EAST AND THE MEDITERRANEAN

In 610 BC Psammetichus I died, leaving his son Wahibre Necho II to carry on his labours. Necho maintained Egypt's commitments to the remnants of the legitimate Assyrian kingdom. When the Medes and the Babylonians took Harran, the Egyptians, who had taken refuge to the west of the Euphrates, crossed back over into Assyria in 609 BC, but were unable to recapture Harran. The city remained in the hands of the Medes, who perhaps saw it as a base for new conquests in the west. Nevertheless, Necho II profited from the vacuum left by the expulsion of the Assyrians from Syria-Palestine: with the expedition of 609/608 BC against Harran, he seized the opportunity to gain control of Palestine. He killed Josiah, king of Judah, who had attempted to block his path at Megiddo. He then intervened in the kingdom of Israel and returned to Judah to depose Josiah's son Jehoahaz, who had come to the throne when his father died. He replaced Jehoahaz with his brother

Eliakim, who then reigned under the new name of Jehoiakim (*II Kings* 23: 29–35). Jerusalem then paid tribute to Egypt and Necho II ruled Syria, at least as far as Carchemish, for nearly four years – until the Chaldaeans had reorganized themselves.

After the fall of Nineveh, the Chaldaeans and the Medes took control of the region, contenting themselves with the spoils from the mountains of Elam and leaving the Babylonians in control of the area around Susa and Assyria. Nabopolassar did not establish himself in the devastated domains of Assyria, and spent the rest of his reign rebuilding his armed forces; he sent his son Nebuchadrezzar to deal with Syria. Necho II had not succeeded in imposing his authority in Syria with any decisive victory, although he had managed to force the Chaldaeans to take refuge east of the Euphrates, while extending his own influence as far as Sidon. But the Egyptian hold over Syria was fragile, relying only on alliances forged under duress, like the situation imposed on Jerusalem. In the spring of 605 BC Nebuchadrezzar captured Carchemish, where the Egyptian troops were wintering. He pursued the fleeing army as far as Hamath, where he overwhelmed them.

The Egyptians were nevertheless allowed something of a respite, for the death of Nabopolassar just at that time meant that Nebuchadrezzar was forced to return to Babylon in order to stake his claim to the throne. In September of 605 BC he became king, and the following year he came back to review in person the tribute that Damascus, Tyre, Sidon and Jerusalem were reluctantly paying him. The king of Ashkelon rose up in rebellion, but his calls for help from the pharaoh were fruitless; the most that Necho II could do was to repel a Babylonian attack on his eastern border in 601 BC, although he did succeed in capturing Gaza. It was not until the end of Necho II's reign that Egypt exceeded this geographical limit, for the pharaoh's ambitions lay in other directions.

Necho II pursued a policy of opening Egypt up to the Greek world, actively encouraging the establishment of Greek colonies. The settlers who came over to Egypt with the Ionian mercenaries created the first genuine Egyptian navy, which provided Egypt the opportunity to compete with its rivals in the Mediterranean and the Red Sea. With this end in view, Necho embarked on a massive building programme in the Wadi Tumilat, employing 12,000 workers to excavate a canal between the Pelusiac branch of the Nile and the Red Sea. The creation of this new trade route meant that a new transit-camp was required for the caravans: he therefore founded a new city called Per-Temu Tjeku, 'the residence of Atum of Tjeku', Tjeku being the ancient name for the region of Wadi Tumilat. The site of the city, about 15 kilometres west of Ismailia, is now known as Tell el-Maskhuta.

The name Per-Temu led to a tradition identifying the city with the Biblical Pithom, but recent excavations at Tell el-Maskhuta have shown that this was incorrect. The foundation of the site certainly dates to the reign of Necho II, but its later history is very confused. The progress of the city tended to mirror the ups and downs of the canal with which it was linked: whenever the canal was repaired and returned to service, the city was also restored and rebuilt. Darius I, Nectanebo I and II, Ptolemy II and Hadrian all undertook building work at the site. Nectanebo I and II took particular pains to embellish the town by transporting various monuments of Ramesses II from Piramesse. For a long time these monuments were wrongly interpreted as conclusive proof of the site's identification with Pithom.

Necho II's new navy is unlikely to have presented a realistic threat to his rivals, but it led to numerous other benefits, including the creation of a new African trade route by the Phoenician mariners whom Necho had recruited. The fleet may in fact have been the only lasting achievement of his reign – his reputation with both contemporaries and subsequent generations was very poor, despite the fact that he appears to have passed on a certain degree of prosperity to his successors. When he died in 595 BC he left behind a son and three daughters. His son, who ruled under the name of Neferibre Psammetichus II, enjoyed only a short reign before dying in 589 BC, but in that brief period he was able to demonstrate sufficient dynamism to justify the parallels between his names and titles and those of his grandfather, Psammetichus I. The brevity of his reign, however, means that no real comparison can be made between his internal policy and that of his namesake. He made sure that Ankhnesneferibre ('Neferibre lives for her'), his daughter by Queen Takhut, was adopted by the Divine Adoratrice Nitocris, eventually succeeding her in 584 BC. Ankhnesneferibre managed to hold this office until the Persian conquest of Egypt in 525 BC, thus perpetuating the Saite administration of Thebes; the splendour of this period can be appreciated at the magnificent tombs of the Stewards of Amun, Shoshenq son of Harsiese (TT 27) and Padineith (TT 197), in the el-Asasif region.

Psammetichus II's pursuit of glory is particularly indicated by his activities outside Egypt, where he seems to have been determined to make up for the negative effects of his father's foreign policy. Without apparently making much use of the new fleet, he involved Egypt once more in the affairs of the kingdom of Judah. The near failure of the Chaldaean campaign against Egypt in 601 BC had inspired Jehoiakim to rebel against Babylon the following year. His son Jehoiachin succeeded him in 598 BC, but by March of the following year Nebuchadrezzar II had captured Jerusalem. Having pillaged the temple and deported

Jehoiachin to Babylon with the nucleus of his court, he then had
Zedekiah, Jehoiachin's uncle, crowned in his place. Jehoiachin remained
in exile at Babylon for thirty-seven years, but during his absence his
followers carried on the struggle against Zedekiah in both Judah and
Israel. In the early years of Zedekiah's reign Egypt constantly urged
Jerusalem to rebel, and Judah was doubtless part of an anti-Babylonian
coalition that was formed in 594 BC. Psammetichus II undertook a
peaceful tour of the region as far as Byblos in 591 BC, and on his return
celebrated the event as if it had been a traditional military campaign.
This show of force must have encouraged Zedekiah to embark upon a
rebellion that was to prove catastrophic for Jerusalem.

The previous year, Psammetichus II had engaged in hostilities with
the land of Kush, where Anlamani had revived the kingdom of Napata.
This was the first confrontation between Egypt and Nubia since the
time of Tantamani. The Egyptian army successfully advanced to Pnubs,
in the area of the Third Cataract, and perhaps even as far south
as Napata. Curiously, however, Psammetichus does not appear to have
capitalized on this victory, and his troops – including numerous Carians
who carved their names on the monuments at Abu Simbel – subsequently
retreated back to the First Cataract. Elephantine continued to be
the southern border of Egypt, while the zone from Elephantine to
Takompso (the so-called Dodekaschoenos) became a kind of no man's
land between the two countries. The reasons for this campaign are
unclear: the official texts describe it as a necessary response to a
Nubian rebellion, but this is clearly nothing but traditional rhetoric.
The campaign was followed by a wave of deliberate damage to the
monuments of Twenty-fifth Dynasty Kushite rulers in Egypt, almost as
if Psammetichus were attempting to remove all traces of his ancestors'
old enemies. He also attacked the memory of Necho II, for motives
which are not clearly understood, except that the reasons must surely
have been more serious than the military setbacks suffered by his father
at the hands of the Chaldaeans.

THE GREEK PRESENCE

Psammetichus II died in February of 589 BC, before his policy in the
Near East had come to fruition. His son, Khaaibre Apries, was at once
forced to deal with the aftermath of Zedekiah's rebellion, in which he
had participated along with Phoenicia. Nebuchadrezzar II advanced on
Jerusalem and laid siege to it for two years. At the same time he secured
control of Syria by capturing Sidon, but was unable to capture Tyre, for
it was being supplied from the sea by Apries. The efficiency of the
new Egyptian fleet was demonstrated by the fact that Tyre managed to

hold off the Babylonians until as late as 573 BC. The Egyptians were rather less successful on land: although they attempted to support Zedekiah they were forced to retreat, and in 587 BC Jerusalem fell again. Zedekiah was eventually captured by the Babylonians at Jericho, and Nebuchadrezzar decided to make an example of him. He forced him to watch the execution of his son, then he put his eyes out and took him into captivity in Babylon. But the war was not yet over – the followers of the prophet Jeremiah assassinated the Babylonian governor whom Nebuchadrezzar had installed on the throne, then they and their leader fled to Egypt before the Babylonians retaliated in 582 BC.

Apries' military concerns continued when the Elephantine garrison revolted upon learning of Nebuchadrezzar II's defeat of Egypt. Although the general Neshor succeeded in quelling this mutiny, it was only a foretaste of the troubles that were to beset the end of Apries' reign. In 570 BC the pharaoh received a call for help from his Libyan ally, Prince Adikran of Cyrene, who was struggling against Dorian invaders. The mercenaries whom Apries sent – his *machimoi*, or 'warriors' – suffered a humiliating defeat, and on their return a battle broke out between the *machimoi* and the Egyptian Greeks. This conflict degenerated into a civil war between the national army and the Greek and Carian mercenaries. The Egyptian soldiers proclaimed the general Amasis as their new king, since he had gained great glory for his role in the campaign against the Nubians. Apries, now reduced to his mercenary troops, eventually confronted Amasis at Momemphis at the end of 570 BC. There Apries was killed and his body was conveyed to Sais, where Amasis buried him with due honour. Nebuchadrezzar II attempted to take advantage of these internal problems to launch an invasion of Egypt in 568 BC, but he was held back by Amasis.

Swept to the throne on a wave of nationalism, Amasis was unable to avoid confronting the problem of the Greeks, both within Egypt and elsewhere. He dealt with the Greeks and Carians living in Egypt by adopting a policy of amalgamating the various foreign communities spread throughout northern Egypt; according to Herodotus he did so by concentrating the foreigners in the city of Naukratis, to the south-east of the future site of Alexandria. Excavation of the site has provided evidence that Naukratis was indeed used for this purpose, and it is apparent that the city was already the home of Greek colonists as early as the reign of Psammetichus I. Amasis awarded important economic and commercial privileges to the foreigners settled at Naukratis. He afforded the city the status of an independent trading post, providing it with its own cult places. This economy based on 'trading posts', which underwent a gradual process of development from then until modern times, formed the foundation for the prosperity of the Delta and contributed greatly to the economic success of Egypt as a whole, which reached something of a peak during the reign of Amasis. It is thought that Egypt's population at this time was probably about 7.5 million, an enormous number compared with the rest of the Mediterranean region, especially considering that Egypt's population was not to exceed 8 million until the nineteenth century.

Amasis has traditionally been remembered as a good-natured and exuberant ruler as well as a wise legislator, but unfortunately the Persian conquerors removed the records of his achievements from almost all the monuments that he built. His qualities as a diplomat are suggested by the fact that he remained on good terms with the Greek world. Military successes over certain towns in Cyprus brought him the use of the powerful Cypriot fleet. This naval power enabled him to trade throughout the Mediterranean and to help his allies against the growing might of the Persians, which was beginning to cause anxiety among his Greek partners. He arranged an alliance with King Croesus of Lydia, and Polycrates, the tyrant of Samos, and he even made terms with his old enemies the Babylonians, who were also allied with Croesus. In 546 BC Lydia finally fell before Cyrus II and seven years later Babylon itself was captured. Egypt's firmest allies still seemed – wrongly as it turned out – to be the Greek cities, whose friendship Amasis cultivated through a series of measures that made him the most philhellenic of the pharaohs, even financing the rebuilding of the temple of Apollo at Delphi after it was destroyed by fire in 548 BC.

But all of these manoeuvres were insufficient to evade one inescapable fact: the Persians, future masters of Asia Minor, were building an empire that was even more powerful than that previously created by the Assyrians. The only group that seemed capable of opposing the Persians were the Greeks, for they were protected both geographically by the sea and tactically by military strategies that were to prove effective in the final battles with Persia. The Egyptians, however, were overtaken by events.

The death of Cyrus II in 529 BC temporarily delayed the invasion of Egypt, but when Amasis died in 526 BC, Psammetichus III succeeded to a throne that was already distinctly shaky. Cambyses II succeeded Cyrus II on the throne at Susa, and in the spring of 525 BC he marched on Egypt, wiping out Psammetichus III's army at Pelusium. The pharaoh took refuge at Memphis – once more the last bastion of resistance – but the city was besieged and finally fell to the Persians. Although Psammetichus III managed to escape again to gather together his last forces, he was eventually recaptured and carried off in chains to Susa. Egypt then became a province of the Achaemenid Empire. Over the next hundred years the Egyptians would still manage a few short bursts of independence, but each of these was only the result of a brief power vacuum between invasions.

OPENING UP TO THE OUTSIDE WORLD

The Nubians and the Saites ruled Egypt for only about two centuries, divided unequally between them. During the Kushite period Egypt rediscovered a kind of national unity; but this was a fragile achievement, in which they were forced to accept that both Saites and Nubians had a right to claim a certain legitimacy for their rule. The Libyan rulers of Sais considered themselves to be the heirs to a throne that Ramesses II's descendants had neglected, while the Kushite dynasty attempted to rediscover the original sources of the Egyptian monarchy in the distant past, for it was undeniable that the Nubians themselves were one of the products of the empire sought by Amun. Between these two forces, Thebes appears to have lost the initiative, both on a political and religious level. Saites and Kushites were moreover agreed on the maintenance of the office of Divine Adoratrice at Thebes, the holder of which was the only person capable of defusing the latent conflict between them.

The Assyrians exacerbated these conflicts by initially installing a Saite ruler – proof of the animosity can be seen in Psammetichus II's final proscriptions against the Nubians almost a century after the removal of the Kushite monarchy. The main beneficiary, however, was Memphis, which once more became the political capital, as it had been in the earliest periods of Egyptian history. The return to Memphis, the archetypal capital, allowed the throne of Egypt to be freshly based on ancient values. This was accompanied by a new surge of investigations into the religious, literary and artistic past, the results of which must have contrasted sharply with the world to which Egypt was opening up, as it welcomed the new masters of the Mediterranean onto its territory. The Egyptians, acting in a way that was to remain natural to them until modern times, first accepted these external influences and then attempted to assimilate the new values, just as they had once before absorbed the culture of Asia. In this way they laid the foundations for a society that, throughout the succeeding centuries, would combine much that was compatible between the two cultures: the strange tomb of Petosiris at Tuna el-Gebel, the paintings of Qaret el-Muzawaqqa in the distant Dakhla Oasis, and the surprising local cultures that sprang up on the Roman *limes*, as at Qasr Dush in Kharga Oasis, where there was a peculiar mixture of Egyptian, Greek, Jewish and Oriental themes. The revival of their national values also helped to dispel the bitter memories of the Assyrian invasion, and this was doubtless one of the reasons why the Saite period was to become a symbol of the lost glory of Egypt. The memories of the Saite dynasty became a refuge of traditional values to which the Egyptians were able to turn as the yoke of each new invader grew too heavy for their shoulders.

15

Persians and Greeks

The defeat of Psammetichus III marked the end of an era in Egyptian foreign policy, and at the same time emphasized Egypt's isolation. At the very moment of confrontation, the Greek allies defected: Phanes of Halicarnassus went over to the enemy at Gaza, and Polycrates of Samos had already betrayed them. The bedouin (known to the Egyptians as 'sandfarers') had been opponents of Egypt since early times, and now they acted as guides for the Persian troops crossing the Sinai.

Quite apart from his military allies, Cambyses II was also welcomed into Egypt by minorities such as the Jewish community at Elephantine, as well as by certain members of the Egyptian aristocracy. It is even possible that the Persian pillaging of Egyptian towns reported by the Greek sources did not actually take place. In any case, the social impact of the invasion was certainly not as serious as later texts suggest, influenced as they no doubt were by anti-Persian propaganda. In fact, the interests of Egypt's new masters seem to have coincided with the traditional feelings of the most privileged classes of native Egyptians. This was to be a constant theme in later Egyptian history: two centuries later Darius III Codoman, and after him Alexander and his heirs, found the same amenable élite group of Egyptians, who were sufficiently interested in maintaining continuity in the government and social system of Egypt that they were prepared to support the illusion of an indigenous administration. One of these officials, called Udjahorresnet, was a typical cultured administrator who espoused the Persian cause. He was a Saite priest and a doctor, and had served as a naval officer in the reigns of Psammetichus III and Amasis. His autobiography, written on a naophorous statue now in the Vatican collection at Rome, describes how he introduced Cambyses to Egyptian culture so that he would be able to take on the appearance of a traditional pharaoh. This was a strategy that was to be adopted by all subsequent foreign rulers of Egypt:

> The Great Chief of all foreign lands, Cambyses, came to Egypt, and the foreign peoples of every foreign land were with him. When he had conquered this land in its entirety, they established themselves in it, and he was Great Ruler of Egypt and Great Chief of all foreign lands. His Majesty assigned to me the office of chief physician. He made me live at his side as companion and administrator of the palace. I composed his titulary, to wit his name of King of Upper and Lower Egypt, Mesutire. (Statue Inscription of Udjahorresnet; Lichtheim 1980a: 37–8)

The Nile valley became a satrapy of the Persian empire and in 522 BC, when Cambyses was obliged to return to Persia to deal with a revolt by Gautama, the pretender to the throne, Egypt was left under the command of the satrap Aryandes. But the Persians clearly did not impose their own style of administration on Egypt. The kings of Susa ruled over Egypt in the guise of pharaohs: like Cambyses II, all of them adopted a complete set of Egyptian titles and ostensibly continued the activities of their Egyptian 'predecessors'.

Udjahorresnet must have been endeavouring to protect the interests of his own city first, for he makes it clear that the newcomers were not showing Sais the respect that its holy sanctuary deserved:

> I let His Majesty know the greatness of Sais, that it is the seat of Neith-the-Great, the mother who bore Ra and inaugurated birth when birth had not yet been . . . I made a petition to the majesty of the King of Upper and Lower Egypt, Cambyses, about all the foreigners who dwelled in the temple of Neith, in order to have them expelled from it, so as to let the temple of Neith be in all its splendour, as it had been before. His Majesty commanded to expel all the foreigners who dwelled in the temple of Neith, to demolish all their houses and all their unclean things that were in this temple.
>
> When they had carried all their personal belongings outside the wall of the temple, His Majesty commanded to cleanse the temple of Neith and to return all its personnel to it . . . and the hour-priests of the temple. His Majesty commanded to give divine offerings to Neith-the-Great, the mother of god, and to the great gods of Sais, as it had been before. His Majesty commanded to perform all their festivals and all their processions, as had been done before. His Majesty did this because I had let His Majesty know the greatness of Sais, that it is the city of all the gods, who dwell there on their seats forever. (Lichtheim 1980a: 38)

This policy regarding Egyptian sanctuaries and national cults was confirmed by the buiding work undertaken by Cambyses II in the Wadi Hammamat and at other Egyptian temples. The solemn burial of an

Apis bull in the sixth year of Cambyses' reign also contradicts the tradition of impiety that later sources ascribe to the Achaemenid ruler. According to the accounts given by Herodotus, Ctesias and especially the *Cambyses Romance* or the *Chronicle* of John of Nikiou (Schwartz 1949a), the principal surviving sources on the period, Cambyses is supposed to have behaved with appalling savagery, culminating in the execution of the Apis bull at Memphis. He is also supposed to have arranged the deportation of masses of opponents, and so on. But these texts were simply repeating the plethora of nationalist propaganda that built up during the period after the end of the Persian domination, when the Greeks, conquerors of the Persians and new masters of Egypt, took great pains to malign their old enemies.

Cambyses II tried unsuccessfully to gain control of Nubia and the oases, and his expedition to Siwa, perhaps seeking confirmation of his rule by the oracle of Amun (a mission in which Alexander was later to succeed), ended in disaster. He is said to have lost a complete army, the traces of which archaeologists may yet discover under the desert sands.

Perhaps the Persian administration's poor reputation was due to the style of government of the satrap Aryandes, who ruled from 522 to 517 BC. When Darius I came to the throne in 522 BC, he must have immediately set off to subdue the Egyptians before they could rise up in revolt. Aryandes seems then to have pursued his own policy in Egypt, striking coins bearing his own image and taking the initiative to capture Cyrene when the Libyans rebelled against their Dorian rulers. However, he does not seem to have shown the same respect for the Egyptians' customs as his sovereign had.

Darius I eventually executed Aryandes and replaced him with Pherendates, simultaneously making appropriate arrangements to reassure public opinion in Egypt: he finished the construction of Necho II's canal between the Pelusiac branch of the Nile and the Red Sea so as to obtain even more economic benefit from Egypt, which was the wealthiest of all the satrapies. Udjahorresnet was commanded to accompany Darius I to Susa, and when he returned was able to describe Egypt's importance to the Persians:

> The majesty of the King of Upper and Lower Egypt, Darius, ever-living, commanded me to return to Egypt – when His Majesty was in Elam and was Great Chief of all foreign lands, and Great Ruler of Egypt – in order to restore the establishment of the House of Life . . . , after it had decayed. The foreigners carried me from country to country. They delivered me to Egypt as commanded by the Lord of the Two Lands.
>
> I did as His Majesty had commanded me. I furnished them with all their staffs consisting of the wellborn, no lowborn among them. I placed them in charge of every learned man . . . His Majesty had commanded to

give them every good thing, in order that they might carry out all their crafts. I supplied them with everything useful to them, with all their equipment that was on record, as they had been before. His Majesty did this because he knew the worth of this guild in making live all that are sick, in making endure forever the names of all their gods, their temples, their offerings, and the conduct of their festivals. (Lichtheim 1980a: 39–40)

Darius re-established the traditional prerogatives of the temple estates, and ordered the construction of the Hibis temple at the Kharga Oasis. He also began a programme of restoration work at Busiris and Elkab and reopened the quarries at Wadi Hammamat. One of the statues that Darius commissioned from Egyptian sculptors has even been found at Susa. He not only undertook the reform of the Egyptian administration and judicial system but introduced a new legal code and began to mint coins locally. He left behind him the memory of the foreign king of Egypt who came closest to understanding the pre-occupations of the Egyptians themselves, and his reign appears to have been a period of great prosperity for Egypt.

But once more events outside Egypt were to determine the fate of the Nile valley. In 490 BC the Greeks defeated the Persians at Marathon, forcing Darius to turn his attention to another front. The cities of the Delta took advantage of this circumstance to launch a revolt in 486 BC. Darius I died before he was able to put down the rebellion; he was succeeded on the throne of Egypt by Xerxes. Crushing the revolt, Xerxes put his own son, Achaemenes, in charge of the satrapy. Achaemenes toughened the administration of the country to such an extent that long afterwards, in the Ptolemaic period, Xerxes' name was written in Egyptian texts with a pejorative determinative normally reserved for conquered enemies. The speed of events, however, was accelerating. In 480 BC Achaemenes took 200 Egyptian vessels to fight on behalf of his brother in the Persian fleet sent against the Greeks. The defeat at Salamis and Xerxes' assassination encouraged the Egyptians to rebel: they took up arms against the Persians during the reign of Artaxerxes I, who had risen to the throne in 465 BC.

Inaros then embarked on his famous struggle with the Persians already described above. Descended from a Libyan dynasty, Inaros was the son of the last Psammetichus. He gathered together the nationalist forces scattered throughout the Delta and declared himself King of Egypt. Prince Amyrtaeus, a descendant of the Saite kings, allied himself with the new king. Between the two of them they succeeded in gaining control of the whole of Lower Egypt down to Memphis, assisted in their struggle by an Athenian squadron.

Inaros finally joined battle with the Persians at Papremis, and this first encounter was successful, resulting in the death of Achaemenes. The rebels then advanced on Memphis, accompanied by their Greek allies. But after a series of skirmishes of which the outcome is not known, the Persians eventually regained the upper hand: the Greeks fled and Inaros was imprisoned on the island of Prosopis, eventually to be executed in Persia in 454 BC. Arsames replaced Achaemenes at the head of the satrapy and Greece made peace with Persia. For a generation Egypt was at peace, and it was during this period of apparent serenity and prosperity that Herodotus made his visit. Arsames allowed the sons of Inaros to maintain their rule in the Delta and he avoided any measures which might have resuscitated the revolt. The Persian officials appointed to govern Egypt became more and more integrated into Egyptian life, even Egyptianizing their own names.

Nevertheless, revolutionary feelings flared up again in Egypt as a result of the struggles for the throne of Susa following the death of Artaxerxes. When Darius II seized power in 424 BC he revived Darius I's conciliatory policy by continuing the decoration of the temple at Hibis. But the support given to him by the Jewish community at Elephantine had the effect of exasperating the 'nationalist' Egyptians, who destroyed the temple at Hibis in the seventeenth year of his reign. The Greeks – particularly the Spartans – gave their support to Sais, which was still the main centre of Egyptian rebellion. The grandson of Amyrtaeus, who bore the same name as his grandfather, led the country into open revolt in 404 BC, after over six years of more or less clandestine opposition. In the same year that Darius II died, Amyrtaeus had himself declared king and founded the Twenty-eighth Dynasty, which consisted only of his own reign. After less than four years, his power was re-cognized as far south as Aswan, and his rule had even been accepted by the Jewish community at Elephantine. Not a single monument bearing his name has survived, however, and practically nothing is known about his reign, which came to an end in 398 BC. The apparent ease with which he took power and the almost complete lack of response from Susa are both explained by the struggle for succession which divided the Persians after the death of Darius II.

In Xenophon's description of the fratricidal struggle between the two sons of Darius II (Artaxerxes II and Cyrus II), it is claimed that Tamos, the defeated leader of Cyrus II's Greek mercenaries, sought refuge in Egypt but was put to death by the pharaoh (whom Xenophon incorrectly calls Psammetichus). This apparently incomprehensible act – in view of the fact that the Egyptians ought to have been the Greeks' natural allies against the Persians – may perhaps be explained as a diplomatic show of goodwill towards Artaxerxes II, the new king of Susa, who was as yet incapable of recapturing Egypt and might thus have been encouraged to steer a more prudent neutral course.

Amyrtaeus II was the first ruler in pharaonic Egypt's last period of national independence, which was to endure for just over half a century, from 404 to 343 BC. During this period the Twenty-eighth Dynasty was followed by the Twenty-ninth, which lasted only twenty years, and the Thirtieth, which was only about double this length. There is little evidence of the manner in which Nepherites I succeeded Amyrtaeus II on the throne in the autumn of 399 BC. Nepherites' previous career is totally unknown, although it must certainly have been a military one. He is usually thought to have been of Libyan descent, since he is known to have come from Mendes, but nothing is known of the circumstances that led to this change of dynasty. Only one surviving document – an Aramaic papyrus at the Brooklyn Museum – gives any indication that the transferral of power was accompanied by violence anywhere in the country. The text describes an open battle between the founder of the Twenty-ninth Dynasty and his predecessor: Nepherites is supposed to have taken Amyrtaeus prisoner and then to have executed him at Memphis before establishing his native city as the new capital. During the 1980s, the excavations of the Brooklyn Museum and the University of New York at Mendes provide evidence of Nepherites I's building activity there, thus backing up the claim that it was the Twenty-ninth Dynasty capital. If this is indeed the case, then Mendes would be expected to include a royal necropolis, though no evidence of such a cemetery has yet emerged.

Nepherites I perhaps had himself crowned at Memphis or Sais – like Nectanebo I later in the dynasty (Traunecker 1979: 420) he would have done so for purely political reasons. His royal titles were also chosen to emphasize his desire to instigate a process of national renewal in imitation of Twenty-sixth Dynasty policy, like that already attempted by Amyrtaeus. Nepherites' Horus name was therefore the same as that of Psammetichus I. His own reign, however, was shorter and less glorious than that of his role model, lasting only six years according to Manetho; the latest surviving text from his reign is dated to his fourth regnal year. On the other hand, the evidence of Nepherites I's building activity is far from negligible: he did a great deal of work in the north, at Tell Timai, Tell Roba, Tell el-Farain, Memphis and Saqqara (where the burial of an Apis bull is recorded in the second year of his reign), and some evidence has survived of a cult dedicated to one of his statues at Akhmim. He is also thought to have been responsible for various sections of the Temple of Amon-Re at Karnak, including the construction of the offering storeroom south of the Sacred Lake and the bark shrine in front of the First Pylon, later finished by Achoris (Traunecker 1979: 423).

When Nepherites I died in the winter of 394–393 BC he left behind two rival factions fighting for power. At first the legitimate party had the upper hand, according to the *Demotic Chronicle* (an early Ptolemaic papyrus inscribed with oracles relating to Twenty-ninth and Thirtieth Dynasty kings), and the son of Nepherites, Manetho's Muthis, reigned for a few months. But his authority was contested by Psammuthis (Pa-sheri-n-Mut: 'The son of Mut'), who usurped the throne, had himself crowned and took the titles 'Ra is powerful' and 'Chosen of Ptah'. The usurper himself, whose impiety is castigated in the *Demotic Chronicle*, only reigned for a single year, eventually giving way to Achoris. Psammuthis' reign was then completely eclipsed as Achoris incorporated it into his own, claiming that his own reign stretched back to the death of Nepherites I. Despite Psammuthis' extremely short reign, there are still traces of his activity – especially at Karnak, where he seems, surprisingly perhaps, to have continued Nepherites' work. He was also active at Akhmim, but there is no trace there of any cult dedicated to him personally, which suggests either that Psammuthis was considered by future generations to have been a usurper or that his successor was very successful in erasing the memory of his reign.

When Achoris rose to the throne he was filled with the desire to prove his legitimacy as ruler, emphasizing his connections with Nepherites I both on his monuments and through his choice of titles, and thus inveigling himself into the heart of the political dynasty. His building work amply confirmed these intentions. The very name of his son, Nepherites II (who succeeded him for a few brief months in the summer of 380 BC, before being deposed by Nectanebo I), must have been intended to give the impression that he was the grandson of the founder of the dynasty. But perhaps this excessive enthusiasm shows that Achoris' origins were in fact less impressive than he wished to suggest by giving himself the title *weḥem meswt* ('He who repeats births'), as Ammenemes I and Sethos I had. Nectanebo I seems to have presented Achoris as a usurper by tracing his own origins back to Nepherites I. No documents have survived to allow this succession problem to be untangled with any certainty, and perhaps the most prudent view is that Achoris and Nectanebo were actually both descendants of Nepherites fighting for their rightful power (Traunecker 1979; 432ff.).

Nevertheless, the fourteen years of Achoris' reign were characterized by a general atmosphere of national renewal. This manifested itself in great building activity at the major temples, including Luxor and Karnak, where he completed the programme of work begun by Nepherites I, as well as Medinet Habu, Elkab, Tod, Medamud and Elephantine, various sites in Middle Egypt, the Serapeum and the temple of Hibis at the Kharga Oasis. The number of statues and objects inscribed with his cartouche, greater in quantity than those left from his predecessors' reigns, seem to confirm this impression. The fact that these items have been found as far away as Phoenicia is also an indication of the Egyptians' reappearance on the international stage.

This, however, was all a long way from the genuine renaissance that had taken place in the Saite period. Although activity had resumed at the great Egyptian quarries, trade was flourishing and Egyptians were once more involved in the politics of the Near East, they were no longer able to play a significant role. They were content instead to ally themselves indirectly with the Greeks in their struggle against the Persians – fear of the Persians had in fact succeeded in temporarily uniting the various peoples of the Mediterranean region. For their part, the Persians no longer regarded Egypt as an independent power – it was simply a rebellious satrapy. Nepherites I had attempted to supply Sparta with equipment and provisions to help them in their war against the common foe, but this consignment was unfortunately lost in transit when it fell into the hands of the Rhodians, who had gone over to the Persians. After this unsuccessful expedition, Egypt ceased to take any further part in the wars with Persia, even in an indirect fashion.

The balance of power in the Mediterranean began to alter as Sparta gradually reduced its involvement in Asia Minor (after the naval battle at Cnidos in 394 BC, and especially after their defeat in 391) and Athens appeared on the scene in support of Cyprus in 390/389 BC. As far as Egypt was concerned, it was only a case of moving from one ally to another, and in fact it was a positive advantage to Egypt that the revolt against the Great King led by Evagoras of Cyprus actually succeeded in drawing the Persian troops further away from the Nile valley. In 389 BC Achoris agreed on a treaty with Athens, giving him a chance to reorganize his forces. This respite lasted until 386 BC, establishing calm over his north Mediterranean front. It ended with the peace of Antalcidas, the terms of which forbade the Greek cities to take up arms against Artaxerxes II. The satrap Pharnabazes was then able to turn his attention to Egypt, since Egypt and Cyprus were the last obstacles to Persian hegemony over the Mediterranean region.

For three years, from 385 to 383 BC, Achoris succeeded in withstanding the Persian armies' attempts to conquer Egypt, which was much better organized than it had been a generation earlier. Instead of being divided among themselves, the Egyptian armies were now united under a single ruler. The Egyptian navy was one of the most powerful of its time, and the army benefited from the support of elite Greek troops. These Greeks, inspired by anti-Persian feelings and commanded by the Athenian general Chabrias, provided a strong defence in the area of the Pelusiac branch of the Nile. Not only were the Persian incursions checked, but the Egyptians also succeeded in regaining a foothold in the Near East, and Evagoras of Cyprus seized the opportunity – while the Persians were occupied with the Egyptians – to establish control over the Mediterranean as far as Tyre.

The Persians then decided to concentrate all their efforts on defeating Cyprus. In 381 BC Tiribazes and Orontes attacked Evagoras, but despite their greater numbers of troops they met with little success. On land, Evagoras managed to cut off their supplies until the starving Persian soldiers rebelled against their leaders. At sea, however, he was less fortunate. He confronted the Persian fleet off Kition and at first had some success, but eventually he was defeated and forced to withdraw as far as Salamis, having lost most of his forces. Orontes at once gave chase and laid siege to Evagoras' own city. Evagoras managed to escape and went to the Egyptian royal court in search of assistance. Achoris, who had already supplied the Cypriots with ships, troops and provisions, judged that the cause was lost. Evagoras nevertheless succeeded in regaining Salamis with a derisory amount of support. It remained only for him to negotiate with the conqueror. Benefiting from the growing divisions between Orontes and Tiribazes, he obtained peace without surrender, thus putting an end to ten years of war.

By the summer of 380 BC the Persians could at last seriously anticipate the recapture of Egypt, having gained all the success they could have hoped for against the Greek cities and on the western front. In addition, the death of Achoris created a particularly favourable situation. There were difficulties with the succession and his son was rapidly deposed by Nectanebo son of Tachos, the ruler of Sebennytos (modern Sammanud), who had been declared king some months earlier. This crisis did not last very long, since Nectanebo had effectively gained control of the whole country by November of 380 BC, but it combined with the political isolation of the pharaoh to temporarily disable Egypt's defences. Another threat to Nectanebo's rule was posed by the removal of the general Chabrias, who had helped him in his rise to power. Not only did the Persians succeed in having Chabrias recalled to Athens in the winter of 380/379 BC, but the Athenian government went so far as to send one of their most brilliant generals, Iphicrates, to lead the Greek auxiliaries in the great Persian force sent against Egypt. These preparations took six years, delayed by dissensions among the Greek and Persian military commanders as well as between the Persians themselves, and it was not until the spring of 373 BC that the Great King's armies finally left northern Palestine, both by land (via the coastal route) and by sea.

The Persian fleet, consisting almost entirely of Greeks, were the first troops to arrive. They did not attempt to enter Egypt by the Pelusiac branch of the Nile, for Nectanebo had reinforced its natural and artificial defences with a series of fortifications and traps. Instead, Iphicrates and Pharnabazes assayed the Mendesian mouth of the Nile (further to the west), which was more poorly defended. This tactic proved to be so successful that after the briefest of battles, they found the path to Memphis opening up before them. Only the mutual mistrust between the Greeks and Persians saved the Egyptians from what must have seemed to be inevitable defeat. Iphicrates wanted to capitalize on his position of strength by marching immediately on Memphis, which he knew to be poorly defended; but Pharnabazes feared that the Greeks were planning to capture Egypt for themselves, and so forced them to wait until the main body of Persian troops had arrived by land. This delay was enough for the pharaoh to rally his troops and launch a direct assault against the invaders. The Great King's army was eventually repelled, partly because the Egyptians were more familiar with the local geography and partly because – the month being July – the annual inundation took place, conveniently transforming the Delta into a marsh.

THE LAST NATIVE DYNASTY

Egypt escaped this fresh invasion and embarked on a relatively long period of peace. The Persians did not return until about thirty years later, in 343 BC. At the same time, the defeat of Pharnabazes led to a breakdown in relations with Iphicrates who, fearing reprisals, fled back to Athens. There he was appointed general of the fleet in 373 BC, to the great chagrin of his former allies. Until 366 BC Egypt stood alone against the Persians: the Greek cities' hands were tied by their agreement with the Great King and everything seemed to point towards a new attempt at the conquest of the Nile valley. But the Achaemenid empire had grown too large for its own good, and the satrapy system exacerbated its centrifugal tendencies. The ageing Artaxerxes II allowed the links between Susa and the provinces to become more relaxed, and during the 370s BC Cappadocia, Caria and the fringes of the empire gradually became semi-autonomous. Cappadocia was the first to openly rebel against Susa in about 368 BC, followed by Phrygia and then Sparta and Athens. Soon the whole of the western Persian Empire, from

Armenia to Phoenicia, was on the verge of breaking away. In less than five years the Great Rebellion of the Satraps had reached its peak, but it was still not time for the whole empire to disintegrate, and unity could be seen to have good points as well as bad. Egypt benefited from this respite, establishing links with the rebellious satraps and even financing some of them, after having restored relations with Sparta and Athens.

In 365 BC Nectanebo I (Plate 24) nominated his son Tachos (Teos) as heir to the throne. Tachos, having been placed in charge of foreign policy, played an active role in the rebellion against the Great King, at first on behalf of his father and later on his own account, from 363 to 361 BC. Tachos even launched a campaign into Syria-Palestine, with the help of two veterans of the earlier Persian wars: the indefatigable Chabrias, who commanded the navy, and Agesilaos, the old king of Sparta, who despite having reached the age of forty-five, set off for Egypt with a contingent of a thousand hoplites. Such a military expedition as this (unthinkable only a generation before) had been made possible by the administrative policies of Nectanebo I, who – like the Saite pharaohs before him – had succeeded in rekindling the nationalist spark in Egypt.

Evidence of Egypt's revival has survived in the abundance and high quality of the artistic and literary output of the time. Nectanebo himself was responsible for the construction of a number of new buildings, as well as a programme of restoration and embellishment at virtually all of the temples in Egypt. It was he who took particular responsibility for the restoration of the temple precincts at Karnak, including the construction of the First Pylon of the temple of Amun. He also erected the first phase of the temple of Isis at Philae, and ordered constructions at Elkab, Hermopolis, Memphis, and the Delta sites of Saft el-Hinna and Tanis. Apart from the construction of temples, his religious policy also extended to the award of tax exemptions and endowments to various temple estates such as those at Edfu and Sais.

At the beginning of 361 BC Tachos began to make preparations for war with Persia: his own troops consisted of *machimoi*, and he extracted heavy taxes from the Egyptians so that there would be sufficient resources in the government coffers to pay the Greek mercenaries. This measure led to a degree of unpopularity that his rivals were very quick to exploit. In 360 BC the Egyptian army set off for Phoenicia, travelling along the coast by land and sea. Tachos himself led the troops into action, accompanied by his grandson, the future Nectanebo II, who was in charge of the *machimoi*; he left the government of Egypt in the hands of his son Tjahepimu. The campaign was beginning to meet with some success when Tjahepimu took advantage of his father's unpopularity to declare his own son, Nectanebo II, king. The army

PLATE 24 *Relief of Nectanebo I. Thirtieth Dynasty, basalt, h. 1.22 m. (Reproduced courtesy of the Trustees of the British Museum, London.)*

immediately rallied around their young commander, Nectanebo, who was also supported by Agesilaos, acting under instructions from Sparta. Tachos fled to the court of the Great King himself, and Chabrias returned to Athens. Only the prince of Mendes opposed the usurper, perhaps in an attempt to protect the interests of the Twenty-ninth Dynasty kings, from whom he was descended. In doing so he thwarted the last attempt by an Egyptian pharaoh to conquer the Near East, for Nectanebo II was obliged to return to Egypt to put down this rebellion against his authority. Thanks to the military talents of Agesilaos, Nectanebo was able to defeat the prince of Mendes in the autumn of 360 BC. Then the old king of Sparta, having successfully raised the money that his city required, departed from Egypt, leaving Nectanebo II as the sole ruler of his country.

During his eighteen-year reign Nectanebo II undertook even more construction and restoration of temples than Nectanebo I, perhaps in an attempt to surpass his predecessors in the eyes of the national priesthood, who were now deriving unprecedented benefits from the system. By this time the priests were the only native Egyptians still holding power in a country where the national policy was controlled by ever-growing numbers of foreigners. Nectanebo II began his reign by officiating over the funeral of an Apis bull at Memphis. He was also responsible for the increasing popularity of another animal cult: that of the Buchis bull, the celebration of which took place at Armant. Like Nectanebo I before him, he showed enthusiasm for every cult at every temple in Egypt, and more than a hundred Egyptian sites show evidence of his attentions.

The internal problems of the Persian empire grew rapidly from the time that Nectanebo II seized power. Just before the death of Artaxerxes II in the first few months of 359 BC, Ochos, the future Artaxerxes III, organized an expedition to regain control of Syria-Palestine, from which Egypt had only recently withdrawn. Was it perhaps his intention to take the campaign down into Egypt itself? Whatever his plans may have been, he was soon on his way back to the capital in response to the Great King's death. For almost a decade he was fully occupied with the problems of maintaining his empire, which was particularly troubled by renewed hostilities in the provinces of Asia Minor. But by 352 BC he had almost succeeded in restoring the ancient Persian dominance over the region. Despite the growing problems posed by Macedonia he had regained control of Asia Minor, which left Egypt – now no longer protected by any alliance – as the only part of the empire still to be reconquered. In the winter of 351/350 BC Artaxerxes III personally led an invasion force against Egypt, but this failed to achieve its purpose.

The defeat of Artaxerxes III had political consequences that spread far beyond the immediate military sphere. The Greek cities, particularly Macedon, deduced that the time had come to launch a united front against the Great King, who had now shown that he was by no means invincible. The first clash took place in Phoenicia: Sidon rebelled, taking up arms in alliance with Egypt. Cyprus openly collaborated with this anti-Persian movement, Cilicia was hovering on the brink of offering support, and the Jews also began to turn their thoughts to revolt. Doubtless the Egyptians could have assumed a commanding role among the group of rebelling provinces, but Nectanebo II was content to despatch 4000 Greek mercenaries to the aid of the people of Sidon when Artaxerxes sent troops from Syria and Cilicia against them in 346 BC. This initial encounter was the rebels' only victory. In 344 BC Cyprus surrendered, with the exception of Salamis, where Pnytagoras was besieged. At the beginning of the same year Artaxerxes III recruited his own force of mercenaries from the Greek cities and sent them to fight against Egypt. He marched unopposed against Sidon, the population of which was well-armed and prepared for battle. The people of Sidon, however, were betrayed by their own king Tennes, who handed over the leading members of the city, only to be executed himself. Braced for a heroic resistance, the citizens of Sidon set fire to their own fleet making flight impossible, so that they perished in the flames of their burning houses. The destruction and pillage of Sidon, involving over 40,000 deaths, persuaded the other Phoenician cities to surrender, and in 343 BC even Pnytagoras submitted to Persian rule. In the autumn of the same year Artaxerxes was able to march on Egypt at the head of an army which was under the firm command of the best generals of the time, including Bagoas and Mentor of Rhodes.

Nectanebo II was ready to resist this new invasion with the help of defensive installations on the Pelusiac branch of the Nile, manned by a relatively modest number of troops amounting to about 100,000 soldiers altogether, 40,000 of which were Greek and Libyan mercenaries (in roughly equal numbers). But the Persians were well-informed of the details of Nectanebo's fortifications, through the knowledge obtained by Greek veterans of the invasion of 350 BC; and the time of year was more propitious than that chosen in the invasion of 373 BC — this time the Nile flood could not come to the aid of the Egyptians. Split into several divisions, the Persian army immediately captured Pelusium and advanced into the Delta region, using captured farmers as guides. Nectanebo II, clearly unequal to the tactical ingenuity of the Greek generals who had always been entrusted with the command of his own troops, was forced to withdraw to Memphis. The Persians then took advantage of the dissension that broke out between the Greeks and Egyptians manning the garrisons to capture Bubastis and various other strongholds. At Memphis Nectanebo recognized that his cause was lost and fled southwards, out of range of his conquerors.

Nectanebo II must have managed to maintain some form of independent rule in the south for at least two more years, as one document found at Edfu is dated to the eighteenth year of his reign. It is generally assumed that he took refuge with one of the princes of Lower Nubia contemporary with King Nastesen of Napata. A stele of Nastesen (now in the Berlin Museum) may well bear the name of Khababash, an ephemeral pharaoh who ruled Egypt in name alone from 338 to 336 BC. Not much is known concerning Khababash, whose reign probably had little more significance than a means of dating a few events, such as the death of an Apis bull at Memphis in his second regnal year and perhaps a few legal acts. If, however, Khababash is to be identified with Kambasuten, a prince of Lower Nubia, he would have eventually come into conflict with Nastesen by espousing the interests of Nectanebo II and then having himself proclaimed pharaoh. The Ptolemaic tradition claims that Khababash launched an anti-Persian campaign into the Delta which may have lasted until as late as the winter of 336/335 BC. The surviving documents are rather inconclusive, and all that can be said for certain is that the defeat and flight of Nectanebo II marked the end of Egypt as an independent entity. The possible survival of national resistance until about 336/335 BC makes no real difference to this fact.

The new conqueror, Artaxerxes III, tore down the principal cities' fortifications and pillaged the temples, forcing the priests to buy back cult items at high prices. He probably did not commit all the atrocities that Greek tradition ascribes to him, for they seem to be modelled too much on the outrages supposedly perpetrated by Cambyses, such as the murder of Apis and Mnevis bulls and the slaughter of the Buchis bull of Mendes. Artaxerxes simply installed a satrap called Pherendates (the namesake of the satrap once installed by Darius I), before returning to Susa, the capital from which the uncontested power of the Achaemenids once more flowed. The Egyptians were no longer masters of their own fate, and their destiny was inextricably linked with that of the Achaemenid Empire.

THE NEW MASTER OF THE UNIVERSE

The new Persian hegemony, which must have seemed to have been re-established for a long time to come, actually lasted for less than a decade. Bagoas had Artaxerxes and almost all his family poisoned in the summer of 338 BC and declared the young Arses to be the new king. Only weeks later, Philip II of Macedon fought and won the battle of Chaironeia against troops from many Greek cities (including Athens, Thebes and Corinth), thus uniting around him all of the Greek armies. The Persian Empire was then beset by a degree of hesitation, until about 336/335 BC – the date when Khababash's revolt is alleged to have taken place. During the summer of 336 BC, Arses met the same fate as his predecessor and Darius III Codoman rose to power. He ruled Egypt as pharaoh for the two remaining years of the Achaemenid Empire. In the spring of 334 BC Alexander crossed the Hellespont; in May he conquered the satraps and by the autumn he had defeated Darius III at Issos. In the autumn of the following year Mazakes, the satrap of Egypt who had managed to protect the country from the incursions of Amyntas, finally handed it over to Alexander without resistance. The oracle of Amun then recognized Alexander as the new Master of the Universe.

Conclusion

I have chosen to end this account of pharaonic history with the conquest of Alexander, since the arrival of the Macedonians marked the end of the political autonomy of Egypt. The Egyptians continued to participate in international affairs, but they did so within a Near Eastern and Mediterranean region that was itself completely transformed. The Egyptians' new rulers – Alexander, the Ptolemies and the Caesars – tipped the balance of world power firmly towards the West. They were only the most recent intruders into a world that had been entered by many outsiders since the beginning of the first millennium BC. Libyans, Ethiopians and Persians had all entered the Nile valley at one time or another, and the inhabitants had grown used to seeing the political initiative seized by foreigners. But the Persians were the only conquerors who deprived the pharaohs of their independence – the others were happy to manipulate the traditional national identity of Egypt of their own ends. Even the Greeks and Romans kept up at least a semblance of this tradition. They preserved the basic framework of Egyptian society, while in practice operating according to the rules of their own cultures. Although the new rulers acted as if they were still intent on maintaining the creation of Ra and continuing to build temples and religious establishments, for 800 years they were effectively hiding themselves behind the pharaohs' mask.

Was the loss of independence a significant watershed in Egyptian history? This is, after all, not the only way of interpreting the situation. It is one thing to argue that the history of Egypt after 332 BC was inseparable from that of the Greek world, but to contend that post-pharaonic Egypt actually lost its identity is quite a different matter. When Alexander conquered Egypt, he was faced with the same problem as his Persian predecessors: his empire had become so extensive that he could not rule the whole entity according to the same set of laws. He therefore had to superimpose his authority on the existing systems. In order to insinuate himself into Egypt's theocratic method of government he was obliged to seek the assistance of the very infrastructure that had supported the pharaohs: the priesthood.

The increasing acquisition of power by the Egyptian priesthood throughout the first millennium BC has already been discussed. This increase of power was accompanied by a strengthening of the national organization of local priesthoods, so that they became a kind of hierarchical administration that was able to survive each successive wave of invaders. Each new ruler not only came to an agreement with the priesthood, he also bolstered his power by organizing an annual council at which the king and the high officials discussed with the priests the major national policies of the time. The decisions of this council were passed on to the local communities, thus ensuring that the king kept control of a population that had long been accustomed to obeying the local religious authorities. There is possible indirect proof of the continuation of such a system in the priests' apparent ability not only to maintain their influence on the government but to regain, in 118 BC, the endowments of the divine estates that had been lost to them before the Ptolemaic period. They managed to hold on to these privileges until the Romans placed them under the authority of a magistrate, the *idiologos*, who was given supreme command of all religious cults throughout the Nile valley. In other words, for a period of almost a century during the Greco-Roman period the priests succeeded in regaining virtually all of the power they had held during the pharaonic period. The Ptolemies' constant attention to religious buildings is clear evidence of this. The largest temples from Philae to the Delta were built or restored during the Ptolemaic period, and as modern visitors pass by their great edifices and sprawling cities (often only partly excavated) throughout the valley and sub-desert zones, they gain the distinct impression that the buildings of the Greco-Roman period were at least as numerous and impressive as those of earlier periods.

If temples were the places where Egyptian culture was ultimately preserved and diffused, then the Greco-Roman period certainly showed an unbroken continuity with the preceding phases. The temple of Hathor at Dendera, for example, was first established in the earliest period of Egyptian history, but the construction of the existing building was begun by Ptolemy XII Neos Dionysos (Auletes) and finished by Antoninus Pius. The temple plan and the programme of decoration at Dendera and other Greco-Roman temples are considered to be typical of the Egyptian temple in general, and the cultural ambience of the Ptolemaic sacred precincts certainly appears to have strayed no further from the model Egyptian temple than the architecture. Even the language in which the Greco-Roman liturgical texts were composed is closer to that of Middle Kingdom Egypt than the vernacular of the Greco-Roman period.

But this desire to preserve the original purity of Egyptian culture eventually reached a state of stagnation. The priests hid themselves away in sterile research into the rituals, adopting a concern for detail and complexity that came perilously close to Byzantinism. The art of the period also reflected the gulf that had developed between the pharaonic fiction and the reality of daily life. Religious art was still rigidly concerned with representations of the past, but the official images began to show the influence of Greek art. The art of the common people further complicated this curious blend through the introduction of a composite iconography based on the most popular religious cults, such as those of Isis and Serapis, which were eventually to dominate the entire Roman empire. These influences slowly led to a civilization that was less and less pharaonic and much more a Mediterranean phenomenon, gradually imposed on cultures from Babylon to Rome over the course of the centuries.

This cosmopolitan society had already been developing in the major Greek centres within Egypt from the sixth century BC onwards, and its growth was accelerated further by the foundation of Alexandria, which was intended to be the second capital of Alexander's empire. The new metropolis took advantage of its political and commercial role to develop into one of the principal intellectual meeting-places of a Mediterranean region in which West was increasingly encountering East. Alexandria was the ultimate destination of the caravans that brought Indian luxury goods from far-off Gerrha via the Persian Gulf, Petra, Dura Europos and the Phoenician coast, thus linking Egypt with Asia Minor and the Silk Route. The Nile valley itself functioned more than ever as a conduit, leading down into Africa via Syene (Aswan) and the oases. Traders also passed across to the Red Sea via the ancient trade routes and the new roads between the port of Berenice and the towns of Koptos and Ptolemais in Middle Egypt, which were as much Greek foundations as Egyptian.

Alexandria was the melting-pot in which Oriental goods jostled with products brought from the West via the great maritime routes leading from Rhodes, Carthage and Rome. The civilization that grew up in Alexandria was a unique mixture of cultures providing the setting for literary works such as Theocritus' *Idylls*, where the celebration of the festival of Adonis and the rich blend of peoples are evoked with great humour. This civilization, which the ancient writers characterized as 'Alexandria ad Aegyptum' (Alexandria-by-Egypt), was to reappear much later in the cosmopolitan city described by Lawrence Durrell.

Egypt might not yet have been reduced to the purely exotic role that it was to play with regard to Rome, but it was certainly already a thing of the past. Appearances were assiduously kept up, and a history of Egypt could be written solely on the basis of the temples built by a succession of pharaohs who spoke only Greek. But it would not be a history of the Egyptian people: such a history ought instead to draw on a variety of sources, blending together the customs of both foreigners and native Egyptians. Who, indeed, were the Egyptian population? There was a vague mass of peasants and cleruchs, immigrants married to native Egyptians, too poor to escape from their ancestral farming techniques and reduced to silence by the combined influence of the traditional priesthood and the Greek administration. But there were also communities of Greeks who controlled commerce and the new methods of exchange on which the banking and finance systems were based. Were the typical Egyptians of the Ptolemaic period illiterate peasants or Hellenistic city-dwellers?

The life-style of Egyptian peasants essentially changed very little from the New Kingdom to the Ptolemaic period, and continued in much the same way until the industrial revolution of the nineteenth century. Life as a peasant at the beginning of the twentieth century was still marked by the same rhythms and subject to the same basic constraints as in ancient times. The modern regularization of the Nile's course and the prevention of the annual flood by means of the Aswan Dam have only resulted in the modification of an apparently unchanging cycle. Potters still fashion ceramic forms similar to those that archaeologists recognize from their excavations, and even the advent of plastic has not produced a radically different material culture.

The other ancient popular culture – the 'Hellenistic' section of society – was by no means exclusive to Egypt and need not be understood or described purely in the context of the Nile valley. As with the later Roman domination of Egypt, a much wider range of sources and approaches, involving several civilizations and various social developments, can be utilized in a study of the Ptolemaic period. These are supplemented by a set of data unique to Egyptology – the documentary sources, the later examples of which (i.e. those of the first millennium BC) are still not completely known. The full corpus of Greco-Roman texts is still being compiled and it is too soon to make social or economic deductions from it. Until these sources have been properly assimilated, the history of the periods which they document will have to continue to be described in terms of political and military events recorded in official texts or the writings of Greek historians. Research into this area has still yielded relatively few results, partly because sources from earlier periods have tended to be more abundant (and

Egyptologists have tended to treat these pharaonic sources as 'loftier' than the later texts), and partly because the later sites were often located in Middle and Lower Egypt, which have tended to be less accessible both in terms of traditional archaeological goals and in purely practical terms. The rescue excavations undertaken in the Delta since the Second World War are now supplying invaluable information concerning the Greco-Roman period.

Greco-Roman Egypt was not the only milieu in which elements of pharaonic Egypt were to survive: the distant kingdom of Napata continued to exist long after Psammetichus II's defeat of the Nubians at Pnubs. The political centre was simply pushed further south from Napata to Meroe, a city which was already flourishing in the seventh century BC; in the third century BC it became the capital of the country known to the Greeks as Ethiopia. Although there are still many gaps in our knowledge of Meroitic civilization, it evidently played a substantial historical role, at least in Lower Nubia and as far north as Aswan in the early Ptolemaic period. Diodorus Siculus mentions a certain Ergamenes, who is perhaps to be identified with Arnekhamani, builder of the temple of the lion-god Apedemak at Mussawarat es-Sufra. This philhellenic ruler seems to have decorated the buildings at Meroe with an Alexandrian style of art, many traces of which have been revealed in excavations at the site. It is also likely that Meroe participated in the Upper Egyptian revolt against Ptolemy V.

The 'island of Meroe' became legendary in Classical literature as an inaccessible place where pharaonic civilization had retained its original purity. The excavation of Meroitic sites, however, has consistently demonstrated that native Nubian traits were in the ascendancy from the mid-second century BC. The Meroitic people abandoned the Egyptian language in favour of their own tongue, although this was still tran-scribed with the help of hieroglyphic signs based on the demotic script. They also adopted an African-style matriarchal regime and set up a dynasty of queens known as the Candaces. It was one of these queens who came into conflict with the prefect Petronius in the reign of Au-gustus, when she successfully protected her territory from the threat of the Roman invaders. Despite an expedition in the time of Nero, information regarding Meroe – then at the height of its powers – was still vague. Sporadic contacts with Rome were maintained until the fourth century AD, but they must still have been weak enough for the Greek stories to continually confuse Ethiopia with India. The Greeks deliberately linked these two civilizations together in the interests of their readers' obsession with exoticism.

It seems that the kingdom of Meroe lasted for almost as long as Egypt itself, finally succumbing in AD 350 to the attacks of the Axumites, who imposed their Christian religion over a region stetching as far north as Meroe's northern neighbours, the Nuba. The civilization which then dominated the Nubian region is poorly known, but it seems to have involved a return to the roots of the Bedja culture. The redoutable Blemmyes were still worshipping in the temple of Isis at Philae until as late as the time of Justinian. The culture of this period in Nubia combined traces of the Egyptian and Meroitic civilizations, and this strange mixture of cultures resisted the onset of Christianity for as long as Egypt itself, which eventually gave up the struggle in about the mid-sixth century AD.

The Meroitic people were apparently convinced that the Ptolemies were the legitimate heirs of the pharaohs. But even the humblest surviving works of art from Nubia show that the original Egyptian model was repeatedly influenced by each of their own distinctive cultures. When Piankhy conquered Egypt he represented himself as an Egyptian rather than a Nubian; this was because the civilization that he symbolized was the product of extreme acculturation.

Alexander's successors and his Roman heirs were obliged to integrate Egypt into their political systems. At first they were content simply to adopt those Egyptian cultural traits that conformed with their political aims, but later they reinterpreted the cultural components on which they were drawing – the official image they projected became more and more distorted as they moved further away from native Egyptian culture. When Hadrian ordered the construction of a model of the Canopus Serapeum within his villa at Tivoli, he was consciously presenting himself as the true pharaoh of Egypt, and his enthusiastic adoption of this title was far more than a capricious whim: it enabled him to universalize his authority, which was henceforth derived from both East and West. Much later in history, when the original essence of Egyptian civilization had been lost, only the symbols – reinterpreted by the cultures that lay at the root of European civilization – would remain, leading eventually to the Christianized obelisks of Mozart's *Magic Flute*. The road to wisdom passes through Egypt.

Appendix:

Chronology of Ancient Egypt

	4500–3150 BC PREDYNASTIC PERIOD
	4500–4000 BC BADARIAN
4000–3500 BC	NAQADA I (Amratian)
3500–3300 BC	NAQADA II (Gerzean A)
3300–3150 BC	NAQADA III (Gerzean B)

	3150–2700 BC THINITE PERIOD
3150–2925 BC	**Dynasty I**
3150–3125 BC	NARMER-MENES
3125–3100 BC	AHA
3100–3055 BC	DJER
3055–3050 BC	WADJIT ('SERPENT')/DJET
3050–2995 BC	DEN/UDIMU
2995–	ANEDJIB/ANDJYEB/ENEZIB
–2950 BC	SEMERKHET
2960–2926 BC	KAʿA
2925–2700 BC	**Dynasty II**
	HETEPSEKHEMWY
	RENEB
	NYNETJER/NUTJEREN
	WENEG
	SENED
	PERIBSEN
	SEKHEMIB
	KHASEKHEM/KHASEKHEMWY

	2700–2190 BC OLD KINGDOM
2700–2625 BC	**Dynasty III**
	NEBKA (= SANAKHT?)

	Djoser
	Sekhemkhet
	Khaba
	Neferka(re)?
	Huni
2625–2510 BC	**Dynasty IV**
	Snofru
	Cheops
	Djedefre
	Chephren
	Baefre(?)
	Mycerinus
	Shepseskaf
2510–2460 BC	**Dynasty V**
	Userkaf
	Sahure
	Neferirkare-Kakai
	Shepseskare
	Neferefre
	Neuserre
	Menkauhor
	Djedkare-Isesi
	Wenis
2460–2200 BC	**Dynasty VI**
	Teti
	Userkare
	Pepy I
	Merenre I
	Pepy II
	Merenre II
	Nitocris

2200–2040 BC FIRST INTERMEDIATE PERIOD

2200–c.2160 BC	**Dynasties VII and VIII**
	Many short-lived kings including Qakare Iby and Khuy.
2160–c.2040 BC	**Dynasties IX and X** (Herakleopolis)
	Meribre Khety I
	Neferkare
	Nebkaure (?) Khety II
	Neferkare Meribre
	Wahkare Khety III
	Merikare
2160–2040 BC	**Dyansty XI** (Thebes)
	Mentuhotpe (I)

	Seherutawy Inyotef I
2118–2069 BC	Wahankh Inyotef II
2069–2061 BC	Nakhtnebtepnefer Inyotef III
2061–2040 BC	Sʿankhibtawy Mentuhotpe II

2040–1674 BC MIDDLE KINGDOM

2040–1991 BC	**Dynasty XI (all Egypt)**
2040–2009 BC	Nebhepetre Mentuhotpe II
2009–1997 BC	Sʿankhkare Mentuhotpe III
1997–1991 BC	Nebtawyre Mentuhotpe IV
1991–1785 BC	**Dynasty XII**
1991–1962 BC	Ammenemes I
1962–1928 BC	Sesostris I
1928–1895 BC	Ammenemes II
1895–1878 BC	Sesostris II
1878–1842 BC	Sesostris III
1842–1797 BC	Ammenemes III
1797–1790 BC	Ammenemes IV
1790–1785 BC	Sobkneferu
1785–1633 BC	**Dynasties XIII and XIV**
	Sekhemre-Khutawy
	Ammenemes V
	Sehetepibre (II)
	Ammenemes VI ('Ameny the Asiatic')
	Hornedjheritef 'the Asiatic'
*c.*1750 BC	Sobkhotep I
	Reniseneb
	Hor I
	Ammenemes VII
	Ugaf
	Sesostris IV
	Khendjer
	Smenkhkare
	Sobkemsaf I
*c.*1745 BC	Sobkhotep III
*c.*1741–1730 BC	Neferhotep I
	Sahathor
	Sobkhotep IV
*c.*1720–1715 BC	Sobkhotep V
	Neferhotep II
	Neferhotep III
	Iaib
*c.*1704–1690 BC	Iy
	Ini
	Dedumesiu I

1674–1553 BC SECOND INTERMEDIATE PERIOD

	Dynasty XIV	Dynasties XV and XVI (Hyksos)	Dynasty XVII (Thebes)
1674 BC	DEDUMESIU I		
		SALITIS	
	DEDUMESIU II		
	SENEBMIU		
	DJEDKARE		
	MONTHUEMSAF		
1650 BC		YAQUB-HAR	
			RAHOTEP
			INYOTEF V
			SOBKEMSAF II
		KHYAN	DJEHUTY
1633 BC	End of Dynasty XIV		MENTUHOTPE VII
			NEBIRYAU I
			INYOTEF VII
		APOPHIS I	
			SENAKHTENRE TAʿA I
			SEQENENRE TAʿA II
1578 BC			KAMOSE
		APOPHIS II	

1552–1069 BC NEW KINGDOM

1552–1314 or 1295 BC	**Dynasty XVIII**
1552–1526 BC	AHMOSE
1526–1506 BC	AMENOPHIS I
1506–1493 BC	TUTHMOSIS I
1493–1479 BC	TUTHMOSIS II
1479–1425 BC	TUTHMOSIS III
1478–1458 BC	HATSHEPSUT
1425–1401 BC	AMENOPHIS II
1401–1390 BC	TUTHMOSIS IV
1390–1352 BC	AMENOPHIS III
1352–1348 BC	AMENOPHIS IV
1348–1338 BC	AKHENATEN
1338–1336 BC	SMENKHKARE(?)
1336–1327 BC	TUTANKHATEN/TUTANKHAMUN
1327–1323 BC	AY
1323–1295 BC	HOREMHEB
1295–1188 BC	**Dynasty XIX**
1295–1294 BC	RAMESSES I
1294–1279 BC	SETHOS I
1279–1212 BC	RAMESSES II

1212–1202 BC	MERNEPTAH	
1202–1199 BC	AMENMESSE	
1202–1196 BC	SETHOS II	
1196–1190 BC	SIPTAH	
1196–1188 BC	TWOSRE	
1188–1069 BC	**Dynasty XX**	
1188–1186 BC	SETHNAKHTE	
1186–1154 BC	RAMESSES III	
1154–1148 BC	RAMESSES IV	
1148–1144 BC	RAMESSES V	
1144–1136 BC	RAMESSES VI	
1136–1128 BC	RAMESSES VII	
1128–1125 BC	RAMESSES VIII	
1125–1107 BC	RAMESSES IX	
1107–1098 BC	RAMESSES X	
1098–1069 BC	RAMESSES XI	

1069–702 BC THIRD INTERMEDIATE PERIOD

1069–945 BC	**Dynasty XXI**	**Theban Chief Priests**
1070–1055 BC		PINUDJEM I (as chief priest)
1069–1043 BC	SMENDES	
1054–1032 BC		PINUDJEM I (as king)
1054–1046 BC		MASAHARTA
1045–992 BC		MENKHEPERRE
1043–1039 BC	AMENEMNISU	
1039–993 BC	PSUSENNES I	
993–984 BC	AMENEMOPE	
992–990 BC		SMENDES
990–969 BC		PINUDJEM II
984–978 BC	OSORKON THE ELDER	
978–959 BC	SIAMUN	
969–945 BC		PSUSENNES
959–945 BC	PSUSENNES II	
945–715 BC	**Dynasty XXII**	**Theban Chief Priests**
945–924 BC	SHOSHENQ I	IUPUT
924–889 BC	OSORKON I	SHOSHENQ
890–889 BC	SHOSHENQ II	SMENDES
889–874 BC	TAKELOT I	IUWELOT
		HARSIESE
870–860 BC	HARSIESE	
874–850 BC	OSORKON II	NIMLOT
850–825 BC	TAKELOT II	OSORKON
		Dynasty XXIII
825–773 BC	SHOSHENQ III	PEDUBASTIS I
787–759 BC		OSORKON III

773–767 BC	PIMAY	
764–757 BC		TAKELOT III
767–730 BC	SHOSHENQ V	
757–754 BC		RUDAMON
754–715 BC		IUPUT II

747–525 BC LATE PERIOD

747–656 BC	**Dynasty XXV**	**Dynasty XXIV**
747–716 BC	PIANKHY	
727–716 BC		TEFNAKHT
716–715 BC		BOCCHORIS
716–702 BC	SHABAKA	
702–690 BC	SHEBITKU	
690–664 BC	TAHARQA	
672–525 BC		**Dynasty XXVI**
672–664 BC		NECHO I
664–	TANTAMANI	PSAMMETICHUS
–656 BC	END OF KUSHITE RULE	
610–595 BC		NECHO II
595–589 BC		PSAMMETICHUS II
589–570 BC		APRIES
570–526 BC		AMASIS
526–525 BC		PSAMMETICHUS III

525–404 BC DYNASTY XXVII (FIRST PERSIAN PERIOD)

525–522 BC	CAMBYSES II
522–486 BC	DARIUS I
486–465 BC	XERXES I
465–424 BC	ARTAXERXES I
424–405 BC	DARIUS II
405–359 BC	ARTAXERXES II

404–343 BC DYNASTIES XXVIII–XXX

	Dynasty XXVIII
404–399 BC	AMYRTAEUS
399–380 BC	**Dynasty XXIX**
399–393 BC	NEPHERITES I
393 BC	PSAMMUTHIS
393–380 BC	ACHORIS
380 BC	NEPHERITES II
380–343 BC	**Dynasty XXX**
380–362 BC	NECTANEBO I

362–360 BC	TACHOS
360–343 BC	NECTANEBO II

343–332 BC SECOND PERSIAN PERIOD

343–338 BC	ARTAXERXES III OCHOS
338–336 BC	ARSES
336–332 BC	DARIUS III CODOMAN
333 BC	KHABABASH (LAST KNOWN INDIGENOUS EGYPTIAN RULER)

332 BC-AD 395 GRECO-ROMAN PERIOD

332–304 BC MACEDONIAN DYNASTY

332–323 BC	ALEXANDER THE GREAT
323–316 BC	PHILIP ARRHIDAEUS
316–304 BC	ALEXANDER IV

304–30 BC PTOLEMAIC PERIOD

30 BC-AD 395 ROMAN PERIOD

Glossary

'**abnormal hieratic**' Regional form of the hieratic script used for non-literary texts during the Third Intermediate Period. It was completely replaced by demotic in the Twenty-sixth Dynasty.

akh One of the three major elements of human identity (along with the *ba* and *ka*), the *akh* was the essence of each individual's immortality, leaving the body at death to join the circumpolar stars. It was represented by the crested ibis hieroglyph.

Amarna Letters Diplomatic correspondence between the pharaohs of the Amarna period (*c.*1370–1330 BC) and various Near Eastern rulers, written in cuneiform on baked clay tablets and discovered at the site of el-Amarna.

ambulatory Roofed colonnade acting as a walkway, usually around the outside edge of a temple or shrine.

astronomical ceiling Ceiling in a tomb or temple decorated with depictions of the Egyptian constellations.

ba One of the three major elements of human identity (along with the *akh* and *ka*), the *ba* was present at the ceremonial weighing of its owner's heart after death. It was represented as a human-headed bird flying between the worlds of the living and the dead. The literal meaning of the term *ba* was 'power' or 'divine essence'; a human had only one *ba* but gods could have several such manifestations.

bark Model boat used to carry the image of a deity at festival times. Special bark shrines were constructed as resting places for the bark between one temple and another or within the precincts of a temple complex.

benben **stone** Sacred stone at Heliopolis which symbolized the first manifestation of the sun-god. The *benben* was the archetypal form of the obelisk and perhaps also of the pyramid.

block statue Schematic cube-shaped representation of a squatting human figure, evidently intended to symbolize the deceased's hope of resurrection.

Book of Caverns Compilation of religious scenes and texts on the walls of New Kingdom royal tombs, depicting the progress of the sun-god Ra through the six caverns of the underworld. Events in the *Book of Caverns* concentrate on the idea of rewarding good and punishing evil.

Book of the Dead   Collection of funerary spells usually written on papyrus and placed with the deceased in the tomb. *Book of the Dead* papyri, dating from the New Kingdom to the Ptolemaic period, were illustrated with vignettes showing scenes of the deceased worshipping gods, undergoing judgement or participating in agricultural work in the afterworld.

Book of Gates   Funerary composition decorating royal sarcophagi and the walls of royal tombs, describing the passage of the sun-god Ra through the twelve gates of the underworld. The earliest example of the *Book of Gates* is in the tomb of Horemheb at the Valley of the Kings.

Book of What is in the Underworld (**Amduat**)   Funerary composition on the walls of New Kingdom royal tombs, consisting of text and painted scenes depicting the progress of the sun-god Ra through the twelve hours of the night. The *Book of What is in the Underworld* culminated in the birth of Khepri, the scarab manifestation of the sun, from the mouth of a snake.

canopic jar   Vessel containing the entrails extracted from a mummified body. There were four canopic jars, each guarded by one of the four Sons of Horus (Imsety, Hapy, Qebehsenuef and Duamutef). The shape of the lids changed from a basic convex form in the Old Kingdom to a human head in the Middle Kingdom and the heads of each of the Sons of Horus from the Nineteenth Dynasty onwards.

cartouche   Sign representing an oval loop of rope within which the king's nomen and prenomen (see below) were each written; used from the Fourth Dynasty onwards. The cartouche was also used for the names of the god Aten and for the Divine Adoratrices in Late Period Thebes.

cataract   Rocky stretch of the Nile prone to rapids. There were six cataracts altogether, interrupting the course of the Nile from Aswan to Khartoum.

Coffin Texts   A collection of over a thousand spells usually inscribed on coffins and sarcophagi during the Middle Kingdom. The spells were based on those in the Pyramid Texts and they were intended to enable the deceased to pass safely to the afterworld.

co-regency   Period during which a king and his successor ruled jointly. During a co-regency the years were dated to the reigns of both kings.

criosphinx   Ram-headed sphinx.

demotic   (Greek: 'popular') Cursive script adapted from Egyptian hieroglyphs, used primarily for legal, administrative and commercial texts on papyri and ostraca from the beginning of the Late Period to the Roman period (*c.*700 BC-AD 450). From the Ptolemaic period onwards demotic was also used for literary and religious compositions, including monumental inscriptions such as the Rosetta Stone.

Divine Adoratrice   Chief priestess of Amun at Thebes from the New Kingdom onwards. In the Twenty-fifth and Twenty-sixth Dynasties the Divine Adoratrice and her 'adopted' successor played a powerful role in the transmission of royal power.

djadjat   Local council of elders or magistrates whose function was to advise the provincial governor.

djed **pillar**   Hieroglyphic symbol meaning 'stability', the iconographic origins of which are unclear; it has been variously interpreted as a tree, a pole to which ears of corn were tied, and the backbone of the god Osiris. It was a powerful prehistoric fetish particularly associated with the the site of Abydos.

Dodekaschoenos   Geographical term referring to the southernmost province of Greco-Roman Egypt. The Dodekaschoenos was the region of Lower Nubia between Aswan and the Wadi Allaqi, covering a distance of twelve *schoeni* (*c.*75 miles).

dromos   Processional way leading to and from temple entrances.

encaustic   Form of painting introduced into Egypt during the late Ptolemaic period, employing hot wax mixed with pigment. The Faiyum 'mummy portraits' of the Roman period were painted in encaustic on wooden panels.

ennead   Group of nine deities, the earliest and most famous of which was the Heliopolitan Ennead, which consists of Ra-Atum, Shu, Tefnut, Geb, Nut, Osiris, Isis, Nephthys and Seth.

Execration Texts   Set of magical texts dating from the late Old Kingdom to the reigns of Sesostris III and Amenemhat III (*c.*1878–1797 BC) in the Middle Kingdom. The Execration Texts were lists of hostile forces that the Egyptians wished to destroy. They were written in the hieratic script on small pottery vessels and on clay figures of bound captives, which were subsequently deliberately broken and concealed near tombs or ritual sites. The names range from deceased Egyptians to foreign princes and peoples.

faience   Fired quartz paste with a vitrified outer layer (also known as 'glazed composition'), used primarily for jewellery and small vessels.

false door   Type of stone or wooden funerary stele bearing texts and painted reliefs which first appears in the *mastaba* tombs and mortuary temples of the Old Kingdom. It allowed the *ka* of the deceased to emerge from the tomb chamber into the chapel to receive offerings. The false door stele often incorporated a statue or relief of the *ka* itself.

Golden Horus name   One of the five elements making up the classic royal titulature from the Twelfth Dynasty onwards.

haty-ʿ   Title given to provincial rulers (nomarchs).

ḥeḳa-djet   'Lord of eternity'; an epithet of the god Osiris.

hieratic   (Greek: 'sacred') Cursive script consisting of simplified forms of Egyptian hieroglyphs, used to write on ostraca and papyri. The earliest surviving hieratic documents date to the Fourth Dynasty, but the origins of hieratic are probably almost as early as the hieroglyphic script itself. Hieratic was used both for religious and secular texts for most of the dynastic period, finally being replaced by demotic in the Late Period.

hieroglyphics   (Greek: 'sacred carved (letters)') Egyptian writing system, used from the late predynastic period (*c.*3100 BC) until the end of the fourth century AD. The hieroglyphic script consisted of pictorial signs arranged in horizontal or vertical lines. Each hieroglyphic sign functioned either as an ideogram or a phonogram, allowing the scribe to build up complex sequences of words and sentences.

Horus name The first (and earliest recorded) epithet in the written sequence of the royal 'fivefold titulature', identifying the king with a particular aspect of the hawk-god Horus and usually written inside a **serekh** (see below).

Hyksos (*ḥekaw-khasut*) Asiatics who infiltrated Egypt during the Middle Kingdom and became rulers of Lower Egypt during the Second Intermediate Period (*c*.1750–1550 BC).

hypostyle hall Large columned hall which was one of the essential elements of an Egyptian temple. It is usually considered to be symbolic of the primeval papyrus swamp.

instruction text Type of 'wisdom literature' that became popular in the Middle Kingdom with such texts as the *Instruction of Ammenemes I* and the *Teaching for Merikare*, consisting of didactic statements on how life should be lived.

Iput-isut ('the most esteemed of places') The original central area of the Temple of Amun at Karnak, stretching from the Festival Hall of Tuthmosis III to the Fourth Pylon, and dating back to at least the Eleventh Dynasty.

ka One of the three major elements of human identity (along with the *akh* and *ba*), the *ka* came into being at the same moment as the body, of which it was the essential life-force or personality. After death it was the *ka* which moved between the tomb chamber and the chapel, emerging through the 'false door' in order to consume the daily offerings. It was represented by the hieroglyph for two raised arms, the plural of which (*kaw*) meant 'sustenance'.

king-list List of pharaohs' names, inscribed on a temple wall (e.g. Karnak and Abydos) or papyrus (e.g. the Turin Canon).

kiosk Small unroofed chapel in which the statues of gods were placed during festivals.

Maat Goddess personifying truth and divine order. The concept of Maat was an essential component of the Egyptians' idea of a balanced universe; it was the duty of the king to maintain Maat on behalf of the gods.

mammisi Term coined by Auguste Mariette to describe the chapel within a temple where the divine birth was celebrated. The Temple of Hathor at Dendera has two *mammisis*, one dating to the Thirtieth Dynasty and the other to the Roman period.

mastaba (Arabic: 'bench') Type of tomb consisting of subterranean chambers surmounted by a mud-brick or stone superstructure, used primarily during the early dynastic period and the Old Kingdom.

merkhet Surveying device used by Egyptian priests and architects to lay the foundations of temples and pyramids.

migdol Type of fortress common in Bronze Age Syria-Palestine.

mortuary temple Temple in which the cult of the deceased king was celebrated. In pyramid complexes the mortuary temple (fulfilling a similar function to the chapel in private tombs) was immediately adjacent to the pyramid and linked with the valley temple by a descending causeway. From the early New Kingdom onwards the mortuary temple was located separately from the royal tomb.

naos   Small shrine or holy of holies, usually made of stone or wood and intended to contain the image of a deity.

nemes **head-dress**   Royal head-dress consisting of a cloth knotted at the back and with two side lappets at the front, like that worn by Tutankhamun on his golden portrait mask.

Nine Bows   Term used by the Egyptian king to refer to the various peoples subject to his will (including the Egyptians themselves).

nome   Ptolemaic term for an Egyptian province, corresponding to the ancient Egyptian word *sepat*. There were forty-two nomes altogether (twenty-two in Upper Egypt and twenty in Lower Egypt), each represented by its own icon, such as the 'white walls' of Memphis, the 'fish' of Mendes and the 'ibis' of Hermopolis. The chief official of each nome, whose powers tended to increase during times of national disunity, was described as a nomarch.

nomen   Royal 'birth-name' of a king and one of the five parts of the king's classic titulature. The second of those written in a cartouche, it was usually accompanied by the phrase *sa Ra* ('Son of Ra'). This name (generally followed by a number, e.g. Ammenemes II or Ramesses III) is the one commonly used by modern Egyptologists to refer to a particular king.

obelisk   Shaft of stone (usually granite) tapering towards the top and surmounted by a pyramidion; first erected as part of the Heliopolitan sun cult. By the Middle Kingdom monolithic obelisks were regularly placed in pairs at the entrance to a temple or tomb chapel.

ogdoad   Group of eight deities, the most important instance of which is the Hermopolitan Ogdoad, consisting of four pairs of male frogs and female snakes personifying the primordial forces of creation.

onomasticon   List of various categories of hieroglyphic words such as plants, animals or towns.

Osirid pillar   Combination of a pillar and the colossal statue of a king, usually placed in rows around the forecourt of a temple.

ostracon   (Greek: 'potsherd') Fragment of pottery or flake of stone bearing a drawing or text, most common in the late New Kingdom.

palace façade   Style of architecture consisting of a series of recessed niches along the frontage of a building. The exteriors of the early *mastaba* tombs at Abydos and Saqqara are decorated in a palace façade style.

palette   In the predynastic period geometrical and animal-shaped stone palettes were used for grinding cosmetics. The protodynastic period was marked by the appearance of large ceremonial palettes bearing carved reliefs commemorating important events such as royal victories or religious ceremonies.

peristyle court   Temple court surrounded by a roofed colonnade on all four sides.

prenomen   Royal 'throne name', one of the five elements of the king's titulature. The prenomen was written inside a cartouche and usually accompanied by the phrase *n-sw-bity* ('He of the Sedge and the Bee') or *neb tawy* ('Lord of the Two Lands').

pylon   Monumental temple gateway consisting of a pair of sloping massifs of masonry, usually supposed to represent the *akhet* ('horizon') hieroglyph. Most major temples incorporated at least one pylon, but the Temple of Amun at Karnak has ten.

pyramidion   Small pyramid-shaped stone usually placed at the apex of pyramids and obelisks. Its shape, modelled on the *benben* stone, symbolized both the primeval mound and the frozen rays of the sun. In the New Kingdom and Late Period, pyramidia were used to decorate the superstructures of private tombs at Saqqara and Thebes.

Pyramid Texts   A set of spells carved on the internal walls of pyramids from the reign of Wenis until the Eighth Dynasty (*c.*2470–2200 BC). The texts deal with the king's safe passage through the perils of the afterworld, as well as other subjects such as myths, funerary ceremonies and temple rituals. The corpus of Pyramid Texts ultimately formed the basis of the Coffin Texts and the *Book of the Dead*.

Ramessid period   Nineteenth and Twentieth Dynasties (*c.*1295–1069 BC), during which most of the rulers were called Ramesses.

Red Crown   (*deshret*) The crown of Lower Egypt.

reserve head   Realistic image of the head of the deceased sculpted in limestone and usually placed near the entrance to the burial chamber. Only about thirty reserve heads have been found, primarily in Fourth Dynasty private *mastaba* tombs at Giza.

satrapy   Term for a province of the Achaemenid Empire. Each satrapy was ruled by a satrap.

Sea Peoples   A mixture of Indo-European peoples (including the Sherden and the Peleset) who migrated southwards across the Mediterranean and through the Levant during the late second millennium BC. Their attempts to invade Egypt during the late Nineteenth and early Twentieth Dynasties were ultimately unsuccessful. The origins and precise nature of the Sea Peoples are a matter of some debate.

sed festival (or *heb-sed*)   Jubilee celebrated by the king, theoretically after thirty years of power (but in practice probably more regularly). In the course of the *sed* festival the king was required to undertake various physical acts to demonstrate his continued vitality.

Serapeum   Set of underground galleries at Saqqara serving as the burial place of the sacred Apis bulls (the personifications of the *ka* of Ptah, the god of Memphis) from the Eighteenth Dynasty onwards. The term Serapeum strictly refers only to the Greco-Roman temple at ground level, which is dedicated to the syncretic god Serapis (a combination of Osiris, the Apis bull and various Hellenistic deities), whose worship was introduced into Egypt in the reign of

Ptolemy I. Although the Saqqara Serapeum is the earliest and best preserved example, the most important Greco-Roman Serapeum was at Alexandria.

serdab (Arabic: 'cellar') Special room in a tomb where the statues of the deceased were kept. it was usually near the tomb chapel and there were often holes or slots in the wall so that the statues (and therefore the *ka* of the deceased) could be given sustenance in the form of offerings.

serekh Hieroglyphic sign in the form of a ceremonial gateway surmounted by a cornice and flanked by buttresses, which was used as a frame for the king's Horus name. The repeated *serekh* was the basic element of palace façade architecture.

shabti (*shawabty, ushabti*) Mummiform figurine, usually of faience, wood or stone, which was intended to undertake specific tasks for the deceased in the afterworld (principally clearing silt from canals). The *shabti* was invariably inscribed with the sixth chapter of the *Book of the Dead*, which is known as the '*shabti* formula'.

shendyt kilt Royal pleated kilt with a distinctive central tab.

speos Rock-cut temple such as Speos Artemidos (at Beni Hasan) and Abu Simbel.

stele Slab of stone or wood bearing inscriptions, reliefs or paintings, usually of a religious or funerary nature.

sun temple Term referring to a variety of sacred buildings dedicated to the worship of the solar deity. The earliest Egyptian sun temple would probably have been at Heliopolis, but the best surviving examples are the Fifth Dynasty sun temples of Neuserre and Userkaf at Abu Ghurob. Both of these resembled pyramid complexes in plan, except that the focus of attention was a colossal obelisk standing in an open courtyard (rather than a pyramidal royal tomb). In the reign of Akhenaten several unusual temples dedicated to the Aten (the sun-disc) were constructed at el-Amarna. The Aten temples consisted of sequences of open courtyards containing numerous open-air altars.

talatat **blocks** (Arabic: 'three hand-breadths') Distinctive small blocks of sandstone bearing relief decoration and deriving from the temples and palaces of the Amarna period. Many *talatat* blocks were reused in the construction of later temples, particularly at Karnak and Hermopolis Magna.

triad Group of three deities, usually comprising mother, father and son (e.g. Amun, Mut and Khons).

Turin Canon King-list written on fragments of a New Kingdom papyrus in the Museo Egizio at Turin.

Two Ladies name One of the elements of the royal 'fivefold titulature', the Two Ladies being the vulture-goddess Nekhbet and the cobra-goddess Wadjet, representing Upper Egypt and Lower Egypt respectively.

uraeus Royal cobra worn on the brow as part of the crown or head-dress.

valley temple Section of the pyramid complex in which the embalming, purification and 'opening of the mouth' ceremonies took place. The valley temple was usually connected to the mortuary temple and pyramid by an ascending causeway.

Weighing of the Heart   Judgement scene from the *Book of the Dead* in which the heart of the deceased was weighed against the feather symbolizing the goddess Maat ('truth') in the presence of the gods, determining whether he could pass through to eternal life in the afterworld. Painted vignettes of the Weighing of the Heart were frequently included in *Book of the Dead* papyri.

White Crown   (*hedjet*) The crown of Upper Egypt, which could be worn alone or combined with the Red Crown of Lower Egypt in the form of the Double Crown (*pshent*).

Bibliography

(This bibliography is not exhaustive, and individual excavation reports and textual corpora have generally been excluded. The list provides the reader with both readily available general works and a selection of the major specialist studies, so that particular points can be explored more deeply. The focus is particularly on research carried out since 1960.)

ABBREVIATIONS

ÄAT *Ägypten und Altes Testament*, Wiesbaden.

AAWLM *Abhandlungen der Akademie der Wissenschaften in Leiden*, Leiden.

AcOr *Acta Orientalia*, Leiden, Copenhagen.

ADAIK *Abhandlungen des Deutschen Archäologischen Instituts Kairo*, Gluckstadt.

ADAW *Abhandlungen der Deutschen Akademie der Wissenschaften zu Berlin*, Berlin.

Aegyptus *Aegyptus. Rivista Italiana di Egittologia e di Papirologia*, Milan.

ÄF *Ägyptologische Forschungen*, Glückstadt, Hamburg, New York.

AoF *Altorientalische Forschungen*, Berlin.

AH *Aegyptiaca Helvetica*, Geneva.

AHAW *Abhandlungen der Heidelberger Akademie der Wissenschaften, Phil.-hist. Klasse*, Heidelberg.

AHS *Alexandria Archaeological and Historical Studies*, Alexandria.

AJA *American Journal of Archaeology*, Boston.

AKAW *Abhandlungen der königlichen Akademie der Wissenschaften*, Berlin.

ÄMA *Ägyptologische Microfiche Archive*, Wiesbaden.

AnAe *Analecta Aegyptiaca*, Copenhagen.

Ann. IPHOS *Annuaire de l'Institut de Philologie et d'Histoire Orientales et Slaves*, Brussels.

AnOr *Analecta Orientalia*, Rome.

APAW *Abhandlungen der Preussischen Akademie der Wissenschaften*, Berlin. [*ADAW* since 1945]

ARCE American Research Center in Egypt, Cairo.

ASAE   Annales du Service des Antiquités de l'Égypte, Cairo.

AV   Archäologische Veröffentlichungen des Deutschen Archäologischen Instituts, Abteilung Kairo, Cairo.

BAE   Bibliotheca Aegyptiaca, Brussels.

BASOR   Bulletin of the American School of Oriental Research, New Haven, CT.

BdE   Bibliothèque d'Études, IFAO, Cairo.

BES   Bulletin of the Egyptological Seminar, New York.

BIE   Bulletin de l'Institut d'Égypte, Cairo.

BIFAO   Bulletin de l'IFAO, Cairo.

BiOr   Bibliotheca Orientalis, Leiden.

BM British Museum, London.

BOREAS   BOREAS, Uppsala Studies in Ancient Mediterranean and Near Eastern Civilizations, Uppsala.

BSEA   British School of Egyptian Archaeology, London.

BSEG   Bulletin de la Societe d'Égyptologie de Genève, Geneva.

BSFE   Bulletin de la Société Française d'Égyptologie, Paris.

BSGE   Bulletin de la Société Géographique d'Égypte, Cairo.

CAH   Cambridge Ancient History, Cambridge.

CASAE   Cahiers Supplementaires des Annales du Service des Antiquités de l'Égypte, Cairo.

CdE   Chronique d'Égypte. Brussels.

CG Catalogue Général, Egyptian Museum, Cairo.

CRAIBL   Comptes Rendus de l'Académie des Inscriptions et Belles Lettres, Paris.

CRIPEL   Cahiers de Recherches de l'Institut de Papyrologie et Egyptologie de Lille, Lille.

DE   Discussions in Egyptology, Oxford.

Doc. FIFAO   Documents de Fouilles de l'Institut Français d'Archéologie Orientale, Cairo.

DÖAW   Denkschrift der Österreichischen Akademie der Wissenschaften, Vienna.

L'égyptologie en 1979   L'égyptologie en 1979. Axes prioritaires de recherche, Colloques internationaux du CNRS, Paris: 1982.

Enchoria: Zeitschrift für Demotistik und Koptologie, Wiesbaden.

ET   Etudes et Travaux, Warsaw.

EVO   Egitto e Vicino Oriente, Rivista della sezione orientalistica dell'Istituto di Storia Antica, Pisa.

FuB   Forschungen und Berichte, Berlin.

GM   Göttinger Miszellen. Göttingen.

GOF   Göttinger Orientforschungen, Wiesbaden.

HÄB   Hildescheimer ägyptologische Beiträge, Hildesheim.

HdO   Handbuch der Orientalistik, Leiden.

HPBM   Hieratic Papyri in the British Museum, London.

IFAO   Institut Français d'Archéologie Orientale, Cairo.

IPHOS   Annuaire de l'Institut de Philologie et d'Histoire Orientales et Slaves. Brussels.

JA *Journal Asiatique*, Paris.

JAOS *Journal of the American Oriental Society*, New Haven, CT.

JARCE *Journal of the American Research Center in Egypt*, Cairo.

JE Journal d'Entrées, Egyptian Museum, Cairo.

JEA *Journal of Egyptian Archaeology*, London.

JEOL *Jaarbericht van het Vooraziatisch-Egyptisch Genootschap 'Ex Oriente Lux'*, Leiden.

JNES *Journal of Near Eastern Studies*, Chicago.

JSSEA *Journal de la SSEA*

KÄT *Kleine Ägyptische Texte*, Wiesbaden.

KRI K. A. Kitchen 1968–88: *Ramesside Inscriptions: Historical and Bio-graphical*. 7 vols. Oxford.

LÄ *Lexikon der Ägyptologie*, Wiesbaden: 1975–87.

LÄS *Leipziger Ägyptologische Studien*, Gluckstadt, Hamburg, New York.

LAPO *Literatures Anciennes du Proche-Orient*, Paris.

MÄS *Munchner Ägyptologische Studien*, Munich and Berlin.

MDAIK *Mitteilungen des Deutschen Archäologischen Instituts*, Cairo.

MIFAO *Mémoires publiés par les membres de l'Institut Français d'Archéologie Orientale*, Cairo.

MIO *Mitteilungen des Instituts für Orientforschung*, Berlin.

MMA Metropolitan Museum of Art, New York.

MNL *Meroitic Newsletter*, Paris.

Mon. Aeg. *Monumenta Aegyptiaca*, Brussels.

MRE *Monographies Reine Elisabeth*, Brussels.

NA *Nyame Akuma*. Khartoum.

NARCE *Newsletter of the American Research Center in Egypt*, Princeton and Cairo.

NAWG *Nachrichten von der Akademie der Wissenschaften zu Göttingen*, Göttingen.

OBO *Orbis Biblicus et Orientalis*, Freiburg.

Oikumene Oikumene, *Studia ad historiam antiquam classicam et orientalem spectantia*, Budapest.

OIP *Oriental Institute Publications*, Chicago.

OLA *Orientalia Lovaniensa Analecta*, Louvain.

OLP *Orientalia Lovaniensa Periodica*, Louvain.

OMRO *Oudheidkundige Mededelingen uit het Rijksmuseum van Oudheden te Leiden*, Leiden.

Or *Orientalia*, Rome.

OrAnt *Oriens Antiquus*, Rome.

PIHAN *Stamboul Publications de l'Institut Historique et Archéologique Neerlandais de Stamboul*, Istanbul.

PM Porter, B. and Moss, R. L. B. 1939–88: *Topographical Bibliography of Ancient Egyptian Hieroglyphic Texts, Reliefs and Paintings*. 8 vols. Oxford.

RAPH *Recherches d'Archéologie, de Philologie et d'Histoire*, IFAO, Cairo.

RdE *Revue d'Égyptologie*, Paris.

REA *Revue des Études Anciennes*, Paris.

REG *Revue des Études Grecques*, Paris.

RIDA   *Revue Internationale du Droit de l'Antiquité*, Paris.

RIHAO   *Revista del Instituto de Historia Antigua Oriental*, Buenos Aires.

RIK   *Ramesside Inscriptions in Karnak*, Oriental Institute, Chicago.

RSO   *Rivista degli Studi Orientali*, Rome.

RT   *Recueil de Travaux Relatifs à la Philologie et à l'Archéologie Égyptiennes et Asyriennes*. Paris.

Saeculum   *Saeculum, Jahrbuch für Universalgeschichte*, Freiburg and Munich.

SAK   *Studien zur Altägyptischen Kultur*, Hamburg.

SAOC   *Studies in Ancient Oriental Civilization*, Oriental Institute, Chicago.

SBAW   *Sitzungsberichte der Bayerischen Akademie der Wissenschaften*, Munich.

Schr. Or.   *Schriften zur Geschichte und Kultur des Alten Orients*, Berlin.

SHAW   *Sitzungsberichte der Heidelberger Akademie der Wissenschaften*, Heidelberg.

SNR   *Sudan Notes and Records*, Khartoum.

Sond. DAIK   *Sonderdrucke des Deutschen Archäologischen Instituts in Kairo*, Cairo.

SSEA   *Society for the Study of Egyptian Antiquities*, Toronto.

Stud. Aeg.   *Studia Aegyptiaca*, Budapest.

TÄB   *Tübinger Ägyptologische Beitrage*, Tübingen.

TAVO   *Tübinger Atlas des Vorderen Orients*, Wiesbaden.

TT   Theban Tomb.

UGAÄ   *Untersuchungen zur Geschichte und Altertumskunde Ägyptens*, Berlin.

Urk.   Sethe, K. et al. 1906–: *Urkunden des ägyptischen Altertums*. Leipzig. *VA Varia Aegyptiaca*, San Antonio, TX.

VIAÄ   *Wien Veröffentlichungen des Instituts fur Archäologie und Ägyptologie*, Vienna.

WdO   *Die Welt des Orients, Wissentschaftliche Beiträge zur Kunde des Morgenlandes*, Wuppertal, Stuttgart, Göttingen.

WZKM   *Wiener Zeitschrift fur die Kunde des Morgenlandes*, Vienna.

WZU Halle   *Wissentschaftliche Zeitschrift der Universität Halle*, Halle.

ZÄS   *Zeitschrift fur Ägyptische Sprache und Altertumskunde*, Leipzig and Berlin.

ZDPV   *Zeitschrift des Deutschen Palästina-Vereins*, Leipzig and Wiesbaden.

Abd el-Razik, Mahmoud 1974: The Dedicatory and Building Texts of Ramesses II in Luxor Temple, I: The Texts. *JEA* 60, 142–60.

Abitz, Friedrich 1984: *König und Gott: Die Götterszenen in den ägyptischen Königsgräbern von Thutmosis IV. bis Ramses III.* Wiesbaden.

—— 1986: *Ramses III. in den Gräbern seiner Söhne.* OBO 72.

Abu-Ghazi, Dia 1968. Bewailing the King in the Pyramid Texts. *BIFAO* 66, 157–64.

Abu Bakr, A. el-M. Y. 1981: Pharaonic Egypt. In G. Mokhtar (ed.), *General History of Africa* II. Paris, London, Berkeley: 84–111.

Adam, Shehata and Vercoutter, Jean 1981: The Importance of Nubia: A Link between Central Africa and the Mediterranean. In G. Mokhtar (ed.), *General History of Africa* II. Paris, London, Berkeley: 226–45.

Adams, Barbara 1974a: *Ancient Hierakonpolis*. Warminster.

—— 1974b: *Ancient Hierakonpolis: Supplement*. Warminster.

—— 1984: *Egyptian Mummies*. Princes Risborough.

Adams, William Y. 1968: Invasion, Diffusion, Evolution. *Antiquity* 42, 194–215.

—— 1980: Du royaume de Kouch à l'avènement de l'Islam. *Courrier UNESCO*, 25–9.

—— 1983: Primis and the 'Aethiopian' Frontier. *JARCE* 20, 93–104.

—— 1984: *Nubia: Corridor to Africa*. London.

—— 1985: Doubts about the 'Lost Pharaohs'. *JNES* 44, 185–92.

Ahlstrom, G. W. and Edelmann, D. 1985: Merneptah's Israel. *JNES* 44, 59–62.

Akhavi, S. 1982: Socialization of Egyptian Workers. *NARCE* 119, 42–6.

Albright, W. 1952: The Smaller Beth Shan Stela of Sethos I (1309–1280 BC). *BASOR* 125, 24–32.

Aldred, Cyril 1969: The 'New Year' Gifts to the Pharaoh. *JEA* 55, 73–81.

—— 1970: The Foreign Gifts Offered to the Pharaoh. *JEA* 56, 105–16.

—— 1971: *Jewels of the Pharaohs: Egyptian Jewellery of the Dynastic Period*. London.

—— 1979b: More Light on the Ramesside Tomb Robberies. In J. Ruffle et al. (ed.), *Glimpses of Ancient Egypt. Studies in Honour of H. W. Fairman*. Warminster: 92–9.

—— 1980: *Egyptian Art*. London.

—— 1984: *The Egyptians*. Revised edition. London.

—— 1988: *Akhenaten: King of Egypt*. London.

Alex, M. 1985: *Klimadaten ausgewählter Stationen des vorderen Orients*. *TAVO* A/14.

Allam, Shafik 1963: *Beiträge zum Hathorkult (bis zum Ende des Mittleren Reiches)*. *MÄS* 4.

—— 1973a: *Das Verfahrensrecht in der altägyptischen Arbeitersiedlung von Deir el-Medinah*. Tübingen.

—— 1973b: *Hieratische Ostraka und Papyri aus der Ramessidenzeit*. Tübingen.

—— 1973c: De la divinité dans le droit pharaonique. *BSFE* 68, 17–30.

—— 1978: Un droit pénal existait-il stricto sensu en Égypte pharaonique? *JEA* 64, 65–8.

—— 1981: Quelques aspects du mariage dans l'Égypte ancienne. *JEA* 67, 116–35.

—— 1983: *Quelques pages de la vie quotidienne en Égypte ancienne*. Cairo.

—— 1984: La problématique des quarante rouleaux de lois. In *Studien zu Sprache und Religion Ägyptens. Festschrift W. Westendorf*. Göttingen: 447–52.

—— 1986: Réflexions sur le 'Code légal' d'Hermopolis dans l'Égypte ancienne. *CdE* 61, 50–75.

Allard-Huard, Léone and Huard, Paul 1985: *Le cheval, le fer et le chameau sur le Nil et au Sahara*. Cairo.

Alpin, Prosper 1581–4: *Histoire Naturelle de l'Égypte, La médecine des Égyptiens, Plantes d'Égypte*. 5 vols. Reprinted 1979–80. Cairo.

Altenmüller, Hartwig 1976: *Grad und Totenreich der alten Ägypter*. Hamburg.

—— 1981: Amenophis I. als Mittler. *MDAIK* 37, 1–7.

—— 1982: Tausret and Sethnacht. *JEA* 68, 107–15.

—— 1983a: Bemerkungen zu den Königsgräbern des Neuen Reiches. *SAK* 10, 25–62.

—— 1983b: Rolle und Bedeutung des Grabes des Königin Tausret im Königsgräbertal von Theben. *BSEG* 8, 3–11.

—— 1984: Der Begräbnistag Sethos' II. *SAK* 11, 37–47.

—— 1985: Das Grab der Königin Tausret (KV 14). Bericht über eine archäologische Unternehmung. *GM* 84, 7–18.

Altenmüller, Harwig and Brunner, Hellmut 1970: *Ägyptologie: Literatur.* 2nd edn. *HdO* I/1.2.

—— 1972: Die Texte zum Begräbnisritual in den Pyramiden des Alten Reiches. Wiesbaden.

Altenmüller, Hartwig and Moussa, Ahmed M. 1982: Die Inschriften der Taharkastele von der Dahschurstrasse. *SAK* 9, 57–84.

Amborn, H. 1976: *Die Bedeutung der Kulturen des Niltals für die Eisenproduktion im subsaharischen Afrika.* Wiesbaden.

Amélineau, E. 1899: *Le tombeau d'Osiris. Monographie de la découverte faite en 1887–1898.* Paris.

Amer, Amin A. A. 1985: Reflexions on the Reign of Ramesses VI. *JEA* 71, 66–70.

Amin, M. A. 1970: Ancient Trade Routes between Egypt and the Sudan, 4000 to 700 BC. *SNR* 51, 23–30.

Andreau, J. and Étienne, Roland 1984: Vingt ans de recherches sur l'archaïsme et la modernité des sociétés antiques. *REA* 86, 55–69.

Andrews, Carol 1987: *Egyptian Mummies.* London.

Anthes, Rudolph 1968: *Die Büste der Königin Nofretete.* 4th edn. Berlin.

Anus, Pierre and Saad, Ramadan 1971: Habitations de prêtres dans le temple d'Amon de Karnak. *Kêmi* 21, 217–38.

Apel, H. 1982: *Verwandschaft, Gott und Geld. Zur Organisation archaischer, ägyptischer und antiker Gesellschaft.* Frankfurt.

Arkell, A. J. 1975: *The Prehistory of the Nile Valley. HdO* VII/1.2.

Armayor, O. K. 1985: *Herodotus' Autopsy of the Fayoum. Lac Moeris and the Labyrinth of Egypt.* Amsterdam.

Arnold, Dieter 1974a: *Der Tempel des Königs Mentuhotep von Deir el-Bahari* I. *AV* 8.

—— 1974b: *Der Tempel des Königs Mentuhotep von Deir el-Bahari* II. *AV* 11.

—— 1981: Uberlegungen zum Problem des Pyramidenbaues. *MDAIK* 37, 15–28.

—— 1987: *Der Pyramidenbezirk des Königs Amenemhet III. in Dahschur I. Die Pyramide. AV* 53.

—— 1991: *Building in Egypt: Pharaonic Stone Masonry.* Oxford.

Artin Pacha, Y. 1909: *Contes populaires du Soudan égyptien recueillis en 1908 sur le Nil Blanc et le Nil Bleu.* Leroux.

Assman, Jan 1970: *Der König als Sonnenpriester. Ein kosmographischer Begleittext zur kultischen Sonnenhymnik in thebanischen Tempeln und Grabern. ADAIK* 7.

—— 1975a: *Ägyptische Hymnen und Gebete. Eingeleitet, übersetzt und erläutert*. Zurich.

—— 1975b: *Zeit und Ewigkeit im alten Ägypten. AHAW* 1.

—— 1977: Die Verborgenheit des Mythos in Ägypten. *GM* 25, 7–44.

—— 1979: Weisheit, Loyalismus und Frömmigkeit. In *Studien zu altägyptischen Lebenslehren. OBO* 28, 11–72.

—— 1980: Die 'loyalistische Lehre' Echnatons. *SAK* 8, 1–32.

—— 1983a: Das Dekorationsprogramm der königlichen Sonnenheiligtümer des Neuen Reiches nach einer Fassung der Spätzeit. *ZÄS* 110, 91–8.

—— 1983b: *Re und Amun. Die Krise des polytheistischen Weltbilds im Ägypten der 18.–20. Dynastie. OBO* 51.

—— 1983c: *Sonnenhymnen in thebanischen Gräbern, Theben* I. Mayence.

—— 1984: *Ägypten. Theologie und Frömmigkeit einer frühen Hochkultur*. Stuttgart.

Assman, Jan et al. (eds) 1977: *Fragen an die altägyptische Literatur: Studien zum Gedenken an Eberhard Otto*. Wiesbaden.

Atzler, Michael 1981: *Untersuchungen zur Herausbildung von Herrschaftsformen in Ägypten. HÄB* 16.

Auffret, Pierre 1981: *Hymnes d'Égypte et d'Israël. Études de structures littéraires. OBO* 34.

Aufrère, Sydney 1982: Contribution à l'étude de la morphologie du protocole 'classique'. *BIFAO* 82, 19–74.

Austin, M. M. 1970: *Greece and Egypt in the Archaic Age*. Cambridge.

Azim, Michel 1978–80a: Découverte de dépôts de fondation d'Horemheb au IXe pylône de Karnak. *Karnak* 7, 93–120.

—— 1978–80b: La structure des pylônes d'Horemheb à Karnak. *Karnak* 7, 127–66.

—— 1985: Le grand pylône de Louqsor: un essai d'analyse architecturale et technique. In F. Geus and F. Thill (eds), *Mélanges offerts à Jean Vercoutter*. Paris: 19–42.

Badawy, Alexandre 1948: *Le dessin architectural chez les anciens Égyptiens: Étude comparative des représentations égyptiennes de construction*. Cairo.

—— 1954: *A History of Egyptian Architecture 1: From the Earliest Times to the End of the Old Kingdom*. Giza.

—— 1958: Politique et architecture dans l'Égypte pharaonique. *CdE* 33, 171–81.

—— 1966: *A History of Egyptian Architecture 2: The First Intermediate Period, the Middle Kingdom and the Second Intermediate Period*. Berkeley, CA.

—— 1968: *A History of Egyptian Architecture 3: The Empire (the New Kingdom)*. Berkeley, CA.

Baedecker, K. 1974: *Egypt and the Sudan. Handbook for Travellers*. 8th edn. Leipzig.

Baer, Klaus 1974: *Rank and Title in the Old Kingdom. The Structure of Egyptian Administration in the Fifth and Sixth Dynasties*. Chicago.

Baikie, J. 1929: *A History of Egypt from the Earliest Times to the End of the XVIIIth Dynasty*. London.

Baillet, J. 1912: *Le régime pharaonique dans ses rapports avec l'évolution de la morale en Égypte*. Blois.

Baines, John 1974: The Inundation Stela of Sebekhotpe VIII. *AcOr* 36, 39–58.

—— 1976: The Sebekhotpe VIII Inundation Stela: an Additional Fragment. *AcOr* 37, 39–58.

—— 1984: Interpretation of Religion: Logic, Discourse, Rationality. *GM* 76, 25–54.

—— 1986: *Fecundity Figures: Egyptian Personification and the Iconology of a Genre*. Warminster.

Baines, John and Málek, Jaromir 1980: *Atlas of Ancient Egypt*. Oxford.

Bakir, Abd el-Monem 1978: *Slavery in Pharaonic Egypt*. CASAE 18.

Ball, John 1942: *Egypt in the Classical Geographers*. Cairo.

Barguet, Paul 1953a: *La Stèle de la Famine à Séhel*. BdE 24.

—— 1953b: La structure du temple Ipet-sout d'Amon à Karnak, du Moyen Empire à Aménophis II. *BIFAO* 52, 145–55.

—— 1962: *Le temple d'Amon-Rê à Karnak: Essai d'exégèse*. RAPH 21.

—— 1967: *Le Livre des Morts des anciens Égyptiens*. Paris.

—— 1975: Le *Livre des Portes* et la transmission du pouvoir royal. *RdE* 27, 30–6.

—— 1976: Note sur le grand temple d'Aton à el-Amarna. *RdE* 28, 148–51.

—— 1986a: Note sur la sortie du roi hors du palais. In *Hommages à François Daumas* I. Montpellier: 51–4.

—— 1986b: *Les textes des sarcophages égyptiens du Moyen Empire*. Paris.

Barta, Wolfgang 1969a: *Das Gespräch eines Mannes mit seinem BA (Papyrus Berlin 3024)*. MÄS 18.

—— 1969b: Falke des Palastes als ältester Königstitel. *MDAIK* 24, 51–7.

—— 1973: *Untersuchungen zum Götterkreis der Neunheit*. MÄS 28.

—— 1975: *Untersuchungen zur Göttlichkeit des regierenden Königs. Ritus und Sakralkönigtum in Altägypten nach Zeugnissen der Frühzeit und des Alten Reiches*. MÄS 32.

—— 1978: Die Sedfest-Darstellung Osorkons II. im Tempel von Bubastis. *SAK* 6, 25–42.

—— 1980a: Die Mondfinsternis im 15. Regierungsjahr Takelots II. *RdE* 32, 3–17.

—— 1980b: Thronbesteigung und Krönungsfeier als unterschiedliche Zeugnisse königlicher Herrschaftsübername. *SAK* 8, 33–53.

—— 1981a: Bemerkungen zur Chronologie der 6. bis 11. Dynastie. *ZÄS* 108, 23–33.

—— 1981b: Bemerkungen zur Chronologie der 21. Dynastie. *MDAIK* 37, 35–40.

—— 1981c: Die Chronologie der 1. bis 5. Dynastie nach den Angaben des rekonstruirten Annalensteins. *ZÄS* 108, 11–13.

—— 1983a: Bemerkungen zur Rekonstruktion der Vorlage des Turiner Königspapyrus. *GM* 64, 11–13.

—— 1983b: Zur Entwicklung des ägyptischen Kalenderwesens. *ZÄS* 110, 16–26.

—— 1984: Anmerkungen zur Chronologie der Dritten Zwischenzeit. *GM* 70, 7–12.

—— 1987a: Zur Konstruktion der ägyptischen Königsnamen. *ZÄS* 114, 3–10.

—— 1987b: Zur Konstruktion der ägyptischen Königsnamen II: Die Horus-, Herrinnen- und Goldnamen von der Frühzeit bis zum Ende des Alten Reiches. *ZÄS* 114, 105–113.

Barucq, André 1962: *L'expression de la louange divine et de la prière dans la Bible et en Égypte*. BdE 33.

Barucq, André and Daumas, François 1980: *Hymnes et prières de l'Égypte ancienne*. Paris.

Bastianini, G. 1975: *Lista dei prefetti d'Egitto dal 30a al 299p*. Bonn.

Batta, E. 1986: *Obelisken und ihre Geschichte in Rom*. Frankfurt.

Baud, Marcelle 1978: *Le caractère du dessin en Égypte ancienne*. Paris.

Baumgartel, E. J. 1981: *The Cultures of Prehistoric Egypt*. London.

Beckerath, Jürgen von. 1964: *Untersuchungen zur politischen Geschichte der zweiten Zwischenzeit in Ägypten*. ÄF 23.

—— 1968: Die 'Stele der Verbannten' im Museum des Louvre. *RdE* 20, 7–36.

—— 1971a: *Abriss der Geschichte des alten Ägyptens*. Munich.

—— 1971b: Ein Denkmal zur Genealogie der XX. Dynastie. *ZÄS* 97, 7–12.

—— 1984a: *Handbuch der ägyptischen Königsnamen*. MÄS 20.

—— 1984b: Bemerkungen zum Turiner Königspapyrus und zu den Dynastien der ägyptischen Geschichte. *SAK* 11, 49–57.

—— 1984c: Bemerkungen zum Problem der Thronfolge in der Mitte der XX. Dynastie. *MDAIK* 40, 1–6.

—— 1984d: Drie Thronbesteigungsdaten der XX. Dynastie. *GM* 79, 7–10.

Bedevian, Armenag K. 1936: *Illustrated Polyglottic Dictionary of Plant Names*. Cairo.

Begelsbacher-Fischer, B. L. 1981: *Untersuchungen zur Götterwelt des Alten Reiches im Spiegel der Privatgräber der IV. und V. Dynastie*. OBO 37.

—— 1985: *Ägypten*. Zurich.

Behrens, H. 1963: Neolitische-frühmetallzeitliche Tierskelettfunde aus dem Nilgebiet und ihre religionsgeschichtliche Bedeutung. *ZÄS* 88, 75–83.

Beinlich, Horst 1976: *Studien zu den 'geographischen Inschriften' (10–14, o.äg.Gau)*. TÄB 2.

—— 1979: Die Nilquellen nach Herodot. *ZÄS* 106, 11–14.

—— 1984: *Die Osirisreliquien. Zum Motiv der Körpergliederung in der altägyptischen Religion*. Wiesbaden.

—— 1987: Der Moeris-See nach Herodot. *GM* 100, 15–18.

Bell, Barbara 1971: The Dark Ages in Ancient History I: The First Dark Age in Egypt. *AJA* 75, 1–26.

Bell, L. 1985: Luxor Temple and the Cult of the Royal Ka. *JNES* 44, 251–94.

Bell, L., Johnson, J. et al. 1984. The Eastern Desert of Upper Egypt: Routes and Inscriptions. *JNES* 43, 27–46.

Bell, Martha 1985. Gurob Tomb 605 and Mycenaean Chronology. BdE 97/1, 61–86.

Bellod, A., Golvin, J.-C. and Traunecker, C. 1983: *Du ciel de Thèbes*. Paris.

Bellion, Madeleine 1987: *Égypte ancienne. Catalogue des manuscrits hiéroglyphiques et hiératiques et des dessins, sur papyrus, cuir ou tissu, publiés ou signalés*. Paris.

Belon du Mans, P. 1970: *Le voyage en Egypte de P. Belon du Mans* [1587]. Cairo.

Berlandini, Jocelyne 1976: Le protocole de Toutankhamon sur les socles du dromos du Xe pylône à Karnak. *GM* 22, 13–20.

—— 1978: Une stèle de donation du dynaste libyen Roudamon. *BIFAO* 78, 147–64.

—— 1979: La pyramide 'ruinée' de Sakkara-Nord et le roi Ikaouhor-Menkaouhor. *RdE* 31, 3–28.

—— 1982: Les tombes amarniennes et d'époque Toutankhamon à Sakkara. Criteres stylistiques. *L'égyptologie en 1979* II, 195–212.

Bierbrier, Morris L. 1972: The Length of the Reign of Sethos I. *JEA* 58, 303.

—— 1975a: The Length of the Reign of Ramesses X. *JEA* 61, 251.

—— 1975b: *The Late New Kingdom in Egypt (c. 1300–664 B.C.). A Genealogical and Chronological Investigation.* Warminster.

—— 1982: *The Tomb-Builders of the Pharaohs.* London.

Bietak, Manfred 1968: *Studien zur Chronologie der nubischen C-Gruppe. Ein Beitrag zur Frühgeschichte Unternubiens.* CG, 70501–70754

—— 1975: *Der Fundort im Rahmen der archäologischen-geographischen Untersuchungen über das ägyptische Ostdelta, Tel el-Dab'a 2.* Vienna.

—— 1979: Urban Archaeology and the 'Town Problem' in Ancient Egypt. In K. Weeks (ed.), *Egyptology and the Social Sciences.* Cairo: 97–144.

—— 1981: *Avaris and Piramesse: Archaeological Exploration in the Eastern Nile Delta.* London.

—— 1984a: *Eine Palastanlage aus der Zeit der späten Mittleren Reiches und andere Forschungsergebnisse aus dem östlichen Nildelta.* Vienna.

—— 1984b: Zum Königsreich des '3-zh-R'' Nehesi. *SAK* 11, 59–75.

Bietak, Manfred and Engelmayer, R. 1963: *Eine frühdynastische Abri-Siedlung mit Felsbildern aus Sayala-Nubien.* Vienna.

Bietak, Manfred and Mlinar, C. 1987: *Ein Friedhof der syrisch-palästinischen mittleren Bronzezeit-Kultur mit einem Totentempel, Tell el-Dab'a 5.* Vienna.

Bisson de la Roque, F. 1950: *Trésor de Tod.* CG, 7050–70754.

Bisson de la Roque, F., Contenau, G. and Chapouthier, F. 1953: *Le Trésor de Tod. Doc. FIFAO* 11.

Björkmann, G. 1971: *Kings at Karnak.* Uppsala.

Blacker, C. and M. Loewe. 1975: *Ancient Cosmologies.* London.

Blanc, Nicole 1978: Peuplement de la vallée du Nil au sud du 23e parallèle. In *Histoire Generale de l'Afrique*: Études et Documents I. Paris, London, Berkeley: 37–64.

Blankenberg-van Delden, C. 1969: *The Large Commemorative Scarabs of Amenhotep III.* Leiden.

—— 1976: More Large Commemorative Scarabs of Amenhotep III. *JEA* 62, 74–80.

—— 1982a: A Genealogical Reconstruction of the Kings and Queens of the Late 17th and Early 18th Dynasties. *GM* 54, 31–46.

—— 1982b: Kamosis. *GM* 60, 7–8.

—— 1982c: Queen Ahmes Merytamon. *GM* 61, 13–16.

Bleeker, C. J. 1967: *Egyptian Festivals, Enactments of Religious Renewal. Studies in the History of Religions. Numen* 13, Supplement. Leiden.

Bleiberg, Edward 1985–6: Historical Texts as Political Propaganda During the New Kingdom. *BES* 7, 5–14.

Blumenthal, Elke 1970: *Untersuchungen zum ägyptischen Konigtum des Mittleren Reiches I: Die Phraseologie.* Berlin.

—— 1980: Die Lehre für Konig Merikare. *ZÄS* 107, 5–41.

—— 1982: Die Prophezeiung des Neferti. *ZÄS* 109, 1–27.

—— 1983: Die erste Koregenz der 12. Dynastie. *ZÄS* 110, 104–21.

—— 1984: Die Lehre des Königs Amenemhets I: I. *ZÄS* 111, 85–107.

—— 1985: Die Lehre des Königs Amenemhets I: II. *ZÄS* 112, 104–15.

Blumenthal, E., I. Müller et al. 1984. *Urkunden der 18. Dynastie. Übersetzung zu den Heften 5–16.* Berlin.

Blunt, H., Albert, J., Seguezzi, S. and von Neitzschitz, G. 1974: *Voyages en Égypte des années 1634–1634 et 1636, Henry Blunt, Jacques Albert, Santo Seguezzi, George von Neitzschitz.* Cairo.

Boardman, J. and Hammond, N. 1982: The Expansion of the Greek World, 8th to 6th Century BC. *CAH* 3/3.

Boessneck, Joachim 1981: *Gemeinsame Anliegen von Ägyptologie und Zoologie aus der Sicht des Zooarchäologen. SBAW* 1981.5.

Boessneck, Joachim and von den Driesch, A. 1982: *Studien an subfossilien Tierknochen aus Ägypten. MÄS* 40.

Bogoslowski, Eugeni S. 1983: Review of J. J. Perepelkin, *Die Revolution Amenhotep IV, 1* (Moscow, 1967). *GM* 61, 53–64.

Bolla-Kotek, S. von. 1969: *Untersuchungen zur Tiermiete und Viehpacht im Altertum.* 2nd edn. Munich.

Bongrani-Fanfoni, L. 1987: Un nuovo documento di Scepenupet Ia e Amenardis Ia. *OrAnt* 26, 65–71.

Bonhème, Marie-Ange 1978: Les désignations de la 'titulature' royale au Nouvel Empire. *BIFAO* 78, 347–88.

—— 1979: Hérihor fut-il effectivement roi? *BIFAO* 79, 267–84.

—— 1987a: *Le Livre des Rois de la troisième periode intermédiaire I: Herihor, XXIe dynastie.* Cairo.

—— 1987b: *Les noms royaux dan l'Égypte de la troisième période inter-médiaire. BdE* 98.

Bonhème, Marie-Ange and Forgeau, Annie 1988: *Pharaon. Les secrets du pouvoir.* Paris.

Bonneau, Danielle 1971a: *Le fisc et le Nil. Incidences des irrégularités de la crue du Nil sur la fiscalité foncière....* Paris.

—— 1971b: Les fêtes de la crue du Nil. Problèmes de lieux, de dates et d'organisation. *RdE* 23, 49–65.

Bonnel, R. G. and Tobin, V. A. 1985: Christ and Osiris. A Comparative Study. In S. Groll (ed.), *Pharaonic Egypt.* Jerusalem: 1–29.

Bonnet, Hans 1971: *Reallexikon der ägyptischen Religionsgeschichte.* 2nd edn. Berlin.

Boreux, Charles 1924–5: *Études de nautique égyptienne, l'art de la navigation en Égypte jusqu'à la fin de l'Ancien Empire. MIFAO* 50.

—— 1926: *L'art égyptien.* Brussels.

—— 1932: *Musée de Louvre: antiquités égyptiennes. Catalogue-guide.* Paris.

Borghouts, J. F. 1978: *Ancient Egyptian Magical Texts.* Leiden.

—— 1986: *Nieuwjaar in het oude Egypte.* Leiden.

Botti, Giuseppe 1967: *L'archivio demotico da Deir el-Medineh. Catalogo Museo Egizio de Torino* I:1. Florence.

Bourguet, Pierre du 1964: *L'art copte, Petit Palais, Paris, 17 juin-15 septembre 1964.* Paris.

—— 1968a: *Histoires et Légendes de l'Égypte mystérieuse.* Paris.

—— 1968b: *L'art copte.* A. Michel.

—— 1973: *L'art égyptien.* Desclee de Brouwer.

Bovier-Lapierre, R. P., Gauthier, H. and Jouguet, P. 1932: *Précis de l'histoire d'Égypte I: Égypte préhistorique pharaonique et gréco-romaine.* Cairo.

Bradbury, Louise 1985: Nefer's Inscription: On the Death Date of Queen Ahmose-Nefertary and the Deed Found Pleasing to the King. *JARCE* 22, 73–95.

Brander, Bruce 1977: *Le Nil.*

Bratton, Fred Gladstone 1972: *A History of Egyptian Archaeology.* New York.

Breasted, James Henry 1906: *Ancient Records of Egypt.* 4 vols. Chicago.

Brémond, Gabriel 1974: *Voyage en Égypte de Gabriel Brémond [1643–6].* Cairo.

Bresciani, Edda 1969: *Letteratura e poesia dell'antico Egitto. Introduzione, traduzione originali e note.* Turin.

—— 1978: *J.-F. Champollion, Lettres à Zelmire. Champollion et son temps* I.

—— 1981: La morte di Cambise ovvero dell'empietà punita: a proposito della 'Cronica Demotica', verso, col. C, 7–8. *EVO* 4, 217–22.

—— 1985: Ugiahorresnet a Menfi. *EVO* 8, 1–6.

Bretten, Michael von. 1976: *Voyages en Égypte de Michael Von Bretten, 1585–1586.* Cairo.

Brewer, D. J. 1985: The Fayum Zooarchaeological Survey: a Preliminary Report. *NARCE* 128, 5–15.

Brinks, Jürgen 1979: *Die Enwicklung der königlichen Grabanlagen des Alten Reiches. Eine strukturelle und historische Analyse altägyptischen Architecktur. HÄB* 10.

—— 1980: *Mastaba und Pyramidentempel – ein struktureller Vergleich. GM* 39, 45–60.

—— 1981: Die Sedfestanlagen der Pyramidentempel. *CdE* 56, 5–14.

—— 1984: Einiges zum Bau der Pyramiden des Alten Reiches. *GM* 78, 33–48.

Brissaud, Philippe 1982: *Les ateliers de potiers de la région de Louqsor. BdE* 78.

Brovarski, Edward J. 1985: Akhmim in the Old Kingdom and First Intermediate Period. *BdE* 97/1, 117–53.

Brunner, Helmut 1957: *Altägyptische Erziehung.* Wiesbaden.

—— 1964: *Die Geburt des Gottkönigs. Studien zur Überlieferung eines altägyptischen Mythos.* Wiesbaden.

—— 1974: Djedefhor in der römischen Kaiserzeit. *Stud. Aeg.* 1, 55–64.

—— 1983: *Grundzüge der altägyptischen Religion.* Darmstadt.

—— 1986: *Grundzüge einer Geschichte der altägyptischen Literatur.* 4th edn. Darmstadt.

Brunner-Traut, Emma 1977: *Altägyptische Tiergeschichte und Fabel, Gestalt und Strahlkraft.* Darmstadt.

—— 1982: *Ägypten. Ein Kunst- und Reiseführer mit Landeskunde.* Stuttgart.

—— 1985: *Lebensweisheit der alten Ägypter.* Freiburg.

—— 1986: *Altägyptische Marchen.* 7th edn. Cologne.

Brussels 1975: *Le règne du soleil. Akhnaton et Néfertiti. Exposition organisée par le Ministère de la Culture aux Musées Royaux d'Art et d'Histoire.*

—— 1986: *La femme aux temps des pharaons. Catalogue de l'exposition aux musées Royaux d'Art et d'Histoire.*

Bucaille, Maurice 1987: *Les momies des pharaons et la médecine. Ramsès II à Paris. Le pharaon et Moïse.* Séguier.

Budge, E. A. Wallis 1912: *Annals of Nubian Kings with a Sketch of the History of the Nubian Kingdom of Napata.* London.

Bureth, P. 1964: *Les titulatures impériales dans les papyrus, les ostraca et les inscriptions d'Égypte.* Brussels.

Burkhardt, Adelheid 1985: *Ägypter und Meroiten im Dodekaschoenos. Untersuchungen zur Typologie und Bedeutung der demotischen Graffiti.* Meroitica 8.

Bury, J., Cook, S. et al. 1969: *The Persian Empire and the West.* CAH 4.

Buttery, A. 1974: *Armies and Enemies of Ancient Egypt and Assyria, 3200 BC to 612 BC.* Goring by Sea.

Butzer, Karl W. 1976: *Early Hydraulic Civilisation in Egypt: a Study in Cultural Ecology.* Chicago.

Butzer, K. W. and Hansen, C. 1968: *Desert and River in Nubia. Geomorphologic and Prehistoric Environment at the Aswan Reservoir.* Madison, WI.

Caillaud, Frédéric 1827: *Voyage à Méroé, au fleuve blanc au delta de Fazoql dans le midi du royaume de Sennar, à Syouah et dans cinq autres oasis.* Paris.

Caminos, Ricardo A. 1958: *The Chronicle of Prince Osorkon.* AnOr 37.

—— 1977: *A Tale of Woe. From a Hieratic Papyrus in the A. S. Pushkin Museum of Fine Arts in Moscow (P. Pushkin 127).* Oxford.

Caminos, Ricardo A. and Fischer, H. G. 1976: *Ancient Egyptian Epigraphy and Paleography. The Recording of Inscriptions and Scenes in Tombs and Temples.* New York.

Cannuyer, Christian 1985: Notules à propos de la stèle du sphinx. VA 1, 83–90.

Cantarelli, L. 1968: *La serie dei prefetti de Egitto.* Rome.

Capart, Jean 1931: *Propos sur l'art égyptien.* Brussels.

Carlton, E. 1977: *Ideology and Social Order.* London.

Carmody, D. K. and Carmody, J. T. 1985: *Shamans, Prophets and Sages.* Belmont, CA.

Carré, Jean-Marie 1956: *Voyageurs et écrivains français en Égypte.* 2nd edn. Cairo.

Carter, Howard 1923–33: *The Tomb of Tut. ankh. Amen.* 3 vols. London.

Cassin, E., Bottéro, J. and Vercoutter, J. 1967: *Die altorientalischen Reiche III: Die erste Halfte des 1. Jahrtausends.* Frankfurt.

Casson, Lionel 1984: *Ancient Trade and Society.* Detroit.

—— 1986: *Ships and Seamanship in the Ancient World.* Detroit.

—— 1988: *Die Pharaonen.* Munich.

Castel, U., Sauneron, N. and Sauneron, S. 1972: *Voyages en Égypte pendant les années 1587–1588: Lichtenstein, Kiechel, Teufel, Fernberger, Lunebau, Miloïti.* Cairo.

Gastellucci, G. Rosati 1980: L'onomastica del Medio Regno come mezzo di datazione. *Aegyptus* 70, 3–72.

Castillos, Juan J. 1982: *A Reappraisal of the Published Evidence on Egyptian predynastic and Early Dynastic Cemeteries.* Toronto.

Cauville, Sylvie 1983: *La théologie d'Osiris à Edfou.* BdE 91.

—— 1984: *Edfou.* Cairo.

Cenival, Françoise de 1972: *Les associations religieuses en Égypte d'après les documents démotiques.* BdE 46.

Cenival, Jean-Louis de 1964: *Architecture universelle: Égypte, époque pharaonique.* Frieburg.

—— 1965: Un nouveau fragment de la Pierre de Palerme. *BSFE* 44, 13–17.

Černý, Jaroslav 1958a: Stela of Ramesses II from Beisan. *Eretz Israel* 5, 75–81.

—— 1958b: Name of the King of the Unfinished Pyramid at Zawiyet el-Aryân. *MDAIK* 16, 25–9.

—— 1961: Note on the Supposed Beginning of a Sothic Period under Sethos I. *JEA* 47, 150–52.

—— 1973a: *A Community of Workmen at Thebes in the Ramesside Period.* BdE 50.

—— 1973b: *The Valley of the Kings. Fragments d'un manuscrit inachevé.* BdE 61.

—— 1979: *Ancient Egyptian Religion.* Originally publ. 1952. London.

Černý, Jaroslav, Clère, J.-J. and Bruyère, B. 1949: *Répertoire onomastique de Deir el-Médineh* I. Doc. FIFAO 12.

Cervíček, P. 1975: Notes on the Chronology of the Nubian Rock Art to the End of the Bronze Age (mid 11th cent. BC). *Études Nubiennes. Colloque de Chantilly.* BdE 77, 35–56.

Champollion, Jean-François 1835–45: *Monuments de l'Égypte et de la Nubie.* 4 vols. Paris.

—— 1972: *Textes et langages de l'Égypte pharaonique. Cent cinquante années de recherches, 1822–1972.* 3 vols. Cairo.

Chappaz, Jena-Luc 1983: Le premier édifice d'Amenophis IV à Karnak. *BSEG* 8, 13–45.

Charlton, Nial 1974: Some Reflections on the History of Pharaonic Egypt. *JEA* 60, 200–5.

Charpentier, G. 1986: *Recueil de matériaux épigraphiques relatifs à la botanique de l'Égypte antique.* Paris.

Cherpion, Nadine 1987: Quelques jalons pour une histoire de la peinture thébaine. *BSFE* 110, 27–47.

Chesneau, J. and Thevet, A. 1984: *Voyages des annees 1549–1552.* Cairo.

Chevereau, Pierre-Marie 1985: *Prosopographie des cadres militaires égyptiens de la Basse Époque. Carrières militaires et carrières sacerdotales en Égypte du XIe au IIe siècle avant J.-C.* Antony.

—— 1987: Contribution à la prosopographie des cadres militaires de l'Ancien Empire et de la Première Périod Intermédiaire. *RdE* 38, 13–48.

Chevrier, Henri 1956: Chronologie des constructions de la salle hypostyle. *ASAE* 54, 35–8.

—— 1964: Technique de la construction dans l'ancienne Égypte I: Murs en briques crues. *RdE* 16, 11–17.

—— 1970: Technique de la construction dans l'ancienne Égypte II: Problèmes posés par les obélisques. *RdE* 22, 15–39.

—— 1971: Technique de la construction dans l'ancienne Égypte III: Grosoeuvre et maçonnerie. *RdE* 23, 67–111.

Christie, Agatha 1973: *Akhnaton. A Play in Three Acts*. London.

Christophe, Louis-A. 1950: Ramsès IV et le Musée du Caire. *Cahiers d'Histoire Égyptienne* 3, 47–67.

—— 1951a: La carrière du prince Mérenptah et les trois régences ramessides. *ASAE* 51, 335–72.

—— 1951b: Notes géographiques. À propos des compagnes de Thoutmosis III. *RdE* 6, 89–114.

—— 1953: Les fondations de Ramsès III entre Memphis et Thebes. *Cahiers d'Histoire Égyptienne* 5, 227–49.

—— 1955: Les quatre plus illustres fils de Chéops. *Cahiers d'Histoire Égyptienne* 7, 213–22.

—— 1956a: Trois monuments inédits mentionnant le grand majordome de Nitocris, Padihorresnet. *BIFAO* 55, 65–84.

—— 1956b: Les trois derniers grands majordomes de la XXVIᵉ dynastie. *ASAE* 54, 83–100.

—— 1956c: Gérard de Nerval au Caire. *La Revue du Caire* 189, 171–97.

—— 1956d: Les reliques égyptiennes de Gérard de Nerval. *La Revue du Caire* 191–2.

—— 1956–7: Les temples d'Abou Simbel et la famille de Ramsès II. *BIE* 37, 107–29.

—— 1957a: Deux voyageurs suisses dans l'Égypte d'il y a cent ans. *La Revue de Caire* 199, 231–52.

—— 1957b: L'organisation de l'armée égyptienne a l'époque ramesside. *La Revue du Caire* 207, 387–405.

—— 1957c: Les divinités du papyrus Harris I et leurs épithètes. *ASAE* 54, 345–89.

—— 1958: Le pylône 'ramesside' d'Edfou. *ASAE* 55, 1–23.

—— 1960–1: Les monuments de Nubie. *La Revue du Caire* 244, 397–415 (Le temple de Debod); 246, 87–108 (De Dehmit à Kalabcha); 348, 257–75 (Kalabcha); 250, 429–48 (De Kalabcha à Gerf-Hussein); 252, 125–42 (Forteresses de Basse-Nubie).

—— 1961a: Le vocabulaire d'architecture monumentale d'après le papyrus Harris I. *Mélanges Maspero* I:6, *MIFAO* 66, 17–29.

—— 1961b: L'Institut d'Égypte et l'archéologie. *La Revue de Caire* 249, 345–54.

—— 1964: L'alun égyptien. Introduction historique. *BSGE* 37, 75–91.

—— 1965–6: Qui, le premier, entra dans le grand temple d'Abou Simbel? *BIE* 47, 37–46.

—— 1967a: Le voyage nubien du colonel Strator (fin octobre-début novembre 1817). *BIFAO* 65, 169–76.

—— 1967b: Le ravitaillement en poissons des artisans de la nécropole thébaine à la fin du règne de Ramsès III. *BIFAO* 65, 177–200.

—— 1977: *Campagne internationale de l'UNESCO pour la sauvegarde des sites et monuments de la Nubie: Bibliographie.* Paris.

Churcher, C. S. 1972: *Late Pleistocene Vertebrates from Archaeological Sites in the Plain of Kom Ombo, Upper Egypt.* Toronto.

Clément, R. 1960: *Les Français d'Égypte aux XVIIᵉ et XVIIIᵉ siècles. RAPH* 15.

Clère, Jacques-Jean 1951: Une statuette du fils âiné du roi Nectanebô. *RdE* 6, 135–56.

—— 1957: Notes sur la chapelle funéraire de Ramsès I à Abydos et sur son inscription dédicatoire. *RdE* 11, 1–38.

—— 1958: Fragments d'une nouvelle représentation égyptienne du monde. *MDAIK* 16, 30–46.

—— 1968: Nouveaux fragments de scènes du jubilé d'Aménophis IV. *RdE* 20, 51–4.

—— 1970: Notes sur l'inscription biographique de Sarenpout 1ᵉʳ à Assouan. *RdE* 22, 41–9.

—— 1975: Un monument de la religion populaire de l'époque ramesside. *RdE* 27, 70–7.

—— 1977: Sur l'existence d'un temple du Nouvel Empire à Dêbôd en Basse-Nubie. In E. Endesfelder et al. (eds), *Ägypten und Kusch. Schur. Or.* 13, 10–14.

—— 1985: Un dépôt de fondation du temple memphite de Sethos 1ᵉʳ. In F. Geus and F. Thill (eds), *Mélanges offerts à Jean Vercoutter.* Paris: 51–7.

Clère, Jacques-Jean and Vandier, J. 1948: *Textes de la première pèriode intermédiaire et de la 11ᵉ dynastie* I. *BAE* 10.

Cline, E. 1987: Amenhotep III and the Aegean: a Reassessment of Egypto-Aegean Relations in the 14th Century B.C. *Or* 56, 1–35.

Clutton-Brock, J. 1981: *Domesticated Animals from Early Times.* London.

Cockburn, A. and Cockburn, E. 1980: *Mummies, Diseases, and Ancient Cultures.* Cambridge.

Collins, Lydia 1976: The Private Tombs of Thebes: Excavations by Sir Robert Mond, 1905 and 1906. *JEA* 62, 18–40.

Combe, E., Bainville, J. and Driault, E. 1933: *Précis de l'histoire d'Égypte 3: L'Égypte ottomane, l'expédition française en Égypte et le règne de Mohamed-Aly (1517–1849).* Cairo.

Condon, Virginia 1978: *Seven Royal Hymns: Papyrus Turin CG 54031. MÄS* 37.

Connoly, R. C., Harrison, R. G. and Ahmed, S. 1976: Serological Evidences for the Parentage of Tut'ankhamun and Smenkhkare. *JEA* 62, 184–6.

Cooney, John D. 1965: *Amarna Reliefs from Hermopolis in American Collections.* New York.

Coppin, Jean 1971: *Les voyages en Égypte de Jean Coppin [1638–46].* Cairo.

Coquin, René-Georges 1972: La christianisation des temples de Karnak. *BIFAO* 72, 169–78.

Corteggiani, Jean-Pierre 1979a: *L'Égypte des pharaons au musée du Caire.* Paris.

—— 1979b: Une stèle héliopolitaine d'époque saïte. In *Hommages Sauneron* I. *BdE* 81, 115–54.

Costa, Pedro 1978: The Frontal Sinuses of the Remains Purported to be Akhenaton. *JEA* 64, 76–9.

Cruz-Uribe, Eugene 1977: On the Wife of Merneptah. *GM* 24, 23–32.

—— 1978: The Father of Ramses I: OI 11456. *JNES* 37, 237–44.

—— 1980: On the Existence of Psammetichus. *Serapis* 5, 35–39.

Cumming, Barbara 1982–4: *Egyptian Historical Records of the Later Eighteenth Dynasty*. Warminster.

Curl, J. S. 1982: *The Egyptian Revival: An Introductory Study of a Recurring Theme in the History of Taste*. London.

Curto, Silvio 1970: *Medicina e demici nell'antico Egitto*. Turin.

—— 1979: *Storia delle Museo Egizio di Torino*. 2nd edn. Turin.

—— 1981: *L'antico Egitto*. Turin.

—— 1984: Some Notes Concerning the Religion and Statues of Divinities of Ancient Egypt. In *Studien zu Sprache und Religion Ägyptens. Festschrift W. Westendorf*. Göttingen: 717–34.

Czermak, Wilhelm 1948: Akten in Keilschrift und das auswärtige Amt des Pharaos. *WZKM* 51, 1–13.

Da Gallipoli, B. A., Rocchetta, A. and Castela, H. 1974: *Voyages en Égypte des années 1597–1601*. Cairo.

Danelius, Eva and Steinitz, Heinz 1967: The Fishes and Other Aquatic Animals on the Punt-Reliefs at Deir el-Bahri. *JEA* 53, 15–24.

Darby, W. and Ghalioungui, P. 1977: *Food: the Gift of Osiris*. London.

Daressy, Georges 1888: Les carrières de Gebelein et le roi Smendès. *RT* 10, 133–8.

—— 1895: Inscriptions du tombeau de Psametik à Saqqarah. *RT* 17, 17–25.

—— 1896a: Inscriptions inédites de la XXIIᵉ dynastie. *RT* 18, 46–53.

—— 1896b: Une inondation à Thèbes sous le règne d'Osorkon II (*sic*). *RT* 18, 181–6.

—— 1899: Les rois Psusennès. *RT* 21, 9–12.

—— 1900: Stèle de l'an II d'Amasis. *RT* 22, 1–9.

—— 1901: Inscriptions de la chapelle d'Amenirtis à Médinet-Habou. *RT* 23, 4–18.

—— 1908: Le roi Auput et son domaine. *RT* 30, 202–8.

—— 1910: Le décret d'Amon en faveur du grand prêtre Pinozem. *RT* 32, 175–86.

—— 1912: Ramsès-Si-Ptah. *RT* 34, 39–52.

—— 1913a: Inscriptions historiques mendésiennes. *RT* 35, 124–9.

—— 1913b: Notes sur les XXIIᵉ, XXIIIᵉ and XXIVᵉ dynasties. *RT* 35, 129–150.

—— 1916: Le classement des rois de la famille des Bubastites. *RT* 38, 9–20.

—— 1923: La crue du Nil de l'an XXIX d'Amasis. *ASAE* 23, 47–8.

Daumas, François 1953: Le trône d'une statuette de Pépi 1ᵉʳ trouvé à Dendera. *BIFAO* 52, 163–72. Reprinted in *BSFE* 12, 36–9.

—— 1958: *Les mammisis des temples égyptiens*. Paris.

—— 1960: La scène de la résurrection au tombeau de Pétosiris. *BIFAO* 59, 63–80.

—— 1965a: *La civilisation de l'Égypte pharaonique*. Paris-Grenoble.

—— 1965b: *Les dieux de l'Égypte*, coll. 'Que sais-je?' no. 1194. Paris.

—— 1967: L'origine d'Amon de Karnak. *BIFAO* 65, 201–14.

—— 1968: *La vie dans l'Égypte ancienne*, coll. 'Que sais-je?' no. 1302. Paris.

—— 1969: Une table d'offrandes de Montouhotep Nebhepetre à Dendara. *MDAIK* 24, 96–9.

—— 1972: Les textes bilingues ou trilingues. In *Textes et langages de l'Égypte pharaonique* III. *BdE* 64/3, 41–5.

—— 1973: Derechef Pépi 1er a Dendara. *RdE* 25, 7–20.

—— 1980: L'interprétation des temples égyptiens anciens à la lumière des temples greco-romains. *Karnak* 6, 261–84.

D'Auria, Sue 1983: The Princess Baketamun. *JEA* 69, 161–2.

Dautzenberg, N. 1983: Zum König Ityi der 1. Dynastie. *GM* 69, 33–6.

—— 1984: Menes im Sothisbuch. *GM* 76, 11–16.

—— 1986a: Zu den Regierungszeiten in Manethos 1. Dynastie. *GM* 92, 23–8.

—— 1986b: Zu den Königen Chaires und Cheneres bei Manetho. *GM* 94, 25–9.

—— 1987a: Die Darstellung der 23. Dynastie bei Manetho. *GM* 96, 22–44.

—— 1987b: Iun-Re: der erste Kronprinz des Chephren? *GM* 99, 13–17.

—— 1988: Ägyptologische Bemerkungen zu Platons Atlantis-Erzählung. *GM* 102, 19–29.

Davey, Christopher J. 1976: The Structural Failure of the Meidum Pyramid. *JEA* 62, 178–9.

David, Ann Rosalie 1981: *A Guide to Religious Ritual at Abydos*. Warminster.

—— 1982: *Ancient Egyptian Religious Beliefs and Practices*. London.

—— 1987: *The Pyramid Builders of Ancient Egypt*. London.

Davis, Whitney M. 1979a: Sources for the Study of Rock Art in the Nile Valley. *GM* 32, 59–74.

—— 1979b: Plato on Egyptian Art. *JEA* 65, 121–7.

—— 1979c: Ancient Naukratis and the Cypriotes in Egypt. *GM* 35, 13–24.

—— 1980: The Cypriotes at Naukratis. *GM* 41, 7–20.

—— 1981: Egypt, Samos and Archaic Style in Greek Sculpture. *JEA* 67, 61–81.

Debono, Fernand 1981: Prehistory in the Nile Valley. In J. Ki-Zerbo (ed.), *General History of Africa* I. Paris, London, Berkeley: 634–55.

Debono, Fernand and Mortensen, Bodil 1978–80: Rapport préliminaire sur les résultats de l'étude des objets de la fouille des installations du Moyen Empire et 'Hyksôs' à l'est du lac sacré de Karnak. *Karnak* 7, 377–84.

—— 1988: *The Predynastic Cemetery at Heliopolis*. *AV* 63.

Decker, Wolfgang 1971: *Die physische Leistung Pharaos, Untersuchungen zu Heldentum, Jagd und Leibesübungen der ägyptischen Könige*. Cologne.

—— 1975: *Quellentexte zum Sport und Körperkulture im alten Ägypten*. St Augustin.

—— 1978: *Annotierte Bibliographie zum Sport im alten Ägypten*. St Augustin.

Delange, Elisabeth 1987: *Catalogue des statues égyptiennes du Moyen Empire*. Paris.

Delaporte, L., Drioton, E. et al. 1948: *Atlas historique* I: *l'Antiquité*. Paris.

Delia, Robert D. 1979: A New Look at Some Old Dates. A Reexamination of Twelfth Dynasty Double Dated Inscriptions. *BES* 1, 15–28.

—— 1982: Doubts about Double Dates and Coregencies. *BES* 4, 55–70.

Deman, A. 1985: Présence des Égyptiens dans la seconde guerre médique (480–479 av. J.-C.). *CdE* 60, 56–75.

Demarée, R. J. and Janssen, J. J. (eds) 1982: *Gleanings from Deir el-Medina*. Leiden.

Denon, Vivant 1801: *Voyage dans la Basse et la Haute Égypte*. Paris.

Derchain, Philippe 1953: La visite de Vespasien au Sérapeum d'Alexandrie. *CdE* 56, 261–79.

—— 1959: Le papyrus Salt 825 (BM 10051) et la cosmologie égyptienne. *BIFAO* 58, 73–80.

—— 1962: Le rôle du roi d'Égypte dans le maintien de l'ordre cosmique. In *Le pouvoir et le Sacré*. Brussels: 61–73.

—— 1965: *Le papyrus Salt 825 (BM 10051), rituel pour la conservation de la vie en Égypte*. Académie Royale de Belgique, Cl. Lettres, *Mémoires* 58/1a.

—— 1966: Ménès, le roi 'Quelqu'un'. *RdE* 18, 31–6.

—— 1970: La réception de Sinouhé à la Cour de Sésostris Ier. *RdE* 22, 79–83.

—— 1977: Geburt und Tod eines Gottes. *GM* 24, 33–4.

—— 1979a: En l'an 363 de Sa Majesté le Roi de Haute et Basse Égypte Râ-Harakhty vivant par-delà le temps et l'espace. *CdE* 53, 48–56.

—— 1979b: Der ägyptische Gott als Person und Funktion. In W. Westendorf (ed.), *Aspekte der spätägyptischen Religion*. Wiesbaden: 43–5.

—— 1980: Comment les Égyptiens écrivaient un traité de la royauté. *BSFE* 87–8, 14–17.

—— 1987: Magie et politique. À propos de l'hymne à Sésostris III. *CdE* 62, 21–9.

Desanges, Jehan E. 1968: Vues grecques sur quelques aspects de la monarchie méroïtique. *BIFAO* 66, 89–104.

Deshayes, Jean 1969: *Les civilisations de l'Orient ancien*. In *Les grandes civilisations*. Arthaud.

Desmond Clark, J. (ed.) 1982: *The Cambridge History of Africa I: From Earliest Times to c. 500 BC*. Cambridge.

Desroches-Noblecourt, Christiane 1946: *Le style égyptien*. Paris.

—— 1962: *L'art égyptien*. Paris.

—— 1963: *Tutankhamen: Life and Death of a Pharaoh*. London.

—— 1964: *Peintures des tombeaux et des temples égyptiens*. Milan.

—— 1972: Un buste monumental d'Aménophis IV, don prestigieux de l'Égypte à la France. *Revue du Louvre* 1972/4–5, 239–50.

—— 1979: Touy, mère de Ramsès II, la reine Tanadjmy et les reliques de l'expérience amarnienne. *L'égyptologie en 1979* II: 227–44.

—— 1984: Le 'bestiaire' symbolique du libérateur Ahmosis. In *Studien zu Sprache und Religion Ägyptens. Festschrift W. Westendorf*. Göttingen: 883–92.

—— 1985: *The Great Pharaoh Ramses II and his Time*. Montreal.

Desroches-Noblecourt, Christiane and Gerster, G. 1968: *The World Saves Abu Simbel*. Vienna.

Devauchelle, Didier and Aly, M. I. 1986: Présentation des stèles nouvellement découvertes au Sérapéum. *BSFE* 106, 31–44.

Dewachter, Michel 1971a: Graffiti des voyageurs du XIXe siècle relevés dans le temps d'Amada en Basse-Nubie. *BIFAO* 69, 131–70.

—— 1971b: Le voyage nubien du comte Carlo Vidua (fin février-fin avril 1820). *BIFAO* 69, 171–90.

—— 1975: Contribution à l'histoire de la cachette royale de Deir el-Bahari. *BSFE* 74, 19–32.

—— 1976: Le roi Sahathor et la famille de Néferhotep 1er. *RdE* 28, 66–73.

—— 1979: Le percement de l'isthme de Suez et l'exploration archeologique. *L'égyptologie en 1979* I, 222–8.

—— 1984: Le roi Sahathor, compléments. *RdE* 35, 195–9.

—— 1986: Le scarabée funéraire de Néchao II et deux amulettes inédites du Musée Jacquemart-André. *RdE* 37, 53–62.

Diakonoff, Igor A. 1982: The Structure of Near Eastern Society Before the Middle of the 2nd Millenium B.C. *Oikumene* 3, 7–100.

Diebner, Bernd J. 1984: Erwägungen zum Thema 'Exodus'. *SAK* 11, 595–630.

Dixon, D. M. 1964: The Origin of the Kingdom of Kush (Napata-Meroë). *JEA* 50, 121–32.

Dodson, Aidan 1981: Nefertiti's Regality: A Comment. *JEA* 67, 179–80.

—— 1985: On the Date of the Unfinished Pyramid of Zawyet El-Aryan. *DE* 3, 21–4.

—— 1986: Was the Sarcophagus of Ramesses III Begun for Sethos II? *JEA* 72, 196–8.

—— 1987a: The Tombs of the Kings of the Thirteenth Dynasty in the Memphite Necropolis. *ZÄS* 114, 36–45.

—— 1987b: Two Thirteenth Dynasty Pyramids at Abusir? *VA* 3, 231–2.

—— 1987c: The Takhats and Some Other Royal Ladies of the Ramesside Period. *JEA* 73, 224–9.

—— 1987d: Psusennes II. *RdE* 38, 49–54.

Donadoni, Sergio 1957: Per la data della 'Stele di Bentresh'. *MDAIK* 15, 47–50.

—— 1977: Sulla situazione giuridica della Nubia nell'impero egiziano. In E. Endesfelder et al. (eds), *Ägypten und Kush. Schr. Or.* 13, 133–8.

—— 1981: *L'Egitto*. Turin.

Donadoni, Sergio (ed.) 1963: *Fonti indirette della storia egiziana*. Rome.

Donner, Herbert 1969: Elemente ägyptischen Totenglauben bei den Aramäern Ägyptens. In *Religions en Égypte hellenistique et romaine*. Strasbourg: 35–44.

Doresse, Jean 1960: *Des hiéroglyphes à la croix: Christianisme et religion pharaonique. PIHAN Stamboul* 7.

Doresse, Marianne 1971: Le dieu voilé dans sa châsse et la fête du début de la décade. *RdE* 23, 113–36.

—— 1973: Le dieu voilé dans sa châsse et la fête du début de la décade. *RdE* 25, 92–135.

—— 1979: Le dieu voilé dans sa châsse et la fête du début de la décade. *RdE* 31, 36–65.

—— 1981: Observations sur la publication des blocs des temples atoniens de Karnak: The Akhenaten Temple Project. *GM* 46, 45–79.

Dormion, G. and Goidin, J.-P. 1986: *Khéops. Nouvelle enquête. Propositions préliminaires*. Paris.

Drenkhahn, Rosemarie 1976: *Die Handwerker und ihre Tätigkeit im altem Ägypten*. Wiesbaden.

—— 1980: *Die Elephantine-Stele des Sethnacht und ihr historischer Hintergrund*. Wiesbaden.

—— 1981: Ein Nachtrag zu Tausret. *GM* 43, 19–22.

Drew-Bear, M. 1979: *Le nome hermopolite: Toponymes et sites*. Missoula.

Drioton, Étienne 1939: Une statue prophylactique de Ramsès III. *ASAE* 39, 57–89.

—— 1953: Un document sur la vie chère à Thèbes au début de la XVIIIᵉ dynastie. *BSFE* 12, 11–25.

—— 1954: Une liste de rois de la IVᵉ dynastie dans l'ouâdi Hammâmât. *BSFE* 16, 41–9.

—— 1957: Le nationalisme au temps des pharaons. *La Revue du Caire* 198, 81–92.

—— 1958: Amon avant la fondation de Thèbes. *BSFE* 26, 33–41.

—— 1969: *L'Égypte pharaonique*. Paris.

Drioton, Étienne and du Bourguet, P. 1965: *Les pharaons à la conquête de l'art*. Paris.

Drioton, Etienne and Vandier, Jean 1962: *L'Égypte. Des origines à la conquête d'Alexandre*. 4th edn. Paris.

Drovetti, Bernardino 1985: *Bernardino Drovetti epistolario 1800–1851*. Milan.

Drower, Margaret S. 1982: Gaston Maspero and the Birth of the Egypt Expoloration Fund (1881–3). *JEA* 68, 299–317.

—— 1985: *Flinders Petrie. A Life in Archaeology*. London.

Dunand, Françoise 1980: Fête, tradition, propagande: les cérémonies en l'honneur de Bérénice, fille de Ptolémée III, en 238 a.C. In J. Vercoutter (ed.), *Livre du Centenaire. MIFAO* 104, 287–301.

—— 1983: Culte royal et culte impérial en Égypte. Continuités et ruptures. *Aegyptiaca Treverensia* 2, 47–56.

Dunham, Dows 1970: *The Barkal Temples*. Boston.

Dupont-Sommer, André 1978: Les dieux et les hommes en l'île d'Éléphantine, près d'Assouan, au temps de l'Empire des Perses. *CRAIBL* 1978, 756–72.

Dymond, D. P. 1974: *Archaeology and History: a Plea for Reconciliation*. London.

Eaton-Krauss, Marianne 1981a: Seti-Merenptah als Kronprinz Merenptahs. *GM* 50, 15–22.

—— 1981b: The Dating of the 'Hierakonpolis-Falcon'. *GM* 42, 15–18.

—— 1981c: Miscellanea Amarniensia. *CdE* 56, 245–64.

—— 1987: The Titulary of Tutankhamun. In J. Osing and G. Dreyer (eds), *Form und Mass. ÄAT* 12, 110–23.

Ebach, J. and Görg, M. 1987: *Beziehung zwischen Israel und Ägypten*. Darmstadt.

Edel, Elmar 1944: Untersuchungen zur Phraseologie der ägyptischen Inschriften des Alten Reiches. *MDAIK* 13, 1–90.

—— 1961–3: *Zu den Inschriften aus den Jahreszeitenreliefs der 'Weltkammer' aus dem Sonnenheiligtum des Niuserre. NAWG.*

—— 1972: *Nj-rmṯw-nswt*: 'A Besitzer von Menschen ist der König'. *GM* 2, 15–18.

—— 1974: Neue Identifikationen topographischer Namen in den konventionellen Namenzusammenstellungen des Neuen Reiches. *GM* 11, 19–22.

—— 1978: Amasis und Nabukadrezar II. *GM* 29, 13–20.

—— 1981: *Hieroglyphische Inschriften des alten Reiches.* Wiesbaden.

—— 1984: Zur Stele Sesostris' I. aus dem Wadi el-Hudi (*ASAE* 39, 197ff.). *GM* 78, 51–4.

—— 1985: Der Seevölkerbericht aus dem 8. Jahre Ramses' III. (*MH* II, 15–18, pl. 46). Übersetzung und Struktur. *BdE* 97/1, 223–37.

Edgerton, William F. 1947: The Nauri Decree of Seti I: a Translation and Analysis of the Legal Portion. *JNES* 6, 219–30.

Edgerton, William F. and Wilson, J. A. 1936: *Historical Records of Ramses III: The Texts in* Medinet Habu *Volumes I and II, Translated with Explanatory Notes. SAOC* 12.

Edwards, Iorweth E. S. 1960: *Oracular Amuletic Decrees of the Late New Kingdom.* 2 vols. *HPBM* 4.

—— 1974: The Collapse of the Meidum Pyramid. *JEA* 60, 251–2.

—— 1975: Something Which Herodotus May Also Have Seen. *RdE* 27, 117–24.

—— 1985: *The Pyramids of Egypt.* 3rd edn. Harmondsworth.

Edwards, Iorweth E. S., Gadd, C. J. and Hammond, N. G. 1971: *Cambridge Ancient History I. 2: The Early History of the Middle East.* 3rd edn. Cambridge.

—— 1973: *Cambridge Ancient History II. 1–2: History of the Middle East and the Aegean Region c.1800-1380 and c.1380-1000.* 3rd edn. Cambridge.

—— 1974: *Cambridge Ancient History I. 1: Prolegomena and Prehistory.* 3rd edn. Cambridge.

—— 1977: *Plates to Volumes I and II.* Cambridge.

Eggebrecht, Arne 1980: *Geschichte der Arbeit 1. Die frühen Hochkulturen: das alte Ägypten.* Cologne.

—— 1982: *Ägypten: Faszination und Abenteuer.* Mayence.

Eiwanger, Josef 1984: *Merimde-Benisalame 1: Die Funde der Uhrschicht. AV* 47.

—— 1988: *Merimde-Benisalame 2: Die Funde der mittleren Merimdekultur. AV* 51.

El-Amir, Mustafa 1964: Monogamy, Polygamy, Endogamy and Consanguinity in Ancient Egyptian Marriage. *BIFAO* 62, 103–8.

El-Baz, F. 1984: *The Geology of Egypt: an Annotated Bibliography.* Leiden.

El-Bedewi, F. A. 1968–9: Search for Presently Unknown Chambers in Chefren Pyramid. *BIE* 50, 65–74.

El-Dawakhly, Zeinab 1966–8: New Lights on the Role of Women in Ancient Egypt. *BIE* 48–9, 79–86.

El-Dissoury, K. T. 1969: *Elephantine in the Old Kingdom.* Chicago.

El-Farag, R. A. 1980: A Stela of Khasekhemui from Abydos. *MDAIK* 36, 77–80.

El-Nadoury, Rashid 1968a: Human Sacrifices in the Ancient Near East. *AHS Alexandrie* 2, 1–10.

—— 1968b: The Origin of the Fortified Enclosures of the Early Egyptian Dynastic Period. *AHS Alexandrie* 2, 11–19.

El-Nadoury, R. and Vercoutter, J. 1981: The Legacy of Pharaonic Egypt. In G. Mokhtas (ed.), *General History of Africa* II. London, Paris, Berkeley: 155–83.

El-Sadeek, W. 1984: Twenty-sixth Dynasty Necropolis at Gizeh. *VIAÄ Wien* 29.

El-Sawi, Ahmed 1983: Ramesses II Completing a Shrine in the Temple of Sety I at Abydos. *SAK* 10, 307–10.

El-Sayed, Ramadan 1974: Quelques éclaircissements sur l'histoire de la XXVIe dynastie, d'après la statue du Caire *CG 658*. *BIFAO* 74, 29–44.

—— 1978: Piankhi, fils de Hérihor. Documents sur sa vie et sur son rôle. *BIFAO* 78, 197–218.

—— 1979a: Stèles de particuliers relatives au culte rendu aux statues royales de la XVIIIe e la XXe dynastie. *BIFAO* 79, 155–66.

—— 1979b: Quelques précisions sur l'histoire de la province d'Edfou à la Deuxième Période Intermédiaire (Études des stèles *JE* 38917 et 46988 du Musée du Caire). *BIFAO* 79, 167–208.

El-Shazly, E. M. 1987: The Ostracinic Branch: a Proposed Old Branch of the River Nile. *DE* 7, 69–78.

El-Yahky, Farid 1984: The Origin and Development of Sanctuaries in Predynastic Egypt. *JSSEA* 14, 70–3.

—— 1985a: The Sahara and Predynastic Egypt: an Overview. *JSSEA* 15, 81–5.

—— 1985b: Clarifications on the Gerzean Boat Scenes. *BIFAO* 85, 187–95.

Endesfelder, Erika 1977: Über die ökonomischen und sozialen Verhältnisse der Rieche von Napata und Meroe. In E. Endesfelder et al. (eds), *Ägypten und Kush*. Schr. Or. 13, 143–64.

—— 1979: Zur Frage der Bewässerung im pharaonischen Ägypten. *ZÄS* 106, 37–51.

Engel, H. 1979: *Die Vorfahren Israels in Ägypten*. Frankfurt.

Engelbach, R. 1940: Material for a Revision of the History of the Heresy Period of the XVIIIth Dynasty. *ASAE* 40, 133–65.

Erichsen, W. 1933: *Papyrus Harris I: Hieroglyphische Transkription*. BAE 5.

Erman, Adolphe 1900: Die Naukratisstele. *ZÄS* 38, 127–33.

—— 1952a: *La religion des Égyptiens*. Payot.

—— 1952b: *L'Égypte des pharaons*. Payot.

Ertman, Earl L. 1979: Some Probable Representations of Ay. *L'égyptologie en 1979* II, 245–8. Reprinted in *GM* 51 (1981), 51–6.

Eyre, Christopher J. 1980: The Reign-length of Ramesses VII. *JEA* 66, 168–70.

—— 1984: Crime and Adultery in Ancient Egypt. *JEA* 70, 92–105.

—— 1987: The Use of Data from Deir el-Medina. *BiOr* 44, 21–36.

Fabri, Felix 1975: *Le voyage en Égypte de Félix Fabri [1483]*. Cairo.

Fagan, Brian M. 1977: *The Rape of the Nile. Tomb Robbers, Tourists, and Archaeologists in Egypt*. London.

Fairman, H. W. 1958: The Kingship Rituals of Egypt. In S. H. Hooke (ed.), *Myth, Ritual and Kingship*. Oxford: 74–104.

Fairservis Jr., W. A. 1983: *Hierakonpolis: The Graffiti and the Origins of Egyptian Hieroglyphic Writing*. Poughkeepsie, NY.

Fakhry, Ahmed 1973: *The Oases of Egypt I: Siwa Oasis*. Cairo.

—— 1974: *The Oases of Egypt II: Bahriya and Farafra Oases*. Cairo.

—— 1975: *The Pyramids*. 4th edn. Chicago.

Falck, M. von, Klie, S. and Schulz, A. 1985: Neufunde ergänzen Königsnamen eines Herrschers der 2. Zwischenzeit. *GM* 87, 15–24.

Faulkner, Raymond O. 1958: The Battle of Kadesh. *MDAIK* 16, 93–111.

—— 1959: Wpwtyw 'Bystanders'. *JEA* 45, 102.

—— 1969: *The Ancient Egyptian Pyramid Texts*. 2 vols. Oxford.

—— 1973–8: *The Egyptian Coffin Texts*. 3 vols. Warminster.

—— 1985: *The Ancient Egyptian Book of the Dead*. London.

Fazzini, Richard A. 1988: *Egypt: Dynasty XXII–XXV*. Leiden.

Fechheimer, H. 1922: *Die Plastik der Ägypter*. Berlin.

Fecht, Gerhard 1958: Zu den Namen ägyptischer Fürsten und Städte in den *Annalen* des Assurbanipal und der *Chronik* des Asarhaddon. *MDAIK* 16, 112–19.

—— 1979: Die Berichte des Hrw = ḥwi.f über seine drei Reisen nach J3m. *ÄAT* 1, 105–34.

—— 1983: Die Israelstele, Gestalt und Aussage. *ÄAT* 5, 106–38.

—— 1984a: Das 'Poème' über die Qadesh-Schlacht. *SAK* 11, 281–333.

—— 1984b: Nachträge zu meinem 'Das "Poème" über die Qadesch-Schlacht'. *GM* 80, 55–8.

—— 1984c: Ramses II. und die Schlacht bei Qadesh (Qidsha). *GM* 80, 23–54.

Federn, Walter 1935: Zur Familiengeschichte der IV. Dynastie Ägyptens. *WZKM* 42, 165–92.

Feucht, Erika 1978: Zwei Reliefs Scheschonqs I. aus El Hibeh. *SAK* 6, 69–77.

—— 1981: Relief Scheschonq I. beim Erschlagen der Feinde aus El-Hibe. *SAK* 9, 105–18.

Finkenstaedt, Elizabeth 1976: The Chronology of Egyptian Predynastic Black-Topped Ware. *ZÄS* 103, 5–8.

—— 1981: Regional Painting Style in Prehistoric Egypt. *ZÄS* 107, 116–20.

—— 1984: Violence and Kingship: The Evidence of the Palettes. *ZÄS* 111, 107–10.

—— 1985: Cognitive vs. Ecological Niches in Prehistoric Egypt. *JARCE* 32, 143–7.

Firchow, Otto 1957: Königsschiff und Sonnenbarke. *WZKM* 54, 34–42.

Fischer, Henry G. 1964: *Inscriptions from the Coptite Nome: Dynasties VI-XI*. *AnOr* 40.

—— 1968: *Dendera in the Third Millenium B.C. Down to the Theban Domination of Upper Egypt*. New York.

—— 1974: Nbty in Old Kingdom Titles and Names. *JEA* 60, 94–9.

—— 1975: Two Tantalizing Biographical Fragments of Historical Interest. *JEA* 61, 33–7.

Fischer-Elfert, Hans-Werner 1983a: The Sufferings of an Army Officer. *GM* 63, 43–6.

—— 1983b: Morphologie, Rhetorik und Genese der Soldatencharakteristik. *GM* 66, 45–66.

—— 1986: *Literarische Ostraka der Ramessidenzeit in Übersetzung. KÄT.*

—— 1987a: *Die satirische Streitschrift des Papyrus Anastasi I. 2: Übersetzung und Kommentierung.* Wiesbaden.

—— 1987b: Der Pharao, die Magier und der General: Die Erzählung des Papyrus Vandier. *BiOr* 44, 5–21.

Flaubert, Gustave 1986: *Voyage en Égypte [1849–50].* Paris.

Foissy-Aufrère, Marie-Pierre 1985: *Égypte & Provence. Civilisation, survivances et 'cabinetz de curiositez'.* Avignon.

Forgeau, Annie 1984: Prêtres isiaques: essai d'anthropologie religieuse. *BIFAO* 84, 155–87.

Foti, L. 1978: Menes in Diodorus I.89. *Oikumene* 2, 113–26.

Fox, Michael V. 1988: *The Song of Songs and the Ancient Egyptian Love Songs.* Madison, WI.

Frandsen, P. J. 1976: Heqareshu and the Family of Tuthmosis IV. *AcOr* 37, 5–10.

—— 1979: Egyptian Imperialism. In M. T. Larsen (ed.), *Power and Propaganda.* Copenhagen: 167–92.

Franke, Detlef 1973: Ein Beitrag zur Diskussion über die asiatische Productionsweise. *GM* 5, 63–72.

Frankfort, Henri 1951: *La royauté et les dieux.* Payot.

Freud, Sigmund 1939: *Moses and Monotheism.* London.

Friedell, E. 1982: *Kulturgeschichte Ägyptens und des Alten Orients.* Munich.

Friedman, Florence 1975: On the Meaning of W3ḏ-wr in Selected Literary Texts. *GM* 17, 15–22.

Froidefond, Christian 1971: *Le mirage égyptien dans la littérature grecque, d'Homère à Aristote.* Aix-en-Provence.

Fuscaldo, P. 1982: La medicina en el antiguo Egipto. *RIHAO* 6, 35–60.

Gaballa, Gaballa Aly 1969: Minor War Scenes of Ramesses II at Karnak. *JEA* 55, 82–8.

Gabolde, Marc 1987: Ay, Toutankhamon et les martelages de la stèle de la restauration de Karnak (CG 34183). *BSEG* 11, 37–62.

Gabra, Gawdat 1981: A Lifesize Statue of Nepherites I from Buto. *SAK* 9, 119–24.

Gale, N. H. and Stos-Gale, Z. A. 1981: Ancient Egyptian Silver. *JEA* 67, 103–15.

Gardiner, Alan H. 1904: The Installation of a Vizier. *RT* 26, 1–19.

—— 1916: The Defeat of the Hyksos by Kamose: The Carnarvon Tablet, No. I. *JEA* 3, 95–110.

—— 1938: The House of Life. *JEA* 24, 157–79.

—— 1948: *Ramesside Administrative Documents.* Oxford.

—— 1952: Some Reflections on the Nauri Decree. *JEA* 38, 24–33.

—— 1955: The Problem of the Month-names. *RdE* 10, 9–31.

—— 1956: The First King Menthotpe of the Eleventh Dynasty. *MDAIK* 14, 42–51.

—— 1959: *The Royal Canon of Turin.* Oxford.

—— 1960: *The Kadesh Inscriptions of Ramesses II.* Oxford.

—— 1961: *Egypt of the Pharaohs.* Oxford.

Garelli, Paul 1982: *Le Proche-Orient asiatique. Des origines aux invasions des Peuples de la Mer.* 2nd edn. Paris.

Garelli, Paul and Nikiprowetzky, V. 1974: *Le Proche-Orient asiatique. Les empires mésopotamiens: Israël.* Paris.

Garnot, Jean Sainte Fare 1942: *L'imakh* et les *imakhous* d'après les *Textes des Pyramides. Annuaire de l'École Pratique des Hautes Études,* section V, 1–32.

—— 1948: *La vie religieuse dans l'ancienne Égypte.* Paris.

—— 1952: Études sur la nécropole de Gîza sous la IVe dynastie. *RdE* 9, 69–79.

—— 1958: Sur le nom de 'l'Horus cobra'. *MDAIK* 16, 138–46.

Gasm El-Seed, A. A. 1985: La tombe de Tanoutamon à El Kurru (Ku. 16). *RdE* 36, 67–72.

Gauthier, Henri 1906: Quelques remarques sur la XIe dynastie. *BIFAO* 5, 23–40.

—— 1907–17: *Le Livre des Rois d'Égypte. Recueil de titres et protocoles royaux, noms propres des rois, reines et princesses.* . . . *MIFAO* 17–21.

—— 1921: Le 'fils royaux de Kouch' et le personnel administratif de l'Éthiopie. *RT* 39, 179–238.

—— 1923: Quelques additions au *Livres des Rois d'Égypte* (Ancien et Moyen Empire). *RT* 40, 177–204.

—— 1925–31: *Dictionnaire des noms géographiques contenus dans les textes hiéroglyphiques.* 7 vols. *IFAO.*

—— 1932: Les deux rois Kamose (XVIIe dynastie). In S. R. K. Glanville (ed.), *Studies Griffith.* Oxford: 3–8.

—— 1934: Un monument nouveau du roi Psamtik II. *ASAE* 34, 129–34.

Gautier, J.-E. and Jequier, G. 1902: *Mémoire sur les fouilles de Licht. MIFAO* 6.

Gavillet, Marguerite 1981: L'évocation du roi dans la littérature royale égyptienne comparée à celle des *Psaumes* royaux et le rapport roi-Dieu. *BSEG* 5, 3–14 and 6, 3–17.

George, Beate and Peterson, B. 1979: *Die Karnak-Zeichnungen von Baltzar Cronstrand 1836–1837.* Stockholm.

Gericke, H. 1984: *Mathematik in Antike und Orient.* Berlin.

Germer, Renate 1979: *Untersuchungen über Arzneipflanzen im alten Ägypten.* Hamburg.

—— 1981: Einige Bemerkungen zum angeblichen Opiumexport von Zypern nach Ägypten. *SAK* 9, 125–30.

Germond, Philippe 1979: Le roi et le retour de l'inondation. *BSEG* 1, 5–12.

Gestermann, Louise 1984: Hathor, Harsomtus aun Mntw-htp.w II. In *Studien zu Sprache und Religion Ägyptens. Festschrift W. Westendorf.* Göttingen: 763–76.

—— 1987: *Kontinuität und Wandel in Politik und Verwaltung des frühen mittleren Reiches in Ägypten. GOF* IV/18.

Geus, Francis 1982: Du Ve millénaire av. J.-C. à l'époque méroitique: les dernières fouilles au Soudan nilotique. *BSFE* 94, 20–30.

Ghali, I. A. 1969: *L'Égypte et les Juifs dans l'antiquite*. Paris.

Ghalioungui, Paul 1973: *The House of Life: Magic and Medical Science in Ancient Egypt*. Amsterdam.

—— 1983: *The Physicians of Pharaonic Egypt*. Mainz am Rhein.

Ghobrial, Monir G. 1967: *The Structural Geology of the Kharga Oasis. Geological Survey Papers* 43. Cairo.

Ghoneim, W. 1977: *Die ökonomische Bedeutung des Rindes im alten Ägypten*. Bonn.

Giammarusti, Antonio and Roccati, Alessandro 1980: *File, Storia e vita di un santuario egizio*. Novara.

Giddy, Lisa L. 1980: Some Exports from the Oases of the Libyan Desert into the Nile Valley: Tomb 131 at Thebes. In J. Vercoutter (ed.), *Livre du Centenaire*. MIFAO 104, 119–25.

—— 1987: *Egyptian Oases: Bahariya, Dakhla, Farafra and Kharga During Pharaonic Times*. Warminster.

Giedion, S. 1966: *La naissance de l'architecture*. Brussels.

Gil-Artagnan, André 1975: Projet *Pount*. Essai de reconstitution d'un navire et d'un navigation antiques. *BSFE* 73, 28–43.

Gilbert, Pierre 1949a: *La poésie égyptienne*. 2nd edn. Brussels.

—— 1949b: *Esquisse d'une histoire de l'Égypte ancienne et de sa culture*. Brussels.

Ginter, Boleslav and Koslowski, J. K. 1979: *Silexindustrien in el-Tarif*. AV 26.

—— 1986: Kulturelle und Paläoklimatische Sequenz in der Fayum-Depression: eine zusammenfassende Darstellung der Forschungsarbeit ... 1979–1981. *MDAIK* 42, 9–24.

Ginter, B., Koslowski, J. K. and Pawlikowski, M. 1985: Field Report from the Survey Conducted in Upper Egypt in 1983. *MDAIK* 41, 15–42.

Gitton, Michel 1967: Un monument de la reine Keñsa à Karnak. *RdE* 19, 161–3.

—— 1974: Le palais de Karnak. *BIFAO* 74, 63–74.

—— 1975a: Les premiers obélisques monolithes, à propos d'un texte de Pline l'Ancien. *BIFAO* 75, 97–102.

—— 1975b: *L'épouse du dieu Ahmès Néfertary*. Paris.

—— 1976: Le rôle des femmes dans le clergé d'Amon à la 18e dynastie. *BSFE* 75, 31–46.

—— 1978: Variation sur le thème de la titulature des reines. *BIFAO* 78, 389–404.

—— 1984: *Les divines épouses de la 18e dynastie*. Paris.

Giveon, Raphael 1965: A Sealing of Khyan from the Shephela of Southern Palestine. *JEA* 51, 202–4.

—— 1967: Royal Seals of the XIIth Dynasty from Western Asia. *RdE* 19, 29–37.

—— 1971: *Les bédouins Shosou des documents égyptiens*. Leiden.

—— 1974: Amenophis III in Athribis. *GM* 9, 25–6.

—— 1977: Remarks on the Transmission of Egyptian Lists of Asiatic Toponyms. In J. Assmann et al. (eds), *Fragen an die altägyptische Literatur. Studien zum Gedenken an Eberhard Otto*. Wiesbaden: 171–84.

—— 1978: *The Impact of Egypt in Canaan: Iconographical and Related Studies.* OBO 20.

—— 1979a: The XIIIth Dynasty in Asia. *RdE* 30, 163–7.

—— 1979b: Remarks on Some Egyptian Toponym Lists Concerning Canaan. *ÄAT* 1, 135–41.

—— 1979c: Western Asiatic Aspects of the Amarna-period: the Monotheism-problem. *L'égyptologie en 1979* II, 249–52.

—— 1980: Resheph in Egypt. *JEA* 66, 144–50.

—— 1981: Ya'qob-har. *GM* 83, 27–30.

—— 1983: A Data Corrected: If It Is Hebrew To You. *GM* 69, 95.

—— 1984: Amenmesse in Canaan? *GM* 83, 27–30.

—— 1986: Cattle: Administration in Middle Kingdom Egypt and Canaan. In *Hommages à François Daumas* 1. Montpelier: 279–84.

Godron, Gérard 1958: Études sur l'époque archaïque. *BIFAO* 57, 143–56.

Goedicke, Hans 1957: Das Verhältnis zwischen königlichen und privaten Darstellungen im Alten Reich. *MDAIK* 15, 57–67.

—— 1960: *Die Stellung des Königs im Alten Reich.* Wiesbaden.

—— 1961: Die Siegelzylinder von Pepi I. *MDAIK* 17, 69–90.

—— 1962: Psammetik I. (und) die Libyer. *MDAIK* 18, 26–49.

—— 1966a: Some Remarks on the 400-Year Stela. *CdE* 41, 23–39.

—— 1966b: An Additional Note on '3 "Foreigner"'. *JEA* 52, 172–4.

—— 1967: *Königliche Dokumente aus dem Alten Reiche.* Wiesbaden.

—— 1969a: Probleme der Herakleopolitenzeit. *MDAIK* 24, 136–43.

—— 1969b: Ägäische Namen in ägyptischen Inschriften. *WZKM* 62, 7–10.

—— 1970: *The Report about The Dispute of a Man with his Ba.* Baltimore.

—— 1974: The Inverted Water. *GM* 10, 13–18.

—— 1977: 727 vor Christus. *WZKM* 69, 1–19.

—— 1979a: 'Irsu the Kharu' in Papyrus Harris. *WZKM* 71, 1–17.

—— 1979b: The Origin of the Royal Administration. *L'égyptologie en 1979* II, 123–30.

—— 1981a: Harkhuf's Travels. *JNES* 40, 1–20.

—— 1981b: The '400-Year Stela' Reconsidered. *BES* 3, 25–43.

—— 1981c: The Campaign of Psammetik II Against Nubia. *MDAIK* 37, 187–98.

—— 1981d: The Chronology of the Palermo and the Turin Canons. *JARCE* 18, 89–90.

—— 1981e: The Palermo Stone and the Archaic Kings of Egypt. *JARCE* 18, 88–9.

—— 1984: *Studies in the Hekanakhte Papers.* Baltimore.

—— 1985a: *Perspectives on the Battle of Kadesh.* Baltimore.

—— 1985b: Rudjedet's Delivery. *VA* 1, 19–26.

—— 1987: Ramesses II and the Wadi Tumilat. *VA* 3, 13–24.

—— 1988: Yam: More. *GM* 101, 35–42.

Goelet Jr., O. 1986: The Term *Stp-s3* in the Old Kingdom and its Later Development. *JARCE* 23, 85–98.

Görg, Manfred 1975: Ninive in Ägypten. *GM* 17, 31–4.

—— 1976: Die Phryger in Hieroglyphen. *GM* 22, 37–8.

—— 1977a: *Zimiu* und *lamassu*. *GM* 23, 35–6.

—— 1977b: Komparatistische Untersuchungen an ägyptischer und israelitischer Literatur. In J. Assmann et al. (eds), *Fragen und die altägyptische Literatur. Studien zum Gedenken an Eberhard Otto*. Wiesbaden: 197–216.

—— 1978: Eine Variante von Mitanni. *GM* 29, 25–6.

—— 1979a: Mitanni in Gruppenschreibung. *GM* 32, 17–20.

—— 1979b: Das Ratespiel um *Mw-qd*. *GM* 32, 21–2.

—— 1979c: Identifikation von Fremdnamen. *ÄAT* 1, 152–73.

—— 1979d: Tuthmosis III. und die Shasou-region. *JNES* 38, 199–202.

—— 1982a: Weitere Belege für Ibirta. *GM* 59, 13–14.

—— 1982b: Ein Siegelamulett Amenophis III. aus Palastina. *GM* 60, 41–2.

—— 1983: Die afrikanischen Namen der Kaimauer von Elephantine. *GM* 67, 39–42.

—— 1984: Weitere Bemerkungen zur Geschenkliste Amenophis III. (EA 14). *GM* 71, 15–16.

Goff, B. L. 1979: *Symbols of Ancient Egypt in the Late Period: Twenty-first Dynasty*. The Hague.

Gohary, J. O. 1979: Nefertiti at Karnak. In J. Ruffle et al. (eds), *Glimpses of Ancient Egypt. Studies in Honour of H. W. Fairman*. Warminster: 30–1.

Golvin, Jean-Claude and Larronde, Jean 1982: Étude des procédés de construction dans l'Égypte ancienne 1: L'édification des murs de grès en grand appareil à l'époque romaine. *ASAE* 68, 165–90.

Golvin, Jean-Claude and Vergnieux, Robert 1986: Étude des procédés de construction dans l'Égypte ancienne 4: Le ravalement des parois, la taille des volumes et des moulures. In *Hommages à François Daumas* I. Montpellier: 299–321.

Gomaa, Farouk 1973: *Chaemwese. Sohn Ramses II. und Hoherpriester von Memphis*. Wiesbaden.

—— 1975: *Die libyschen Fürstentümer des Deltas vom Tode Osorkons II. bis zur Wiedervereinigung Ägyptens durch Psammetik I*. Wiesbaden.

—— 1980: *Ägypten während der Ersten Zwischenzeit*. TAVO B/27.

—— 1986: *Die Besiedlung Ägyptens während des mittleren Reiches 1: Oberägypten*. TAVO B 66/1.

—— 1987: *Die Besiedlung Ägyptens während des mittleren Reiches 2: Unterägypten und die angrenzenden Gebiete*. TAVO B 66/2.

Goneim, Zakaria 1957: *Excavations at Saqqara: Horus Sekhem-Khet. The Unnifished Step Pyramid at Saqqara I*. Cairo.

—— 1959: La pyramide ensevelie. *La Revue du Caire* 232, 450–71.

Gonzales, Antonius 1977: *Le voyage en Égypte du Père Antonius Gonzales, 1665–1666*. Cairo.

Gottschalk, G. 1979: *Die grossen Pharaonen: Ihr Leben, ihre Zeit, ihre Kunstwerke. . . .* Munich.

Goyon, Georges 1970: Nouvelles observations relatives à l'orientation de la pyramide de Khéops. *RdE* 22, 85–98.

—— 1971a: Les navires de transport de la chaussée monumentale d'Ounas. *BIFAO* 69, 11–42.

—— 1971b: Les ports des pyramides et le grand canal de Memphis. *RdE* 23, 137–53.

—— 1974: Kerkasôre et l'ancien observatoire d'Eudoxe. *BIFAO* 74, 135–48.

—— 1976: Un procédé de travail du granit par l'action thermique chez les anciens Égyptiens. *RdE* 28, 74–86.

—— 1979: Est-ce enfin Sakhebou? In J. Vercoutter (ed.), *Hommages Sauneron* I. *BdE* 81, 43–50.

Goyon, Jean-Claude 1972: *Rituels funéraires de l'ancienne Égypte.* . . . Paris.

—— 1978–80: Une dalle aux noms de Menkheperrê, fils de Pinedjem 1er, d'Isetemkheb et de Smendès (CSX 1305). *Karnak* 7, 275–80.

—— 1983: Inscriptions tardives du temple de Mout à Karnak. *JARCE* 20, 47–64.

Goyon, Jean-Claude and Josset-Goyon, P. 1988: *Un corpus pour l'éternité.* Paris.

Graefe, Erhart 1979a: Zu Pjj, der angeblichen Nebenfrau des Achanjati. *GM* 33, 17–18.

—— 1979b: La structure administrative de l'institution de l'Épouse Divine d'Amon. *L'égyptologie en 1979* II, 131–4.

—— 1981: *Untersuchungen zur Verwaltung und Geschichte der Institution der Gottesgemahlin des Amun vom Begin des Neuen Reiches bis zur Spätzeit.* Wiesbaden.

—— 1984: Der Pyramidenbesuch des Guilielmus de Boldensele im Jahre 1335. *SAK* 11, 569–84.

Grapow, Hermann 1949: *Studien zu den Annalen Thutmosis des Dritten und zu ihnen verwandten historischen Berichten des Neuen Reiches. ADAW* 1947/2.

Gratien, Brigitte 1978: *Les cultures Kerma. Essai de classification.* Lille.

Grdseloff, Bernhard 1942: *Les débuts du culte de Rechef en Égypte.* Cairo.

Green, Michael 1983: The Syrian and Lebanese Topographical Data in the Story of Sinuhe. *CdE* 58, 38–59.

—— 1987: Review of A. Nibbi, *Wenamun and Alashiya Reconsidered. BiOr* 44, 99–103.

Grelot, P. 1972 *Documents araméens d'Égypte.* Paris.

Grene, B. 1987: *Herodotus: the History.* Chicago.

Grenier, Jean-Claude 1979: Djédem dans les textes du temple de Tôd. In J. Vercoutter (ed.), *Hommages Sauneron* I. *BdE* 81, 381–90.

—— 1983: La stèle funéraire du dernier taureau Bouchis. *BIFAO* 83, 197–208.

—— 1987: Le protocole pharaonique des Empereurs romains (Analyse formelle et signification historique). *RdE* 38, 81–104.

Greven, L. 1985: *Der Ka in Theologie und Königskult der Ägypter des Alten Reiches. ÄF* 17.

Griaule, Marcel 1966: *Dieu d'eau.* Paris.

Grieshammer, Reinhard 1979: Gott und dans Negative nach Quellen der ägyptischen Spätzeit. In W. Westendorf (ed.), *Aspekte der spätägyptischen Religion.* Wiesbaden: 79–92.

—— 1982: Maat und Sädäq. Zum Kulturzusammenhang zwischen Ägypten und Kanaan. *GM* 55, 35–42.

Griffith, F. L. 1985: *Stories of the High Priest of Memphis. The Seton of Herodotus and the Demotic Tales of Khamuas.* Originally publ. 1900. Oxford.

—— 1927: The Abydos Decree of Seti I at Naure. *JEA* 13, 193–208.

Griffiths, John Gwyn 1960: *The Conflict of Horus and Seth, from Egyptian and Classical Sources. A Study in Ancient Mythology.* Liverpool.

—— 1980: *The Origins of Osiris and His Cult.* Leiden.

Grimal, Nicolas 1980: Bibliothèques et propagande royale à l'époque éthiopienne. In J. Vercoutter (ed.), *Livre du Centenaire. MIFAO* 104, 37–48.

—— 1981a: *La stèle triomphale de Pi('ankh)y au Musée du Caire. JE 48862 et 47086–47089. MIFAO* 105.

—— 1981b: *Quatre stèles napatéennes au Musée du Caire. JE 48863–48866. MIFAO* 106.

—— 1985: Les 'noyés' de Balat. In *Mélanges offerts à Jean Vercoutter.* Paris: 111–12.

—— 1986: *Les termes de la propagande royale égyptienne. De la XIXᵉ dynastie à la conquête d'Alexandre.* Paris.

Grimm, Alfred 1983a: Ein Porträt der Hatschepsut als Gottesfrau und Königin. *GM* 65, 33–8.

—— 1983b: Zu einer getilgten Darstellung der Hatschepsut im Tempel von Deir el-Bahari. *GM* 68, 93–4.

—— 1984: Ein Statuentorso des Hakoris aus Ahnas el-Medineh im ägyptischen Museum zu Kairo. *GM* 77, 14–18.

—— 1984–5: König Hakoris als Sonnenpriester. Ein Porträt aus El-Tôd im ägyptischen Museum zu Kairo. *BSEG* 9–10, 109–12.

—— 1985a: Das Fragment einer Liste fremdländischer Tiere, Pflanzen und Städte aus dem Totentempel des Königs Djedkare-Asosi. *SAK* 12, 29–42.

—— 1985b: Ein zweites Sedfest des Königs Adjib. *VA* 1, 91–8.

Groff, William 1899: Moïse et les magiciens à la Cour du pharaon d'après la tradition chrétienne et les textes démotiques. *RT* 21, 219–22.

—— 1902: Études sur certains rapports entre l'Égypte et la Bible. *RT* 24, 121–34.

Grzymski, K. A. 1982: *Medewi*/Bedewi and *Md̲s*/Bedja. *GM* 58, 27–30.

Gundlach, Rolf 1977: Der Denkstein des Königs Ahmose. Zur Inhaltsstruktur der Königsnovelle. In J. Assmann et al. (eds), *Fragen an die altägyptische Literatur. Studien zum Gedenken an Eberhard Otto.* Wiesbaden: 217–40.

—— 1979: Der Obelisk Thutmosis' I. *ÄAT* 1, 192–226.

—— 1981: Mentuhotep IV. and Min: Analyse der Inschriften M 110, M 191 and M 192a aus dem Wâdi Hammâmât. *SAK* 8, 89–114.

—— 1982: Sur Relevanz geschichtswissenschaftlicher Theorien für die Ägyptologie. *GM* 55, 43–58.

—— 1987: Die Felsstelen Amenophis' III. am 1. Katarakt (Zur Aussagenstruktur königlicher historischer Texte). In J. Osing and G. Dreyer (eds), *Form und Mass. ÄAT* 12, 180–217.

Gunn, Battiscombe 1943: Notes on the Naucratis Stela. *JEA* 29, 55–9.

Gunn, Battiscombe and Gardiner, A. H. 1918: New Renderings of Egyptian Texts II: The Expulsion of the Hyksos. *JEA* 5, 36–56.

Gutgesell, Manfred 1982: Die Struktur der pharaonischen Wirtschaft: Eine Erwiderung. *GM* 56, 95–109.

—— 1983: Die Entstehung des Pirvateigentums an Produktionsmitteln im alten Ägypten. *GM* 66, 67–80.

Haag, M. 1984: *Guide to Cairo Including the Pyramids and Saqqara*. London.

Habachi, Labib 1954a: Khatâ 'na-Qantîr: Importance. *ASAE* 52, 443–562.

—— 1954b: La libération de l'Égypte de l'occupation hyksôs. À propos de la découverte de la stèle de Kamosé à Karnak. *La Revue du Caire* 33/175, 52–8.

—— 1957a: The Graffiti and Work of the Viceroys of Kush in the Region of Aswan. *Kush* 5, 13–36. Reprinted in L. Habachi (ed.), *Sixteen Studies on Lower Nubia*. *CASAE* 23 (1981), 26–63.

—— 1957b: A Statue of Bakennifi, Nomarch of Athribis During the Invasion of Egypt by Assurbanipal. *MDAIK* 15, 68–77.

—— 1959: The First Two Viceroys of Kush and Their Family. *Kush* 7, 45–63.

—— 1963: King Nebhepetre Menthuhotpe: His Monuments, Place in History, Deification and Unusual Representations in the Form of Gods. *MDAIK* 19, 16–52.

—— 1966: The Qantir Stela of the Vizier Rahotep and the Statue Ruler-of-Rulers. In *Festgabe für Dr. Walter Will, Ehrensenator der Universität München, zum 70. Geburtstag am 12. November 1966*. Cologne: 67–77.

—— 1967: Setau, the Famous Viceroy of Ramesses II and his Career. *Cahiers d'Histoire Égyptienne* 10, 51–68. Reprinted in L. Habachi (ed.), *Sixteen Studies on Lower Nubia*. *CASAE* 23 (1981), 121–38.

—— 1969a: *Features of the Deification of Ramesses II*. *ADAIK* 5. Reprinted in L. Habachi (ed.), *Sixteen Studies on Lower Nubia*. *CASAE* 23 (1981), 219–46.

—— 1969b: La reine Touy, femme de Séthi, et ses proches parents inconnus. *RdE* 21, 27–47.

—— 1969c: The Administration of Nubia During the New Kingdom with Special Reference to Discoveries Made During the Last Few Years. In *Symposium international sur La Nubie*. Cairo: 65–78.

—— 1971: The Jubilee of Ramesses' II and Amenophis' III with Reference to Certain Aspects of their Celebration. *ZÄS* 97, 64–72.

—— 1972: *The Second Stela of Kamose and his Struggle against the Hyksos Ruler and His Capital*. *ADAIK* 8.

—— 1974a: Sethos I's Devotion to Seth and Avaris. *ZÄS* 100, 95–102.

—— 1974b: Amenophis III et Amenhotep, fils de Hapou, à Athribis. *RdE* 26, 21–33.

—— 1974c: Psammétique II dans la région de la Première Catracte. *OrAnt* 13, 317–26.

—— 1977a: Mentuhotpe, the Vizier and Son-in-law of Taharqa. In E. Endesfelder et al. (eds), *Äegypten und Kush*. *Schr. Or.* 13, 165–70.

—— 1977b: *The Obelisks of Egypt: Skyscrapers of the Past*. Cairo.

—— 1979: Unknown or Little-known Monuments of Tutankhamun and of His Viziers. In J. Ruffle et al. (eds), *Glimpses of Ancient Egypt: Studies in Honour of H. W. Fairman*. Warminster: 32–41.

—— 1980: The Military Posts of Ramesses II on the Coastal Road and the Western Part of the Delta. *BIFAO* 80, 13–30.

—— 1981a: Identification of Heqaib and Sabni with Owners of Tombs in Qubbet el-Hawa and their Relationship with Nubia. In L. Habachi (ed.), *Sixteen Studies on Lower Nubia. CASAE* 23, 11–27.

—— 1981b: Viceroys of Kush During the Reigns of Sethos I and Ramesses II and the Order in which They Assumed Their Function. In L. Habachi (ed.), *Sixteen Studies on Lower Nubia. CASAE* 23, 139–54.

—— 1981c: Viceroys of Kush during the New Kingdom. In L. Habachi (ed.), *Sixteen Studies on Lower Nubia. CASAE* 23, 155–68.

—— 1982: Athribis in the XXVIth Dynasty. *BIFAO* 82, 213–35.

—— 1985: *The Sanctuary of Heqaib. AV* 33.

Haeny, Gerhardt 1979a: New Kingdom Architecture. In K. Weeks (ed.), *Egyptology and the Social Sciences*. Cairo: 85–94.

—— 1979b: La fonction religieuse des 'Châteaux de millions d'années. *L'égyptologie en 1979* I, 111–16.

—— 1985: A Short Architectural History of Philae. *BIFAO* 85, 197–233.

Hahn, I. 1978: Representation of Society in the Old Testament and the Asiatic Mode of Production. *Oikumene* 2, 27–41.

Haider, P. W. 1984: Die hethitische Stadt Arushna in ägyptischen Ortsnamenlisten des Neuen Reiches. *GM* 72, 9–14.

Hakem, A. M. Ali, Hrbek, I. and Vercoutter, J. 1980: The civilization of Napata and Meroe. In G. Mokhtar (ed.), *General History of Africa* II. Paris, London, Berkel: 298–325.

Hall, E. S. 1986: *The Pharaoh Smites his Enemies*. Munich.

Hamza, Mahmoud 1937: The Statue of Meneptah I Found at Athar en-Nabi and the Route of Pi'ankhy from Memphis to Heliopolis. *ASAE* 37, 233–42.

Hani, Jean 1972: *La religion égyptienne dans la pensée de Plutarque*. Lille.

Hanke, R. 1978: *Amarna-Reliefs aus Hermopolis. Neue Veröffentlichungen und Studien*. Hildesheim.

Harant, Christopher 1972: *Le voyage en Égypte de Christopher Harant [1598]*. Cairo.

Harari, Ibram 1974: Le principe juridique de l'organisation sociale dans le décret de Séti Ier à Nauri. In *Le Droit égyptien ancien*. Brussels: 57–73.

—— 1979: Les administrateurs itinerants en Égypte ancienne. *L'égyptologie en 1979* II, 135–40.

Hari, Robert 1976a: La reine d'Horemheb était-elle la soeur de Néfertiti? *CdE* 51, 29–46.

—— 1976b: Un nouvel élément de la corégence Amenophis III-Akhenaton. *CdE* 51, 252–60.

—— 1978: La succession de Toutankhamon. *BSFE* 82, 8–21.

—— 1979: La persécution des hérétiques. *L'égyptologie en 1979* II, 259–62.

—— 1981: Sésostris et les historiens antiques. *BSEG* 5, 15–21.

—— 1984a: La 'Damnatio memoriae' amarnienne. In *Mélanges Adolphe Gutbub*. Montpellier: 95–102.

—— 1984b: La religion amarnienne et la tradition polythéiste. In *Studien zu Sprache und Religion Ägyptens. Festschrift W. Westendorf*. Göttingen: 1039–55.

—— 1984–5: Quelques remarques sur l'abandon d'Akhetaton. *BSEG* 9–10, 113–17.

Harris, J. R. 1971: *The Legacy of Egypt*. 2nd edn. London.

—— 1973a: Nefernefruaten. *GM* 4, 15–18.

—— 1973b: The Date of the 'Restauration' Stele of Tutankhamun. *GM* 5, 9–12.

—— 1974: Nefernefruaten Regnans. *AcOr* 36, 11–21.

—— 1977: Akhenaten or Nefertiti? *AcOr* 38, 5–10.

Harris, J. R. and Wente, E. F. 1980: *An X-ray Atlas of the Royal Mummies*. Chicago and London.

Hartleben, H. 1983: *Champollion: Sa vie et son oeuvre*. Paris.

Hartog, François 1980: *Le miroir d'Hérodote: Essai sur la représentation de l'autre*. Paris.

Hasitzka, M. and Satzinger, H. 1988: *Urkunden der 18. Dynastie, Indices zu den Heften 1–22. Corrigenda zu den Heften 5–16*. Berlin.

Hassan, Fekri A. 1980: Radiocarbon Chronology of Archaic Egypt. *JNES* 39, 203–8.

Hassan, Sélim n.d.: *Le sphinx, son histoire à la lumière des fouilles récentes*.

Haycock, B. 1965: The Kingship of Kush in the Sudan. *Comparative Studies in Society and History* 7, 461–80.

—— 1968: Towards a Better Understanding of the Kingdom of Kush (Napata-Meroe). *SNR* 49, 1–16.

Hayen, H. 1986: Die Sahara: Eine vergessene Wagenprovinz. In W. Treue (ed.), *Achse, Rad und Wagen Fünftausend Jahre Kultur-und Technikgeschichte*. Göttingen.

Hayes, W. C. 1942: *Ostraka and Name Stones from the Tomb of Sen-Mut (No. 71) at Thebes*. New York.

Heerma van Voss, M. 1982: *Ägypten, die 21. Dynastie. Iconography of Religions* 19/9.

Hegyi, D. 1983: Athen und die Achaemeniden in der zweiten Halfte des 5. Jahrhunderts v.u.Z. *Oikumene* 4, 53–9.

Helck, Wolfgang 1939: *Der Einfluss der Militärführer in der 18. ägyptischen Dynastie*. Berlin.

—— 1955–8: *Urkunden des ägyptischen Altertums IV: Urkunden der 18. Dynastie*. Berlin.

—— 1956a: Wirtschaftliche Bemerkungen zum privaten Grabbesitz im Alten Reich. *MDAIK* 14, 63–75.

—— 1956b: *Untersuchungen zu Manetho und der ägyptischen Königslisten. UGAÄ* 18.

—— 1957: Bemerkungen zu den Pyramidenstädten im Alten Reich. *MDAIK* 15, 91–111.

—— 1966: Zum Kult an Königsstatuen. *JNES* 25, 32–41.

—— 1969: *Der Text der 'Lehre Amenemhets I. für seinen Sohn*. Wiesbaden.

—— 1970: *Die Prophezeiung des Nfr.ti*. Wiesbaden.

—— 1971: *Die Beziehung Ägyptens zu Vorderasien im 3. und 2. Jahrtausend v. Chr*. 2nd edn. Wiesbaden.

—— 1975a: *Wirtschaftsgeschichte des alten Ägypten im 3. and 2. Jahrtausend vor Chr. HdO* I/1.5.

—— 1975b: *Historisch-biographische Texte der 2. Zwischenzeit und neue Texte der 18. Dynastie*. Wiesbaden.

—— 1975c: Abgeschlagene Hände als Siegeszeichen. *GM* 18, 23–4.

—— 1976a: Die Seevölker in der ägyptischen Quellen. *Jahrbericht des Instituts für Vorgeschichte der Universität Frankfurt am Main*, 7–21.

—— 1976b: Zum Datum der Eroberung von Auaris. *GM* 19, 33–4.

—— 1977a: *Die Lehre für König Merikare*. Wiesbaden.

—— 1977b: Das Verfassen einer Königsinschrift. In J. Assman et al. (eds), *Fragen an die altägyptische Literatur. Studien zum Gedenken an Eberhard Otto*. Wiesbaden: 241–56.

—— 1979a: Die Datierung der Gefässaufschriften aus der Djorserpyramide. *ZÄS* 106, 120–32.

—— 1979b: Die Vorgänger König Suppiluliumas I. *ÄAT* 1, 238–46.

—— 1980: Ein 'Feldzug' unter Amenophis IV. gegen Nubien. *SAK* 8, 117–26.

—— 1981a: *Geschichte des alten Ägypten*. 2nd edn. *HdO* I/1.3.

—— 1981b: Probleme der Königsfolge in der Übergangszeit von 18. zu 19. Dynastie. *MDAIK* 37, 207–16.

—— 1981c: Wo errichtete Thutmosis III. seine Siegesstele am Euphrat? *CdE* 56, 241–4.

—— 1981–2: Zu den Königinnen Amenophis' II. *GM* 53, 23–6.

—— 1983a: Zur Verfolgung einer Prinzessin unter Amenophis III. *GM* 62, 23–4.

—— 1983b: Schwachstellen der Chronologie-Diskussion. *GM* 67, 43–50.

—— 1983c: Chronologische Swachstellen II. *GM* 69, 37–42.

—— 1983d: *Ägypten. Die Mythologie der alten Ägypter, Wörterbuch der Mytologien* I.1.

—— 1984a: Chronologische Schwastellen III. *GM* 70, 31–2.

—— 1984b: Der 'König von Ober- und Unterägypten'. In *Studien zu Sprache und Religion Ägyptens. Festschrift W. Westendorf*. Göttingen: 251–6.

—— 1984c: *Übersetzung zu den Heften 17–22 der Urk. IV*. Originally publ. 1961. Berlin.

—— 1986a: Der Aufstand des Tetian. *SAK* 13, 125–34.

—— 1986b: *Politische Gegensätze im alten Ägypten. Ein Versuch. HÄB* 23.

—— 1987: *Untersuchungen zur Thinitenzeit*. Wiesbaden.

Helck, Wolfgang and Otto, Eberhardt 1956: *Kleines Wörterbuch der Ägyptologie*. Wiesbaden.

Helck, Wolfgang, Otto, Eberhardt and Westendorf, Wolfhardt 1972–86: *Lexikon der Ägyptologie*. 6 vols. Wiesbaden.

Henfling, Edwin 1984: Das Eine und das Viele. In *Studien zu Sprache und Religion Ägyptens. Festschrift W. Westendorf*. Göttingen: 735–40.

Henige, David 1981: Generation-counting and Late New Kingdom Chronology. *JEA* 67: 182.

Herreros, E. G. de 1923: *Quatre voyageurs espagnols à Alexandrie*. Alexandria.

Hickmann, Hans 1961: Ägypten. In H. Besseler and M. Schneider (eds), *Musikgeschichte in Bildern II: Musik der Altertums* I. Leipzig.

Hinkel, Friedrich W. 1977: *The Archaeological Map of the Sudan 1: a Guide to its Use and Explanation of its Principles*. Berlin.

—— 1984: Die meroitischen Pyramiden: Formen, Kriterien und Bauweisen. *Meroitica* 7, 310–31.

Hintze, Fritz 1974: Zur statistischen Untersuchung afrikanischer Orts- und Völkernamen aus ägyptischen Texten. *MNL* 14, 4–19.

Hintze, Fritz and Hintze, Ursula 1967: *Les civilisations du Soudan antique.* Leipzig.

Hobbs, A. and Adzigian, J. 1981: *A Complete Guide to Egypt and the Archaeological Sites.* New York.

Hodjash, Svetlana and Berlev, O. D. 1982: *The Egyptian Reliefs and Stelae in the Pushkin Museum of Fine Arts, Moscow.* Leningrad.

Hölbl, Günther 1981: Die Ausbreitung ägyptischen Kulturgutes in den ägäischen Raum vom 8. bis zum 6. JH. v. Chr. *Or* 50, 186–92.

Hoffman, Michael A. 1979: *Egypt Before the Pharaohs.* London.

Hoffman, M. A., Hamroush, H. A. and Allen, R. O. 1986: A Model of Urban Development for the Hierakonpolis Region from Predynastic through Old Kingdom Times. *JARCE* 23, 175–87.

Hoffmeier, James K. 1983: Some Egyptian Motifs Related to Warfare and Enemies and Their Old Testament Counterparts. *Ancient World* 6, 53–70.

—— 1985: *'Sacred' in the Vocabulary of Ancient Egypt: The Term Dsr with Special References to Dynasties I–XX.* OBO 59.

Hofmann, Inge 1979: *Der Sudan als ägyptische Kolonie im Altertum. VIAÄ Wien 5.*

—— 1981a: Kambysis in Ägypten. *SAK* 9, 179–200.

—— 1981b: Kuschiten in Palästina. *GM* 46, 9–10.

—— 1984: Meriotische Herrscher. *Meroitica* 7, 242–4.

Hofmann, Inge, Tomandl, H. and Zach, M. 1984a: Bewohner Kordofans auf ägyptischen Darstellungen? *GM* 75, 15–18.

—— 1984b: Eduard Freiherr von Callots Bericht über Meroe. *GM* 79, 85–90.

Hofmann, Inge and Vorblicher, A. 1979: *Der Äthiopenlogos bei Herodot.* Vienna.

Holm-Rasmussen, T. 1977: Nectanebos II and Temple M at Karnak (North). *GM* 26, 37–42.

—— 1979: On the Statue Cult of Nektanebos II. *AcOr* 40, 21–5.

Holmes, D. 1985: Inter-regional Variability in Egyptian Predynastic Lithic Assemblages. *Wepwawet* 1, 16.

Hopfner, Thomas 1922–5: *Fontes Historiae Religionis Aegyptiacae.* 5 vols. Bonn.

Hornung, Erik 1956: Chaotische Bereiche in der geordneten Welt. *ZÄS* 81, 28–32.

—— 1957: Zur geschichtlichen Rolle des Königs in der 18. Dynastie. *MDAIK,* 15, 120–33.

—— 1964: *Untersuchungen zur Chronologie und Geschichte des Neuen Reiches.* Wiesbaden.

—— 1966: *Geschichte als Fest. Zwei Vorträge zum Geschichtsbilde der frühen Menschheit.* Darmstadt.

—— 1967: Der Mensch als 'Bild Gottes' in Ägypten. In O. Loretz (ed.), *Die Gottebenbildlichkeit des Menschen.* Munich: 123–56.

—— 1971: Politische Planung and Realität im alten Ägypten. *Saeculum* 22, 48–58.

—— 1979: Chronologie in Bewegung. *ÄAT* 1, 247–52.

—— 1983: Die Israelstele des Merenptah. *ÄAT* 5, 224–33.

—— 1984: *Götterwort und Götterbild im alten Ägypten*. In H.-J. Klimkeit (ed.), *Götterbild in Kunst und Schrift. Studium Universale* 2.

Hornung, Erik 1983. *Conceptions of God in Ancient Egypt: The One and the Many*. London.

Hornung, Erik and Staehelin, E. 1974: *Studien zum Sedfest*. Geneva.

Huard, Paul 1965: Recherches sur les traits culturels des chasseurs anciens du Sahara centre-oriental et du nil. *RdE* 17, 21–80.

—— 1966: Contribution saharienne à l'étude de questions intéressant l'Égypte ancienne. *BSFE* 45, 5–18.

Huard, Paul and Leclant, J. 1973: Figurations de pièges des chasseurs anciens du Nil et du Sahara. *RdE* 25, 136–77.

—— 1980: *La culture des chasseurs du Nil et du Sahara*. Algiers.

Hugot, H.-J. 1974: *Le Sahara avant le désert*. Toulouse.

Humbert, Jean 1987: Panorama de quatre siècles d'égyptomanie. *BSFE* 110, 48–77.

Huntington, R. and Metcalf, P. 1979: *Celebration of Death: The Anthropology of Mortuary Ritual*. Cambridge.

Irby, C. and Mangles, J. 1985: *Travels in Egypt and Nubia, Syria and Asia Minor during the Years 1817 and 1818*. Originally publ. 1823. London.

Irmscher, J. 1968–9: Winckelmann and Egypt. *BIE* 50, 5–10.

Isler, M. 1985: On Pyramid Building. *JARCE* 22, 129–42.

Iversen, Erik 1968: *Obelisks in Exile I: Rome*. Copenhagen.

—— 1972: *Obelisks in Exile II: Istanbul and England*.

—— 1975: *Canon and Proportions in Egyptian Art*. Warminster.

—— 1979: Remarks on Some Passages from the Shabaka Stone. *ÄAT* 1, 253–62.

—— 1985: *Egyptian and Hermetic Doctrine*. Copenhagen.

Jacobsohn, H. 1939: *Die dogmatische Stellung des Königs in der Theologie der alten Ägypten*. *ÄF* 8.

Jacq, Christian 1986: *Le voyage dans l'autre monde selon l'Égypte ancienne. Épreuves et métamorphoses du mort d'après les Textes des Pyramides et les Textes des Sarcophages*. Paris.

Jacquet-Gordon, Helen 1960: The Inscription on the Philadelphia-Cairo Statue of Osorkon II. *JEA* 46, 12–23.

—— 1967: The Illusory Year 36 of Osorkon I. *JEA* 53, 63–8.

—— 1981: Fragments of a Topographical List Dating to the Reign of Thutmosis I. *BIFAO du Centenaire*, 41–6.

Jaeger, Bertrand 1982: *Essai de classification et datation des scarabées Menkheperre*. OBO, Arch. 2.

James, Peter (ed.) 1991: *Centuries of Darkness: A Challenge to the Conventional Chronology of Old World Archaeology*. London.

James, S. 1986: *Missing Pharaohs, Missing Tombs*. Horam.

James, T. G. H. 1962: *The Hekanakhte Papers and other Early Middle Kingdom Documents*. New York.

—— 1982: *Excavating in Egypt: The Egypt Exploration Society 1882–1982*. London.

—— 1984a: *Pharaoh's People: Scenes from Life in Imperial Egypt*. London.

—— 1984b: *The British Museum and Ancient Egypt*. London.

James, T. G. H. and Davies, W. 1982: *Egyptian Sculpture*. London.

Jansen, H. L. 1971: *Ägyptische Religion. Handbuch der Religionen* I. Göttingen.

Janssen, Jac J. 1975: *Commodity Prices from the Ramessid Period. An Economic Study of the Village of Necropolis Workmen at Thebes*. Leiden.

—— 1978: Year 8 of Ramesses VI Attested. *GM* 29, 45–6.

—— 1981: Die Struktur der pharaonischen Wirtschaft. *GM* 48, 59–77.

—— 1982: Gift-giving in Ancient Egypt as an Economic Feature. *JEA* 68, 253–8.

—— 1986: Agrarian Administration in Egypt During the Twentieth Dynasty. *BiOr* 43, 351–66.

Jansen-Winkeln, Karl 1987a: Thronname und Begräbnis Takeloths I. *VA* 3, 253–8.

—— 1987b: Zum militärischen Befehlsbereich der Hohenpriester des Amun. *GM* 99, 19–22.

—— 1988: Weiteres zum Grab Osorkons II. *GM* 102, 31–9.

Jasnow, Richard 1983: Evidence for the Deification of Thutmosis III in the Ptolemaic Period. *GM* 64, 33–4.

Jeffreys, David G. 1981: The Threat to Ancient Memphis During this Century. In N. Grimal (ed.), *Prospection et sauvegarde des antiquités de l'Égypte. BdE* 88, 187–8.

—— 1985: *Survey of Memphis I: the Archaeological Report*. London.

Jelgersma, H. C. 1981–2: The Influence of Negro Culture on Egyptian Art. *JEOL* 27, 43–6.

Jenkins, Nancy 1980: *The Boat Beneath the Pyramid: King Cheops' Royal Ship*. London.

Jenni, H. 1986: *Das Dekorationsprogramm des Sarkophages Nektanebos' II*. Geneva.

Jequier, Gustave 1922: *Les temples ramessides et saïtes, de la XIXe dynastie à la XXe dynastie*. Paris.

—— 1925: *Histoire de la civilisation égyptienne, des origines à la conquête d'Alexandre*. Paris.

—— 1932: Les femmes de Pépi II. In S. R. K. Glanville (ed.), *Studies Griffith*. Oxford: 9–12.

Jirku, Aanton 1941: Der Name der palästinischen Stadt Bet-Šᶜan und siene ägyptische Wiedergabe. *WZKM* 48, 49–50.

Johnson, Janet H. 1983: The Demotic Chronicle as a Statement of a Theory of Kingship. *JSSEA* 13, 61–72.

—— 1984: Is the Demotic Chronicle an Anti-Greek Tract? In H. J. Thissen and K.-T. Zauzich (eds), *Grammata Demotika. Festschrift E. Lüddeckens*. Würtzburg: 107–24.

Jomard, M. 1981: *Voyage à l'oasis de Syouah*. Originally publ. 1923. Paris.

Jonckheere, Frans 1958: *Les médicins de l'Égypte pharaonique. Essai de prosopographie.* Brussels.

Jonquière, C. de la n.d.: *L'expédition d'Égypte.* Paris.

Jouguet, Pierre 1926–61: *L'impérialisme macédonien et l'hellénisation de l'Orient.* Paris.

Jüngst, H. 1982: Zur Interpretation einiger Metallarbeiterszenen auf Wandbilder alt-ägyptischer Gräber. *GM* 59, 15–28.

Junker, H. 1941: *Die politische Lehre von Memphis. APAW* 1941/6.

Kaczmarczyk, A. and Hedges, R. E. M. 1983: *Ancient Egyptian Faience: An Analytical Survey of Egyptian Faience from Predynastic to Roman Times.* Warminster.

Kadry, Ahmed 1980: Remains of a Kiosk of Psammetikhos II on Philae Island. *MDAIK* 36, 293–8.

—— 1981: Some Comments on the Qadesh Battle. *BIFAO du Centenaire*, 47–55.

—— 1982: Semenkhkare, the Ephemeral King. *ASAE* 68, 191–4.

—— 1983: The Theocratic Symptoms at the End of the New Kingdom in Ancient Egypt. *JSSEA* 13, 35–43.

—— 1986: The Social Status and Education of Military Scribes in Egypt during the 18th Dynasty. *Oikumene* 5, 155–62.

Kaiser, Werner 1956: Zu den Sonnenheiligtümer der 5. Dynastie. *MDAIK* 14, 104–16.

—— 1958: Zur vorgeschichtlichen Bedeutung von Hierakonpolis. *MDAIK* 16, 183–92.

—— 1969: Zu den königlichen Tabelzirken der 1. und 2. Dynastie in Abydos und zur Baugeschichte des Djoser-Grabmals. *MDAIK* 25, 1–21.

—— 1981: Zu den Königsgräbern der 1. Dynastie in Umm el-Qaab. *MDAIK* 37, 247–54.

—— 1985a: Ein Kultbezirk des Königs Den in Sakkara. *MDAIK* 41, 47–60.

—— 1985b: Zur Südausdehnung der vorgeschichtlichen Deltakulturen und zur frühen Entwicklung Oberägyptens. *MDAIK* 41, 61–87.

—— 1987: Zum Friedhof der Naqadakultur von Minshat Abu Omar. *ASAE* 71, 119–25.

Kakosy, Laszlo 1964: *Urzeitmythen und Historiographie im alten Ägypten, Neve Beiträge zur Geschichte der alten Welt I: Alter Orient und Griechenland.* Berlin.

—— 1977a: The Primordial Birth of the King. *Stud. Aeg.* 3, 67–71.

—— 1977b: Osiris als Gott des Kampfes. In J. Assmann et al. (eds), *Fragen an die altagyptische Literatur. Studien zum Gedenken an Eberhard Otto.* Wiesbaden: 258–88.

—— 1981: Die weltanschauliche Krise des Neuen Reiches [*ZÄS* 100 (1973), 35–40]. *Stud. Aeg.* 7, 263–8.

—— 1986: *The Battle Reliefs of King Sety I. RIK* 4, *OIP* 107.

Kamel, Ibrahim 1979: Studies for Discussion about King Ahmose's Tomb. *ASAE* 68, 115–30.

Kamil, Jill 1976: *Luxor: A Guide to Ancient Thebes.* 2nd edn. London.

—— 1978: *A Guide to the Necropolis of Sakkara and the Site of Memphis.* London.

—— 1983: *Upper Egypt: Historical Outline and Descriptive Guide to the Ancient Sites.* New York.

Kamish, M. 1985: Foreigners at Memphis in the Middle of the Eighteenth Dynasty. *Wepwawet*, 1, 12–13.

Kanawati, Naguib 1974a: The Financial Resources of the Viziers of the Old Kingdom and the Historical Implications. *AHS Alexandrie* 5, 1–20.

—— 1974b: Notes on the Genealogy of the Late Sixth Dynasty. *AHS Alexandrie* 5, 52–8.

—— 1977: *The Egyptian Administration in the Old Kingdom: Evidence on its Economic Decline.* Warminster.

—— 1979: The Overseer of Commissions in the Nine Provinces. *L'égyptologie en 1979* II, 141–2.

—— 1980: *Governmental Reforms in the Old Kingdom Egypt.* Warminster.

—— 1981: Deux conspirations contre Pépy Iᵉʳ. *CdE* 56, 203–17.

—— 1984: New Evidence on the Reign of Userkaf? *GM* 83, 31–8.

Känel, Frédérique von 1979: Akhmîm et le IXᵉ nome de Haute Égypte. In *L'égyptologie en 1979* I, 235–8.

—— 1984a: *Les prêtres-ouab de Sekhmet et les conjurateurs de Serket.* Paris.

—— 1984b: Les courtisans de Psousennès et leurs tombes à Tanis. *BSFE* 100, 31–43.

—— 1987:'*La nèpe et le scorpion'. Une monographie sur la déesse Serket.* Geneva.

Kaplony, Peter 1963a: *Die Inschriften der ägyptischen Frühzeit.* Wiesbaden.

—— 1963b: Gottespalast und Götterfestungen in den ägyptischen Frühzeit. *ZÄS* 88, 5–16.

—— 1964: *Die Inschriften der ägyptischen Früzeit. Supplement.* Wiesbaden.

—— 1965: Bemerkungen zu einigen Steingefässe mit archaischen Königsnamen. *MDAIK* 20, 1–46.

—— 1967: *Kleine Beiträge zu den Inschriften der ägyptischen Frühzeit.* Wiesbaden.

—— 1968: *Steingefässe mit Inschriften der Frühzeit und des Alten Reiches.* Brussels.

—— 1971: Ägyptisches Königtum in der Spätzeit. *CdE* 46, 250–74.

—— 1977: *Die Rollsiegel des Alten Reiches I: Allgemeiner Teil mit Studien zum Königtum des Alten Reiches.* Brussels.

—— 1981: *Die Rollseigel im Alten Reich 2: Test und Tafeln.* Brussels.

Kaplony-Heckel, Ursula 1963: *Die demotischen Tempeleide.* Wiesbaden.

Kayser, Hans 1969: *Ägyptisches Kunsthandwerk: Bibliothek für Kunst und Antiquitäten-freunde* 26. Brunswick.

Kees, Hermann 1954: Zu den Annaleninschrift des Hohenpriesters Osorkon vom 11. Jahre Takeloths II. *MIO* 2, 353–62.

—— 1958: Die weisse Kapelle Sesostris' I. in Karnak und das Sedfest. *MDAIK* 16, 194–213.

—— 1964: *Die Hohenpriester des Amun von Karnak von Herihor bis zum*

Ende der Äthiopenzeit. Leiden.

Kemp, Barry J. 1976: The Window of Appearance at El-Amarna and the Basic Structure of this City. *JEA* 62, 81–99.

—— 1978a: A Further Note on the Palace of Apries at Memphis. *GM* 29, 61–2.

—— 1978b: Inperialism and Empire in New Kingdom Egypt. In P. D. A. Garnsey and C. R. Whittaker (eds), *Imperialism in the Ancient World*. Cambridge: 7–57, 284ff.

—— 1982: Automatic Analysis of Predynastic Cemeteries: A New Method for an Old Problem. *JEA* 68, 5–15.

—— 1985: The Location of the Early Town at Dendera. *MDAIK* 41, 89–98.

—— 1987: The Amarna Workmen's Village in Retrospect. *JEA* 73, 21–50.

Kemp, B. and Merrillees, R. 1980: *Minoan Pottery in Second Millenium Egypt*. Mainz am Rhein.

Kendall, Timothy 1982: *Kush: Lost Kingdom of the Nile*. Brockton, Mass.

Kessler, Dieter 1981: *Historische Topographie der Region zwischen Mallawi und Samalut*. *TAVO* B/30. Wiesbaden.

—— 1982: Zu den Feldzügen des Tefnachte, Namlot und Pije. *SAK* 9, 227–52.

—— 1984: Nachtrag zur archäologischen und historischen Karte der Region zwischen Mallawi und Samalut. *SAK* 11, 506–20.

—— 1987: Zur Bedeutung der Szenen des täglichen Lebens in den Privatgräbern (I): Die Szenen des Schiffsbaues und der Schiffahrt. *ZÄS* 114, 59–88.

Khalidi, T. 1984: *Land Tenure and Social Transformation in the Middle East*. Beirut.

Khonsu 1979: *The Temple of Khonsu* 1: Plates 1–110. *Scenes of King Herihor in the Court, with Translations of Texts*. OIP 100.

—— 1981: *The Temple of Khonsu* 2: Plates 111–207. *Scenes and Inscriptions in the Court and the First Hypostyle Hall . . .* OIP 103.

Khoury, René 1977: Quelques notes additionnelles au *Voyage en Égypte* de Pierre Belon (1547). *BIFAO* 77, 261–70.

Kienitz, Friedrich K. 1953: *Die politische Geschichte Ägyptens vom 7. bis zum 4. Jahrhundert vor der Zeitwende*. Berlin.

—— 1967: Die saïtische Renaissance. In E. Cassin, J. Bottéro and J. Vercoutter (eds), *Die altorientalischen Reiche III: Die erste Halfte des 1. Jahrhunderts*. Frankfurt.

Kirk, G. S. 1970: *Myth: Its Meaning and Functions in Ancient and Other Cultures*. Cambridge.

Kischkewitz, Hannelore 1977: Zur temporären Einwohnung des Gottes im König. In E. Endesfelder et al. (eds), *Ägypten und Kush*. Schr. Or. 13, 207–12.

Kitchen, Kenneth A. 1972: Ramesses VII and the Twentieth Dynasty. *JEA* 58, 182–94.

—— 1975–6: The Great Biographical Stela of Setau, Viceroy of Nubia. *OLP* 6/7, 295–302.

—— 1977a: Historical Observations on Ramesside Nubia. In E. Endesfelder et al. (eds), *Agypten und Kush*. Schr. Or. 13, 213–26.

—— 1977b: On the Princedoms of Late-Libyan Egypt. *CdE* 52, 40–8.

—— 1982a: *Pharaoh Triumphant: The Life and Times of Ramesses II King of Egypt*. Warminster.

—— 1982b: The Twentieth Dynasty Revisited. *JEA* 68, 116–25.

—— 1982–3: Further Thoughts on Egyptian Chronology in the Third Intermediate Period. *RdE* 34, 59–69.

—— 1983: Egypt, the Levant and Assyria in 701 BC. *ÄAT* 5, 243–53.

—— 1984: Family Relationship of Ramesses IX and the Late Twentieth Dynasty. *SAK* 11, 127–34.

—— 1985: Les suites des guerres libyennes de Ramses III. *RdE* 36, 177–9.

—— 1986: *The Third Intermediate Period in Egypt (1100–650 B.C.)*. Warminster.

—— 1987a: The Titularies of the Ramesside Kings as Expression of their Ideal Kingship. *ASAE* 71, 131–41.

—— 1987b: Amenmesses in Northern Egypt. *GM* 99, 23–5.

Kleindienst, M. R. 1985: Dakhleh Oasis Project. The Paleolithic: A Report on the 1986 Season. *JSSEA* 15, 136–7.

Klemm, Rosemarie and Klemm, Dietrich 1981: *Die Steine der Pharaonen*. Munich.

Klengel, Horst 1977: Das Land Kusch in den Keilschrifttexten von Amarna. In E. Endesfelder et al. (eds), *Ägypten und Kusch*. Schr. Or. 13, 227–32.

Klunzinger, C. B. 1980: *Bilder aus Oberägypten, der Wüste und dem Roten Meere*. Originally publ. 1878.

Knauf, E. A. and Lenzen, C. J. 1987: Notes on Syrian Toponyms in Egyptian Sources II. *GM* 98, 49–54.

Köhler, U. 1974: Die Anfänge der deutschen Ägyptologie: Heinrich Brugsch. Eine Einschätzung. *GM* 12, 29–42.

Koenig, Yvan 1983: Livraison d'or et de galène au trésor du temple d'Amon sous la XXe dynastie: document A, partie inférieure. *BIFAO* 83, 249–55.

—— 1985: Égypte et Israël: quelques points de contact. *JA* 273, 1–10.

Kornfeld, Walter 1967: Aramäische Sarkophage in Assuan. *WZKM* 61, 9–16.

Korostovtsev, Michail A. 1977: À propos du genre 'historique' dans la littérature de l'ancienne Égypte. In J. Assmann et al. (eds), *Fragen an die altägyptische Literatur. Studien zum Gedanken an Eberhard Otto*. Wiesbaden: 315–24.

Krauss, Rolf 1981a: Necho II. alias Nechepso. *GM* 42, 49–60.

—— 1981b: Sothis, Elephantine und die altägyptische Chronologie. *GM* 50, 71–80.

—— 1981c: Zur historischen Einordnung Amenmesses und zur Chronologie der 19./20. Dynastie. *GM* 45, 27–34.

—— 1981d: *Das Ende der Amarnazeit. Beiträge zur Geschichte und Chronologie des Neuen Reiches*. 2nd edn. *HÄB* 7.

—— 1982: Talfestdaten: eine Korrektur. *GM* 54, 53–4.

—— 1983: Zu den Familienbeziehungen der Königin Tachat. *GM* 61, 51–2.

—— 1984: Korrekturen und Ergänzungen zur Chronologie des Mittleren Reiches und Neuen Reiches: Ein Zwischenbericht. *GM* 70, 37–44.

—— 1985: *Sothis- und Monddaten. Studien zur astronomischen und technischen Chronologie Altägyptens. HÄB* 20.

—— 1986: Kija: ursprüngliche Besitzerin der Kanopen aus KV 55. *MDAIK* 42, 67–80.

Krebs, Walter 1976: Unterägypten und die Reichseinigung. *ZÄS* 103, 76–8.

—— 1977: Die neolitischen Rinderhirten der Sashara und die Masai. In E. Endesfelden et al. (eds), *Ägypten und Kusch. Schr. Or.* 13, 265–78.

Kruchten, Jean-Marie 1979: Retribution de l'armée d'après le décret d'Horemheb. *L'égyptologie en 1979* II, 143–8.

—— 1981a: *Le décret d'Horemheb. Traduction, commentaire épigraphique, philogique et institutionnel.* Brussels.

—— 1981b: Comment on écrit l'histoire égyptienne: la fin de la XIXe dynastie vue d'après la section 'historique' du papyrus Harris I. *IPHOS* 25, 51–64.

—— 1982: Convention et innovation dans un texte royal du début de l'époque ramesside: la stèle de l'an 1 de Sethi Ier découverte à Beith-San. *IPHOS* 26, 21–62.

—— 1986: *Le grand texte oraculaire de Djehoutymose, intendant du domaine d'Amon sous le pontificat de Pindejem II. MRE* 5.

Krzyzaniak, Lech 1977: *Early Farming Cultures on the Lower Nile.* Warsaw.

—— 1983: Les débuts de la domestication des animaux et des plantes dans les pays du Nil. *BSFE* 96, 4–13.

Krzyzaniak, Lech and Kobusiewicz, M. 1984: *Origin and Early Development of Food-Producing Cultures in North-Eastern Africa.* Posnan.

Kuchman Sabbahy, Lisa 1981: The Titulary of Queens *nbt* and *ḫnwt*. *GM* 52, 37–42.

—— 1984: ʿnḫ-n.s.-Ppy, ʿnḫ-n.s.-Mry-Rʿ I and II, and the Title *w3ḏs ḏti*. *GM* 72, 33–6.

Kühnert-Eggerbrecht, E. 1969: *Die Axt als Waffe and Werkzeug im alten Ägypten. MÄS* 15.

Kuhlmann, Klaus P. 1981a: Ptolemais, Queen of Nectabebo I. Notes on the Inscription of an Unknown Princess of the XXXth Dynasty. *MDAIK* 37, 267–80.

—— 1981b: Zur *srḫ*-Symbolik bei Thronen. *GM* 50, 39–46.

—— 1982: Archäologische Forschungen im Raum von Achmim. *MDAIK* 38, 347–54.

Kuhlmann, K. P. and Schenkel, W. 1983: *Das Grab des Ibi, Obergutsverwalters der Gottesgemahlin des Amun (Thebanisches Grab Nr. 36). AV* 15.

Kurth, Dieter 1987: Zu den Darstellungen Pepi I. im Hathortempel von Dendera. In W. Helck (ed.), *Temple und Kult.* Wiesbaden.

Labib, Mahfouz 1961: *Pèlerins et voyageurs au mont Sinaï. RAPH* 25.

Labib, Pahor 1936: *Die Herrschaft der Hyksos.* Glückstadt.

Labrousse, Audran, Lauer, J.-P. and Leclant, J. 1977: *Le temple haut du complexe funéraire du roi Ounas: Mission archéologique de Saqqarah* II. *BdE* 73.

Lacaze, G., Masson, O. and Yoyotte, J. 1984: Deux documents memphites copiés par J.-M. Vansleb au XVIIe siècle. *RdE* 35, 127–37.

Lacovara, Peter 1985: Archeology and the Decay of Mudbrick Structures in Egypt. *NARCE* 128, 20–8.

Lacovara, Peter and Reeves, C.-N. 1987: The Colossal Statue of Mycerinus

Reconsidered. *RdE* 38, 111–15.

Lalouette, Claire 1981a: *L'art égyptien*. Paris.

—— 1981b: *La littérature égyptienne*. Paris.

—— 1984: *Textes sacrés et textes profanes de l'ancienne Égypte* I. Paris.

—— 1985: *L'empire des Ramsès*. Paris.

—— 1986: *Thebès ou la naissance d'un empire*. Paris.

—— 1987: *Textes sacrés et textes profanes de l'ancienne Égypte* II. Paris.

Lane, Edward William 1978: *An Account of the Manners and Customs of the Modern Egyptians, Written in Egypt During the Years 1833–1835*. Cairo.

Lane, Mary-Ellen 1985: *A Guide to the Antiquities of the Fayyum*. Cairo.

Lange, Kurt and Hirmer, Max 1978: *Ägypten. Architektur, Plastik, Malerei in drei Jahrtausenden*. Munich.

Larson, John A. 1975–6: The Date of the Regnal Year Change in the Reign of Ramesses II. *Serapis* 3, 17–22.

Lauer, Jean-Philippe 1929: Études sur quelques monuments de la IIIᵉ dynastie (pyramide à degrés de Saqqarah). *ASAE* 29, 99–129.

—— 1948: *Études complémentaires sur les monuments du roi Zoser à Saqqarah* I. Cairo.

—— 1956: Sur le dualisme de la monarchie égyptienne et son expression architecturale sous les premières dynasties. *BIFAO* 55, 153–72.

—— 1957: Évolution de la tombe royale égyptienne jusqu'à la pyramide à degrés. *MDAIK* 15, 148–65.

—— 1960a: *Observations sur les pyramides*. BdE 30.

—— 1960b: Žbynek Žaba: l'orientation astronomique dans l'ancienne Égypte et la précession de l'axe du monde. *BIFAO* 60, 171–84.

—— 1961: Au sujet du nom gravé sur la plaquette d'ivoire de la pyramide de l'Horus Sekhemkhet. *BIFAO* 61, 25–8.

—— 1962a: Sur l'âge et l'attribution possible de l'excavation monumentale de Zaouiêt el-Aryan. *RdE* 14, 21–36.

—— 1962b: *Histoire monumentale des pyramides d'Égypte I: Les pyramides à degrés (IIIᵉ dynastie)*. BdE 39.

—— 1966a: Quelques remarques sur la 1ʳᵉ dynastie. *BIFAO* 64, 169–84.

—— 1966b: Nouvelles remarques sur les pyramides à degrés de la IIIᵉ dynastie. *Or* 35, 440–8.

—— 1966–8: Recherche et découverte du tombeau sud de l'Horus Sekhem-Khet à Saqqarah. *BIE* 48–9, 121–36. Reprinted in *RdE* 20, 97–107.

—— 1967: Sur la pyramide de Meïdoum et les deux pyramides du roi Snefrou à Dahchour. *Or* 36, 239–54.

—— 1969a: Remarques sur le complexes funéraires royaux de la fin de la IVᵉ dynastie. *Or* 38, 560–78.

—— 1969b: À propos des vestiges des murs à redans encadrés par les 'Tombs of the Courtiers' et des 'forts' d'Abydos. *MDAIK* 25, 79–84.

—— 1972: *Les pyramides de Sakkarah*. Cairo.

—— 1973: Remarques sur la planification de la construction de la grande pyramide. *BIFAO* 73, 127–42.

—— 1976: À propos du prétendu désastre de la pyramide de Meïdoum. *CdE* 51, 72–89.

—— 1977: *Saqqarah. La nécropole royale de Memphis. Quarante siècles d'histoire, cent vingt-cing ans de recherches.* Paris.

—— 1979: Le développement des complexes funéraires royaux en Égypte depuis les temps prédynastiques jusqu'à la fin de l'Ancien Empire. *BIFAO* 79, 355–94.

—— 1980: Le premier temple de culte funéraire en Égypte. *BIFAO* 80, 45–68.

—— 1981: La signification et le rôle des fausses-portes de palais dans les tombeaux du type de Négadah. *MDAIK* 37, 281–8.

—— 1984–5: Considérations sur l'évolution de la tombe royale sous la Ier dynastie. *BSEG* 9–10, 141–52.

—— 1988: *Saqqarah, une vie. Entretiens avec Philippe Flandrin.* Rivages.

Lauer, Jean-Philippe and Leclant, J. 1969: Découverte de statues de prisonniers au temple de la pyramide de Pépi Ier. *RdE* 21, 55–62.

—— 1972: *Le temple haut du complexe funéraire du roi Téti: Mission archéologique de Saqqarah* I. *BdE* 51.

Lauffray, Jean 1973: *Karnak d'Égypte: Domaine du divin.* Paris.

—— 1979: Urbanisme et architecture du domaine d'Aton à Karnak d'après les 'talatat' du IXe pylône. *L'égyptologie en 1979* II, 265–70.

Leahy, Anthony 1979: Nespamedu, 'King' of Thinis. *GM* 35, 31–40.

—— 1984a: Saite Royal Sculpture: A Review. *GM* 80, 59–76.

—— 1984b: Tanutamon, Son of Shabako? *GM* 83, 43–6.

Leblanc, Christian 1979: Les piliers dits 'osiriaques' dans la contexte des temples de culte royal. *L'égyptologie en 1979* I, 133–4.

—— 1980: Piliers et colosses de type 'osiriaque' dans le contexte des temples de culte royale. *BIFAO* 80, 69–90.

—— 1982: Le culte rendu aux colosses 'osiriaques' durnat le Nouvel Empire. *BIFAO* 82, 295–311.

—— 1986: Henout-taouy et la tombe No. 73 de la Vallée des Reines. *BIFAO* 86, 203–26.

Leca, Ange-Pierre 1977: *Les momies.* Paris.

Leclant, Jean 1949: Nouveaux documents relatifs à l'an VI de Taharqa. *Kêmi* 10, 28–42.

—— 1954: *Enquête sur les sacerdoces et les sanctuaires égyptiens à l'époque dite 'éthiopienne' (XXVe dynastie).* *BdE* 17.

—— 1956: La 'mascarade' des boeufs gras et le triomphe de l'Égypte. *MDAIK* 14, 129–45.

—— 1957: Tefnout et les Divines Adoratrices thébaines. *MDAIK* 15, 166–71.

—— 1961a: *Mentouemhat, quatrième prophete d'Amon, prince de la ville.* *BdE* 35.

—— 1961b: Le voyage de Jean-Nicolas Huyot en Égypte (1818–1819) et les manuscrits de Nestor Lhôte. *BSFE* 32, 35–42.

—— 1961c: Sur un contrepoids de *menat* au nom de Taharqa: allaitement et 'apparition' royale. *BdE* 32, 251–84.

—— 1965: *Recherches sur les monuments thébains de la XXVe dynastie dite éthiopienne.* *BdE* 36.

—— 1969: Espace et temps, ordre et chaos dans l'Égypte pharaonique. *Revue de Synthèse* 55–6, 217–39.

—— 1978a: *Le temps des pyramides. De la Préhistoire aux Hyksos (1560 av. J.-C.).* Paris.

—— 1978b: L'exploration des côtes de la mer Rouge. À la quête de Pount et des secrets de la mer Erythrée. *Annales d'Éthiopie* 11, 69–75.

—— 1978c: Le nom de Chypre dans les textes hiéroglyphiques. *Colloques internationaux du CNRS no. 578, Salamine de Chypre. Histoire et archeologie*, 131–5.

—— 1979: *L'Empire des Conquérants. L'Égypte au Nouvel Empire (1560–1070)*. Paris.

—— 1980a: *L'Égypte du crépuscule. De Tanis à Meroë (1070 av. J.-C. – IVe siècle ap. J.-C.)*. Paris.

—— 1980b: *Égypte pharaonique et Afrique*. Paris.

—— 1980c: Les 'empires' et l'impérialisme de l'Égypte pharaonique. In M. Duverger (ed.), *Le concept d'Empire*. Paris: 49–68.

—— 1981a: The Empire of Kush: Napata and Meroe. In G. Mokhtar (ed.), *General History of Africa* II. Paris, London, Berkeley: 278–97.

—— 1981b: La 'famille libyenne' au temple haut de Pépi Ier. In J. Vercoutter (ed.), *Livre de Centenaire. MIFAO* 104, 49–54.

—— 1981c: Recherches récentes sur l'histoire de l'Égypte pharaonique. *REA* 83, 5–15.

—— 1984a: Textes de la Pyramide de Pépi Ier, VII: une nouvelle mention des *Fnhw* dans les *Textes des Pyramides*. *SAK* 11, 455–60.

—— 1984b: Taharqa à Sedeinga. In *Studien zu Sprache und Religion Ägyptens. Festschrift W. Westendorf*. Göttingen: 1113–17.

—— 1985: Recherches récentes sur les textes des Pyramides et les pyramides à textes de Saqqarah. *Bulletin de la Classe des Lettres et Sciences Morales et Politiques de l'Académie Royale de Belgique* 71, 295–305.

—— 1987: Le rayonnement de l'Égypte au temps des rois tanites et libyens. In *Tanis: L'or des pharaons*. Paris.

Leclant, Jean and Clerc, Gisèle 1967–88: Fouilles et travaux en Égypte et au Soudan. Annual reports in *Or*.

Lecorsu, France 1966: Une description inédite d'Abou Simbel: le manuscrit du Colonel Straton. *BSFE* 45, 19–32.

Lefebvre, Gustave 1927: Stèle de l'an V de Meneptah. *ASAE* 27, 19–30.

—— 1929a: *Histoire des grands prêtres d'Amon de Karnak jusqu'à la XXIe dynastie*. Paris.

—— 1929b: *Inscriptions concernant les grands prêtres d'Amon Romé-Roy et Amenhotep*. Paris.

—— 1940: Deux mots de la Ier dynastie, aux inscriptions du tombeau 'de Hemaka' a Saqqarah. *RdE* 4, 222–3.

—— 1951: Inscription dédicatoire de la chapelle funéraire de Ramsès I à Abydos. *ASAE* 51, 167–200.

—— 1976: *Romans et contes égyptiens de l'époque pharaonique. Traduction avec introduction, notices et commentaires*. Paris.

Legrain, Georges 1914: *Louqsor sans les pharaons. Légendes et chansons populaires de la Haute Égypte*. Paris and Brussels.

—— 1929: *Les temples de Karnak. Fragment du dernier ouvrage de G. Legrain, Directeur des travaux du Service des Antiquités de l'Égypte*. Paris and Brussels.

Lehner, Mark 1983: Some Observations on the Layout of the Khufu and Khafre

Pyramids. *JARCE* 20, 7–26.

—— 1985: *The Pyramid Tomb of Hetep-heres and the Satellite Pyramid of Khufu*. Mainz am Rhein.

—— 1986: The Giza Plateau Mapping Project. *NARCE* 131, 23–57.

Lello, G. 1978: Thutmose III's First Lunar Date. *JNES* 37, 327–30.

Lenzen, C. J. and Knauf, E. A. 1987: Notes on Syrian Toponyms in Egyptian Sources I. *GM* 96, 59–64.

Leprohon, Ronald J. 1983: Intef III and Amenemhat III at Elephantine. *Ancient World* 6, 103–7.

Lepsius, C. R. 1849–56: *Denkmäler aus Ägypten und Äthiopien*. . . . 12 vols. Leipzig.

Leroy, Christian 1975: Voyageurs et marins dans l'antiquité. *REG* 88, 178–81.

Leroy-Molinghen, A. 1985: Homère et Thèbes aux cent portes. *CdE* 60, 131–7.

Lesko, Leonard H. 1980: The Wars of Ramses III. *Serapis* 6, 83–6.

Letellier, Bernadette 1979: La cour à péristyle de Thoutmosis IV à Karnak (et la 'cour des fêtes' de Thoutmosis II). In J. Vercoutter (ed.), *Hommages Sauneron* I. *BdE* 81, 51–72.

Lévêque, Pierre (ed.) 1987: *Les premières civilisations I: Des despotismes orientaux à la cité grecque*. Paris.

Lexa, Frantisek 1925: *La magie dans l'Égypte ancienne, de l'Ancien Empire jusqu'à l'époque copte*. 3 vols. Paris.

—— 1926: *Papyrus Insinger. Les enseignements moraux d'un scribe égyptien du premier siècle apres J.-C*. . . . Paris.

Lichtheim, Miriam 1973: *Ancient Egyptian Literature. A Book of Readings I: The Old and Middle Kingdom*. Berkeley, CA.

—— 1976: *Ancient Egyptian Literature. A Book of Readings II: The New Kingdom*. Berkeley, CA.

—— 1980a: *Ancient Egyptian Literature. A Book of Readings III: The Late Period*. Berkeley, CA.

—— 1980b: Some Corrections to my *Ancient Egyptian Literature, I–III*. *GM* 41, 67–74.

—— 1983: *Late Egyptian Wisdom Literature in the International Context. A Study of Demotic Instructions*. OBO 52.

Limme, Luc 1972: Les oasis de Khargeh et Dakhleh d'après les documents égyptiens de l'époque pharaonique. *CRIPEL* 1, 41–58.

Lincoln, B. 1981: *Priests, Warriors and Cattle. A Study in the Ecology of Religions*. Berkeley, CA.

Lindblad, Ingegerd 1984: *Royal Sculpture of the Early Eighteenth Dynasty in Egypt. Medelhavsmuseet Memoir 5*. Stockholm.

Lipińska, Jadwiga 1967: Names and History of the Sanctuaries Built by Tuthmosis III at Deir el-Bahri. *JEA* 53, 25–33.

Lipke, P. 1984: *The Royal Ship of Cheops: A Retrospectival Account of the Discovery, Restoration, and Reconstruction*. Oxford.

Littauer, M. A. and Crouwel, J. H. 1979: *Wheeled Vehicles and Ridden Animals in the Ancient Near East*. Leiden.

Lloyd, Allan B. 1975: *Herodutus Book II.1: An Introduction*. Leiden.

—— 1976: *Herodotus Book II.2: Commentary 1–98*. Leiden.

—— 1982: The Inscription of Udjahorresnet: A Collaborator's Testament. *JEA* 68, 166–80.

Loeben, Christian E. 1986: Eine Bestattung der grossen königlichen Gemahlin Nofrete in Amarna? Die Totenfigur der Norfrete. *MDAIK* 42, 99–108.

Lohr, B. 1974: Ahanjati in Heliopolis. *GM* 11, 33–38.

Long, R. D. 1976: Ancient Egyptian Chronology, Radiocarbon Dating and Calibration. *ZÄS* 103, 30–48.

Lopez, Jesus 1973: L'auteur de l'*Enseignement pour Mérikarê*. *RdE* 25, 178–91.

Loprieno, Antonio 1981–2: Methodologische Anmerkungen zur Rolle der Dialekte in der ägyptischen Sprachentwicklung. *GM* 53, 75–95.

Lorent, J. A. 1861: *Égypten. Alhambra. Algier. Tlemsen. Reisebilder aus den Anfängen der Photographie*. Mannheim: 1985.

Lorton, David 1974a: *The Juridical Terminology of International Relations in Egyptian Texts Through Dyn. XVIII*. Baltimore.

—— 1974b: Terminology Related to the Laws of Warfare in Dynasty XVIII. *JARCE* 11, 53–68.

—— 1979: Towards a Constitutional Approach to Ancient Egyptian Kingship. *JAOS* 99, 460–5.

—— 1986a: Review of A. Nibbi, *Ancient Egypt and Some Eastern Neighbours, Ancient Babylon Reconsidered, Wenamun and Alashiya Reconsidered*. *DE* 6, 89–100.

—— 1986b: Terms of Coregency in the Middle Kingdom. *VA* 2, 113–20.

—— 1986c: The King and the Law. *VA* 2, 53–62.

—— 1987a: The Internal History of the Herakleopolitan Period. *DE* 7, 21–8.

—— 1987b: Egypt's Easternmost Delta Before the New Kingdom. *DE* 7, 9–12.

—— 1987c: Why 'Menes'? *VA* 3, 33–8.

Luckenbill, D. D. 1926: *Ancient Records of Assyria and Babylonia, I. Historical Records of Assyria*. Chicago.

Luft, Ulricht 1978: *Beiträge zur Historisierung der Götterwelt und der Mythenschreibung*. Stud. Aeg. 4.

—— 1982: Illahunstudien I: Zu der Chronologie und den Beamten in den Briefen aus Illahun. *Oikumene* 3, 101–56.

—— 1986a: Illahunstudien III: Zur Sozialen Stellung des Totenpriesters im Mittleren Reiches. *Oikumene* 5, 117–53.

—— 1986b: Noch einmal zum Ebers-Kalander. *GM* 92, 69–77.

—— 1987: Der Tagesbeginn in Ägypten. *AoF* 14, 3–11.

Lurie, I. 1971: *Studien zum altägyptischen Recht*. Weimar.

Macadam, M. F. L. 1949: *The Temples of Kawa I: The Inscriptions*. Oxford.

—— 1955: *The Temples of Kawa II: History and Archaeology of the Site*. Oxford.

Malaise, Michel 1981: Aton, le sceptre Ouas et la fête Sed. *GM* 50, 47–64.

Málek, Jaromir 1982: The Original Version of the Royal Canon of Turin. *JEA* 68, 93–106.

Malinine, Michel 1953: *Choix de textes juridiques en hiératique 'anormal' et en démotique (25ᵉ–27ᵉ dynasties) 1: Traduction et commentaire philologique*. Paris.

—— 1983: *Choix de textes juidiques en hiératique anormal et en demotique 2:*

Transcriptions. RAPH 18.

Manniche, Lise 1988: *Lost Tombs.* London.

Manuelian, Peter der 1983: Prologomena zur Untersuchung saïtischer 'Kopien'. *SAK* 10, 221–46.

—— 1987: *Studies in the Reign of Amenophis II. HÄB* 26.

Martin, Geoffrey T. 1976: La découverte du tombeau d'Horemheb à Saqqarah. *BSFE* 77–8, 11–25.

—— 1979: Queen Mutnodjmet at Memphis and El-Amarna. *L'égyptologie en 1979* II, 275–8.

—— 1984: *Corpus of Reliefs of the New Kingdom from the Memphite Necropolis and Lower Egypt.* London.

—— 1991: *The Hidden Tombs of Memphis.* London.

Martin, Maurice 1979: Souvenirs d'un compagnon de voyage de Paul Lucas en Égypte (1707). In J. Vercoutter (ed.), *Hommages Sauneron* II. *BdE* 82, 471–6.

Martin-Pardey, Éva 1988: *Untersuchungen zur ägyptischen Provinzialverwaltung bis zum Ende des Alten Reiches.* Hildesheim.

Mary, Sherry I. 1979: Kia, the Second Pharaoh. *L'égyptologie en 1979* II, 279–80.

Maspero, Gaston 1895: *Histoire ancienne des peuples de l'Orient Classique I: Les origins. Égypte & Chaldée.* Paris.

—— 1897: *Histoire ancienne des peuples de l'Orient Classique II: Les premières mêlées des peuples.* Paris.

—— 1899: *Histoire ancienne des peuples de l'Orient Classique III: Les Empires.* Paris.

—— 1914: Chansons populaires recueillies dans la Haute Égypte de 1900 à 1914 pendant les inspections du Service des Antiquités. *ASAE* 14, 97–290.

Masson, Olivier 1969: Les Cariens en Égypte. *BSFE* 56, 25–36.

—— 1971: Les Chypriotes en Égypte. *BSFE* 60, 28–46.

Mathieu, Bernard 1987: Le voyage de Platon en Égypte. *ASAE* 71, 153–67.

Matzker, I. 1986: *Die letzten Könige der 12. Dynastie.* Frankfurt.

Maury, Bernard 1979: Toponymie traditionnelle de l'ancienne piste joignant Kharga à Dakhla. In J. Vercoutter (ed.), *Hommages Sauneron* II. *BdE* 82, 365–76.

Mayer, L. 1802: *Vues en Égypte, d'après les dessins originaux en la possession de Sir R. Ainslee, pris durant son ambassade à Constantinople. . . .* London.

Maystre, Charles 1950: Le compte des épagomènes dans les chronologies individuelles. *RdE* 7, 85–8.

McFarlane, A. 1987: The First Nomarch at Akhmim: The Identification of a Sixth Dynasty Biographical Inscription. *GM* 100, 63–72.

McQuitty, W. 1976: *Island of Isis: Philae Temple of the Nile.* London.

Mattha, G. 1975: *The Demotic Legal Code of Hermopolis West. BdE* 45.

Meeks, Dimitri 1963: Les 'quatre *ka*' du demiurge memphite. *RdE* 15, 35–47.

—— 1971: Génies, anges et démons en Égypte. In *Génies, anges et démons. Sources Orientales* 8, 18–14.

—— n.d. Pureté et purification en Égypte. In *Dictionnaire de la Bible, Supplément* 9, col. 430–52.

Megally, Mounir 1977: *Recherches sur l'économie, l'administration et la comptabilité égyptienne à la XVIIIe dyn. d'après la pap. E 3226 du Louvre.* BdE 71.

Mekhitarian, Arpag 1978: *Egyptian Painting.* 2nd edn. London.

Mellaart, James 1965/78: *Earliest Civilizations of the Near East.* London.

Meltzer, Edward S. 1970: Archaic Sovereign as Primeval God? *ZÄS* 98, 84.

—— 1978: The Parentage of Tutʿankhamun and Smenkhareʿ. *JEA* 64, 134–5.

Menassa, Leïla and Laferrière, Pierre 1974: *La Sâqia. Technique et vocabulaire de la roue à eau égyptienne.* BdE 67.

Mendelssohn, K. 1973: A Building Disaster at the Meidum Pyramid. *JEA* 59, 60–71.

—— 1976: Reply to Mr C. J. Davey's Comments (*JEA* 62, 178–9). *JEA* 62, 179–81.

Menu, Bernadette 1970: *Le régime juridique des terres et du personnel attaché à la terre dans le Papyrus Wilbour.* Lille.

—— 1981: Considérations sur le droit pénal au Moyen Empire égyptien dans le P. Brooklyn 35.1446. *BIFAO du Centenaire,* 57–76.

—— 1982: *Recherches sur l'histoire juridique, économique et sociale de l'ancienne Égypte.* Versailles.

—— 1984: *Droit – économie – société de l'Égypte ancienne (Chronique bibliographique 1967–1982).* Versailles.

—— 1986: Les récits de créations en Égypte ancienne. *Foi et Vie* LXXXV/5, 67–77.

—— 1987a: *L'obélisque de la Concorde.* Versailles.

—— 1987b: Les cosmogonies de l'ancienne Égypte. In *La creation dans l'Orient ancien.* Paris.

Merkelbach, Reinholdt 1962: *Roman und Mysterium in der Antike.* Munich.

Mesnil du Buisson, C. du 1969: Le décor asiatique du couteau de Gebel el-Arak. *BIFAO* 68, 63–84.

Meulenaere, Herman de 1958a: *Herodotos over de 26ste dynastie.* Louvain.

—— 1958b: Le vizir Harsiêsis de la 30e dynastie. *MDAIK* 16, 230–6.

—— 1985: Les grands prêtres de Ptah à l'époque saïto-perse. In F. Geus and F. Thill (eds), *Mélanges offerts à Jean Vercoutter.* Paris: 263–6.

—— 1986: Un général du Delta, gouverneur de la Haute Égypte. *CdE* 61, 203–10.

Meyer, C. 1982: *Senenmut: Eine prosopographische Untersuchung.* Hamburg.

Meyer, Eduard 1973: *Fremdvölkerdarstellungen altägyptischer Denkmäler. Sammlung photographischer Aufnahmen aus den Jahren 1912–1913.* ÄMA 2.

Michalowski, Kazimierz 1968: *L'art de l'ancienne Égypte.* Paris.

—— 1980: Les contacts culturels dans le monde méditerranéen. In J. Vercoutter (ed.), *Livre du Centenaire.* MIFAO 104, 303–6.

Midant-Reynes, Béatrice 1986: L'industrie lithique en Égypte: à propos des fouilles de Balat (Oasis de Dakhla). *BSFE* 102, 27–39.

—— 1987: Contribution à l'étude de la société prédynastique: le cas du couteau 'Ripple-flake'. *SAK* 14, 185–224.

Millard, A. R. 1979: The Scythian Problem. In J. Ruffle et al. (eds), *Glimpses of*

Ancient Egypt. Studies in Honour of H. W. Fairman. Warminster: 119–22.

Millet, Nicholas B. 1981: Social and Political Organization in Meroe. *ZÄS* 108, 124–41.

Mills, Anthony J. 1975: Approach to Third Millenium Nubia. In *Études Nubiennes, colloque de Chantilly. BdE* 77, 199–204.

Minae, A. T. 1984: *Architecture as Environmental Communication. Approach to Semiotics* 69. Berlin.

Minutoli, H. von 1982: *Reise zum Tempel des Jupiter Ammon in der Libyschen Wuste und nach Ober-Ägypten in den Jahren 1820–1821.* Originally publ. 1824. Berlin.

Mohammed, M. Abd el-Qader 1966: The Hittite Provincial Administration of Conquered Territories. *ASAE* 59, 109–42.

Mokhtar, Mohamed Gamal el-Din 1983: *Ihnâsya el-Medina (Herakleopolis Magna): Its Importance and Its Role in Pharaonic Egypt. BdE* 40.

Mokhtar, Mohamed Gamal el-Din (ed.) 1981: *General History of Africa* II. Paris, London, Berkeley.

Monconys, Balthasar de 1973: *Le voyage en Egypte de Balthasar de Monconys [1646].* Cairo.

Monnet Saleh, Janine 1955: Un monument de la corégence des Divines Adoratrices Nitocris et Ankhenesneferibrê. *RdE* 10, 37–47.

—— 1965: Remarques sur la famille et les successeurs de Ramsès III. *BIFAO* 63, 209–36.

—— 1969: Forteresses ou villages protégés thinites? *BIFAO* 67, 173–88.

—— 1980: Égypte et Nubbie antique: approche d'une colonisation. *BSEG* 3, 39–49.

—— 1983: Les représentations de temples sur plates-formes à pieux de la poterie gerzéenne d'Égypte. *BIFAO* 83, 263–9.

—— 1986: Interprétation globale des documents concernant l'unification de l'Égypte. *BIFAO* 86, 227–38.

—— 1987: Remarques sur les représentations de la peinture d'Hiérakonpolis (Tombe No. 100). *JEA* 73, 51–8.

Montenat, C. 1986: Un aperçu des industries préhistoriques du golfe de Suez et du littoral égyptien de la Mer Rouge. *BIFAO* 86, 239–56.

Montet, Pierre 1925: *Les scènes de la vie privée dans les tombeaux égyptiens de l'Ancien Empire.* Paris.

—— 1946: *La vie quotidienne en Égypte au temps des Ramsès.* Paris.

—— 1947: *La nécropole royale de Tanis I: Les constructions et le tombeau d'Osorkon II à Tanis.* Paris.

—— 1951a: *La nécropole royale de Tanis II: Les constructions et le tombeau de Psousennès à Tanis.* Paris.

—— 1951b: Le roi Ougaf à Médamoud. *RdE* 8, 163–70.

—— 1952: *Les énigmes de Tanis. Douze années de fouilles dans une capitale oubliée du delta égyptien.* Paris.

—— 1956: *Isis. Ou à la recherche de l'Égypte ensevelie.* Paris.

—— 1957: Le tombeau d'Ousirmare Chechanq fils de Bastit (Chechanq III) à Tanis. *BSFE* 23, 7–13.

—— 1960: *La nécropole royale de Tanis III: Les constructions et le tombeau de*

Chéchanq III à Tanis. Paris.

—— 1962: La date du sphinx A 23 du Louvre. *BSFE* 33, 6–8.

—— 1984: *Vies des pharaons illustres.* Paris.

Morenz, Siegfried 1962: *La religion égyptienne, essai d'interpretation.* Paris.

—— 1971: Traditionen um Cheops. Beiträge, zur uberlieferungsgeschichtlichen Methode in der Ägyptologie, I. *ZÄS* 97, 111–18.

—— 1972: Traditionen um Menes. Beiträge zur uberlieferungsgeschichtlichen Methode in der Ägyptologie, II. *ZÄS* 99, 10–16.

Moret, Alexandre 1901: Le titre 'Horus d'Or' dans le protocole pharaonique. *RT* 23, 23–32.

—— 1903: *Du caractère religieux la royauté pharaonique.* Paris.

—— 1923: *Des clans aux empires.* Paris.

—— 1925: La compagne de Séti Ier au nord du Carmel d'après les fouilles de M. Fischer. *Revue de l'Égypte Ancienne* I, 18–30.

—— 1926: *Le Nil et la civilisation égyptienne.* Paris.

—— 1927: *La mise à mort du dieu en Égypte.* Paris.

Morisson, Anthoine 1976: *Le voyage en Égypte d'Anthoine Morisson [1697].* Cairo.

Morkot, R. G. 1986: Violent Images of Queenship and the Royal Cult. *Wepwawet* 1, 1–9.

—— 1987: Studies in New Kingdom Nubia 1. Politics, Economics and Ideology: Egyptian Imperialism in Nubia. *Wepwawet* 3, 29–49.

Moscati, S. 1963: *Historical Art in the Ancient Near East.* Rome.

Moscati, S. (ed.) 1988: *I Fenici.* Venice.

Moursi, Mohamed I. 1972: *Die Hohenpriester des Sonnengottes von der Frühzeit Ägyptens bis zum Ende des Neuen Reiches.* MÄS 26.

—— 1983: Corpus der Mnevis-Stelen und Untersuchungen zum Kult der Mnevis-Stiere in Heliopolis. *SAK* 10, 247–68.

Moussa, Ahmed Mahmoud 1981: A Stela of Taharqa from the Desert Road at Dahshur. *MDAIK* 37, 331–8.

Moussa, Ahmed Mahmoud and Altenmüller, H. 1975: Ein Denkmal zum Kult des Königs Unas am Ende der 12. Dynastie. *MDAIK* 31, 93–7.

Mrsich, T. 1968: *Untersuchungen zur Hausurkunde des Alten Reiches. Ein Beitrag zum ägyptischen Stiftungsrecht.* MÄS 13.

Müller, Ingeborg 1977: Der Vizekönig Merimose. In E. Endesfelder et al. (eds), *Ägypten und Kusch.* Schr. Or. 13, 325–30.

Müller, Maya 1979: Die Darstellung der Königfamilie in Amarna. *L'égyptologie en 1979* II, 281–4.

—— 1986: Zum Werkvarfahren an thebanischen Grabwänden des Neuen Reiches. *SAK* 13, 149–64.

Müller-Wollermann, Renate 1983: Bemerkungen zu den sogenannten Tributen. *GM* 66, 81–93.

Munier, Henri and Wiet, Gaston 1932: *Précis de l'histoire d'Égypte II: L'Égypte byzantine et musulmane.* Cairo.

Munro, Irmtraut 1986: Zusammenstellung von Datierungskriterien für Inschriften der Amarna-Zeit nach J. J. Perepelkin *Die Revolution Amenophis' IV. GM* 94, 81–7.

—— 1988: Zum Kult des Ahmose in Abydos. Ein weiterer Beleg aus der Ramessidenzeit. *GM* 101, 57–62.

Munro, Peter 1978: Der König als Kind. *SAK* 6, 131–7.

—— 1984: Die Nacht vor der Thronbesteigung. Zum ältesten Teil des Mundöffnungsrituals. In *Studien zu Sprache und Religion Ägyptens, Festschrift W. Westendorf.* Göttingen: 907–28.

—— 1987: Review of Y. Y. Perepelkin, *The Revolution of Amenhotep IV. BiOr* 44, 137–43.

Munro-Hay, S. C. 1982–3: Kings and Kingdoms of Nubia. *RSO* 29, 87–138.

Münster, M. 1968: *Untersuchungen zur Göttin Isis vom Alten Reich bis zum Ende des Neuen Reiches. MÄS* 11.

Murnane, William J. 1970: The Hypothetical Coregency Between Amenhotep III and Akhenaten: Two Observations: *Serapis* 2, 17–21.

—— 1975–6: The Accession Date of Sethos I. *Serapis* 3, 23–34.

—— 1976: The Earlier Reign of Ramesses II: Two Addenda. *GM* 19, 41–44.

—— 1977: *Ancient Egyptian Coregencies. SAOC* 40.

—— 1980a: *United with Eternity: A Concise Guide to the Monuments of Medinet Habu.* Chicago and Cairo.

—— 1980b: Unpublished Fragments of Hatshepsut's Historical Inscription from Her Sanctuary at Karnak. *Serapis* 6, 91–102.

—— 1981a: In Defense of the Middle Kingdom Double Dates. *BES* 3, 73–81.

—— 1981b: The Sed Festival: A Problem in Historical Method. *MDAIK* 37, 369–76.

—— 1985a: *The Road to Kadesh: Historical Interpretation of the Battle Reliefs of King Sety I at Karnak. SAOK* 42.

—— 1985b: Tutankhamun on the Eighth Pylon at Karnak. *VA* 1, 59–68.

Muszynski, Michel 1977: Les 'associations religieuses' en Égypte, d'après les sources hiéroglyphiques, démotiques et grecques. *OLP* 8, 145–74.

Mysliwiec, Carol 1978: Le naos de Pithom. *BIFAO* 78, 171–96.

—— 1979: Amon, Atoum and Aton: The Evolution of Heliopolitan Influences in Thebes. *L'égyptologie en 1979* II, 285–90.

—— 1985: *XVIIIth Dynasty Before the Amarna Period. Iconography of Religions* 16/5. Leiden.

NaʿAman, Nadav 1982: The Town of Ibirta and the Relations of the 'Apiru and the Shosou'. *GM* 57, 27–34.

—— 1983: The Town of Malahu. *GM* 63, 46–52.

Naville, Édouard 1903: La pierre de Palerme. *RT* 25, 64–81.

—— 1930: *Details releves dans les ruines de quelques temples égyptiens.* Paris.

Neher, A. 1956: *Moïse et la vacation juive.* Paris.

Nibbi, Alessandra 1974: Further Remarks on *w3d-wr*, Sea Peoples and Keftiu. *GM* 10, 35–40.

—— 1975a: *Ym* and the Wadi Tumilat. *GM* 15, 35–8.

—— 1975b: The Wadi Tumilat, Atika and *mw-qd. GM* 16, 33–8.

—— 1975c: Henu of the Eleventh Dynasty and *w3d-wr. GM* 17, 39–44.

—— 1976a: Remarks on the Two Stelae from the Wadi Gasus. *JEA* 62, 45–56.

—— 1976b: *ḫbsḏ* from the Sinai. *GM* 19, 45–8.

—— 1976c: A Further Note on *ḫbsꜣ. GM* 20, 37–9.

—— 1976d: *ḥbsḏ* Again. *GM* 22, 51–2.

—— 1979a: Some Rapidly Disappearing and Unrecorded Sites in the Eastern Delta. *GM* 35, 41–6.

—— 1979b: Some Evidence from Scientists Indicating the Vegetation of Lower and Middle Egypt During the Pharaonic Period. *L'égyptologie en 1979* I, 247–54.

—— 1979c: The 'Trees and Towns' Palette. *ASAE* 63, 143–54.

—— 1981: The Hieroglyph Signs *gs* and *km* and their Relationship. *GM* 52, 43–54.

—— 1981–2: The *nhsy. w* of the Dahsur Decree of Pepi I. *GM* 53, 27–32.

—— 1982a: A Note on the *Lexikon* Entry: Meer. *GM* 58, 53–8.

—— 1982b: The Chief Obstacle to Understanding the Wars of Ramesses III. *GM* 59, 51–60.

—— 1982c: Egitto e Bibbia sulla base della stele de Piankhi. *Liber Annuus* 39, 7–58.

—— 1983: A Further Note on the *km* Hieroglyph. *GM* 63, 77–80.

—— 1984: The Sea Peoples: Some Problems Concerning Historical Method. *Terra Antiqua Balcanica* II. *Annales de l'Université de Sofia* 77/2, 310–19.

—— 1985: The Lebanon (sic) and Djahy in the Egyptian Texts. *DE* 1, 17–26.

—— 1986a: Hatiba of Alashiya and a Correction to My Proposed Area for that Country. *DE* 5, 47–54.

—— 1986b: *Lapwings and Libyans in Ancient Egypt*. Oxford.

—— 1988: Byblos (sic) and Wenamun: a Reply to Some Recent Unrealistic Criticism. *DE* 11, 31–42.

Niccacci, Alviero 1977: Il messagio de Tefnakht. *Liver Annuus* 27, 213–28.

Nims, Charles F. 1973: The Transition from the Traditional to the New Style of Wall Relief under Amenhotep IV. *JNES* 32, 181–7.

Niwinski, Andrzej 1984a: Three More Remarks in the Discussion of the History of the Twenty-First Dynasty. *BES* 6, 81–8.

—— 1984b: The Bab El-Gusus Tomb and the Royal Cache in Deir el-Bahri. *JEA* 70, 73–81.

—— 1985: Zur Datierung und Herkunft der altägyptischen Särge. *BiOr* 42, 508–25.

Noth, M. 1938: Die Wege des Pharaonenheeres in Palästina und Syrien. *ZDPV* 61, 26–65.

—— 1943: Die Annalen Thutmose III. als Geschichtsquelle. *ZDPV* 66, 156–74.

Ockinga, Boyo 1983: Zum Fortleben des 'Amarna-Loyalismus' in der Ramessidenzeit. *WdO* 14, 207–15.

—— 1987: On the Interpretation of the Kadesh Record. *CdE* 62, 38–48.

O'Connor, David 1984: Kerma and Egypt: The Significance of the Monumental Buildings, Kerma I, II, and XI. *JARCE* 31, 65–108.

—— 1985: The Chronology of Scarabs of the Middle Kingdom and the Second Intermediate Period. *JSSEA* 15, 1–41.

—— 1986: The Locations of Yam and Kush and their Historical Implications. *JARCE* 23, 27–50.

—— 1987: The Location of Irem. *JEA* 73, 99–136.

O'Mara, Patrick 1985a: *Some Indirect Sothic and Lunar Dates from the Late Middle Kingdom in Egypt.* Cambria, CA.

—— 1985b: *Additional Unlabeled Lunar Dates from the Old Kingdom in Egypt.* Cambria, CA.

—— 1986a: Is the Cairo Stone a Fake? An Example of Proof by Default. *DE* 4, 33–40.

—— 1986b: Historiographies (Ancient and Modern) of the Archaic Period. Part I: Should We Examine the Foundations? A Revisionist Approach. *DE* 6, 33–46.

—— 1987: Historiographies (Ancient and Modern) of the Archaic Period. Part II: Resolving the Palermo Stone as a Rational Structure. *DE* 7, 37–50.

—— 1988: Was the Sed Festival Periodic in Early Egyptian History? (I). *DE* 11, 21–30.

Onasch, Christian 1977: Kusch in der Sicht von Ägyptern und Griechen. In E. Endesfelder et al. (eds), *Ägypten und Kusch. Schr. Or.* 13, 331–6.

Osing, Jurgen 1977: Zur Korregenz Amenophis III.–Amenophis IV. *GM* 26, 53–4.

—— 1978: Zu einigen ägyptischen Namen in keilschriftlicher Umschreibung. *GM* 27, 37–42.

—— 1979: Zu einer Fremdvölkerliste Ramses' II. in Karnak. *GM* 36, 37–9.

—— 1980: Zum ägyptischen Namen für Zypern. *GM* 40, 45–52.

—— 1981: Zu einer Fremdvölker-Kachel aus Medinet Habu. *MDAIK* 37, 389–92.

—— 1982: Strukturen in Fremdländerlisten. *JEA* 68, 77–80.

—— 1986: Notizen zu den Oasen Charga und Dachla. *GM* 92, 79–85.

Otto, Eberhardt 1954: *Die biographischen Inschriften der ägyptischen Spätzeit. Ihr geistgeschichtliche und litterarische Bedeutung.* Leiden.

—— 1956: Prolegomena zur Frage der Gesetzgebung und Rechtssprechung in Ägypten. *MDAIK* 14, 150–9.

—— 1957: Zwei Bemerkungen zum Königskult der Spätzeit. *MDAIK* 15, 193–207.

—— 1958: *Das Verhältnis von Rite und Mythus im ägyptischen.* SHAW 1958/1.

—— 1960: Der Gebrauch des Königstitel *bitj.* *ZÄS* 85, 143–52.

—— 1964: *Gott und Mensch, nach den ägyptischen Tempelinschriften der griechischen-römischen Zeit. Eine Untersuchung zur Phraseologie....* *ADAW* 1964/1.

—— 1966: Geschichtsbild und Geschichtsschreibung in Ägypten. *WdO* 3, 161–76.

—— 1969a: *Wesen und Wandel der altägyptischen Kultur.* Berlin and Heidelberg.

—— 1969b: Ligitimation des Herrschers im pharaonischen Ägypten. *Saeculum* 20, 385–411.

—— 1969c: Das 'goldene Zeitalter' in einem ägyptischen Text. In *Religions en Égypte hellénistique et romaine.* Paris: 93–108.

—— 1970: Weltanschauliche und politische Tendenzschriften. *HdO* I, 139–47.

—— 1971: Gott als Retter Ägyptens. In *Tradition und Glaube. Das frühe*

Christentum in seiner Umwelt. Göttingen: 9–22.

—— 1979: Israel under the Assyrians. In M. T. Larsen (ed.), *Power and Propaganda. Mesopotamia* 7, 251–62.

Padro I Parcerisa, J. 1987: Le rôle de l'Égypte dans les relations commerciales d'Orient et d'Occident au Premier Millénaire. *ASAE* 71, 213–22.

Padro I Parcerisa, J. and F. Molina 1986: Un vase de l'époque des Hyksos trouvé à Almunecar (province de Grenade, Espagne). In *Hommages à François Daumas* 2, 517–24.

Palanque, C. 1903: *Le Nil à l'époque pharaonique. Son rôle et son culte en Égypte*. Paris.

Palerne, Jean 1971: *Le voyage en Égypte de Jean Palerne, Forésien [1581]*. Cairo.

Pantalacci, Laure 1985: Un décret de Pépi II en faveur des gouverneurs de l'oasis de Dakhla. *BIFAO* 85, 245–54.

Parant, Robert 1974: Recherches sur le droit pénal égyptien. Intention coupable et responsabilité pénale. In *Le Droit égyptien ancien*. Brussels: 25–55.

—— 1982: *L'affaire Sinouhé. Tentative d'approache de la justice répressive égyptienne au début du II millénaire avant J.-C.*. Aurillac.

Paris. 1967: *Toutankhamon et son temps*. Petit Palais.

—— 1976: *Ramsès le Grand*. Galeries Nationales du Grand Palais.

—— 1982: *Naissance de l'Écriture. Cunéiformes et hiéroglyphes*. Galeries Nationales du Grand Palais.

—— 1988: *Les premiers hommes au pays de la Bible. Préhistoire en Israël*. CNRS-DGRCST.

Parker, Richard A. 1952: Sothic Dates and Calendar 'Adjustment'. *RdE* 9, 101–8.

—— 1957a: The Length of Reign of Ramesses X. *RdE* 11, 163–4.

—— 1957b: The Length of Reign of Amasis and the Beginning of the Twenty-sixth Synasty. *MDAIK* 15, 208–12.

—— 1970: The Beginning of the Lunar Month in Ancient Egypt. *JNES* 29, 217–20.

Parker, Richard A., Leclant, J. and Goyon, J.-C. 1979: *The Edifice of Taharqa by the Sacred Lake of Karnak. BES* 8.

Parthey, G. 1858: *Ägypten beim Geographen von Ravenna*. Berlin.

Paulissen, E., van Vermeersch, P. and Neer, W. 1985: Late Palaeolithic Sites at Qena. *NA* 26, 7–13.

Peet, T. E. 1930: *The Great Tomb-Robberies of the Twentieth Egyptian Dynasty*. Oxford.

Perdu, Olivier 1977: Khenemet-nefer-hedjet: une princesse et deux reines du Moyen Empire. *RdE* 29, 68–85.

—— 1985: Le monument de Samtoutefnakht à Naples (première partie). *RdE* 36, 89–113.

—— 1986: Stèles royales de la XXVIe dynastie. *BSFE* 105, 23–38.

Peremans, W. and Van't Dack, E. 1986: À propos d'une prosopographie de l'Égypte basée sur les sources démotiques. *Enchoria* 14, 79–86.

Perepelkin, J. J. 1983: *Privateigentum in der Vorstellung des ägyptischen Alten Reiches*. Tübingen.

Pestman, P. W. 1974: Le démotique comme langue juridique. In *Le Droit égyptien ancien*. Brussels: 75–85.

—— 1977: *Recueil de textes démotiques et bilingues*. Leiden.

—— 1982: The 'Last Will of Naunakhte' and the Accession Date of Ramesses V. In R. J. Demarée and J. J. Janssen (eds), *Gleanings from Deir el-Medina*. Leiden: 173–82.

—— 1984: Remarks on the Legal Manual of Hermopolis: A Review Article. *Enchoria* 12, 33–42.

Petrie, W. M. F. 1974: *Illahun, Kahun and Gurob*. Originally publ. 1891. London.

—— 1953: *Ceremonial Slate Palettes*. BSEA 66.

Piankoff, Alexandre 1948: Le nom du roi Sethos en égyptien. *BIFAO* 47, 175–7.

—— 1959: Les tombeaux de la Vallée des Rois avant et après l'hérésie amarnienne. *BSFE* 28–9, 7–14.

—— 1964: Les grandes compositions religieuses du Nouvel Empire et la reforme d'Amarna. *BIFAO* 62, 207–18.

Pickavance, Kathleen M. 1981: The Pyramids of Snofru at Dahshûr: Three Seventeenth-Century Travellers. *JEA* 67, 136–42.

Pirenne, Jacques 1962: La théorie des trois cycles de l'histoire égyptienne antique. *BSFE* 34–5, 11–12.

—— 1972: La population égyptienne a-t-elle participé à l'administration locale? *RdE* 24, 136–41.

Pirenne, Jacques and Théodoridès, Aristides 1966: *Droit égyptien, introduction bibliographique à l'histoire du Droit et à l'ethnologie juridique*. Brussels.

Pococke, R. 1743–5: *A Description of the East and Some Other Countries*. 2 vols. London.

Pohl, A. 1957: Einige Gedanken zur ḫabiru-Frage. *WZKM* 54, 157–60.

Polacek, Adalbert 1974: Le décret d'Horemheb à Karnak: essai d'analyse socio-juridique. In *Le Droit égyptien ancien*. Brussels: 87–111.

Posener, Georges 1934a: À propos de la stèle de Bentresh. *BIFAO* 34, 75–81.

—— 1934b: Notes sur la stèle de Naucratis. *ASAE* 34, 143–8.

—— 1940: *Princes et pays d'Asie et de Nubie*. Brussels.

—— 1947: Les douanes de la Méditerranée dans l'Égypte saïte. *Revue de Philologie* 21, 117–31.

—— 1957: Les Asiatiques en Égypte sous les XIIe et XIIIe dynasties. *Syria* 34, 145–63.

—— 1960: *De la divinité du pharaon*. Cahiers de la Societe Asiatique 15.

—— 1969a: *Littérature et politique dans l'Égypte de la XIIe dynastie*. Paris.

—— 1969b: Achoris. *RdE* 21, 148–50.

—— 1974: *Mwḳd* V. GM 11, 39–40.

—— 1976: *L'enseignement loyaliste. Sagesse égyptienne du Moyen Empire*. Paris.

—— 1977: L'or de Pount. *Ägypten und Kusch*. Schr. Or. 13, 337–42.

—— 1980: *La première domination perse en Égypte, recueil d'inscriptions hiéroglyphiques*. BdE 11. Originally publ. 1936. Cairo.

—— 1986: Du nouveau sur Kombabos. *RdE* 37, 91–6.

Posener, G., Sauneron, S. and Yoyotte, J. 1962: *Dictionary of Egyptian Civilisation*. London.

Posener-Kriéger, Paule 1976: *Les archives du temple funéraire de Néferirkarê-Kakaï (les papyrus d'Abousir)*. BdE 65.

Preáux, Claire 1978: *Le monde hellénistique, la Grece et l'Orient (323–146 av. J.-C.)*. Paris.

Priese, Karl-Heinz 1970a: Der Beginn der kuschitischen Herrschaft in Ägypten. *ZÄS* 98, 16–32.

—— 1970b: Zur Sprache der ägyptischen Inschriften der Könige von Kusch. *ZÄS* 98, 99–124.

—— 1973: Zur Entstehung der meriotischen Schrift. *Meroitica* 1, 273–306.

Pritchard, James B. 1955: *Ancient Near Eastern Texts Relating to the Old Testament*. Princeton.

Quaegebeur, Jan 1975: *Le dieu égyptien Shaï dans la religion et l'onomastique*. OLA 2.

—— 1986: Aménophis, nom royal et nom divin: questions méthodologiques. *RdE* 37, 97–106.

Quezel, P. and Babero. M. 1988: *Carte de la végétation potentielle de la region méditerranéenne 1: Méditerranée orientale*. Paris.

Quirke, S. 1986: The Regular Titles of the Late Middle Kingdom. *RdE* 37, 107–30.

—— 1990: *The Administration of Egypt in the Late Middle Kingdom: the Hieratic Documents*. New Malden.

Radwan, Ali 1975: Der Königsname. *SAK* 2, 213–34.

—— 1981: Zwei Stelen aus dem 47. Jahre Thutmosis' III. *MDAIK* 37, 403–8.

—— 1983: *Die Kupfer- und Bronzegafässe Ägyptens. Von den Anfängen bis zum Beginn der Spätzeit*. Munich.

Ragab, H. 1980: *Le papyrus*. Cairo.

Rainey, Anson F. 1976: Taharqa and Syntax. *Tel Aviv* 3, 38–41.

Ranke, Hermann 1932: Istar als Heilgöttin in Ägypten. In S. R. K. Glanville (ed.), *Studies Griffith*. Oxford: 412–18.

—— 1936: *The Art of Ancient Egypt: Architecture, Sculpture, Painting, Applied Art*. Vienna.

Ratié, Suzanne 1979: *La reine Hatchepsout. Sources et problèmes*. Leiden.

—— 1980: Attributs et destinée de la princesse Neferuré. *BSEG* 4, 77–82.

—— 1986: Quelques problèmes soulevés par la persécution de Toutankhamon. In *Hommages à François Daumas* 2. Montpellier: 545–50.

Raven, Maarten J. 1982: The 30th Dynasty Nespamedu Family. *OMRO* 61, 19–32.

—— 1983: Wax in Egyptian Magic and Symbolism. *OMRO* 64, 7–47.

Ray, John D. 1974: Pharaoh Nechepso. *JEA* 60, 255–6.

—— 1982: The Carian Inscriptions from Egypt. *JEA* 68, 181–98.

—— 1986: Psammuthis and Hakoris. *JEA* 72, 149–58.

Redford, Donald B. 1967a: *History and Chronology of the Eighteenth Dynasty of Egypt. Seven Studies*. Toronto.

—— 1967b: The Father of Khnumhotpe II of Beni Hasan. *JEA* 53, 158–9.

—— 1971: The Earliest Years of Ramesses II, and the Building of the

Ramesside Court at Luxor. *JEA* 57, 110–19.

—— 1972: Studies in Relations Between Palestine and Egypt During the First Millenium B. C. I: The Taxation System of Solomon. In *Story of the Ancient Palestinian World*, 141–56.

—— 1979a: The Historical Retrospective at the Beginning of Thutmose III's Annals. *ÄAT* 1, 338–42.

—— 1979b: The Historiography of Ancient Egypt. In K. Weeks (ed.), *Egyptology and the Social Sciences*. Cairo: 3–20.

—— 1983: Notes on the History of Ancient Buto. *BES* 5, 67–94.

—— 1984a: *Akhenaten: The Heretic King*. Princeton.

—— 1984b: The Meaning and Use of the Term *gnwt* 'Annals'. In *Studien zu Sprache und Religion Ägyptens. Festschrift W. Westendorf*. Göttingen: 327–41.

—— 1985: Saïs and the Kushite Invasions of the Eight Century B.C. *JARCE* 22, 5–15.

—— 1986a: Egypt and Western Asia in the Old Kingdom. *JARCE* 23, 125–43.

—— 1986b: New Light on Temple J at Karnak. *Or* 55, 1–15.

—— 1986c: *Pharaonic King-lists, Annals and Day-books. A Contribution to the Study of Egyptian Sense of History*. Toronto.

Reeves, C. N. 1978: A Further Occurence of Nefertiti as *ḥmt nsw ʿ3t. GM* 30, 61–70.

—— 1979: A Fragment of Fifth Dynasty Annals at University College, London. *GM* 32, 47–52.

—— 1981a: The Tomb of Tuthmosis IV: Two Questionable Attributions. *GM* 44, 49–56.

—— 1981b: A Reappraisal of Tomb 55 in the Valley of the Kings. *JEA* 67, 48–55.

—— 1982a: Akhenaten After All? *GM* 54, 61–72.

—— 1982b: Tuthmosis IV as 'Great-Grandfather' of Tut'ankhamun. *GM* 56, 65–70.

Reinecke, Walter Friedrich 1977: Ein Nubienfeldzug unter Königin Hatschepsut. In E. Endesfelder et al. (eds), *Ägypten und Kusch. Schr. Or.* 13, 369–76.

—— 1979: Die mathematischen Kenntnisse der ägyptischen Verwaltungsbeamten. *L'égyptologie en 1979* II, 159–66.

Reiser, E. 1972: *Der königliche Harim im alten Ägypten und seine Verwaltung*. Vienna.

Reymond, E. A. E. 1986: The King's Effigy. In *Hommages à François Daumas* 2. Montpellier: 551–7.

Richards, J. and Ryan, N. 1985: *Data Processing in Archaeology*. Cambridge.

Ridley, R. T. 1983: The Discovery of the Pyramid Texts. *ZÄS* 110, 74–80.

Riedel, Oskar M. 1981: Das Transportproblem beim Bau der grossen Pyramiden. *GM* 52, 67–74.

—— 1981–2: Nachtrag zu: 'Das Transportproblem beim Bau der grossen Pyramiden' aus Heft 52. *GM* 53, 47–50.

—— 1985: *Der Pyramidenbau und seine Transportprobleme. Die Maschinen des Herodots*. Vienna.

Riederer, Josef 1987: Die chemische Analyse in der archäologischen Forschung. *GM* 100, 91–5.

Ries, Julien 1986: *Théologies royales en Égypte et au Proche-Orient ancien et hellénisation des cultes orientaux.* Louvain.

Rinaldi, C. 1983: *Le piramidi. Un' indagine sulle tecniche costrottive.* Milan.

Ritner, Robert K. 1980: Khababash and the Satrap Stele: A Grammatical Rejoinder. *ZÄS* 107, 135–7.

Rizkana, Ibrahim and Seeher, Jurgen 1984: New Light on the Relation of Maadi to the Upper Egyptian Cultural Sequence. *MDAIK* 40, 237–52.

—— 1985: The Chippped Stones at Maadi. Preliminary Reassessment of a Predynastic Industry and its Long-Distance Relations. *MDAIK* 41, 235–55.

—— 1988: *Maadi II. The Lithic Industries of the Predynastic Settlement. AV* 65.

Rizqallah, F. and Rizqallah, K. 1978: *La préparation du pain dans un village du Delta égyptien (province de Charqia). BdE* 76.

Roberts, David 1946–9: *Egypt and Nubia.* London.

Robins, Gay 1978: Amenhotep I and the Child Amenemhat. *GM* 30, 71–6.

—— 1981a: The Value of the Estimated Ages of the Royal Mummies at Death as Historical Evidence. *GM* 45, 63–8.

—— 1981b: ḥmt nsw wrt Meritaton. *GM* 52, 75–82.

—— 1982a: Ahhotpe I, II and III. *GM* 56, 71–8.

—— 1982b: Meritamun, Daughter of Ahmose, and Meritamun, Daughter of Thutmose III. *GM* 56, 79–88.

—— 1982c: *S3t nsw nt ḫt.f Tj'3. GM* 57, 55–6.

—— 1983: A Critical Examination of the Theory that the Right to the Throne of Ancient Egypt Passed Through the Female Line in the 18th Dynasty. *GM* 62, 67–78.

—— 1987: The Role of the Royal Family in the 18th Dynasty Up to the Reign of Amenhotpe III, 2: Royal Children. *Wepwawet* 3, 15–17.

—— 1988: Ancient Egyptian Sexuality. *DE* 11, 61–72.

Robins, G. and Shute, C. C. D. 1985: Wisdom from Egypt and Greece. *DE* 1, 35–42.

—— 1987: *The Rhind Mathematical Papyrus. An Ancient Egyptian Text.* London.

Rocatti, Alessandro 1982: *La littérature historique sous l'Ancien Empire égyptien.* Paris.

—— 1984: Les papyrus de Turin. *BSFE* 99, 9–27.

—— n.d.: *Il Museo Egizio di Torino.* Rome.

Rocatti, Alessandro (ed.) 1987: *La Magia in Egitto.* Milan.

Rocchetta, A. 1974: *Voyages en Égypte des Années 1597–1601.* Paris.

Rocco, D. 1982: Los Habiru. Nuevos enfoques para un viejo problema. *RIHAO* 6, 113–24.

Roeder, Gunther 1926: Ramses II. als Gott. Nach den Hildesheimer Denkstein aus Horbêt. *ZÄS* 61, 57–67.

—— 1956: Amarna-Blöcke aus Hermopolis. *MDAIK* 14, 160–74.

—— 1959: *Die ägyptische Götterwelt.* Zurich and Stuttgart.

—— 1960a: *Mythen und Legenden um ägyptische Gottheiten und Pharaonen.*

Zurich and Stuttgart.

—— 1960b: *Kulte, Orakel und Naturverehrung im alten Ägypten*. Zurich und Stuttgart.

Römer, M. 1975: Bemerkungen zum Argumentationsgang von Erik Hornung 'Der Eine und die Vielen'. *GM* 17, 47–66.

Rössler-Köhler, Ursula 1984: Der König als Kind, Königsname und Maat-Opfer. Einige Überlegungen zu unterschiedlichen Materialen. In *Studien zu Sprache und Religion Ägyptens. Festschrift W. Westendorf*. Göttingen: 929–45.

Rössler-Köhler, Ursula and Kurth, D. 1988: *Zur Archäologie des 12. oberägyptischen Gaues. Bericht über zwei Surveys der Jahre 1980 und 1981*. Wiesbaden.

Romano, James F. 1983: A Relief of King Ahmose and Early Eighteenth Century Archaism. *BES* 5, 103–11.

—— 1985: Review of I. Lindbad, *Royal Sculpture of the Early 18th Dynasty*. *BiOr* 42, 614–19.

Romano, J. F. and von Bothmer, D. 1979: *The Luxor Museum of Ancient Egyptian Art: Catalogue*. Cairo.

Romer, John 1974: Tuthmosis I and Bîban el-Molûk: Some Problems of Attribution. *JEA* 60, 119–33.

—— 1984: *Ancient Lives: The Story of the Pharaohs' Tombmakers*. London.

Rose, J. 1985: 'The Songs of Re'. *Cartouches of the Kings of Egypt*. Warrington.

Rosenvasser, Abraham 1972: The Stele Aksha 505 and the Cult of Ramesses II as a God in the Army. *RIHAO* 1, 99–114.

—— 1978: La estela del ano 400. *RIHAO* 4, 63–85.

Roth, Ann Macy 1977–8: Ahhotep I and Ahhotep II. *Serapis* 4, 31–40.

Rousseau, Jean 1988: Les calendriers de Djoser. *DE* 11, 73–86.

Roux, Georges 1985: *La Mésopotamie. Essai d'histoire politique, économique et culturelle*. Paris.

Ruffle, John et al. (eds) 1979: *Glimpses of Ancient Egypt. Studies in Honour of H. W. Fairman*. Warminster.

Rühlmann, Gerhard 1971: Deine Feinde fallen unter deinen Sohlen: Bemerkungen zu einem altorientalischen Machtsymbol. *WZU Halle* 20, 61–84.

Russmann, Edna R. 1974: *The Representation of the King, XXVth Dynasty*. Brussels.

—— 1979: Some Reflections on the Regalia of the Kushite Kings of Egypt. *Meroitica* 5, 49–54.

Ruszczyc, Barbara 1977: Taharqa à Tell Atrib. In E. Endesfelder et al. (eds), *Ägypten und Kusch. Schr. Or.* 13, 391–6.

Sa'ad, Ramadan M. 1975: Fragments d'un monument de Toutânkhamon retrouvés dans le IXe pylône de Karnak. *Karnak* 5, 93–109.

Sa'ad, Ramadan M. and Manniche, Lise 1971: A Unique Offering List of Amenophis IV Recently Found at Karnak. *JEA* 57, 70–2.

Sadek, Ashraf I. 1979: Glimpses of Popular Religion in the New Kingdom Egypt I: Mourning for Amenophis I at Deir el-Medina. *GM* 36, 51–6.

Säve-Söderbergh, Torgny 1946: Zu den äthiopischen Episoden bei Herodot. *Eranos Rudbergianus* 44, 68–80.

Saffirio, L. 1981: Popoli dell' antica età della pietra in Egitto e Nubia. *Aegyptus* 71, 3–64.

—— 1982: Popoli del' antica età della pietra in Egitto e Nubia. *Aegyptus* 72, 3–42.

Said, Edward 1980: *L'Orientalisme. L'Orient créé par l'Occident*. Paris.

Said, Rushdi and Faure, H. 1981: Chronological Framework: African Pluvial and Glacial Epochs. In J. Ki-Zerbo (ed.), *General History of Africa* I. Paris, London, Berkeley: 359–99.

Said, Rushdi and Yousri, Fouad 1963–4: Origin and Pleistocene History of River Nile Near Cairo, Egypt. *BIE* 45, 1–30.

Sainte Fare Garnot, Jean 1948: *La vie religieuse dans l'ancienne Égypte*. Paris.

Saleh, Abd el-Aziz 1972: The *gnbtyw* of Thutmosis III's *Annals* and the South Arabian *Geb(b)anitae* of the Classical Writers. *BIFAO* 72, 245–62.

—— 1981: Notes on the Ancient Egyptian *t3-ntr* 'God's-land'. *BIFAO du Centenaire*, 107–18.

Salman, A. B. 1984: *Bibliography of Geology and Related Sciences Concerning Western Desert Egypt (1732–1984)*. Cairo.

Salmon, Georges 1905–23: *Silvestre de Sacy (1758–1838) I-II. Bibliothèque des arabisants français, 1–2*. Cairo.

Salmon, Pierre 1965: *La politique égyptienne d'Athènes*. Brussels.

Sammarco, A. 1935: *Précis de l'histoire d'Égypte IV: Les règnes de 'Abbas, de Sa'id et d'Isma'il (1848–1879)*. Rome.

Samson, Julia Ellen 1976: Royal Names in Amarna History. *CdE* 51, 30–8.

—— 1978: *Amarna, City of Akhenaton and Nefertiti*. Warminster.

—— 1979a: Akhenaten's Successor. *GM* 32, 53–8.

—— 1979b: The History of the Mystery of Akhenaten's Successor. *L'égyptologie en 1979* II, 291–8.

—— 1981–2: Akhenaten's Coregent Ankhheperure-Nefernefruaten. *GM* 53, 51–4.

—— 1982a: Akhenaten's Coregent and Successor. *GM* 57, 57–60.

—— 1982b: Nefernefruaten-Nefertiti 'Beloved of Akhenaten'. Ankhkheperure Nefernefruaten 'Beloved of Akhenaten'. Ankhkheperure Smenkhkare. *GM* 57, 61–8.

—— 1985: *Nefertiti and Cleopatra: Queen-monarchs of Ancient Egypt*. London.

Sandars, N. K. 1985: *The Sea Peoples: Warriors of the Mediterranean*. London.

Sandman, Maj 1938: *Texts from the Time of Akhenaten*. BAE 8.

Sandys, G. and Lithgow, W. 1973: *Voyages en Égypte des années 1611 et 1612, Georges Sandys et William Lithgow*. Paris.

Saout, Françoise le. 1978–80a: Reconstitution des murs de la Cour de la Cachette. *Karnak* 7, 213–58.

—— 1978–80b: Nouveaux fragments au nom d'Horemheb. *Karnak* 7, 259–64.

—— 1978–80c: À propos d'un colosse de Ramsès II à Karnak. *Karnak* 7, 267–74.

Saout, Françoise le, M'Arouf, F. A.-el-H. and Thomas Zimmer 1987: Le Moyen Empire à Karnak: Varia 1. *Karnak* 8, 293–323.

Saout, Francoise le and Traunecker, C. 1978–80: Les travaux au IXe pylône de Karnak: annexe épigraphique. *Karnak* 7, 67–74.

Satzinger, Helmut 1984: Zu den neubabylonischen Transkriptionen ägyptischer Personnennamen. *GM* 73, 89–90.

Sauneron, Serge 1950: Trois personnages du scandale d'Éléphantine. *RdE* 7, 53–62.

—— 1952: La forme égyptienne du nom Teshub. *BIFAO* 51, 57–9.

—— 1954: La justice à la porte des temples (à propos du nom ègyptien des propylées). *BIFAO* 54, 117–28.

—— 1955: Quelques sanctuaires égyptiens des oasis de Dakhleh et de Khargeh. *Cahiers d'Histoire Égyptienne* 7, 279–99.

—— 1959: Les songes et leur interprétation dans l'Égypte ancienne. *Sources Orientales* 2, 18–61.

—— 1966: Une visite à Soleb en 1850. *BIFAO* 64, 193–6.

—— 1968a: *L'égyptologie. Que sais-je?* Paris.

—— 1968b: Les désillusions de la guerre asiatique (Papyrus Deir el-Médineh 25). *Kêmi* 18, 17–27.

—— 1971: Deux épisodes de l'exploration des pyramides. *Beiträge zur ägyptischen Bauforschung und Altertumskunde* 12, 113–19.

—— 1974: *Villes et Légendes d'Égypte (1–45)*. Cairo.

—— 1988: *Les prêtres de l'ancienne Égypte*. 2nd edn. Paris.

Sauneron, Serge and Stierlin, H. 1975: *Derniers temples d'Égypte: Edfou et Philae*. Paris.

Sauneron, Serge and Yoyotte, Jean 1950: Traces d'établissements asiatiques en Moyenne Égypte sous Ramsès II. *RdE* 7, 67–70.

—— 1952: La campagne nubienne de Psammétique II et sa signification historique. *BIFAO* 50, 157–207.

Sayed, Abd el-Monem A. H. 1977: Discovery of the Site of the 12th Dynasty Port at Wâdi Gawâsîs on the Red Sea Shore. *RdE* 29, 138–78.

—— 1983: New Light on the Recently Discovered Port on the Red Sea Shore. *CdE* 58, 23–37.

Scamuzzi, Ernesto 1966: *L'art égyptien au Musée de Turin*. Paris.

Schaedel, H. 1936: *Die Listen des grossen Papyrus Harris: Ihre wissenschaftliche und politische Ausdeutung. LÄS* 6.

Schäfer, A. 1986: Zur Entstehung der Mitregenschaft als Legitimationsprinzip von Herrschaft. *ZÄS* 113, 44–55.

Schäfer, Heinrich 1901: *Die äthiopische Königsinschrift der Berliner Museums*. Leipzig.

—— 1974: *Principles of Egyptian Art*. Oxford.

Schäfer, Heinrich and Andrae, W. 1925: *Die Kunst des alten Orients*. Berlin.

Scharff, Alexander 1936: *Der historische Abschnitt der Lehre für König Merikarê*. Munich.

Scheel, Bernd 1985: Studien zum Metallhandwerk im Alten Ägypten I: Handlungen und Beischriften in den Bildprogrammen des Gräber des Alten Reiches. *SAK* 12, 117–78.

—— 1986: Studien zur Metallhandwerk im Alten Ägypten II: Handlungen und Beischriften in den Bildprogrammen der Gräber des Mittleren Reiches. *SAK* 13, 181–206.

—— 1988: Anmerkungen zur Kupferverhüttung und Kupferraffination im Alten Ägypten. *DE* 11, 87–97.

Schenkel, Wolfgang 1974: Die Einführung der künstlichen Felderbewässerung im alten Ägypten. *GM* 11, 41–6.

—— 1977: Zur Frage der Vorlagen spätzeitlicher 'Kopien'. In J. Assmann et al. (eds), *Fragen an die altägyptische Literatur. Studien zum Gedenken an Eberhard Otto*. Wiesbaden: 417–42.

—— 1978: *Die Bewässerungsrevolution im alten Ägypten. DAIK* 6.

—— 1979: Atlantis: die 'namenlose' Insel. *GM* 36, 57–60.

—— 1986: Das Wort fur 'König (von Oberägypten)'. *GM* 94, 57–73.

Schild, Romauld and Wendorf, Fred 1977: *The Prehistory of Dakhla Oasis and Adjacent Desert*. Warsaw.

Schlögl, Hermann A. 1985: *Echnaton-Tutanchamun: Fakte und Texte*. 2nd edn. Wiesbaden.

—— 1986: *Amenophis IV. Echnaton. Mit Selbstzeugnissen und Bilddokumenten dargestellt*. Reinbek.

Schlott-Schwab, A. 1981: *Die Ausmasse Ägyptens nach altägyptischen Texten. ÄAT* 3.

—— 1983: Weitere Gedanken zur Entstehung des altägyptischen Staates. *GM* 67, 69–80.

Schmidt, Klaus 1984: Zur Frage der ökonomischen Grundlagen frühbronzezeitlicher Seidlungen im Südsinai. *MDAIK* 40, 261–4.

Schmitz, Bettina 1978: Untersuchungen zu zwei Königinen der frühen 18. Dynastie, Ahhotep und Ahmose. *CdE* 53, 207–21.

Scholtz, Piotr 1984: Fürstin Iti: 'Schönheit aus Punt'. *SAK* 11, 529–56.

Schott, Erika 1972: Bücher und Bibliotheken im alten Ägypten. *GM* 1, 24–7.

—— 1977: Bücher und Bibliotheken im alten Ägypten. *GM* 25, 73–80.

Schott, Siegfried 1945: *Mythe und Mythenbildung im alten Ägypten. UGAÄ* 15.

—— 1950: *Altägyptische Fesdaten. AAWLM* 10.

—— 1956a: *Zum Krönungstag der Königin Hatschepsût. NAWG* 1956/4.

—— 1956b: *Les chants d'amour de l'Égypte ancienne*. Paris.

—— 1957: *Die Reinigung Pharaohs in einem memphitischen Tempel*. Göttingen.

—— 1959: Altägyptische Vorstellungen vom Weltende. *Analecta Biblica* 12, 319–30.

—— 1964: *Der Denkstein Sethos I. für die Kapelle Ramses' I. in Abydos*. Göttingen.

—— 1965: Aufnahmen vom Hungersnotrelief aus dem Aufweg der Unaspyramide. *RdE* 17, 7–13.

—— 1969: Le temple du sphinx à Giza et les deux axes du monde égyptien. *BSFE* 53–4, 31–41.

Schuller-Götzburg, T. V. 1986: Zur Familiengeschichte der 11. Dynastie. *GM* 90, 67–70.

Schulman, Alan R. 1964: *Military Rank, Title and Organization in the*

Egyptian New Kingdom. MÄS 6.

—— 1966: A Problem of Pedubasts. *JARCE* 5, 33–41.

—— 1979a: Diplomatic Marriage in the Egyptian New Kingdom. *JNES* 38, 177–94.

—— 1979b: The Nubian War of Akhenaton. *L'égyptologie en 1979* II, 299–316.

—— 1980: Chariots, Chariotry and the Hyksos. *JSSEA* 10, 105–53.

—— 1984: Reshep at Zagazig: A New Document. In *Studien zu Sprache und Religion Ägyptens. Festschrift W. Westendorf*. Göttingen: 855–63.

—— 1986: The Curious Case of Hadad the Edomite. In L. H. Lesko (ed.), *Egyptological Studies in Honour of Richard A. Parker*. Chicago: 122–35.

Schulze, Peter H. 1976: *Herrin beider Länder Hatschepsut (Frau, Gott und Pharao)*. Bergisch Gladbach.

—— 1980: *Auf den Schwingen des Horusfalken. Die Geburt der ägyptischen Hochkultur*. Bergisch Gladbach.

—— 1983: *Der Sturz des göttlichen Falken. Revolution im alten Ägypten*. Bergisch Gladbach.

Schwaller de Lubicz, R. A. 1949: *Le temple dans l'Homme*. Cairo.

—— 1982: *Les temples de Karnak. Contribution à l'étude de la pensée pharaonique*. Paris.

Schwartz, Jacques 1949a: Les conquérants perses et la littérature égyptienne. *BIFAO* 48, 65–80.

—— 1949b: Le 'Cycle de Pétoubastis' et les commentaires égyptiens de l'*Exode*. *BIFAO* 49, 67–83.

—— 1951: Hérodote et l'Égypte. *Revue Archéologique* 37, 143–50.

Schwarz, J.-C. 1979: La médicine dentaire dans l'Égypte ancienne. *BSEG* 2, 37–43.

Schweitzer, Ursula 1948: *Löwe und Sphinx im alten Ägypten*. ÄF 15.

Sée, Geneviève 1973: *Naissance de l'urbanisme dans la vallée du Nil*. Paris.

—— 1974: *Grandes villes de l'Égypte antique*. Paris.

Seele, K. C. 1940: *The Coregency of Ramses II with Seti I and the Date of the Great Hypostyle Hall at Karnak*. Chicago.

Seidl, Erwin 1964: *Altägyptisches Recht*. Leiden.

Sethe, Kurt 1896: *Die Thronwirren unter den Nachfolgern Königs Thutmosis' I. Die Prinzenliste von Medinet Habu, Untersuchungen 1*. Leipzig.

—— 1912: *Die Einsetzung des Veziers unter der 18. Dynastie*. Berlin.

—— 1930: *Urkunden der ägyptischen Altertums IV: Urkunden der 18. Dynastie*. Leipzig.

—— 1935: *Urkunden der ägyptischen Altertums VII: Urkunden des Mittleren Reiches*. Leipzig.

—— 1984: *Übersetzung zu den Heften 1-4 der Urk. IV*. Originally publ. 1914. Leipzig.

Settgast, Jürgen 1963: Materialen zur Ersten Zwischenzeit I. *MDAIK* 19, 7–15.

—— 1969: Zu ungewöhnlichen Darstellungen von Bogenschützen. *MDAIK* 25, 136–8.

Severyns, A. 1960: *Grèce et Proche-Orient avant Homère*. Brussels.

Seyfried, Karl Joachim 1976: Nachträge zu Yoyotte 'Les Sementiou . . .'. *BSFE* 73, 44–55.

—— 1981: *Beiträge zu den Expeditionen des Mittleren Reiches in der Ostwüste. HÄB* 15.

—— 1987: Bemerkungen zur Erweiterung der unterirdischen Anlagen einiger Gräber des Neuen Reiches in Thebes: Versuch einer Deutung. *ASAE* 71, 229–49.

Shaw, Ian M. E. 1984: The Egyptian Archaic Period: A Reappraisal of the C-14 Dates (I). *GM* 78, 79–86.

—— 1985: Egyptian Chronology and the Irish Oak Calibration. *JNES* 44, 295–318.

Sherif, Negm el-Dim Mohamed 1981: Nubia before Napata (3100 to 750). In G. Mokhtar (ed.), *General History of Africa* II, Paris, London, Berkeley: 245–77.

Sherman, E. J. 1982: Ancient Egyptian Biographies of the Late Period (380 BCE through 246 BCE). *NARCE* 119, 38–41.

Siliotti, A. 1985: *Viaggiatori veneti alla scoperta dell-Egitto. Itinerari de storia e arte.* Venice.

Silverman, David 1969: Pygmies and Dwarves in the Old Kingdom. *Serapis* 1, 53–62.

Simpson, William Kelly 1965: The Stela of Amun-wosre, Governor of Upper Egypt in the Reign of Ammenemes I or II. *JEA* 51, 63–8.

—— 1974: Polygamy in Egypt in the Middle Kingdom. *JEA* 60, 100–105.

—— 1980: Mariette and Verdi's Aïda. *BES* 2, 111–20.

—— 1981: Textual Notes on the Elephantine Building Text of Sesostris I and the Zizina Fragment from the Tomb of Horemheb. *GM* 45, 69–70.

—— 1982a: Egyptian Sculpture and Two-dimensional Representation as Propaganda. *JEA* 68, 266–71.

—— 1982b: A Relief of a Divine Votaress in Boston. *CdE* 57, 231–5.

Sledzianowski, B. 1973: Alessandra Nibbi, *The Sea Peoples*: A Reexamination of the Egyptian Sources. *GM* 5, 59–62.

Slíwa, Joachim 1974: Some Remarks Concerning Victorious Ruler Representations in Egyptian Art. *FuB* 16, 97–117.

Smith, Harry S. 1972: Dates of the Obsequies of the Mother of Apis. *RdE* 24, 176–87.

—— 1979: The Excavation of the Anubieion at Saqqara: A Contribution to Memphite Topography and Stratigraphy (from 400 BC–641 AD). *L'egyptologie en 1979* I, 279–82.

Smith, Harry S. and Smith, A. 1976: A Reconsideration of the Kamose Texts. *ZÄS* 103, 48–76.

Smith, Harry S. and Hall, R. M. 1983: *Ancient Centres of Egyptian Civilization.* London.

Smith, Mark J. 1980: A Second Dynasty King in a Demotic Papyrus of the Roman Period. *JEA* 66, 173.

Smith, R. W. and Redford, D. 1976: *The Akhenaten Temple Project 1: Initial Discoveries.* Warminster.

—— 1988: *The Akhenaten Temple Project 2: The Temple Rwd-Mnw and the Inscriptions*. Warminster.

Smith, W. S. 1978: *A History of Egyptian Sculpture and Painting in the Old Kingdom*. London and Boston.

Soukiassian, Georges 1981: Une étape de la proscription de Seth. *GM* 44, 59–68.

Sourouzian, Hourig 1981: L'apparition du pylône. *BIFAO du Centenaire*, 141–52.

—— 1983: Henout-mi-Rê, fille de Ramses II et grande épouse du roi. *ASAE* 69, 365–71.

Spalinger Anthony J. 1973: The Year 712 BC and Its Implications for Egyptian History. *JARCE* 10, 95–101.

—— 1974a: Assurbanipal and Egypt: a Source Study. *JAOS* 94, 316–28.

—— 1974b: Some Notes on the Battle of Megiddo and Reflections on Egyptian Military Writing. *MDAIK* 30, 221–9.

—— 1974c: Esarhaddon and Egypt: an Analysis of the First Invasion of Egypt. *Or* 43, 295–326.

—— 1977a: A Critical Analysis of the 'Annals' of Thutmose III (*Stücke* V–VII). *JARCE* 14, 42–54.

—— 1977b: Egypt and Babylonia: A Survey (c.620 BC–550 BC). *SAK* 5, 221–44.

—— 1978a: A New Reference to an Egyptian Campaign of Thutmose III in Asia. *JNES* 37, 35–41.

—— 1978b: The Date of the Death of Gyges and its Historical Implications. *JAOS* 98, 400–9.

—— 1978c: A Canaanite Ritual Found in Egyptian Reliefs. *JSSEA* 8, 47–60.

—— 1978d: The Foreign Policy of Egypt Preceding the Assyrian Conquest. *CdE* 53, 22–47.

—— 1978e: The Concept of the Monarchy During the Saite Epoch: an Essay of Synthesis. *Or* 47, 12–36.

—— 1978f: The Reign of King Chabbash: an Interpretation. *ZÄS* 105, 142–54.

—— 1979a: Egyptian-Hittite Relations at the Close of the Amarna Period and Some Notes on Hittite Military Stragegy in North Syria. *BES* 1, 55–90.

—— 1979b: Some Additional Remarks on the Battle of Megiddo. *GM* 33, 47–54.

—— 1979c: The Northern Wars of Seti I: an Integrative Study. *JARCE* 16, 29–47.

—— 1979d: Traces of the Early Career of Ramesses II. *JNES* 38, 271–86.

—— 1979e: Some Notes on the Libyans of the Old Kingdom and Later Historical Reflexes. *JSSEA* 9, 125–62.

—— 1979f: Traces of the Early Career of Seti I. *JSSEA* 9, 227–40.

—— 1980a: Addenda to 'The Reign of King Chabbas: An Interpretation' (*ZÄS* 105, 1978, pp. 142–154). *ZÄS* 107, 87.

—— 1980b: Remarks on the Family of Queen ḫꜥ.s.nbw and the Problem of Kinship in Dynasty XIII. *RdE* 32, 95–116.

—— 1980c: Historical Observations on the Military Reliefs of Abu Simbel and

Other Ramesside Temples in Nubia. *JEA* 66, 83–99.

—— 1981a: Considerations on the Hittite Treaty Between Egypt and Hatti. *SAK* 9, 299–358.

—— 1981b: Notes on the Military in Egypt During the XXVth Dynasty. *JSSEA* 11, 37–58.

—— 1983: The Historical Implications of the Year 9 Campaign of Amenophis II. *JSSEA* 13, 89–101.

—— 1986a: Baking During the Reign of Seti I. *BIFAO* 86, 307–52.

—— 1986b: Foods in P. Bulaq 18. *SAK* 13, 207–48.

—— 1987: The Grain System of Dynasty 18. *SAK* 14, 283–311.

Spanel, D. 1984: The Date of Ankhtifi of Mo'alla. *GM* 78, 87–94.

Speke, J. H. 1865: *Les sources du Nil. Journal de voyage du capitaine J. H. Speke.* . . . Paris.

Spencer, P. A. and Spencer, A. J. 1986: Notes on Late Libyan Egypt. *JEA* 72, 198–201.

Spiegel, Joachim 1957a: Der 'Ruf' des Königs. *WZKM* 54, 191–203.

—— 1957b: Zur Kunstentwicklung der zweiten Hälfte des Alten Reiches. *MDAIK* 15, 225–61.

Stadelmann, Rainer 1965: Ein Beitrag zum Brief des Hyksos Apophis. *MDAIK* 20, 62–9.

—— 1980: Snofru und die Pyramiden von Meidum und Dahschur. *MDAIK* 36, 437–49.

—— 1981a: Die lange Regierung Ramses' II. *MDAIK* 37, 457–64.

—— 1981b: La ville de pyramide à l'Ancien Empire. *RdE* 33, 67–77.

—— 1983: Das vermeintliche Sonnenheiligtum im Norden des Djoserbezirkes. *ASAE* 69, 373–8.

—— 1984: Khaefkhufu = Chephren. Beiträge zur Geschichte der 4. Dynastie. *SAK* 11, 165–72.

—— 1985: *Die ägyptischen Pyramiden. Vom Ziegelbau zum Weltwunder.* Mainz.

—— 1987: Königinnengrab und Pyramidenbezirk im Alten Reich. *ASAE* 71, 251–60.

Staehelin, Elisabeth 1966: *Untersuchungen zur ägyptischen Tracht im Alten Reich. MÄS* 8.

Steindorff, Georg 1932: Nubien, Nubier und die sogenannten Troglodyten. In S. R. K. Glanville (ed.), *Studies Griffith.* Oxford: 358–68.

Steinmann, Frank 1980: Untersuchungen zu den in der handwerklich-künstlerichen Produktion beschäftigten Personen und Berufsgruppen des Neuen Reichs. *ZÄS* 107, 137–57.

—— 1982: Untersuchungen zu den in der handwerklich-künstlerichen Produktion beschäftigten Personen und Berufsgruppen des Neuen Reichs. *ZÄS* 109, 66–72 and 149–56.

—— 1984: Untersuchungen zu den in der handwerklich-künstlerichen Produktion beschäftigten Personen und Berufsgruppen des Neuen Reichs. *ZÄS* 111, 30–40.

Stewart, H. M. 1960: Some pre-ʿAmarnah Sun-hymns. *JEA* 46, 83–90.

Stierlin, Henri 1984: *Égypte. Des origines à l'Islam.* Paris.

Stork, Lothar 1973: Gab es in Ägypten einen rituellen Königsmord? *GM 5*, 31–2.

—— 1979: Beginn und Ende einer Reise nach Punt: das Wadi Tumilat. *GM 35*, 93–8.

—— 1981a: Zur Etymologie von ḫ3b 'Flusspferd'. *GM 43*, 61–2.

—— 1981b: Er ist ein Gott, während ich ein Herrscher bin. Die Anfechtung der Hyksossuzeränität unter Kamose. *GM 43*, 63–6.

—— 1981c: Was störte der Hyksos Apophis am Gebrüll der thebanischen Nilpferde? *GM 43*, 67–8.

Strange, John 1973: A 'New' Proposal for the Identity of Keftiu/Caphtor. A Preliminary Account. *GM 8*, 47–52.

Strauss-Seeber, Cornelia 1987: Zum Statuenprogramm Ramses' II. im Luxortempel. In W. Helck (ed.), *Tempel und Kult*. Wiesbaden: 24–42.

Strouhal, Eugen 1979: Queen Mutnodjmet at Memphis: Anthropological and Paleopathological Evidence. *L'égyptologie en 1979* II, 317–22.

Strudwick, Nigel 1985: *The Administration of Egypt in the Old Kingdom*. London.

Suys, Émile 1933: *Étude sur le conte du fellah plaideur, récit égyptien du Moyen Empire. AnOr 5*.

Swelim, Nabil M. A. 1971: The Funerary Complex of Horus Neter-khet at Sakkara. *AHS Alexandrie 4*, 30–8.

—— 1974: Horus Senerka: an Essay on the Fall of the First Dynasty. *AHS Alexandrie 5*, 67–78.

—— 1983: *Some Problems on the History of the Third Dynasty. AHS Alexandrie 7*.

Symeonoglou, S. 1985: *The Topography of Thebes: From the Bronze Age to Modern Times*. Princeton.

Szafranski, Zbigniew 1979: Problem of Power-concentration in Hands of One Family in Edfu at the Time of Sebekhetep IV. Genealogical Tree. Preliminary Study. *L'égyptologie en 1979* II: 173–6.

—— 1983: Some Remarks about the Process of Democratization of the Egyptian Religion in the Second Intermediate Period. *ET 12*, 53–66.

—— 1985: Buried Statues of Mentuhotep II Nebhepetre and Amenophis I at Deir el-Bahari. *MDAIK 41*, 257–64.

Tagher, Jacques 1950: Fouilleurs et antiquaires en Égypte au XIXe siècle. *Cahiers d'Histoire Égyptienne 3*, 72–86.

Tawfik, Sayed 1981: Aton Studies 6. Was Nefernefruaten the Immediate Successor of Akhenaten? *MDAIK 37*, 469–74.

Teeter, Emily 1986: The Search for Truth: a Preliminary Report on the Presentation of Maat. *NARCE 134*, 3–13.

Tefnin, Roland 1979a: *La statuaire d'Hatschepsout*. Brussels.

—— 1979b: Image et histoire. Réflexions sur l'usage documentaire de l'image égyptienne. *CdE 54*, 218–44.

—— 1981: Image, écriture, récit. À propos des représentations de la bataille de Qadech. *GM 47*, 55–78.

—— 1986: Réflexions sur l'esthétique amarnienne, à propos d'une nouvelle tête de princesse. *SAK 13*, 255–62.

Thausing, Gertrud 1948: Zur Frage der 'juristischen Person' im ägyptischen Recht. *WZKM* 51, 14–20.

Théodoridès, Aristide 1967: À propos de la loi dans l'Égypte pharaonique. *RIDA* 14, 107–52.

—— 1971: The Concept of Law in Ancient Egypt. In J. R. Harris (ed.), *The Legacy of Egypt*. 2nd edn. Oxford: 291–322.

—— 1973: Les Égyptiens anciens, 'citoyens' or 'sujets de Pharaon'? *RIDA* 20, 51–112.

—— 1974: Le problème du droit égyptien ancien. In *Le Droit égyptien ancien*. Brussels.

Thissen, Heinz-J. 1984a: Ziegelfabrikation nach demotischen Texten. *Enchoria* 12, 51–6.

—— 1984b: *Die Lehre des Anchscheschongi (P. BM 10508). Einleitung, Übersetzung, Indices*. Bonn.

Thomas, Elizabeth 1959: Ramesses III: Notes and Queries. *JEA* 45, 101–2.

—— 1967: Was Queen Mutnedjmet the Owner of Tomb 33 in the Valley of the Queens? *JEA* 53, 161–3.

Thomas, A. P. 1980: The Tomb of Queen Ahmose(?) Merytamen, Theban tomb 320. *Serapis* 6, 171–81.

—— 1981: *Gurob*. 2 vols. Warminster.

Tietze, C. 1985: Amarna: Analyse der Wohnhauser und soziale Struktur der Stadtbewohner. *ZÄS* 112, 48–84.

—— 1986: Amarna II. *ZÄS* 113, 55–78.

Tomandl, Herbert 1984: Der Gefangenfries am Thronuntersatz aus dem Amuntempel von Napata. *GM* 82, 65–72.

—— 1986: Die Thronuntersätze vom Amuntempel in Meroe und Jebel Barkal. Ein ikonographischer Vergleigh. *VA* 2, 63–72.

Török, Laszlo 1979: The Art of the Ballana Culture and Its Relation to Late Antique Art. *Meroitica* 5, 85–100.

—— 1984a: Economy in the Empire of Kush: a Review of the Written Evidence. *ZÄS* 111, 45–69.

—— 1984b: Meroitic Architecture: Contributions to Problems of Chronology and Style. *Meroitica* 7, 351–66.

—— 1987: *The Royal Crowns of Kush. A Study in Middle Nile Valley Regalia and Iconography in the 1st Millennia B.C. and A.D.* Oxford.

Touny, A. D. and Wenig, S. 1969: *Der Sport im alten Ägypten*. Leipzig.

Traunecker, Claude 1975: Une Stèle commémorant la construction de l'enceinte d'un temple de Montou. *Karnak* 5, 141–58.

—— 1979: Essai sur l'histoire de la XXIXe dynastie. *BIFAO* 79, 395–436.

—— 1980: Un nouveau document sur Darius Ier à Karnak. *Karnak* 6, 209–13.

—— 1984: Données nouvelles sur le début du règne d'Amenophis IV et son oeuvre à Karnak. *JSSEA* 14, 60–9.

—— 1986: Amenophis IV et Nefertiti: Le couple royal d'après les talatates du IXe pylone de Karnak. *BSFE* 107, 17–44.

—— 1987: Les 'temples hauts' de Basse Époque: un aspect du fonctionnement économique des temples. *RdE* 38, 147–62.

Traunecker, Claude and Traunecker, Françoise 1984–5: Sur la salle dite 'du couronnement' à Tell el-Amarna. *BSEG* 9–10, 285–307.

Traunecker, Claude and Golvin, J.-C. 1984: *Karnak. Résurrection d'un site.* Paris.

Traunecker, C., Le Saout, F. and Masson, O. 1981: *La chapelle d'Achôris à Karnak II.* Cairo.

Trench, Jorge A. 1988: Geometrical Model for the Ascending and Descending Corridors of the Great Pyramid. *GM* 102, 85–94.

Trigger, Bruce G. 1979a: The Narmer Palette in Cross-cultural Perspective. *ÄAT* 1, 409–19.

—— 1979b: Egypt and the Comparative Study of Early Civilizations. In K. Weeks (ed.), *Egyptology and the Social Sciences.* Cairo: 23–56.

—— 1981: Akhenaten and Durkheim. *BIFAO du Centenaire*, 165–84.

Trigger, Bruce G., Kemp, B. and O'Connor, D. 1983: *Ancient Egypt: A Social History.* Cambridge.

Troy, Lana 1979: Ahhotep: a Source Evaluation. *GM* 35, 81–92.

—— 1981: One Merytamun Too Many. An Exercise in Critical Method. *GM* 50, 81–96.

Tulhoff, A. 1984: *Tutmosis III. 1490–1436 v. Chr. Das ägyptische Weltreich auf dem Höhepunkt der Macht.* Munich.

Uphill, Eric P. 1965: The Egyptian Sed-festival Rites. *JNES* 24, 365–83.

—— 1965–6: The Nine Bows. *JEOL* 19, 393–420.

—— 1975: The Office *sd3wty bity*. *JEA* 61, 250.

—— 1984a: *The Temples of Per Ramesses.* Warminster.

—— 1984b: The Sequence of Kings for the First Dynasty. In *Studien zu Sprache und Religion Ägyptens. Festschrift W. Westendorf.* Göttingen: 653–67.

Vahala, Frantisek 1970: Der Elephant in Ägypten und Nubien. *ZÄS* 98, 81–3.

Valbelle, Dominique 1979: Modalités d'une enquête ponctuelle sur la vie quotidienne. *L'égyptologie en 1979* II, 177–8.

—— 1985a: *'Les ouvriers de la tomb'. Deir el-Médineh à l'époque ramesside.* BdE 96.

—— 1985b: Eléments sur la démographie et la paysage urbains, d'après les papyrus documentaires d'époque pharaonique. *CRIPEL* 7, 75–90.

—— 1987: Les recensements dans l'Égypte pharaonique des troisième et deuxième millénaires. *CRIPEL* 9, 33–52.

Valloggia, Michel 1964: Remarques sur les noms de la reine Sebek-Ka-Re Neferou-Sebek. *RdE* 16, 45–53.

—— 1969: Amenemhat IV et sa corégence avec Amenemhat III. *RdE* 21, 107–33.

—— 1974: Les vizirs des XIe et XIIe dynasties. *BIFAO* 74, 123–34.

—— 1976: *Recherche sur les 'messages' (upwtjw) dans les sources égyptiennes profanes.* Geneva.

—— 1981: This sur la route des oasis. *BIFAO du Centenaire*, 185–90.

—— 1986: *Balat I: Le mastaba de Medou-nefer.* Cairo.

Van den Boorn, G. P. F. 1982: On the Date of the Duties of the Vizier. *Or* 51, 369–81.

Van der Plas, Dirk 1986: *L'Hymne à la crue du Nil, Egyptologische Uitgaven IV.* Leiden.

Vandersleyen, Claude 1967: Une tempête sous le règne d'Amosis. *RdE* 19, 123–59.

—— 1971a: *Les guerres d'Amosis, fondateur de la XVIIIe dynastie. MRE* 1.

—— 1971b: Des obstacles que constituent les cataractes du Nil. *BIFAO* 69, 253–66.

—— 1975–6: Aménophis III incarnant le dieu Neferhotep. *OLP* 6/7, 535–42.

—— 1980: Les deux Ahhotep. *SAK* 8, 233–42.

—— 1981: Sources égyptiennes pour l'Éthiopie des Grecs. *BIFAO du Centenaire*, 191–6.

—— 1983a: Un seul roi Taa sous la 17e Dynastie. *GM* 63, 67–70.

—— 1983b: L'identité d'Ahmès Sapaïr. *SAK* 10, 311–24.

—— 1985: *Das alte Ägypten. Propyläen Kunstgeschichte* 18.

—— 1987: Une tête de Chéfren en granit rose. *RdE* 38, 94–7.

Van de Walle, Baudouin 1976: La découverte d'Amarna et d'Akhenaton. *RdE* 28, 7–24.

—— 1979: Les textes d'Amarna se réfèrent-ils à une doctrine morale? *OBO* 28, 353–62.

Vandier, Jacques 1936: *La famine dans l'Égypte ancienne. RAPH* 7.

—— 1949: *La religion égyptienne.* 2nd edn. Paris.

—— 1950: *Mo'alla. La tombe d'Ankhtifi et la tombe de Sébekhotep. BdE* 18.

—— 1952: *Manuel d'archéologie égyptienne I: Les époques de formations. La préhistoire: les trois premières dynasties.* Paris.

—— 1954: *Manuel d'archéologie égyptienne II: Les grandes époques. L'architecture funéraire.* Paris.

—— 1955a: *Manuel d'archéologie égyptienne II: Les grandes époques. L'architecture religieuse et civile.* Paris.

—— 1955b: Hémen et Taharqa. *RdE* 10, 73–9.

—— 1958: *Manuel d'archéologie égyptienne III: Les grandes époques. La statuaire.* Paris.

—— 1964: *Manuel d'archéologie égyptienne IV: Bas-reliefs et peintures, scènes de la vie quotidienne 1.* Paris.

—— 1969: *Manuel d'archéologie égyptienne V: Bas-reliefs et peintures, scènes de la vie quotidienne 2.* Paris.

—— 1971: Ramsès-Siptah. *RdE* 23, 165–91.

—— 1978: *Manuel d'archéologie égyptienne VI: Bas-reliefs et peintures, scènes de la vie agricole à l'Ancien et au Moyen Empire.* Paris.

Van Dijk, Jacobus 1979: The Luxor Building Inscription of Ramesses III. *GM* 33, 19–30.

Van Dijk, Jacobus and Eaton-Krauss, M. 1986: Tutankhamun at Memphis. *MDAIK* 42, 35–44.

Van Ghistele, Joos 1976: *Le voyage en Égypte de Joos van Ghistele, 1482–1483.* Cairo.

Van Seters, John 1954: A Date for the *Admonitions* in the Second Intermediate Period. *JEA* 50, 13–23.

—— 1967: *The Hyksos: a New Investigation.* New Haven, Conn.

—— 1983: *In Search of History. Historiography in the Ancient World and the Origins of Biblical History.* London.

Van Siclen, Charles Cornell 1973: The Accession Date of Amenhotep III and the Jubilee. *JNES* 32, 290–300.

—— 1984: The Date of the Granite Bark Shrine of Tuthmosis III. *GM* 79, 53–4.

—— 1985: Amenhotep II at Dendera (Lunet). *VA* 1, 69–73.

—— 1987a: Amenhotep II and the Mut Temple Complex at Karnak. *VA* 3, 281–2.

—— 1987b: Amenhotep II, Shabako, and the Roman Camp at Luxor. *VA* 3, 157–65.

Varille, Alexandre 1947: *À propos des pyramides de Snefrou*. Cairo.

Veniet, M. 1982: Greek Pottery in Egypt. *NARCE* 117, 30–1.

Venit, Marjorie Susan 1984: Early Attic Black Figure Vases in Egypt. *JARCE* 31, 141–54.

—— 1985a: Laconian Black Figure in Egypt. *AJA* 89, 391–8.

—— 1985b: Two Early Corinthian Alabastra in Alexandria. *JEA* 71, 183–9.

Ventura, Raphael 1983: More Chronological Evidence from Turin Papyrus Cat. 1907 + 1908. *JNES* 42, 271–8.

Vercoutter, Jean 1947: Les Haou-nebout. *BIFAO* 46, 125–58.

—— 1949: Les Haou-nebout. *BIFAO* 48, 107–209.

—— 1963: Journal du voyage en Basse Nubie de Linant de Bellefonds (1821–1822). *BSFE* 37–8, 39–64.

—— 1964a: Journal du voyage en Basse Nubie de Linant de Bellefonds (1821–1822). *BSFE* 41, 23–32.

—— 1964b: La stèle de Mirgissa IM 209 et la localisation d'Iken (Kor ou Mirgissa?) *RdE* 16, 179–91.

—— 1972a: La XVIIIe dynastie à Saï et en Haute Nubie. *CRIPEL* 1, 9–38.

—— 1972b: Une campagne militaire de Séti Ier en Haute Nubie. Stèle de Saï S 579. *RdE* 24, 201–8.

—— 1975: Le roi Ougaf et la XIIIe dynastie sur la IIe Cataracte (stèle de Mirgissa IM 375). *RdE* 27, 222–34.

—— 1976: Égyptologie et climatologie. Les crues du Nil à Semneh. *CRIPEL* 4, 141–72.

—— 1979a: L'image du noir dans l'Égypte ancienne (des origines à la XXVe dynastie). *Meroitica* 5, 19–22.

—— 1979b: Balat sur la route de l'Oasis. *L'égyptologie en 1979* I, 283–8.

—— 1980a: Le pays Irem et la pénétration égyptienne en Afrique (Stèle de Saï S. 579). In J. Vercoutter (ed.), *Livre du Centenaire*. MIFAO 104, 157–78.

—— 1980b: Le peuplement de l'Égypte ancienne. In *Histoire Generale de l'Afrique: Études et Documents* 1. Paris, London, Berkeley: 15–36.

—— 1981: Discovery and diffusion of metals and development of social systems up to the fifth century before our era. In J. Ki-Zerbo (ed.), *General History of Africa* I. Paris, London, Berkeley: 706–29.

—— 1984: L'Égypte et le Soudan nilotique, problèmes historiques et archéologiques. *BOREAS* 13, 115–24.

—— 1987: L'Égypte jusqu'à la fin du Nouvel Empire. In P. Lévêque (ed.), *Les premieres civilisations I: Des despotismes orientaux à la cité grecque*. Paris.

Vergote, Joseph 1961: *Toutankhamon dans les archives hittites*. PIHAN Stamboul 12.

—— 1980: À propos du nom de Moïse. *BSEG* 4, 89–95.

Verhoeven, U. 1984: *Grillen, Kochen, Backen im Alltag und im Ritual Altägyptens. Ein lexicographischer Beitrag, Rites Égyptiens* 4.

Verner, Miroslav 1979: Neue Schriftliche Quelle aus Abusir. *L'égyptologie en 1979* II, 179–82.

—— 1980: Die Königsmutter Chentkaus von Abusir und einige Bemerkungen zur Geschichte der 5. Dynastie. *SAK* 8, 243–68.

—— 1982: Eine zweite unvollendete Pyramide in Abusir. *ZÄS* 109, 75–8.

—— 1985a: Les sculptures de Reneferef découvertes à Abousir. *BIFAO* 85, 267–80.

—— 1985b: Les statuettes de prisonniers en bois d'Abousir. *RdE* 36, 145–52.

—— 1985c: Un roi de la Ve dynastie: Reneferef ou Renefer? *BIFAO* 85, 281–4.

—— 1986: Supplément aux sculptures de Reneferef découvertes à Abousir. *BIFAO* 86, 361–6.

Verner, M. and V. Hasek. 1981: Die Anwendung geophysikalischer Methoden bei der archäologischen Forschung in Abusir. *ZÄS* 108, 68–84.

Vernus, Pascal 1970: Quelques exemples du type du 'parvenu' dans l'Égypte ancienne. *BSFE* 59, 31–47.

—— 1975: Inscriptions de la Troisième Période Intermédiaire I–II. *BIFAO* 75, 1–72.

—— 1976: Inscriptions de la Troisième Période Intermédiaire III. *BIFAO* 76, 1–15.

—— 1977: Le dieu personnel dans l'Égypte pharaonique. In *Collogues de la Société Ernest Renan*, 143–57.

—— 1978: Un témoignage culturel du conflit avec les Éthiopiens. *GM* 29, 145–8.

—— 1980: Inscriptions de la Troisième Période Intermédiaire. Le texte oraculaire remployé dans le passage axial du IIIe pylône de Karnak. *Karnak* 6, 215–33.

—— 1982: La stèle du roi Sekhemsankhtaouyré Neferhotep Iykhernofert et la domination Hyksôs (Stèle Caire JE 59635). *ASAE* 68, 129–35.

—— 1985: Le concept de monarchie dans l'Égypte ancienne. In E. Le Roy Ladurie (ed.), *Les monarchies.*

Vikentiev, Vladimir 1930: *La Haute crue de Nil et l'averse de l'an 6 de Taharqa.* Cairo.

Villamont, de 1971: *Voyages en Égypte des années 1589, 1590 & 1591.* Cairo.

Vittmann, Günther 1974: Was There a Coregency of Ahmose with Amenophis I? *JEA* 60, 250–1.

—— 1983: Zur Familie der Fürsten von Athribis in der Spätzeit. *SAK* 10, 333–40.

—— 1984: Zu einigen keilschriftlichen Umschreibungen ägyptischer Personennamen. *GM* 70, 65–6.

Vleemings, Sven P. 1980: The Sale of a Slave in the Time of Pharaoh Py. *OMRO* 61, 1–18.

Volkoff, Olog V. 1967: *Comment on visitait la vallée du Nil: les 'guides' de l'Égypte. RAPH* 28.

——1970: *À la recherche de manuscrits en Égypte. RAPH* 30.

—— 1971: *Le Caire 969–1969. Histoire de la ville des 'Mille et Une Nuits'.* Cairo.

—— 1972: *Voyageurs russes in Égypte. RAPH* 32.

—— 1981: Notes additionnelles au Voyage en Égypte de Jean Coppin (1638–1646). *BIFAO du Centenaire,* 471–504.

Volney, C. F. 1807: *Voyage en Syrie et en Égypte pendant les années 1783, 84 et 85.* Paris.

Volten, Axel 1945: *Zwei altägyptische politische Schriften. Die Lehre für König Merikarê (Pap. Carlsberg VI) and die Lehre des Königs Amenemhet. AnAe* 4.

Vycichl, Werner 1972: Die ägyptische Bezeichnung für den 'Kriegsgefangenen' (*Sqr'nh*). *GM* 2, 43–6.

—— 1977: Heliodors *Aithiopika* und die Volkesstämme des Reiches Meroë. In E. Endesfelder et al. (eds), *Ägypten und Kusch. Schr. Or.* 13, 447–58.

—— 1982a: Eine weitere Bezeichnung für den 'Kriegsgefangenen'. *GM* 54, 75–6.

—— 1982b: Le nom des Hyksos. *BSEG* 6, 103–11.

Wagner, Guy 1977: Nouvelles inscriptions d'Akôris. In J. Vercoutter (ed.), *Hommages Sauneron* II. *BdE* 82, 51–6.

—— 1979: Nouveaux toponymes des oasis transcrits en grec, grécisés ou arabisés. *L'égyptologie en 1979* I, 293–6.

Wainwright, G. A. 1952: Asiatic Keftiu. *AJA* 56, 196–212.

Walbank, F. W. 1979: Egypt in Polybius. In J. Ruffle et al. (eds), *Glimpses of Ancient Egypt. Studies in Honour of H. W. Fairman.* Warminster: 180–9.

Wallet-Lebrun, Christiane 1982. Notes sur le temple d'Amon-Rê à Karnak 1: L'emplacement insolite des obélisques d'Hatshepsout. *BIFAO* 82, 355–62.

—— 1984: Notes sur le temple d'Amon-Rê à Karnak 2: Les *w3d_* thoutmosides entre les IVe et V^e pylônes. *BIFAO* 84, 317–33.

Ward, William A. 1981: Middle Egyptian *sm3yt*, 'Archive'. *JEA* 67, 171–3.

—— 1982: *Index of Egyptian Administrative and Religious Titles of the Middle Kingdom.* Beirut.

Warren, Peter 1985: The Aegean and Egypt: Matters for Research. *DE* 2, 61–4.

Watterson, Barbara 1984: *The Gods of Ancient Egypt.* London.

Way, T. von der 1984: *Die Textüberliefrung Ramses II. Sur Qades-Schlacht. Analyse und Struktur. HÄB* 22.

Weeks, Kent 1979: *Egyptology and the Social Sciences.* Cairo.

—— 1985: *An Historical Bibliography of Egyptian Prehistory. ARCE Catalog* 6.

Wegner, Josef W. and Wegner, Gary 1986: Reexamining the Bent Pyramid. *VA* 2, 209–18.

Weill, Raymond 1900: L'art de la fortification dans la haute antiquité égyptienne. *JA* 15, 80–142 and 200–53.

—— 1904: *Recueil des inscriptions égyptiennes du Sinaï.* Paris.

—— 1907: Notes sur les monuments de la période thinite. *RT* 29, 26–53.

—— 1912: *Les décrets royaux de l'Ancien Empire égyptien. Étude sur les décrets royaux trouvés à Koptos (campagne de 1910 et 1911). . . .* Paris.

—— 1926–8: *Bases, méthodes et résultats de la chronologie égyptienne*. Paris.

—— 1928: Le roi Neterkhet-Zeser et l'officier Imhotep à la pyramide à degrés de Saqqarah. *Revue de l'Égypte Ancienne* 2/1–2, 99–120.

—— 1929: Les successeurs de la XIIe dynastie à Médamoud. *Revue de l'Égypte Ancienne* 2/3–4, 144–71.

—— 1938a: Notes sur les monuments de la pyramide à degrés de Saqqara d'après les publications d'ensemble. *RdE* 3, 115–27.

—— 1938b: Le problème du site d'Avaris. *RdE* 3, 166.

—— 1938c: Sharouhen dans les textes de Ras-Shamra. *RdE* 3, 167.

—— 1938d: Le dieu cananéen Hwrwn sous les traits de Horus-faucon chez les Ramessides. *RdE* 3, 167–8.

—— 1938e: Un nouvel Antef de la XIe dynastie. *RdE* 3, 169–70.

—— 1940: Sekhemre-Souaztaoui Sebekhotep à El Kab. Un nouveau roi, Sekhemre-Sankhtaoui Neferhotep, à El Kab et à Karnak. *RdE* 4, 218–20.

—— 1946a: Les ports antiques submergés de la Méditerranée orientale et le déplacement du niveau marin. *RdE* 5, 137–87.

——1946b: Le ‛*pr-w* du Nouvel Empire sont le *habiri* des textes accadiens: ces *habiri* (exactement *hapiri*) ne sont pas de 'Hébreux'. *RdE* 5, 251–2.

—— 1948: Notes sur l'histoire primitive des grandes religions égyptiennes. *BIFAO* 47, 59–150.

—— 1949: Un nouveau pharaon de l'époque tardive en Moyenne Égypte et l'Horus de Deir el-Gebrâwi, XIIe nome. *BIFAO* 49, 57–65.

—— 1950a: Les nouvelles propositions de reconstruction historique et chronologique du Moyen Empire. *RdE* 7, 89–105.

—— 1950b: Le roi Hotepibre Amou-se-Hornezherit. *RdE* 7, 194.

—— 1951: Une question inattendue: comment les rois de l'Ancien Empire ont-ils été conduits à faire les Grandes Pyramides? *RdE* 6, 232–4.

—— 1961: *Recherches sur la Ier dynastie et les temps prépharaoniques*. BdE 38.

Weinstein, James M. 1981: The Egyptian Empire in Palestine: a Reassessment. *BASOR* 241, 1–28.

Wendorf, Fred 1982: Food Production in the Paleolithic. Excavations at Wadi Kubbaniya: 1981. *NARCE* 116, 13–21.

Wendorf, F. and Schild, R. 1984: *Cattle-keepers of the Eastern Sahara. The Neolithic of Bir Kiseiba*. Dallas.

Wenig, Stefen 1973: Nochmals zur 1. und 2. Nebendynastie von Napata. *Meroitica* 1, 147–60.

—— 1978: *Africa in Antiquity. The Arts of Ancient Nubia and the Sudan*. 2 vols. Brooklyn, NY.

Werbrouck, Marcelle 1938: *Les pleureuses dans l'Égypte ancienne*. Brussels.

Werner, E. K. 1982: The Amarna Period of the Eighteenth Dynasty. Egypt Bibliography Supplement 1980–1981. *NARCE* 120, 3–21.

—— 1984: The Amarna Period of the Eighteenth Dynasty. Egypt Bibliography Supplement 1982–1983. *NARCE* 126, 21–39.

Wessetzky, Vilmos 1973: Die ägyptische Tempelbibliothek. *ZÄS* 100, 54–9.

—— 1977: An der Grenze von Literatur und Geschichte. In J. Assmann et al. (eds), *Fragen an die altägyptische Literatur: Studien Zum Gedenken an Eberhard Otto*. Wiesbaden: 499–502.

—— 1984: Die Bücherliste des Tempels von Edfu und Imhotep. *GM* 83, 85–90.

Westendorf, Wolfhart 1974: Das Eine und die Vielen. Zur Schematisierung der altägyptischen Religion trotz ihrer Komplexität. *GM* 13, 59–61.

—— 1976: Achenatens angebliche Selbstverbannung nach Amarna. *GM* 20, 55–8.

—— 1979: *Aspekte der spätägyptischen Religion. GOF* IV/9.

—— 1983a: Raum und Zeit als Entsprechungen der beiden Ewigkeiten. *ÄAT* 5, 422–35.

—— 1983b: Die Geburt der Zeit aus dem Raum. *GM* 63, 71–6.

Wiesner, J. n.d.: *L'art égyptien*. Paris.

Wifall, Walter 1981: The Foreign Nations: Israel's Nine Bows. *BES* 3, 113–24.

Wild, Henri 1972: Une statue de la XIIᵉ dynastie utilisée par le roi hermopolitain Thot-em-hat de la XXIIIᵉ. *RdE* 24, 209–15.

Wild, J. 1973: *Voyages en Égypte de J. Wild [1606–10]*. Trans. by O. V. Volkoff. Cairo.

Wildung, Dietrich 1969a: *Die Rolle ägyptischer Könige im Bewusstsein ihrer Nachwelt* I. MÄS 17.

—— 1969b: Zur Deutung der Pyramide von Medûm. *RdE* 21, 133–45.

—— 1969c: Zur Frühgeschichte des Amun-tempels von Karnak. *MDAIK* 25, 212–19.

—— 1972: Ramses, die grosse Sonne Ägyptens. *ZÄS* 99, 33–41.

—— 1974: Aufbau und Zwechbestimmung der Königsliste von Karnak. *GM* 9, 41–8.

—— 1977: *Egyptian Saints. Deification in Pharaonic Egypt*. New York.

—— 1984a: *L'Age d'Or de l'Égypte, le Moyen Empire*. Paris.

—— 1984b: Zur Formgeschichte der Landeskronen. In *Studien zu Sprache und Religion Ägyptens. Festschrift W. Westendorf*. Göttingen: 967–80.

—— 1985: *Ni-user-re Sonnenkönig-Sonnegott. SAS* 1.

Wilkinson, R. H. 1985: The Horus Name and the Form and Significance of the Serekh in the Royal Egyptian Titulary. *JSSEA* 15, 98–104.

Willems, H. O. 1983–4: The Nomarchs of the Hare Nome and Early Middle Kingdom History. *JEOL* 28, 80–102.

Williams, Bruce 1985: A Chronology of Meriotic Occupation Below the Fourth Cataract. *JARCE* 22, 149–95.

Williams, R. J. 1964: Literature as a Medium of Political Propaganda in Ancient Egypt. In W. S. McCullough (ed.), *The Seed of Wisdom*. Toronto: 14–30.

Wilson, John A. 1930: The Language of the Historical Texts Commemorating Ramses III, in Medinet Habu Studies 1928/1929. *OIC* 7, 24–33.

—— 1973: Akh-en-Aton and Nefert-iti. *JNES* 32, 235–41.

Wilson, S. 1983: *Saints and Their Cults: Studies in Religious Sociology, Folklore and History*. Cambridge.

Winter, Erich 1957: Zur Deutung der Sonnenheiligtümer der 5. Dynastie. *WZKM* 54, 222–33.

Wittfogel, K. A. 1976: *Oriental Despotism: A Comparative Study of Total Power*. New Haven, Conn.

Wolf, W. 1986: *Die Welt der Ägypter*. Essen.

Wright, G. R. 1979: The Passage on the Sea. *GM* 33, 55–68.

Yeiven, S. 1965: Who Were the *Mntyw*? *JEA* 51, 204–6.

—— 1976: Canaanite Ritual Vessels in Egyptian Cultic Practices. *JEA* 62, 110–14.

Youssef, Ahmed Abd el-Hamid 1964: Merenptah's Fourth Year Text at Amada. *ASAE* 58, 273–80.

Yoyotte, Jean 1950a: Les filles de Téti et la reine Seshé du papyrus Ebers. *RdE* 7, 184–5.

—— 1950b: Les grands dieux et la religion officielle sous Séti Ier et Ramsès II. *BSFE* 3, 17–22.

—— 1951a: Le martelage des noms royaux éthiopiens par Psammétique II. *RdE* 8, 215–39.

—— 1951b: Un document relatif aux rapports de la Libye et de la Nubie. *BSFE* 6, 9–14.

—— 1952: Un corps de police de l'Égypte pharaonique. *RdE* 9, 139–51.

—— 1953: Pour une localisation du pays de *Iam*. *BIFAO* 52, 173–8.

—— 1958: À propos de la parenté féminine du roi Téti (IVe dynastie). *BIFAO* 57, 91–8.

—— 1960a: Néchao. In *Supplément au Dictionnaire de la Bible* VI. Paris: 363–94.

—— 1960b: Le talisman de la victoire d'Osorkon. *BSFE* 31, 13–22.

—— 1961: Les principautés du Delta au temps de l'anarchie libyennes, études d'histoire politique. *MIFAO* 66, 121–81.

—— 1962: Processions géographiques mentionnant le Fayoum et ses localités. *BIFAO* 61, 79–138.

—— 1972a: Petoubastis III. RdE 24, 216–23.

—— 1972b: Les Adoratrices de la IIIe Periode Intermédiaire, à propos d'un chef-d'oeuvre rapporté par Champollion. *BSFE* 64, 31–52.

—— 1972c: Une statue de Darius découverte à Suse. *JA* 1972, 235–66.

—— 1975: Les *Sementiou* et l'exploitation des régions minières de l'Ancien Empire. *BSFE* 73, 44–55.

—— 1976–7: 'Osorkon fils de Mehytouskhe', un pharaon oublié? *BSFE* 77–8, 39–54.

—— 1977: Une notice biographique du roi Osiris. *BIFAO* 77, 145–50.

—— 1980a: Une monumentale litanie de granit: les Sekhmet d'Aménophis III et la conjuration permanente de la déesse dangereuse. *BSFE* 87–8, 46–75.

—— 1981: Pharaonic Egypt: society, economy and culture. In G. Mokhtar (ed.), *General History of Africa* II, 136–54.

—— 1980–1: Héra d'Héliopolis et le sacrifice humain. *Annuaire de l'École Pratique des Hautes Études*, section V, 89, 31–102.

—— 1981: Le général Thouti et la perception des tributs syriens. *BSFE* 91, 33–51.

—— 1982–3: Le dieu Horemheb. *RdE* 34, 148–9.

—— 1987: 'Tanis', suivi de 'Pharaons, guerriers libyens et grands prêtres'. In *La Troisième Période Intermédiaire*. Paris: 25–72.

Yoyotte, Jean and López, Jesus 1969: L'organisation de l'armée et les titulatures de soldat au Nouvel Empire égyptien. *BiOr* 26, 3–19.

Yoyotte, Jean and Sauneron, Serge 1949: Le martelage des noms royaux éthiopiens et la campagne nubienne de Psammetik II. *BSFE* 2, 45–49.

Yoyotte, Jean et al. (eds) 1987: *Tanis, l'or des Pharaons*. Galeries Nationales du Grand Palais. Paris.

Yurco, Frank J. 1977–8: Meryet-Amun: Wife of Ramesses II or Amenhotep I? A Review. *Serapis* 4, 57–64.

—— 1980: Sennacherib's Third Campaign and the Coregency of Shabaka and Shebitku. *Serapis* 6, 221–40.

—— 1986: Merenptah's Canaanite Campaign. *JARCE* 23, 189–215.

Žabkar, Louis V. 1972: The Egyptian Name of the Fortress of Semna South. *JEA* 58, 83–90.

—— 1975: Semna South: the Southern Fortress. *JEA* 61, 42–4.

Zadok, Ran 1977: On Some Egyptians in First-millenium Mesopotamia. *GM* 26, 63–8.

—— 1983: On Some Egyptians in Babylonian Documents. *GM* 64, 73–5.

Zauzich, Karl-Theodore 1978: Neue Namen für die Konige Harmachis und Anchmachis. *GM* 29, 157–8.

Zayed, Abd el-Hamid and Devisse, J. 1981: Egypt's Relations with the Rest of Africa. In G. Mokhtar (ed.), *General History of Africa* II, Paris, London, Berkeley: 136–54.

Zibelius, Karola 1979: Zu Form und Inhalt der Ortsnamen des alten Reiches. *ÄAT* 1, 456–77.

—— 1981–2: Zur Entstehung des altägyptischen Staates. *GM* 53, 63–74.

Ziegler, Christiane 1987: Les arts du métal à la Troisième Période Intermédiaire. In J. Yoyotte et al. (eds), *Tanis, l'or des pharaons*. Paris: 85–101.

Ziegler, K., Sontheimer, W. and Gärtner, G. 1979: *Der Kleine Pauly. Lexikon der Antike, auf der Gundlage von Pauly's Realencyclopädie der klassischen Altertumwïssenschaft*. 5 vols.

Zimmer, Thierry 1988: Les voyageurs modernes à Karnak: rapport préliminaire. *Karnak* 8, 391–406.

Ziskind, J. R. 1973: The International Legal Status of the Sea in Antiquity. *AcOr* 35, 35–49.

Zivie, Alain-Pierre 1972: Un monument associant les noms de Ramsès Ier et de Sethi Ier. *BIFAO* 72, 99–114.

—— 1975: Quelques remarques sur un monument nouveau de Mérenptah. *GM* 18, 45–50.

—— 1979: Du bon usage des traditions littéraires et des légendes populaires: à propos du Caire et de sa région. *L'égyptologie en 1979* I, 303–4.

—— 1981: Du côté de Babylone. Traditions littéraires et légendes au secours de l'archéologie. In J. Vercoutter (ed.), *Livre de Centenaire*. MIFAO 104, 311–17.

Zivie, Christiane M. 1972: Nitocris, Rhodopis et la troisième pyramide de Giza. *BIFAO* 72, 115–38.

—— 1974a: Princes et rois du Nouvel Empire à Gîza. *Stud. Aeg.* 1, 421–33.

—— 1974b: Les colonnes du 'Temple de l'Est' à Tanis: épithètes royales at noms divins. *BIFAO* 74, 93–122.

—— 1976: *Giza au deuxième millénaire*. Cairo.

—— 1980: La Stèle d'Aménophis II à Giza. À propos d'une interprétation récente. *SAK* 8, 269–84.

—— 1981: Bousiris du Létopolite. In J. Vercoutter (ed.), *Livre du Centenaire*. *MIFAO* 104, 91–107.

A Guide to Further Reading

Kent R. Weeks
American University in Cairo

References that appear in the Bibliography are cited here by author and date of publication. Other references, usually to more recent works, are given in full. With very few exceptions, entries are limited to works in English, but it must be noted that much of the best work being done today is published in German or French. Journal abbreviations are explained in pp. 404ff.

A complete survey of Egyptological literature, providing abstracts (that are frequently in English, no matter what the language of the work abstracted) of about 1,200 books and articles annually, is available in the *Annual Egyptological Bibliography*, published since 1947 by the International Association of Egyptologists and the Nederlands Instituut voor het Nabije Oosten, Leiden. It is currently edited by L. M. J. Zonhoven. In addition, the appearance of the *Lexikon der Ägyptologie* (Helck, Otto, Westendorf, 1972–1986) has made even obscure Egyptological data accessible. Articles are in German, French or English, and each is written by an expert in the field. A seventh volume (1992) indexes the *Lexikon* in all three languages.

A very useful, general, one-volume introduction to Egypt's culture in English is Baines and Malek (1980). More detailed descriptions of archaeological sites may conveniently be found in Veronica Seton-Williams and Peter Stocks, *Blue Guide: Egypt* (3rd edn, London: Black and New York: Norton, 1993).

INTRODUCTION

In addition to Fagan (1977), Iversen (1968, 1972), James (1982), Redford (1979b) and Sauneron (1968a), four other works are excellent for the history of Egyptology. Peter Clayton, *The Rediscovery of Ancient Egypt: Artists and Travellers in the 19th Century* (London: Thames and Hudson, 1982) is a well-illustrated survey. Leslie Greener, *The Discovery of Egypt* (London: Cassell and New York: Viking, 1966), although covering Egyptology only up to 1950, is thorough and eminently readable. Jean Vercoutter, *The Search for Ancient Egypt* (London: Thames and Hudson, 1992) provides a good review of the material, with numerous colour plates. John A. Wilson, *Signs and Wonders Upon Pharaoh: A History of American Egyptology* (Chicago: University of Chicago Press, 1964) is an excellent book with coverage much broader than its title suggests. In addition to Curl (1982), which studies Egyptian influences in European arts and crafts, one may consult Richard G. Carrott, *The Egyptian Revival: Its Sources, Monuments and Meaning, 1808–1858* (Berkeley: University of California Press, 1978) for Egyptian influences in nineteenth-century America. The basis of Egyptian chronology is discussed by Redford (1986c).

1 FROM PREHISTORY TO HISTORY

Long neglected, Egypt's prehistoric period and first two dynasties are now fields of great activity: scarcely a year goes by without major revisions of chronology or cultures, and syntheses and theories change very rapidly. The works of B. Adams (1974a,b), Hassan (1980) and Hoffman (1979) are all important. Bruce Trigger, 'The Rise of Egyptian Civilisation', in: Trigger, Kemp and O'Connor (1983) is an excellent brief survey of the material. Weeks (1985) surveys the vast literature. One also should consult Barbara Adams, *Predynastic Egypt* (Shire Egyptology, 7) (Aylesbury, England: Shire, 1988); Winifred Needler, *Predynastic and Archaic Egypt in the Brooklyn Museum* (Wilbour Monographs, 9) (Brooklyn: Brooklyn Museum, 1984); A. J. Spencer, *Early Egypt: The Rise of Civilisation in the Nile Valley* (London: British Museum Press, 1993). Fred Wendorf is the foremost expert on Palaeolithic and early Neolithnic Egypt; any of his numerous works deserve study.

2 RELIGION AND HISTORY

The literature on Egyptian religion is vast. Works by Hornung (1983); Morenz (1962, available in English as: *Egyptian Religion* [Ithaca: Cornell University Press, 1973]); and, more recently, Stephen Quirke, *Ancient Egyptian Religion* (London: British Museum Press, 1992) are good introductions. Also of particular interest are James P. Allen, *Genesis in Egypt: The Philosophy of Ancient Egyptian Creation Accounts* (*Yale Egyptological Series*, 2) (New Haven: Yale University Press, 1988); and James P. Allen, J. Assmann, et al., *Religion and Philosophy in Ancient Egypt* (*Yale Egyptological Series*, 3) (New Haven: Yale University Press, 1989).

3 THE THINITE PERIOD

In addition to Spencer and Needler, cited above in para. 1, Butzer (1976), and the chronological studies of Shaw (1984, 1985), one should consult Bruce G. Trigger, *Early Civilizations: Ancient Egypt in Context* (Cairo: American

University in Cairo Press, 1993); Bruce G. Trigger, 'Egypt: A Fledgling Nation', *JSSEA* 17 (1987): 58–66; Kathryn Bard, 'Toward an Interpretation of the Role of Ideology in the Evolution of Complex Society in Egypt', *Journal of Anthropological Archaeology* 11 (1992): 1–24.

4 THE OLD KINGDOM

Baer (1974), Kanawati (1977, 1980) and Strudwick (1985) are now complemented by Christopher Eyre, 'Work and the Organization of Work in the Old Kingdom', in: Marvin Powell, *Labor in the Ancient Near East* (New Haven: American Oriental Society, 1987), pp. 5–47. The continuing work of Mark Lehner in the workman's village at Giza (1983, 1985, 1986, and several forthcoming studies) is especially important for socio-cultural studies. A brief but useful and well-illustrated survey of the period is Jaromir Malek and Werner Forman, *In the Shadow of the Pyramids: Egypt during the Old Kingdom* (Norman: University of Oklahoma Press, 1986). One also should consult the appropriate chapters of Barry J. Kemp, *Ancient Egypt: Anatomy of a Civilization* (London: Routledge, 1989).

5 FUNERARY IDEAS

W. S. Smith (1978 reprint of 1946 edn), and W. S. Smith, *The Art and Architecture of Ancient Egypt*, rev., with additions by William Kelly Simpson (New Haven: Yale University Press, 1981, and soon to appear in a new edition) remain basic references. Yvonne Harpur, *Decoration in Egyptian Tombs of the Old Kingdom: Studies in Orientation and Scene Content* (London: Kegan Paul, 1987), though rather technical, usefully updates some of Smith's data. Faulkner (1969) and Lichtheim (1973) provide reliable translations of important texts. Architecture is treated in Edwards (1985) and Giedion (1966), and important new commentary is to be found in Arnold (1991) and in Stadelmann (1985). (One hopes that Stadelmann's excellent book will soon appear in an English edition.)

6 THE STRUGGLE FOR POWER; 7 THE MIDDLE KINGDOM;
8 THE INVASION

Dynasties 7–11 have been extensively studied, but most recent major work is in German or French. For the First Intermediate Period, however, one should note Fischer (1964, 1968), James (1962) and W. S. Smith (cited above in para. 5). Valuable data on Middle Kingdom history may be drawn from the appropriate chapters in the *Cambridge Ancient History*, 3rd edn (Edwards, Gadd and Hammond, 1971); on literature from Lichtheim (1973); on government from Quirke (1990); on architecture from Badawy (1966); and on society and economy from James (1962). In addition to James, one also should consult Klaus Baer, 'An Eleventh Dynasty Farmer's Letter to His Family', *JAOS* 83 (1963): 1–19. A brief but useful and up-to-date survey of these periods is: Donald B. Redford, *Egypt, Canaan, and Israel in Ancient Times* (Princeton: Princeton University Press, 1992 and Cairo: American University in Cairo Press, 1993), chapters 3–6. So, too, is Barry J. Kemp, 'Old Kingdom, Middle Kingdom and Second Intermediate Period, *c.* 2686–1552 BC', in Trigger, Kemp and O'Connor (1983). Also of importance is Manfred Bietak's excellent report on his work in the Eastern Delta (Bietak, 1981). An excellent survey of the art of the period and its cultural context continues to be William C. Hayes, *The Scepter of Egypt* (2 vols, New York: Metropolitan Museum of Art, 1952–59). For Egypt's relations with Nubian cultures, see W. Y. Adams (1984) and Bruce G. Trigger, *Nubia Under the Pharaohs* (London: Thames and Hudson, 1976).

9   THE TUTHMOSIDS

The first part of the New Kingdom is a period of great building activity at home and of extensive contacts abroad. In many ways, it is the most impressive period in Egypt's history, and a very large body of data is available for its study. Thus, books and articles tend to be more highly specialized than for some earlier periods, and it is difficult to recommend studies having general coverage. Certainly, one would want to put Charles Nims, *Thebes of the Pharaohs* (London: Elek Books, 1965) on the list, as well as the appropriate chapters of Hayes and the *Cambridge Ancient History* (both cited above). Redford (1967a) and Kemp (cited above, para. 4), continue to be very useful general sources. Manuelian (1987), Peter Dorman, *The Monuments of Senenmut: Problems in Historical Methodology* (London: Kegan Paul, 1988), and Betsy Bryan, *The Reign of Tuthmosis IV* (Baltimore: Johns Hopkins University Press, 1991), are more recent studies that deal with particular individuals and their world.

10   AKHENATEN

The large body of materials covering the Amarna Period is now conveniently indexed in Geoffrey T. Martin, *A Bibliography of the Amarna Period and its Aftermath: The Reigns of Akhenaten, Smenkhkare, Tutankhamun and Ay* (London: Kegan Paul, 1991). Redford (1984a) and Aldred (1988) are the two best general surveys. The catalogue of a superb exhibition of art that toured in the United States is *Egypt's Dazzling Sun: Amenhotep III and His World* (Cleveland: Cleveland Museum of Art and Indiana University Press, 1992). It contains a number of useful essays on the period. Many books have been written about Tutankhamun; one of the most useful is the well-illustrated and well-written survey by C. N. Reeves, *The Complete Tutankhamun: The King, The Tomb, The Royal Treasure* (London: Thames and Hudson, and Cairo: American University in Cairo Press, 1990).

11   THE RAMESSID PERIOD

Kitchen (1982a) offers an excellent historical survey, as do the relevant chapters of Redford (cited above, para. 9). Harris and Wente (1980) is an important survey of the royal mummies; Murnane (1980a and 1985a) of Egypt's Asiatic empire. Janssen (1975, 1986) is important for the economy. The workmen's village at Deir el-Medineh, one of the most fascinating sites in all of Egypt, has been described by Bierbrier (1982), Černý (1973a,b), John Romer (1984), and, in a broader context, by T. G. H. James, *Pharaoh's People: Scenes from Life in Imperial Egypt* (London: Bodley Head, 1984). For the Valley of the Kings, see John Romer, *Valley of the Kings* (New York: Morrow, 1981), and Erik Hornung, *The Valley of the Kings: Horizon of Eternity* (New York: Timkin, 1990).

12   THE DOMAIN OF AMUN

The Centre Franco-égyptien has worked at Karnak for most of this century, and it is to their work that one must turn for the best data on that complex of temples. See, e.g., Barguet (1962), Vandier (1955a), and Traunecker and Golvin (1984). The Epigraphic Survey of the University of Chicago's Oriental Institute has published the inscriptions in several parts of Karnak's Temple of Amun and, more recently, in parts of Luxor Temple. One may also consult Lanny Bell, 'Luxor Temple and the Cult of the Royal Ka', *JNES* 44 (1985): 251–94; Eberhard Otto, *Egyptian Art: The Cults of Osiris and Amun* (New York: Abrams, 1967, and, with a slightly different subtitle, London: Thames and Hudson, 1968). Sauneron (1988; the 1960 edn was transl., rather poorly, as: *The Priests of Ancient Egypt*. New York: Grove, 1969) can still be a useful reference.

13   THE THIRD INTERMEDIATE PERIOD;   14   NUBIANS AND SAITES; 15   PERSIANS AND GREEKS

This is a complicated time in Egypt's history, but help can be found in Bierbrier (1975b), Kitchen (1986), Fazzini (1988); and in the more specialized studies of Spalinger (cited in the Bibliography). One also may profitably check Russman

(1974, 1979) and Samson (1985). Two excellent recent volumes are: Janet H. Johnson (ed.), *Life in a Multi-Cultural Society: Egypt from Cambyses to Constantine and Beyond* (SAOC, 51) (Chicago, 1992); and Alan K. Bowman, *Egypt After the Pharaohs: 332 BC–AD 642* (Berkeley: University of California Press, 1986).

Index

Second Dyn II
Hetepsekhemwy